G

M000278941

# The German Army on the Somme
## 1914 - 1916

*To my wife Laurie, who lights up my life.*

# The German Army on the Somme

# 1914-1916

JACK SHELDON

Pen & Sword
**MILITARY**

First published in Great Britain in 2005 by
Pen & Sword Military
an imprint of
Pen & Sword Books Ltd
47 Church Street
Barnsley
South Yorkshire
S70 2AS

Copyright © Jack Sheldon, 2005

ISBN 1 84415 269 3

The right of Jack Sheldon to be identified as Author
of this work has been asserted by him in accordance
with the Copyright, Designs and Patents Act 1988.

*All rights reserved. No part of this book may be reproduced or
transmitted in any form or by any means, electronic or mechanical
including photocopying, recording or by any information storage
and retrieval system, without permission from the Publisher in writing.*

Typeset in 10pt Ellington by Pen & Sword Books Limited

*Pen & Sword Books Ltd incorporates the imprints of*
Pen & Sword Aviation, Pen & Sword Maritime, Pen & Sword Military,
Wharncliffe Local History, Pen & Sword Select,
Pen & Sword Military Classics and Leo Cooper.

# Contents

# Foreword by Professor Richard Holmes

There is no shortage of books on the battle of the Somme: indeed, Martin Middlebrook's seminal *The First Day on the Somme* and Gary Sheffield's admirable short history *The Somme* have bracketed my working life, so to speak. But it seems to me that there are two difficulties with even the best books on the battle. First, it was a coalition campaign. Perhaps one-third of the Allied soldiers who fought on the Somme were French, as were 200,000 of the well over 600,000 Allied casualties. And both French and British soldiers fought an enemy who is remarkably badly-documented in English. Of course we all read the section on the German army with which the official historian closes each of his chapters, and we are also all too eager to quote General von Kuhl's deductions about the battle. But the real German army of the Somme, shoved back inch by inch, fighting manfully, across that strip of murdered nature between Albert and Bapaume between July and November 1916, is often reduced to snatches from the German official history or quotes from Ernst Junger.

The chief merit of this much-needed book is that Jack Sheldon has done what all good historians ought, and has gone back to the sources. Although the Prussian archives at Potsdam were badly damaged in the Second World War, the Bavarian archives at Munich survived intact, and there are also many relevant documents in the Württemberg archives at Stuttgart. Moreover, although almost all these are accessible only to German-speakers, a whole raft of regimental histories had been written long before the Second World War. These documents form the basis for this study, which, in my view, takes us as close as we will ever get to understanding the soldier in field grey who fought my grandfather's generation on the Somme.

Four general points emerge from Jack Sheldon's story. The first is that the Somme had not always been a quiet sector before the first British arrived in the summer of 1915. The French had mounted determined attacks during the battle of Serre in 1915, enabling the Germans to emphasise the importance of deep dug-outs with two entrances, and for at least one corps to distil the lessons of the fighting into an *aide mémoire* posted in each dugout. The Germans used the period between the arrival of the British and the beginning of the Battle of the Somme to lay out their positions in depth; infantrymen working so hard that, as one divisional commander put it, engineers were only needed in the role of foremen...' On 1st July 1916 the British attacked defenders who were expecting their assault ('all possible defensive preparations for the attack were made') and were led by officers who had thought hard about how best to break it.

Next, German accounts show just how much British and German performance depended on skilled and determined junior leadership. Thus Reserve Leutnant Vulpius describes setting off on his own with seven British prisoners, realising that he was doomed if a counter-attack came but reflecting that: 'Luck is one of the greatest soldierly virtues.' Hauptmann von Wurmb's decisive action recaptured the Schwaben redoubt on 1st July. The officer who led the successful counter-attack on High Wood in the middle of the same month tells us how he got last-minute intelligence just short of the wood, briefed his men fully about situation and mission, and then took the wood and a hundred prisoners for a relatively light cost in casualties. Conversely, Reserve Leutnant

Ballheimer recounts how his counter-attack was mounted with 'total lack of clarity about the situation' and failed: he and his comrades were captured. A regimental commander took the view that once his position was surrounded, German artillery had fallen silent and there seemed no chance of a counterattack he had run out of options: 'After repeated consultations with my officers I decided to surrender.'

Thirdly, although a German lieutenant colonel calls the personal behaviour of British officers 'beyond all praise,' they were often seen as badly-trained: 'it is noticeable that the British officer lacks thorough, detailed training: he appears to be more of a sportsman.' Indeed, many Germans concluded that there were serious errors in the way the British actually fought the battle. One gunner officer thought that the British advanced in 'hordes' on 1 July, and on 18 August; a medical officer saw British infantry suffer severely because they believed that shelling had extinguished all traces of life' and attacked hidden machine guns. There were times when the British seemed unable to orchestrate the battle. A captured Australian captain complained that when his division attacked on 29th July 'the higher command and control must have been extremely poor' because there was no way of controlling friendly artillery fire.

And lastly, these accounts emphasise that towards the end of the battle the fighting became an attritional struggle on a landscape mauled by the power of the gun. A gunner officer described his gun position as 'a scene of the most terrible devastation – a crater field strewn randomly everywhere with charred shell-carrying baskets, torn open cartridges and duds. There were also...shell holes so large that they would have comfortably accommodated a complete gun!' A platoon commander describes living under the 'hail of iron' as shellfire lacerated his platoon: 'Peters dead – Jönsson dead – Unteroffizier Krützfeld wounded – Nagel dead.' It is small wonder that some men were pushed beyond the levels of human endurance: one officer saw a neighbouring regiment 'streaming backwards in disorder. The commander has apparently lost control over his men.' But others found drink and sleep a great restorative: 'I swallowed two complete mess tins full of tea and rum in one great draught and fell asleep,' records an infantryman.

Historians will probably continue to squabble about who actually won the battle of the Somme as long as they discuss anything. Jack Sheldon observes that the Allies did not succeed in breaking through on the Somme, nor did they destroy the morale of the German army. But he agrees that it was never the same afterwards, and quotes a Bavarian general who acknowledged that: 'The monster of the modern overwhelming machine of war gobbled up our finest men.' But in one sense to talk of victory and defeat is to miss the point. As this book makes so very clear, the Somme was a supreme test of human qualities, and the soldiers on both sides displayed them more abundantly than their political leaders deserved, or those who were not there could ever really recognise. Jack Sheldon has sought to do justice to the Sommekämpfer in field grey, just as I have done my best for Tommy Atkins, who was both his adversary and, in the shared agony of one of history's fiercest battles, also his comrade. And when I read this penetrating and harrowing collection I see how much we have needed it, and for so long.

Richard Holmes, May 2005

# Introduction and Acknowledgments

This book has had a long period of gestation. My interest in military history was first aroused in the late 1960s when I was lucky enough to be taught at the Royal Military Academy, Sandhurst by a brilliant group of historians led by that distinguished and gallant Commando, the late Brigadier Peter Young DSO MC. The standard of teaching and the enthusiasm for the subject they engendered was extremely high: no surprise, bearing in mind that the department included David Chandler and John Keegan, to name but two highly influential members. Once I was commissioned, it was natural for me to continue my studies by tackling the long and impressive history of my own regiment and its forbears. We regularly celebrated the part we played at the battles of Quebec and Waterloo, but on 1st July each year we also commemorated the Battle of the Somme, where we had furnished seventeen battalions and won two Victoria Crosses.

The result was that words and phrases from the Somme Day Citation and the personal accounts in the various regimental histories were seared into my brain from an early age: 'Lieutenant Colonel Green personally counted eight machine guns firing on the battalion front...They advanced until almost all of them became casualties...Many men were killed on the wire while attempting to force a way through...The German line was seen to be heavily manned, about a man a yard...In spite of the barrage, these men opened heavy machine gun and rifle fire on the first two waves, causing many casualties...The mud and filth in the trenches was indescribable...the wounded were propped against the parapets and I saw them slipping down into the slime...and being choked in it...The attack is unsuccessful and we hold no part of the enemy line...all the officers of the company are missing...Two companies got in but were reported as bombed back...Truly a fitting scene for Dante's conception of hell...'

This was strong stuff. It created in me a great curiosity to learn about the battle and to find out more about the German army, whose activities made up half of the story. This proved to be far from easy, because in most accounts written in English, no matter how good, the activities of the German army are only lightly sketched in. Scarcely any provide more than that which may be obtained from reading the official histories. More than twenty years ago I began visiting the battlefields and obtained something of a feel for the ground, then luck played a part once more and I was selected to attend the two year General Staff Course at the German Command and Staff College in Hamburg. This gave me both the German language and a comprehensive understanding of the workings of the German General Staff, whose origins pre-date all other such institutions. I still lacked an incentive to exploit this knowledge, but that came during the 1990s when the Battleground Europe series of guidebooks started to appear and I got into correspondence with Nigel Cave, the series editor. It was Nigel who pointed out the need for the current book and encouraged me, through his enthusiasm, to start delving into the libraries and the records of the imperial German army.

As I began to read into the subject, it became apparent that a wealth of material was available. The Royal Air Force bombed the Prussian archives in Potsdam in April 1945, burning the entire contents, but fortunately, between the wars, hundreds and hundreds of regimental histories had already been written. In addition the records of the Bavarian regiments were stored largely intact in Munich and those of the Württemberg regiments, less the documents which fell victim to a waste paper drive during the Second World War, could be consulted in Stuttgart. Corps and divisions from the south and south-west of Germany played a prominent part in the operations in the region of the Somme from 1914 onwards, so in many cases I was able to go back to original documents, reports and maps. This research convinced me that not everything in the accepted version of events accords with all the records. It soon became clear, too, that luck played no part in, nor was there anything accidental about, the blow dealt out to the British army from Gommecourt to Fricourt on 1st July 1916; that although the Battle of the Somme was frequently a close-run affair, poor Allied coordination and persistence in attacking weakly on narrow fronts played into the hands of the German commanders, who were able to rush forward reserves, husband their resources, maintain the overall integrity of their defence and so continue a successful delaying battle until the onset of winter ultimately neutralised the considerable Allied superiority in men and matériel. But to understand why the Old Front Line ran where it did and how the German army prepared itself for the trial of the 1916 battle, it is necessary to follow the story on the Somme as it unfolded from autumn 1914, so that is where the account begins.

This book could not have been written without the assistance of numerous other people. My first debt is to the historians and diarists, the writers of reports and chroniclers of events, who have left a huge legacy of material in the German language. Nigel Cave, my editor, has provided unswerving support and enthusiasm for the project and I am grateful to Professor Richard Holmes, who has done so much in recent years to make military history accessible to all, for the Foreword. My research would have been completely impossible without the aid of Kapitän zur See Dr. Jörg Duppler, former Director of the Bundeswehr Militärgeschichtliches Forschungsamt, Potsdam and the staff of the magnificent library there, who spent hours searching out rare books for me. Dr Achim Fuchs of the Kriegsarchiv, Munich has provided me with a great deal of assistance, as has the staff of the Hauptstaatsarchiv, Stuttgart. My thanks are due also to Lieutenant Colonel Phillip Robinson RE in the United Kingdom, Ralph Whitehead in New York State, Alex Fasse, Dieter Challie and Norbert Krüger in Germany for advice and assistance with material, Arlene King for her unstinting hospitality and use of the documents archived at the Newfoundland Memorial, Beaumont Hamel and Colonel Tom Thaler of the United States Marine Corps who read the text and commented. If I have unknowingly accidentally infringed copyright during the writing of this book, I would request that my apologies be accepted. My special thanks go also to my wife Laurie, who shares my interest in the Western Front, walks the ground with me and drew the maps for this book. During the collection and translation of material, not to mention the writing of the book, she has had to put up with lengthy absences and I am constantly grateful for her patience, love and support.

What follows is a series of snapshots of an army, which has spent too long in the shadows. In my selection of eyewitness accounts, I have tried to show it in the round; the good things as well as the bad. I hope that the hundreds of thousands of Sommekämpfer in field grey would have thought that the portrayal was fair and that it did them justice. Throughout, I have tried to be as accurate as is possible after an interval of ninety years, but there are bound to be some errors in the text, for which I naturally take full responsibility.

Jack Sheldon<br>
Vercors<br>
France<br>
October 2004

**Author's Note**

*Certain eyewitness accounts and other descriptions in the text are linked to a particular locality on the battlefield. Each chapter includes a map of the area. The figures on each map relate to the numbers in bold associated with that section of the relevant chapter. In some cases different witnesses were located in the same area, so they share a number.*

*The Germans never differentiated between English, Scottish, Irish or Welsh soldiers and units, referring to them all as Engländer. In order to avoid endless footnotes, whenever witnesses refer, for example, to 'Englishmen in kilts', or 'Englishmen from Northern Ireland', Engländer has been translated throughout as 'British'.*

*German time, which was one hour ahead of British time, is used throughout the book.*

CHAPTER ONE

# September – December 1914

War came in earnest to the unspoilt, prosperous farming area of the Somme in the closing days of September 1914, just as the baking heat of summer gave way to fine and sunny days, but increasingly fresh and chilly nights. The previous month had seen a certain amount of manoeuvring and some skirmishes, but no really large scale operations. The Germans had lost the strategic initiative on the Marne, but they still nursed hopes of swift victory on the Western Front. For much of the remainder of the year the course of the campaign centred on German attempts to concentrate overwhelming force on the allied left flank and the allies' countermoves. The consequent strategic realignment and the move north of the newly created Sixth Army under Crown Prince Rupprecht of Bavaria overwhelmed the logistical system and the creaking infrastructure; in particular the limitations of the railway systems of the occupied areas of Belgium and France caused chronic delays and major disruption. The inevitable consequences were supply shortages and piecemeal, haphazard deployment of forces in hasty, ill-prepared operations, which ultimately ended in stalemate. All these difficulties can be seen in microcosm in the experiences in the region of the Somme of the men of the I and II Bavarian Army Corps, the XXI Army Corps and the XIV Reserve Corps, who fresh from their heavy but successful battles south of Metz and Nancy in August, were to play such a large role in the battles of the subsequent two years.

In mid-September, under great pressure from Falkenhayn, Crown Prince Rupprecht set about to do his best to achieve the mission he had been given, 'To bring about the decision on the northern flank of the enemy and to provide right flank protection; depending on the circumstances it is to be accepted that troops will have to be thrown into the battle on arrival'.[1] The Crown Prince did everything in his power and that of his staff to expedite the move and to ensure that he was concentrated before beginning operations, but within a week the countering of the corresponding movements of the reconstituted French Second Army under Castelnau, meant that battle was joined incrementally from south to north, beginning in the Chaulnes – Lihon area south west of Péronne on the 24th September and spreading rapidly northwards until the Guard Corps was fighting for Serre by the 5th and Hébuterne by the 7th October. The outcome of this initial phase of operations was the rough trace of the line which, with slight variations, was that assaulted by the allied armies on 1st July 1916. Setting off on a circuitous journey, with numerous checks and hold-ups, the redeployment began, then battle was joined near Chaulnes on 24th September.

*Oberleutnant Roth Adjutant Infantry Regiment 138 [2]*

"The situation was completely unclear. The Regiment knew nothing of the withdrawal from the Marne. Only the presence of numerous trains full of wounded that we came across during our journey through Belgium and the tales of the wounded from the battle for Noyon indicated that bitter fighting was in progress and that it awaited us. The overall appreciation of the situation was that we were on the extreme flank of the battle, that only enemy cavalry was deployed in front of us and that we merely had to march off and roll up the French northern flank. This opinion was voiced regularly during the battles of the coming days and was reflected in the orders of the higher commanders. I well remember one order from Supreme Army Headquarters which read more or less, 'To the Bavarian Army with XXI Corps falls the happy duty of bringing about the final decision of the war by rolling up the French northern flank.'"

*Oberstleutnant Randebrock 2nd Battalion Infantry Regiment 17 [3]*

"It was a beautiful clear autumn morning. The flat land stretched away as far as the eye could see, field after field of sugar beet, punctuated by numerous villages and the high trees of the parks of the chateaus. Everywhere hares raced away in front of the companies and coveys of partridges rose out of every field. What a great place for hunting. In Lorraine we had always fought in hilly country, covered in woods large and small. If we came under artillery fire we could quickly disappear into a hollow or a wood. Here, in this billiard-table place, there was no cover to be had. We expected to come under artillery fire at any moment, but all was calm."

*Reserve Hauptmann Karl Weber 5th Company Bavarian Infantry Regiment 16 [4] 1*

"At 5pm [24th September] we received an order which said (roughly), 'The enemy cavalry forces have been defeated. The Army Corps is to go into bivouac. HQ 2nd Infantry Brigade and Infantry Regiment 2 in Lihons and Rosières. Infantry Regiment 16 in Vermandovillers (3rd Battalion) and Chaulnes (1st and 2nd Battalions). It must be assumed that there is a possibility that these bivouacs will have to be fought for.' Bivouacs which had to be fought for came low in our estimation. As darkness fell the 1st and 2nd Battalions shook out left and right of the road Vermandovillers-Chaulnes and advanced with scouts forward. All conversation was in whispers. All noise was reduced to a minimum and the battalions arrived about one kilometre from the little town of Chaulnes, whose church tower was burning like a torch. There must have been a battle here, but nobody knew anything about it. A cavalry patrol coming the other way reported that Chaulnes was free of enemy, so the

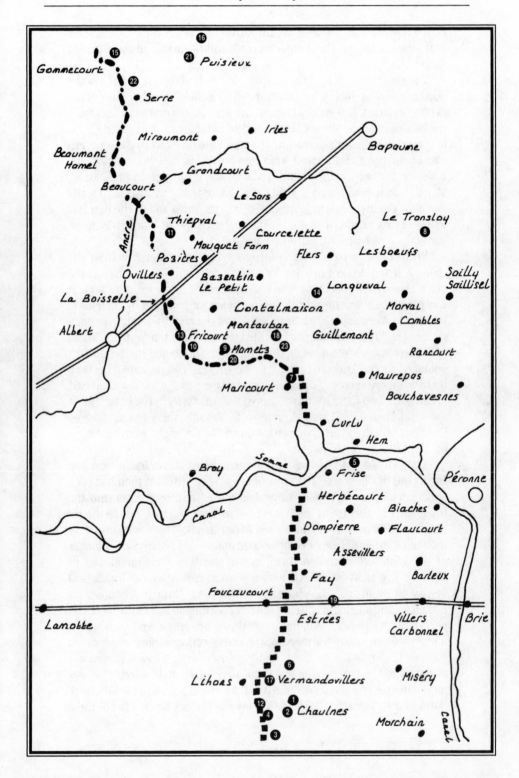

march was resumed on the road and patrols, including the billeters, were sent forward, so that the companies could follow them into the different parts of the town.

"The companies, with 5th Company in the lead, had just reached the northern edge of the town unscathed and its leading elements were at the market square, when suddenly rapid fire was opened on the patrols from the houses and from the wall of the park of the chateau. Fortunately most of it was too high...I dispensed with a move into bivouacs in the southern part of the town and instead went to report to Battalion Headquarters. Based on an order which had arrived in the meantime from division, Major Haas forbade street fighting at night, ordering us instead to settle down for the night on the northern edge of the town and in the first few houses of its northern section. The highest state of alarm was to be maintained and security patrols pushed out.

"Because the patrols were continually coming under fire from the chateau, it was decided to bring forward an artillery piece and flatten the place, thus driving off those who were disturbing the peace. Of course it was pitch black and the gunners were somewhat bemused by their task, which was to engage the chateau walls and the chateau itself over open sights at eighty metres range. I pointed out the direction to them. 'Stand by!' There was a violent crash, then nothing. Finally the shell exploded, doubtless several kilometres south of the village. 'OK, Repeat!' This time there was more success. The shell flattened the gates to the park and part of the wall. Two more rounds produced a similar effect. The enemy must have had enough and they disappeared. Proudly the gunners dragged their howitzer away and we settled down for the night from midnight on...

"At dawn the 1st and 2nd Battalions received the order to clear the enemy out of Chaulnes. The execution was more difficult than had been anticipated; apparently the enemy had moved reinforcements into the town during the night and these were now putting up obstinate resistance...By midday Chaulnes was in our hands. There were of course individual riflemen concealed in isolated houses and cellars and a number of the 16th fell victim to them, not to mention the Commander of Infantry Regiment 35 which had also attacked. After the attack and despite being warned, he chose to lead his men through Chaulnes on horseback and so met his fate. It did not take long to deal with these last pockets of resistance. Amongst the thirty prisoners who were taken during the street battles there was a young officer whose conduct, in contrast to that of his men, was hardly praiseworthy. He was hauled out of bed, where apparently he had spent the entire battle asleep. He was most amusing and highly delighted that he would be coming to 'Münken' [München = Munich]. 'The French army can kiss my arse!' I heard these

very words myself otherwise I should not have believed it..."
A little to the south the French were strenuously contesting possession of Hallu, Chilly and Maucourt. In the fluid, confused, swirling fighting there were many cameos of a style of soldiering which would soon disappear for ever. Cavalry patrols jingled and clattered round the countryside, reconnoitring and raiding, infantry manoeuvred in massed close formation, shaking out only in the final stages of an attack and all this activity was given close support by field artillery armed with their 105 mm guns. One such action occurred on 25th September.

*Reserve Vizewachtmeister B. Gelderblom 4th Battery Field Artillery Regiment 15⁵ 2.*

"A messenger rushed in suddenly: 'Battery advance to Hallu with all speed!' – 'Battery mount up...Trot...Gallop!' We bounced and lurched along the rough track. Everywhere faces beamed at the forthcoming prospect. Now we could do something to help and we would do it, cost it what it would! The village came into view behind the corner of a wood. Small white clouds floated above it; great black clouds shot up as though whipped into the sky, hovered for an instant and fell back. The village was under heavy artillery fire! The horses foamed and panted. Dead French and German soldiers lay along the road. We reached the edge of the village and could breathe more easily, because no fire was landing along the road hard up against the houses, which were giving us cover. Hauptmann Wagner ordered me to make my way along to the other edge and see what help I could offer the infantry with my section. We left at the gallop, accompanied by horse holders. Hardly had we emerged from the shelter of the houses when the hiss and crack of rifle and machine gun fire began to sing the old familiar tune. There could be no question of getting the horses further forward, so we dismounted, the horses headed into cover and we rushed forward from cover to cover until we reached the firing line. Our infantry was lining a hedge and had dug in a little. An officer briefed me: 'The French have established themselves in the farm and the copse. 1,200 metres right is an enemy battery. 500 metres forward of our position is the enemy front line. We must have support, or we cannot advance'. A thousand thoughts raced through my mind: How could a section close up on a complete battery in the open? How could we get into a firing position and what should be engaged first? Two gaps in the hedge might have been made to take guns – but how to get there? It was unthinkable to try it in harness.

"In a series of dashes we made it back to the village, where the horse holders were waiting. A small infantry reserve was also present. The horse holders moved the guns forward to the very limit of the cover. From there the guns were moved forward by the gunners and the infantrymen. I crawled forward once more to the hedge to observe. The area teemed with targets. If only the guns would arrive! ...Finally after extreme exertions of pushing and pulling on ropes they were there.  Over open sights, one gun was laid on the battery and the other on the firing line. The aim of the gunners was brilliant.  Shot after shot was on target and everyone worked with a will.  The battery commander arrived with a second section.  The enemy fire slackened, the battery that we had taken in the flank fell silent and the first of the enemy infantry was in headlong flight.  Large numbers went down in the shrapnel and machine gun fire, others took cover in the farmyard and behind stacks of straw and barns...A company that marched forward in close order was shattered with a few rounds at 1,800 metres.  Our infantry went forward and without incurring too many casualties occupied the village of Chilly. Unfortunately the presence to the left and right of dug in French troops precluded further progress...During the afternoon the final two guns of the battery arrived in the area of the hedge and that evening we completely shot up the teams which were intended to recover the enemy guns."

Further south the first of several serious attempts to capture the village of Fouquescourt took place.  During the night, after strenuous marching, the men of Infantry Regiment 138 were bivouacked in Fransart for the night 25th – 26th September, when suddenly there was a great commotion:

*Gefreiter Schmidt 5th Company Infantry Regiment 138*[6] **3.**

"We had hardly laid down to rest when we were roused from the sleep of the dead by shouts of, 'Everyone out! The enemy is attacking!' All hell had broken loose.  The enemy artillery was bringing fire down on the village and shells were crashing and bursting in the roofs and walls, sending wood, stones, tiles, smoke and earth spinning up into the air.  In the midst of all the chaos, the riflemen were rolling up their coats and groundsheets, section commanders were calling their sections together before doubling them to the appointed assembly area behind the village. Oberst Berger, the regimental commander, quickly gave out orders to advance.  The 2nd Battalion was to advance in company columns, echeloned right, in the direction of the village to our front.  This was followed by an order to the companies to push the leading sections forward in a skirmish line.  At this moment the sun began to break through the early morning fog and this was accompanied by murderous enemy fire.  One of our batteries, which had been at readiness between the houses, galloped forward through enemy artillery fire, into a fire position amidst the fields of sugar beet.  Bouncing and swaying they advanced; each bursting shell sending a number of sugar beet up into the air.

"Hardly had our line of skirmishers reached the edge of the village, when our Oberst rode past us.  Our company gathered at the entrance to the village, whilst the first section of 1 Platoon covered down to the right.

Shortly after this the whole platoon was directed to move round to the right. Doubling forward across the exposed road they headed for cover behind a haystack, but as they were running forward someone shouted, 'There's a sunken road!' and everyone raced towards it. Later our second and third platoons also gathered in the sunken road. Leutnant Guittienne lay on top of the embankment and observed the enemy. A little later he gave the order 'Fix bayonets!' It was clear to all of us why. If the enemy attempted to break through, he would be resisted fiercely. Sometime later an enemy rider appeared from a wood to our right and entered the road along which we were lying. He was shot at from close range, at which he wheeled his horse swiftly and disappeared back into the wood."

As the day progressed the battle for the village intensified. The outcome hung constantly in the balance as first one side then the other gained an advantage. Some idea of the nature of the battle may be gained from the description given of it by the commander of Infantry Regiment 138.

*Oberst Roth Infantry Regiment 138*[7] **3.**

"Gradually the situation in Fouquescourt, in which the whole of 59 Brigade was wedged, became ever more critical. Enemy artillery fire increased noticeably, coming down from three sides. The French infantry attempted repeatedly to thrust against the village from west and northwest, but they were beaten back by the men of 1st Company, Infantry Regiment 138 who had established themselves in orchards on the edge of the village. Two good examples of the confused situation then occurred. A French higher staff arrived at full gallop on the hill south of Méharicourt about 1,500 metres from us. The clerical staff jumped down from their horses and started assembling map tables. The party's entire attention seemed to be directed towards Maucourt and Chilly. None of the officers seemed to realise that we had already occupied Fouquescourt off to their flank. I assumed that a French cavalry division was about to advance and ordered the 5th Company to prepare to fire volleys. Advancing French artillery appeared, then it was a matter of opening fire. Within seconds, the French were back behind the hill. Almost at the same moment a French despatch rider came hurtling at full tilt, message in hand, for Fouquescourt. I was delighted by the thought of a useful capture, so ordered everyone into cover and not to open fire. Then unfortunately, fire came from one of the companies a little more to the rear. The Frenchman hauled his mount around, still at a mad gallop, and, lying along his horse's neck, escaped back to Méharicourt.

"Suddenly there was an enormous roar and the ear-splitting impact of a heavy shell landing in the road in the midst of the parked vehicles of the machine gun company. The ground shook, windows rattled and tiles rained down. For several minutes the street was shrouded in clouds of dust, from which could be heard the moans of the wounded. The horses, maddened by fear, threatened to bolt, but the drivers, sticking it out bravely by their waggons, exerted all their strength and held them back. Where was the gunfire coming from – from the rear? Out of the question, but a few minutes later came another impact among the machine gun company, with the same result. The bucking horses were quietened once more and none of the drivers deserted his post, even though the next shell might get him. There could be no finer memorial for Hauptmann Treichel, the peacetime commander of this company, who had already fallen on 19th August, than this calmness under fire!

"The artillery fire was indeed coming from the rear. A shell splinter proved that it was our artillery that was firing at us. What now? regimental and brigade HQs consulted, the fire had to be stopped, but how? All links to the rear had been broken. There was only one possibility – ride! Hauptmann Lotz, the brigade adjutant, was despatched, but a further blast blew him off his horse. I then requested the permission of the brigade commander, General von Wurmb, to ride to the rear. He shook my hand, agreeing. Undaunted, Hauptmann Lotz linked up with me, as did my faithful groom, Hans Stemmler of 7th Company. We waited until the next of the shells, which were landing at regular intervals, had exploded, then we rode for our lives. My horse must have realised what was at stake and he careered madly across country through shell holes, up hill and down dale in the direction of Fransart, accompanied by the howling, whizzing and cracking of artillery shells and small arms fire, which were landing all around us. After about two kilometres we were through the worst and we paused for breath – luck was with us! My groom's horse had been hit by a shell splinter, but had come through it well... In a wood northeast of Fransart, Oberst von Elstorff, the commander of 65 Brigade, directed us to the artillery commander and within a few minutes we had succeeded in getting the fire on Fouquescourt lifted. A weight fell from our shoulders.

"Whose fault was it? An artillery observation officer believed that he had seen 59 Brigade flooding back out of Fouquescourt, so the artillery commander had brought down fire on the eastern exit to the village: full marks for the accuracy of our artillery. We rode on to the Divisional staff in Hattencourt and had a comical, but potentially deadly encounter. A gunner officer, who believed us to be a British patrol, jumped out at us deathly pale and trembling with excitement, pistol drawn..."

All this fighting was taking a high toll in casualties, which in turn was straining the medical units to the limit. There was a lack both of trained personnel and matériel. The casualty evacuation chain at this time was at best rudimentary and in any case overwhelmed by the numbers involved and the near impossibility of arranging and organising suitable transport. As always it was the front line troops who had to bear the brunt of these deficiencies, just as here at Chilly on 26th September:

*Oberstleutnant Randebrock 2nd Battalion Infantry Regiment 17*[8] **4.**

"Hauptmann Stifft and I sat on a bench near the church. Suddenly a shell landed about twenty paces from us. A second hit the roof of the church and covered us with splinters from the slate roof. That was the start of fourteen evil days, during which we had to endure very heavy fire from dawn to dusk. Stifft and I left the dangerous neighbourhood of the church and went on to the main street. Oertzen came up to me and asked me to come to the room where the wounded were being tended. I took all the chocolate and cigars I had and went into the house which had been converted into a dressing station. In the first room lay the dying, about twenty of them. It was a shocking sight. In a second room, a large chamber, lay the lightly wounded. The first had no fewer than four wounds. 'With three bullets in me I carried on', he said, 'but the fourth went right through my knee and I could do no more.' There were at least 160 men in this room. You could cut the air with a knife! In the midst of this scene of misery, working in his shirtsleeves, sweating profusely and with bloodied hands, which he rubbed across his forehead, was our young doctor. He was already utterly exhausted, but he could not pause in his work even for an instant, because the other two doctors had somehow gone astray and did not arrive until midday.

"Whilst I was going from stretcher to stretcher talking to the men, a shell suddenly landed right in the middle of the room, directly amongst this dreadful agony, and seriously wounded a medical orderly. There was no halting the men after that. 'We need to get out of here', they said to one another. All those still able to walk leapt up and headed hurriedly for the door. Many were too weak to move, but many others were able to walk the two kilometres to Hallu despite their severe wounds. Because no waggons were available, I directed that wheelbarrows and other makeshift means of carriage be brought and gradually the men were transported to the rear on them. Shells fell constantly in thinly walled half-timbered houses, which collapsed with great crashes. Shrapnel shell after shrapnel shell burst in the air, sending its death-dealing contents cascading down. Day after day the scene was unchanged. Hardly had the first grey of dawn lit the sky, when the artillery opened up and continued until the stars could be seen in the skies above. Every minute of the day, the dead and wounded were being transported along the village street to the aid post, which was itself hit twice by shells, despite the fact that it flew the Red Cross flag."

Further to the north men of the élite Bavarian Infantry-Leibregiment moved across the vital Somme crossing at Brie, south of Péronne, despatching Graf Armansperg and his company to hold the Somme bridge between Hem and Feuillères. In the event it was a short-lived mission. The men of the II Bavarian Army Corps and their screening cavalry had received a rude shock north of the river Somme when they were taken hard in the flank by French territorial forces, were checked and forced into a temporary partial withdrawal.

*Hauptmann Graf Armansperg Bavarian Infantry Leibregiment* [9] **5. & 6.**

"About 7.00 pm on the 25th September 1914 Leutnant Eduard Feilitzsch 4th Company Bavarian Infantry-Leibregiment arrived bearing orders from the 2nd Division. The Company was to pull back to Herbécourt with the 4th Company and to link up with Bavarian Infantry Regiment 20. It was now dark... I gave orders that the platoons were to withdraw individually across the bridge in the order Roid, Bavarian Infantry Regiment 1, Barth, Reitzenstein and were to assemble in Feuillères north. The clean break was achieved without casualties, despite the fact that the French were pressing forward...In Herbécourt I heard from some cavalrymen that I Army Corps had had a very heavy battle the previous day and that the right flank had even been forced back. Bavarian Infantry Regiment 20 was entrenched to the west of Herbécourt, but it was possible that the village would be evacuated tonight...The whole time long columns of German riders came through heading east. These included mounted artillery, which looked ghostly in the darkness. The cavalryman would have appreciated the night time security which my company could have provided, but because neither 4th Company nor Bavarian Infantry Regiment 20 was there, I decided on my own responsibility to seek out the regiment, as far as possible avoiding contact with the enemy.

"My aim was to head for Belloy, where the staff of the 2nd Division was located, via Asseviillers. My little command had now grown considerably, comprising as it did the 3rd Company Bavarian Infantry-Leibregiment, Two platoons of the 1st Company Bavarian Infantry-Leibregiment and Chevaulegers [Light Horse], with a total of nine vehicles. It was a beautifully clear starry night. A cyclist sent on ahead reported that Belloy was overflowing, so I marched to Barleux, where we succeeded in getting everyone shelter in several barns. I continued on to make contact with the HKK [Army Cavalry Headquarters], where I was warmly received and discovered for sure that I should be safe for the night in Barleux. Where on earth the 1st Division was, nobody knew. I discovered very clearly during these days how very little even the higher staffs knew about the situation; how everything was shrouded in uncertainty. It was also pointless to ask the officers and men at the front. They know absolutely nothing. All I could do was to go from one place to another and gradually build up a picture...At 8.00am on 26th September the 9th Cavalry Division headed off for battle near Flaucourt...I headed for Villers

Carbonnel, met up with HQ 9th Cavalry Division and many cavalrymen, then continued to Berny.  There I heard from two wounded men of Bavarian Infantry Regiment 2 that 3 Infantry Brigade was along the line Fay-Assevillers and that the 1st Division was south of that, so I headed off towards Ablaincourt.

"From high ground near Berny it was possible to see that the battlefield was as flat as a pancake.  From the north and west came the roar of guns and the crack of shrapnel.  GHQ was said to be in Fresnes, so I raced there by bicycle, met up with Aviator Erhard, who said that in the course of heavy fighting the previous day Bavarian Infantry Regiment 2 had taken serious casualties.  In Fresnes Chateau I enjoyed a glass of red wine with a Prussian leutnant of hussars and a young signals officer, who told me that the 1st Division was in Ablaincourt.  How very beautiful Fresnes Chateau was.  Someone was playing Mozart sonatas, which though elsewhere would have been wonderful, was a useless activity here...I went on to Ablaincourt ...explained my adventure to the staff who told me that the regiment was now in Vermandovillers north and that the 2nd Battalion was holding the wood to the west.  I directed the company to get something to eat in Ablaincourt, so that the men would have something in their stomachs if they had to fight then, widely spaced by platoons, the company crossed the open ground between Ablaincourt and Vermandovillers which was under observation and artillery fire by the enemy...This move took place without casualties and the company reassembled behind the northernmost houses of Vermandovillers.

"I was received with open arms by the battalion and regiment who were delighted that at least one of the detached companies was still intact...I had to report my excursion immediately to Generals Pechmann and Rauchenberger, who were generous with their praise and promised me the Iron Cross...As it began to go dark [on 26th September], the French directed an amazing weight of fire against our 2nd Battalion in Sternwald [Star Wood*] and immediately after that the French columns stormed forward to attack.  There was a hail of fire from rifles, machine guns and artillery pieces.  The 5th Company was rushed forward to plug a gap and this was followed up by the 1st Company.  My company was assembled ready to move in a dark lane in the village; I needed only to give the order to fix bayonets and to march off.  The shooting died away, the French attack had been driven off with heavy losses, but the 5th Company had suffered badly too.  Leutnant Basson was dead, as were several other men.

"An anxious night followed.  Outside our brave lads lay in their trenches, rifles by their sides, ready to endure renewed attacks.  Again and again there was a sudden crackling of rifle fire; then Tann moved the regimental band forward and soon could be heard rising above the blood soaked battlefield the sound of our Regimental March, followed by 'Wacht

---

* Star Wood was located just to the west of Vermandovillers. It took its name from the distinctive pattern of tracks and bridleways within it.

am Rhein' and 'Deutschland, Deutschland über alles'. Spirits rose at once and many even began to join in and sing enthusiastically. The wounded pulled themselves upright to listen to these well loved tunes. Dear Fatherland, I thought, you may remain calm.[10] Come what may, no enemy was going to break through here...

"So dawn broke on a foggy morning. Once again came the sudden crackle of rapid fire, yet again the French thrust was halted. All around the ground was littered with the red trousers of the dead. Riedheim pulled a clever trick. He was unsure if the advancing troops were German or French, so he leapt up and shouted 'En avant!' As the assault force began to react to this, he shouted 'Rapid Fire!' and mowed the lot down with his machine gun..."

The short-term situation north of the river Somme was turning rather more in favour of the Germans as increasing numbers of units and formations of II Bavarian Army Corps were fed into the battle. The 4th Bavarian Infantry Division clashed with the French territorial forces in an encounter battle, which was decided in favour of the former. Leaving screening forces on its northern flank, it pressed westwards in the direction of Albert along the line Sailly, Combles, Guillemont and Montauban. To its south, with its left flank anchored on the Somme, the 3rd Bavarian Infantry Division probed forward along the axis Bouchavesnes, Leforest and Hardecourt, but this advance faltered in the face of increasing enemy resistance in and around Maricourt, and it turned to the left flank units of the 4th Bavarian Infantry Division for assistance. What followed was a typical example of over-hasty, uncoordinated and clumsy action during which all the gallantry in the world on behalf of the attackers was no match for well-placed, roughly dug in French infantry and well-handled artillery.

*Oberst Otto Schulz Bavarian Infantry Regiment 22*[11] *7.*

"The journey from Metz was so slow that we fell a day's march behind our schedule and had to make it up by mean of forced marches. Nevertheless Bavarian Infantry Regiment 22 arrived at the front internally cohesive and ready to do battle...During the evening of the 26th September it arrived at Maurepas after a march of fifty one kilometres. The 3rd Battalion Bavarian Infantry Regiment 22 (Hauptmann Käfferlein) was subordinated on the 27th September to Bavarian Infantry Regiment 17, which had advanced to the south west of Maurepas. The 2nd Battalion Bavarian Infantry Regiment 22 (Major Nägelsbach) was under the command of Bavarian Infantry Regiment 18 which had the mission of taking Hardecourt and advancing on Maricourt. The 1st Battalion and the Machine Gun Company were despatched to act as reserve to 6 Bavarian Infantry Brigade. I myself headed for the staff of 6 Brigade and rode with it to the area of Hardecourt from where Generalmajor Weiss-Jonsk (Commander, Bavarian Infantry Regiment 18) was directing the battle for Maricourt, Hardecourt having already been captured. The attack on Maricourt failed and the 2nd Battalion Bavarian Infantry Regiment 22 became involved in heavy fighting in the woods to the northeast of Maricourt.

"Generalmajor Claus (Commander, 6 Brigade) wanted to deploy my 1st Battalion, but General Weiss-Jonsk instead arranged for the Battalion to be used further north with 5 Reserve Brigade and to launch an attack on the right by-passing Maricourt. General Claus agreed and formed a new battlegroup from 1st Battalion Bavarian Infantry Regiment 22, 1st Battalion Bavarian Reserve Infantry Regiment 5 and 1st and 3rd Battalions Bavarian Reserve Infantry Regiment 8. This was placed under my command and entitled 'Group Schulz'. I received the mission to advance on Montauban via Guillemont and to capture it. Guillemont was not defended by the enemy and so was taken without a fight. Because the advance was to continue in a westerly direction, I advanced two up: 1st Battalion Bavarian Reserve Infantry Regiment 5 right and 2nd Battalion Bavarian Infantry Regiment 22 left. 1st and 3rd Battalions Bavarian Reserve Infantry Regiment 8 were under my personal control. I then launched an attack on Trônes Wood, which was occupied [by the French] throughout its length. Battery Schöpf was subordinated to me and brought fire down on Trônes Wood. After a lengthy fire fight the lines of infantry stormed the wood, which was up to 500 metres deep, drove the enemy out and pushed on to its western edge.

"The battalions then regrouped for an attack on Bernafay Wood which was 250-300 metres distant. There was a need for an even longer bombardment and then the battalions, reinforced by elements of Bavarian Reserve Infantry Regiment 8, stormed it. There was a hard fight for a brick works to the south, during the capture of which Leutnant Krieger and 2nd Company distinguished themselves. Montauban, about half a kilometre further on, appeared to be strongly held. The fire of my riflemen, who were lining the western edge of Bernafay Wood, was returned in such a volume that there could be no question of launching a successful attack without careful preparation. At this moment (7.05 pm) an order arrived from General Claus. In connection with the intention of enveloping Maricourt, we were to attack the line Carnoy – Hill 122 north of Maricourt. My analysis, and his own opinion during the preparations for this attack, convinced him that it would be impossible whilst Montauban was in enemy hands. Because darkness was falling and the fact that the attack on Montauban would be considerably easier once 4th Infantry Division (only 7 Infantry Brigade plus artillery) had reached Longueval and pushed further forward to Bazentin le Petit, thus threatening the enemy's left flank, the attack on Montauban was postponed until the following day. Our artillery engaged Montauban for a while and then all was calm. The command post of Group Schulz was withdrawn from a track junction on the eastern edge of Trônes Wood to Guillemont.

"The first task of the group on 28th September was the capture of Montauban. The command post was advanced to Trônes Wood. 1st Battalion Bavarian Reserve Infantry Regiment 5 and 1st Battalion Bavarian Infantry Regiment 22, who had reconnoitred the ground during the night, stayed in the lead and opened fire as dawn broke. In addition to our field artillery, the heavy artillery also bombarded Montauban. I had despatched Leutnant Munzinger to the 4th Infantry Division, requesting them to participate in the attack. Generalleutnant Graf Montgelas agreed 'possible' assistance. Until the arrival of XIV Reserve Corps he could not take part in an attack, because his 7 Infantry Brigade was currently the only infantry flank protection for the entire German army.

"Montauban, which stretched out west to east, presented only a narrow front to the east, against which we concentrated overwhelming firepower. The subsequent attack succeeded. Companies which enveloped the village to the north forced their way in and captured it after intense street fighting. It had been occupied by 3rd Battalion 69th Regiment of the Line (From XX Corps, with which we had fought in Lorraine). In one farmyard an entire company, including its commander, was captured. The enemy artillery, which had now located us, brought down heavy fire on us from Carnoy and Maricourt. When at 3.00 pm the 4th Infantry Division moved, I ordered an immediate attack [southwards] refusing my right flank along the road Montauban – Carnoy and with my left directed against the western end of Maricourt. Although I had personally agreed everything with General Weiss-Jonsk, his forces did not launch simultaneously with mine. My left flank quickly came under fire from the direction of Maricourt and turned to face this threat. This meant that my line of infantry became thinner, despite the fact that, bit by bit, I fed in almost all my men. My right flank was stalled midway between Montauban and Carnoy, about one hundred metres from the enemy. My left was almost a kilometre from Maricourt. Because the 4th Infantry Division had held back and it was already dark, I called off the attack and ordered my front line to dig in. In order to be immediately on the spot in case of an enemy night counter attack, I maintained my command post on the track junction east of Trônes Wood during the night.

"In the early morning of 29th September I moved my command post to Montauban, initially into the only house on the southern edge which was not destroyed. The enemy artillery quickly located us (apparently informed by a spy). It opened fire from the line Mametz-Carnoy-Maricourt and drove us out. The fire pursued us as I moved successively to the middle of the village, then the northern edge then to the southern edge once more. I then moved to a quarry north of the village and finally found a peaceful spot. I then had the village searched, had all the men found brought to a closed room and guarded. In a cellar a telephone line and a French artillery uniform were discovered. I was now no longer pestered by enemy artillery and I moved my command post back to the undamaged house and remained there during the night and on 30th September.

"During the evening an order arrived from 6 Infantry Brigade to capture Carnoy during the night. During a telephone conversation which I conducted with 6th Infantry Brigade at 3.00 am it was agreed that the operation would be undertaken at dawn. I discussed this with Oberstleutnant Deboi (Commander Bavarian Reserve Infantry Regiment 5), who in the meantime had called forward additional elements of his regiment and was to command the operation...At dawn on 30th September Bavarian Reserve Infantry Regiment 5 began the attack against Carnoy. In order to make the attack easier, I arranged for Bavarian Reserve Infantry Regiment 8 (under Oberst Gloss) to advance simultaneously on the left against the line Hill 122 – Maricourt... Bavarian Reserve Infantry Regiment 5 soon came up against a trench line 150 metres north of Carnoy and captured it after a short battle without significant casualties. The enemy artillery, which by now (7.00 am) had been informed about the surprise attack, brought down heavy fire on Carnoy. Carnoy was therefore not entered by Bavarian Reserve Infantry Regiment 5. Battalion Eckert, on the right flank, by-passed the village to its right and left. The task to take Carnoy was effectively completed. But the aim of all this was to take Maricourt. This village would be untenable if my Group succeeded in pushing on further to reach the road half a kilometre south of Carnoy which led to Maricourt. In order to be able to counter interference from Mametz, I reinforced the right flank with a half battalion from the 2nd Battalion Bavarian Infantry Regiment 17 (Ruchte).

"It appeared that the road which led west out of Maricourt was the main enemy position. It seemed to be strongly held, so I reinforced Bavarian Reserve Infantry Regiment 8 with several companies of Bavarian Infantry Regiment 22. Along the entire front, I worked my regiments forward until they were 100 – 200 metres from the road, which my artillery kept under constant fire. The attack appeared to be going to succeed so I ordered it to be carried out. On the right flank my infantrymen were fifty metres from the enemy, in the centre and left flank 100 – 200 metres away. They fixed bayonets and charged. Numerous Frenchmen left the position, others raised their hands, but then the enemy artillery brought down heavy fire on the attackers. In a worthy attempt to support the attack, our artillery brought down fire, but it dropped short and hit our infantry from behind. This was unbearable for the troops and caused them to pull back. The enemy artillery increased its fire, causing heavy casualties amongst the retreating men. The withdrawal came to a halt at the start line of the attack south of Montauban. Renewed heavy artillery fire caused further withdrawals. Only in Montauban and along the track from Montauban–Hardecourt did we officers succeed by vigorous intervention in preventing further retreat. The stragglers were assembled north of Montauban and a defensive front was established, from which we would have beaten off the enemy attack which was to be expected. None occurred, the French chose instead to harry us with artillery. Their heavy artillery switched its fire to the [Bavarian] Field Artillery Regiment 11 (4th Infantry Division), which was deployed north west of Montauban, and destroyed a number of guns.

"During the afternoon a mounted Unteroffizier led a further 118 stragglers and shirkers to me. Some of them had slight wounds whose origin was suspicious. Not everyone who wore field grey was a hero. Oberleutnant Schöpf received the Max-Joseph-Order and once someone other than Generalleutant Breitkopf was in command of the 3rd Infantry Division, I received the Iron Cross First Class...The Germans never took Maricourt because there was never a coordinated attack mounted against it."

Further north, too, the casualties were beginning to mount as French resistance increased and the Germans began to learn the cost of attacking even improvised trench lines.

### *Oberstleutnant Winterstein Field Artillery Regiment 15*[12] **8.**

"On the 27th September we assembled near Rocquiny and headed across the battlefield of the previous day towards Le Transloy. The traces of the battle were to be seen everywhere, most noticeably a great many dead French soldiers. On a hill near Flers all three batteries came into action and we fought on until, with evening, the light began to fade. In the course of this action 1st Battery engaged an enemy squadron near Warlencourt in the flank and forced it to turn and flee. In contrast to the earlier situation, the enemy cavalry was more active. After repeated changes of firing positions near Le Sars and Martinpuich, we arrived in bivouac in Le Transloy towards 10.00 pm. Due to the fires the village was brightly lit. 600 men had been buried in the course of the day in the churchyard that we passed and there were still piles of unburied dead lying all around..."

With I & II Bavarian Corps fully engaged, it was now time for the Reserve XIV Corps to enter the fray. These were the men of the 26th and 28th Reserve Infantry Divisions from Württemberg and Baden respectively, whose military prowess was to prove such a thorn in the side of first the French and then the British during the next two years. It entered the battle in the Bapaume area on the 28th September and advanced with the Roman road Bapaume – Albert – Amiens as its axis, aiming to close up on the Ancre and continue the advance westwards.

*Leutnant Koehler 51 Reserve Infantry Brigade*[13]

"The enemy was located either side of the Route Nationale, but their exact locations and strength were unknown. It was certainly assumed that they would offer serious resistance on the outskirts of Bapaume. Our Corps formed the right wing of the Army. It advanced with the 26th Reserve Division north of the road to Bapaume, which was inclusive to it and the 28th Reserve Division, whose advance guard was near Haplincourt, with its main body in assembly areas around Bertincourt, south of the road. The advance guard of our Division was in the area of Beugny and was commanded by Exzellenz [General] von Auwärter, whilst the main body to which we belonged and which was commanded by our General was located, as has already been stated, near Boursies. Army Cavalry Corps I, which had arrived in the area before us, was to provide flank protection to the right...The intention was for Infantry Regiment 180 to attack Lagnicourt, whilst the whole of Reserve Infantry Regiment 121 took up a position behind the right flank at the northern corner of the trees of Louverval. There was good observation from the ridge north of Louverval.

"As far as the eye could see the countryside rolled away in a series of ridges divided by broad folds in the ground. The prosperous countryside, whose fields had not yet been touched by war, stretched out like a multi-coloured carpet out of which rose numerous tree-girt villages. A characteristically fragrant slight haze which hung over all the outlines and colours of the area, giving it a rather gentle, picturesque look, was flooded by the bright light of the morning sun, which shone down out of a cloudless sky. In long, thin lines which quickly disappeared and then some way off reappeared, only to vanish once more, Infantry Regiment 180 climbed out of the hollow so as to launch the attack on Lagnicourt. The artillery took up positions north of Lagnicourt. The brigade staff was located nearby and further north could be seen the staff of the Guards Cavalry Division, whose rear elements were just passing us. No shots were fired; it was almost like an exercise...Our commander had directed a ruthless pursuit in a westerly direction, but when we arrived at the outskirts of Biefvillers the enemy greeted us with hot rifle and machine-gun fire. Soon his artillery joined in.

"The French seemed to be in positions on the hills 1,500 metres west of the village. Infantry Regiment 180 attacked immediately and Reserve Infantry Regiment 121, which had just deployed, received the order from the General to link up as soon as possible to the left with the 180th. It had already begun to get dark. The enemy, which apparently comprised cycle troops and cavalry, once more did not stay to receive the attack. We watched the cavalry mount up, not without engaging them with our machine guns which, despite the range, emptied a few saddles, but it was not possible to force the enemy to halt. Nothing came of the planned pursuit either, because in the meantime orders had arrived from division not to drive further westwards, but to divert south westwards and occupy accommodation in Warlencourt, Le Sars and Martinpuich... The beautiful day was followed by an ideal moonlit night. We moved through gleaming, silvery fields towards houses shining whitely and through the dark shadows of beautiful trees, enfolded, despite general weariness, by the magic of indescribable beauty. To this was added the feeling of a job well done. Despite enemy attempts to halt us, we had advanced more than forty five kilometres this day. The quarters were not brilliant, but the food was really quite good and with the feeling, 'Just a few more days like today and we shall have taken Amiens and be marching on Paris', we laid down to rest just before midnight."

To the south of the Bapaume – Albert road, the 28th Reserve Division was also making good progress. No really serious French resistance was met until the attempt was made to storm Fricourt, but nevertheless there were some set backs, and individual deaths which left their mark on the advancing troops. The 28th September had seen Reserve Infantry Regiment 40 taking the lead for most of the day. Towards evening orders were given out near Mametz for a possible further advance on Fricourt:

*Leutnant P. Müller Reserve Infantry Regiment 40*[14]  **9.**

"The Oberstleutnant had just given me my orders, repeating several times the boundary between the leading battalions, when there was an ear-splitting crash. A shrapnel round had burst just over our heads. Oberstleutnant John von Freyend collapsed, falling to his right. I tried to catch him in my arms and to support him. As he slid down, his helmet remained caught on a twig, then it fell to the ground. Now I could see that the helmet had been pierced by a ball, which had entered his right temple, causing instant death. No word, not a sigh, just a slight grimace and it was all over. Oberstleutnant John von Freyend, our courageous leader in the strenuous and hard fighting in the Vosges, was no more. He had truly kept the word which he had given us when we marched away from Mannheim that he would be the first in the field and the last to his quarters to take his rest. He was a father to all his soldiers and he was deeply mourned by us all."

Despite this blow, the advance resumed on 29th September and for the first time both sides clashed over Fricourt.

*Oberleutnant Gutsch Reserve Infantry Regiment 40*[15]  **10.**

"Major Käther and I raced breathlessly after the line of advancing troops.  Having crossed the hollow, we looked back to see one of the battalion commanders and his adjutant also running down into the hollow.  Suddenly a shell burst right in front of the two running men and covered them in a black cloud of smoke, debris and fragments.  We thought that we had lost this battalion staff as well, but both officers emerged unhurt from the cloud, running towards us, whilst the enemy continued to bring down shells into the hollow.  We were pleased that we had left the wood edge when we did, because the enemy began to bring it under heavy artillery fire.  We were now lying in the support line, just behind a slight crest, from which we could raise ourselves to observe forward.  We were not spared artillery fire here either.  It was brought down accurately on our line.  The fifth man to my right was hit in the head by a dud shell.  Without a sound a brave man of the 40th died a hero's death, with a shell sticking in his head...In Fricourt itself there was heavy enemy fire.  Several houses went up in flames, lighting up the area during the night.  As darkness fell, the regimental staff went forward to Fricourt so as to be able to direct the battle better.  We met up with the brigade staff in the chateau.  Fricourt, in flames, with bullets flying around and our men drawn up in defensive positions for the night, presented a weirdly beautiful aspect.  We felt ourselves to be victors.  We had once more advanced several kilometres, despite heavy enemy counter fire.  We were all filled with the hope that in the coming days we should be advancing to further victories.  Things were to turn out differently."

North of the road it was another early start for the men of 26th Reserve Infantry Division.  They had so far endured less hard fighting than their comrades to the south, but they too were finally halted by increasing French resistance.

*Leutnant Koehler 51 Reserve Infantry Brigade*[16]  **11.**

"51 Reserve Infantry Brigade, in accordance with the divisional order, was to be at the disposal of the division east of Courcelette and north of Martinpuich by 6.00 am and by daybreak was to have occupied Thiepval with one battalion.  This occupation was carried out initially by 2nd Battalion Reserve Infantry Regiment 121 commanded by Major Bürger.  He had been ordered to occupy crossings over the Ancre and on the far side of the Ancre to reconnoitre forward to the line Hamel – Mesnil – Aveluy Wood.  The first part of this task was accomplished without difficulty.  The French did not defend Thiepval, but on the other hand they had constructed fortifications in Thiepval Wood and the Ancre crossings proved to be blocked by barbed wire and various other obstacles.  It was not possible, therefore, for patrols to push on over the Ancre...As we entered Thiepval the population of just about 200 was in a state of understandable panic.  A number of anxious women were assembled in the priest's house.  The first of our troops who had entered Thiepval in the morning had taken their men away and from the cries that met us, a bloodbath amongst these civilian captives was the very least that the women were expecting. They were very relieved to discover that their menfolk were fit and well in the village church. In general, the population was fearful rather than hostile. They hoped, as did we, that their village would soon be outside the battle area and the youthful priest even gave us some good information about the ground in the Ancre Valley.

"Up to this point everything had gone to plan. Further operations, however, turned out to be rather difficult. When 8th Company Infantry Regiment 180 attempted to advance on Authuille, it came up against such strong resistance that it was forced to halt about a kilometre southwest of Thiepval and our General, who was moving with the commander of 52 Brigade along the road to Authuille in order to have a better view of the ground, came under heavy shrapnel fire from the direction of Mesnil. Fortunately the French artillery concentrated its efforts shortly afterwards on a herd of cows grazing nearby. They must have been amazed by the steadfastness of these troops!

"Every one of us who was in the park and château of Thiepval on this day will always have pleasant, somewhat nostalgic, memories of this property. In the excellently maintained park, dotted with magnificent trees, which was entered via great wrought iron gates, the château rose behind a broad expanse of lawn. It was not especially large or imposing, but it was very pleasing. Its interior bore witness to the best of French taste and refined elegance. The beautiful library, whose desk the owner seemed only just to have left, the roomy dining room with its wood carvings, its massive fireplace, the comfortable furniture and its magnificent carpet, the clean domestic rooms and airy bedrooms – all pointed to a noble enjoyment of life. The brigade staff and some officers of the 180th were sitting around the round table of the dining room, whilst a warming fire crackled in the grate, when suddenly a Prussian cavalry brigade entered Thiepval. A really pleasant evening developed with comrades who were, however, somewhat astounded to be suddenly so close to the enemy; they had assumed that the enemy was located further to the west.

"The poetry of this wartime evening was abruptly interrupted. A Vizewachtmeister, who was to have reconnoitred the Ancre crossings, entered excitedly with the news that the French, advancing from the direction of Hamel, were already on this side of the Ancre in considerable strength. Oberstleutnant Fromm, commander of 3rd Battalion Infantry Regiment 180, which together with the 9th and 11th Companies had returned to Brigade as evening approached, received from our General the order to take his men and drive the advancing enemy back. The companies disappeared into the night and all was quiet. After the long

day we attempted to get some sleep.  Suddenly between about 2.00 am
and 3.00 am, general alert!  Wild small arms fire rattled in Thiepval
Wood.  The rifle bullets cracked against the walls of the houses. An
Unteroffizier who had taken part in the operation returned and related
that the two companies had been captured and that the enemy were very
numerous.  This was unpleasant news for the cavalry, who rapidly
withdrew, leaving the commander, at his request, their machine guns.
Everything was prepared for defence; we awaited the enemy. Instead of
them Oberstleutnant Fromm with his two companies returned safe and
sound.  The French had in fact surrounded him and wanted to take his
party prisoner as they approached the Ancre bridges.  However he
answered their demand for his surrender with a determined 'Jamais!'
[Never!] and, despite overwhelming fire from various directions, had
brought himself and his companies back with only slight casualties."
The following day there was extremely heavy fighting in and around Fricourt.  By
the end of the day, the village and its surrounding ground of tactical importance
had been subject to several French counter attacks and all the units of 28th Reserve
Infantry Division were hanging on grimly.  Included amongst them was Reserve
Jäger Battalion 8.  These Jäger units were manned by countrymen, foresters and
hunters, all of whom had highly developed fieldcraft and shooting skills.  They
were specially trained to accompany cavalry, but were also used as normal
infantry, where their élite nature meant that they generally performed to an
extremely high standard.  Here around Fricourt they were tested to the limit.

*Oberjäger Balfranz Reserve Jäger Battalion 8*[17] **10.**

"On the 30th September the commander received the order to defend
the position to the last man...This was done and  despite the heavy fire
throughout the night nearly every man had produced a shell scrape as
protection against fire.  As far as possible, and despite the unfavourable
chalky soil, this work was continued.  About 9.00 am Oberjäger Probst
approached my cover, both hands pressed against his left side.  At this
point he sank to his knees.  Remaining under cover, I shouted to him to get
himself into cover as soon as possible, because the whole area was being
swept by fire. 'Just a minute!' he said, 'I can't go on!' Hardly had he laid
down when an enemy bullet smashed both his knees.  Despite the fire I
leapt forward to drag him into my scrape, but with the last of his strength,
he resisted, saying, 'Leave me here. I've had it. Save yourself and go back!'
A bullet passed through my jacket and ammunition pouch and I jumped
back in my hole.  I tied my handkerchief to my bayonet and dashed
forward, waving this at the enemy.  Amazingly I was not shot at.  He said
to me, 'Give my best wishes to my father in Brodenach in the Moselle
Valley, to Leutnant Müller and the rest of the company!'  He reached out
and shook my hand; his face was already that of a corpse and I jumped

back in my scrape once more. As I later discovered, Leutnant Müller had already been dead for an hour. Occasionally I heard Oberjäger Probst cry out once more, apparently because he was being hit again. A viciously heavy fire fight cut off all contact with him.

"Only once it went dark was I able to make contact with him once more. He was dead. He had pulled down his chinstrap and pushed his head deep inside his shako. Even in death he seemed to want to minimise the appalling picture he presented...Towards 3.00 pm, whilst observing the enemy position 900 metres away through a telescope, I saw an enemy infantryman stand bolt upright and climb out of the trench. He must have thought that we could not reach him at that range. I handed the telescope to my number two to carry on observing, then I took aim and fired. My comrade reported a hit. I assumed that the man was seriously wounded and requested my platoon commander to forbid further firing at the wounded man. After about two minutes the wounded Frenchman had worked his way up onto the parapet of the trench, whence he could be pulled down into it.

"Towards 5.00 pm my platoon commander, Feldwebel Kiel, was hit in the back by a ricochet. Several times he demanded that I finish him off. 'A bullet, just give me a bullet!' I dashed over to him to bandage him up, but it was impossible to join him in the tiny scrape. When it went dark, he was recovered by the stretcher bearers. Despite having a hole the size of a fist in his back and his lung laid bare, he was fully recovered after six weeks. About 5.30 pm my section commander, Hamann, was seriously wounded and, at the request of the others, I assumed command. A little later my close, unique friend and pal, Gefreiter Werkle from Ottweiler, was seriously wounded in the head. I bandaged him hastily. As he breathed the blood ran down into his air passages and he gave out a death rattle. I gave up all hope for him and went back in my hole."

Gradually night fell on the battlefield around Fricourt, the firing fell away and thoughts turned to feeding the inner man. The intensity of the battle and speed of movement of the past few days had generally disrupted the normal smooth working of rationing and replenishment of the rifle companies, but they were filled with men of resource.

*Radfahrer Wilhelm Klein 5th Coy Reserve Infantry Regiment 111*[18] **10.**

"We had spent the first night in our initial trenches near Fricourt. There had been no rations because our field kitchens had not found us. It was the same the next day. I was with the left flank group of the Company about 500 metres from the south western corner of the village. My bike was lying behind the trench. I had a packet of cocoa, ground coffee and sugar on my luggage carrier. Towards evening I said to my mates: 'How about brewing up some coffee? – but somebody will have to fetch water and wood.' I was not able to leave because at any moment I might be sent for by the company commander to carry a report. Wehrmann Stehle offered to go and find the necessary items and disappeared. Soon he returned heavy laden with a milk churn of water, two saucepans, a can of petrol and cotton waste. Soon a chimney-like shaft appeared on the rear wall of the trench and a saucepan was stuffed with cotton waste, which was soaked with petrol. Two bayonets were laid on it and a saucepan of water on top of that. Between us and the enemy we had hung a groundsheet so that the French could not see the light of the fire. The whole section waited intently for the coffee to be ready. The water was coming up to the boil and I had just scattered coffee in the water when a voice called quietly, 'Is that a fire down there? – Put it out at once.' It was our company commander, Leutnant Eisenlohr, who was visiting the trenches during the twilight. I replied, 'I'm brewing coffee, sir.' Reply: 'Put the fire out at once, the enemy will see it.' In the twilight the company commander could see neither the groundsheet, nor the fact that the enemy could not see it, so I did not carry out the order immediately, but replied. 'Sir, the coffee is nearly brewed!' 'Fire out immediately', he ordered again. I hung on until the coffee boiled properly. In the meantime the company commander arrived to stamp out the fire with his boot. Just in the nick of time, I whipped the saucepan away as his boot came down and extinguished the fire. The coffee was saved and the ticking off we received was worth it, because we had some excellent coffee with plenty of sugar. The following night the field kitchens arrived in Fricourt and we could go and fetch warm food. During 1915 the company field kitchen was established in a cellar a hundred metres from company HQ, so we could even go and fetch food during the day until, during the Battle of the Somme, the British shot everything to bits."

Already by the beginning of October the front-line positions were starting to solidify as men dug and held where their advance had been checked. These initial scrapes and trenches were rarely optimally placed and casualties continued to mount among the front line forces.

*Oberjäger Balfranz Reserve Jäger Battalion 8*[19] **10.**

   "Between 5.00 and 6.00 am on 1st October I was on sentry duty, when suddenly out of the mist to our front I saw a line of enemy moving past us, parallel to our position. I quietly raised the alarm and we were soon ready to fire. At the agreed signal the first shots were fired and this led to a dreadful exchange of small arms fire. A little while later we received reinforcements from Reserve Infantry Regiment 111 and two replacements arrived in my section. I placed them in the trench of some men who had been wounded. One, a short man with a goatee beard, was shot dead through the head a few moments later. We had had no warm food for three days. In a quiet moment I climbed out of my hole and, gathering knapsacks and weapons, piled them around my trench for flank protection. During the day the food in these knapsacks stood me in good stead. In the knapsack of the soldier who had been killed that morning I found, amongst other things, a letter from his wife in Burladingen (Hohenzollern) in which she wrote that he was to be of good courage because she and their little one went to church every morning to pray for his safe return."

Five kilometres away at Maricourt, where all attempts to take the village had been thwarted by a dogged French defence, the regimental commander of Bavarian Infantry Regiment 22 was having to face up to some bitter truths.

*Oberst Otto Schulz Bavarian Infantry Regiment 22*[20] **7.**

"Much of the self confidence and moral strength engendered by the battles in Lorraine (19th and 20th August) which were brilliantly carried out by the troops were squandered pointlessly [during the battle for Maricourt]...The deficiencies of the railway line Metz-Luxemburg forced a halt of several days in Metz. Through energetic attention to administration and tough training exercises the regimental commanders of the 3rd Infantry Division succeeded in restoring discipline and efficiency amongst their troops. As a result the troops carried out the forced marches after the rail journey to Picardy with few falling out.

"But the enemy had changed too. The battles in Lorraine had given our troops a feeling of superiority. They received an extremely rude shock when they had to accept near Maricourt that the French, even though they were from the same corps that we had brushed aside in Lorraine, had changed. They were tough, daring and self-confident. The Miracle of the Marne had so raised the morale of the French that the order to withdraw must be regarded as a crime against all things German. Against such an opponent, ill prepared, uncoordinated and over-hasty minor attacks were dashed to pieces around Maricourt. They even led in the case of individual units, for example my 2nd Battalion, which was subordinated to Bavarian Infantry Regiment 18, to unexpected setbacks, whilst further strengthening the self confidence of the enemy.

"The piecemeal throwing in of troops damaged their efficiency considerably. As a result the only successes in the Battle of the Somme 1914, which involved the taking of ground, were the capture of Hardecourt by the 18th Bavarian Infantry Regiment (under Weiss-Jonak), the conquest after heavy fighting of Trônes Wood, Bernafay Wood and Montauban Wood by my detachment and the capture of Curlu by my re-united 22nd [Bavarian] Infantry Regiment on 1st October. We were agreeably pleased that the divisional commander effectively absented himself entirely from the battles of the 1st October, leaving the higher

direction to Generalleutnant von Claus, who had made himself fully
conversant with the situation..."

The situation was little brighter where the Württemberg regiments, overlooking
the Ancre, were engaged in hard fighting for the heights and the woods leading
down to the river. Far from rolling up the French with their right flank in the air,
they were in increasing danger of being outflanked themselves.

*Leutnant Koehler 51 Reserve Infantry Brigade*[21]

"It cannot be said that we were particularly encouraged by the situation
in which we found ourselves. We felt that we were well placed to handle
a French attack, but it was not without concern that we observed how the
envelopment of our right flank made constant progress. Every day we
could tell from the roar of the guns and the clouds of the bursting artillery
shells that the French had pushed further forward. Finally we observed
them far to our right rear, approximately in the area of Sapignies.
Trusting in our Army High Command as we did, we were convinced that
they would soon be drawing the short straw, but still a load fell from our
shoulders when the following message suddenly arrived: 'At 12.00 am on
the 2nd October the Guards Corps will arrive in Bapaume from the south
and will then advance on the right of XIV Corps'. With watches in our
hands we awaited the approach of the happy hour. Day by day we
observed with pleasure how the points of impact crept backwards and so
we were able to monitor the progress of the Guards. We derived the same
pleasurable fulfilment of expectations from the Prussian thrusts as we
had from our own advance. Nobody doubted that as soon as the Guards
had drawn level with us our attack would be resumed. As is well known,
we were unfortunately deceiving ourselves."

Although it was becoming clear that there was no easy or simple way of continuing
to advance westwards, all along the line local attacks continued to rage. Down in
the southern sector, Infantry Regiment 17 was involved in an extremely costly
attempt to take Maucourt, south west of Chaulnes, on the 7th October. All the
companies were launched in the direction of the village, but it was soon clear to
Oberstleutnant Randebock, Commanding Officer of 3rd Battalion Infantry
Regiment 17, that things were not going according to plan. To the left, Infantry
Regiment 131 also made no progress. At 3.00 pm the final reserve, two companies
of Infantry Regiment 97 and a sabre squadron of Dragoon Regiment 7, was
deployed. It made no difference. When it went dark the survivors were ordered
back to the start line and the moon rose on the battlefield, lighting up the bodies
of the dead and the tireless work of the stretcher bearers and medical orderlies.

*Oberstleutnant Randebock 3rd Battalion Infantry Regiment 17*[22] **12.**

"From the front, Reserve Leutnant Thamm came running. He had been
hit in the neck by a shrapnel ball and was bleeding profusely. Then from

all sides reports reached me: Hauptmann Wilde dead, Leutnant Holtey seriously wounded, Hauptmann Wittich dead, Reserve Leutnant Zacher seriously wounded, Feldwebel Seiler wounded etc. There was not a single officer left in the firing line; hardly a man was still firing...[When it was dark] I went forward across the battlefield, right up to the furthest point where the men had fallen. They were lying so close, they almost touched. In one place I counted thirty in a row. Almost all had been killed by head wounds. In their midst lay Hauptmann Wilde, his Pickelhaube next to him. There was an entry wound in the centre of his forehead, a small dark mark, surrounded by three or four spots of blood. I tore off a sugar beet leaf and wiped the blood away. Now he lay peacefully, just as he had lain so often near me in bivouac. Some of the men brought his body back.

"In the garden of the notary I selected a beautiful spot beneath a lime tree. Here his grave was dug. His batman, who had been lying behind him, explained to me that Wilde had seized the weapon of a wounded man and pushed on with the attack. That was when he was shot and killed. He must have died immediately, because his arms were still bent as though he was holding a rifle. I removed the Iron Cross from his body. I had personally presented it to him only two days earlier. Then he had been red with embarrassment, saying that he had still done nothing to deserve it. He really was a great man. In accordance with the old soldier's custom, the men had prepared a cross with the inscription: 'To their beloved and courageous Hauptmann – 11th Company, Infantry Regiment 17.' This they had placed on his grave and hung his Pickelhaube from it.

"When all had left the scene, I stayed behind and stood for a while by the grave, deep in thought. Then I too turned to go. At the point where the path curved away, I turned round once more and was confronted by a magical scene, as though from a fairy tale. The grave lay in the shadow of some low bushes and nothing could be seen either of the cross or the Pickelhaube itself. The eagle on it, which glistened and gleamed in the moonlight, seemed to be hovering in the air, enfolding this hero's grave beneath its protective wings, whilst its gilded spike, pointing towards the star-studded heavens, glowed and blazed as though it was lighting the way for the ascending soul of the warrior who was at rest beneath it."

With the fighting still mired around Fricourt, it was decided to adopt the somewhat desperate expedient of launching a silent night attack against Bécourt during the evening of the 7th October, with a view to breaking through towards Albert. There had been no artillery preparation and no opportunity for prior reconnaissance by the participating troops. It was a disaster waiting to happen and things began to go wrong from the start.

*Leutnant Bohl 1st Company Reserve Infantry Regiment 40* [23] **13.**

"The 1st Battalion deployed at 9.30 pm ready for the attack. The colours were uncased in the centre of the line. The battalion, commanded by Hauptmann von Schmidt, formed the left wing of the detachment, on the left flank of that was 1st Company, under Oberleutnant Morlock. We set off in a pitch black night, pushing forward silently over stubble fields, ever onwards, ever more expectantly, when suddenly we were challenged in German by a patrol and finally established that instead of approaching Bécourt, we were in front of La Boisselle, which was already occupied by a battalion of Württemberg Regiment 120. So we had either been set off in the wrong direction, or we had lost our ordered heading in the dark. The battalion was reorganised, re-launched immediately and this time, with stretched nerves, we correctly approached the wood which lay behind Bécourt.

"When we were about 400 – 500metres from the edge of the wood, which was looming out of the dark, we suddenly came under a great weight of fire from our left flank. The commander of 1st Company ordered us to incline left and in double time we set off for the enemy firing at us from the flank. The sudden move to the left meant that part of my platoon lost contact and continued towards Bécourt with the rest of the battalion. The part which had gone left advanced to a slope, where the French had occupied some already dug trenches and were firing like madmen, at the cost of some casualties. In the meantime the battalion had entered the wood to our front, but the situation was unclear to us. The 1st Company was pinned down by the enemy and because of the heavy fire could neither advance through it nor withdraw from the slope. At this point the battalion commander, Hauptmann von Schmidt, arrived at the 1st Company, directed that the enemy was to be kept occupied here and ordered me to take one section of my Platoon along the open flank of the company as far as Bécourt Wood in order to establish what was happening.

"In the continuing heavy shooting it was naturally impossible for orders to be heard, so I just pulled the first eight men of my right flank back down the slope by their legs. Two of them rolled back lifelessly. I headed off with six men and arrived unscathed at the edge of the well-known Bécourt Wood where, remarkably, everything was as quiet as the grave. The edge of the wood, which was enclosed by an impenetrable hedge, was unoccupied. We forced a way through and I deployed my six men in a hasty position near the gap in a rough position which had been prepared by the French and was equipped with plentiful rifle and machine-gun ammunition. Of the machine guns, only a few stands remained. I made my way along the hedge to the tip of the wood to observe and to await events. Suddenly I heard voices coming towards me from the direction of Bécourt. Luckily they were on the other side of the hedge. It was three Frenchmen, apparently officers, and I, standing immobile in the tip of my wood, was only hidden from them by the hedge. They spoke animatedly about the immediate re-occupation of the position and disappeared once more in different directions. I soon noticed that French infantry had crept into position and were occupying the slope in extension of the position occupied by 1st Company, which was still engaged in a fire fight about 500 metres away.

"It now seemed to me appropriate to withdraw my patrol with all speed from its position. This decision was given further urgency when suddenly we heard activity to our rear from approximately the direction of the wood park. The French were advancing noisily into the wood, doubtless with the aim of re-occupying the wood edge. Had the attack on Bécourt failed therefore? Running like the devil we headed out from the hedge and the wood. We too were spotted and, running as hard as we could towards the company, we were driven on like hares by fire from the rear and flank. Nevertheless all seven of us got through in one piece back to the company, even though we had had take to avoiding action at the precise moment when the battalion commander decided to withdraw the 1st Company from the slope and cost what it may to get it to follow the 1st Battalion to Bécourt.

"I gave a report on the situation, stating that the only chance of avoiding enemy cross fire from the French, who were occupying both the slope and the wood edge, which were at right angles to one another, was to proceed in a wide arc. In view of this Hauptmann Schmidt ordered our company commander to withdraw the men individually from the slope, which was still under fire, to the next reachable cover and there to await further orders...The disengagement of the 1st Company from the enemy was carried out as ordered about 3.00 am. Due to the darkness and in the fog of the early morning many men got lost. When I myself, with a few of my own men, arrived in the first available cover, it was already occupied by men of other companies and regiments who had got split up one way or another during the course of the fighting in the wood, or who had become disorientated and lost their way whilst crawling backwards and forwards in the wood until finally they had no idea about who was shooting at them..."

About 400 German soldiers were captured as a result of this farce. It effectively spelt the end of mobile operations in this area. In order to avoid having their colours fall into the hands of the enemy, the standard bearers of Reserve Infantry Regiment 111 buried them. As a result of this a divisional order was issued banning the carrying of colours during night attacks. Extraordinarily enough, given the heavy fighting in this area during subsequent years, the colours of the 111th were found after the war by German prisoners of war engaged on battlefield clearance. Casualties at this time were by no means confined to the infantry units. The French army was already making use of its heavy guns in a harassing and counter-battery role and this led to an incident which dealt 1st Battalion of Bavarian Field Artillery Regiment 11 a heavy blow. The final round of an enemy half hour retaliatory bombardment on the observation post at the windmill at Montauban was a direct hit, which blew off the roof and buried the occupants. Although Major Friedl escaped with minor bruising to the chest and shock and his Adjutant, Leutnant von Stubenrauch, escaped unhurt, the commander of 1st Battery, Oberleutnant Grodhaus, and the observation post NCO, Unteroffizier Fischer, were both dead when they were removed from the rubble.

*Oberleutnant Gruber Bavarian Field Artillery Regiment 11*[24] **14.**

"During the evening of the following day, good old Grodhaus and Unteroffizier Fischer were buried in Longueval churchyard. It was a peculiar business. Almost all the officers of the regiment were crowded around in front of the two open graves. The scene was lit by stable lanterns and two votive candles from the church. The moon rose, then there was a roar of guns, because almost simultaneously I Corps launched an attack. It was a soldier's death, a soldier's fate. In death as in life the two brave comrades lay alongside one another, just as they had been observing the enemy together only a few hours previously. The regimental commander gave a moving graveside oration. Leutnant von Stubenrauch, who had so narrowly escaped death, wrote in his diary, 'I wonder who will be next?'"

Further to the north, the Guards had succeeded in pressing the French line back and were engaged in digging in around the Gommecourt-Hebuterne area, where they were to spend several weeks in minor line-straightening operations with the French.

*Oberleutnant von Stoesel 2nd Battalion Grenadier Guard Regiment 3*[25] **15.**

"During the night 7-8th October 1914, the 2nd Company was occupying trenches near Gommecourt. A building, Maison Pilier, lay between the trench lines, about 180 metres in front of ours and 120 metres from the French. We maintained an advanced position in the house and this duty was taken over at 12.30 am by Unteroffizier Hirschberg and twelve men of the 2nd Company. The following morning the French brought down artillery fire against the house from 10.00 am to 12.30 pm, then launched a thirty to forty man attack against it. Unteroffizier Hirschberg and his twelve men beat this off. The house came under further fire with high explosive and shrapnel. At about 1.30 pm there was a further attack by about two sections. Unteroffizier Hirschberg drove this attack off as well. The French artillery opened up yet again and this lasted until 3.15 pm.

"This firing brought down the gable end of the house and collapsed the stairs, so that the advance post was trapped temporarily in the cellar. There was no communication between the German trenches and the house so it was not possible to send forward reinforcements or to replenish ammunition. By now the advance post had shot off most of its ammunition. Then about 4.30 pm the French launched a fresh attack against the house with about forty men. Hirschberg allowed the French to get to about fifty metres, then ordered fire to be opened and shot the French officer dead himself. Once again the attack was beaten off. The French brought artillery fire down on the house once more and despatched a patrol to the house at around 9.30 pm. As the NCO commander of this patrol approached the house, he was stabbed to death by Gefreiter Zillich. During the night Unteroffizier Hirschberg was relieved. Maison Pilier was later abandoned by our troops and shot to ruins."

With ambushes and surprise attacks the order of the day, it was inevitable that mistakes and peculiar incidents would occur. The diarist of the Queen Elisabeth Grenadier Guard Regiment Nr 3 recorded one such on the 9th October at Gommecourt.

"At 6.00 am a furious fire fight broke out. First it was confined to the infantry then the artillery joined in. Bullets cracked around the village in all directions and in between shrapnel shells burst. Everyone thought that the French were attacking! The alarm was raised everywhere. A little while later the fire died away. Rather later it transpired that a sentry had mistaken a number of cows which were grazing between the lines for an enemy patrol and had opened fire on them. Naturally the fire was taken up by the neighbouring section. The French, feeling nervous, assumed that a German attack was on the way and opened fire all along the line, so a few cows had caused, 'active operations on the Western Front'." [26]

Such incidents caused little harm generally, but the same could not be said of an unfortunate event the following week near Bucquoy on the 14th October.

*Leutnant von Breska 11th Company Grenadier Guard Regiment 3*[27]   **16.**

"Having had a sleep during the afternoon, we were sitting over a cup of coffee about 5 pm. The French artillery fire, which for days had not landed on Louvière Farm, drew closer. Suddenly a shell landed in a stable in which a platoon was resting. The circumstances were as unfavourable as possible. The shell went through a small window and burst inside. Result: nine killed and fifteen wounded, including naturally some of the best men. We had not yet realised what had happened, when suddenly a shell landed in the hall outside the room where we were drinking coffee. We were luckier. The shell exploded as it hit the roof. The fragments penetrated the roof, the floor and came sideways through our door. Fähnrich von Francois, who was sitting next to me, received a small

splinter in the ball of his foot.  We jumped up from the table and headed
for the door, but were hit by a cloud of dust and fragments of chalk.  There
was an awful smell.  As soon as things cleared we went outside and moved
the men into better protected places.  I then took cover in a dugout with
Hauptmann von Berg.  After the first excitement had died down and once
we were convinced that the next shell was not going to be directed at the
farm, we looked after the wounded.  Unfortunately some were rather
badly hurt.  Fusilier Pierre, who had already received the Iron Cross, died
during the evening.  Anyway we bandaged everyone up and moved them
into safe accommodation.  A cyclist summoned doctors and wagons – the
telephone had been destroyed – and within a few hours we got everyone
away."

As the battle lines settled down, supply difficulties meant that foraging and
improvisation was essential until the hold-ups in the supply chain could be
rectified.  Human nature being what it is the system was not always as well
controlled as it might have been.  Naturally it was not only the troops who had it
hard.  The harvest had been disrupted, there had been widespread requisitioning or
seizures of food supplies and many animals had been killed or slaughtered for the
invading armies.  As a result the local population also went hungry at times.

*Major von Fahland Field Artillery Regiment 15*[28] **2.**

   "One day in Hallu a large store of eggs was discovered.  There were said
   to be 100,000.  They were concealed beneath straw and when this was
   used up, they came to light one day.  Initially it was a wasteful free-for-all;
   gunners were seen carrying them off in their helmets.  When there were
   very few eggs left, a guard was finally posted on them.  We at least had
   superb egg-based meals for a considerable time.  From time to time there
   was a shortage of oats.  The batteries were forced to do their own
   threshing.  Threshing machines which we came across were pressed into
   service and taken with us whenever we changed location."

*Hauptmann Wagner Field Artillery Regiment 15*[29] **2.**

   "The road to Hallu was paved with golden egg yolks!  The first time that
   the midday meal was issued, a large number of local women appeared
   with their children.  We handed out food to these hungry souls as long as
   the supplies lasted... in order to elicit our sympathy the children were
   ostentatiously and constantly pushed to the front, but because there were
   too few of these little mites, they were passed on at each corner and used
   by the neighbours to beg for food.  It was a case of pass the parcel."

With the weather deteriorating as the autumn progressed, the provision of
adequate supplies of food and drink to maintain the health and morale of the men

holding out in the exposed forward positions became a major preoccupation for regimental officers.

*Hauptmann Dittmann  3rd Company Reserve Infantry Regiment 111*[30] **10.**

"When in October 1914 the nights began to get cold and the food also arrived on the position cold and covered in a thick layer of fat, I requested over the telephone that we be sent red wine or schnaps to ward off the risk of diarrhoea.  There was no easy way of heating food on the position, because fires were banned in case they attracted the attention of the enemy.  Anyway the following night the ration party arrived with several bottles.  The contents were divided up evenly and I shared a bottle with my telephonist.  When we were relieved after three weeks' hard fighting, we found out that we had been drinking the pure alcohol intended for heating food.  The supply officer, Leutnant Essig, said to me:  'We all noticed that only the 3rd Company was drinking the stove alcohol, rather than heating the food with it!'"

It is not clear if the men of the Elisabeth Regiment [Grenadier Guard Regiment 3] resorted to the same expedient, but such were the conditions in the northern section of the battlefield that they might have been forgiven for doing so.

*Leutnant von Breska 11th Company Grenadier Guard Regiment 3*[31] **15.**

"The night down by the wire obstacle was frightful.  The trench was half full of water, so I let some of the men lie down on straw behind it.  Where the trench was in a better condition everyone lay down in it once straw had been laid down and this kept them out of the wind at least. Next morning the straw was soaked right through.  Some of the men had to keep watch, some had a protective role and others patrolled hourly to maintain contact with the Alexander Regiment [Grenadier Guard Regiment 1] near Gommecourt and the 2nd Foot Guards on Hill 125.  I checked from time to time, but was satisfied that we were really alert.  The fact that I was personally sharing all the misery of the night seemed to increase everybody's resistance considerably.  I regularly received replies to my questions, such as, 'Well Herr Leutnant that's the way it has to be. This is war', or, 'Having stood it for three nights, we can manage these few hours as well'.  Towards dawn, two recruits reported sick and I sent them down to the farm.  The others stuck it out well.  For hours I wandered along in the teeming rain on the soggy ground behind the trench, but luckily the tracks formed by the patrols were well trodden.  When I finally took a rest my coat and equipment were so saturated that I could only take a break in a kneeling position, like a dog on all fours."

Not everyone had it so bad and at this stage of the war the artillery units, in particular, were often fortunate enough to find themselves good and comfortable billets.

*Hauptmann Wagner Field Artillery Regiment 15[32]* **17.**

"The observation binoculars were mounted in the crown of a willow tree. To our front and surrounded by trees and orchards lay hotly disputed Lihons and the nearby Lihu Farm. Behind the observation post, in the sunken road with its slippery carpet of rotting fruit and brown leaves, the Bavarians left us a dugout which they had built. It was cut back into the embankment. It was roofed and to the rear it was equipped with a door and a window. The men from Munich had also donated its furnishings – chair, table, crockery and pictures. They had only taken 'their' stove with them. To the left of this cave led the way to the Brandenburg Landsturm battery. I cannot remember if they were still wearing blue uniforms...To the right and through a rustling field of sugar beet was the brilliantly constructed and camouflaged battery position. Behind this again, shaded by its poplar trees, was Bovent Farm, looking for all the world like a painting by a Dutch master. There in the clean, tiled living room, we officers spent the nights amongst friendly people and developed a taste for cider.

"Further north the Bavarians were still holding the line and so each day a smartly uniformed mounted postman came past and collected our mail from us. Along the front all was still. Only in the evening might we hear two distant drumbeats. This would be followed by the weak sound of two shells descending from the heavens on their way to their intended target of Ablaincourt, but often they fell as duds, short. Every night one platoon was told off for digging duties in the park at Vermandovillers. Our courageous medical sergeant used to go along too in order to be able to tend them. Because he never had anything to do, he used to risk taking a 'front line' nap. When he awoke one morning, he found to his considerable shock that a dud had landed between his legs. It was only somewhat later that he discovered that the sneaky gunners had put it there!"

One problem which manifested itself early was that of battlefield hygiene. Already the intensity of the initial battles and the near impossibility of moving freely in No Man's Land meant that unusual expedients had to be resorted to in order to deal with the thousands of unburied bodies which littered the battlefield. Sometimes, as in the Hill 110 area south of Fricourt, this had unforeseen consequences.

*Vizefeldwebel Behringer 3rd Company Reserve Infantry Regiment 111[33]* **10.**

"During October 1914, it was not possible for us to recover for all the bodies of our comrades that lay between the two positions. It all took time. In order to reduce the risk of infection, all the corpses that were strewn around were covered with chloride of lime. A medical detachment arrived one night to carry out this duty in front of our thick barbed wire obstacle, (which at that time consisted of a trip wire!). Conscientiously all the bodies received a goodly portion.

"But dear oh dear! One of our patrols was lying silently out in No Man's Land observing. The medical personnel came across them and prepared to give them a good sprinkling too. The first member of the patrol to have powder poured on him bawled, 'Pack it in you clot, or you'll get the butt of my rifle in your crotch!' As a result of this friendly greeting a fire fight broke out, but we had no casualties."

As the autumn wore on the German army became ever more cunning in its ability to scrounge and scavenge. It was often said that it was easy to tell where an infantry company had been in billet or bivouac from the number of empty bottles they left behind. This was certainly true of the men of Reserve Infantry Regiment 40, who made a significant discovery in early November.

### *Leutnant Bohl 1st Company Reserve Infantry Regiment 40*[34] 18.

"1st Company arrived in Montauban on the 5th November. I, together with the 1st Platoon which I was to lead until May 1915, occupied what allegedly had previously been a large lumber store. I had stressed heavily to my platoon the need to maintain very high standards of discipline, because Divisional Orders had directed that the civil occupants of our billets, 'were to be treated with every courtesy'. Apparently the owner of this particular building, though innocent of any crime, had recently been shot by the Germans. I became aware that the locals were furtively, but actively, entering and leaving our billet by its rear entrance, but I took little notice, because we were due to move forward onto our position as it went dark. However, my 1st Platoon was rather more attentive! They followed their instincts. If this was meant to be a disused lumber store, how come there was a constant stream of French people carrying baskets and bags in and out of it? Wherever the vultures gather, there must be a carcase! So it proved when the platoon started to sniff around.

"When, about one and a half hours before we were due to depart, I returned to our quarters I was greeted by my 'sentry', who stood there with cheeks glowing red and slurred in my ear, 'We've found a wine cellar. Your water bottle's already filled with champagne.' From the cellar of the house to our storeroom, the entire platoon was sitting lined up on the stairs and across the floor. Just like builders passing bricks, the full bottles flew silently from hand to hand from the hole punched in the cellar wall direct into knapsacks or to be poured into water bottles and thirsty throats. Along with wine, cognac and champagne a uniform suddenly appeared from the cellar. I recognised immediately that it was that of a fireman and thus harmless, but I called for it to be sent over to me.

"In the meantime, naturally, the civilians who 'were to be treated with every courtesy' became aware of what was happening to their hoard. They rushed into the house yelling and cursing and finally brought the mayor of Montauban to the scene. He, drawing upon all the authority of his office, attempted to call me to account, but he drew a blank. I addressed the amazed gentleman with a torrent of Parisian gutter slang, rendering him speechless, then before he could gather his wits, I turned on him angrily, telling him that a hidden military uniform and equipment had been found in the cellar and that unless he and all the other inhabitants, 'to whom every courtesy was due', did not mind their Ps and Qs, they would all be arrested summarily. That had the desired effect and, thank heavens, the time for our departure was upon us.

"Had only the 1st Platoon been involved it would still have been possible to say that the 1st Company was present and correct, but news of the find had spread like wildfire, attracting brotherly support. With headgear on at all angles and some reversed, with shining, grinning faces, 1st Company poured out onto the square weaving their way into lines. Their equipment was hung about them any old way and the corks of their water bottles had come adrift due to the running, so that wine, cognac and even champagne was slopping and foaming all over the place. My true and faithful men reported to me that the needs of their platoon commander had been catered for and that two bottles of champagne and a bottle of rum had been placed in the care of the field kitchen for me. What possible objection could I raise against such a selfless action?

"Our company commander, Oberleutant Morlock, cursed and fumed, but never succeeded in creating order out of chaos, so in the end he could do nothing but laugh it off and lead his merry band forward to confront the ferocious foe. The company did not create the impression that they were marching to meet a soldierly fate; rather more that that they were ambling home after an afternoon in the pub. I had a terrible job that night to keep my soldiers awake. One sentry would be finding his eyelids too heavy to keep open, whilst the man next to him would be seeing double. It was in any case always the devil's own job during the period of transition to the unaccustomed trenches, when everyone was seeing ghosts in front of the positions, to maintain a reliable standard of wakefulness and alertness. So I spent the night running guiltily up and down the position, acting as an extra pair of eyes, shaking and pummelling my all-to-peacefully inclined warriors to keep the ever-encroaching sleep at bay. In the end it all turned out well. Out of the sinister black night dawned the grey of a foggy November day. It really was the morning after the night before. That Friday morning, 6th November, the platoon commanders of 1st Company Reserve Infantry Regiment 40 breakfasted on champagne, rather than coffee. The commanders of the 2nd and 3rd Platoons, Brosamer and Krauss – both of whom were unfortunately killed later – were guests at my noble feast and we were not over-concerned with the fact that the French artillery blessed the early morn with a shower of shells. The reports of the guns were just like a slightly livelier version of the sound of champagne corks popping..."

As the days grew shorter in late October and early November, it was already clear that the front-line troops would have to settle in for a lengthy period in their current positions. The early trenches began to develop into local networks on the ground of tactical importance. There were still wide gaps, which could only be covered by fire by day and patrol activity at night, but gradually the front-line was assuming its permanent shape. The French brought up increasing amounts of heavy artillery, the villages were pounded, the buildings smashed and the animals killed or driven away. The local inhabitants, who like all countryfolk, were reluctant to be parted from their farms and land, became an increasing problem. It was impossible to guarantee their safety and nearly as hard for them to obtain supplies of food and drink. In Thiepval the priest and a substantial number of villagers were still there at the end of October. Finally 26th Reserve Division arranged for their evacuation and on the 1st November, thirty-five men, forty-five women and twenty-five children were transported to the rear via Courcelette. The officers and men of Infantry Regiment 180 now had the deserted village to themselves and continued under the watchful eye of Oberstleutnant von Hoff, their third commander of the war, to develop the position. Nothing escaped his gimlet eye. Regimental orders on the 7th November included:

"I forbid the assembly or movement of parties larger than section strength in Thiepval. There must be no marching in step. Talking and words of command are forbidden...Private devotions and services in Thiepval church are forbidden. These are to be held in small groups in dugouts or cellars, or better still in Courcelette after relief...If cooking takes place in houses in Thiepval, care is to be taken that smoke from chimneys cannot be detected at a distance..."[35] **11.**

Three days later a full tour of inspection of the trench system yielded thirteen areas for immediate improvement, which provide an interesting guide as to how far the position was already developed.

"1. Stones and white chalky soil are exposed on parapets and piles of earth, even where these could just as easily be covered with brown earth or turf.

2. In some places communications trenches have not reached a depth of 1.70 metres.

3. All trenches, without exception, are to be lined with bricks. There is sufficient material available for this.

4. In many cases overhead cover of dugouts and machine gun positions is no thicker than a few centimetres.

5. Here and there in the trenches and alcoves there are accumulations of urine and the trenches leading to the latrines are littered with great piles of faeces in places.

6. Many of the trench junctions lack signposts to indicate where the trenches run.

7. In many sectors there is a lack of clarity about inter-subunit boundaries and arcs of fire which will not endanger neighbouring troops.

8. Faltering responses lead to the conclusion that not all soldiers are acquainted with the ranges to reference points to their front.

9. In many cases where shelters have been dug into the walls of the trench just below the parapet and filled with straw, the individual is raised so high that he is insufficiently protected.

10. All advanced listening posts must be linked to the main position by sufficiently deep communication trenches. Barbed wire, chain link fencing, knife rests and similar material must be kept immediately available, so that these trenches are not available to enemy patrols to close up on the position.

11. I recommend that listening posts be linked to their companies by bell pulls, because alarm shots may not be heard above the noise of enemy fire.

12. The wire obstacle is too low in many places. Every opportunity is to be taken to raise it to one metre during foggy weather or at night. The current one is inadequate.

13. Earth which has been thrown up is frequently too high and too sharply angled. Its surface does not match the colour of the surrounding ground sufficiently.

I expect all sector and company commanders to use all means and all their energy to ensure that these points are corrected..."[36]

Meanwhile, down at Deniécourt in the Santerre, life was taking on a regular and comfortable routine of its own for the men of Field Artillery Regiment 15 from Alsace.

*Hauptmann Wagner Field Artillery Regiment 15*[37] **19.**

"The setting sun glowed in shades of gold and copper over the park and the wood. The 'evening blessing' poured down over the poor little church in Soyécourt. Black plumes of smoke rose up against the red sky from the crashing impacts, paused for a moment and sank down once more like black veils. Then a pair of shells followed by another growled their way over towards Estrées. Their impact could be heard in the far distance. The good old 90 millimetre guns put in another appearance, their shells rushing noisily over the wood. Then an almost ceremonial silence prevailed. Fine clouds of dust rose in the air. The branches and twigs stirred in the evening breeze. Tired leaves fluttered down to the ground. Now and then a vehicle rattled on its way. There remained a few awkward considerations: how to justify this or that shell from the gigantic daily quota of five rounds. A few instructions were passed to our oh-so-primitive flash ranging point on top of the summerhouse, then there was a final tour of the battery and the soldiers' cookhouse in the conservatory on the edge of the lawn. Once that was complete, duty was over for the day.

"With electric torches we lit our way through the carefully blacked-out chateau. There awaited us our batmen: Levy, the former ladies' tailor in his cook's whites and Lorbach, our ever-cheerful singer from Cologne. The fire was lit in the magnificent salon and candles glittered on the table at which we sat, almost as in peacetime, to take our evening meal. The portraits of the Kergolays and Herlévilles, which were admired by both the commander and we leutnants, stared at us with living eyes from their golden frames...The food and drink may have been simple, but the atmosphere was happy and festive. Every evening the magic of the old refined culture which enfolded us released us from the imperatives of war. Then, when with the fire and candles burning low, Gelderblom entertained us with his violin, within us and around us the war lost its meaning.... The hauptmann laid his head to rest in the charming former boudoir of a very pampered lady, but we leutnants and the doctor were not badly off either. We could all have used a little more sleep, but each day the war began again at dawn and we had to concern ourselves with the French and other matters..."

As the year drew towards its close, the French made a huge effort to dislodge the invaders. All along the line and especially between the middle of the month and Christmas, there were heavy local battles for possession of key features and villages. Ammunition shortages, particularly for the artillery, had long made themselves felt. At times the infantry practically had to beg for fire support. On the 17th December, Montauban came under heavy attack.

*Fernsprechunteroffizier Elperstedt 3rd Battalion Reserve Infantry Regiment 40*[38] **18.**

"The heavy shells crashed down, enveloping Montauban with smoke. With a deafening roar the town hall blew up, sending debris flying and leaving windows and door frames hanging in the poplar trees. Hissing and roaring, shells slammed into the ground and mud, stones and dust rained down, taking your breath away. The storm of heavy artillery fire made communication with the front line almost impossible. The cables had been cut long before...Receiver in hand, I contacted the artillery. 'This is Hauptmann Leinekugel,' came the reply.

'This is the signaller 3rd Battalion Reserve Infantry Regiment 40. Herr Hauptmann there is a large group of Frenchmen attacking in Carnoy

Copse. Please open fire.'

'We must save ammunition, but if it is urgently necessary, we shall open fire.'

'Herr Hauptmann, the target is worth it.'

'OK.  Keep a good look out.'

'Yes, Sir'

I then heard: 'Number One Gun – fire!'

I called out, 'Fifty metres short!'

'Number Two Gun – fire!'

'On target!'

'Battery – Fire for effect!'

"This was followed by several salvoes, which roared over our heads, smoking out the copse. The Poilus scattered like a swarm of wasps, offering a good target to our machine gunners and riflemen."

Around Ovillers, Mametz and Fricourt the battle raged for several days, flaring up constantly between the 17th and 21st December and leaving both sides with thousands of casualties.  On the 21st yet another attack was halted.  This had cost the French 400 – 500 killed and a great many wounded.  There was an informal truce between Mametz and Montauban.

*Leutnant Westermann Company Commander 6th Company Reserve Infantry Regiment 40*[39] **20.**

"Suddenly I spotted a Red Cross flag some way off behind the rise.  I hurried forward to my company.  I stood everyone to and forbade anyone to look over the parapet, because I had to be extremely careful.  The French had a habit of using all sorts of tricks to assist their advances and were certainly not over fussy about the means they were prepared to employ.  I assumed that they might be planning to overrun us, relying on the fact that the 'barbarians' would respect the international significance of the Red Cross flag, or that they might believe that they could establish the strength of our position by observing any of our men curious enough to allow themselves to be seen.  Hence my strict order in all circumstances to remain under cover and to await further direction.  In the meantime the waving Red Cross flag drew nearer and became ever more distinct.  I then informed my platoon commanders that I would go over to the other side, but that if there was any hostile act towards me they were to open fire at once without considering me, because at all costs we could not allow the position to be overrun.  In the same way fire was to be opened if I was to give the signal from over there.  If in fact the enemy intentions were peaceful, I did not want to lose the opportunity to get to know the enemy position and the earthworks in particular by daylight.

"Once I had disappeared over the parapet and had made sure that I took obvious care in passing the wire obstacle – in fact it had been long since shot away, but I did not want the enemy to know that – I had two men from the left of the company also advance under the Red Cross flag. These were Unteroffiziers Riesner and Stoss. We met about a hundred metres forward of our position and halted until a French medical orderly gave a hand signal. I also waved to him, indicating that he could come forward. At this he signalled to his rear and four men appeared with two stretchers. They now came up to us and I asked them in French how they intended to proceed. The medical team replied that they wished to recover some seriously wounded men, who had been lying helplessly and groaning loudly in No Man's Land since the previous morning. I gave my approval for this and guaranteed them a short ceasefire. We shook hands on this, I stated my respect of the French medical services for the way they were acting and told them that they could have done the same thing the previous day because my response would have been the same, despite the recent days of fighting. He could also pass on to his friends that the 'Boches' were anything but barbarians. Whilst the French recovered five wounded men, I had a good look round and made some useful observations. I was particularly interested in the earthworks which were right in front of us. Once the French had returned to their position, we also went back to our trenches having made a number of extremely helpful discoveries. The battle was resumed gradually..."

As the fighting reduced in intensity after the 21st December, some of the front-line troops were fortunate enough to be relieved. One soldier, who had survived vicious fighting during the recent past, could hardly wait to write to his family to pass on all his news.

*Musketier Xaver Schilling 8th Company Reserve Infantry Regiment 111*[40] **10.**

"My loved ones at home!

"To God be all praise and thanks! We were relieved today. No more trenches! It was relief from very hell. I do not want to cause you unnecessary anxiety, so the fact that I thoughtlessly wrote on a card to Marie that we had had a hard few days has bothered me. You have perhaps been upset over nothing and that is pointless. Now listen! Up until the 17th it was relatively peaceful... then at 6.00am I was on forward sentry and heard a trumpet call from the French. We had never heard such a thing before! At the same time came flashes of light, flares and shouting. Our sentries fired and the others, drunk with sleep, stood to arms. The stars seemed to be falling from heaven, but it was the first of the shells landing very close. 'Urra! Urra!' they shouted from across the way. Incredible though it seemed to me, the French were really advancing. We could see them clearly illuminated by our searchlights, but they pushed ever closer. We were dazzled by the flash of the shells and deafened by the explosions. Our lads all ducked as each landed – a pointless thing to do, because it would have been too late...our knees trembled, not from fear but excitement and tension. Shells landed to the left and right and we were deluged by earth. A loud shout to the others, 'I'm in one piece, are you still OK?' 'I'm fine.' They came ever closer, their bayonets flashing eerily. Now with finger on the trigger, flash, reload, flash, reload and so on without stopping. They advanced to within thirty metres, but then there were no more of them. The attack fizzled out.

"That morning the ground in front of us was covered with the dead. There was no more sign of the infantry, but the artillery started up, shell after shell. It was revenge for the failed attack...Eventually we had to abandon our firing shields. Cowering helplessly in the trench we let the terrible fire pass over our heads. We were in that position from 6.30 am to 12.30 pm. It was a terrible time. Next to us the wounded were shouting for help. The detonation of the countless shells fused into one monotonous tone that sounded in our ears like the clanging of a huge bell. Splinters flew in all directions, sweeping away our firing shields and showering down on us...We just lay on the ground and prayed. There was little of our trench left: shot up, collapsed, the dugouts crushed. It was the same the following day. The enemy was bent on our destruction. We were helpless. Where was our artillery? Why did it fire so little?... And so it continued for four days! By the end we were reduced to a tiny group. There were only fifteen left from one platoon...By the fourth day all that remained was one short section of trench, a hole in the ground that was so far untouched. The six or eight of us who were left huddled together in it. There was hardly a commander to be seen. On one occasion our Oberstleutnant von Schweinichen, a grey old man, ran along the trench under heavy artillery fire. 'Courage lads, we are going to hold this position!' Four officers of our battalion, who were in a dugout, were torn apart by the same shell."

Then suddenly Christmas was upon them. Up near Gommecourt the Guards had had a much quieter time than those engaged further south. The last serious attack had occurred on the19th November, so they had had plenty of time to prepare to mark the festive season appropriately. The novel situation and surroundings and the effort made a deep and lasting impression on those involved.

*Major Thilo von Bose Grenadier Guard Regiment 2*[41] **21.**

"The Christmas festivities began on the 21st December, with a church parade held in the school at Puisieux. Company parties, featuring decorated and candle-lit Christmas trees, completed the celebrations. A great many presents had arrived in good time from the Ersatz Battalion and members of the Alexander [Grenadier Guard Regiment 1] Regimental Association, so a good selection could be laid out for every man. Sunny and frosty weather lifted the spirits. The good old Christmas carols rang

out and more than ever thoughts returned to loved ones at home. Sadly so
many of these had to pass this Christmas mourning their fallen and
worrying about their wounded sons, brothers, fathers and husbands! It
was hard too for many individuals to think of faithful comrades who were
no longer numbered among the living. Yet each could draw inner strength
from the knowledge of duty done, of the horror of war kept well away
from the homeland. Following the arrival of a draft, comprising mostly
recovered wounded and including Leutnants von Ompteda and Findeklee
on 22nd, the 1st Battalion celebrated Christmas on the 23rd, also in
Puisieux."

*Grenadier Badendieck 5th Company Grenadier Guard Regiment 1*[42] **20.**

"Our people had decorated the hall of our girls' boarding school very
attractively and a volunteer choir sang. The Leutnant gave an address and
there were speeches. Every man received a package of presents and two
mugs full of a drink, which the Feldwebel insisted was real beer. Then
there was punch and three sweet, round, fatty pancakes each. Did we not
live like the Gods in France? On the stroke of 12 o'clock we also received
our presents from 'over there': six heavy 'iron rations' of an especially
festive calibre. Our artillery had orders today only to fire in the case of an
attack. And so a great feeling of well-being prevailed!"
Perhaps also reflecting the tacit 'live and let live' policy which had prevailed in this
area for the past six weeks, Christmas still had one further surprise in store for the
Guards.

*Grenadier Thimian 2nd Company Grenadier Guard Regiment 1*[43] **22.**

"After we had been relieved, there were numerous parcels and letters,
and our regimental Christmas continued with all sorts of good and useful
presents. In the evening we had a company service. So moving were the
words of Leutnant Freiherr von Ompteda's address that there was hardly
a dry eye in the house. During the afternoon of the 24th, the whole
battalion came together to celebrate Christmas and that was even better.
Then we brewed hot toddy and ate our cakes. It would have been too
difficult to try to carry everything back to our trenches. At ten o'clock in
the evening we took up our positions. It was a clear starry night, frosty
and freezing cold. From midnight I was on sentry duty; then my mind
was filled with longing for home, where the family would be gathered
round the Christmas tree waiting for those of us away on active service.
Up until the afternoon of Christmas Day, everything was noticeably quiet,
then occurred something I shall never forget. I was on guard, when I
suddenly noticed that a Frenchman had climbed onto the parapet of his
trench. I had just taken aim when I noticed that one of our men had
climbed out too. The two of them advanced step by step towards each

other and shook hands. Then others from both sides followed their example. The Frenchmen, who were mostly old, looked ill-nourished and poorly clothed. They begged for tobacco. We chatted for forty five minutes then we all returned quietly to our respective trenches."

So the Guards and others lucky enough to be out of the line and in comfortable billets were able to make the best of a difficult situation. It was a somewhat more austere occasion for those down around Montauban, where Christmas came straight after bitter fighting and there was certainly no thought of truces – just of home.

*Hauptmann Tüchert 4th Company Reserve Infantry Regiment 40*[44] **23.**

"Out on the firing step stands the sentry, his rifle at the ready – Bright flashes light up the horizon and further flashes come from the direction of Bouillon Farm. Zii-pp, Zii-pp! Crack! Crash! Thud! Thud! Two Christmas greetings arrive from the enemy guns in the wreckage of Mametz – quiet descends once more. Beneath in the dugout Heinrich from Ebersbach has exchanged the burnt out candles on the Christmas tree with new ones, whilst Otto, the oldest present, reads the letter from his wife for the tenth time. Chuckling happily to himself he strokes his patriarchal beard then, drawing closer to the Christmas tree, he gazes, lost in thought, at the photographs of his dear wife and four children that were enclosed in the letter. By now he is oblivious to the others. He is thinking of the little ones smiling happily and dancing round the candle-bedecked tree. He hears their shouts of joy, their clear high voices. Now Fritz and Otto are playing with their new train set, little Karl is turning the pages of a picture book and Liesl stands there hugging her teddy bear. Happy, happy children, who know nothing of war.

"Suddenly more serious, his thoughts turn to his beloved wife. He sees the tears in her eyes; tears of bitter, frustrated anger; worrying, yearning, hoping, 'Oh let him return home once more' – Listen! Now he can hear them singing; yes they are singing their old Christmas carols in voices of angels – Silent Night, Holy Night! He can hold back no longer, the old warrior can sense the tender hand of his wife, he has forgotten the war and breaking the silence of the dugout, he sings with his children: Silent Night, Holy Night! And as for his three comrades in the dugout, whose thoughts tonight are also back at home, they too join in this hymn of peace – sixty metres from the enemy lines ... Outside up on the firing step stands the sentry, protecting them all."

Ultimately all Christmases which soldiers have to spend away from family and friends are a disappointment. However much effort is made to provide the best possible Christmas cheer, there is always something lacking and perhaps the whole of Christmas 1914 was best summed up by this little observation.

*Unteroffizier Esperstedt Reserve Infantry Regiment 40*[45] **22.**

"There in the trench, standing in a small niche which had been carved out of the earth, stood a little fir tree. Its branches, poor, withered things, had been decorated with baubles made from moulded ration bread. From a hole in the ground, a muffled voice called 'Happy Christmas'. I returned the greeting then trudged on musing – the little tree, comrades dead and gone, Happy Christmas? – I couldn't make rhyme or reason of it at all."

And so the first year of the war drew to a close. It had been a year of hopes dashed, opportunities missed and unparalleled bloody fighting. Nobody, apart from the casualties, had made it home 'before the leaves fell.' Nobody had a solution to the current stalemate and the future, here on the Somme as elsewhere, was shrouded in uncertainty. For the Guards there was a tragic sting in the tail. On New Year's Eve Grenadier Guard Regiment 1 marked the turn of the year with a service in the church at Bucquoy.

*Rittmeister von Graese Grenadier Guard Regiment 1*[46] **16.**

"During the sermon, enemy artillery fire landed around the church, so that Divisional Padre Paeßold had to cut his sermon short. The men were ordered to return to their quarters without forming up, because it was obvious that the church was the target of the enemy artillery. We had just crossed the square in front of the church when a shell exploded at the corner of our house. Loud shouts could be heard from the thick cloud of smoke which covered the whole square. On leaving the house we stumbled over a musician from the Elisabeth Regiment [Grenadier Guard Regiment 3], whose head had been literally torn off. As the smoke cleared we discovered twenty killed and sixty wounded – all hit by this single shell...It was a painful way to end the year...

"Shortly before midnight we crept through the trenches from sentry to sentry. Single shots whistled back and forth, interspersed with rifle grenades. Then suddenly as the clock showed 12 o'clock the New Year was toasted in a loud, spreading avalanche of sound, which raced like wildfire up and down the line, surely echoing from the coast of Flanders to the southern tip of Alsace. God be with you, New Year of the war! Will you bring us peace? When? For whom? Would we, faithfully holding the line here, live to see it? This New Year's Eve in the trenches made a wonderful impression. It was atmospheric, almost peaceful. What an array of nostalgic thoughts and dreams of the future filled our hearts at such a time, what thoughts of love raced silently homewards! Our snatched slumbers were filled with dreams and beloved images of home...".

1. Kronprinz Rupprecht: 'Mein Kriegstagebuch' Bd I p 127
2. Lasch: History IR 138 pp 79-80
3. Held: History IR 17 p 61
4. Kriegsarchiv, München HS 1984
5. Wagner: History FAR 15 p 83-84
6. Lasch: op. cit. p 86
7. ibid. pp 86-87
8. Held: op. cit. 17 pp 67-68
9. Kriegsarchiv, München HS2073
10. 'Dear Fatherland you may remain calm', which sounds rather stilted out of context, is, in fact, a quotation from the song 'Wacht am Rhein.'
11. Kriegsarchiv, München HS 1984
12. Wagner: History FAR 15 p 340
13. Hauptstaatsarchiv, Stuttgart M410 Bü 140/8
14. Gallion: History RIR 40 p 38
15. ibid. pp 38-39
16. Hauptstaatsarchiv, Stuttgart M410 Bü 140/8
17. Jecklin: History RJägBatl 8 pp 48-49
18. Bachelin: History RIR 111 pp 234-244
19. Jecklin: op. cit. pp 49-50
20. Kriegsarchiv, München HS 1984
21. Hauptstaatsarchiv, Stuttgart M410 Bü 140/8
22. Held: op. cit. pp 73-74
23. Gallion: op. cit. pp 42-43
24. Waldenfels: History Bav FAR 11 p 53
25. ibid. p 111
26. Rosenberg-Lipinsky: History GardeGrenRegt 3 p111
27. ibid. p116
28. Wagner: op. cit. p 72
29. ibid.  p81
30. Bachelin: op. cit. p 244
31. Rosenberg-Lipinsky: op. cit. p 121
32. Wagner: op. cit. p 84-85
33. Bachelin: op. cit. p 244
34. Gallion: op. cit. pp 46-48
35. Hauptstaatsarchiv, Stuttgart M99 Bü 141/2
36. Hauptstaatsarchiv, Stuttgart M99 Bü 141/3
37. Wagner: op. cit. pp 85-86
38. Gallion: op. cit. p 53
39. ibid.  p 55
40. Bachelin: op. cit. pp 251-252
41. Bose: History GGR 1 p 144
42. ibid. pp 145-146
43. ibid. p 145
44. Gallion: op. cit. pp 56-57
45. ibid. p 57
46. Bose: op. cit. p 146

CHAPTER TWO

# January – December 1915

The end of the First Battle of Ypres, in November 1914, meant that the entire Western Front had solidified into stalemate. As far as the Germans were concerned, the priority for the time being was the Eastern Front. In the west they generally only reacted to Allied initiatives and because the bulk of operations took place further north, the Somme front was something of a backwater throughout the year.

January 1915 had opened with a period of frosty weather which, though extremely cold, meant at least that the ground was firmer and the trenches remained in a reasonable state of repair. This was followed by very wet weather, which caused enormous damage to unrevetted trench walls and to the advanced saps, which had been driven forward all along the front towards the French lines. The pouring rain played havoc with these primitive earthworks, so work had to go on day and night to try to maintain them. The clay in the base of the trenches was soon puddled by the tramp of feet and became impervious. Very quickly all the trenches were deep in water and mud, the sides fell in and within a few days it was impossible to move along the communication trenches at all. The conditions that month were truly appalling.

*Reserve Leutnant Franz Demmel 5th Company Bavarian Infantry-Leibregiment[1] 1.*

"When on the 5th January we moved to reoccupy our old positions [near Maricourt] as the Communication Trench Company, the weather was frightful. En route and in the communication trenches, the water was knee-deep in places. In the so-called shelters, the water dripped so much and so constantly that many simply avoided them, preferring to take their chances outside. Although night after night we and our comrades from Bavarian Infantry Regiment 16 were ordered forward to work on the front line trenches, it was almost impossible to detect any signs of success. The only saving grace was that it was just the same for the French soldiers. Often enough we could see that the ration parties were forced in the twilight to make their way across country outside the trenches, because over there, just as for us, to move through the trenches with food containers, weapons, loaves of army bread and similar items, was simply impossible. Who would hold it against us that in such situations we both acted as though we had seen nothing? If this unspoken agreement during this most trying and difficult of times was suddenly to be broken, by either side, then it would be clear that fresh troops had moved in.

"We were the Wood Company from the 15th to the 20th January and that was somewhat better. The rain had eased a bit and the shelters were more stable and dryer. Sentry duty, which this over-extended position demanded, became bearable. From the 25th to the 31st January we were once again the forward company. We were lucky in that it coincided with a period of sharp frost, so thanks to nature and without intervention by us, the trenches became more passable than they would have been even with the most assiduous spadework. The Kaiser's birthday on the 27th January was a noteworthy occasion. It could not be allowed to pass without trace and so at exactly 12 o'clock the infantry along the entire line, as far as we could hear, opened up rapid small arms fire on the enemy trenches. This was followed by a cannonade from the artillery, so it would have been possible to have believed that a violent attack was about to take place. But, with the exception of a few nervous shots, the French let it pass without undertaking any sort of response."

*Leutnant Fritsch Field Artillery Regiment 67[2]* **2.**

"It had been raining the entire day and the snow had melted. I was manning the telephone in a dugout [near Hallu] and it was 9.50 pm. I suddenly heard a loud rushing noise as though a powerful stream was flowing past the door. I tried to see what it was, but a clod of earth had jammed the door. At the same moment water began streaming in through cracks in the door, so fast that in three minutes I was standing up to my thighs in water. When I set about smashing the door in with a carbine, the water was suddenly up to my neck. I grabbed the telephone and climbed out and onto the parapet. There we stood, fully exposed to the elements, clothing soaked and with no cover at all. We then began to dig in once more, but we could not do much work, our clothing was so stiff. Towards morning it began to freeze and all our weapons rusted.

"There we lay from 11.00 pm to 3.00 pm the following day. It was absolutely the worst situation that I have so far had to endure throughout the war. We had nothing to eat, because everything had been swept away. That morning nobody could get through to us to bring us anything, because the communication trenches were full of water. Our telephone link to Chaulnes had been severed by shell fire, so that afternoon at 3.00 pm I set off to fix it. The Frenchmen opened up on me at a range of about 150 metres, but I had no choice but to run upright across country. It was a life or death race along the line of the cable. I could see the earth being kicked up by bullets to my left and right, but God was protecting me. An infantry leutnant had instructed me to take cover every fifty metres, but each time I got up, the firing began again. At least the danger grew less as I covered more ground and finally, having fixed the fault, I got through."

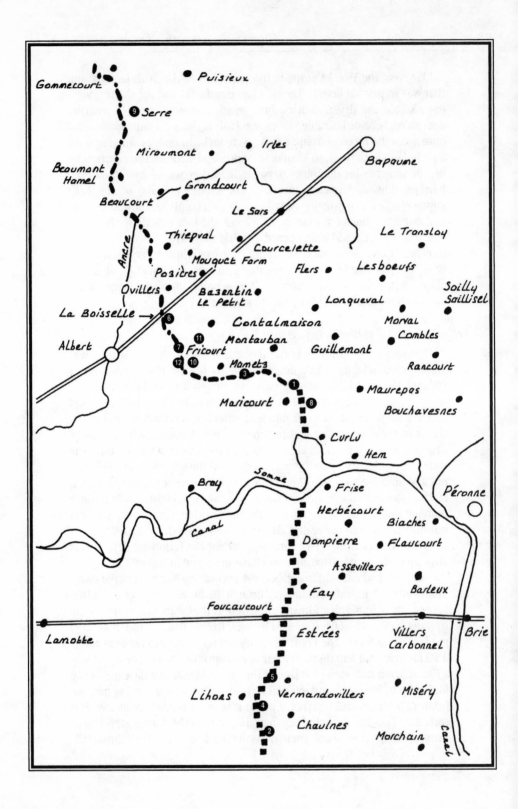

On the night of the19th – 20 th January, Reserve Infantry Regiment 40 was stood to all night, because German airmen had reported large troop concentrations around Carnoy. Hand grenades at the ready, bayonets fixed, the men waited in vain throughout the long night, despite the fact that the rain was lashing down constantly. By the morning of the 20th January, the situation was awful. Everyone and everything was soaked through. Uniforms were plastered with mud, offering no protection; the dugouts were leaking and looked ready to collapse. The bread was damp and the food cold. Then during the early hours of the following night it seemed as though something was happening at last. The atmosphere was extremely tense.

*Unteroffizier Schultz 2nd Company Reserve Infantry Regiment 40*[3] **3.**

"During this rainy night, the sentry suddenly heard scratching and rustling in the barbed wire obstacle. Because he believed that an enemy patrol was attempting to cut a lane through the obstacle, he stood the whole company to. A patrol of volunteers was sent forward in the direction of the sound and everyone waited, nerves strained, for its return. The 'captured item' which they brought back was only an old umbrella which had probably been used by a listening post as protection against the rain, but had been blown into the obstacle by a gust of wind!"

Ever since the autumn attacks had stalled, both sides used nightly patrols to cover gaps in the defences and to maintain contact with neighbouring units. Gradually, however, the patrols became more aggressive in intent, being launched with ever-increasing frequency against enemy standing patrols, listening posts and front line trenches. Like many of the techniques and tactics of the period, the patrols tended to be hastily improvised. Some were successful, others less so. In comparison with the complex operations and trench raids launched as the year progressed, these early night time activities were simple, almost naïve, in their conception and conduct. Nevertheless, they offered an opportunity for lessons to be learned and techniques to be honed. They also provided the volunteers, with whom all such German operations were conducted, with an opportunity for aggressive action and to have their efforts rewarded. The following minor action earned Unteroffizier Koch an Iron Cross 1st Class and the other participants the Iron Cross 2nd Class.

*Landwehr Leutnant Rust Infantry Regiment 60*[4] **4.**

"On the 17th January, we noticed that the enemy trenches were more densely occupied than usual. We had to find out if there was a particular reason for this; if, for example, a French attack had to be anticipated. Volunteers forward! Koch was the first and he was joined by his friend Unteroffizier Wozniakowski and Musketier Selden from the 5th Company. Rifles were left behind, daggers were carried in boot tops and a number of hand grenades were carried. Crawling along the line of the railway embankment, past the French sentry, they reached the densely occupied trench.  Go! – It was the work of a moment to throw hand grenades into the middle of the Frenchmen, where they exploded, sending splinters flying in all directions.  Loud shouts, confusion and frenzied shooting was the surprised response of the French troops.  The sentry, up on the embankment, took fright and blazed away aimlessly into the darkness.  The company, which was occupying an advanced strong point, could clearly hear the exploding grenades, the shouting and the shooting and began to fear for our brave lads, but they all returned safely.  The noise that the French infantry was making alerted their artillery into carrying out their plan of engaging our positions; especially that of the 5th Company, as swiftly as possible.  Unfortunately they were not totally without success, because they landed a shell right in a dugout where Koch was giving a report to the company commander, killing or wounding several men.

"The French army could not be allowed to get away with that.  Hardly had the enemy fire died away, than Koch and his two comrades went forward again with a fresh supply of grenades, even though they knew that the Frenchmen, who were still shooting, would be keeping an even better look out.  They were about halfway to the French position when Koch was wounded by a rifle shot through the shoulder and had to return. This did not stop his assistants from closing up to the French trench and throwing more grenades amongst the French soldiers as revenge for the blood of their comrades. Miraculously, they returned once more uninjured. The following morning a white flag was seen fluttering lustily from the French barbed wire obstacle, where Musketier Selden had tied it as a visiting card and token of German courage."

The battles of the previous year had left No Man's Land strewn with thousands of unburied bodies. Whenever possible, these had been dealt with, but in many areas, especially where the opposing lines were close together and the ground between was swept by small arms fire, it had proved impossible to find a solution to the problem. Not only was it bad for morale, but the presence of these putrefying remains attracted plagues of rats which gorged on the decayed flesh, threatening serious outbreaks of disease.  In February, Reserve Infantry Regiment 269 took over positions near Vermandovillers, which had been the scene of intense fighting the previous autumn. Having arrived, the men were engaged in revetting their trenches, when they suddenly became aware of the situation and decided to do something about it as and when they could.

*Reserve Unteroffizier Kurt Herzfeldt 7th Company Reserve Infantry Regiment 269*[5] **5.**

"I looked over to Gefreiter Bommel. He was standing behind an armoured shield, observing the area to the front. 'What's going on then?' I asked.  Silently he gestured at the spyhole...'Dead comrades!' he said, gallantly mastering his revulsion. I put the telescope to my eye and looked over the parapet. The French trench ran in a wide curve between Lihu Copse and Frenchman's Copse. No Man's Land varied between 180 and 300 metres wide and was composed of the yellow clay of a sugar beet field. Half rotted, yellowing sugar beet leaves moved in the wind. In amongst them, looking just like carelessly discarded bundles of clothes, were, indeed, dead comrades. I counted more than twenty from my vantage point. The calfskin knapsacks of those who had fallen hard up against the enemy wire must have been torn open and plundered, because their flaps were open. These field grey soldiers had died a hero's death in October 1914, during a misbegotten assault on the village of Lihons and the surrounding trench system, which failed utterly. Since then the corpses of our comrades from Infantry Regiments 17 and 131 had laid there rotting in the open...Missing! Who knew their names?...Crack, crack! A few copper-jacketed bullets whipped overhead, jerking us back to brutal reality..."

*Feldwebel Manthey 1st Company Reserve Infantry Regiment 269*[6] **5.**

"At 8.00 am on the 11th February there was dense fog...There were about a hundred corpses from the battles of October 1914 lying in front of our position and the wind frequently blew an appalling stink from them at us. I exploited the foggy day by rounding up every spare man of the 3rd Platoon of the Company who had a spade and led them forward of the position. We were able to bury thirty-six Germans. In thirty cases, by examining personal marks or names inside uniform jackets, we were able to identify the individuals. They were our comrades from Infantry Regiments 17 and 131. We later marked all valuables and personal property with the names of those concerned and forwarded them to Division."

*Musketier Wassilowski 6th Company Reserve Infantry Regiment 269*[7] **5.**

Between our position and that of the enemy lay a great many corpses from the War of Movement. We all wanted nothing more than to be able to bury them. Attempts to get the French to acquiesce were in vain, being answered with hand and rifle grenades. They were a disrespectful bunch. We did not reply in kind. Early one foggy morning Hauptmann von Borch gave us permission to go forward into No Man's Land, with four men from each section and recover personal equipment and possessions. A few rushes and we arrived at the first of the dead. We covered him with earth and placed his shako on the grave; these men were from a Jäger battalion. We also did our duty by three other comrades, busying ourselves with the collection of as many pieces of equipment and personal effects as possible. We also kept in mind the 'trench rumour' that there was a large reward on offer for the recovery of the body of a fallen major, but we did not find any trace of him..."

No sooner had the line reached at the end of the battles of 1914 solidified into the opposing positions, which were to remain virtually unchanged for the next twenty months, than solutions began to be sought to end the tactical stalemate. Much of the active war moved underground, where a constant struggle, in appalling conditions, for mastery of the terrain took place. The Somme sector saw a great deal of such activity. In the north this took place, notably, around Beaumont Hamel, La Boisselle, Fricourt and Mametz, where the battle went on ceaselessly, sometimes as much as fifty, sixty or even seventy metres below ground. Further south, a battle for underground supremacy also raged around Dompierre, Vermandovillers and elsewhere. This type of warfare put the individual under an appalling strain. The work itself was extremely hard, the conditions bad and there was a constant risk of being blown up.

The early days of the New Year saw a continuation of intense fighting which had begun around Christmas for the Granathof [Shell Farm], a large property on the southern tip of La Boisselle. Although the place was of little tactical significance, its control became a matter of honour, thus assuming a disproportionate importance. The sappers of Bavarian Engineer Regiment 1 played a large part in these initial battles. From the end of December 1914, they were engaged in driving no fewer than eight shallow galleries forward towards the farm. As early as 5th January, the French sappers could be heard working near to one of these galleries and by the end of the day it had been charged with 300 kilograms of high explosive, tamped back for nine metres and blown. This not only crushed the French gallery, but also destroyed a German gallery, which was located seven metres away and damaged a second.

During the coming two weeks, new galleries were started and others blown, whenever the nearby presence of French sappers could be established. Attempts were made to blow up the Granathof itself, to prevent the French sappers from working. Then on 12th January the French soldiers were dealt a serious blow, when a 600 kilogram charge was detonated. As a result of the enormous explosion, over forty French soldiers were killed. One eyewitness described seeing the air full of dismembered bodies and flying limbs, ten dead soldiers landed right in front of the German trenches and one unfortunate man was blown no less than 150 metres through the air, complete with rifle and bayonet.[8] By the time the fighting died down on 20th January, Reserve Infantry Regiment 120 had launched a final surprise attack on 18th January, which led to the complete annihilation of the 7th and 8th Companies of the French Infantry Regiment 65. Three officers and 104 men were captured. The remaining members of the two companies were killed; the property, which was laid waste, nevertheless continued to be hotly disputed throughout the year and to be the scene of constant mining and counter-mining activity[9]. (The area around the Granathof was later known to the British as the Glory Hole.) Generalleutnant von Auwärter, commander of 52 Reserve

Infantry Brigade, was so impressed with the work of the Bavarian sappers, who had contributed so much to this local victory, that he published a special Order of the Day, praising their work. Although the initial frenetic activity reduced in intensity around the Granathof, it did not fade away completely and there was one incident here in early March, which made a deep impression on all concerned. **6.**

"It was during the night of the 8th/9th March, Unteroffizier Nagel was working with his section at the face, when suddenly a draught of fresh air was noticed throughout the thirty-five metre length of the gallery. He immediately informed the duty officer, Offizierstellvertreter Heinz, who went down to the gallery to check on this strange event. He discovered a gap, only a few centimetres wide, which led to an adjacent space containing cool, fresh air. Heinz immediately set to work to enlarge the gap, so that he could illuminate the space carefully with a hand torch. In so doing, he discovered a great pile of packets, stacked high, with tamping in position behind them. One packet was taken and quickly examined. It was filled with a well-known type of French explosive called 'Geddite'. There could be no more doubt; the sappers had come across a French mine which was ready to be blown. Because it might explode at any minute, Heinz ordered the gallery itself, plus adjacent ones, which were threatened with crushing, to be cleared and he alerted the infantrymen who were manning the position. Everyone waited, nerves tensed, but there was no explosion. Then Heinz took a courageous decision. The risk of explosion was to be dealt with by dismantling the charge. The call went out through the ranks of the sappers for volunteers. Without batting an eyelid, Unteroffizier Nagel and Pioniers Amann, Bauer, Gottsman, Hirn, Heinrich, and Karl Hoffmann offered their services. They were joined by Musketier Lanzen of Reserve Infantry Regiment 119 who, displaying an outstanding example of comradely solidarity with the engineers, wished to participate in this dangerous task.

"Silently, the eight soldiers raced to follow their officer, in single file, through the dark gallery. They were soon at the spot. The hole was attacked with a pick. There was the sound of stone cracking and falling down, then the hole was large enough to climb through. The engineers stood before the enemy charge; through the darkness Death stared them in the face. At any moment a French engineer officer might press the button and then the nine men...but enough of these black thoughts...Let's get to work. Wordlessly the packets are passed from hand to hand. The men all work silently and determinedly. There is not a sound in this sinister place, save that of their laboured breathing. So it continues for fifteen minutes...thirty minutes...forty five minutes...The sappers are bathed in sweat, but the stack has shrunk in size. Suddenly several filled sandbags appear and beneath them four mighty wooden boxes... Let's get them

out... Suddenly one of the pioneers calls out aloud, excitedly: 'Look! There
are the firing cables!' Nine pairs of eyes follow his pointing finger and, in
the light of a pocket torch, the two copper firing wires can be seen,
glinting treacherously...threatening death... 'Pass the wire cutters!' Deftly
the wires are cut with a few swift snips. The danger is past. Silently, Death
stalks off...

"The exhausted men breathe deeply. Slowly the realisation of their
achievement sinks in. They have spent forty-five minutes on a powder keg:
a few thousand seconds, a fraction of only one of which would have
sufficed to prevent any one of them from ever seeing daylight again..." [10]

On this occasion, fortune was smiling on them, but the boot was on the other foot
a month later, when the French engineers succeeded in blowing up a large mine on
the vital ground of Hill 110, just south of Fricourt, at 11.00 am on the 12th
April. Intense artillery fire had begun at 10.00 am on the Quarry Position, then
came the explosion, which produced a crater twenty metres wide and eight metres
deep. It destroyed a section of trench and the entrance to an important German
gallery. Subsequent attempts by the French troops to storm and occupy the crater
failed. They were finally ejected by means of a hand grenade attack.

*Dr Niedenthal Medical Officer 1st Battalion Reserve Infantry Regiment 110*[11] **7.**

"Returning to my dugout, I noticed on my watch that it was about
10.00 am. Suddenly the air was filled with roaring, whizzing, thumps
and crashes, which put all the noise of battle of the previous days into the
shade. Suddenly the entire hill began to sway and shake and the roofs of
the dugouts to collapse. Despite the shells which were still falling,
everyone hurried up to the surface. The French engineers had managed to
blow their mine first. All the careful weeks of work by our brave infantry
and engineers had been destroyed and with it the lives of fifteen of our
courageous men. They were never seen again. As fast as the concentration
of shells had begun, it ceased. Duty called above, but all the
communication trenches had been wrecked, so we had to head off up the
hill across country. There we were met with a scene of utter desolation,
destruction and misery. The crater, which the Frenchmen had blown, lay
in the middle of the Quarry Position. The mine had crushed the biggest
dugout, burying twelve reservists, the Feldwebel and the platoon
commander. Despite the weight of fire from the French artillery, the men
set-to tirelessly to free their comrades. The first man we came across
during the digging was the platoon commander, Reserve Leutnant
Weymann. He was stone dead and in his eyes, with their blank stare, could
be read all the terror of death from asphyxiation. The Feldwebel lay dead
above him. Gradually we were able to force a way into the depths and,
initially, we were overjoyed to see the twelve reservists sitting in a line
along the wall, as though they were asleep. Well they certainly were, but

it was an eternal sleep that they were slumbering..."
This type of incident became an all-too-frequent occurrence as the war
underground ebbed and flowed, absorbing increasing amounts of effort and
generating increasingly large explosions. Around the Granathof in La Boisselle
alone, between April 1915 and January 1916, there were sixty-one explosions,
some involving charges as large as 20,000 – 25,000 kilograms of explosive.12
Above ground, as the year progressed, trench routines became well established.
Wherever the situation it was relatively quiet, the unspoken policy of 'live and let
live' made the monotonous task of enduring foul weather and dispiriting living
conditions more bearable, but life was never easy or simple. Furthermore, it would
be wrong to assume that only the soldiers manning the front line trenches had a
hard time of it. Throughout the forward area, life was tough and dangerous, not
least for those charged with the unglamorous, but vital, task of supply and
replenishment.

*Trainfahrer Zabel Reserve Infantry Regiment 269*[13] **5.**

"The drivers often had greater dangers to endure than the front line
soldier in his trench. The soldier could take cover and only had to consider
his own defence, but what of the driver? His first concern was his horses,
his second his wagon, his third and crucial, his load and last of all himself.
He was also forced to use pre-designated routes, which were well known
to the enemy and were under fire constantly. He could not jump left or
right into the ditches by the road and wait until the fire was lifted; he had
to get forward out of the line of fire... One evening I decided to relieve an
old friend of his difficult duty of driving a load of wire up to the position
and so made the journey for him. It was my baptism of fire. This evening
the French were giving it everything that they had. All along the round
bullets were whistling past our ears, but fortunately neither we, nor the
horses, suffered much. The wagons, however, were hit repeatedly and
afterwards they were riddled with bullets."

*Unteroffizier Shultz Reserve Infantry Regiment 40*[14] **3.**

"Collection of water and rations was a story in itself. Because there
were no communication trenches, it all had to be done across country. In
order to orientate the carrying parties during their return from the field
kitchen, small lanterns were hung on poles and raised above the parapet.
This indicated where the personnel could slide down into the trench. One
particularly unpleasant evening, Kriegsfreiwilliger B had been detailed off
as a carrier and it was not possible to place the lanterns in position. On his
return to the position, comrade B moved with the others along the line of
the trench calling, 'Can I slide down here?' At one point a sentry replied,
'Just drop down!' Upon hearing this, B slid down into the trench, but oh
dear me!  Instead of finding himself in the trench, our friend had fallen

down up to his armpits in a latrine that the sappers had produced. Amidst general hilarity, the unhappy warrior had to be freed from his trap. As a result of the delightful scent he was exuding, he was allocated a personal dugout and his clothes were sent back to Flers to be boiled, hopefully not in the field kitchen. Right up until the moment of relief some days later, B lived the life of a hermit in his dugout, clad only in underclothes and socks..."

The spring brought a new development, which was to be the main preoccupation of the field artillery thereafter. This was the division of the front into defensive fire zones. With the aim of bringing down a curtain of fire, which would counter enemy attempts to attack, every battery was made responsible for a designated area. Every aspect of the target was checked and studied – range, bearing and so forth. All this material was carefully recorded, so that the guns could be laid on these targets rapidly and also were able to engage them at night. There were continual exercises, against the stop watch, to minimise response times. This was coupled with the deployment of artillery liaison officers to the infantry in the forward trenches.

*Landwehr Leutnant M. Gerster Reserve Infantry Regiment 119*[15]

"Up to this point the infantry never knew which element of the artillery was responsible for their support in the event of an attack. This now changed. The entire front was divided into defensive fire zones and each officer in the front line had to know which battery had the task of bringing down a wall of fire to seal off his sector and how to get in contact with it by the swiftest means. Special batteries were designated to fire on opportunity targets which appeared suddenly. In view of the small number of batteries available to the Division, the battery defensive fire zones were extraordinarily large, which would have meant that unless reinforcements had been made available, the effectiveness of the artillery would have been severely weakened. In order both to train the infantry to make quick decisions, as well as to test the alertness of telephonists and the emergency readiness of the artillery, so-called fire control exercises were carried out. That is to say that the infantry, having had a target indicated to them, had to know how to bring down fire on a particular point as quickly as possible.

"The importance of infantry-artillery links was recognised ever more. As a result the communications system was subject to constant improvement. Rocket signals, semaphore flags and light signals by night, which were received by artillery observation points, served this purpose. In order to counter infantry prejudice and to explain its potential, artillery officers had to give presentations about their arm of service. In addition infantry officers and NCOs were directed to visit the artillery in order to convince themselves, with their own eyes, that the artillery could not fulfil exaggerated infantry demands and, furthermore, to teach them independently to be able to direct fire from the front line trenches, when no artillery liaison officer was present. Over the months these measures led to perfect cooperation between the two arms of service, to trust of the artillery by the infantry, which was not shaken by the occasional unavoidable dropping short of shells. In this way the foundation for the effective countering of an enemy attack was laid."

The requirement to provide legions of liaison officers offered a useful, rare opportunity to promote deserving vizefeldwebels and officer cadets to the rank of reserve leutnant. As a result the battalions and batteries benefited from the addition of numerous high quality junior officers, who provided the backbone of their units during the coming months.[16] The provision of first class, flexible and responsive artillery remained a major pre-occupation throughout the year, as did the deployment to front line positions of large numbers of grenade launchers and trench mortars, the latter beginning to appear in quantity from April onwards. But, as always, the major task of the forward troops was to dig and go on digging; to attempt to render their positions invulnerable to either surprise or sustained attack; to labour hard and to endure the ceaseless unpleasantness of lengthy periods of trench duty.

*Reserve Leutnant Heizmann Reserve Infantry Regiment 109*[17] **6.**

"When we mention La Boisselle, we should not only describe the dangers. We should also praise the efforts the regiment made to develop the position. Over time, at the cost of strenuous labour, which robbed us of our nights, we produced a first-class trench system... which in our sector, not including the long communication trench to Contalmaison, eventually reached twenty-seven kilometres. Let us recall the names of the trenches. How often did you stand in the Regimental Crater, ready to go forward and man the trenches... or set off on the march for a rest! I saw you there, fetching rations and mail, or waiting to collect trench stores. Did you count the number of seriously wounded men, whom we lifted into the ambulances, or those who went hunting rats with carbines? Did you trudge, heavy laden, with coils of wire or drills, through North, Star, or House Trenches, to the position on the National Road, or over the Grand Duke Frederick Bridge in the Appendix to help the right flank company erect obstacles? Did you haul shuttering timber, knife rests, trench mortars and sandbags through the Middle Way or Emperor Street to the Granathof? How often did you have to seek shelter with a comrade when you were passing the church and it came under fire? Didn't you have to carry fascines, hurdles and mortar rounds through Observers' Way, Hedgerow Way, Nail, Beier and Fusilier Trenches to the front?... Do you remember digging the deep trench which ran from Businessman's Trench to Sap Three... which we named in honour of our recently fallen company commander, 'Waldmannweg' [Waldmann Way]?... How we sweated, what labour it cost, to link up the saps in the left hand sector! What care we took over dugouts for the regiment, battalion, kitchens, aid post and the mortar pits! We made every piece of ground into a fortress..."

*Reserve Leutnant Franz Demmel 5th Company Bavarian Infantry Leibregiment*[18] **8.**

"On Easter Sunday, the 4th April, we marked the day in the morning with a church service, then in the evening we marched to our position, this time in the so-called 'Hollow Copse', opposite Maricourt and not far from Hardecourt. The dugouts were well made and practically shell proof, which was just as well, because there was much artillery fire. We had one man killed during the relief. Our comrade Schönig, a regular member of the regiment, was killed by a shrapnel ball, just after he had gone on sentry duty. We mourned him as a kindly man, keen to do his duty and buried him in a small hollow near the position.

"The weather was very bad and the rats gave us a lot of trouble in the dugouts. Every time when we came off sentry duty, or had returned from digging, dog tired and just wanting to lie down straight away for a few hours sleep, we were plagued by these beasts, half the size of rabbits, which came creeping up to sniff around for anything edible in our knapsacks, which we used as pillows. They were not shy about using our faces as a shortcut, they scrabbled their way up the sleeves of our jackets and began to nibble away wherever they liked. These bloody creatures could drive a man to despair and for every dozen that we beat to death or shot, another dozen members of this noble race would take their place..."

After more than three months of relative quiet along the front, the situation suddenly changed in June, when the French army decided to try to reduce the salient formed around Toutvent Farm, to the west of Serre, where the previous year the Prussian Guards had pushed forward and established the current line. Capture of the ridge, upon which Serre stood, would have had serious consequences for the German army. Although this was not an attack to compare with the heavy fighting around Souchez and Lorette further north and might have been intended as a diversion, it was certainly significant locally and it demanded all the resources of the 52nd Infantry Division and the 26th Reserve Division to counter it. It was clear that the attack had been the subject of detailed planning and comprehensive preparation. From the end of May, the German troops had been picking up various signs that something was in the wind. There had been an increase in French aerial activity and a decrease in patrol activity. Guns were ranged in, troop movements took place and saps and communication trenches were pushed forward in the threatened area. All these observations were confirmed by German air reconnaissance, but the intensity of the attack, when it occurred, nevertheless came as a rude shock.

There was a noticeable increase in artillery fire during the night of the 3rd/4th

June and this continued throughout the next day. The Germans launched a captive balloon to aid spotting and later that day they had the good fortune to shoot down two enemy aircraft, one of which came down between the lines. As Sunday the 6th June wore on, extremely heavy artillery fire came down throughout the 52nd Division sector, falling especially heavily on Infantry Regiment 170, which held that part of the salient where the main blow was due to fall. Writing later, General der Infanterie Freiherr von Soden, then Commander of the 26th Reserve Division, remarked, 'There had been plenty of time to organise an appropriate response, [but] at the time nobody fully appreciated the devastating effect of concentrated artillery fire against the forward trenches, which comprised the main line of resistance.'[19] By dint of stripping out every sub unit which could be spared, his Division managed to pull together a total of the equivalent of three battalions as immediate reserves, extra ammunition was dumped forward and headquarters and staffs were reorganised to face the attack, which was expected to occur on the 6th June. Nothing happened, but the German positions were kept under – what at the time was considered to be – an appalling weight of fire. That evening, the 52nd Division reported tersely, 'Trenches utterly smashed. Expect attack tomorrow. Request artillery support.'[20]

German reserves began moving to the support of 52nd Infantry Division and all guns within range brought down supporting fire. After much confusion, by 11.30 am the following day it had become clear that, exploiting dense early morning mist, the French troops had stormed and taken Toutvent Farm, then had advanced towards Serre, but had been repulsed after bitter fighting at close quarters. For the next week, the French Second Army constantly moved up fresh regiments, renewed the assault four times altogether and beat off a strong German counter-attack on the 12th June, but finally called off the attack on the 13th. German resistance was stiffening, they had suffered heavy losses and there was no longer any realistic prospect of achieving the aim of taking the high ground around Serre.

*Reserve Vizefeldwebel Müller 10th Company Infantry Regiment 66*[21]  **9.**

   "After the 12th June, the Frenchmen did not dare to attack again. The occasional eruption of artillery or small arms fire indicated rather more that they feared a counterattack from our side, than that they themselves were inclined to advance. In the meantime the new trench of Infantry Regiment 190, which led to Serre, had been further developed, so that the 5th and 10th Companies now enjoyed left flank protection...We discovered the effectiveness of our artillery fire against the enemy positions from a statement made by a deserter, who suddenly leapt over our barricade on the 12th June. The final days that we spent in the position passed with no upsurge in fighting. The French will to attack was broken. From our observation posts, they could clearly be seen digging in, in the trenches that they had occupied. They themselves rejected any possibility of gaining further ground. The attempted breakthrough could clearly be seen to have failed. The vital parts of the German positions had been maintained, even in the face of an immense weight of enemy fire..." Nevertheless, as a result of the skilful use of artillery and heavy mortars, the French army had achieved, albeit at a high cost, the breaking of the German first line on a two and a half kilometre front. In so doing they created a gap, which only the tough resistance put up by the men of the 52nd Infantry Division, first class work by the supporting artillery of 26th Reserve Division and the heroic intervention of its hastily procured infantry reserves, prevented from being expanded considerably. This battle, short and sharp though it was, was of the first importance to the units of XIV Reserve Corps, who drew from it numerous lessons which they applied subsequently, as they further developed their defensive positions and put in place the command and control methods and tactics with which they would fight the Battle of the Somme the following year.

*Generalleutnant Freiherr von Soden Commander 26th Reserve Infantry Division*[22]

"For the 26th Reserve Division, the Battle of Serre was an extremely instructive preparation for the Battle of the Somme, during which experiences gained at Serre were of the greatest value."

*Pfarrer Kortheuer Divisional Padre 52nd Infantry Division*[23]  **9.**

"They were hard days, but great days. Of course, we left a sector of trench line in the hands of the enemy. We had serious casualties. The rows of crosses around Louvière Farm, behind the front and in cemeteries of the villages where we were billeted bear witness to that. But what did the enemy achieve in return for this enormous effort? Before the battle he occupied the heights around Hébuterne and we the valley. Now the French trenches run along the valley bottom. Without interference, we have been able to construct a new and improved trench line on the Serre heights. 150,000 shells were fired in vain at our lines; we used only a third of that quantity and caused the enemy a bloody casualty list. During the morning of the 9th June, the inhabitants of Bucquoy were gathered in their Sunday best at the Puisieux end of the village, awaiting the arrival of their fellow countrymen. They did indeed come, but they were 200 prisoners of war, who had fallen into our hands, despite the overwhelming strength they had brought to bear. No, the battles around Serre, hard-fought though they were, proved yet again that the Germans, faithful to their cause, are still standing firm in France."

The German army was much given to detailed examination of battles, engagements and procedures, which it kept under constant review. It was brutally honest and detailed in its reporting; the lessons learned were absorbed, approved at high level and distributed for attention and action swiftly, generally right down to company level. This meant that important information and directives were kept current and were known to all officers in the field.  During the second half of 1915 and first half of 1916, as will be seen, a constant stream of information, directives and exhortations was issued.  As an example, within only two weeks of the end of the fighting around Serre, reports had gone up the chain of command to Second Army Headquarters and the Army Commander, General von Below himself, had released this operational instruction [Army – Oberkommando 2 Ia No 96] on 27th June.[24]

> "Deep dugouts, proof against even direct hits by heavy artillery, which are now available almost everywhere, carry with them a danger that cannot be treated lightly.  They make the swift occupation of the firing step, in the event of a surprise attack, more difficult.  This was highlighted during the recent battles near Hébuterne.  There can be no doubt that the French army succeeded in several places in breaking into our position, almost without being engaged, whilst some of our troops were still sheltering in the dugouts, where they were then taken prisoner.
>
> "In order to prevent this, the entrances to dugouts are to be widened and they are to be equipped with two entrances.  The desire to dig unnecessarily deep is also to be discouraged.  A depth of three metres is sufficient to provide protection from a direct hit of up to 155 millimetre calibre.
>
> "The main point, however, is to make certain that the men in the dugouts are warned of an enemy attack in sufficient time and that they then exit the dugouts as quickly as possible.  A wide variety of means may be employed in order to raise the alarm: bells, drums, voice tubes, shouting down etc.  To ensure that the procedure will work when it is needed, the alarm system must be exercised.  In the same way, the men must be drilled intensively to pour out of the dugouts swiftly and to race to their positions.  The regiments are to lay down the necessary words of command for this procedure.
>
> "One essential pre-requisite, in order to remove any doubt about the matter, is to establish who is in charge of each dugout, so that, if in the event of an enemy attack, certain groups do not man their battle positions in time, the relevant commander can be court-martialled.  I require the necessary action to be taken with the utmost urgency.
>
> Signed: von Below"

Positional warfare, such as that which occurred throughout much of the year, laid stress on the virtues of endurance and resistance, provided few opportunities for displays of soldierly daring which were much admired by this army.  But as a result of a successful patrol on the 26th June the Commander of Reserve Infantry Regiment 109 published the following order:

> "Kriegsfreiwilliger Eder, 1st Company, is today singled out for his especially courageous behaviour.  Last night he pulled down a French flag which was attached to a flagpole by the French positions.  As a result of his

proven bravery in the face of the enemy, he has been promoted to Gefreiter."[25]

But if patrol activity served to keep the offensive spirit alive, the monotony and drudgery of life in the trenches continued to be broken most often by flurries of activity associated with mine warfare.

*Reserve Leutnant Hibschenberger 10th Company Reserve Infantry Regiment 110*[26] **10.**

"In careful work lasting many months, we had pushed forward a large and extensive minefield and, in the course of hard struggles, gradually gained the upper hand. The craters lay cheek by jowl with one another. There were barely enough letters in the alphabet to designate all of them. Approximately twenty interconnected galleries, about ten – twenty metres deep, led away towards the enemy from all points of the position. As a result we had pushed the French troops back off the crest and made life constantly difficult for them. Consequently they wanted to recapture the Crater Field at all costs. An attack preceded by a six-hour artillery bombardment was unsuccessful. Perhaps double the preparation might work. This occurred on the 19th July. About 9.00 am, fire was brought down by heavy artillery on the rearward edge of the Quarry Position. These were 280 millimetre shells with delay fuzes. Leutnant Meyer, the artillery observer, who was with me on the position, photographed the results, which produced holes like small craters. Already that morning five enemy detachments were reported to be on the march in the direction of Hill 110. Unfortunately they were not engaged.

"Suddenly, at 10.00 am, all the enemy batteries opened drumfire of a previously unknown intensity. This lasted for ten hours, with pauses. Estimates were that the enemy had fired 23,000 shells of all calibres and 3,000 mortar rounds against a 200 metre front. The fire was directed by aviators and an observation balloon. Heavy calibre fire was directed against the engineer park and the Second Position at the Quarry as far as Sap Two. Mined dugouts, five metres deep, were crushed; many men were buried alive and all the earth mortars and grenade launchers were destroyed. The engineer park blew up when 400 kilograms of blasting explosive was hit. The enemy mortar bombs and field artillery shells gave off a stink like phosphorous, which irritated the mucous membranes and produced nausea. Of course, all means of communications were destroyed. The whole position was a mass of craters and the trenches were completely flattened. However the mine galleries remained intact, so I was able to move to all parts of my company. This enabled me to keep morale up, give the necessary direction and make important observations.

"When, at around 2.00 pm, the fire slackened, I ordered the remaining dugouts on the Second Position to be cleared. There were already French soldiers in the Quarry. With Pioniers Santa and Boyle and my soldiers

Schroth and Brückner, I attempted to get to the Crater Field. Our machine gun on the eastern corner of the Quarry was still in one piece. Enemy aviators, who were circling very low above the Quarry, had already spotted us and artillery fire came down on the position with renewed intensity. I need hardly mention that our artillery did not stand idly by. They brought down fire brilliantly on the French front line trenches. It was a vision of hell. Shortly before 7.00 pm the fire was lifted to the rear, a sure sign of the imminence of the attack. Our machine gun was already in action. The French broke in as far as Mine Gallery Thirteen, but we pushed them out with hand grenades and I was able to reoccupy the old position around Crater M. The French had broken into the quarry by Crater A and had pushed on to the Thüringer Sap. Sections led by Kleinophorst and Elsner threw them out of Crater A and Fremgen's section cleared Thüringer Way. After a bitter hand to hand struggle lasting thirty minutes, the entire position was back in our hands. Despite ten hours of preparatory fire and the use of poisonous gases, the 10th Company had succeeded in smashing the attack alone. The French had achieved nothing at all. Our mine system was completely intact. Damage to material, however was immense; it was a terrible scene of destruction. This day of glory for the 10th Company had come at a high price. Nine men had been killed and twenty-five wounded; most of them seriously. As far as the French were concerned, we found one officer, one officer cadet and thirty-two men dead on the position. Four wounded men were captured. All were from the 6th and 7th Companies of Infantry Regiment 403.

"So the 19th July ended in an honourable victory. It was followed by a hard night. The position had to be cleared and reconstructed. The wounded had to be taken to the rear and the dead recovered. To that was added the uncertainty as to whether the enemy would come again. The company undertook this work after enduring ten hours of drumfire and beating off an attack. These brave and courageous Landwehr and Landsturm men deserve the highest praise and I think of them with pride."

On the 2nd August, the first day of the second year of war for the men of XIV Reserve Corps, there was a solemn ceremony in Bapaume as a memorial to the dead of the Corps was unveiled and dedicated in the presence of the Grand Duke of Baden. It was placed near to the memorial to the French fallen of the war of 1870/71. An eyewitness from Reserve Infantry Regiment 109 described the scene:[27]

"Grey rain clouds hung in the sky. In the little town of Bapaume, there was festive bustle. In colours of red and black or yellow and red, the pennants and standards fluttered alongside the imperial colours.

Everywhere there was a ceremonial stillness. A long procession moved in the direction of the cemetery near the town. There a memorial to our dead had been erected. It was massive and yet modest, beautifully wrought, but not pretentious. It was a tall obelisk, sculpted in shell limestone, mounted on a base in the form of a truncated, stepped pyramid and surmounted by a large sphere, the symbol of beginning and completion. It stood there, surrounded by a hedge of close clipped bushes, at the end of one of the silent avenues of lime trees, which divided the cemetery in the form of a cross. Few words were inscribed on the memorial and its decoration was of the simplest: the Iron Cross and beneath it an inscription composed by His Excellency, Generalleutnant von Stein:

> 'Wir neigen das Haupt vor unseren Toten
> Die furchtlos und treu ihr Leben boten
> Was sterblich war, brachten wir hier zu Ruh'
> Ihr Geist zog befreit der Heimat zu'

> 'We bow our heads before the graves
> Of these brave men whose lives they gave
> Their mortal remains lie here at rest
> Their spirits recalled to the Homeland's breast'

> 'Through this memorial the XIV Reserve Corps acknowledges its debt to those of its Comrades who fell around Bapaume."[28]

The first seven months of the year had continued much as the previous one had ended. The Poilus of the French army had faced the Feldgrauen of the Germany army from fixed positions across a No Man's Land which been disputed repeatedly as local fighting flared up and died away. It had all become routine, but then in the closing days of July came a development in the northern sector of the Somme, which was a total, almost unbelievable, surprise to the Germans.

### Landwehr Leutnant M. Gerster Reserve Infantry Regiment 119[29]

"Already by the second half of July, Reserve Infantry Regiment 121, which had high points of observation at its disposal, noted a great deal of movement behind the enemy lines. This increased continually. On the roads from Bray to Corbie, from Engelbelmer to Hedauville and Hedauville to Mailly, batteries of four to six guns were seen moving by day, as were individual guns with strong teams of horses, motor transport, numerous supply vehicles and others of all kinds. In between came formed bodies of troops: infantry in company, battalion and regimental strength accompanied by cavalry. Large scale troop movements and reliefs seemed to be underway. Suddenly a new battery firing from the flank opened up. The firing signature and explosions on impact sounded different. The infantry had developed a sharp ear for such things during the course of the months.

"The entire style of firing was quite different. Instead of high explosive, the new opponents made use of a great deal of airburst shrapnel. The shooting was less accurate; rather there was an emphasis on an aimless strewing of shells all over the area equally. The previous opponents had ranged in their guns with a terrible accuracy, which the new ones lacked. Soon new calibres were being discovered. The French 75 millimetre shell disappeared. On 30th July, the casing of an 83 millimetre shrapnel round, on 8th August a 155 millimetre and on the 12th August a 77 millimetre round were found. The new shells were made of drawn steel, with thicker walls than the French ones. They had different, wider driving bands and sloping marks from the rifling. For the first time shells with burning fuzes appeared, the factory markings indicating English or United States [origin]. There could be no more doubt. The British artillery had relieved the French.

"What, however, was the position with the infantry? On the 1st August a steel-jacketed round was discovered in Thiepval A. It had five rifling grooves, with a left hand spin, so it could only have come from a British weapon. The French had for the most part kept quiet at night. Suddenly sentries were maintaining a lively rate of fire, which from early morning until it was light, grew into the planned firing of salvoes; so much so, that it seemed as though an infantry battle was taking place. The number of enemy machine guns increased alarmingly. Instead of the slow tack-tack of the French machine guns, which fell silent after twenty-five rounds until a new strip could be loaded, there was a new, seemingly never-ending, chatter of new weapons which fired right across the front and at night menaced the approach routes. On 2nd August white illuminating cartridges like ours appeared. The parachute flares had disappeared.

"Initially nobody wanted to believe that the British had arrived. Where had the British suddenly produced an army large enough to relieve the French on such a scale? The wildest rumours flew through the air. It was rumoured that following the breakthrough battles in the east, the Western Front would now be torn apart. The strategists, of whom there was rarely any lack in the trenches, just as in the taverns back home, demonstrated with logical precision that we Germans would now break through around Albert, thrust forward to Abbeville via Amiens and so split the British from the French. The really clever ones, especially those who belonged to the artillery, who allegedly could hear the grass grow, even knew exactly how many corps and guns we would deploy. For the time being the enemy simply deployed more and more forces. The first of the British, who was seen on 1st August at Thiepval Wood, was taken for a Frenchman in a field grey kepi. By 2nd August, patrols of Reserve Infantry Regiment 99, operating forward of the mill in Hamel, were describing the new opponents as definitely British. On the other hand, as late as the 4th August, Reserve Infantry Regiment 121 reported that their patrols, operating the previous night, had heard French being spoken in the trenches and that they had definitely recognised the singing of the French marching song 'Sambre et Meuse', the Alsace 'Marseillaise'. On the same day, information arrived from General Headquarters that the 52nd Infantry Division on the right flank of the 26th Reserve Division had reported the presence of the British, then at 2.00 pm, Reserve Infantry Regiment 121 observed clearly a man in the enemy trench, 'with a round, stiff, sand-coloured forage cap and a brown suit.'

"There was still some doubt. Perhaps we were opposed by a mixed force of French and British? It was essential, therefore, to confirm the situation by means of the capture of prisoners. The divisional order to bring in a prisoner dead or alive was hardly necessary. Even without it, our patrols were as hell bent as the devil after some poor soul, on running to earth the slightest shred of evidence. But the enemy still did not dare to enter No Man's Land. In the meantime, observation of the enemy relief continued. The new uniform of the British soldier was observed ever more frequently. On the 5th August, Reserve Infantry Regiment 121 reported that the men in the enemy trench were dressed in brown uniforms and were carrying short rifles. In Sector Thiepval B, a Feldwebelleutnant, who had had taken part in the China campaign, shot an opponent who had shown himself from the knees up. He had clearly recognised the British uniform of grey-green colour, with its breast pockets and pleated jacket. However in Thiepval C, the 2nd Battalion Reserve Infantry Regiment 121 still felt that they had French opposite them. On 7th August, Reserve Infantry Regiment 121 recognised men in the village street in earth coloured uniforms, but others in the cemetery in blue uniforms. Reserve Infantry Regiment 99 reported that an officer's patrol, which moved along the enemy wire obstacle, was in no doubt that they had heard French spoken and French national songs sung and whistled. In order to dismiss all doubts, division directed that proposals for trench raids were to be forwarded. Reserve Infantry Regiment 99 suggested an operation against the station master's house in the Ancre valley, Reserve Infantry Regiment 121 one against the so-called 'Cattle-Shed Copse' opposite Thiepval and a second against an advanced section of trench which made up the enemy position opposite the 'Granatloch'.

"By 9th August these proved to be unnecessary. In the mist a member from the enemy trench garrison, who had been working on the barbed obstacle, lost his sense of direction. He appeared in front of the German trench, where he was spotted by a group of watchful and decisive defenders of the Beaumont Mill sector and was captured before he could escape.  He was British. The French army had been relieved along the entire corps frontage, because the same night the 28th Reserve Division captured a prisoner from the Scottish Black Watch Regiment, which was deployed at the Granathof.  Reserve Infantry Regiment 99 was full of glee at having captured the first British prisoner in the divisional sector and the success further spurred on the patrols of the other regiments. On 13th August, Reserve Infantry Regiment 119, which was deployed on the right of the brigade shot two members of a strong enemy patrol from the 1st Royal Irish Fusiliers and took them prisoner.  On 24th August, Reserve Infantry Regiment 99, also operating in the Mill sector, clashed with a British patrol. Casualties occurred on both sides and during the same night a patrol from Reserve Infantry Regiment 121 shot a member of a British listening post. The man could not be recovered and was left lying by the enemy wire obstacle.  However, they captured two British weapons that the enemy dropped whilst making their escape".

*Unteroffizier Schmid 5th Battery Bavarian Field Artillery Regiment 1*[30]  **11.**

"For some days we had apparently had the British opposite us and they brought us under accurate fire. They had a new calibre of piece – 83 millimetres – which fired a sulphur gas shell.* At 11.30 am the bombardment opened and lasted until 3.00 pm.  They fired well, landing shells two to three metres from the guns and also close to the dugouts. I was surrounded by newly-joined men from Munich. The colour drained from their faces and they offered up their final prayers.  None believed that he would escape with his life. I tried to keep their courage up by telling jokes and stories, but I was not very successful.  As a last resort I took out my faithful harmonica and began to blow a tune: 'Muß i denn zum Städtle hinaus.'  Some of them started to take notice and began to whistle along with me for all they were worth.[31] Finally everything calmed down."

There was a swift reaction to the change.  New directives were sent out to the units of XIV Corps, regimental policy towards the new arrivals was published and within a few days an intelligence report, produced as a result of the interrogation of two prisoners captured from 6th Battalion Black Watch and 1st Battalion East Lancashire Regiment respectively, was circulated.[32] This confirmed the relief of the French army by the British and provided a useful, detailed and accurate insight into the recent history, organisation of the battalions themselves and their higher formations.

*Headquarters XIV Reserve Corps Operations Branch Order 854 dated 5th August 1915*[33]

"British troops have been spotted in a number of places opposite the

---

* Schmid is mistaken. The British Army had no gas shells at this time. He was describing the products of combustion when a standard shell, filled with Lyddite, exploded.

52nd Infantry Division, the 26th Reserve Division and the right flank of the 28th Reserve Division. It is possible that French troops are being relieved by British ones. I wish to make the following points clear, for the forthcoming battles with the British.

"The British companies are in the habit of carrying white flags with them. These they raise when they believe that they are no longer able to hold out. Our troops have earlier been taken in by this. They have launched themselves forward, in order to take prisoners and have suffered heavy casualties from adjoining British companies who have not shown a white flag. In battle, therefore, no notice is to be taken of isolated enemy signals of surrender.

"During certain attacks, large numbers of British soldiers have approached our trenches, apparently unarmed, as though they were going to come over to us. These have been mostly coloured soldiers, such as Indians, and they have been received as deserters. Once they were in the trenches, they began suddenly to continue the attack with grenades and knives, whilst other British infantry arrived to consolidate the position.

"Would-be deserters, who appear in large numbers on our front, are to be fired upon with no more ado. If it is observed that they really are carrying no weapons, it is to be made clear that they are to halt beyond the wire obstacle and to approach individually. This is to be made known to all soldiers.
      Signed: von Stein"

*Infantry Regiment 180 Order No 2355 dated 9th August 1915*[34]
      "Comrades!
      "It has been established beyond doubt, that we now have British soldiers opposite us.

"The British soldier is well known as a daring and brave man, whom we therefore do not want to underestimate. The British soldier only pretends to surrender (even if he has already been wounded), in order to take the next opportunity to stab his opponent to death with a knife. So exercise extreme caution when handling prisoners.

"Should the enemy dare to go over to the attack, he will find that we are equipped to deal with him. We must bend all our efforts to the further development of our position.

"We do not want to let up in our efforts to try to bring in prisoners, because it is of extreme importance for us to be aware, constantly, about whom is opposite us.
      "This order is to be made known to all personnel.
            Signed: von Boronsky"

The relief complete, the two sides settled down opposite one another. The British army was less well disposed towards 'live and let live' than the French troops had been, but although mining, countermining, patrolling, raiding and constant exchanges of artillery fire took place, there were no more significant operations that year on the Somme.

*Landwehr Leutnant M. Gerster Reserve Infantry Regiment 119*[35]

"The lengthy period of positional warfare brought with it a thorough reorganisation and an increase in the means of close quarter battle. Heavy and medium mortars had proved their worth everywhere where the trenches were located near to one another. This was the case at Thiepval, where there was much patrol activity and the accumulation of mortars served the tactical purposes of destroying obstacles and enemy trenches, or opening the way for our assaulting troops to the positions that were due to be attacked. The old makeshift light mortars disappeared, to be replaced by the Lance mortars, which proved to have a long range and to be easily transportable. In August the earth mortars with which the 28th Reserve Division had had good experiences near La Boisselle, made their first appearance in the Brigade area. These were the old type with guide rails, upon which the beer barrel-like rounds were launched steeply towards the enemy. The enemy took it badly when on the 19th August Reserve Infantry Regiment 121 first used the new weapon against them, replying with heavy artillery fire against its presumed firing point. Later this primitive model was replaced by the Albrecht model, which performed brilliantly everywhere.

"The makeshift hand grenades available on the outbreak of war disappeared gradually. Factory-made types replaced them: the discus grenade, which gradually disappeared too; the ball-shaped grenade, later relieved by the lighter egg grenade, which could be thrown further and the stick grenade. The safety device of the stick grenade was a constant source of concern and anger for the company commanders. Despite all care, again and again the firing cord was accidentally caught and pulled on exiting dugouts, or when passing along trenches revetted with wooden hurdles. This ignited the grenade without the carrier being aware of the fact, thus putting him in mortal danger. The star screw catch, which was introduced after much experimentation, finally produced a splendid solution to a problem which was far from insignificant for the infantry. The old ballista system, which launched rocks at the enemy, was given a modern reincarnation in the form of the Bosch grenade launcher. This was the source of great fun for the engineers and infantry who operated it. It certainly did little damage to the enemy, but it annoyed them and was a nuisance."

In the meantime, the focus of allied offensive activity moved north to the sector between Arras and La Bassée. German reserves had to be created from units stationed on the Somme and these were engaged in the heavy fighting further north. If the small-scale action around Serre the previous June had provided useful pointers for the development of positions and improvement of means of command and control and tactics, the fighting around Arras produced a mass of information, which was immediately processed and circulated down to company level in the form of directives and memoranda, such as that of Operations Branch VI Army Corps redistributed by the 12th Infantry Division on 28th October,[36]

"The battles around Arras have shown us that a well-constructed position, even one which has been subject to preparatory fire lasting for days, including the heaviest possible drum fire, can be held against repeated assaults, provided that the garrison remains absolutely calm and is led by energetic officers of iron will, who would prefer to die in the defensive line with their men rather than yield.

"The first position must comprise three lines of trenches, separated by about 100 –150 metres. The main essential is to have a broad, strongly constructed obstacle, separated into several distinct rows, to the front. Such obstacles have withstood the very heaviest enemy artillery fire. Swiftly constructed, weak obstacles which lack depth and hasty obstacles are, on the other hand, totally worthless. All enemy infantry attacks wither away before well made obstacles, even if the distance from the start line is very close. Each trench of the first position must be equally strong and thoroughly prepared for defence. This means that all three require a wire obstacle and each must be stocked with ammunition for the close quarter battle (rifle ammunition, hand grenades, signal flares etc). They must also have digging implements, all types of defence stores, rations and water. It is not a good idea to keep all these stocks in the very front line; they must be distributed in all three trenches. Special attention is to be paid to constant re-supply, especially of grenades.

"The first trench must be so well equipped with bullet-proof observation and listening posts that a strong enemy attack can be beaten off, even when casualties have been taken. An overlarge garrison simply invites heavy casualties. The strength in which the second and third trenches can be held depends upon the number of troops available. Regimental and brigade reserves must be able to reach these places in a timely manner.

"Correct use of the machine guns is of fundamental importance. If they are properly placed off to a flank, preferably not in the front-line trench, but in an elevated position and properly handled, their effect can be practically devastating. If they are placed in prepared positions, they will be lost if these places are buried by shell fire. The best plan is to keep them as well protected as possible, then to bring them into action from behind the parapet.

"Communication trenches must not be dug at right angles to the main trenches. They must zigzag, or at least be equipped with short saps left and right. This means that the enemy, who prefers to attack at the junction points of the main trenches and these communication trenches, is immediately confronted by another line of resistance. Prepared hasty obstacles designed to block the trenches are to be held ready at all necessary places.

"The French troops attack immediately behind their barrage. It is difficult to spot this short interlude available to us to man our defences, but it is essential to do so, in order to avoid being overrun. Swift counterattacks are frequently the only means of regaining the front-line trench. If the enemy breaks into the position, counter-attack immediately. This was almost always successful, whereas attempts to recapture ground later failed in many cases – so keep reserves close by.

"Co-location of infantry regimental commanders and artillery group commanders has proved to be very effective.

"The first pre-requisite for the commander to be able to influence the battle is to maintain communication to all subordinate forces. In the front-line trenches, voice tubes have proved to be best, followed by bells and gongs. Further to the rear, there must be constant efforts to maintain telephone links. The most resistant means has proved to be armoured cable laid two to three metres deep. However this takes a long time to lay and it is difficult to repair. In many places, in particular those which are not subject to long periods of drumfire, lightweight cable laid above ground has proved to be effective, because it is easily repairable. All vital links must, in any case, be laid in triplicate. It is impossible to counter the fact that even the best link will fail during heavy fire, so stout hearted men must be held in readiness to act as runners. Without them, the commander can exert no influence over the course of the battle.

"Links to neighbours (artillery and infantry) must not fail. They were always good to I Bavarian Reserve Corps, but often failed with the left hand division of IV Army Corps. Even when the other side makes mistakes, our side must constantly strive to rebuild the link. Do not select paths which are under fire, even if this means diversions. Make immediate use of neighbours who still have communications for relay purposes.

"In all reports there must be strict differentiation between events which have been observed directly and those which have been reported from other places. No matter how hard the battle, reports must be properly assessed. Incorrect or exaggerated reports can lead the high command to draw false conclusion, which can have the most serious consequences.

"All commanders stress unanimously that the arrival of the rations had an immediate positive effect on the morale of their men and their ability to go on resisting. Warm food is to be brought forward to the front-line at least once per day. To this end, regiments should designate particular officers and carrying parties. Use of non-deployed elements has proved effective in some cases. In others, elements of the engineer company were used. There must be dumps of solid fuel in all first position trenches. At times of tension, the men need more to drink and less to eat than normal. If conditions allow, delivery of mail into the front line has a stimulating effect and is good for morale.

"If the artillery has ranged in its defensive fire zones accurately and has exercised the use of alarm signals carefully with the infantry, it is often the case that enemy infantry attacks can be nipped in the bud, especially when it has been possible to fire on concentrations of troops in the enemy trenches. Our artillery achieved this brilliantly at Arras.

"Engineers are best held back. If they are then used at night after the initial attacks, to make good damage to the defensive positions, they can render the best possible service to the infantry.

"Commanders must pay the greatest attention to the care and evacuation of the wounded. Stretcherbearers from the medical companies must use every opportunity to go to the front line and recover the wounded. Wherever this duty is done with care and energy, the trust of the men in their commanders and ability to resist is enhanced.

"It has been noticeably advantageous to appoint an experienced and energetic mounted officer and to provide him with manpower from the Divisional cavalry regiment to gather together small groups and stragglers behind the front and to despatch them forward to their units. It is also a good plan to control the villages behind the lines (Battle Police), the transport lines and quartermasters' areas (officer in a motor vehicle) to keep an eye open for soldiers who have gathered there unnecessarily.

"Bids have been submitted to raise the first line ammunition stocks of the field artillery batteries to 1,500 rounds. Nevertheless it must be impressed on the field artillery that it must be sparing in its use of ammunition.

"All other individual lessons learned relate to the local conditions, which must always be taken into account as swiftly as possible."

    Signed: Châles de Beaulieu
    Authenticated: von Maskowski
    Major

XIV Reserve Corps also summarised these lessons for the individual soldier and printed a notice for display in all dugouts:[37]

Notice
For every dugout in the front line

1. Our infantry is superior to any enemy, which it resists courageously or attacks valiantly.
2. Our dugouts will resist the heaviest and lengthiest artillery fire, but you need to leave yours in a timely fashion and race to the parapet when the enemy attacks. Anyone who remains inside risks death from hand grenades or the effects of gas. So: everyone out!
3. Don't store your rifles and hand grenades in the entrances to the dugouts, where they can easily become buried. Take them with you into the dugout! The same applies to machine guns.
4. Don't be afraid of gas attacks – even if they darken the sky. The gas will pass over to the rear quickly. Put on your protective equipment and light fires of old wooden boxes in front of you! Only troops who have lost their heads during a gas attack have been thrown back by the enemy; those who have stood firm have beaten back attacks.
5. Use your rifle initially from the parapet! Only throw grenades when the enemy has closed right up. They are often thrown too soon.
6. If the enemy breaks into the trench, continue the fight with hand grenades! Help will arrive immediately from the flanks and rear and everyone must go to the aid of their neighbours if the enemy breaks in there.
7. If there is an enemy breakthrough, don't lose your head! Only feeble troops surrender. Brave troops conduct a fighting withdrawal. In this way courageous companies have taken thousands of prisoners during the recent battles.
8. Soldiers will always be re-supplied with food and drink, even if the battle lasts for days.

The Commanding General
von Stein

1st and 2nd Battalions of the Prussian Reserve Infantry Regiment 99, which was the only Regiment not from Württemberg to form part of the 26th Reserve Division, were engaged fully in the autumn fighting. Generalleutnant Freiherr von Soden, the divisional commander, seized on this fact, exploiting fully the practical experience that they had gained. Further emphasis was placed on infantry-artillery cooperation and a great deal of work was done to improve proficiency with hand grenades, which had tended to be an engineer speciality up until that time.

*Landwehr Leutnant M. Gerster Reserve Infantry Regiment 119*[38]
    "The importance of the hand grenade in the close quarter battle was repeatedly drummed into every single man during the course of thorough

training. Troops returning from Arras demonstrated grenade fighting to others. They were shown how to beat off attacks, by using masses of grenades simultaneously. This produced a drumfire-like effect and created a type of area defensive fire. The technique of bombing from traverse to traverse to wrest back, bit by bit from the enemy, a trench which he had forced his way into, was also demonstrated. Each man had to throw live grenades. The companies also trained grenade teams, which specialised in the technique of rolling up an enemy which was defending a trench. The troops soon developed an interest in the competitive possibilities of the new weapon, so during sports days, which the battalions which had been relieved organised behind the front, competitions for accuracy and length attracted a great number of participants."

*Generalleutnant Freiherr von Soden Commander 26th Reserve Division*[39]

"This period of relative calm at the front was fully exploited by the carrying out of carefully planned work, which bore fruit during the Battle of the Somme. The First Position developed into three lines of trenches. Further to the rear were the Second and Third Positions, which were developed by reinforcement troops. The mined dugouts were driven deeper and deeper, to a depth of up to eight metres or more and they were also equipped with two or more entrances. The infantryman became so at home with this type of work that engineers were only needed in the role of foremen...Progress was made with the provision of water supplies and the discovery of sources by divining... and electricity was supplied increasingly to the tunnels and dugouts... The Third Line of the First Position, the so-called Intermediate Position, was further strengthened by the development of Soden Redoubt, the Grallsburg, Old-Württemberg Redoubt, Schwaben Redoubt and through the fortification of Mouquet Farm... Sources of intelligence improved. These included radio intercept and listening in to telephone conversations by means of the installation of 'Moritz' and 'Arend' stations. All the time that the enemy was unaware of the potential of these stations, we were in a position to listen in to every enemy order and we got to know every company commander by name..."

Streams of intelligence reports and summaries were produced and given wide distribution. Much of the material comprised basic background intelligence, but translations of captured British and French documents were also grist to the mill, as were detailed prisoner interrogation reports and the occasional unusual item. Temporary Lieutenant Colonel Harold Evans Walter, 8th Battalion Lincolnshire Regiment,[40] who was captured at Loos on 26th September, was found to be carrying a poem on his person. This was very cleverly and wittily translated into rhyming and scanning German and distributed successively by Second Army on 18th November, XIV Reserve Corps on 23rd November and 26th Reserve Division down to company level on 24th November. It is not known if this was done as an example of British military cynicism regarding politicians, or just to raise a smile.

> *Lloyd George no doubt, when his life ebbs out*
> *Will in a fiery chariot*
> *Ride in state on a red-hot plate*
> *Between Satan and Judas Iscariot*
>
> *Ananias that day to the Devil will say*
> *My claim to precedence now fails*
> *So move me up higher, away from the fire*
> *And make way for that Liar from Wales"*[41]

Just as earlier when the French army was occupying the whole of the Somme region, life had once more taken on a routine quality. This showed itself in a number of ways, but especially manifested itself in the way the opposing artillery operated.

*Landwehr Leutnant M Gerster Reserve Infantry Regiment 119*[42]

"This was a period of quiet... during which time there were no large scale military operations... It was of course not really peaceful. Nightly fights between patrols flared repeatedly along the brigade sector. Later these grew into trench raids and involved substantial numbers of assaulting troops and large quantities of ammunition. The enemy artillery brought down fire of varying intensity, first on this point, then on that, attempted to interfere with work, or bring the traffic to a standstill. At other times, in conjunction with the trench mortars, it would flatten a section of trench, causing casualties and damage. Our artillery replied, when ammunition was available to them and calls for help from the infantry became too loud. The delightful phrase 'Revenge Fire' was coined, being applied, in particular, when the villages in the rear, where the troops rested and where the higher headquarters were located, came under fire. Gradually a type of unwritten understanding developed between the artillery of the two sides and they stuck to it. If the enemy fired on Pozières and Grandcourt, we fired on Authuille and Hamel. If we brought down fire on Aveluy and Mesnil, revenge arrived in Martinpuich and Courcelette. If the guns of 28th Reserve Division questioned the busy traffic at Albert Station, the enemy replied to ensure that we did not lack for anything at Irles Halt. Days such as 1st November, when only four shells fell on the brigade sector, were indeed a rarity. On the other hand there were ever more days when more than 1,000 shells landed unpleasantly."

The primacy of the artillery on the battlefield was well established by now. It was clear that only by fully exploiting its potential could the German defenders hope to hold off a determined attack. This in turn demanded the best possible liaison between artillery and infantry and above all excellent communications so that the fire of the guns could be controlled at as high a level as possible, in order to ensure that in an emergency all guns within range could be called upon to respond. The means of communication available in 1915–16 made this extremely difficult to achieve, so it remained a major preoccupation of all commanders throughout the period. Following an incident on 23rd December, which had not been well handled, the commander of Reserve Field Artillery Regiment 26 spent the Christmas period reflecting on the problem and committing his thoughts to paper.

### *Major Bornemann Reserve Field Artillery Regiment 26*[43]

"In general it may be stated that formal links to the infantry are all in place, thanks to the presence of the artillery liaison officers. On the other hand, it appears that insufficient attention has been paid to fostering personal relationships; yet this area demands the greatest attention if mutual understanding and cooperation between the two arms is to be improved.

"<u>Background.</u> A mine was being detonated in Beaumont North and the artillery liaison officer was informed by the engineer commander. The liaison officer correctly brought a battery to standby, but failed to inform the artillery battalion. In consequence, nobody but the liaison officer and the battery knew that a mine was about to explode. This was a serious error, which should have been avoided at all costs. Following the explosion the enemy position behind the blown mine and the communication trenches leading to it ought to have been brought under harassing fire, because there would have been many valuable targets. But this was not the only reason that not informing Battalion was an error of judgement. It meant, in addition, that neither the battalion nor the neighbouring sectors could prepare themselves for the consequences of the explosion.

"From 12.00 pm onwards on 23rd December the enemy artillery brought down fire on Beaumont itself and part of Sectors Beaumont North and Beaumont South. From all the reports that were made as a result of this incident and also from experience gained during similar occurrences, it is without doubt the case that the observation from the observation posts, as well their interface with the guns, is deemed to have decreased in importance because it is assumed that the liaison officers with the infantry will see and report everything of significance. <u>This is completely false</u>. In this respect it has been reconfirmed that all battery observation posts must be manned constantly by day and also that it is the duty of every section commander, battery commander and, above all, every observer, to order fire to be opened on his own initiative if it seems at all to be necessary. The principle must be: rather too many rounds expended, than over concern with ammunition usage, which means that there is too little weight of fire employed on suitable targets. In addition, it has been observed that too little reporting occurs, on the assumption that command posts are long since fully in the picture. It is the duty of the observer to keep all relevant posts up to date. This is to be done by the provision of accurate reports, which make clear which sectors are under enemy fire. These reports must be relayed from the batteries to the battalions and from there to the regiment. If necessary, the reports should go direct to the regiment. There have been far too many failures in this regard.  It is fundamentally wrong to wait until demands for situation reports come from the rear. Every command post should try to compete with every other to be first with the information.  It is for the reporter himself to decide what should be passed on, but rather report too much, than risk a report being missed, in the mistaken belief that it may already be known about.

"Effect of Fire. According to the statements of prisoners, our artillery only causes the enemy slight casualties, mainly because the same places are continually engaged in the same pattern. In the recent past, our fire plans have directed concentrations almost exclusively against the enemy forward positions, directly opposite. It can be assumed, with certainty, that our operating methods have not gone unnoticed by the enemy and that he has aimed off for them correspondingly. So we must strive to ensure that we bring variety into our operating methods, so that we may reasonably assume that we are causing the enemy casualties. We must not restrict ourselves to firing at the trenches opposite, but must also bring down fire on all targets within range, so that the enemy is unable to feel comfortable anywhere and, in particular, so that we can disrupt the work of enemy artillery observers who are deployed everywhere.

"As an example, assume that we are bombarding Beaumont itself, Beaumont North and Beaumont South: the 2nd Battalion brings down flanking fire on the relevant trenches. 1st Battalion remains free to engage the Sugar Refinery, Auchonvillers, Flower Pot Copse and known observation posts.  To make this possible, every gun in range must participate.  This should be possible when there is no other call for defensive fire, or the front line trench may not be engaged, because it is unoccupied or only weakly held.

"It is not possible to confine our activities to concentrations of fire. The amount of ammunition available will not allow it. Concentrations should bring success against particular points, but other places, such as those listed above, also need to be engaged. Concentrations have a localised effect. But if we restrict ourselves to those alone, the enemy will be able to do as he pleases elsewhere. So when particular points are engaged, some guns must be ranged at the same time against other worthwhile targets. This isolated fire should serve both to disrupt the enemy and convince our own infantry that we will not cease fire until the enemy does.

"Our response fire must be brought down as swiftly as possible. That increases the trust the infantry has in us. As was mentioned earlier, the sense of responsibility on the part of the battery commanders and all others authorised to call for fire, must not only not be restrained, on the contrary, it must be promoted. That is to say every valuable target must be engaged, without consideration about ammunition expenditure. The regiment will take responsibility for that. When, as has happened, for example, a battery commander detects an enemy battery within range, it is to be engaged immediately with at least 200 rounds, without prior consultation. It must be mentioned, however, that experience has shown that it is a sound idea to have the presence of the enemy artillery confirmed by survey.

"The regiment has requested that our aviators cooperate more with the field artillery than they have done hitherto; that in principle they direct fire on at least one target per flight. These could be roads or engineer parks and, later, mobile targets. This will only be possible if battery commanders prepare suitably gridded target sketches of the observable terrain. The regiment will check this work later. Whenever enemy aircraft are over the position, then the principles remain as they always have been. That is to say, our positions must not be betrayed too early, in order that we may be fully battle ready at moments of danger. Because our aviators are now stationed closer to the front, it will be possible to call for support in a shorter space of time than used to be the case. The appearance of enemy aircraft is to be reported without delay.

"The group commanders have total control over the ammunition allocated to them. If there is a reason to exceed this usage, this can occur immediately on the responsibility of the group commander. The regiment can be requested later to replenish from stocks under its control and, where this is insufficient, ammunition will be demanded from higher authority."

This was a serious subject for consideration on Christmas Day, but then Christmas 1915 was altogether a more serious, sombre time than it had been a year previously. Yes, there were Christmas trees and celebrations in the dugouts; yes, presents arrived from family and well-wishers, but very few troops could be spared from front line duties to go to the rear for the traditional church services and general festivities. Instead there was patrol activity up and down the line. Men of the 7th Company Reserve Infantry Regiment 119 under Unteroffizier Lehmann, clashed with the British up near Beaumont Hamel in a sharp action on 23rd December[44] and, whilst 2nd Battalion Reserve Infantry Regiment 111 was lucky enough to spend Christmas in Le Sars, where they were showered with gifts by the Lord Mayor of Konstanz, Herr Dietrich,[45] for the majority the festive season was spent in far from festive surroundings.

Some of the men of Reserve Infantry Regiment 110, which had continued to have a hard autumn, disputing possession of Hill 110 and other key points around Fricourt with their opponents, spent Christmas planning and practising for a major trench raid, which was scheduled after one or two false starts for 6.00 pm on the 29th December. It was to be conducted by two officers and forty five men. Its target was a group of farm buildings along the road Bray – Fricourt, west of Hill 110 and the aim was to capture prisoners. It was to be a complex operation, contrasting very sharply with the amateurish efforts which had been a constant in the life of the front line soldiers in the earlier part of the year. It involved not only the use of a heavy artillery bombardment, but also featured the firing of firing gas shells as a deception measure. No effort was spared and the volunteers were rehearsed intensively in their roles.

*Reserve Leutnant Vulpius Reserve Infantry Regiment 110* [46] **12.**

"The weather around Christmas was foul. The damp, west wind, which had been blowing gas back over us, obstinately refused to slacken. Although it would otherwise have been pleasant to be whiling away the time in our favourite Bazentin, it would have been better to have had the operation behind us. Our comrades looked on us with pity: rather as at experimental rabbits. This was, after all, one of the very first of this type of raid, which was to involve lengthy artillery preparation and gas shells, but we were full of confidence after Hauptmann Wagener had laid everything out clearly and crisply.

"Finally we had gas weather on 29th December and we marched up to our positions...We had a final briefing, then waited with dry mouths. The artillery preparation would be beginning shortly. Night fell on cloudy skies. Then, at exactly 5.00 pm, there was a roaring and growling overhead and shells could be seen arching through the sky like shooting stars, to land over there and begin the violent process of destruction... The bombardment went on for forty-five minutes, rising finally to a peak of drumfire. We stood there like spectators at a public entertainment. It had now gone dark. The luminous figures and hands on the watch moved round to 5.50 pm. 'Go.' We hare along the embankment of the road, until we reach our target fifty metres away. 'Down!' The heavy mortars thunder and roar, recognisable from the patterns of light they trace against the dark sky. A curtain of fire crashes down, sending millions of sparks flying upwards. A thought runs through my tense mind: it is just like the golden rain when the bridge at Heidelberg is being illuminated! - 5.58 pm – 59 – Stand by! 6.00 pm. OK let's go! Damn it, a mortar round is arriving late. 'Take Cover!' Fragments fly in all directions. One man is wounded and has to withdraw. He is the only casualty of the entire raid. We take only five seconds to reach the trench. The mortars have done a great job of flattening the obstacle, but we still have a metaphorical stone in our shoe: a stinging stink of gas! It takes so long to disperse. 'Mask up!' Moments later I order them to be removed. It is completely impossible in these stupid objects to take a single step – better to have stinging eyes.

"We dash over the front line trench, which one group secures. Now into the buildings! The fire lifts forward. Explosions and flares provide some light. One roof has been blown off completely and lies wrecked on top of the ruins... We press on, leaving another group at a trench junction. There are dead men in a crushed dugout. Pistol shots ring out from the far side of the buildings. I peer around the corner of a wall and am confronted by the black entrance to a cellar. Caution – there could be men from Partenheimer's patrol about. I bawl down the password: *'Gandenberger!'* An unrecognisable English voice replies. Right let's sort that out. A hand grenade is flung down, explodes with a fearful crash, black smoke rises, followed by pitiful cries. We could despatch the lot of them, but we need live prisoners. I still have four men with me, including the lanky Kriegsfreiwilliger Eisenstraud and Roth of the 1st Company, tough men both, who guard the junction with a communication trench. I scratch together my few words of English. 'Are you wounded?' – 'Yes, yes!' 'You will be well treated if you come out immediately.' No success. Signal flares shoot up, indicating that we need to think about withdrawing. 'Right! Either you come up, or you will get a second grenade!' This works. In a long line, they climb out, hands up in the air, faces creased with anxiety and without weapons. They include a callow young corporal from a suburb of London. Their lieutenant went on leave yesterday – pity! Ever more emerge, twelve, thirteen, rather too many! It's just as well they are not a daring lot. 'If anyone makes a wrong move, he's a dead man!' With my back to a wall I shine a light on their faces and point my revolver. 'Good comrade, no weapons, good friend!' [sic] One of them falls to his knees, pointing at his bleeding hand and plucks at my arm.

"My men head off. Finally there are still seven lads standing in front of me. If a counterattack is launched from the communication trench, we have had it, but nothing happens. Luck is one of the greatest soldierly virtues. I cannot see a single one of my men and I can hardly lead off, so I attempt to impose my will: 'My entire company is just round the corner. Our forces have already reached Albert. You see those poplars over there?' A few appear lit up in the flash of an explosion. 'Right, head in that direction. That is the German trench. Any one trying to escape will be shot!' 'Yes, yes!' and, truthfully, they trotted off in that direction in single file, with two men supporting a seriously injured comrade – the hand grenade had torn open his stomach – bringing up the rear. I followed on, revolver raised, looking behind me at each step: They must be coming! – Nothing.

"We left the enemy trench and linked up with the others. It was a comfortable trip back through No Man's Land, because our artillery was still coming down on the enemy positions and the British had forgotten about defensive fire. Then I could not believe my eyes: a Tommy lit a cigarette for his escort and there they were, both smoking! Their good treatment led them to take a risk. One or two tried to run for it, but a couple of prods with the bayonet put paid to that idea. A giant of a man was standing in our trench and he lowered each newcomer down into it with an elegant swing. We carried the seriously wounded man down into a dugout and let him drink calmly. Our men were as gentle as nurses with him, but it was a hopeless case. I counted the heads of my dear comrades. All present and correct! Then I counted the almost equally dear prisoners. Partenheimer's patrol had had great success, swiftly overcoming resistance and taking prisoners. Altogether there were twenty of them... We marched to the rear in a sort of 'victory procession', with one Tommy between each two of our men. We were bursting with pride as we marched along our way, singing, to Bazentin, with the Tommies, who were quite happy to cling on to the evil enemy. There was a surprise at the entrance to the village. The entire garrison was lining the route and greeted us with the light of countless electric torches. It was a triumphant little scene. The prisoners were brought into the church. They were brimming over with gratitude. Goodness knows what they had been told about the Huns! One of them tore the cockade from his headdress and gave it to me, 'Because you did not kill me!'"

So 1915 drew to a close. For the German army it had been a long, monotonous, year, marked more by endless labour and tedious fatigues than clashes with the enemy. In fact, most of the time, their greatest enemy was staleness and boredom. Nevertheless, the soldiers manning the trenches had learned how to make themselves as safe and comfortable as the conditions would allow. They were much better equipped to cope with the demands of trench warfare and their weaponry, accommodation and living arrangements were an infinite improvement on the improvisations of December 1914. In short, they now accepted that the war on the Western Front was not going to be brought to a conclusion in the near future and, just as important, they had learned to endure. They had gained enormously in experience, drawing and applying the critical lessons obtained in the hard schools of the fighting for Serre and the battles north of Arras. At the beginning of the year there had been general uncertainty about what the future would hold. This time it was at least clear that the New Year would bring more of the same, but that they were now strongly placed to resist whatever pressure the enemy chose to bring to bear on them.

1 Anon: History 5th Coy BILR pp 66-67
2 Seneca: History FAR 67 p 69
3 Gallion: History RIR 40 p 60
4 Cron: History IR 60 p 69
5 Eder: History RIR 269 p 13
6 ibid. p 16
7 ibid. pp 16-17
8 Lehmann: History BPiR p 122
9 Fromm: History RIR 120 pp 17-19
10 Bathe: 'Männer am Feind' pp 77-79
11 Anon: History RIR 110 pp 73-74
12 Frisch: History RIR 109 p 59
13 Eder: op. cit. pp 19-20
14 Gallion: op .cit. p 62
15 Hauptstaatsarchiv, Stuttgart M410 Bü 260
16 Kuchtner: History BFAR 9 p 84
17 Frisch: op. cit. pp 53-54
18 Anon: History 5th Coy BILR pp 71-72
19 Soden: History 26th Res Div p 81
20 ibid. p 82
21 Korfes: History IR 66 p 154
22 Soden: op. cit. p 85
23 Korfes: op. cit. p 155
24 Kriegsarchiv München 8 RIR Bd 21
25 Frisch: op. cit. p 65
26 Anon: History RIR 110 pp 79-81
27 Frisch: op. cit. p 68
28 This memorial was moved to the German war cemetery at Villers-au-Flos in 1932.
29 Hauptstaatsarchiv, Stuttgart M410 Bü 260
30 Xylander: History BFAR 1 p 104
31 It was still a good tune forty-five years later when Elvis Presley used it for 'Wooden Heart'.
32 Hauptstaatsarchiv, Stuttgart M107 Bü 41/22
33 Hauptstaatsarchiv, Stuttgart M99 Bü 141/91
34 Hauptstaatsarchiv, Stuttgart M99 Bü 141/105
35 Hauptstaatsarchiv, Stuttgart M410 Bü 260
36 Kriegsarchiv München 6 RIR Bd 8
37 Hauptstaatsarchiv, Stuttgart M107 Bü 41/119
38 Hauptstaatsarchiv, Stuttgart M410 Bü 260
39 Soden: op. cit. p 90
40 Lt. Col. HE Walter was captured at Loos, died of wounds on 29th September 1915 and is buried at Douai Communal Cemetery. He was last seen by his Battalion on the edge of Bois Hugo, a few hundred metres north of Hill 70. 'He stood', said Second Lieutenant Cragg, 'not knowing what fear was, in the midst of a hot fire at close range, forty yards off, calling on us to charge. Just as he led us, he fell.' The Lincolns lost 22 officers and 471 other ranks in this action.
41 Hauptstaatsarchiv, Stuttgart M104 Bü 41/51
42 Hauptstaatsarchiv, Stuttgart M410 Bü 260
43 Hauptstaatsarchiv, Stuttgart M179 Bü 16
44 Gerster: History RIR 119 p 43
45 Bachelin: History RIR 111 pp 82-83
46 Anon: History RIR 110 pp 91-93

CHAPTER THREE

# 1st January – 30th June 1916

U p and down the line 1916 opened with a renewal of the battle, not only against the enemy, but also against the mud. Trying to maintain the trench system and to keep the routes clear was even more difficult than it had been a year earlier, because the trench network was so much more complex and long by this stage of the war. Once more the walls of the communications trenches slumped and they filled with water, thus rendering them impassable, but much the same applied to the second and third line trenches of the First Position. With every available man working as hard as he was able, it was not possible during the early part of the year to do more than maintain a single front line trench open. Nevertheless living conditions, both at the front and in the billets behind the lines, were a substantial improvement over those which had obtained the previous winter. Almost all dugouts were fitted with heating stoves and the various corps and divisions supplemented fuel supplies from Germany by employing some troops locally as charcoal burners.

*Landwehr Leutnant M. Gerster Reserve Infantry Regiment 119*[1]

"Already in November the winter rains had set in unusually heavily. In December there was even more precipitation. Very soon the ground, where it did not consist entirely of chalk, was so soaked that the high walls of the trenches collapsed. All attempts by the troops to counter the new enemy with revetments made of hurdles and wooden frameworks were in vain. Already, after only a few days, the communication trenches and the second and third trenches of the First Position were reduced to muddy ditches with deep puddles. With ceaseless effort the front line trench was maintained in good condition. Only when the storm abated was it possible to open up the main communication trenches and the second trench. All troops in rear were called forward to assist, so there could be no question at all of rest. Troops from XVIII Corps and Infantry Regiments 115 and 117 were also used for trench digging; for the most part in the Second Position, however. Even though the winter was bad, the troops in the front line had deep dry dugouts with stoves and fuel, so they were at least able to get dry and were accommodated warmly. Nevertheless during very bad weather in certain really vile dugouts, some companies never got out of wet boots and clothing for weeks at a time. During the first winter of the war there was only one trench to maintain, but now the work was tripled. As a result and despite the greatest administrative care the army could arrange, the strain was extraordinarily great. But the troops stuck it out with remarkable patience; the occasional moaning heard being just as normal to the daily life of a soldier as the creaking of a mill."

Behind the lines, corps and divisional slaughterhouses, butchery departments, bakeries and mineral water bottling plants had sprung up everywhere. These were frequently large-scale operations. In order to deliver the daily ration of 350 grams of uncooked meat per man, one of the Bavarian corps estimated that it slaughtered and butchered an average of forty beef cattle and fifty to ninety pigs per day, with peaks on occasions of sixty cattle and one hundred and sixty pigs. A comparison with civilian slaughterhouses back in Bavaria which served towns of between 10,000 and 150,000 inhabitants, showed that only those of Augsburg and Würzburg were busier. Offal was issued freely as a ration supplement and all by-products were shipped back to Germany.[2] The German army on the Somme had become both self-sufficient and thoroughly dug-in, in every sense of the word. The engineer commander of 26th Reserve Division calculated that by now the total length of trench line in the divisional sector was 200 kilometres, that there were 1,500 mined dugouts and no fewer than 150 bullet proof observation posts.[3]

During early January, it had become increasingly clear that some of the French forward positions south of the Somme were only very weakly held, so the 11th Division planned an operation to capture Frise and the positions running southwards from there.  During a conference on the 11th January it transpired that there was a lack of resources to attempt too ambitious an operation, but that a local success would enable the German lines to be shortened usefully. The village was strongly defended to the south where it was overlooked from high ground, but the approach on its eastern side appeared to be more promising. There was sufficient time for extensive reconnaissance by the battalion and company commanders who would be participating and the assault forces were also withdrawn from the line for comprehensive rehearsals, which were further prolonged, to the point of boredom, by the need to wait for a favourable wind to permit the attack to be preceded by the release of gas. Finally the weather forecast was favourable on the 24th January and the attacking forces of Infantry Regiments 38 and 51 moved into position.

Unfortunately the promised winds failed to materialise, so a hastily-organised dumping programme made increased conventional ammunition available to the artillery and it was finally decided to launch the attack on 28th January, supported by sixty batteries and fifty nine mortars. To the south, other formations of the VI Army Corps, in particular the Bavarian 10th Infantry Division, launched simultaneous deceptions, which helped to disguise the true objectives and to enable the 11th Division to succeed completely in its assault. Fire was brought down from 8.30 am on the 28th January all along the front and the feint operations were launched during the early afternoon. The experience of Bavarian

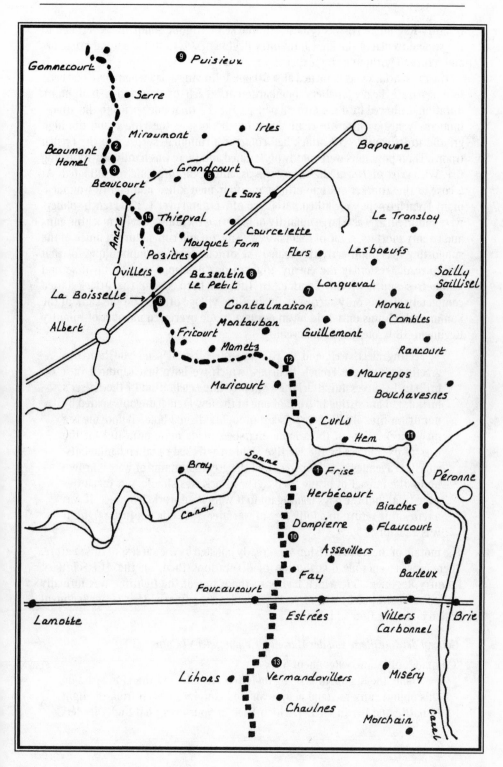

Infantry Regiment 16 was typical. It attacked with one company, penetrated to the second trench of the French Infantry Regiment 74, captured several prisoners and returned without a single casualty.[4]

The main attack was launched at 4.30 pm, following a day when there had been four separate heavy artillery bombardments, each of one and a half hours duration, followed by a ten minute pause. For the final hour prior to the attack, immensely heavy drumfire came down on the area of the village and the high ground to its south. The attack had come as a complete surprise to the French troops. Their positions were totally obliterated and there was hardly any returning fire. With cries of 'Hurra' the village was assaulted, captured and consolidated. At a cost to the attackers of one officer and four men killed and eighty wounded, many French troops were killed, seventeen officers and over 1,300 French soldiers were captured, as was a large quantity of matériel, including twelve machine guns and twenty mortars, some of them heavy.[5] The 'tip and run' nature of much of the supporting deception activity enabled the official French communiqué for that day to read, 'Yesterday the enemy attacked our positions on a front of several kilometres south of the Somme. In the southern sector the attack failed completely. It was only successful against the village of Frise on the bank of the Somme, which was only held by an outpost.'[6] One overjoyed member of Infantry Regiment 38 wrote home that evening,

> 'Feeling alert, well and in the best of spirits, I send you heartiest greetings from the French trenches, which we have just captured in a brilliantly successful attack in a slightly late celebration of the Kaiser's birthday. I am sitting in front of one of the few French dugouts spared by our drum fire. By the way it is a thoroughly dismal hole. Before me is a magnificent view of the Somme marshes, made more beautiful for the eyes of us soldiers by the warlike sight of wrecked canal embankments, smashed avenues of poplar trees and the great fountains of water thrown up by the impact of heavy shells...The attack was simple, our casualties were light, but the days leading up to it were hard work. For once, it was a refreshing return to a jolly sort of warfare. This was not just a fight, it was a victory.'[7] 1.

The morale of the 11th Division was greatly boosted by the success of this venture. There was a generous distribution of decorations then, on the 4th February, Infantry Regiment 51, which had born the brunt of the fighting, was formally visited and reviewed by the Corps Commander, who then addressed the Regiment drawn up in a hollow square.

*General der Kavallerie von der Marwitz, Commander VI Corps* [8]

"Comrades of Infantry Regiment 51!

> "Today the Regiment is being reviewed. I could not, therefore, pass up this opportunity to stand before you and convince myself from the light of battle and joy in victory which I see in your eyes, that under leaders

such as you have and under the command of Oberstleutnant Schwerk, the man who is as a father to you all and to whom quite rightly you accord the highest respect, that I could at any future time entrust you with similar difficult missions.

"But not all of you could answer his name at this regimental roll call! Even though the casualties are light in comparison with that which has been achieved, at an individual level, they are no less painful. Some amongst you must now declare *'Ich hatt' einen Kameraden'* [I had a comrade][9] and perhaps now be realising sadly that you will never again befriend a better man. We wish all the wounded, from the bottom of our hearts, a speedy recovery; for those, however, who sealed their oath of allegiance with their death on the battlefield, I call out aloud, 'Honour their memory!'

"What sort of an operation was it that we now have behind us? You all know that the position that we inherited here from the I Bavarian Corps was shaped by the battles, which were fought here in September and October 1914. As a result, the village of Frise, which is squeezed in by the banks of the river and the Somme canal, remained in French hands. If we were now to succeed in capturing this village, our line would be shortened significantly and we should be able to economise on forces. In addition, no operation of any size had been launched in the Second Army area for fifteen months; only through patrol operations did we establish that we were up against the III French Corps, our old enemies from Souchez. So it was high time for us to show the enemy once more, that the old Prussian offensive spirit was alive and well in our troops and that the enemy press was lying when it maintained that our troops had lost this spirit. On the 28th and 29th January, you made this abundantly clear to the French.

"If the village was to be captured, the high ground to its south had to be secured first. That essentially was your task and you succeeded brilliantly. You have experienced how our artillery brought fire down on the enemy for eight hours and have seen, when the time of your attack came, how outstanding the effect of our artillery fire was. You were able to penetrate the first and second enemy trenches without difficulty. Only when you reached the third trench did you find enemy troops and you simply captured them. As a result you added a fresh laurel leaf to your Regimental wreath of glory. The communiqué from Supreme Headquarters expressly states that this feat of arms was the work of Silesian regiments; back home the province is looking on with pride at its sons.

"The Fatherland and your Supreme Commander thank you for your devotion to duty, for your courage and your sacrificial bravery. I am certain that you will remain true to your Supreme Commander and in future hold fast to the loyalty you displayed on the 28th January 1916. Confirm that to me with a cheer, (Regiment, Present Arms!), 'His Majesty, the Kaiser, *Hurra!*'"

Mining and counter-mining continued with unabated intensity. Two German engineers were killed on New Year's Eve, when a small charge was blown in a gallery of the minefield located on Redan Ridge just north of Beaumont Hamel. This was followed two days later by a massive British 20,000 kilogram charge which blew a giant crater in the Albert - Bapaume road at La Boisselle.[10] Thereafter, up and down the entire front, especially where the German engineers confronted their British counterparts, the activity was frequently frenetic, as the two sides sought to gain an advantage. On Redan Ridge, for example, there was a German explosion on 2nd January, followed a week later by explosions on the 8th and 9th January, which checked the British miners, but not for long. British camouflets fired on the 16th, 17th and 18th January blew in a fifteen metre length of the German gallery, but there were no casualties. The work went on; mines and camouflets were blown by the two sides successively on the 24th and 27th January, followed by others on the 4th, 21st and 25th February, but without causing much damage. The infantry on both sides came to regard the activity as almost routine and the German defensive gallery which ran along parallel to the front line served as an effective barrier to a surprise attack on the main position. Then on the 2nd March, there was an altogether more nerve-wracking incident for the men of Reserve Infantry Regiment 119 and their supporting engineers.

"For several days we had heard a pair of enemy miners at work, so the charging of a half-complete mine chamber was ordered. The carriers laboured to move the anonymous boxes, which concealed death. Slowly the chamber was filled. The work was punctuated by listening pauses. The charge was almost complete. Suddenly, what was that? There was no sound, no thuds any more. Had the British sensed the danger and suspended the work? Or...Suddenly the engineer manning the listening apparatus felt the blood rushing into his head. The temperature underground seemed to have become unbearable. Oh God! The British are loading. The equipment amplified the rustling which must have been coming from the movement backwards and forwards. Now it had become a life or death race. Swiftly the loading was completed. The detonators were placed and the firing cables were run out. Now began the work of tamping. Sandbags and beams were used to block the gallery back: five, ten, twenty metres. The overpressure from exploding gases is terrible. Insufficient tamping is a disaster, because the material is flung out in a terrible spray which blows back into our own mine system and trenches.

"Now night had fallen. Still the work went on at a feverish pace. Up above the night sentries were coming on duty. Flares shot up into the sky like meteorites, before falling down to extinguish themselves in the enemy wire obstacle. Patrol activities began in the neighbouring sectors, but it was quiet today in the minefield. Here death lay in wait. The clock moved on towards midnight. The mine gallery is charged and ready for firing. One of the engineers informs the company commander. The soldiers manning the trench know what they have to do. The artillery stands by ready to fire. The engineer leutnant sits in a dugout and connects the firing cables to a small four-cornered box. Carefully he tests the circuit and the trembling magnetic needle protrudes. A sapper mounts the dark stairs and reports that everything is ready to fire and that all the galleries and shafts have been cleared of workers.

"Slowly the officer withdraws the spring-loaded firing mechanism out of the box. His watch lies in front of him. The blast is scheduled for exactly midnight. Outside and to the sides of the site of the explosion, a hundred eyes bore into the night; calloused, cramped hands grip cold weapons; mortars and earth mortars await the instant when they can launch their bombs into the enemy trenches, which following the shock of the explosion will be filled with enemy troops. Midnight! The button is pressed! The clockwork mechanism in the box whirs. All the lights go out. The dugout sways and threatens to collapse. The very earth quakes. The ground heaves up like a wave above the seat of the explosion and falls back once more. A light cloud of dust seems to be hovering over the site. Suddenly blue flames rush skywards out of a crater, dancing and flickering on the ground and roaring upwards into the sky. This lasts for several seconds! Over there in the enemy trench, two long blue flames like snakes' tongues, lunge forwards seeking victims. No Man's Land is lit up by this ghostly light. Shots crash out. A machine gun starts to chatter. Can we hear shrieks?

"Total darkness descends once more! On the eastern horizon flashes can be seen and then comes the howl of howitzer shells boring down and exploding on the British lines. The murderous bombs of the mortars and earth mortars shoot up in the air like rockets, their trajectories marked like meteors in the sky. A vision of hell unfolds. The fire concentration lasts for five minutes then everything is quiet. What has happened? Apparently the enemy had also prepared a charge. We had fired ours first and the explosion had blown his charge violently to the rear...For two weeks all was quiet in the minefield."[11] 2.

There was also a great deal of low-level patrol activity, but increasingly night time operations in No Man's Land took the form of complex and ambitious trench raids. This was not all one way traffic; frequently the British army, who learned quickly, managed to the turn the tables on the German soldiers, but generally speaking the innovations and therefore most of the success of these operations went their way. Between the 1st of February and the 30th April the 26th Reserve Division alone brought in, dead or alive, six officers and fifty other ranks and were thus able by means of prisoner interrogation to remain fully informed about all developments opposite its positions.[12]

Its other formations enjoyed similar success, so by a few weeks into 1916, it had became clear that XIV Reserve Corps was the pace setter on the Somme front, as far as patrolling and trench raiding was concerned. Apparently in response to a tasking by Second Army dated the 29th February, General von Stein signed a report entitled 'Patrolling Experiences'.[13] This was clearly copied out to all major Headquarters within the Army, because it was renumbered by VI Corps and sent down to its own units a short time later. This is a fascinating document, because it indicates the extent to which the German army had had to keep its techniques under constant review, in order to retain the initiative in this type of warfare, once the relief of the French army by the British was completed in the summer of 1915. It also shows how very sophisticated this type of operation had become by this stage of the war and how much attention to detail was required if success was to be assured.

"Patrolling Experiences. There is no set template for patrol operations. This aspect of the art of war is also a variable one. As soon as the enemy establishes the cause of his misfortune, he seeks the means to prevent a repetition. Once he has found a solution, it is necessary to introduce changes to the way such operations are prepared and conducted. In that which follows, will be found an explanation as to how the patrolling methods of XIV Reserve Corps have gradually evolved since the arrival of the British army along the front.

"When, during the summer of last year, the French army deployed along the Reserve Corps front was relieved by the British army, our troops soon noticed that the new opponents were pursuing a very active patrolling policy, which threatened to rob them of their mastery of the terrain between the two positions. We responded by patrolling very aggressively. Very quickly the German patrols, with their long experience of trench warfare and detailed knowledge of the ground, were able to gain the upper hand and to begin bringing in members of the British patrols dead or alive. In consequence, the British further strengthened their already strong patrols. Sometimes these were found to be forty men strong. Because they continued to have men captured, the British reduced the intensity of their patrolling somewhat. The few patrols that did venture out almost always had strong flank protection and rearguards.

"In order to be able to go on capturing prisoners and other trophies, we adopted a new procedure. By bringing fire down on the enemy wire obstacle using mortars or earth mortars and, more rarely, artillery, we lured out the British to carry out nightly repair work. They would then be ambushed by our patrols, which were lying in wait for them and some of them would be captured. During all these clashes, our men proved to be superior in their use of hand grenades. Gradually this procedure began to fail. The British either ceased trying to improve their wire, or they introduced ever larger protection parties. This, more or less, brought the capture of prisoners in No Man's Land to an end, so we then decided to seek out the enemy in his own trenches. It had previously already proved possible on numerous occasions for small patrols to break in as far as the second or third trenches and to bring back prisoners or captured materiel. British sentries who attempted to intervene were dealt with. The improvements to the way enemy sentry duty was carried out, forced us to organise patrol operations on a larger scale.

"The break-in point and wire obstacles were smashed up with artillery and mortar fire, generally towards evening whilst it was still light. In one divisional area, the destruction of the wire obstacle sometimes occurred some days before the operation. Infantry patrols went forward as it grew dark. Our own artillery had the tasks of neutralising adjacent sectors and enemy batteries which might attempt to intervene as well as isolating the target of the attack by defensive fire. During the first of these attacks, the enemy artillery failed utterly. It opened fire too late, too little and frequently at the wrong targets such as villages behind the front. Gradually it learnt. Defensive fire was far better placed during recent operations. The operations are now better timed during the night, rather than in the evening. The 52nd Infantry Division has already achieved good results in this way. The enemy artillery must be confused by diversions.

"Operational aims. Most operations have the same objectives. To cause enemy casualties, capture prisoners and war materiel, demoralise the enemy and raise the self confidence and will to win of our own troops. In addition, some operations will attempt to ascertain if the enemy has installed gas cylinders and sometimes attempts will be made to interrupt enemy mining activity by destroying the entrances to galleries.

"Selection of the break-in point. Special operations, such as determining the presence of gas cylinders or destroying mine entrances leave little room for manoeuvre in the selection of the break-in point, but in all other cases, the following conditions must be fulfilled: Ease of isolating the point by defensive fire, use of covered approaches to and from the target to lessen exposure to artillery and enfilading machine gun fire. Selection of a starting point in our own position, upon which the enemy artillery has either not ranged in his guns at all, or with only partial success...

"Infantry: There must be exact knowledge of both positions and No Man's Land based on previous patrolling.

"In addition, observation through telescopes from rear positions and from the flanks is required, as is study of sketches, panoramas and aerial photographs. The entire operation must be rehearsed on a training facility in the rear area. This should be constructed to be as similar to the target as possible. Every man must know the location of the enemy machine guns.

"Participation.  Only volunteers led by officers experienced in patrolling should be used. The strength of fighting patrols must match the local conditions and size of the task. Within the Reserve Corps this has varied from twenty to one hundred and twenty men. Officers and plenty of NCOs are always used. If there is a heavy preparatory bombardment of the target area, a hard close-quarter battle is not to be expected. It is recommended not to make patrols too large.  Depending on the distance between the two positions, rearguards, flank protection and relays are to be pushed forward into No Man's Land, or held ready in the front line trench.

"Weapons and Equipment.  All participants are to carry good hand grenades. Some of the men should carry rifles and bayonets. The remainder should be equipped with specialised close quarter weapons (pistols, daggers and knives, clubs and sharpened spades). Some regiments use recognition signs such as white armbands, or crosses front and rear. Other units are against any form of aids to recognition. Belt hooks on uniform jackets tend to snag in wire obstacles and are better removed. Puttees and lace up boots are frequently preferred to jackboots, which tend to be pulled off in mud. Everything which could lead to the identification of a unit must be left behind; i.e. all written items, epaulettes and other badges. Unit stamps on clothing and equipment must be obliterated. Some of the men must carry wire cutters and wiring gloves. Some tent halves to carry away dead, wounded and captured equipment are required. If gas shells are used, gasmasks must be carried hung around the neck and tucked into open jackets. No headdress is worn, so as to facilitate masking up. Walking and running in gas masks in the dark must be practised.

"Further preparations.  Arrange for gaps to be made in our own wire obstacle, or prepare Russian saps, which run beneath it.  The gaps should be marked with white cloths.  The overall commander and each patrol leader must observe the ranging in of the artillery and mortars.    All participants may also observe unobtrusively. The aim here is to increase their confidence in the fire to be brought down by the supporting arms and also to enable them to put forward any special requests that they may have. During rehearsals on the training area, all participants receive supplementary rations.

"Conduct. The ground and the distance separating the two positions determine whether the patrols form up in the front line trenches or in No Man's Land. In the case of the latter, there must be flank protection. Sentries in areas where experience shows that they will come under enemy artillery fire, must be placed in bullet proof shelters, where they can observe to the flanks and rear. Our artillery protects the operation by bringing down defensive fire. The assault begins when the commander gives a previously arranged signal. In many cases the patrols advance frontally on the objectives or outflank them, in order to penetrate as quickly as possible to the second and third trenches, which is frequently the first place where the position is manned. Particular trenches are swiftly checked and all resistance is snuffed out. Demands for surrender are shouted in the defenders' own language down dugouts, cellars and mine shafts. If they attempt to resist, do not emerge, or do not respond immediately, hand grenades are thrown in. The patrols do not enter mine galleries. The orders for the patrol operation must make it clear if they are permitted to enter dugouts.

"The withdrawal is carried out as swiftly as possible. The period spent in the enemy trenches should not exceed a quarter of an hour. The signal to pull back is given by the commander by whistle, hooter, or similar device. Some units use light signals, but there is a danger of confusion, if the enemy makes use of a similar signal. In fact flares are better used simultaneously at other points for deception purposes. It is important that the glare of these flares does not illuminate the patrol area. Whether the withdrawal route is the same as that used for the approach, or different, is decided on a case-by-case basis and as a result of consideration about where enemy fire is to be expected. Small patrols and medical orderlies man the re-entry points by our own trenches. The dugouts where the patrols reorganise are decided in advance and made known. This is where immediate roll calls occur and casualties are established. At least one dugout is equipped and manned as a medical aid post. The overall commander is informed as soon as all the participants are accounted for.

"Engineers. It is recommended to reinforce patrols with engineers. They can assist in dealing with obstacles and in grenade battles. The 28th Reserve Division has had success with the use of improvised explosive charges against enemy troops sheltering in mine galleries or deep dugouts. ([These comprise] twelve heavy home-made grenades fitted with twelve detonators and a metre length of safety fuse). They may only be thrown once our own troops have cleared the objective. On the 22nd February on the west front of Fricourt*, part of an enemy mine gallery was so damaged by these charges that the enemy has still not resumed work in this part of the mine field.

"Mortars. Their main task is to blow gaps in the wire obstacle. The production of each gap requires two medium mortars and 30 – 40 rounds altogether. Heavy mortars must be employed against particularly stout obstacles. The mortars must not be permitted to open fire from the starting point of the operation. Ranging can be spread over several days.

*This heavily mined area was known to the Germans as the Kniewerk; to the Allies as the Tambour Position.

The enemy must already be used to mortar fire along the entire front, so that he does not pay special attention to this. Numerous alternative firing points for the mortars must be prepared. The distance between the enemy and our own positions is widest along the 52nd Infantry Division front. In order to shorten the assault distances, the division holds its patrols ready to assault as close as possible to the enemy position. Therefore this must be engaged with the greatest possible accuracy. Mortars are more accurate than the artillery. In order to be protected from flying splinters, patrols must take cover in abandoned dugouts, old trenches, deep shell holes or similar. The division only engages the objective with heavy, medium and Albrecht mortars. So far this procedure has been successful, but it could lead to harder close-quarter fighting on the objective, than would be the case if it had been engaged with heavy artillery. In order to reduce as far as possible enemy's ability to take counter measures, the mortars fire at maximum rate.

"Artillery: On the Objective. Employ light and heavy field howitzers to prepare the ground for the assault. If the presence of especially strong dugouts is suspected, it is advisable, but not absolutely necessary, to use mortars. The ammunition requirement for a target 200 metres wide by 150 metres deep is about 2 – 300 rounds of heavy ammunition and about the same quantity of light ammunition. The rate of fire per half hour for a light field howitzer battery is 300 rounds. The preliminary bombardment should be as short as possible and not exceed three quarters of an hour. It is better to strive for twenty minutes. These figures provide a guide as to the number of batteries required

"Defensive Fire. This should prevent the enemy from evacuating the objective, reinforcements from arriving and fire from being opened from the trenches in rear and to the flanks. This fire commences with the start of the operation and continues until the operation commander has had the safe return of the patrols reported to him. The number of batteries required depends on the trench system involved. If the objective is thoroughly smashed up, then there should be few casualties during the close quarter battle. Such casualties can only be produced by the enemy artillery or through fire from trenches to the flanks or rear which overlook the objective. Machine guns are particularly dangerous in this regard. If the objective can be enfiladed from neighbouring sectors, these flanking positions must be brought under heavy fire. If they are very close to the objective, so that they cannot be fired on during the assault, they must be bombarded just as heavily as the objective before the attack. If there is no possibility of enfilading fire, neutralisation by field guns is sufficient. If there are enemy trenches which overlook the objective and from which machine gun fire is to be expected (though this generally is not a favourable situation), they must be covered by defensive fire from heavy howitzers or field guns. If no machine guns are anticipated, field gun fire is sufficient.

"Gas Shells. Choking agents fired in conjunction with fragmentation ammunition are suitable for use when the position is being softened up. Troops not hit by fragments, will be rendered unfit for battle by the choking agent. Shells filled with choking agents were employed by the 28th Division during the operation against the Kronenwerk [Crown Position] on the 9th February and the British ran about the position like headless chickens, offering no resistance. Our patrols, which entered the trenches immediately after the last of the shells had fallen, had to mask up. A Vizefeldwebel who failed to do this collapsed, but recovered quickly after he was hauled out of the trench. After about two minutes masks could be removed. If choking agents are used when the wind direction is unfavourable, it is recommended to cease firing this type of ammunition ten minutes before our infantrymen are scheduled to break in. If the wind direction is favourable, tear gas shells are suitable for use in neutralising flanking positions. This must be mixed with some high explosive, because experience has shown that individual machine guns may still be fired from areas subjected to tear gas fire. The Reserve Corps has no experience about the neutralisation of enemy artillery with gas shells.

"Enemy Artillery. The enemy artillery must be prevented from bringing down defensive fire on our withdrawing troops. If the operation is a complete surprise to the enemy, comes at a difficult moment and at a place where his artillery is not ranged in, or only partially, and if the operation is conducted swiftly, our attacking groups may well be back in our own trenches before the enemy artillery has opened fire. If it is necessary to select an objective where the enemy is well ranged in – which is always the case with mine fields - or if the enemy batteries open up unexpectedly early, our artillery held in reserve for this purpose must intervene immediately. In most cases it has proved possible to silence the enemy batteries. This will not always be successful; in which case there will be casualties. It is of the utmost importance, by means of decoy operations in numerous other places, to distract the enemy artillery away from the area of the patrol operation. It is recommended to conduct these decoys with flares and artillery fire simultaneously. Mines exploding also deceive the enemy.

"Telephones. The commander of the operation must be linked by telephone to the artillery commander, the sector commander and the front line trenches. If the width of No Man's Land permits assaulting troops to be pushed up near to the enemy position [prior to the operation], it is recommended to run a telephone line forward and to man it with a small patrol, which can keep the commander informed immediately about unforeseen incidents.

"Machine Guns. These are useful for bringing enfilade fire down on enemy trenches.

"Praise and Iron Crosses. The troops must be so schooled that they themselves demand to go on patrol operations. They must strive to achieve their ambition of capturing as many prisoners and as much materiel as possible and, through their skill, suffer as few casualties as possible. A short report is to be made to Corps detailing every daring example of patrolling. The participants will be publicly praised in a Corps Order of the Day and they will each receive a signed certificate of recognition. If the patrol has been successful, if enemy soldiers have been recovered dead or alive, or if there have been important seizures of materiel, the participants will receive the Iron Cross or other decorations. Whenever there has been a particularly successful patrol operation, there is always a large scale distribution of Iron Crosses. Example: For the operation against the farm buildings near Fricourt on 29th December 1915, two officers and one NCO received the Iron Cross 1st Class, whilst five NCOs and thirty-nine men were awarded the Iron Cross 2nd Class.

Signed: von Stein"

That was the theory distilled out of hard-won experience, but it is also instructive to compare its prescriptions with extracts from the plan for a highly successful trench raid conducted by 2nd Battalion Reserve Infantry Regiment 119 on Target Area 47 in the Beaumont Hamel area near Y Ravine, during the night of 6th and 7th April. Launched along the eastern edge of what is now the Newfoundland Memorial, this seventy-five man raid led by Leutnants Kaiser, Burger and Sternfeld, was well planned, well executed and an undoubted feather in the cap of the Regiment. **3.**

"Execution of the Operation

"On the day of the operation, the patrol groups are to be ready to move in the dugouts of Leiling Mulde [Leiling Hollow] from 8.00 pm. All members of the patrols are to understand that they may not remain in the enemy trenches for longer than fifteen minutes after they leave [the start line] in the sunken road. Commanders of patrols will give the signal to withdraw by means of whistle blasts.

"Equipment to be carried by the patrols is to be directed by Oberleutnant Künlen. The commanders are to report to him, on the basis of a personally conducted inspection, that no man is wearing any form of insignia or carrying any written item on his person. The patrols are to wear white armbands on both arms. The leading members of each patrol group are to carry small yellow flags so that they can identify themselves to one another in the event of a clash in the trenches.

"Upon return each man is to return to the dugout whence he began the operation. Leutnant Sieber is to prepare a list of those returning and report to the overall commander. Prisoners and captured items are initially to be taken to dugouts I – IV then, as soon as the enemy artillery fire slackens, they are to be brought to the Sector Staff of Beaumont South.

"In dugouts V & VI a further rearguard, comprising four sections of the 8th Company under the command of Leutnant Sieber 8th Company, is to be held in readiness. Leutnant Sieber himself will be located in dugout II from 10.00 pm. The companies of the battalion are to be at readiness in their dugouts. They are to remain, with gas masks hung ready for use, at battle readiness until the state of alert is lifted. Sentries in the left half of B5, B6, B7 and B8 are only to be placed in bullet proof observation posts.

"Artillery The artillery is to prepare the break in point A-E for the assault, to neutralise flanking forces from Target Areas 43-46 and 47 Advanced Post, to lay down a barrage behind the break in point and to simulate an attack from B8 to Advanced Post 47 by means of the most powerful and heavy bombardment possible of the Advanced Post 47 and Target Area 48. The sections of trench immediately (up to fifty metres) right and left of the break in point, as well as the third sap to the east of the sunken road are (with the exception of clearance of obstacles) to be bombarded to the same extent as the break in point.

"No Man's Land, especially the bank in front of 46 and the sunken road, is to be cleared of possible enemy patrols at the start of the bombardment by the use of shrapnel. In order to deceive the enemy as to the break in point, the fire on neighbouring sectors 43 – 48 is to continue from the beginning of fire preparation until the patrols return and during the outward and inward moves, from 10.30 – 10.35 & 10.50 – 11.10 pm, it is to increase to the highest possible intensity. The most probable points for enfilade in Target Areas 45 and 46 are to be engaged with howitzer fire. During the break in of the patrols, the dugouts behind 47 are to be engaged by heavy howitzers, the second and third trenches on Target Areas 47 and 48 are to be fired on with light and heavy howitzers.

"Mortars and Earth Mortars Every available mortar is to be directed against the break in point. At least six medium or heavy mortars are to be employed on the task of shooting three lanes in the enemy obstacle. The four earth mortars in B8 are to bring down the heaviest possible deception fire on Advanced Post 47 from 10.00 – 11.00 pm. Registration of mortars is to occur as long as possible before the operation; at least eight days previously. Mortars and earth mortars are to fire simultaneously and also against neighbouring sectors in order to deceive the enemy. The registration is to be spread over several days, so as not to draw the enemy's attention to the point of assault through unusual mortar fire.

"Dress and Equipment    Field caps are to be worn.  No shoulderboards or insignia.  Identification marks on equipment are to be rendered illegible.  No written material in pockets.  Belt hooks are to be removed from jackets.  As a recognition mark, all participants are to stitch white bands to both right and left arms. Two first field dressings are to be carried in the front jacket pockets.  Gas masks are not to be taken.  Each man is to carry six hand grenades (four stick grenades on the waist belt), two egg shaped grenades in the jacket pockets (tear-off hooks for these on waist belt).  Two men of each patrol are to carry rifles, the remainder are to carry pistols, model 08, each with a filled reserve magazine and daggers.(Pistols are to be carried in open holsters and secured round the neck with the strap from a bread pouch.)

"In addition:    four men per patrol      wire cutters

two men per patrol       rolled tent halves

two men per patrol       axes

two men per patrol       sharpened trench spades

Commanders of each patrol are to carry small yellow flags with which to identify themselves in the event of a clash in the trenches.  Commanders and NCOs are to have whistles, electric torches and watches with luminous figures.  The three commanders are also to carry signalling horns.  Commanders are to report the return of their patrols to the commander of the rearguard.  The patrols are then to move, as quickly as possibly, the rearguard last, to their departure dugouts, where they are to remain with any prisoners and captured equipment until they receive further orders from the command post.  Prisoners are to be guarded carefully and any documents are to be taken from them immediately.  Each man is to give his name to the Control NCO located in the dugout.  He in turn is to transmit this immediately to the Control Officer (Dugout II).

"The individual officers' patrols and the designated sub-patrols are to make every effort to stick together during the operation.  Shouts of 'Hurra'[14] and all other unnecessary noise are to be avoided during the break in and withdrawal, in order not to betray the break in points.  The password is to be given immediately on demand.  Possible casualties and their equipment are to be recovered at all costs.  Wounded are to be brought in the first instance to the aid post established in dugout VII (Manned by Assistanzarzt Dr. Pietzcker with two medical orderlies and two additional stretcher bearers).  As soon as the order has been given by the command post, any wounded and prisoners are to be taken to the rear through the 2nd trench of B6 and Sommergraben to the orderly room of 5th Coy by the churchyard in Beaumont.  An advanced dressing station is to be established there under the command of Oberarzt Dr. Kötzle, with two medical orderlies and two stretcher bearers."[15]

The raid, which was planned and executed absolutely in line with the latest best practice, hit 2nd Battalion South Wales Borderers, which had only been in the line for three days, extremely hard. Altogether, the British 29th Division suffered 112 casualties as a result of this raid: one officer and thirty-three other ranks were killed, eight officers and forty-two other ranks wounded and twenty-eight other ranks missing, (nineteen of whom were captured).[16] The cost to Reserve Infantry Regiment 119 was three men killed by a grenade explosion and one man seriously wounded, but successfully evacuated. The British army sought retribution during the major three-objective raid on the 30th April, in an attack on the 1st and 10th Companies Reserve Infantry Regiment 119, but it telegraphed its intentions to the alert defenders, who shot the attack to a standstill with pre-arranged artillery and small arms fire as soon as it was launched. In his after action report, the battalion commander drew attention to all the deficiencies in the preparation and conduct of the operation:

*Hauptmann von Breuning Commander 2nd Battalion Reserve Infantry Regiment 119*[17] **3.**

"For more than a week the behaviour of the enemy had made it clear that he was planning something against the sector. Almost daily he ranged in his heavy guns against different points. There was a great deal of aerial activity and patrolling ceased. It could not have been a full scale attack, because otherwise more heavy and super-heavy artillery would have been involved. Our patrols also established that he was strengthening his obstacle, so the sole possibility was a trench raid. The only remaining question was, against which sector was it planned?...The ground most favours an assault against the right hand 'Pincer'. There are covered approaches and it is not enfiladed from anywhere. It only presents a narrow front and cannot expect fire support from the flanks. On the evening of [27th April], the sector commander informed the commander of Artillery Group A that the right hand Pincer was in special danger and an increased state of alert was maintained throughout the night...On the 28th April it was striking that there was heavy fire against the left flank and a great deal of shrapnel fire on the obstacle, which was somewhat damaged. It was repaired and the attack did not occur... A daylight patrol on 29th April discovered and recovered two short arrows, surmounted by shiny bottles in front of the 1st Company, which they discovered pointed the way to a small hollow in the ground, which offered a covered approach... For the night 29th – 30th April, there was once again an increased state of alert, then the tip of the wood was very noticeably hit with 240 millimetre shells and heavy mortars... After it went dark, all was quiet, but at 12.30 am there was suddenly extremely heavy artillery and mortar fire and at the same time machine-gun fire... Two of our patrols went forward immediately... to meet the enemy in No Man's Land if possible... Red flares called for immediate defensive fire from our artillery... [and] the patrols later confirmed that it came down exactly as intended."

For the next hour there followed a carefully monitored and controlled artillery fire fight, with all sub-sector commanders and observers reporting the origin and intensity of the incoming fire, so that the artillery group commander could switch his guns between fire missions and engage new targets with his stand by batteries as required. At around 1.30 am, the artillery was ordered to reduce the rate of fire dramatically, but to be ready to re-engage if an enemy assault did in fact occur. At the same time all the companies in the sector launched additional patrols forward. By 2.00 am, the patrols were back in; those that had spent the entire time forward, reporting that the British had indeed tried for some time to launch the raid, but that they could not get forward through the defensive barrage. Communications and coordination of the defensive battle, right down to platoon level, had been first class. Despite the expenditure by the British army of 4,000 – 5,000 artillery shells and mortar bombs, casualties amongst the defenders had been negligible and the damage to the trenches was quickly repaired. These raiders still had much to learn.

One constant theme during the first part of the year was the continuing improvement to the defensive positions, including increasing use of concrete to provide shell- and bullet-proof protection. Nothing was left to chance. There might have been little fighting in the area, but the work of improving the positions never ceased. One particularly well-known field fortification developed during this period was that which became known to the British as the Schwaben Redoubt. This defensive work was destined to play a significant role in the main battle which was to follow. As a result much myth and misinformation attaches to it, so it is important to understand its layout and construction. Fortunately a great many maps, sketches and diagrams, which show the Redoubt at various times, have survived.[18]

By early 1915, trenches were beginning to snake across the high ground dominating the terrain between the fortified villages which constituted the front line. This included a small network centred on high ground approximately 700 metres north of Thiepval village. At the time this was known as the Schwaben Schanze [Schwabian Earthworks]. There were links to Mouquet Farm via the Auwärtergraben [Auwärter Trench], which was named after the Brigade Commander, 52 Reserve Infantry Brigade of 26th Reserve Division. The Teufelsgraben [Devil's Trench] ran forward southwest to act as a communication trench to the front line opposite Thiepval Wood and a further trench, named Martinspfad [Martin's Path], led south to Thiepval village.

As 1915 wore on, it was decide to complete the third line of trenches of the First Position and to develop it further into the so-called Zwischenstellung [Intermediate Position]. This was when the line of field fortifications such as the Soden, Grallsburg, Old Württemberg, Schwaben, Stuff and Goat Redoubts was developed. The size of each depended on the terrain and the role of the relevant fort. In the case of Schwaben Redoubt, the aim was to dominate the high ground between Thiepval and Saint Pierre Divion and to provide both depth to the First

Position and overhead fire to the flanks and above the trenches opposite Thiepval Wood. It was roughly triangular in shape, its frontage was approximately 500 metres and its most important features were two parallel trenches, about thirty metres apart, which ran northwest from the Thiepval – Grandcourt road at a point about 250 metres north of Thiepval cemetery.

The first trench was named the Kampfgraben [Battle Trench] and the second the Wohngraben [Accommodation Trench]. The Kampfgraben had twenty traverses and nine mined dugouts, each with two entrances. The Wohngraben had fifteen traverses and eight mined dugouts, six with two entrances and two with three entrances. One of these eight dugouts served as an aid post and a second as a company command post. There were also three dugouts, one of which was a battalion command post, in Auwärtergraben where it ran through the Redoubt. None of the dugouts listed above was linked to any other and there were no other underground features whatsoever. In particular, there were no great subterranean installations and no tunnels connected the Redoubt with Saint Pierre Divion. The Redoubt had a searchlight position, a signalling station and it provided battle positions for three machine guns and four '*Musketen*' [heavy automatic rifles, with a two man crew]. It was a key point in the defensive system and those who constructed it and manned it were in no doubt about its importance.

*Hauptmann Herbert von Wurmb 3rd Company Bavarian Reserve Infantry Regiment 8*[19] **4.**

> "The Schwaben Redoubt was a point of decisive importance. If the enemy succeeded in establishing himself here on a long term basis, not only would the whole position of the 26th Reserve Division on the southern bank of the Ancre have been extraordinarily endangered, but also the entire operational viability of the divisional artillery on the northern bank would have been called into question, because from the Redoubt all the batteries there would have been in full view."

The more time went by and building materials were available in quantity, the more elaborate the defences became. The experiences gained during the battles for Serre and Arras the previous year and information yielded by current operations around Verdun, proved to be extremely useful. Obvious signs of a forthcoming allied offensive lent new urgency to the work and only the highest standards were acceptable.

*Generalleutnant Freiherr von Soden, Commander 26th Reserve Division*[20]

> "[There was] feverish development of the positions, including the Intermediate Position and the Second and Third Positions, especially the Grallsburg and Schwaben Redoubt. The Ancre Valley obstacle was strengthened. Stop lines were constructed, as were additional communications trenches. Numerous new battery positions were constructed, ready to accommodate reinforcing batteries. Dugouts were improved, deepened to at least seven metres and equipped with two or three exits. Specially organised concrete squads built sector observation

posts. The wire obstacles were strengthened and mine galleries were extended, as was the telephone network. There was an increase in the number of 'Moritz' [telephone intercept] stations and great attention was paid to telephone security. Church bells, sirens and gongs were installed to warn of gas attacks. Draught horses and stores were moved back out of villages within artillery range. Civilians were moved to the rear and large quantities of ammunition, including hand grenades, were placed in shell-proof shelters, as far forward as the frontline itself."

The engineers carried out detailed surveys, designed new trenches and dugouts, produced working drawings of concrete emplacements of various kinds and inspected the work of the infantry regiments incessantly and critically. On the 15th and 19th May the engineer commander at Second Army conducted a complete inspection of the First Position in the 26th Reserve Division area. This followed an earlier visit at the beginning of March. Reports were circulated as a result of these inspections and units had to respond swiftly to correct and report on the rectification of deficiencies. Some idea of the attention to detail involved may be seen in these extracts from the report on the May visits:[21]

"The network of approach trenches needs to be expanded in certain places. For example:

a)   "The Borriesweg [Borries Way] and Kurzgraben [Short Trench] (north of Serre) lead from the Intermediate Position to the 3rd trench of the first position, but because they merge for about forty metres before they reach the junction with the 3rd trench, they do not constitute two independent links, separate from one another. This can be rectified easily by producing separate junctions for each trench with the 3rd trench.

b)   Two approach trenches begin at the Puisieux-Serre road. At least one of them must be lengthened to the rear, up to a point in the second position south of Puisieux. If the planned new Lehmgraben [Clay Trench] is built, this requirement will be met.

Where roads cross, the approach trenches must be continued (by tunnelling under or overbridging). This is lacking, for example, at several crossings on the Puisieux-Serre Road.

c)   The number of signposts needs to be increased in certain places, for example, in the 2nd and 3rd trenches in Beaumont....

The number and method of construction of observation posts varies widely. Shell proof, concreted posts are only available in sufficient quantity in the sector of Reserve Infantry Regiment 119. There are also some nearly shell proof posts with three layers of railway line in the sector of Infantry Regiment 180. In the sector of Reserve Infantry Regiment 121, almost all posts are only splinter-proof. Here an improvement through the use of shell-proof structures is imperative. In the sector of Reserve Infantry Regiment 99, posts with a double layer of railway lines are very numerous, but their ability to resist [shells] seems, however, to be questionable. Several posts have already been knocked out by hits.[22] In view of the importance of concrete shell-proof observation posts to guarantee observation during heavy artillery fire, it must be urgently recommended that each infantry regiment trains concrete squads. The engineer companies are largely occupied with mine warfare and are not in a position to be solely responsible for concrete constructions. The speaking tubes which run from the observation posts to the nearest dugouts were in some cases unusable. They need to be repaired. In those places where these tubes lie openly on the floor of the trench, their survival under shellfire is questionable. It is recommended that earth borers supplied by the engineers be used to drill holes between observation posts and dugouts, so that the speaking tubes can be placed in shell-proof surroundings."

This sort of staff work was replicated in other places, attention being paid to the smallest relevant detail, as here in a directive concerning observation posts from the engineer commander of the 10th Bavarian Infantry Division, [23]

"Apart from ensuring that there is a good field of view, the main point to be considered when constructing concrete observation posts is that of unobtrusiveness. Insufficient attention is still being paid to this requirement. Before a start is made with construction, the worksite is to be masked. In wooded areas, a hedge, at least twenty metres long, is to be put in place. Where the ground is open, an unobtrusive, gently rising fold in the ground is to be produced. Once the observation point is finished, in the first case ivy is to be planted, which will entwine itself around it; in the second, it is to be painted to blend in with its surroundings. In order to prepare for the eventuality that an exploding shell will block the observation slits, the roof is to be equipped with an opening protected by an iron plate, which can be opened to permit observation by use of a mirror..."

Meanwhile the work of intelligence gathering, patrolling and raiding continued with undiminished intensity. It was critical for staffs in higher headquarters to be kept abreast of all new developments and changes in the Allied order of battle; prisoner interrogations, which almost invariably yielded a great deal of operational intelligence, provided one of the surest means of achieving this. The British army was beginning to respond more effectively to these operations, however, so successes were sometimes hard bought.

*Landwehr Leutnant M Gerster Reserve Infantry Regiment 119*[24]

"The signs of a British offensive in our area increased day by day and the first storm signals became ever clearer. That they would come was certain, only the extent of the operation was unclear. On the 12th April, Supreme Headquarters was still predicting a British thrust limited to north of the Ancre, where the British divisions were packed closely together. In fact, in the middle of April, 52nd Infantry Division was facing odds of six or eight to one. On the right of the brigade, daring patrol work brought Reserve Infantry Regiment 119 the good fortune to discover the presence of 87 Brigade, 29th Division, which only days earlier had arrived from Suez. Left of the brigade, 56 Reserve Infantry Brigade identified the 8th British Division. On the other hand, patrols of 5th Company Reserve Infantry Regiment 99, which clashed with the enemy in front of C3 on the 3rd April and C1 on the 10th April, enjoyed no such success.

"The enemy seemed finally to have got the measure of our trench raid tactics and suddenly turned them against us. Generally he just suffered reverses, but occasionally, however, he succeeded in forcing a way into our lines and capturing prisoners. Initially this caused fury and a tendency to blame subordinate commanders and forward troops, but it was soon realised that sufficient expenditure of ammunition in support of a courageous assaulting force meant that such break-ins would almost always succeed. When on the 24th April, 3rd Battalion Reserve Infantry Regiment 99 had been relieved by the 1st Battalion, the enemy suddenly brought down drum-like fire on the position, cut gaps in the obstacle, forced a way into the trench and made off with thirteen prisoners. The success of his first operation encouraged him to repeat the attempt on 30th April. All of a sudden, artillery fire swept violently along the entire brigade front. Under the protection of shrapnel shells, the British assaulted the German line at three points. On the right flank, concentrated defensive fire had been called for in time and the British patrol was driven off with heavy casualties. In the centre the British closed up to the wire obstacle in front of 10th Company Reserve Infantry Regiment 119. The one seriously wounded and four dead that the company was able to recover, belonged to 87 Brigade, 29th Division. On the left flank of C6, the 12th Company Reserve Infantry Regiment 99 met the attackers with hand grenades, forced them to withdraw and captured a British soldier from 15th Lancashire Regt [sic],[25] 96 Brigade."

*Hauptmann Wagener 8th Company Reserve Infantry Regiment 110*[26] **5.**

"In May 1916, I was commanding 8th Company Reserve Infantry Regiment 110, when towards the end of the month the Regiment was ordered, at all costs, if necessary by means of trench raids, to bring in a number of prisoners from the British unit opposite the regiment. I received the mission to launch a raid directed at the so-called Besenhecke [Broom Hedge] sector of the Bécourt area at the head of a 200 man strong company, which was put together for this purpose. A combination of unfortunate circumstances caused an attempt at 3.00 am on the 4th June to fail. We lost about twenty men killed and wounded; and one man fell into enemy hands. Nevertheless, with the enthusiastic agreement of the entire company, we attacked again that same evening. I led the first attacking assault group myself. After a hard fight, during which we once more lost leaders and men, we succeeded in bringing seventeen British soldiers back to our trenches. The prisoners belonged to the British 34th Division, which had been deployed to this position shortly before. They made an outstanding impression and recounted that their division had received training in the attack before they were sent forward. During both these operations there was extraordinarily heavy enemy artillery fire."

*Generalleutnant Freiherr von Soden Commander 26th Reserve Division*[27]

"Numerous small-scale operations to bring in prisoners and unsettle the enemy took place. These were mostly still blessed with good fortune and succeeded in taking large numbers of prisoners. So, for example, on the 8th May a raid by Reserve Infantry Regiment 99 against the forward edge of Thiepval Wood, led to the capture of twenty eight men of 1st Dorsets of the 32nd Division. It was proved repeatedly that such operations could not expect success, unless there was the expenditure of at least 10,000 artillery rounds. A well-planned and prepared operation of Reserve Infantry Regiment 119 on the 10th/11th June against the village of Hamel failed – apparently because our own artillery fired short and prevented the assaulting force from getting forward. We have to accept casualties from our own gunfire; they cannot be avoided completely."

On the 26th May, considering rightly that attack is the best form of defence, General von Below, Commander Second Army, repeated a proposal which he had originally put forward in March, to disrupt the British preparations on the Somme by means of spoiling attack. Its aim would be to attack the Allies on a twenty kilometre front from St Pierre Divion in the north to Foucaucourt in the south. The scheme involved an attack to a depth of twenty five kilometres in a series of phases, tackling the British forces north of the Somme initially, then following up south of the river. 'As far as timings for the two or three phase attack are concerned,' he wrote, 'the attack cannot begin soon enough. The British have been reinforced so strongly north of the Somme that there can hardly be any remaining doubt concerning their plans for an offensive...Whether they intend to attack in the next few days, or if they are waiting for further reinforcements, or an improvement in the training of their troops, cannot be determined. If we launch an attack in the next few weeks, it is entirely possible that we shall pre-empt the British and throw their plans into confusion...'

On the 2nd June, despite the fact that there had been no response to his proposal from Supreme Headquarters, von Below returned to his theme, stressing that the situation looked even more threatening and urging at least an attack between St Pierre Divion and Ovillers. It is impossible to say if this urging would have had any effect on General von Falkenhayn, because the opening of the Brusilov offensive, Russia's last great effort of the war, on the 4th June, finally put paid to any hope that somehow, despite continuing offensive operations in the Verdun area, reserves might be found for a possible Somme attack. Falkenhayn himself returned to the point in his own memoirs, 'The intention to nip the preparations for the British relief attack in the bud by means of a powerful counter thrust had to be dropped. The army reserves of troops and munitions which had been retained for this purpose were weakened considerably by the need to send forces to the east.' But it must be remembered that he was then looking to excuse his underestimation of the Somme threat and to attempt to justify the chronic lack of reserves when the blow finally fell.

As a result of a full staff appreciation of the situation, it was decided that the defensive *Schwerpunkt* [main effort] was to be north of the River Somme. This appreciation has not survived, but it is quite clear that the heavy commitment of the French army at Verdun led the Germans to believe that they would not be capable of playing a significant part in any battle which might occur in the Somme region. It may well be that they were reinforced in this view as a result of information, or possibly misinformation, that they received from clandestine sources. In accordance with German doctrine of risk – taking to permit reinforcement of the Schwerpunkt, in mid June the 10th Bavarian Infantry Division was pulled out of the line south of the Somme and its individual regiments were moved north to undertake reinforcing missions. An intelligence report from Second Army, dated the 10th June, read in part, '...according to a report of a reliable agent, the great British offensive will take place after Whitsun'.[30]   It is interesting, also, to note that an order, dated the 24th June, issued by Bavarian Reserve Infantry Regiment 8 for the move into reserve behind 26th Reserve Division, specifically states, 'It has been established from reports by agents, that an attack by British and French units is to be expected shortly on both banks of the Somme...'.[31] It would seem, therefore, quite likely that information supplied by spies played an important part in building up the intelligence picture at the time.[32]

The loss of the 10th Bavarian Division forced XVII Corps south of the river to undergo a major reorganisation, which meant that individual formations had to take over wider sectors of the line. The French seemed to have got wind of the ensuing comprehensive regrouping and, by means of increased artillery fire, interfered considerably with the relocation of the units. Some regiments were convinced that the counter-moves had been betrayed to the French through

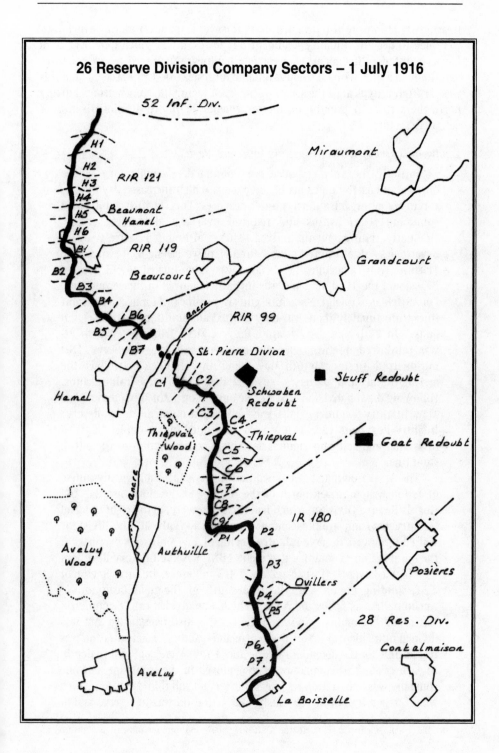

**26 Reserve Division Company Sectors – 1 July 1916**

treachery.[33] They were also troubled about the over-extended frontages which they were had to occupy. Infantry Regiment 61, for example, which took over from Bavarian Infantry Regiment 16 west of Chaulnes, was forced to use all three battalions in a line, with no troops available for reserve or depth tasks[34] – and this was far from untypical in the sector of the front facing the French army. Further north the arrival, or promise of, reinforcements facilitated a rationalisation of defensive sectors.

### Landwehr Leutnant M. Gerster Reserve Infanterie Regiment 119[35]

"Initially the only response our commanders could make to the obvious offensive intentions of the enemy, which increased day by day, was to review organisational countermeasures. This clarified complicated command relationships and reduced overlarge defensive sectors. Gradually reinforcements arrived. These, although relatively weak, nevertheless significantly raised our defensive strength. To this end, Machine Gun Detachment Fasbender was subordinated to 52 Reserve Brigade on the 10th May and was initially deployed in the second line. On 25th May, six Belgian machine guns were allocated for use in the front line. Unfortunately there was only limited ammunition for the Belgian guns. On 12th May, 3rd Battalion Reserve Field Artillery Regiment 26 was reinforced by two light gun batteries and two old heavy 150 millimetre batteries. By 6th May, the enemy, who had not missed the arrival of the new batteries, engaged them with large calibre guns. Following the sub-division of Sector Beaumont on 12th May, on the 22nd May, Infantry Regiment 180 was relieved around Serre by Reserve Infantry Regiment 121. This was accompanied by a complete shift in divisional and company boundaries and a reorganisation of the entire front line.

"The Army Command calculated that the most probable enemy course of action was an attack north of the Ancre and therefore inserted 2nd Guards Reserve Division, which had been in reserve, to the right of 52nd Infantry Division around Gommecourt. As a result, all the divisions shifted sideways. Reserve Infantry Regiment 121 only took over part of the old position of Infantry Regiment 180. Reserve Infantry Regiment 119 handed over the former sectors B 1-3 to Reserve Infantry Regiment 121, holding on only to the line south of the road Beaumont – Auchonvillers as far as the Ancre, which was divided into Beaumont – North and Beaumont – South. Thiepval was also reorganised and was divided into Thiepval – North, – Centre and – South.* Each battalion was responsible for the defence of one sector. Forces were deployed in depth. In each case, three companies were deployed in the front line and one company was in battalion reserve in the second and third trenches, which were further developed vigorously. One battalion was in reserve and at

---

*Once the redeployment was complete, the front line sub-sectors were renumbered as shown on the map relating to 1st July 1916.

rest. On the 23rd May, the Division also moved the 26th Division Recruit Depot forward into the divisional area in order to have a further reserve readily available and to be able to occupy the Second Position.

"Because it was intended that Infantry Regiment 180 would relieve Reserve Infantry Regiment 109, which was occupying Ovillers to the south of Reserve Infantry Regiment 99, on 24th May, Sector Beaumont was allocated to 51 Reserve Infantry Brigade and Reserve Infantry Regiment 119 left the Brigade for the second time. For a while 52 Reserve Infantry Brigade only had the Thiepval sector to defend. This was occupied by Reserve Infantry Regiment 99, whose 4th Battalion had returned to it on 17th May. The relief in Ovillers began during the night of 7th/8th June and was completed on the 9th June. Infantry Regiment 180 discovered that its new position was a well-constructed system of trenches with deep, spacious, mined dugouts in which they could face the coming attack with confidence. The extension to the south of the Brigade front necessitated a regrouping of the artillery. Reserve Field Artillery Battalion 27, which was newly trained, was allocated to 52 Reserve Infantry Brigade. Whereas Ovillers offered accommodation for 2,500 men in the first position, Thiepval, which was stronger and better developed, had space for 3,900 men. There were few dugouts in the Intermediate and Second Positions. Mouquet Farm only had space for 100 men and in the second position, across the entire width, there were only 200 places in each regimental area. That was not much. A high price was paid further south in July for this deficiency. Further reinforcements and reserves arrived on 13th June: A battalion of Bavarian Reserve Infantry Regiment 8, 3rd Company Foot Artillery Battalion 51, a company of the Bavarian Reinforcement Battalion 5 and Bavarian Engineer Company 20, which, however, moved over to 28th Reserve Division on the18th June."

Naturally these developments in the German lines was of considerable interest to the British army, which was also concerned to probe the strength of the positions, test the alertness and effectiveness of defensive counter measures and maintain and improve the offensive spirit of its own troops. In consequence, several British raids were launched during June.

*Landwehr Leutnant M. Gerster Reserve Infantry Regiment 119*[36]

"Following on from an abortive operation against C2 on 3rd June, the British attempted another raid on a wide front, making use of a great deal of ammunition. At 1.00 am on 6th June, they brought down concentrations of fire along the entire line from Serre to La Boisselle. This fell particularly heavily around St Pierre Divion and in the Ancre Valley, increasing to drumfire in Sector Thiepval – South. In this area a strong British patrol succeeded in forcing a way into C8 and capturing a junior

NCO and ten men of 8th Company Reserve Infantry Regiment 99 in the Staufenring. In imitation of our approach to patrol operations, the British had removed all marks which might have led to the identification of the units involved. So, an examination of a corpse which lay at the break in point of the wire obstacle did not permit determination of the unit concerned. Simultaneously the enemy attacked left and right of the brigade and broke into our positions. Although he had to withdraw from Reserve Infantry Regiment 119 without capturing a prisoner, some from Reserve Infantry Regiment 110 fell into his hands at La Boisselle. According to estimates made by our artillery, the enemy expended around 12,000 rounds in a very short period of time. The entire horizon was filled with the muzzle flashes of the British batteries. As a result, Thiepval Wood and the hills around Mesnil were cast in shadow against the light background, whilst along the entire German line there were flashes of light as the shrapnel and roaring high explosive shells burst. Satisfied with the success of this dress rehearsal for the great offensive, the British infantry did not leave their trenches again."

With the signs of the forthcoming major offensive now quite unmistakeable, the defenders made their final preparations. All that could have been done physically to prepare their positions to withstand the onslaught had been done. Headquarters elements of the regiments, brigades and divisions settled into their forward battle positions. There now remained the need to determine the exact time of the assault and to prepare the men mentally and spiritually for the onslaught that they were about to face.

*Gefreiter Adolf Griesbaum Reserve Infantry Regiment 111*[37] **6.**

"We were billeted in a small village behind the front on the highest state of readiness. At any time we might receive the order to march forward. We knew that we faced a testing time. We had to prepare ourselves – perhaps for our departure from this life. Then I heard that there was the opportunity to go to confession in the little village church. I went there swiftly. The priest was not sitting as usual in the confessional, but stood in the middle of the church. Soon I could be counted amongst those happy warriors who could go into battle, his soul strengthened for the fight. There was no question of having to confess, but we were allowed to! There then followed the days of the bombardment. Day followed day, until at long last the great offensive began. It took all of our strength to endure this trial. Thankfully my heart was strong and composed, because I almost met my end. Returning from the Nestlerhöhlen, [east of Fricourt] I was buried by a large shell. Only gradually did I come round. My comrades had already gone on ahead. With superhuman strength I managed to free myself and escaped with two wounds."

Up and down the line during these final days of June, men waited for the inevitable bombardment to begin. Whether they were manning the front line, or were occupying rather more comfortable billets in the villages to the rear, the presence from horizon to horizon of observation balloons and the constant activity of the dominant allied aircraft left them in no doubt that battle would soon be joined. The tension in the air was almost tangible. All knew that they faced an extremely dangerous and trying period of time, but few can have appreciated the weight of attack that was just about to descend on them.

*General der Infanterie Hermann von Kuhl* [38]

"On 24th June, the overwhelmingly strong French and British artillery brought down a preparatory bombardment on German positions astride the Somme on a forty kilometre front from Gommecourt (south of Arras) to Chaulnes. Ceaselessly, day and night, this hurricane of fire swept away the thin line of German defences. The expenditure of extraordinary quantities of ammunition was designed to turn the German defences into a heap of ruins. The wire obstacles were swept away, the trenches levelled, the dugouts crushed or buried, the approach routes were destroyed and telephone links were cut. In short, the positions were turned into crater fields. The response of the German artillery, which was greatly outnumbered, became ever weaker. It was a miracle that despite the nerve-shattering racket and under this hail of shells, there were still men capable of conducting a defence when the moment of the infantry attacks arrived."

*Landwehr Leutnant M. Gerster Reserve Infantry Regiment 119* [39]

"The night of 23rd/24th June passed noticeably quietly. Dawn broke, heralding a sunny day of azure-blue skies. The troops had just finished preparing their morning coffee. The night sentries were about to lie down and sleep, the scattered day time sentries went on duty and the miners got ready to continue their daily underground work. Then, at 5.00 am, a storm of artillery broke with a crash along the entire line. As far as the eye could see clouds of shrapnel filled the sky, like dust blown on the wind. The bursts were constantly renewed and toil as it might, the morning breeze could not sweep the sky clear. All around there was howling, snarling and hissing. With a sharp ringing sound, the death-dealing shells burst, spewing their leaden fragments against our line. The balls fell like hail on the roofs of the half-destroyed villages, whistled through the branches of the still-green trees and beat down hard on the parched ground, whipping up small clouds of smoke and dust from the earth. Large calibre shells droned through the air like giant bumblebees, crashing, smashing and boring down into the earth. Occasionally small calibre high explosive shells broke the pattern.

"What was it? The men of the trench garrison pricked up their ears in collective astonishment. The sentries in their secure bullet-proof positions kept a sharp eye open for the enemy. The British wire seemed to be intact. Had the Tommies gone off their heads? Did they believe that they could wear us down with shrapnel? We, who had dug ourselves deep into the earth? We who had moled down into the innards of the enemy's territory? The very thought made the infantry smile. But the shooting gradually became unpleasant. Nobody could take a step along the trenches. All work, all movement became impossible. Strangely, in Pozières North and in the Thiepval Sector, a comparative calm soon prevailed. The entire force of the furious enemy artillery poured down on Ovillers South, against which the British immediately employed their mortars, swiftly causing heavy damage to obstacles and trenches. Following on from the violent shock of the first whirlwind of fire, behind which one could conjure up visions of endlessly toiling, sweat-streaked British artillerymen, came calmly-directed, well-aimed individual fire, which gave the impression that the British batteries were engaging in target practice against individual sections of the front. During the afternoon the intensity of the fire increased once more, concentrating on Thiepval and Schwaben Redoubt which lay behind it. On the other hand, the Ovillers Sector was largely left alone and the miners were able to continue with the work of constructing dugouts. Now the barking of the light field guns intermingled with the roaring growl of the heavy shells, which plunged into the ruins of the villages and the Schwaben Redoubt, sending columns of black, brown or poisonous yellow smoke and fountains of earth up into the sky. Amazingly, the frontline trench suffered less than the rear and communication trenches, whose intersections seemed to have been singled out in particular.

"Was it chance, or did the power of the endless shocks cause the dust in the air to coalesce? The clear sky soon clouded over, a light rain damped down the clouds of smoke from the exploding shells, thus making observation easier. At the same time the bombarded trenches which were full of powdered, loose soil were turned into muddy puddles, thus adding to the misery of the trench garrisons. Towards evening there was a pause in the firing. The enemy artillery fell almost completely silent, so that the support columns, which were ready to move, were able with the approach of sunset to begin to make their way to the forward positions, bringing food and ammunition. However, towards evening, numerous enemy aviators took to the air in order to observe the rear areas. With an enormous crash, down came the bombardment once more along the entire line, hitting the columns with a terrible hail of lead and preventing them from reaching the front line."

The situation was similar south of the River Somme, where the men of Infantry

Regiment 128 counted with absolute certainty no fewer than forty French batteries firing on their divisional sector. This fire was being directed from the air and from a huge number of captive balloons. There were sixteen immediately to their front, and using a telescope they counted a total of eighty more stretching away to the north.[40] This accurate fire was taking a heavy toll on the positions and the defenders, but it was not only the front line that was suffering. Behind the lines, villages, which thus far had been largely spared and in which life had carried on fairly normally, suddenly found that the war had caught up with them.

*Vizefeldwebel Weickel Reserve Infantry Regiment 109*[41] **7.**

"It was 5 pm on 22nd June 1916 when the first shells burst in our pleasant little village of Longueval, which lay about four and a half kilometres behind the front. It was almost like the overture to the most dreadful theatre production that the world had ever seen. A soldier was killed, a French female inhabitant and a child wounded. The following day, the 23rd June, a further bombardment was expected. The place lay eerily still and empty. The village streets were ghostly and deserted, because the order had been given that all, soldiers and civilians alike, were to stay under cover. The situation was very different to the way the childlike, active imagination of the French had imagined it and so frequently described it, quietly and out loud – if only the British – the liberators – would come! Day by day and week by week they had longed for the glorious day. Now in practice everything looked very different.

"The memorable day of 24th June dawned. It was the start of the great British offensive. At 5.00 am drumfire was opened on the front. From 10.00 am onwards, our village too came under fire from heavy and super-heavy calibre shells. Twelve observation balloons could be seen in the sky in the direction of Montauban. Almost every round landed on the village. The destructive shells arrived in short and long bursts. One of the very first shells demonstrated their destructiveness, tearing down completely as it did, the side wall of a tall house. Staircase, rooms, furniture, stoves; all were exposed to view. Two days later it was all one great heap of ruins. Now there was an end to the relative comfort and quiet. No more were there good quarters with big wide beds. Now everyone, soldiers and civilians, were all crowded, silent and serious, on straw palliasses in the poorly candle-lit cellars. Whenever there was a break in the firing, we crept carefully up the stairs and looked around to see if the house was still standing, if it was on fire and to breathe fresh air and see the sun. But we were always ready to leap back into cover, because the shells arrived extremely quickly.

"The deafening din went on endlessly, the roaring of the heavy guns never ceased. There could no longer be any doubt. This was deadly serious. It was a matter of life and death and the enemy was going all out for destruction. Terrible battles were being fought out not far away from us and would in all probability soon sweep over us. By then there could be no question of the civilians remaining here. Their wish – 'If only the British would come' – would certainly take another form. The artillery fire continued then suddenly, on the 26th June, came word by telephone that the local commander was to make plans for the evacuation of the civil population; he being in the best position to judge the matter. There was still no definite order, but there was really not the slightest doubt that the evacuation would have to take place very soon. In order to be ready, even during the night, I made quiet arrangements for planks to be sawn up to serve as benches on the large transport waggons. In the same way, horses and harnesses were prepared, so that everything would be ready swiftly when the moment came.

"These precautions were fully justified! Night fell and the fire increased ever more in intensity. Some houses caught fire and were burning out of control, because the water mains were destroyed by shells right at the start of the bombardment... the situation got worse and worse in our village. Then we received an order, by radio, that by 6.00 am in the grey light of dawn, the place was to be evacuated, without any exception. With the agreement of the local commander I summoned the French mayor and three inhabitants and passed on the order to them. Even though their fate was a terrible blow to them it had to be, for their own security. There was not time for lengthy discussions. We had less than three hours at our disposal, so the little group dispersed to carry out this difficult task. It was heartbreaking for them as they made their way back to the cellars, the refuges of the villagers, by the red glow in the sky.

"The people set about the painful task feverishly. Crying and wailing they went to their houses, where they desperately went through their belongings. Drawers and cupboards were pulled open. Clothing, hats, coats, underwear, crockery lay all over the floors as they desperately tried to decide in their confusion what to take with them. By the light of the burning houses, these miserable beings gathered at the assembly points. Some had put on their best clothes, whilst others were clutching, in small bundles, the items they wished to save. Even the civilians knew that it would all be over after this. Their property and possessions would all be lost, victims of the battle. Their homes, their barns, their cattle; they had to leave them all and they would never see them again!

"The loading point was designated as the village exit in the direction of Flers. It was 5.30 am. It was a scene of complete chaos. The large wagon arrived to carry away the old people, the children, the sick and the lame. I wanted to leave the organisation of this to the mayor, but it was impossible. In this dreadful hour, all ideas of brotherly love and equality went out of the window, as the lovely young daughters of the richest man in the village settled themselves comfortably in the waggon, with the permission of the mayor, whilst several of the old, infirm women stood helplessly by the wagon, waiting in vain for a place. So I stepped in to take over the selection of people and allocation of places. Above all the attractive, healthy young women were invited to vacate the waggon; their places being given to the elderly and the children. It was simply a shocking spectacle.

Finally everything was ready for the move out. There were still a few arrangements to be made, when daybreak brought with it the first of the shells. Crrrumppp! Three came down very close to us! The crowd stirred nervously and fearfully. But, thank heavens, the blast went sideways. Now it was time for them to be gone. We could no longer be held responsible for the lives of civilians. At 6.00 am the order was given: 'Move!' So the crowd of people, wretched and poor, shuffled away from their home, their native soil, never to see it again! They left for an uncertain future. If they ever returned it would never be the same. There would be no trace of the familiar places, just a desolate smashed up heap of ruins, because the little village of Longueval has simply disappeared."

Even the bombardment had its lighter moments, especially during the early days, before the constant strain caused by the seemingly-endless torrent of shells started fully to take its toll on everyone's nerves. Already after only two days, there were tales of misfortune or lucky escapes to be found all over the area under attack.

*Musketier W. Stöckle 8th Company Reserve Infantry Regiment 111*[42]   **8.**

"It was during the hot sticky afternoon of 25th June 1916 as the enemy was building up to the preparatory drum fire before the Somme offensive. We were in Bazentin le Petit and contrary to the usual habits of the Tommies, were on the receiving end of a dozen shells in the village. Because we had no underground shelters there, there was some confusion and we stayed in our billets ready to run for it if necessary. Suddenly there was a roaring in the air and an explosion as a shell landed in the middle of our garden. At the same time a long, rounded splinter whizzed through the air and landed in front of our door. Our Leutnant, who had an original taste in souvenirs, spotted at once that it would make an excellent ashtray, so he called out to his batman, 'Fritz, hop out and bring that 'ashtray' here!' Fritz, for his part, felt that the situation in the courtyard was somewhat dangerous, but on the other hand as an old soldier he knew that every order was holy, so he opted for the following compromise, 'Wouldn't the Herr Leutnant like to hold on a little? The British would be bound to send over even more 'ash trays', so that by evening the Herr Leutnant would be able to chose from a much larger selection!' Fritz never confided in us if he had learned this type of politeness when he was serving customers in a shop."

*Leutnant Ebeling 3rd Battalion Reserve Infantry Regiment 15*[43]  **9.**

"Day dawned [26th June]. A British aviator cruised in circles above us. Three companies had already disappeared into Puisieux. Suddenly a signaller dashed out of a dugout and shouted: 'The village is about to be fired on!' Too late! Immediately afterwards a hail of heavy shells came down on the 10th, 11th and 12th Companies. Only the 9th was spared and that was because it was last on the march by a wide margin and had not yet arrived at the village. The pilot had informed his artillery about the battalion. His radio message had been intercepted by our signallers. Unfortunately it took some time to translate. In proportion to the huge weight of fire which came down the casualties were quite bearable."

*Hauptmann Hensel 9th Company Infantry Regiment 60*[44]  **10.**

"After we had taken over the position [near Dompierre], the bombardment increased day by day and hour by hour, until gentle harassing fire had been transformed into drumfire.* The 9th Company held the centre of the line, about 100 metres from the French. The position comprised the battle trench, with an accommodation trench which contained most of the dugouts, just to the rear. We occupied four large mine craters just to our front. Morale was excellent. Everyone knew that hard days lay ahead; knew too that each would do his duty. The bombardment damaged the trenches to such an extent that clearance work was no longer feasible. At night sufficient work took place to ensure that it was possible to move around the position to some extent. During the mornings after a short time everything was levelled once more and the position was only marked by a line of craters. The company was stood-to constantly...So the days passed until the 27th June. Casualties gradually began to make themselves felt. Hot food was no longer getting forward and we had to resort to iron rations. Everyone hoped with each passing hour that the attack would be launched and that the drumfire would cease.

"On the 27th there was a storm of small arms fire. Red signal rockets were launched constantly as a signal to the artillery. The guns and mortars opened up promptly. Everyone was in his alert position and night was lit up like day. Across the whole company front, advancing French troops, launched to test how ready for attack the position was, presented a fantastic target. The ensuing fire and casualties showed them that there was still some way to go. They jumped back in their trenches and soon the French artillery alone was hammering away angrily at the position. The 28th saw a further increase in fire. Everyone was longing for the attack to begin, but the day passed off normally. That evening, just before midnight, the two platoon commanders, Leutnant von der Au and Offizierstellvertreter Biandt were sitting having a discussion with the

---

*Trommelfeuer [drumfire] was a term coined by the Germans to describe a barrage of such extraordinary intensity that the explosions of individual shells could no longer be discerned distinctly. Instead the noise was similiar to that of a grotesquely amplified drum roll.

company commander when, just as on the previous evening, all hell broke loose. Hats on and we were ready. Equipment was carried day and night. No sooner had we reached the top step of the dugout than a runner appeared and shouted that the French were in the trench. So forwards we went from the accommodation trench to the battle trench in order to launch a counter-attack.

"Offizierstellvertreter Biandt, in his well known daring way, jumped out of the cover and raced over the top through the withering fire to his Platoon. The communication trench between the two trenches was at least not occupied. Without opposition we rushed forward and saw that the French were attacking in approximately company strength. Our fire was reinforced strongly by the artillery and mortars. The 210 millimetre shells and heavy mortar rounds landed right in front of our position, so that fragments whistled past our noses. Now we had to find out where the French were. Crater by crater, we worked our way over to our right flank, but finally we established that the French had not got in to the position. At the cost of some casualties, we had beaten off the attack..."

*Reserve Leutnant Wilhelm Geiger Reserve Infantry Regiment 111*[45] **6.**

"During the drumfire which preceded the Battle of the Somme, the Headquarters of the 2nd Battalion was smashed. The staff was located in the poorly protected narrow and low passage which led to the Regimental Aid Post. The guns thundered and roared endlessly. All day long it went on, with only brief pauses. During one such pause, the battalion staff was sitting in this passageway. The Hauptmann, his batman and the senior doctor were on one side, then came the adjutant, the communication trench officer and the two doctors on the other. Finally right at the end sat the telephonists. The adjutant's chair was an old chaise longue which had been rescued from Fricourt and next to it hung the telephone. I was fit to drop with tiredness and wanted to snatch some sleep before the deadly dance started up again outside. Good old Jansen, the communication trench officer, took my place at the telephone. I took a cover down to the end of the passageway and lay down by the telephonists. A sandbag was my pillow and my coat the blanket for this brief rest on the ground. I had not even fallen asleep when there was a terrible crash. All the lights went out. There were shouts in the dark and a choking cloud of explosive gases. The doctors and I raced to the other end of the dugout. There the Hauptmann, the senior doctor and the Hauptmann's batman lay wounded under splintered beams and there sat Jansen on my chair, bent forward, dead with a splinter in his head. His hand still held the pencil that he was using to write a letter to his wife. It was, I believe, their sixth wedding anniversary! Hardly a moment earlier it had been me sitting in that same chair. It got him, not me. Luck?"

By the end of the fourth day of the bombardment, the unprecedented nature and severity of the preparations for the allied assault was causing disquiet at Headquarters Second Army. General von Below did not mince his words in his evening report on 28th June, but it availed him nothing, neither did his request for further infantry and artillery reinforcements. He was, however, able to make use of the individual units of the 10th Bavarian Infantry Division to relieve those defenders who had been hit hardest so far by the bombardment. Eight further artillery batteries were allocated to him, as were four additional reinforcement companies, but this amounted to a few drops of water on a hot stone. Second Army was going to have to meet the forthcoming attack from its own resources.

*Evening Report, Second Army 28th June 1916* [46]

"Enemy activity opposite XIV Reserve Corps (North of the Somme) and XVII Army Corps (South of the Somme) resembles, ever more closely, tactics of wearing down and attrition. It must be assumed that the bombardment, which has now lasted for five days, and which from time to time increases to drumfire, before reducing to calmer, observed fire by the heaviest calibre weapons on different sectors of our positions, will continue for some time. The enemy's gas tactics, which are being aided by the prevailing west winds, of releasing constantly repeated small clouds of gas, is aimed also at gradual attrition. Because of technical mistakes, the enemy has so far achieved little through the use [of gas]. It is a different matter with the artillery. The enormous enemy superiority in heavy and long-range batteries, which the Army has so far been unable to counter, is proving very painful. Our artillery would have been adequate to respond to an assault launched after a one-day heavy bombardment of our trenches. Because of the procedure which he has adopted, the enemy is in a position to flatten our positions and smash our dugouts, through the application of days of fire with 280 and 300 millimetre guns. This means that our infantry is suffering heavy losses day after day, whilst the enemy is able to preserve his manpower. His main forces, which outnumber our infantry many times over, are for the time being probably outside the beaten area of our guns, or protected by overhead cover, which our heavy field howitzers cannot penetrate; whilst the few 210 millimetre mortars are nowhere near sufficient to cover a forty-five to fifty kilometre frontage".

Down to the south, in front of the French sector, the bombardment was certainly having a serious effect. The geography was less favourable to the defence, there had been a greater turnover of defending formations and the trenches and dugouts themselves were generally fewer in number and less well constructed than those further to the north. Casualties were mounting and men of the 10th Bavarian Infantry Division found themselves being plugged in to fill gaps in the defences, frequently in a thoroughly piecemeal way, which was shortly to have serious consequences for them.

*Reserve Leutnant Gruber Machine Gun Company Bavarian Reserve Infantry Regiment 6*[17] **11.**

"During the afternoon [28th June], we saw a pitiful little procession coming from the direction of Cléry and Hem. These were the inhabitants, who had been turned out of the homes which they had thus far occupied, only a few kilometres behind the lines. Women, children and the elderly were departing in a long line, one behind the other. They were all carrying heavy packages or pulling their possession along in childrens' prams or hand carts. Suddenly French artillery rounds crashed down in the middle of this sad little group. But one of their observation officers must have spotted the error, because the fire ceased as soon as it had begun. At 11.00 pm the Machine Gun Company received the order to head for Cléry-East and to report to Major Bezzel there. We did not relish this task, because Cléry, like all other villages near the front, was subject to nightly harassing fire and it seemed very doubtful to us that we should be able to enter the place at all. In fact it was only due to a great stroke of fortune that the majority of our men were not killed near Cléry church. The rain had stopped, but it was difficult to distinguish anything in the dark.

"Towards midnight we and our weapons, which had been made ready, were assembled at the canal in Feuillaucourt and, about 3.00 am on the 29th, I left the canal with about seventy gunners. We intended to avoid using roads, set off across country, but quickly lost direction in the dark, so we had to try to pick up the road to our right, which led over the hill to Cléry. Despite lively harassing fire, we arrived unscathed at the corner of the park in Cléry, where our guide awaited us. Unfortunately he did not know where the Company was. Consequently we stumbled over ruined walls, wires and dead horses all along the line of the main street until we reached the square in front of the church. Here we were hit by a burst of artillery fire and were just able in time to take cover in an adjacent cellar. I left my overheated, sweating men to get their breath back, then went to find the company, which was located about 300 metres in front of the church. In the meantime it had become light and the harassing fire ceased. Each gun team went and occupied a cellar, where they settled in peacefully and prepared a meal from food left behind by the occupants. This was done with great keenness, because each man realised that we might not receive anything else for a long while. To add to our cup of joy, despite the fact that it had been under lively artillery fire, some cases of Munich export beer were found at Cléry station and we rescued them with a barrow. The day was fine and sunny and we were able to enjoy the view down into the valley of the Somme from the lovely gardens..."

*Reserve Hauptmann Klug 5th Company Bavarian Reserve Regiment 6*[48] **12.**

"During the night 28th/29th June, I received an order to advance with my company into Bayernwald [Bavarian Wood]. I succeeded in carrying out this order before it became light. The company was accommodated in the communication trench which linked to Bayernwald and in rough fox holes. I was subordinated to the Battalion Command Post of the Prussian Infantry Regiment 62, which was located in the wood. Towards midnight on the 29th, I was ordered to move my company up to the frontline itself and to relieve the Prussian company which was stationed left and right of the road to Montauban in Position M. The platoons were led forward by one guide apiece from the company which was to be relieved. One of these platoons was led astray and only linked up later with the company. Despite the drumfire, the relief took place without significant casualties. The Prussian company, which we relieved, had been reduced in number to approximately thirty men due to the drumfire and mortar fire in particular. It had already given up the first and second trenches, inasmuch as it was still possible to speak of 'trenches'. Throughout the entire company area there were only three dugouts which offered some guarantee of protection. In order to enter the company commander's dugout, it was necessary to climb over dead and unburied Prussian soldiers. It took until long into the night to re-establish sentry positions in the front line trench. The only contact was with the 12th Company to the south. One platoon of this company lost its way shortly before dawn and ended up in our position. The link back to battalion headquarters in Bayernwald was still working. Food was got through to us from there, but no water; the carriers could not pass the drumfire..."

South of the river, the German artillery was having an extremely hard time of it, because the odds were stacked heavily in favour of the French artillery units, which outnumbered and out-gunned them throughout the area. Battery positions were systematically wrecked and all movement and activity behind the lines became almost impossible. Riding forward to conduct a reconnaissance in the Vermandovillers area, the Assistant Adjutant of Field Artillery Regiment 42 was caught by a concentration of fire and wounded. He then attempted to obtain medical attention in a nearby farmyard, which had been taken over as a dressing station. His wounds were dressed in due course and he waited to be seen by a doctor.

*Reserve Leutnant Deloch Field Artillery Regiment 42*[49] **13.**

"The doctor never arrived to give me a tetanus injection, because suddenly a heavy shell crashed down on the farmyard, with all the usual unpleasant consequences for roof and windows. I saw quickly that it was no use expecting anything more here. Quickly putting on my cap, throwing my jacket and braces across my arm, and using my free hand to hold up my trousers, I joined in the general panic. Out in the open once more, I was fortunate enough to link up with my horse. I then dressed swiftly and rode off for home happily, where I was able to get some proper treatment from the doctor."

The defenders still needed desperately to know when the attack was due to begin. Numerous allied soldiers were captured during these final few days and there was at least one case of desertion by a British soldier in the Beaumont Hamel area. Subsequent interrogations provided information concerning the extent, the date and time of the attack, which was flashed to units and formations throughout the area, as were intercepts from the 'Moritz' listening stations. It was still hard for the German army to form an exact picture, especially because prisoners taken early in the bombardment had been briefed that the attack would follow five days of fire preparation. Nevertheless, by the time the attack came, all tactical surprise, less that of firing mines at strategic points, was lost.

'According to a message of HQ XIV Reserve Corps dated 24th June, (received 26th June) a statement by a British soldier captured near Gommecourt, [indicates that] a major assault will occur in two to three days at the latest. It will be preceded by four to five days of artillery preparation then the infantry will attack. The front will have a width of forty eight kilometres. Gas will be used in certain places.'[50] 'According to statements by prisoners of war, the main attack was to be expected at 4.00 am on the 27th June. In expectation of the enemy, the entire line stood-to, but the general assault did not occur.'[51] This assessment was probably based, at least in part, on the interrogation of Private Victor Wheat of C Company 5th Battalion North Staffordshire Regiment, who had been part of a wiring party, which had come under machine-gun fire during the night of 23rd/24th June. He was badly wounded and left by his comrades to make his own way back to his trench. Weakened and disorientated, he lost his way and fetched up in front of the German wire. There he was captured. His wounds were dressed and he was interrogated. The interrogator noted that he was weak from loss of blood, that his statements were made when he was almost incapacitated through shock and that he [the interrogator] was inclined to the view that this fact added veracity to the prisoner's statements, which apart from providing details of the British organisation continued:

'The British attack will take place in two to three days at the latest. There will be a four to five day bombardment before the infantry attack. The attack will start in this area [Gommecourt] and stretch [south] on a front of thirty miles. Gas will be used only against individual points, where its use is deemed to be necessary... The attack will begin in a few days, probably on Wednesday and will be on a front of thirty to fifty miles. He only had exact knowledge of his own brigade [137 brigade, 46th Division] plans. Gommecourt was to be bypassed to its north and south. The assault was to be pushed forward to the wood behind the fourth trench. [He knew this because] it had all been rehearsed about four days ago in an area of trenches near a copse behind the lines at St Leger... This attack will be led by 6th Battalion North Staffordshire Regiment, because the 5th Battalion had attacked first at Loos... The soldiers have little faith in the success of this attack. Their general had made a poor fist of commanding at Loos...'[52]

'It was known from prisoners that the general Franco-British assault was to take place on 29th June at 5.00 am. Once more all possible defensive preparations for the attack were made. All the front line infantry was longing for the close-quarter battle to come. The effect of the four-day bombardment was boundless bitterness and rage at the soulless machinery of war, which slowly gnawed away at the best that a soldier had to offer, namely confidence in his personal strength and superiority. Once more in the early hours of the 29th everyone stood-to, full of eagerness and trust that they would be able to pay the attackers back in full for the evil recent days'.[53] There are several candidates who might have led the Germans to this conclusion. These include Privates Coones and Barrow of 1st Battalion Newfoundland Regiment, captured along with the severely wounded Captain Butler and one other man, during a catastrophic attempt at a raid and a prisoner snatch during the night of 27th/28th June, which was shot to pieces by artillery, mortar and small arms fire. Apart from providing a great deal of background intelligence, the two stated during their interrogation on the morning of the 28th June that, 'The general attack is expected to take place after artillery and gas preparation lasting four to five days.'[54] Altogether that night, the 29th Division had despatched four strong patrols forward. One of them included a more likely source: Private Josef Lipmann, W Company 2nd Battalion Royal Fusiliers, who deserted from a seventeen man patrol.[55]

Lipmann was twenty-three years old, a carpenter by trade, who had volunteered in August 1914. His parents were Russian. He was born in Russia, but had been living in England for two years before the war. He spent nine months in Gallipoli with the 29th Division, where he became completely disenchanted with the war. According to his interrogator, 'because he had known since the Friday of the previous week, that following drum fire lasting five days and four nights and starting on Saturday morning, the great general offensive of the British would be launched between 5.00 am and 6.00 am on Thursday morning, this prisoner decided some days ago to take the next opportunity to desert...He volunteered for this patrol, with the definite intention of finding an opportunity to desert. In this he succeeded, because he can speak a few words of German and was able to make our troops understand, through a few broken phrases, that he was coming over with friendly intentions...'[56]

Lipmann provided his interrogators with a large amount of additional information. This included names of formations which would be participating in the attack, the colour coding of flares, which would be used to signal to the artillery, the sequence of events before the attack and the tactics that would be used by his own unit. The extension of the bombardment by two days, nullified the value of the timings which he had betrayed but, thoroughly alerted, the 'Moritz' station near Contalmaison made up for the deficiency in the early hours of the 1st July when it intercepted an order from the British 34th Division, which made it quite clear that the offensive was about to begin.[57]

That still lay in the future. In the meantime, there were two more days and nights of intense bombardment for the defenders to endure.

*Landwehr Leutnant M. Gerster Reserve Infantry Regiment 119*[58]

"If the 'Toffee Apples' were intended to destroy the obstacle and flatten the trenches completely, the enemy visualised the use of the 'torpedo mortars' more for the destruction of dugouts. Low flying aircraft searched systematically for places where there was any sign of life in the trenches and for where mined dugouts protected the garrison. With dreadful accuracy, they directed the fire of the heavy mortars on such places. As a result soon no infantryman would emerge from a dug out, as long as an aviator circled above him. With brown groundsheets smeared with mud and earth, they attempted to camouflage the dark entrance holes with their surroundings, in order not to give away the positions to sharp-eyed observers in the air. In certain Target Areas, up to a dozen mortars were massed. As a result there was an unbroken stream of calls for assistance from the front line to engage these terrible means of destruction with counter fire. The artillery declared that it was unable to respond to the wishes of the infantry, if it was to preserve its guns and so remain ready to fire defensively once the general attack came.... The actual front line trench no longer existed, instead crater overlapped crater where it had once been. Half collapsed holes indicated where the dugouts which still remained were located. The staircases were buried beneath piles of earth, which had fallen down from above. As a result the troops had to scramble up a smooth steep slope, which offered almost no footholds, in order to climb up to daylight.

"The obstacle had been swept away. Tangles of wire wrapped around steel supports still showed in some places, where there was once strong protection. Wherever artillery and mortar fire had not already ploughed it up, where the deeply driven wooden and steel stakes still stood, shrapnel fire had swept away the last traces of barbed wire. Where earlier protected sentry positions and shell proof observation posts had stood, rubble heaps, railway lines and concrete blocks were all that was left. How little human hands could do against the work of the machinery of destruction! Where the front line trench once ran, shreds of corrugated iron, splinters of timber shuttering, empty food tins, smashed weapons and the kit and equipment of the dead and wounded lay everywhere... Of course seven days' drum fire had not left the defenders untouched. The feeling of powerlessness against this storm of steel depressed even the strongest.

"Despite all efforts, the rations were inadequate. The uninterrupted high state of readiness, which had to be maintained because of the entire situation, as well as the frequent gas attacks, hindered the troops from getting the sleep that they needed because of the nerve-shattering artillery fire. Tired and indifferent to everything, the troops sat it out on wooden benches or lay on the hard metal beds, staring into the darkness when the tallow lights were extinguished by the overpressure of the explosions. Nobody had washed for days. Black stubble stood out on the pale haggard faces, whilst the eyes of some flashed strangely as though they had looked beyond the portals of the other side. Some trembled when the sound of death roared around the underground protected places. Whose heart was not in his mouth at times during this appalling storm of steel? All longed for an end to it one way or the other. All were seized by a deep bitterness at the inhuman machine of destruction which hammered endlessly. A searing rage against the enemy burned in their minds."

As the bombardment inexorably ground on, the strain of the endless drum fire was taking its toll on the hard-pressed defenders. Casualties were continuing to mount, defences and dugouts were smashed or blown in, forward supply of food and water was faltering in places and sleep was a near-impossibility. In these circumstances, men were thrown back on their own resources and drew strength from a variety of sources. For some of the more devout, their religion was a great source of comfort and inner strength in adversity. Others railed against the enemy, longing to be in action against them and to be able to take revenge for the dreadful ordeal that they were now enduring. Most were simply resigned to do what they had to, to take their share of the dangerous lookout duty from the head of the stairs leading to their dugouts and otherwise grimly to stick out the dreary and dangerous days and nights, trusting that the construction of their dugouts was sturdy enough to withstand the appalling explosions of the super-heavy calibre howitzer rounds directed against them.

*Feldwebel Schumacher 3rd Company Reserve Infantry Regiment 111*[59]

"Our soldiers did not just take knowledge of war and technology into the field with them. They knew that technical means alone were not decisive, but that the stout heart of he who walked quietly and confidently in faith would not fail in the most trying of times. His heart would be strengthened by living faith, which was a source of strength for all soldiers. I know that there was prayer in the trenches and the dugouts. Many a time I came across a man on sentry, his rosary in his hand and his thoughts directed to the strict fulfilment of his duties. Often I have said to myself: 'So long as this spirit is present amongst our troops, the enemy need have no thought of a breakthrough'. All disputes between branches of the church were forgotten. Whenever we had to accord the final honours to a comrade, there was no distinction between protestant and catholic. We reached out to one another across all religious barriers. With thanks, I think back to the tireless work of our padres, who engaged themselves fully in the task of making us equal to our stern soldierly duties."

*Unteroffizier Friedrich Hinkel 7th Company Reserve Infantry Regiment 99*[60] **14.**

"The enemy began to hammer at our trenches and links to the rear with an iron hail of fire of all calibres. Artillery fire! Seven long days there was ceaseless artillery fire, which rose ever more frequently to the intensity of drum fire. Then on the 27th and the 28th there were gas attacks on our trenches. The torture and the fatigue, not to mention the strain on the nerves, were indescribable! There was just one single heart-felt prayer on our lips: 'Oh God, free us from this ordeal; give us release through battle, grant us victory; Lord God! Just let them come!' and this determination increased with the fall of each shell. You made a good job of it, you British! Seven days and nights you rapped and hammered on our door! Now your reception was going to match your turbulent longing to enter!"

1. Hauptstaatsarchiv, Stuttgart M410 Bü 260
2. Dellmensingen: 'Das Bayernbuch vom Weltkriege' pp 236-237
3. Soden: History 26 Res Div p 93
4. Lutz: History BIR 16 p 38
5. Nollau: History IR 51 p 84
6. Lutz: History BIR 16 p 38
7. Burchardi: History Füs R 38 p 173
8. Nollau: op. cit. pp 86-87
9. This is the first line of a poem of 1809 by Ludwig Uhland which was, and still is, played or sung at military funerals and commemorations, where it is the equivalent of 'Last Post'.
10. Anon: History RIR 110 p 105
11. Gerster: History RIR 119 pp 46-48
12. Soden: op. cit. p 95
13. Kriegsarchiv München BRIR 8 Bd 21
14. The origins of the battle cry '*Hurra*' dated back in various linguistic forms for hundreds of years in the German Army. Its First World War form of '*Hurra*' had been unchanged since 1800 and its use was actually a standard procedure in the attack: hence the stress here on not using it, to preserve secrecy.
15. Hauptstaatsarchiv, Stuttgart M107 Bü 42

16. Gerster: History RIR 119 p 48
17. Hauptstaatsarchiv, Stuttgart M107 Bü 42/142
18. The layout on 31 Jul 15 is clearly shown in a diagram contained in Hauptstaatsarchiv, Stuttgart M410 Bü 140 (Skizze 8) and there are several versions of the final Jul 16 state of the Redoubt, including a very large scale (1:2,500) map, in the Kriegsarchiv, München : See RIR 8 (WK) and HS2205. The location and extent of the major tunnel complex in St Pierre Divion is shown on numerous diagrams, including  8 RIR Bd 4 'Kräfteverteilung C1 – C2' 8 Jul 16 and 15 Jul 16 (1:5000)
19. Kriegsarchiv München HS 1984
20. Soden: op. cit. p 98
21. Hauptstaatsarchiv, Stuttgart M43 Bü17
22. An example of this type of observation post can still be seen today in the former area of RIR 99.  It is located at a place which the British called 'The Pope's Nose', which is in a field by the track leading to St Pierre Divion, a short distance north of the Ulster Tower. This post did indeed lose its overhead cover.  It is mistaken frequently for the remains of a German machine-gun position.
23. Kriegsarchiv München BRIR 8 Bd 3
24. Hauptstaatsarchiv, Stuttgart M410 Bü 140
25. The regiment involved was clearly 15th Bn Lancashire Fusiliers of 96 Brigade
26. Müller-Loebnitz: 'Die Badener im Weltkrieg' p 205
27. Soden: op.cit. p 98
28. Grote: 'Somme' p 15
29. Grote: op. cit. p 16
30. Hauptstaatsarchiv, Stuttgart M410 Bü 239
31. Kriegsarchiv München BRIR 8 Bd 3
32. A personal memoir of  General von Bram held in the Kriegsarchiv München [HS 2205] includes the following statement concerning 25th June: 'Statements from prisoners, deserters, reports from agents, small scale enemy patrol operations, all confirmed the general assumption that a major British offensive was imminent.'  In addition, Crown Prince Rupprecht of Bavaria's diary entry for 26th June (Mein Kriegstagebuch 1. Band p 486) states, 'Reports from the Military Attaché in Madrid and an agent agree that the enemy offensive will begin on 1st July.'
33. Keiser: History IR 61 p 157
34. ibid. p 158
35. Hauptstaatsarchiv, Stuttgart M410 Bü 260
36. Hauptstaatsarchiv, Stuttgart M410 Bü 260
37. Bachelin: History RIR 111 p 286
38. v. Kuhl: Der Weltkrieg 1914/18 Bd 1 p 491
39. Hauptstaatsarchiv, Stuttgart M410 Bü 140
40. Richter: History IR 128 I. Teil pp 215-216
41. Frisch: History RIR 109 pp 139-141
42. Bachelin: op. cit. p 284
43. Forstner: History RIR 15 p 301
44. Cron: History IR 60 p 140
45. Bachelin: op. cit. pp 287-288
46. Grote: op. cit. pp 32 - 33
47. Bezzel: History BRIR 6 pp 82-83
48. ibid. pp 85-86
49. Schoenfelder: History FAR 42 p 139
50. Hauptstaatsarchiv, Stuttgart M43/19 RIR 99
51. Hauptstaatsarchiv, Stuttgart M410 Bü 140
52. Kriegsarchiv München BRIR 8 Bd 4
53. Hauptstaatsarchiv, Stuttgart M410 Bü 140
54. Kriegsarchiv München BRIR 8 Bd 4

55. There are references in Schwarte, GenLt Max *Der Weltkampf um Ehre und Recht: Der deutsche Landkrieg* p 548 to other deserters: 'Deserters to the 26th Reserve Division predicted that the attack would begin 27th June at 4.00 am (British time)...' This is almost certainly an error. There is no mention of any such event in the History of the 26th Res Div, which does, however, attribute this information to the interrogation of a prisoner, who was certainly Private Wheat, although his unit is mistakenly given as 5th [Loyal] North Lancashire. The main points of the interrogation of Private Wheat were received by Divisions during the afternoon of 26th June and were relayed by telephone down to Regiments. The information reached RIR 99, for example at 5.00 pm [See Haupt-staatsarchiv Stuttgart M43/19 RIR 99].  Schwarte continues: 'On the 29th a deserter came across. He gave information that the attack would take place north of the Somme on the 30th at 0930 (German time) and two hours later south of the Somme.' The individual is not named.  The author does not even indicate his nationality, or where the alleged desertion occurred.  In view of the fact that Schwarte was probably wrong about the 27th June, there must be some doubt about the second story.  The Battle Log of RIR 99, referred to above, shows, however, that the Regiment received the 'Lipmann warning' at 9.10 pm on the 28th June and a second short-notice warning at 2.13 am on 29th June, following prisoner interrogation, that there would be a British attack in about Brigade strength in the La Boisselle area at 2.30 am that same day. Finally the RIR 99 log also contains an obscure reference to a message received at 5.06 am on the 30th June from 'Ovillers North': 'Statement of a British officer captured near the 'Appendix' [located at La Boisselle], that the British attack will begin at 4.00 am British, 5.00 am German time.' It is possible that this message may be based on the same unnamed source quoted by Cron Oberstleutnant a. D. Hermann in his *Infanterie-Regiment Markgraf Karl (7.Brandenburgisches) Nr. 60 in dem großen Kriege 1914-1918* p 141, 'From deserters it had become known that the attack was planned for 4.00 am 29th June, but that it had been postponed to 8.00 am on 30th June...'

56. Kriegsarchiv München BRIR 8 Bd 4
57. Soden: op. cit. p 108
58. Hauptstaatsarchiv, Stuttgart M410 Bü 140
59. Bachelin: *op. cit.* pp 283-284
60. Müller: History RIR 99 p 107

# CHAPTER 4

# 1st July 1916

Dawn broke on a perfect summer's day on 1st July. Allied artillery and mortar fire rained down at an unprecedented rate, even by the standards of the past week. The nervous tension in the dugouts of the waiting German defenders was almost tangible. They knew beyond doubt that the long-awaited offensive was about to begin. They knew too that they had one chance and one chance only when the barrage lifted: if they wanted to live, they had to win the race to their parapet. If they were out of their dugouts, complete with their weapons and spare ammunition, before the attackers arrived, they would probably prevail. Caught underground, death or capture was their inevitable fate. They fastened on their equipment and checked and rechecked their weapons. All along the line, from Gommecourt to Chaulnes, sentries crouching in the entrances to their dugouts strained to detect a slackening in the fire, then suddenly, at 8.20 am German time, the artillery fire lifted and there was an almighty roar, as a gigantic charge exploded beneath the men of 9th Company Reserve Infantry Regiment 119 who were manning trenches on Hawthorn Ridge overlooking Beaumont Hamel. The After Action Report of 3rd Battalion Reserve Infantry Regiment 119[1] 1. noted:

"At 8.15 am [this is an error, 8.20 am German time, 7.20 British time], a mine with an extraordinarily large charge was blown under the projecting 'nose' in the middle of B1. Almost all of 1st Platoon (Leutnant Renz) and elements on the left of the 2nd Platoon (Leutnant Böhm) were crushed and buried in their dugouts by the explosion. All the entrances to the 3rd Platoon dugouts (Leutnant Breitmeyer) and some of those belonging to the dugouts of the 2nd Platoon (Leutnant Böhm) were buried by falling rock. Only very few men of the 9th Company, those on the left flank and the right flank where the machine guns were located, succeeded in getting straight out into the open and occupying their battle positions. The enormous crater was about fifty metres long and fifteen metres deep. Within a few moments further men managed to dig themselves out, so that the 9th Company had about two sections ready to do battle."

All around, the layer of white chalk gave the impression that there had been a snowstorm. Flares calling for artillery defensive fire shot upwards.

The defenders were beginning to react, but not before some British troops had stormed into the trenches of 3rd Platoon to the left of the crater. Inside one of the dugouts, which had four entrances, three of which were blocked and only a small hole remained of the fourth, the occupants, who included Leutnant Breitmeyer and the company commander, Reserve Oberleutnant Mühlbayer, worked feverishly to escape. Before the sentry could enlarge the hole fully, he was bayoneted and fell back dead down the stairs. Standing by him, Vizefeldwebel Davidsohn shot his assailant in the face with a flare.[2] Hand grenades and smoke bombs were thrown into the dugout and demands for its surrender were shouted down. The defenders, in hope and expectation of reinforcement and support from elsewhere, did not deign to reply and soon a pitched battle for possession of the crater and its surroundings was in full flow.

Further north, at Gommecourt, the barrage lifted a few minutes later. There was absolutely no surprise here. Not only did the defenders know that the attack was coming, they also had a clear idea about its aims, as a result of intelligence gleaned a few days previously from the interrogation of the captured Private Wheat, who was a member of 5th Battalion North Staffordshire Regiment of the 46th (North Midland) Division. The German defences north of the village in the area of Reserve Infantry Regiment 91 had been considerably weakened by the bombardment. The barbed wire obstacle was badly damaged and the trenches were blown in and flattened. However, almost all of the dugouts and hence the soldiers had survived the bombardment.[3] Here the assault succeeded in breaking into the forward trenches, but vigorous local counterattacks swiftly restored the situation. South of the village the main weight of the attack fell on Sectors G5, N1 and N2, [the three sectors immediately south and southeast of the village] which were defended by Infantry Regiment 170. The British troops from the 56th (London) Division succeeded in breaching the defences, which led to hard, confused fighting and a violent reaction from the defenders. Infantry Regiment 170 appealed to Reserve Infantry Regiment 55 for assistance, reporting, 'Enemy attack in Target Areas 16/18 at 08.35 am; gas attack against Sector North at 9.05; attack at 9.15 am against Sector 19. At 9.30 the enemy broke into G5 and is threatening the right flank. We are holding the third trench.'[4] At 9.30 am a Regimental order was given to 3rd Battalion Reserve Infantry Regiment 55: 'Major Tauscher and his Battalion, including the Construction Company, are to attack, via the 2nd Guards position, the enemy which has broken into G5 and drive them out. Report when ready. Machine guns will be made available. The battalion commander is to be on Hill 147'.[5]

Help was on the way. The ensuing battle, which involved hand to hand fighting, lasted until the late afternoon, but finally the defenders prevailed; the attackers being killed or driven out. It was a hard but successful day and especially so for the machine gun crews, which had been deployed in a reinforcing role in G5 just south of the village.

*Leutnant Koch Machine Gun Scharfschützen-Trupp 73*[6]   **2.**

"It should also be noted that the two gunners of Machine Gun 8, who were still unhurt after the weapon had been overrun in the first rush, immediately and without being prevented by the British, dragged the gun

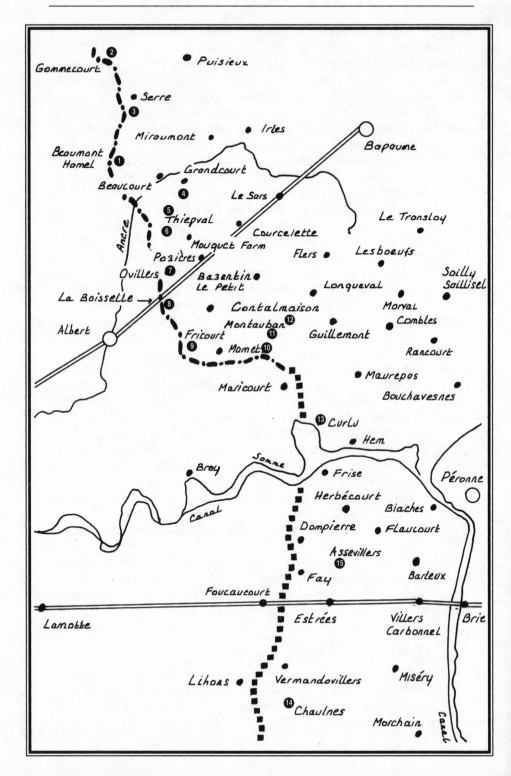

into a dugout, covered it with a groundsheet and sat on it. So they were able later, at a suitable moment, to bring the gun into action against the withdrawing enemy. The weapon commander, Gefreiter Füchte, noticed... two forms suddenly in a thick cloud of gas. [This must have been smoke or dust. The only release of cylinder gas anywhere on the British sector that day was at Fricourt.] He jumped onto the shot-up parapet and killed a British officer, before being killed himself by a hand grenade. His courageous behaviour made it possible for the gunners to bring the weapon into action. Unteroffizier Schultheiss got his gun into action in G5 in good time and caused heavy casualties to the enemy. Gefreiter Freiburger acted as Gunner 3. Gunners Haupt, Meyer, Hast and Gefreiter Berkefeld attended to ammunition resupply. Suddenly the enemy appeared in their rear and threw hand grenades. Freiberger was severely wounded; Haupt, Meyer and Hast were wounded too. The British called upon Unteroffizier Schultheiss to surrender. Schultheiss, who was being resupplied with ammunition by Berkefeld, refused. He swung his gun round and fired to the rear until both men, who were attacked from all sides with hand grenades, were killed. Weapon 7 was located to the right of Weapon 6 and was commanded by Gefreiter Niemeyer. Niemeyer succeeded in beating off the enemy, both those to his front as well as those who had broken into the trench to one side and his rear. He caused the enemy many casualties and prevented enemy exploitation to the right. When Niemeyer was killed by a shot to the head, Hennig continued to operate the gun with great success against the fleeing masses of British. Examination of the corpses showed that he had fired with great calmness and excellent dispersion of fire."

Altogether during the fight for Gommecourt, Reserve Infantry Regiments 55 and 91 lost three officers and 182 men, but lying before the position of Reserve Infantry Regiment 91 were 700 dead British soldiers and as many as 2,000 in front of Reserve Infantry Regiment 55.[7] A little further to the south, a major disaster for the British army was unfolding to the west of the village of Serre where, it will be remembered, there had been a hard-fought battle the previous year. Here the defenders had learned and applied critical lessons. They were now occupying the vital high ground around Serre. It was critical to the integrity of the entire defence north of the Ancre that this place did not fall, so the German army had spent over a year turning it into a virtually impregnable fortress. Promptly at 8.30 am, the Pals Battalions of the 31st Division went over the top into a maelstrom of fire. Incredible to relate, thanks to fortuitous selection of a partially covered approach route, a handful of them actually penetrated as far as Serre village itself, but none lived to tell the tale. The attack was simply ripped to shreds by the men of Infantry Regiment 169 from Baden, ably assisted by machine gunners from Infantry Regiment 66, which was located slightly to the north.

*Unteroffizier Otto Lais Infantry Regiment 169*[8] **3.**

"Wild firing slammed into the masses of the enemy. All around us was the rushing, whistling and roaring of a storm; a hurricane, as the destructive British shells rushed towards our artillery which was firing courageously, our reserves and our rear areas. Throughout all this racket, this rumbling, growling, bursting, cracking and wild banging and crashing of small arms, could be heard the heavy, hard and regular Tack! Tack! of the machine guns... That one firing slower, this other with a faster rhythm – it was the precision work of fine material and skill – and both were playing a gruesome tune to the enemy, whilst providing their own comrades and the men manning the automatic rifles a high degree of security and reassurance.

"The machine gunners, who lived a privileged life at quiet times and were envied for being able to avoid jobs such as carrying heavy mortar rounds forward, were earning their pay today. Belt after belt was fired. 250 rounds – 1,000 – 3,000. 'Pass up the spare barrels!' shouts the gun commander. Barrels are changed – fire on! 5,000 rounds. The barrel must be changed again. It's red hot and the cooling water is boiling – the hands working the weapon are scorched and burned – 'Keep firing!' urges the gun commander, 'or shoot yourself!' The cooling water turns to seething steam with the continuous firing. In the heat of battle, the steam overflow pipe slips out of its fixing on the water jacket. With a great hiss, a jet of steam goes up, providing a superb target for the enemy. It is the greatest good fortune that they have the sun in their eyes and we have it at our backs. The enemy closes up nearer. We fire on endlessly. There is less steam. A further barrel change is urgent. The cooling water has almost steamed away. 'Where's the water?' bawls the gunner. 'Get the mineral water out of the dugout!' 'There's none left Unteroffizier!' It all went during the eight day bombardment.

"The British keep charging forward. Despite the fact that hundreds are already lying dead in the shell holes to our front, fresh waves keep emerging from the assault trenches over there. We have got to fire! A gunner rushes into the crater with the water container and urinates into it. A second pisses into it too – quick, refill! The British have closed to grenade throwing range and hand grenades fly backwards and forwards. The barrel change is complete, the water jacket refilled. Load! Hand and rifle grenades burst close to the weapon. Just keep calm, get the tangle sorted out and load! Speak loudly, slowly and clearly to yourself. 'Forward! – Down! – Back! (Working parts forward – Belt on – Working parts back). The same again! – Safety catch to the right! – Fire!'...Tack! - Tack! Tack! - Tack!...Once more rapid fire slams into the clay pit to our front. High pillars of steam rise from all the machine guns. Most of the steam hoses have been torn off or shot away. Skin hangs in ribbons from the fingers of the burnt hands of the gunners and gun commanders! Constant pressure by their left thumbs on the triggers has turned them into swollen, shapeless lumps of flesh. Their hands rest, as though cramped, on the vibrating weapons.

"18,000 rounds! The other platoon weapon has a stoppage. Gunner Schwarz falls shot through the head, over the belt he is feeding. The belt twists, feeds rounds into the gun crookedly and they jam! Next man forward! The dead man is removed. The gunner strips the feed mechanism, removes the rounds and reloads. Fire; pause; barrel change; fetch ammunition; lay the dead and wounded on the floor of the crater. That is the hard, unrelenting tempo of the morning of 1st July 1916. The sound of machine gun fire can be heard right across the divisional front. The youth of England, the finest regiments of Scotland [Lais is mistaken. No Scottish regiments attacked Serre that day] bled to death in front of Serre. The weapon which was commanded by Unteroffizier Koch from Pforzheim and which was stationed directly on the Serre-Mailly road fires off a last belt! It has fired no fewer 20,000 rounds at the British!"[9]

South of Serre, on the slopes of Redan Ridge below Soden Redoubt, the men of Reserve Infantry Regiment 121 had prepared an unpleasant surprise for any would-be attacker. The Heidenkopf [Quadrilateral], which jutted forward from the German front line had been prepared as a massive booby trap for attacking infantry. It came under heavy artillery fire during the bombardment, was completely evacuated on 28th June, but was reoccupied by a skeleton group of defenders in time for 1st July. There was a realisation that this area could not be held in the short term in the event of a major attack. So the idea developed to lure a large number of attackers into it and to blow them up by means of hidden mines. In the event the plan was much less successful than intended, because the Heidenkopf was not attacked directly. Instead the main British attack swept around it and in fact at least one of the charges may have been set off prematurely, blowing up or burying some of the defenders. Finally the mines were blown, but they achieved comparatively little, except to be the subject of a detailed report by the German engineers later:[10]

[At 8.25 am] it was noted that ...strong British forces were massing around the Heidenkopf [Quadrilateral] and that they suddenly paused in their forward movement. There was no trace of the later fate of the guards of the Heidenkopf and mined dug out. After recapture only the Officer in charge was found and he was lying dead in Bayerngraben [Bavarian Trench]...During the nights which followed the attack, engineer patrols established the extent of the explosion. There were great surface changes. Four large craters surrounded the flattened Quadrilateral Trench. Detonation in all four of the chambers was successful. The weight of the charges was: Ia = 1500kg; Ib = 1500kg; IIa = 1500kg; IIb = 1250kg.

"For the three craters on the right, the dimensions were the same. They measured twenty-five metres in diameter and ten to fifteen metres in depth. The left hand crater was somewhat smaller. The extent to which casualties were caused could be established from the many British dead who were killed by falling rock. The British troops seem to have been especially surprised by the two left hand craters. Our underground installations are still more or less in order. The communication dug out (Stollen II) [Mined dugout II] is already useable once more from Bavarian Trench to the Heidenkopf. For the time being, it is being used as an access route to a forward double sentry post which has been established at the staircase entrance in the old Heidenkopf.

"The British did not actually attack the Heidenkopf. They pushed on left and right of it to Bavarian Trench. As was later established, none of the British remained in the Heidenkopf itself; this despite the fact that they established themselves temporarily behind it in Bavarian Trench. It was only in consequence of the lack of clarity and the confusion caused in the massed British ranks by the German fire that they closed in on the area of the Heidenkopf. Nevertheless, the explosion, which took place ten to fifteen minutes after the first British line had broken in, caused casualties. No doubt the British had suspected the presence of hidden mines in the Heidenkopf. They attempted, therefore, to bypass it to the sides and to enter it from the rear. What led the British to this assumption is impossible to say. Possibly it was the conclusion they drew from the shape of the Heidenkopf. The section of trench which sticks out well forward of the main line could have suggested that it would be cleared during an attack and be used as a trap for the advancing enemy. It is almost impossible to believe that they had exact knowledge of the location of the hidden mines. This particular case underlines the fact that hidden mines should not be laid in obvious parts of the position. As soon as the enemy develops a suspicion he can divert around the feared place.

"This was the reason why he by-passed the open Beaumont North minefield, attacking only to the left and right of it. Hidden mines have proved themselves to be technically hard to employ. If they are laid sufficiently powerful to be effective, their explosion is inconsistent with the most reliable trench defence. In view of the resultant rock fall, nearby trenches can only be occupied after a successful explosion. It is really extremely difficult to judge the correct moment for the explosion. In the current case, observers could not do their work reliably, despite all the preparations. News concerning the British advance reached the firing point only in a roundabout way. Strictly speaking the explosion occurred far too late. The Heidenkopf experience demonstrates that it is not worth placing hidden charges in developed minefields. The simplest and most effective way to use these minefields is to bring them into use as accommodation for the reinforced trench garrison. They perform

outstanding service as stores for hand grenades, matériel and rations. The
blowing of individual positions is to be condemned..."

Elsewhere, throughout most of the length of Redan Ridge, the attackers were
beaten back, mown down by interlocking machine gun fire from depth positions
and the flanks, without ever penetrating the German positions. Here and there
minor incursions were achieved, but within an hour of the start of the attack, the
entire position, less the Heidenkopf, was back in the hands of Reserve Infantry
Regiment 121. During the course of the morning it was decided to recapture the
Heidenkopf too. Reinforcements arrived from the 3rd Battalion Reserve Infantry
Regiment 121 and a platoon, commanded by Leutnant Hoppe, came over from the
neighbouring Infantry Regiment 169 to help. The clearance operation began and
step by step the British troops were forced back out. It was a slow process.
Casualties were heavy on both sides, because the British built and manned a series
of barricades, defended by Lewis gun teams and yielded ground only slowly. Late
in the day, as it began to go dark, there was only one small pocket of resistance left.
This, too, was attacked and eliminated. Those British soldiers, who did not escape
back to their original lines, were captured. Only relatively few prisoners were
taken on 1st July, but a systematic search of the recaptured area and the cratered
zone in front of the position the following day yielded many more. In the end 200
men were sent to the rear.

The Heidenkopf itself was a shambles. There were corpses everywhere, both
British and German, some of them heaped high. Smashed and abandoned
equipment lay all around in a scene of total devastation. This small area alone
claimed the lives of about 150 men of Reserve Infantry Regiment 121 and nearly
500 British soldiers, but there were also 1,200 dead piled up in front of the 1st
Battalion and 576 in front of the 2nd Battalion. The German defenders were
struck by the quality of men who attacked them and how well they were equipped;
remarking, in particular, on the fact that each carried washing and shaving
equipment and that those taken prisoner had no sooner been taken into a dugout
than they began to shave![11] Back at the area south of the Beaumont Hamel –
Auchonvillers road, the scene in and around Hawthorn Crater was one of complete
bloody carnage. The men of the mauled 9th Company of Reserve Infantry
Regiment 119 were able to play little part in the fighting, but adjoining
companies wrought enormous execution in the ranks of the attackers. For a while,
the situation around the newly blown crater was extremely tense, but reserves
began to arrive in short order, as platoons of the 7th and 12th Companies,
accompanied by two 'musketen' [automatic rifles], raced forward from the third
trench to the threatened place and occupied a rough firing line in shell holes
overlooking the road. The attack was in any case withering away, thanks to rapid
fire from machine guns of Reserve Infantry Regiment 121 located in the so-called
'Bergwerk' [Mine] behind Beaumont village. There followed a short period of close
quarter fighting. A British aircraft flew over and dropped bombs on the
reinforcements from the 12th Company, without achieving much, an increasing

number of trapped soldiers from the 9th Company managed to dig themselves free and gradually the situation here on the right flank of Reserve Infantry Regiment 119 swung completely in favour of the defenders.[12]

500 metres to the south, the defenders of the Leilingschlucht [Y Ravine] sector could not have been better placed to repel the heavy attacks which were about to be launched. The roar of the mine blowing up provided them with the best possible warning. They then benefited greatly from the extraordinary error made by the British VIII Corps in that arrangements had been made to lift almost all the suppressive fire from 0820. As a result, the garrison, which thanks to the geography of the area barely suffered at all during the bombardment, was able to take up its firing positions in a completely calm and methodical manner. Here there was no need for them to win a race to the parapet. They and all the other troops manning the positions down to the Ancre Valley had been given a generous start. Their barbed wire obstacle was largely intact. The machine guns were set up carefully and riflemen adopted optimum fire positions. Extra ammunition was carried up and prepared, then section and platoon commanders issued final orders. The commanding officer of 3rd Battalion Reserve Infantry Regiment 119 later reported, 'The enemy attacked all along the line in great strength. The entire garrison was able to occupy battle positions and then to open fire. The telephone link to the artillery was destroyed, so it was not possible to call for defensive fire by this means. The sector command staff and the companies fired red flares into the air, but when it came the defensive fire was weak and far from comprehensive.'[13] In the circumstances, it was just as well for the defenders that this area was covered with a very large number of well placed machine guns. Quite apart from those located in and around the first position, a line of eight weapons spaced out in depth and occupying concealed, mined out positions just to the north of Station Road, which ran from Beaumont village to Beaumont station, wreaked havoc. It is extremely doubtful if the attackers located any of these weapons, or were even aware that they were being engaged by them. Within minutes of the start of the attack, the survivors were pinned down in shell holes in front of the German First Position.

The Battle Log of the 3rd Battalion Reserve Infantry Regiment 119 describes, in a few terse entries, the methodical destruction of the first wave of attackers from the British 29th Division. Because the timing of the blowing of the mine is given as 8.15 am, it is possible that the remainder of the timings are also five minutes ahead of the actual timings involved:

| | |
|---|---|
| '8.15 am | Mine blown in B1. |
| 8.20 am | B1-B3 under attack. |
| 8.30 am | The British are lying down 100 metres short of the first trench of B3. Own machine guns have opened fire. |
| 8.35 am | B2 reports: Attack stalled. Masses of British soldiers are lying in the hollow in front of Target Area 46. Machine guns are being moved forward from the second to the first trench. |

8.40 am          B2 reports:  The British are lying in front of the first trench and
                 are being shot to pieces.  No defensive fire is coming down in the
                 hollow in front of Target Area 46; a battalion is gathering there
                 to launch an attack.
                 Sector Order: Destroy them with machine gun fire...'[14]

As the morning wore on, any minor incursions into the line had all been mopped
up. The well-known tragedy of the destruction of 1st Battalion Essex Regiment and
1st Battalion Newfoundland Regiment just to the south of Y Ravine had come and
gone, without any detectable difference in tone in the German battle log. Early
problems with defensive fire had been largely resolved. It was soon coming down
where it was needed and the defending infantry had had the situation under
control from very early on in the attack. If attackers appeared to their front they
simply shot them to a standstill. By 2.00 pm calm prevailed all along the
Regimental front, which was covered from end to end by the dead and dying
attackers. Their own casualties for the period since the start of the bombardment
were only seven officers and 144 men killed, twenty-four of whom were buried
alive; six officers and 266 other ranks were wounded.

Reserve Infantry Regiment 99, which had the task of defending the strategically
vital Thiepval Ridge, had a much harder, more trying, time of it.  Here the stakes
could not have been higher.  Both sides were well aware of that fact and initially
the British obtained an advantage.  Men of the 36th Ulster Division charged with
capturing the vital Schwaben Redoubt and pressing on towards Grandcourt,
behaved very boldly.  No Man's Land was quite narrow to the north of Thiepval
village, the neutralising barrage, fired partly by first class French batteries, was
effective up to the last minute and the first wave of the assaulting force made good
use of the cover it provided, by crawling forward to within forty – fifty metres of
the German front line before the attack proper was due to begin.  As a result, here
the attackers won the race to the parapet. 'The enemy attack on C2 and C3 was
conducted with such aggression that the two machine guns could only fire for a
short time before they were both overrun. More than half of both teams were killed
or wounded by artillery fire. The remaining weapons in C1, C4 and the
Strassburger Steige [Strasbourg Slope] were operated with outstanding effect.
Despite some stoppages, which were merely attributed to the ammunition, they
fired almost ceaselessly. The Russian machine gun in the Schwaben Redoubt did
not come into action, because a direct hit shortly before the assault buried the gun
and three quarters of its crew.  Both the Platoon Commander and his runner, who
hurried to the spot to dig them out, were killed by shrapnel. The Fasbender platoon
in Schwaben Redoubt was ordered to occupy the front line position in the Redoubt.
During the attack the German weapons on the left flank of C3 and the right of C4
were put out of action by direct hits.  The crews moved to the intact German
weapons and also manned a captured British machine gun, with which they
immediately opened fire on the advancing British soldiers'.[15]

The breakthrough point had been selected skilfully, because the southern part of

C3 was largely in dead ground from C4. This also favoured the further advance to Schwaben Redoubt. In sub-sectors C2 and C3, every man not killed or wounded was captured, but such was the generally confused nature of the fighting that some of the prisoners escaped. According to Oberstleutnant Bram, Commander of Bavarian Reserve Infantry Regiment 8, Reserve Leutnant Schmidt of 7th Company Reserve Infantry Regiment 99, who was deployed in C4, reported that, 'a number of Bavarians arrived in his location. No sooner had they been captured, than they had escaped. The British had already taken their watches, money and rings. Once they had been equipped with weapons taken from the wounded, they played a full part in the fighting'.[16] Hauptmann Schorer, Commander of 4th Company Bavarian Reserve Infantry Regiment 8, was captured with some of his men in Schwaben Redoubt. He was less lucky, being killed by German artillery fire on the way to the British lines.

Initially the situation north of Thiepval was obscure. So swiftly had the forward defenders of Sectors C2 and C3 been overwhelmed, that it was some time before the situation was fully clarified. A further complication came about because an early report received in the Divisional Headquarters stated, 'Our own troops are attacking in the direction of Authuille'.[17] In reality, what had been observed was the sight of German prisoners being conducted to the rear. However, an observation post of Reserve Infantry Regiment 119 on the northern bank of the Ancre eventually spotted that the British had succeeded in overrunning the Schwaben Redoubt.[18] The information was passed directly to the Divisional Commander of the 26th Reserve Division, who lost no time in issuing the order for a counterattack. Had telephone links been available to the 2nd Recruit Company of Infantry Regiment 180, which was occupying the Second Position, there might have been less delay.

*Leutnant Scheurlen 2nd Recruit Company Infantry Regiment 180*[19] **4.**

> "About 9.00 am British officers were seen orientating themselves with the aid of maps and detachments of British soldiers were observed. Some were digging in and others were advancing into the area in front of Schnürlen's Company (1st Recruit Company Infantry Regiment 180). Fire brought to bear by Schnürlen's Company and one weapon of the 1st Machine Gun Company Reserve Infantry Regiment 119 caused the enemy to pull back into the Hansastellung [Hanseatic Position] and Schwaben Redoubt."

The possibility of such a dangerous development had been foreseen. In keeping with normal practice, counter-attack plans would almost certainly have been laid in advance and a Warning Order had been sent down through the chain of command on 27th June: 'At 12.00 midday today the Brigade [52 Reserve] received Operation Order No. 2453 from [26th Reserve] Division that Sector Thiepval North is to be reinforced as necessary. If the enemy gets established there, he is to be ejected at once. Further elements of 1st Battalion Bavarian Reserve Infantry

Regiment 8 can be made available to replace troops moved forward out of the Intermediate or Second Position for this purpose...'[20] This order had led to the reinforcement of the Second Position by elements of Bavarian Reserve Infantry Regiment 8 and the Recruit Companies of Infantry Regiment 180[21] and the placement of 4th Company Bavarian Reserve Infantry Regiment 8 in Schwaben Redoubt, which brought the number of defenders up to between 400 and 500 – not too large a number for a stronghold with a 500 metre frontage.

From the start the entire counter-attack proved to be far from simple to mount. Even the distribution of the order was difficult, because there were no telephone links to the dispersed battalions of Bavarian Reserve Infantry Regiment 8. However Reserve Leutnant Trainé of the Württemberg Reserve Dragoons was available at Divisional Headquarters for such an eventuality and he took the orders in person.[22] The counter-attack was planned to be conducted by three groups, under the overall command of Oberstleutnant Bram, Commander of Bavarian Reserve Infantry Regiment 8. The grouping was intended to be as follows:[23]

Group 1

Major Prager Commanding Officer 1st Battalion Bavarian Reserve Infantry Regiment 8. 2nd Company Bavarian Reserve Infantry Regiment 8, 1st and 2nd Recruit Companies Infantry Regiment 180, Engineer Company Schofeld and 1st Machine Gun Company Reserve Infantry Regiment 119. (Attack from the northern section of the Second Position against Schwaben Redoubt.)

Group 2

Major Beyerköhler Commanding Officer 3rd Battalion Bavarian Reserve Infantry Regiment 8. 3rd, 11th and 12th Companies Bavarian Reserve Infantry Regiment 8. Machine Gun Sharp Shooter Troop 89. (Attack towards Schwaben Redoubt from Hill 153.)

Group 3

Major Roesch Commanding Officer 2nd Battalion Bavarian Reserve Infantry Regiment 8. 2nd Battalion Bavarian Reserve Infantry Regiment 8. (Attack on Schwaben Redoubt via Stuff Redoubt.)

At 9.55 am, Major Roesch received the following order directly from Headquarters 26th Reserve Division:[24] 'Enemy has forced his way into Schwaben Redoubt. 2nd Battalion Bavarian Reserve Infantry Regiment 8, with 1st Machine Gun Company and one platoon of the 'Musketen' Company is subordinated to 52 Reserve Infantry Brigade. The Battalion is to move immediately, dealing with any enemy encountered, to the Ancre Valley and is to advance to the Second Position via Stallmulde [Stable Hollow]*. Sector South I to South III is to be occupied and held, with main effort on the right flank. 52 Reserve Infantry Brigade will be kept informed from here. Signed: Freiherr von Soden'. The Battalion, which had been standing by in Irles since 5.30 am ready to move, set off, but such was the weight of artillery fire directed against the rear areas that it was not until 3.00 pm that it reached Stable Hollow near Grandcourt.

*Stallmulde = Stable Hollow was the name given to the lower section and one branch of the major reentrant located between Grandcourt and Miraumont and referred to by the British as Boom Ravine.

The serious news concerning the loss of Schwaben Redoubt swiftly reached Headquarters XIV Reserve Corps, where Generalleutnant von Stein lost no time in ordering a speeding up of the attack. By 10.45 am an amendment to the 26th Reserve Division Operation Order had been received and was being processed at Headquarters 52 Reserve Infantry Brigade: 'The Corps Commander has ordered that Schwaben Redoubt is to be recaptured at all costs. To that end the arrival of 2nd Battalion Bavarian Reserve Infantry Regiment 8 is not to be awaited. Rather the attack is to be launched with forces from the Second Position.'[25] The Brigade Commander carried out a quick appreciation and issued the following order at 10.50 am to 1st Battalion Bavarian Reserve Infantry Regiment 8: 'The British have forced their way into the Hanseatic Position and Schwaben Redoubt. Major Prager, with Companies Schmeißer, Schnürlen, Hudelmeier and Engineer Company Schofeld, together with 1st Machine Gun Company of Reserve Infantry Regiment 119 and Sharp Shooter Troop 89, are to conduct this attack from the right flank of the Second Position. Major Beyerköhler will advance on Schwaben Redoubt from Hill 153 with three companies.'[26]

Meanwhile time passed as efforts were made to get the necessary orders to all those concerned and the designated units struggled to their start lines through churned up, 'unbelievably muddy', ground[27] and extraordinarily heavy artillery fire. Oberstleutnant Bram finally arrived at 2.00 pm at Stuff Redoubt to take control of the operation. More than two and a half hours had elapsed since he had received his orders at Headquarters 26th Reserve Division; heavy artillery fire having forced him to move on foot from Pys via Courcelette, where he had received a further briefing from Generalleutnant von Auwärter. It hardly mattered. Group 1 under Major Prager still had not received the order to attack. That did not finally arrive until well after 3.00 pm, but prior to that Major Prager had already been developing his own plans. Initially he had intended to make use of both the Recruit Companies, but once he finally saw the order, he stood down 1st Recruit Company at 3.13 pm.[28] Group 2 under Major Beyerköhler, which had received its orders at 11.30 am, was furthest advanced, but still not in position and Group 3 under Major Roesch was struggling to make its way forward.[29] In fact this Battalion had suffered heavy casualties as a result of artillery fire and was scattered. The 8th Company lost all contact during the advance and ended up in the area of 51 Reserve Infantry Brigade, whence it was despatched with forty engineers to reinforce Saint Pierre Divion. This was just an extreme example. The three assault groups were never united and so the attack never had any chance of developing synergy.[30]

Elsewhere a vicious hand-to-hand battle was being conducted by the surviving defenders from 26th Reserve Division and the men of the 36th Ulster Division. Communications were made difficult because of damage to cables, but at 2.58 pm. Reserve Infantry Regiment 99 received a situation report from Thiepval North, which had had to be relayed through Headquarters 52 Reserve Infantry Brigade. The information, which concerned the furthest advance made that day by the 36th

Division, was by that time stale, but it provided the Commander, Major von Fabeck, with important background information, which later led to the launch of a crucial two-section patrol towards Schwaben Redoubt. Considering the dramatic events being reported, the tone of the regimental Battle Log is strangely matter of fact. 'C1 is firmly under our control. Front line trench in C2 is in British hands. In C3 the British have broken through as far as Schwaben Redoubt. Isolated small groups have pushed forward to the area of the Artillery Hollow, Grandcourt. Apparently this is an enemy assault group which has broken through and, somewhat helplessly, is digging in on the western slope of the Artillery Hollow...'[31]

Back at Stuff Redoubt, Oberstleutnant Bram had considerable difficulty in orientating himself, due to battlefield obscuration, but the reports he had received, the promptings of higher headquarters for swift action and his own sightings of British patrols to his front, left him in no doubt that speed was of the essence. He established his headquarters on the steps of a dugout full of wounded men and prepared short supplementary orders, which he sent to Groups 1 and 3, specifying 4.00 pm as the start of the assault. He was able to speak personally to Major Beyerköhler, which was extremely helpful, as were his discussions with Hauptmann Graf Preysing, from Reserve Field Artillery Regiment 26, who was coordinating the artillery support for the counter-attack.[32] There was still no sign or message from Group 3. Runners had been sent, but they had either been killed or had got lost. Bram decide to press on and ordered Major Beyerköhler to launch his assault at 4.00 pm as planned.

At 3.40 pm orders from Major Prager, issued at 3.15 pm reached the 2nd Recruit Company. The men fixed bayonets, gaps were cut through their barbed wire and a few minutes later the Recruit Company set out in two waves to clear the enemy from the Hanseatic Position.[33] Major Beyerköhler took this as the signal to start and, with a quick handshake for Hauptmann Wurmb, his Group began the attack as well. It was initially an unequal struggle against the British defenders, who were able to bring machine gun and mortar fire to bear on the attackers; in addition uncertainty over the timing of the attack and a false report that the Schwaben Redoubt had already been recaptured had prejudiced effective artillery preparation.[34]

*Leutnant Scheurlen 2nd Recruit Company Infantry Regiment 180[35]* **4.**

"After the first wave had crossed the Artillery Hollow, Grandcourt, the second wave left the trenches. Although the right half of the first wave succeeded in forcing a way into the Hanseatic Position, the left half had to wait until the support of the second wave enabled it to get further forward. Despite heavy rifle and machine-gun fire, this part of the Company also succeeded in working its way forward to within 100 metres of the Hanseatic Position, albeit at the cost of heavy casualties (twenty three killed and 100 wounded). In so doing, Offizierstellvertreter Rädle, (who was severely wounded in the upper arm by a shell splinter), together with his platoon, took twenty prisoners and two Lewis guns. Simultaneously Unteroffizier Stumpf and four men (Gessmann, Reng Georg, Bregizer and Dötlinger) launched an assault on about twenty British soldiers, who were attempting to hold out in shell holes in front of the Hanseatic Position. He captured one officer and two men. The remainder were killed."

On the eastern side of the Artillery Hollow, the Bavarians were also making some progress. A daring attack with grenades by a section from the 3rd Company led by Unteroffizier Haas, cleared the way forward to the junction of Stuff Trench and Lach Way on the Thiepval-Grandcourt road, Vizefeldwebel Stolz took Captain Craig, a British MP, prisoner,[36] but thereafter resistance stiffened further. Three British machine guns were in action, fire was coming from three sides and casualties were mounting. The attack began to stall. Generalleutnant Freiherr von Soden, the Divisional Commander, intervened at this point, sending a sharply worded order to Oberstleutnant Bram to inject new life into the attack.[37] Relayed at 5.02 pm via Goat Redoubt, by 52 Reserve Infantry Brigade, it read, 'The Adjutant [Oberleutnant Grabinger], 3rd Battalion Bavarian Reserve Infantry Regiment 8, is to despatch, immediately, two patrols bearing written orders to Oberstleutnant Bram in Stuff Redoubt, stating that the Division expects and expressly orders Bavarian Reserve Infantry Regiment 8: to recapture the entirety of Schwaben Redoubt, to occupy it and to bring relief to the hard-pressed parts of Reserve Infantry Regiment 99. This is a direct order.'[38]

Major Beyerköhler was killed in close-quarter fighting around 5.00 pm and Hauptmann Wurmb, Commander of the 3rd Company, assumed command of Group 2.

*Hauptmann Herbert von Wurmb Bavarian Reserve Infantry Regiment 8*[39] **4.**

"At about 5.00 pm, Major Beyerköhler, the commander of our Group, had gone on ahead. Suddenly a member of his staff called out, 'Herr Major, a British soldier!' 'What's that you say – a British soldier?' replied the Commander. 'Pass me a rifle!' He aimed at a British soldier who was very close to him, but that man was a second quicker than he. Mortally wounded, the kindly Beyerköhler slumped to the ground. His batman was quick to avenge him by shooting this assailant with his master's bloodstained rifle, but the Regiment mourned the passing of this outstanding Battalion Commander ever after. One morning earlier as I was returning from the Schwaben Redoubt with him, he had said to me. 'When the war is over, I am going to take my pension. You young men must carry on the work.' 'All too soon and far from home they had to bury him here.'[40] I took over command of the assaulting Group from Beyerköhler and Leutnant Zimmermann from our Sharp Shooter Troop 89 acted as Adjutant. My faithful servant Adam Kneibert from Sippersfeld near Kaiserslautern was hit in the chest by a British bullet not half a pace behind me. Carried in a tent half, his breath coming in gasps, he was taken away after I had bid him a heartfelt farewell and passed on my best wishes to his wife."

By 7.00 pm, Wurmb's Group, which was bearing almost the entire weight of the counter-attack, was down to around forty effectives. At this point a fighting patrol from Reserve Infantry Regiment 99 intervened. 'The attack on Schwaben Redoubt stalls short of the position. A patrol, comprising two sections of 14th Company Reserve Infantry Regiment 99 commanded by Offizierstellvertreter Lunau, has the mission from the Regiment to establish how far forward the British have penetrated. Without further orders, Offizierstellvertreter Lunau launches an attack on the British who have captured a section of the right flank of the Intermediate Position approximately 150 metres wide. In so doing he captures an enemy machine gun and clears the trench of enemy. He presses on, ejects the enemy from the Lachweg and Martinspfad [Martin's Path] and advances to the Wohngraben [Accommodation Trench] of Schwaben Redoubt. In so doing he captures a further three machine guns and a machine-gun sledge. One of these machine guns had held up several Bavarian companies for a number of hours, preventing them from advancing. The attack of 14th Company Reserve Infantry Regiment 99 cleared the way to Schwaben Redoubt for the Bavarians.'[41] In all, Lunau, aided by Vizefeldwebel Koch and Kriegsfreiwilliger Pfeifer in particular, succeeded in clearing the enemy out of 1,100 metres of trench.[42] Just as Lunau was fighting his way forward, orders reached 1st Recruit Company Infantry Regiment 180 to move forward to the Hanseatic Position and to continue the advance on the Schwaben Redoubt with the men of Bavarian Reserve Infantry Regiment 8, but the attempt was shot to pieces.

*Leutnant Arnold 1st Recruit Company Infantry Regiment 180*[43] **4.**

"At 7.00 pm, the company received the order to move to the Hanseatic Position and from there, together with Company Hudelmeier and the Bavarian troops, to capture Schwaben Redoubt...The company advanced in three waves in the direction of the Hanseatic Position: First wave, Leutnant Arnold; second wave Unteroffizier Seitz; third wave Leutnant Schnürlen. There was 100 metre spacing between the waves. The first wave crossed the Artillery Hollow, Grandcourt, but as it moved up onto the heights it received such a hail of machine gun and rifle fire that further advance was out of the question for the time being. As the third wave appeared, heavy enemy artillery fire came down, causing the company very heavy casualties. Leutnant Schnürlen was killed, so despite being wounded in the arm, [I] took over the company, rallying the remnants in the Artillery Hollow."

This company took no further part in the counter-attack, Leutnant Arnold had to go to the rear later to have his wound dressed, but the survivors were called forward during the early hours of 2 July to Schwaben Redoubt by an order from Major Prager which took nearly five hours to reach them. As the evening wore on, the position of the men of the 36th Division was increasingly precarious, but that of the attackers was scarcely less so. It was impossible for British reinforcements and extremely difficult for German reinforcements to get forward and supplies of some types of ammunition were running low. At 7.39 pm a situation report from Oberstleutnant Bram arrived at Headquarters 52 Reserve brigade: 'The enemy is occupying an area astride Auwärter Trench, both sides of the road Thiepval-Grandcourt, front facing east. The left wing of our assault force is in the area of Bulgarengraben [Bulgarian Trench]. Fresh orders have been sent to Group Prager to attack Schwaben Redoubt from the north-east, but there is still no contact with this group. The whereabouts of the 6th, 7th and 8th Companies Bavarian Reserve Infantry Regiment 8 are unknown, as is that of the staff of the 2nd Battalion. There are no reserves left to assault Schwaben Redoubt. Thirty men of the Recruit Company have been given the mission of establishing contact between the 1st and 3rd Battalions Bavarian Reserve Infantry Regiment 8. Support is requested.'[44]

The situation called for clear heads and decisive action. Some additional forces from 1st Company Infantry Regiment 185 were made available. They were held back in Stuff Redoubt as a reserve, but as men of the scattered companies of 2nd Battalion Bavarian Reserve Infantry Regiment 8 straggled in, Oberstleutnant Bram fed them into the battle, so gradually the attackers gained the upper hand. In response to an order at 8.00 pm from 52 Reserve Brigade, Oberstleutnant Bram made contact with Artillery Group Berta to agree the time for the assault on Schwaben Redoubt, so that this could be preceded by comprehensive artillery fire preparation.[45] In a message timed at 9.27 pm, Generalleutnant von Auwärter guaranteed Oberstleutnant Bram a one hour bombardment by as many batteries as the Artillery Group Commander could concentrate. In the meantime, the indefatigable Hauptmann Wurmb's little group continued to push forward. There were innumerable feats of gallantry on both sides, but the pressure on the hard-pressed defenders grew inexorably, in particular at around 10.00 pm when all the German batteries within range began to bring down effective fire on the Redoubt.[46]

Towards 11.00 pm the final assault on Schwaben Redoubt was launched successfully. The number of attackers was a fraction of that really required for such a task, but they were equal to it. Hauptmann Wurmb's men pressed forward into the Redoubt, pretending to be a much larger force than it actually was, by making maximum noise through battlecries of *'Hurra'* and a great deal of firing. Leutnant Zimmerman was sent to mop up in one direction, whilst Wurmb's remaining men, having dealt with further pockets of resistance, managed finally to link up with Offizierstellvertreter Lunau. Together the group grenaded its way forward along Auwärter Trench. Death, wounds and guarding prisoners further sapped the strength of the attackers, who by this point were reduced to a handful. It was now pitch black, but by shouting and singing *Die Wacht am Rhein*,[47] they were eventually able to find Zimmermann and his men and to organise themselves for hasty defence.[48] Altogether they had captured about one hundred prisoners and numerous machine guns. 'The British corpses of 700 courageous members of the

Ulster Division littered the Redoubt, every foot of which was soaked in blood.'[49]
*Hauptmann Herbert von Wurmb Bavarian Reserve Infantry Regiment 8*[50] **5**.

"Towards 11.30 pm we saw dense lines of troops withdrawing on a
broad front. We could hardly believe our eyes. Could they possibly be
advancing lines of German troops? But when single flares were fired by
our neighbouring battalion in Thiepval we recognised the steel helmets:
British soldiers! 'Rapid Fire!' I shouted loudly through the night to my
machine gun crews. The enemy had been thrown back. Schwaben
Redoubt was ours!... A tiny band had succeeded in throwing out a much
stronger force. It demonstrated that old truth in the Art of War: 'Only the
will to win gains victories'."

Heading the long list of honours won for this absolutely vital action were those
awarded to Oberstleutnant Bram and Hauptmann von Wurmb, who each received
the Knight's Cross of the Royal Bavarian Military Max - Joseph Order for their roles
in the recapture of the Redoubt. This was an exceedingly rare honour. Its bestow-
al on these two key figures was a fair reflection of their achievement. Had they
failed, the entire course of the next three months might have been very different.
In Sector Thiepval Centre the day had developed quite differently. Here the attackers had been hammered by effective artillery fire, but the Albrecht mortars had
done their work well and the positions were defended with great resolution.
Thiepval village itself, after two years of occupation, was a formidable obstacle; its
numerous machine guns extremely well sited. Machine gun 9 in the Brewery
Position fired 18,000 rounds that day. This was because it was in a position to
engage in enfilade the advancing and retreating waves of enemy in front of C2 and
C3 from early morning to late evening. The effect of the machine guns was quite
outstanding.

The greatest number of casualties was achieved by the machine guns in the area
in front of sub-sectors C2 and C3, because five machine guns were able to bring the
area under enfilade fire during the attacks against Thiepval Centre. The thousands
of British corpses lying around there bore witness to the number of enemy
casualties caused by the combined rifle and machine-gun fire. Statements of
British prisoners of war and the British newspapers, which frequently and
specifically mentioned the fighting around Thiepval, underlined the adverse effect
on morale of the action here. According to the policy laid down by the Ministry of
War, a stockpile of 4,500 rounds per machine gun is deemed to be sufficient. In
the light of experience gained during the recent battles, this amount is far from
adequate. When attacks follow one another in swift succession, 4,000 – 5,000
rounds are quickly fired. This is particularly the case when, as at Thiepval, the
machine guns are sited not only to fire frontally, but also to the flanks. Experience
has shown that resupply of small arms ammunition during battles is extremely
difficult. There simply are not the soldiers available. In addition the approach
routes are kept under constant artillery fire. This makes the supply of ready-use
machine-gun ammunition even more difficult. In order to make full use of the

machine guns, at least 8,000 rounds per weapon are required'.[51]

But it was not just the work of the machine gunners that did the damage around Thiepval. The regiment estimated that individual riflemen fired an average of no fewer than 350 rounds per man. All in all, the expenditure of ammunition was prodigious. The presence of the British thrust in and beyond Schwaben Redoubt had to be countered by thinning out the first two trenches in C4, bending back the right flank of the 7th Company along the line of Marktgasse [Market Alley] and arranging for constant artillery defensive fire to be supplemented by direct small arms fire on the British from a line of barricades.

*Unteroffizier Hinkel 7th Company Reserve Infantry Regiment 99*[52]   **6.**

"The 7th Company was surrounded. The situation was extremely critical, as the remnants of the right hand neighbouring company and a few Bavarians arrived on our positions, very downcast and giving all up for lost. This, as I later discovered, had a disheartening effect on many of us. Only the unparalleled courage and totally wild commitment of Offizierstellvertreter Gelzenleichter, the commander of our right flank platoon, saved us and, therefore, quite possibly Thiepval, by his example. Unfortunately, he paid with his life for the courage and enthusiasm his deeds restored in his men. I myself moved from the left to the right flank, but only for a short while, because I was then sent to form a blocking position in Marktgasse [Market Alley] where it intersected the road to the churchyard. We subsequently endured an awful time of it. Thirsty, hungry, listless and played out, the long, but largely uneventful waiting time got on our nerves. Added to that was hellish artillery fire, initially also from howitzers and mortars, which came down incessantly on the lost trenches. British aviators circled above, seeking out the exact positions where the men in field grey were still holding out and firing at our little group: fortunately without causing any damage. Wherever a [British] steel helmet showed itself, it was dealt with, just as in a hare shoot. These lads did not seem to know where they were in our trenches and so we allowed some groups to approach us calmly before despatching them with hand grenades. At long last it began to go dark and the battle, which had rather petered out, flared back into life, as many British soldiers tried under the mantle of darkness to regain their position and fell victim to our well-aimed fire. Perhaps they were pulling back in fear of our counter-attack...With two Gefreiters I went some distance along Marktgasse in the direction of Battalion Headquarters. We eliminated some groups of British soldiers with our hand grenades and drove others off. We then returned, to avoid clashing with the Bavarians who were mopping up in the trenches. Back in our original positions we did not lack for work. Individually, in small groups and then in hordes, they raced backwards out of Schwaben Redoubt. Once more our machine guns clattered away and our rifles glowed red hot. Many an Irish mother's son lay down to the eternal sleep from which there is no awakening. Our men were seized by the same recklessness which had gripped them that morning. Unfortunately we lacked the hand grenades fully to exploit the situation...otherwise, I have no doubt that we should have cleared the enemy that same night out of our entire position as far as the Ancre...The 1st July had long slipped into the past before we regained our old positions at the front. The dawn of a new day revealed to us, in the form of great piles of dead and wounded, some of the success of the violent work we had achieved in conjunction with our machine guns..."

Occupying the most southerly section of the frontage of the 26th Reserve Division was Infantry Regiment 180, which had spent the previous year, up until the major operational reorganisation of June 1916, turning Serre into an impregnable fortress. Now it found itself entrusted with the defence of a sector running from Thiepval South, to the Albert-Bapaume road at Ovillers. The position here was well developed, so its casualties during the bombardment, though not insignificant at ninety-five killed, 187 wounded and two missing,[53] had no influence over its ability to counter the attack of the 8th British Division. At 5.45 am the regiment received the news that the assault was imminent, so there was ample time for those manning the dugouts to prepare to race to their battle positions. 'If the British believe that their fire has shaken and unnerved us, they have deceived themselves', was the note in their war diary at the beginning of the assault. It continued, 'the British attacked Sector Ovillers South in overwhelming strength. The assault unfolded as a series of waves, up to seven of them, which followed in quick succession. Artillery defensive fire came down promptly and the attack in front of the right flank of P5 and in front of P6 and P7 [The area referred to was Mash Valley] withered away in the combined fire of rifle, machine gun and artillery fire. The enemy suffered extraordinarily bloody casualties.'[54]

*Oberstleutnant Alfred Vischer Commander Infantry Regiment 180*[55] **7.**

"Simultaneously with this assault against Ovillers South, the British also attacked P4 and Hill 141 to the north of it. The attack against P4 stalled when one of the first shells of the artillery defensive fire landed in amongst the initial wave of infantrymen. The enemy then attempted to use the sunken road as an approach route, but were prevented from doing so by the fire of a machine gun, which had been hastily brought into action from behind the parados of the first trench of the position. The [enemy] detachment, which was crammed together in the sunken road and which numbered between 150 to 200 men, was literally mown down. The enemy had placed a machine gun to cover its advance along the sunken road, but one of our patrols succeeded in shooting its crew and capturing the machine gun."

The situation was slightly different on the right flank of Infantry Regiment 180.

Here, shortly after 9.00 am, 3rd Company was reporting that there had been a penetration by the enemy in Sectors C8 and C9 held by Reserve Infantry Regiment 99, which threatened to permit the enemy to outflank P1. The 3rd Company beat off a frontal attack and within thirty minutes, the 7th Company rushed forward to stabilise the position and the trench leading north was barricaded. Hard fighting continued and pressure on the right flank of Infantry Regiment 180 increased. Casualties mounted towards the end of the morning, but by shortly after 1.00 pm, Reserve Infantry Regiment 99 had agreed to launch a joint counterattack and this began at 1.45 pm. It was a hard fight with grenades as the two assault groups bombed towards one another. At 4.10 pm, the British were still in possession of one hundred metres of trench in P1. By 4.40 pm, the two groups linked up in the Hindenburg Stellung [Hindenburg Position], but never in fact succeeded in eliminating the men of the British 32nd Division which had captured and subsequently held, the Granatloch. The Germans blamed the fact that they ran out of grenades, but the dash in the attack, which won the race to the parapet here and the subsequent dogged and heroic defence put up by men of the Highland Light Infantry, was largely responsible.

Fighting continued into the evening to eject the enemy remaining in some pockets of resistance in Thiepval South, but as it finally went dark, there was no doubt at all that Infantry Regiment 180 was in total and complete control of every part of its own area of responsibility. The fighting on the 1st July had cost Infantry Regiment 180 seventy nine killed, 181 wounded and thirteen missing,[56] but it had inflicted well over 5,000 casualties on its attackers, a ratio of nearly twenty to one. Justifiably satisfied with the way the day had gone, proud of the fighting prowess of his Division and relieved too, that all the intensive planning and preparation had paid off when its greatest trial came, Generalleutnant Freiherr von Soden lost no time in reporting to the King of Württemberg, 'The entire position of the 26th Reserve Division is completely in our hands'.[57] With the only significant exception of the Granatloch, this was nothing less than the truth. The fighting that day had cost the division dear, but it had achieved a stunning defensive victory.

South of the Albert-Bapaume road, the story was more mixed. The positions of Reserve Infantry Regiments 110 and 111 around La Boisselle and Fricourt respectively had suffered serious damage during the bombardment. The commander of Reserve Infantry Regiment 110, Oberst Freiherr von Vietinghoff, suffering from the effects of explosive gases when his Command Post was destroyed by a heavy shell on 29th June had had to pull back to his Reserve Headquarters in Contalmaison.[58] There were further unpleasant shocks when, at 8.28 am on 1st July, huge mines were detonated at La Boisselle Hollow [Y Sap] and Schwaben Höhe [Lochnagar], north and south of the Roman road. Further to the south, other mines went up forward of the Kniewerk [Tambour] position to the west of Fricourt and up on Hill 110. On the Schwaben Höhe the mighty explosion, which created one of the largest craters on the Western Front, blew almost the whole of 5th Company Reserve Infantry Regiment 110 into eternity and enabled troops from the 34th Division to penetrate the German position. A smart counterattack by the Regiment's 4th Company had largely restored the situation by midday; the attackers were restricted to clinging on to the crater itself. In general, however, a combination of lack of surprise and the great distance of open ground, which the gallant men of the British 34th Division had to cover under the fire of the dominating German positions, turned the advance of its twelve battalions into a crazy and pointless form of mass suicide. The defenders could hardly credit the scene which unfolded in front of them as they poured fire into oncoming waves.

*Oberleutnant Kienitz Machine Gun Company Reserve Infantry Regiment* 110[59]   **8.**

"Silently our machine guns and the infantrymen waited until our opponents came closer. Then, when they were only a few metres from the trenches, the serried ranks of the enemy were sprayed with a hurricane of defensive fire from the machine guns and the aimed fire of the individual riflemen. Standing exposed on the parapet, some individuals hurled hand grenades at the enemy who had taken cover to the front. Within moments it seemed as though the battle had died away completely. But then, initially in small groups, but later in huge masses, the enemy began to pull back towards Bécourt, until finally it seemed as though every man in the entire field was attempting to flee back to his jumping-off point. The fire of our infantrymen and machine guns pursued them, hitting them hard; whilst some of our men daringly charged the British troops, capturing prisoners. Our weapons fired away ceaselessly for two hours, then the battle died away in Bécourt Hollow [Sausage Valley]."

The attackers enjoyed rather more success a little further to the south, where a penetration towards Contalmaison was made at the junction of Reserve Infantry Regiments 110 and 111, which was held by the 2nd Company Reserve Infantry Regiment 110 and 4th Company Reserve Infantry Regiment 111 respectively.

*Landwehr Leutnant Alfred Frick 6th Battery Reserve Field Artillery Regiment 28*[60]   **8.**

"The British, who advanced in hordes, managed to obtain a foothold in our lines; some detachments went quite a distance, forcing their way into the so-called 'Völkerbereitschaft', about 500 metres from Contalmaison. This meant that they were in rear of Fröhlich's 3rd Battery and the 'Sharp Corner' staff located there. Runners, telephonists and men from the Construction Company were formed into a defence platoon and set off under the command of Leutnant Strüvy of 3rd Battery Reserve Field Artillery Regiment 29. One gun of this battery was also hauled out of its position [in support]. This little united force succeeded in ejecting the bold intruders, but large masses of them were established in the so-called Pioniergraben [Engineer's Trench] north of Fricourt. The route to this place had cost them dear in casualties. Under the illusion that the dreadful drum fire had smashed all resistance, the British and Canadian

[sic] troops had advanced in close order. Not infrequently their commanders were mounted! The fifteen remaining undamaged machine guns in the sector of Reserve Infantry Regiment 110 poured fire into the oncoming columns, so that the assaulting forces went down like ripe corn before the scythe. In consequence, the enemy casualties were simply enormous."

The 8th Company Reserve Infantry Regiment 110 had suffered heavy losses during the bombardment and by 30th June was reduced to 80 effectives. Leaving twenty men and a machine gun under Reserve Leutnant Wölfle behind to cover a gap of 150 metres between it and Reserve Infantry Regiment 111, it pulled back and was relieved by the 2nd Company Reserve Regiment 110. Exploiting this situation during the morning of 1st July, the attackers were able, albeit at a high cost, to outflank the 2nd Company and to attack it from the rear. As a result the entire Company was killed or captured. A machine gun which had been placed under command of Leutnant Hausse in the Second Position to provide depth fire suffered mechanical failure after firing only one shot. Hausse destroyed it with a hand grenade and raced off to try to bring a second weapon into action. In this he failed, because two critically placed guns had also been hit and knocked out. Despite a heroic defence by Wölfle's little band, every one of whom was killed, followed by local counter attacks launched by men of the two Regiments, the situation for the defence around Fricourt gradually became critical as the day progressed and British successes around Mametz in the area of Reserve Infantry Regiment 109 meant that the left forward companies of Reserve Infantry Regiment 111 were progressively outflanked.

Geographically, the section of the German lines which ran away eastwards towards Montauban was intrinsically weaker than was the case further north. Here there were none of the mutually supporting spurs, which made the advance elsewhere so difficult and, for some inexplicable reason, the re-engineering of the line which took place north of Fricourt during late 1915 and the first half of 1916, does not seem to have been driven forward with the same energy and sense of urgency in this area. In addition, around the village of Fricourt, early morning fog, coupled with the use of gas and smoke by the British, had substantially reduced the visibility. The lift of the artillery in this area, following the firing of the mines, had a substantial effect on the defending guns, which had already suffered greatly during the preliminary bombardment. Faced with weak defensive fire, a gap between formations and a local failure of machine-gun fire, it is easy to see why the penetration referred to above occurred. To the west of Fricourt village, the firing of the mines on the Tambour position was followed by an assault which was partly countered through the firing of a defensive German mine by the Bavarian engineers, which blew up eighty of the attackers.[61] In this area, the defenders put up a ferocious battle, which cost the repeated attacking waves of the British 21st Division high casualties. Up above Fricourt on Hill 110, despite repeated attacks, the defence held firmly; the machine guns in particular, took a heavy toll throughout the day.

*Rudolf Stadelbacher & Otto Schüsele Machine Gun Company Reserve Infantry Regiment 111*[62] **9.**

"We were deployed in the front line trench of the gravel pit on Hill 110 near Fricourt and so had good fields of fire and observation over Fricourt Station, Fricourt itself and Bécourt. We were able from this position to keep a close watch on the preparations for the Battle of the Somme through binoculars and also, thanks to buried cables, were able to pass the information on. The bombardment began on 24 June and lasted 168 hours. We did not escape unscathed and in fact suffered considerably during it. On one occasion the British fired at our dugout with a 210 millimetre shell. It penetrated and remained wedged under the stairwell as a dud. Unteroffizier Schüsele tried at once to displace the object which had been hanging there and the shell was dislodged. Completely unshaken, Schüsele took it in his arms and aided by Stadelbacher and Strumpfler moved it upstairs and left it in the trench so that it could be buried at a convenient moment. When early 1 July the enemy lifted the fire, we knew that the attack was not far off. Schüsele then discovered that we had insufficient water for the machine gun and said 'I'll go and get some water! Who's coming too?' Stadelbacher spoke up and we went and fetched about fifty litres of water from a damaged well in Fricourt. Going there was an unpleasant experience, but we returned safely to our dugout.

'Right,' said Schüsler, 'Let's get a dixie of water on the stove and make some coffee!' This we did and had another cup of coffee with biscuits. After that we put another pan on the stove and boiled up the last tins of rice and beef. We had had no bread left for several days. That was a good nutritious preparation for battle. In the meantime the enemy had launched a gas attack. Schüsele was on guard and the machine gun was ready to fire. As the gas slowly drifted away, we saw the enemy assault out of all trenches. Our machine gun was in full working order. There was nothing to stop us opening fire. Schüsele acted as gunner and I was his Number 2. Stadelbacher handled ammunition resupply. Unteroffizier Ehret from Sharp Shooter Troop 131 acted as observer. So we put down a hail of fire on the attacking enemy. Two companies of British who attempted to assault from the area of Fricourt Station were quickly caught by our machine gun and suffered dreadful casualties. We were not untouched, suffering two wounded and one killed.

"On one occasion a shell burst right in front of the machine gun and blew it into the trench. That did not stop us however. Altogether we fired 22,000 rounds during the day. As the assault eased, we could see that we were already surrounded. Our telephones were still working. Schüsele rang up the Regiment and received the order, 'Hold the position until it gets dark, then reinforcements will arrive'. During the night we received the order to withdraw and despite the fact that the British were so close that we could hear them talking, we got through unharmed to the Regimental staff in Bazentin Wood. We were each given a bottle of sparkling mineral water there, which cheered us up, then we moved off to the Divisional Intermediate Position, where we stuck it out until we were relieved."

In the area of Reserve Regiment 109, the signal for the attack was the firing of mines on its extreme right flank. Its companies, severely weakened by the preliminary bombardment (so much so, that two of them were to have been relieved by companies of Infantry Regiment 23 that night), waited to counter the assault. But here the artillery had done its work. The positions were badly damaged; the wire largely destroyed. There was no great expanse of No Man's Land to cross and the use of Russian saps* meant that the attackers were able to break into the positions of 1st and 2nd Companies Reserve Infantry Regiment 109 in the first rush, whilst the remaining defenders were still sheltering from the final shells of the bombardment. There were many casualties amongst the defenders and for once the immediate counter-attack, launched by the 3rd Company was beaten back. Already within a few minutes the defenders were having to yield ground; the 4th Company were back in the third trench before 9.00 am, by which time the commander of the 1st Battalion, Hauptmann von Schirach, was already severely wounded and out of the battle.[63]

It was a similar story on the left flank, where the 3rd Battalion was also forced to give ground from the start of the attack. As the day wore on, the situation deteriorated, despite efforts to rush reinforcements from the 2nd Battalion forward and, in any case, Allied success against the German 12th Division around Montauban was exposing the flank of the Regiment to direct fire and the threat of encirclement. Nevertheless, the afternoon passed in bitter fighting here as machine gunners checked the advancing attackers' repeated attempts to close in on the area of the Headquarters of the 3rd Battalion. At 3.00 pm, after pressure lasting for hours, the members of the staff of the 3rd Battalion were taken prisoner. Despite all local efforts to make a stand, the whole position was beginning to unravel until, at around 8.00 pm, the survivors of the attempt to hold on to Mametz village were forced back to the Second Position near Bazentin le Petit. There were thirty-two of them. This dreadful day in the history of the Regiment had cost them fourteen officers killed, six wounded and twenty-four missing. There were also ninety-four other ranks killed, 261 wounded and 1,749 missing. It was October before the reconstituted regiment returned to the battle in the Grandcourt area.

The day ended just as badly for the men of Bavarian Reserve Infantry Regiment 6, who were spread out in a large arc from south west of Montauban to Curlu. They had been unfortunate enough to have been rushed into the front line positions of the 12th Infantry Division in a piecemeal, uncoordinated, manner to replace the enormous losses suffered by the forward companies of Infantry Regiments 62 and 63 during the bombardment. Instead of being deployed as a single entity, the twelve companies were split up and initially put under command

---

* A 'Russian sap' is the name given to a tunnel driven towards, or parallel to, the enemy lines, which is so shallow that only a few centimetres of soil separate it from the surface. This thin overhead cover can be blown off when required, surprising the enemy and producing a ready-made trench. This can then be used to provide a covered approach or a jumping-off trench for an attack..

of officers from the two Prussian regiments. This meant that there were no clear orders, chain of command, communications, rationing or ammunition resupply. After a fight against overwhelming odds, by the evening 1st July their total losses amounted to thirty-five officers and 1,774 other ranks. When, following yet another mine explosion at Casino Point, the attack itself was launched, the 8th Company of the Regiment was in position just to the east of Kleinbahnmulde [Train Alley], due south of Montauban, squarely in line with the assault of the British 30th Division and at the boundary between the British 21 and 55 Brigades. They, like all the other companies, had found that the relief in the line towards the end of the bombardment was completely chaotic and those who were not killed were all captured.

*Offizierstellvertreter Josef Busl 3rd Platoon 8th Company Bavarian Reserve Infantry Regiment 6*[64]**10**.

"On 29th June the order came to relieve Infantry Regiment 62 in the front line south of the narrow-gauge railway Montauban-Carnoy and west of Hardecourt. I went ahead to arrange the handover and my Platoon was led by Unteroffizier Gareis (†1st July 1916). Having been resupplied in the quarry at Montauban, the platoon arrived at the designated place around 5.50 am after an extremely strenuous march through heavy artillery and machine gun fire.

"As a result of the lengthy bombardment, the position was severely damaged. The trenches were partially levelled and the fire positions barely useable. Only three to four dugouts were available to the platoon. Despite the fact that our men were totally exhausted after the continuous strain of the days since 22 June, they set to immediately to clear out the position. During the evening a further dugout was crushed and eight men were lost. Because of the appalling weight of fire, no rations other than coffee could be brought forward...All the signs indicated that the expected attack would take place on 1 July. From 5.00 am the heaviest artillery and mortar fire imaginable came down on our positions, collapsing yet another dugout. Towards 6.00 am we thought that we could detect gas, but we were soon able to unmask.

"The infantry attack began shortly after 7.00 am [sic]. Although the enemy made progress on our flanks, our frontal fire held them back for a long time. After I was wounded at around 8.30 am, Vizefeldwebel Dratz took over the platoon and Unteroffizer Löb, one of the few remaining NCOs, the left hand half platoon. The latter was able to carry on putting down rapid fire until 10.15 am. In places where the drumfire had torn great holes, the enemy succeeded in advancing. Here too our men succeeded for a while in keeping them in check with hand grenades. However the overwhelming strength of the enemy meant that the platoon was nearing the end of its ability to resist. About two thirds of the platoon of six NCOs and fifty six men were dead. During the attack the spirit of the men never drooped. On the contrary they were relieved when the enemy began his attack after the days of drum fire. The platoon performed extremely well; the light of battle shone in their eyes. I was severely wounded in the head and shoulder and was captured by the British. Contrary to the later account of a British officer, Captain Horn, our men did not give in easily. On the contrary they were at the very focus of the battle, at the break-in point. Heroically they blunted the first attack, until they had to yield in the face of overwhelming infantry and artillery."

The companies of Bavarian Reserve Infantry Regiment 6 had found themselves in a thoroughly confused situation, but during the final hours of the bombardment their commander had been placed in a near-impossible position by the commander of 12th Division. On the 30th June, he was ordered to relieve the commander of Infantry Regiment 62 in his dugout south of Bernafay Wood and to assume command of the sector. That evening, at 11.00 pm, he rode to Moislains to try to locate Headquarters 12th Division, which had recently moved to a new location somewhere in the rear. He had hoped to receive a briefing at the Headquarters, but nobody had any information about its whereabouts. So he moved to Ginchy with a skeleton staff and met up with two guides from Infantry Regiment 62 at 2.00 am on 1st July.

*Oberst Leibrock Commander Bavarian Infantry Regiment 6*[65] **11.**

"About 4.00 am my staff and I reached the dugout, which was still in reasonable condition. Apart from the regimental staff, the dugout also housed the Artillery Liaison Officer, Hauptmann Ottens, of Field Artillery Regiment 22 and his Adjutant, a group of runners whose task it was to carry messages across country to the telephone exchange, a section of infantry pioneers, who were working on improving the dugout and lastly a machine gun and its crew. All these personnel were from Infantry Regiment 62. Oberstleutnant von Poser, commander of Infantry Regiment 62, briefed me on the unfavourable position of the dugout, which had no links via communication trenches forward. He also stated that telephone links to the two right hand battalion sectors and the telephone exchange had been broken for a considerable time. There was, however, a telephone link with the left hand battalion in Bayernwald [Bavarian Wood] and one between the telephone exchange in Bernafay Wood and division. He had had a sharp disagreement with the divisional commander regarding the unsuitable location of the dugout, but without success. The artillery liaison officer, Hauptmann Ottens, complained that despite the fact that very frequent and very urgent demands had been made for a supply of telephone cable, they had so far received nothing.

"During the move forward to the dugout, enemy artillery fire was generally moderate; it was heavier on the two woods and between the woods and the dugout. By about 4.30 am the handover of the regimental sector was complete and around 5.00 am the weight of fire increased sharply. It appeared that the enemy was unsure of the exact location of the dugout, because most of the heavy shells fell immediately in rear of it...About 8.00 am Hauptmann Bruck reported from his command post that the Frenchmen had broken into Bayernwald and that confused fighting was currently taking place. Later this report was corrected. British, not French, troops were involved and support was required urgently. The left flank was severely threatened and the position had partly given way. Around 10.00 am, Hauptmann Horn reported that the enemy had broken into Bayernwald and also into the western part of Montauban.

"Because I had no telephone contact with Sectors g – k and had also received no reports from there, I believed that the there had only been a partial penetration in Bruck's battalion area. I reported in these terms to 12th Infantry Division and requested that the divisional reserve be placed at my disposal. The journey by the runners to and fro between the dugout and the telephone exchange took a lot of time. Low flying aircraft were also firing at my men and when I received the agreement of the division to my request, my orders to the divisional reserve in Guillemont had to be given in the same way via the telephone exchange. I directed its commander immediately to despatch four companies to Bayernwald, where they would be subordinated to Hauptmann Bruck. In the meantime enemy aircraft flew low, sometimes less than a hundred metres above the dugout, so I directed that the men who were sheltering in the Quergraben [Cross Trench] behind the dugout to come inside. They were likely to be spotted in that trench, which was only lightly camouflaged with branches and they could achieve nothing there. About 11.00 am a single British soldier was reported to be behind the dugout. Initially he refused to surrender, maintaining instead that the men in the dugout were his prisoners. However he was soon brought into the dugout as a prisoner. The artillery fire had slackened noticeably at this point. Most of it was falling on the wood.

"The British soldier explained that the British attack had thrown the Germans back and that the men of Reserve Infantry Regiment 109 to the right of Bavarian Reserve Infantry Regiment 6 had put their hands up. The British had been in rear of the dugout for a considerable time. Because the effect of this news on our men would be bad, I declared this to be impossible. The fact, however, that this British soldier was wandering around alone behind the dugout, the fact that there was no contact with the battalion sectors on the right and the report from Hauptmann Bruck, led me to fear the worst. In the meantime Hauptmann Bruck reported that the situation in the Bayernwald had apparently improved and that he hoped to be able to hold the wood if the reinforcements arrived promptly. At the same time he requested that his Battalion be relieved because it was at the end of its tether. This report led me to hope that the attack had also stalled on the right and that a German counter-attack was to be expected, even though the German artillery had more or less fallen silent. The noise the shells made rushing over the dugout meant that we could tell that they came from the enemy side...Our observers now reported that our men were standing by the second trench in front of Bayernwald and were engaging the enemy.

"A little later they reported that the British were indeed behind the dugout. I went out myself to take a look. Hardly had I put my head up when I received a burst of small arms fire from the rear. I could not be absolutely certain about the situation, but it was at least clear that it was not our men standing around firing from the Second Trench, but rather the British digging in. I could also make out a group of British infantry, sixty to seventy strong, occupying shell craters behind the dugout. The commander of the machine gun, an Unteroffizier from Infantry Regiment 62, had made several attempts to bring his gun into action. He and his deputy, a Gefreiter, were wounded in the attempt. There was only one route out of the bunker and that was up a staircase into Quergraben, so it was a simple matter for the British to prevent all such attempts by bringing down overwhelming fire. The enemy had by now worked their way so far forward towards the dugout that they could throw grenades into the Quergraben. Officers with revolvers and men with rifles stood ready to defend the lower end of the staircase, but the British succeeded in throwing several grenades into the entrance of the staircase, whence they bounced down into the dugout. I ordered the maps and documents to be burned.

"Casualties had risen to two dead and seven wounded. This included the British prisoner, who was severely wounded by a hand grenade. The dead, wounded and those tending them took up so much space, that it was impossible to move about within the dugout. The British continued to throw grenades into the entrance. The men attempted to avoid them and pressed to the rear. It was impossible to see what was happening and every attempt to coordinate the fire of the weapons was in vain. The men of Infantry Regiment 62 only obeyed orders with reluctance. They were obviously morally and physically exhausted. The presence of unknown superiors played a role here. They did not command the same respect and the novel, unusual and hopeless situation caused discipline to slip. I telephoned Hauptmann Bruck once more, explaining that we were cut off by British infantry, who were attacking with hand grenades and requested him to despatch a company to drive them away. He explained that that would be impossible. All his men were engaged and the reserves had not yet arrived. It was quite out of the question to withdraw men from the firing line. It seemed to me ever more probable that, as the British prisoner had stated, there had been a British breakthrough. In this situation, I felt that further sacrifice was pointless and, because the German artillery was completely silent, that there was no chance of a counter-attack. After repeated consultations with my officers I decided to surrender. It was probably about 3.00 pm by this time."

The German artillery had suffered considerably in this area from the effective counter-battery work of the French artillery, in particular. This undoubtedly contributed to the relative ease with which the Allies were able to drive home their attacks, but it would be wrong and unjust to assume that the German artillerymen just gave up the unequal struggle. Within the limits of the guns and ammunition available to them, they fought as hard as they could.

*Reserve Leutnant Holdermann 3rd Baden Field Artillery Regiment 50*[66] **12.**

"The incredible din, which could never be surpassed, left no doubt that the assault would follow. Knell was observing, Schumacher and I were on the gun position. The Hauptmann, off to the right, was occupying a dugout by the sunken road to Ginchy. It was pointless for us to be all massed in one place. Sure enough they came. The attack was reported at 8.00 am [*sic*]. It had been preceded by the release of clouds of gas. Visibility was poor, but we fired as fast as we could. By 9.00 am the observer had a clear view. The British masses (apparently missed by our defensive fire) had overrun the first trenches... and were digging in. It was lucky that the talk was of 'digging in' and initially there was no further move forward. This would certainly have been possible, because there was hardly any infantry left and the artillery fire was scattered thinly. Despite the bombardment we were ready to fire. We had had three seriously wounded. It was a hot fight. Shells were landing all over the copse, sending branches and twigs flying everywhere. A direct hit landed on a pile of fifty rounds of ammunition and set them off. Fragments from the explosion of our own ammunition endangered the wood for a complete hour. On the gun position, we had no idea about what was going on. We just reacted to the information of our observer that we were shooting too short... During the afternoon we had great success against very clear targets. Three British companies were destroyed as they tried to advance, as were a battery moving into position in Shell Wood and reserves in Schrapnellwald. That evening things were quieter, but there had been great changes to our copse. Three guns had been knocked out and could not be recovered... No communication trenches leading forward were left; entire battalions had to spread out and head for the front across country... Scenes of battle of the greatest interest were to be seen everywhere. We were quite exhausted, but this first onslaught did not really enjoy success,

* Shrapnell Wood, known to the British as German's Wood, was located south–south-east of Montauban.

despite the fact that there were advances to the right and left and some batteries were captured. We could say happily that this was due in large part to the staunch way we fired. Much the same applies to the gun batteries to our front which fired an enormous amount, despite being under constant fire from the enemy, who had known for a long time the exact range to their positions and were able, therefore, to bring accurate fire down and so cause heavy casualties."

The one flicker of success for the Bavarians occurred in and around Curlu, which was attacked by men of the French 37th Regiment of 11th Division to cries of *'Vive la France!'*[67] This fortified village, though damaged, was still reasonably defensible, so the attackers came under heavy machine gun fire from cellars, the cemetery and the church, taking heavy losses on the western edge of the village. There were further attempts during the day to capture the village, but finally, to save casualties, because it was obvious that progress on either side of the village would lead to its inevitable fall, the attacks were suspended in favour of an artillery bombardment. At the end of this further bombardment, the previously attractive village presented a dismal scene of destruction. The cemetery itself was a particularly disgusting sight. Graves were unearthed, coffins were strewn around and broken, shrouds had been torn from long-dead corpses and crosses were smashed and leaning at wild angles. Adjacent to it, the church lay in ruins, its bell tower collapsed.[68] The war diary of Bavarian Reserve Infantry Regiment 6 recorded tersely the events of the day here as follows:

"Start of heavy drumfire on 1July : 6.00 am.

Defensive fire on western edge of village.

Defensive positions in Curlu occupied.

First attack on Curlu : 9.00 am.

Recapture of Curlu, as far as its western edge, by 4th Company, a section of light mortars and one machine gun detachment of Infantry Regiment 63.

Second and third attacks on Curlu beaten off.

Drumfire on Curlu from 4.00 pm, including super-heavy calibre.

Evacuation of Curlu on order of 1st Battalion Infantry Regiment 63, evening."[69]13.

Thanks to this order, a few men of the regiment withdrew to fight another day. Nevertheless, despite the fight put up by some elements of Bavarian Reserve Infantry Regiment 6 in defence of Curlu, to state that Oberst Leibrock was bitter about the way the majority of his regiment was thrown into the line like lambs to the slaughter is dramatically to understate his seething, continuing rage about the way he felt it had been sacrificed. The period he spent as a prisoner of war gave him ample opportunity to reflect on and to analyse the events of those turbulent few days. He was especially anxious that no judgment be made about the performance of his regiment, unless the reader was in full possession of the facts, a summary of which he published after the war.

*Oberst Leibrock Commander Bavarian Reserve Infantry Regiment 6*[70]

"1. Bavarian Reserve Infantry Regiment 6 was not subordinated to the 28th Prussian Reserve Division and the 12th Prussian Infantry Division until the enemy had, with the assistance of aerial observation, already commenced the systematic bombardment of the places of accommodation and work.

2. There was insufficient material for the construction of dugouts and obstacles. This meant that full use could not be made of the work force.

3. The places of accommodation and work of the battalions and companies were changed frequently and eventually work could only occur at night. The consequent lack of rest and recovery affected the quality of the work.

4. The splintering of the regiment, due to the way it was deployed as a work force, felt very unpleasant and it was later the principal cause of the catastrophe when the regiment was deployed tactically. The battalions of my regiment had been removed from my orders and utilised for external duties for more than a week. This made the conduct of internal administration extremely problematic. Tactically, ten companies and the sharp shooter section were subordinated from the start to Prussian commanders and the two remaining infantry companies and the machine gun detachments of my regiment were also deployed elsewhere during the enemy attack.

5. When on 1 July I arrived in the front line to carry out the duties of Sector Commander, the destruction of the telephone lines and poor state of the Regimental dugout meant that I could only make contact with the four companies of my regiment which were subordinated to Hauptmann Bruck of Infantry Regiment 62. Resupply of rations and ammunition was in the hands of officers who were not known personally to me or my subordinates. There was a complete and utter lack of the independent, autonomous cooperation of all personnel, upon which, quite correctly, great stress and value had been laid during training and the preceding years of war, because it is the main factor contributing to battleworthiness. Even after our division had been broken up, if the regiment had at least been deployed complete, then the regiments of 12th Infantry Division could have fought in their narrower sectors with their task made easier and with a greater sense of responsibility. Whether, or to what extent, this would have influenced the overall outcome of the day, I cannot judge. There may indeed have been other reasons for the actual deployment of forces, of which I have no knowledge.

6. As far as I am aware from the statements of officers who were captured at the same time as me, the individual parts of the regiment gave all that was humanly possible in terms of courage and the endurance of the strain and privations they had suffered. Although I have laid stress in this description on the coincidence of negative factors, the reason, apart

from the duty to report truthfully, is mainly the regret that despite the absolutely amazing display of gallantry, tough endurance and the appalling casualties, which the enemy reports will describe as the wiping out of the regiment, it was not possible to beat off the enemy attack."

The comment is often made that the German army had lost the initiative by the end of the first day of fighting on the Somme, but as the experience of Bavarian Reserve Infantry Regiment 6 demonstrates, this can in fact be dated back at least to the moment when the intensity of the preliminary bombardment fixed the defenders in position and prevented them from as much as conducting reliefs in the line in a coherent manner. Already a sense of desperation was entering into the way the defence was being conducted. The coming days would provide innumerable examples of formations and units being broken up and rushed forward, so that gaps in the line could be plugged somehow: regardless of the consequences for the individuals or sub units involved.

South of the river a day of almost unrelieved disaster for the German army was unfolding. Here the Army High Command had misread the situation and had discounted the possibility of any significant French assault. The defending formations had been forced to hold over-extended frontages, in positions which had been subject to extremely effective fire by the French artillery. Losses in men and equipment had been severe. Away to the north the defenders generally began the day with their machine guns and mortars intact. Here, many had already been destroyed or buried. Much of the Germany artillery was also destroyed or suppressed, so when the assault began, two hours later than the one north of the river and aided by persistent morning mist, it enjoyed a large measure of surprise and immediate success. Here the French army had deployed about ten heavy batteries per kilometre of front, subjecting the area to be attacked to a devastatingly accurate barrage of fire, as the German gunners found to their cost. Quite apart from observers operating in aircraft, who flew so low over Estrées that their faces could clearly be seen, the French army launched and maintained no fewer than eighteen captive balloons opposite the 11th Division.[71] As a result, the positions of all the German batteries were known with great accuracy and they suffered accordingly.

The 11th Infantry Division, on the other hand, was supported only by Field Artillery Regiments 6 and 42, who were reinforced later during the bombardment by 4th and 5th Batteries Reserve Field Artillery Regiment 40. The guns were organised into Artillery Group North and Artillery Group South, commanded by the commanders of Field Artillery Regiments 6 and 42 respectively. What made things worse for the German gunners was the almost total lack of heavy batteries of their own with which to bring down counter-battery fire. For a time the Group Commanders could call on the services of 4th Battery Reserve Foot Artillery Regiment 20 (Heavy Howitzers), 3rd Battery Foot Artillery Regiment 28 (Heavy Howitzers) and Foot Artillery Battery 684 (150 millimetre guns), but they did not have exclusive use of them, nor were the numbers anything like equal to the daunting task which faced them.[72] Throughout the bombardment the gun positions were singled out for attack and, when on 30th June the German batteries of Artillery Group North, based behind Estrées, Soyécourt and Fay, fired systematically at the French front line, 2nd Battery Field Artillery Regiment 6 was hit in response by no fewer than 2,000 heavy calibre rounds, which wrecked the position and knocked out three of its guns. This incident was followed by another, when a direct hit on one of the 90 millimetre guns, stationed in Fay, killed seven out of the eight man crew and left the sole survivor, seriously wounded, lying next to the destroyed gun. This was entirely typical. By 1st July, 4th Battery Field Artillery Regiment 6, for example, which was located in the park of the château at Deniécourt, had been engaged by 15,000 rounds of all calibres.[73]

In the final lead up to the attack, the batteries were drenched with gas and further neutralised by high explosive shells.

*Oberleutnant Niemeyer Commander 4th Battery Reserve Field Artillery Regiment 40*[74] **14.**

"By 1st July the battery had been fighting for three days, without suffering damage to men or material. But then, early that day, the enemy attack began. From 6.30 am to 7.30 am, the battery came under heavy fire from gas shells, which burst ceaselessly in front and behind the position. One gas shell hit the third gun, penetrated the protective shield and exploded against a pile of howitzer shells prepared for use in our defensive fire zone. The gas cloud and explosion of the shells which had been hit knocked out the entire crew. During the rescue operation, which began immediately, the gas masks proved to be entirely reliable, provided that the users remained calm and worked at a moderate rate. Four members of the crew were killed outright and the gun commander, who had been gassed badly, did not regain consciousness before he was taken to the rear that evening. Five men, who had also been wounded by fragments, were rendered unconscious by the gas, but they recovered after artificial respiration had been applied. In the meantime the battery maintained a rapid rate of defensive fire. Numerous enemy aircraft circled above the battery, without being engaged...Between approximately 9.00 am and 10.00 am, the battery came under heavy gunfire from weapons of 75 – 150 millimetre calibre. This was so accurate that, within half an hour, a second hit on the third gun damaged the sight mechanism and set its protective roof on fire. The communication trenches were also blown in in three places and, finally, at 10.30 am, the first gun was absolutely wrecked by a direct hit. The gun commander and three men were killed instantly; Leutnant Neidhardt and three gunners were wounded."

By around 11.00 am the German artillery had virtually fallen silent, the First Position of the 121st Division had been breached comprehensively and the villages of Frise, Dompierre and Becquincourt had fallen. Further to the south, the men of the French XXXVth Corps had reached Fay and the assault was already being pressed against the line between Herbécourt and Assevillers, a position almost two and a half thousand metres wide, which was defended by 3rd Battalion Infantry Regiment 60.[75] There were gaps all along the line. Grenadier Regiment 11 was out of touch with Reserve Infantry Regiment 7. There was a gap of at least two hundred metres between the two units, so reserves were hastily pulled together from throughout the Division and sent to provide at least some cover. Infantry Regiment 60 had only three machine guns still in working order when the blow fell on them. The remnants of their over-extended forward companies were simply overrun in the wreckage of their trenches. Here and there pockets of resistance held out throughout the day, before being overwhelmed. Fighting continued throughout the day, Assevillers fell at around 4.00 pm and a little later, at 5.30 pm, Herbécourt was assaulted directly from the northwest. A vigorous counter-attack, which benefited from a short, but effective, fire plan, was launched a little later by 1st Battalion Infantry Regiment 60, reinforced by some remnants of Reserve Infantry Regiment 7 and two companies of engineers. Showing great aggression, the German soldiers swept around and into Assevillers, recapturing it from French colonial troops from Senegal at some cost to themselves.

This was a hand-to-hand battle with the French soldiers, whose wounded continued the battle, as did prisoners, who concealed weapons on their persons. The mopping up was a bloody affair for both sides, during which Leutnant Lindner particularly distinguished himself and impressed his comrades. **15.**

> "During the attack on Assevillers, Leutnant Lindner was wounded in the left forearm. Having had it bandaged hastily, he continued forward with his men, considering that losing the use of his left hand would not prevent him from doing his duty. The edge of the village was stormed. The black troops yielded in the face of a close-quarter battle and pulled back into barricaded farmyards, which we attacked one after the other. Leutnant Lindner was pinned down with his men before one of these fortified farms. Taking a quick decision, he set fire to one of the gates. Before the beams were even burnt through, with a mighty heave, Lindner and his men pushed in the burning gate and stormed in. The black men had no place to retreat and a bitter bayonet fight broke out. After a few moments, Lindner's wounded left arm let him down. A black soldier, as tall as a tree, lunged at his abdomen with his bayonet. Lindner attempted to fend off the blow with the carbine he held in his right hand, but it was too late. He was stabbed in the right hand and a shot, which the black soldier fired simultaneously, smashed into his right arm. His comrades flattened the black man and soon the farmyard was in the hands of the 60th. Lindner lay wounded for a long time in the village, with his wounds hastily dressed, before he was finally evacuated. His right arm had to be amputated because gangrene had set in."[76]

On 22 June the 11th Division had been moved forward into the line on the left flank of the 121st Division, which was located immediately south of the Somme.

Grenadier Regiment 10 held the line between Fay and Estrées and Infantry
Regiment 51, the sector south of there as far as Sternwald [Star Wood], near
Vermandovillers. Luckily for Infantry Regiment 51, the unit which had
distinguished itself earlier in the year during the capture of Frise, the French
assault went in to their north, so although they took some casualties from the
artillery fire, their day passed relatively quietly. It was a different story for
Grenadier Regiment 10, which was the most southerly German Regiment to be
attacked on 1 July. During the previous night, their positions had been subjected
to a torrent of fire, which had damaged so many dugouts that the survivors were
forced to cluster in mine galleries where these existed. As the moment of the
assault approached, the regiment was under gas attack, its trenches were almost
unrecognisable and all the communication trenches to the rear had been destroyed.
Evacuation of the wounded and forward supply of ammunition and rations had
become quite impossible. Maintaining observation of the enemy positions became
tantamount to committing suicide, yet there were numerous heroes, who insisted
on continuing to risk their lives in pursuance of this critical duty.

One important observation post in the area of the 11th Company, just to the
north of Fay, was well known to the Frenchmen, who kept it under constant fire,
killing or wounding numerous men. At this point Landsturmmann Stolpe stepped
forward and insisted to his platoon commander, Leutnant von Uechritz, that he be
allowed to assume the duty. Refusing the counter offer of acting as sentry
elsewhere, he stated, 'Herr Leutnant, every man must do his duty where he belongs
and duty calls me to this place'.[77] Unfortunately the story does not have a happy
ending. The courageous Stolpe was killed a few minutes later. As it became light,
the drumfire increased to maximum intensity and the whole area was enveloped
in gas. A contact patrol despatched to the Wasserburg area by Hauptmann
Reymann at 6.20 am reported 'Due to gas, the visibility is down to three metres'.
Later in the morning the visibility improved somewhat, then, at around 10.00
am, one large and two small mines were blown in sectors E1 and E2 near Fay,
which were held by the 11th and 10th Companies respectively. As a result, an
unknown number of the men sheltering in the German mine galleries, which were
crushed by these explosions, met their death before the main attack actually
began. More gas was fired and shortly afterwards, artillery observers were
reporting, 'Enemy attack underway. It has already reached the third trench in
places. Enemy digging in and preparing communications trenches to the rear.'[78]

Thereafter matters went from bad to worse in this area. The forward positions
had been overwhelmed so swiftly that no information reached the command posts
to the rear, which were in any case drenched with gas throughout the morning. To
add to the appalling difficulties, at 10.30 am, just after six prisoners from the
French 219th Infantry Regiment had been brought to Hauptmann Reymann's
headquarters in Sector E, the dugout containing the staff and the telephone
exchange were crushed by a large calibre shell. Leutnant Hochbaum managed to
free himself, then with the assistance of some men who were hurrying past,

succeeded in saving the Artillery Liaison Officer from Field Artillery Regiment 6, Reserve Leutnant Knoth, Reserve Leutnant Mattenklott and one of the telephonists, who were lying near the entrance. Fire then broke out in the dugout, killing the majority of the men who had been trapped by falling roof supports.[79] Isolated groups of defenders fought on as long as they could before being destroyed or by-passed, unable to do anything to prevent the further advance north east towards Assevillers. By about 2.00 pm, everyone and everything that was not killed, destroyed or buried had fallen into the hands of the French attackers.

Gradually reports concerning the unfolding crisis began arriving at the Headquarters of Major Freiherr von der Goltz in Belloy. Once the extent of the reverses became clear, he acted rapidly to contact elements of Fusilier Regiment 38, which were available to act as the local reserve. They were called forward during the late morning to man the Second Position to the south of Assevillers.

*Leutnant Jürgens Adjutant 1st Battalion Fusilier Regiment 38*[80] **15.**

"On the morning of 1 July it was noticeable that there was very little artillery fire; just the occasional shrapnel round, which burst over our village of Villers Carbonnel. Whilst the staff of the 1st Battalion was having lunch in a cellar, an order arrived that the Battalion was immediately to occupy the Second Position south of Assevillers. The battalion commander would receive more detailed orders from Grenadier Regiment 10 in Belloy. Once runners had been despatched to the companies, the staff set off... Heavy fire was landing on the village exit in the direction of Estrées. One shell came down right in the midst of a section of the Field Recruit Depot... so we had to press on over dead and wounded across the road into a field of ripening corn, where we spread out and headed for Belloy. The companies deployed tactically and followed with large gaps between them. The sun burned down out of a cloudless sky. The many enemy captive balloons seemed to be very close by, observing everything. We, on the other hand, had only one balloon in the sky and we watched as an enemy aircraft circled above it and sent a shower of sparks pouring down on it. Then we saw our last balloon fall burning to the ground. A black column of smoke saluted its dying throes.

"Belloy looked terrible. Every house bore the marks of the bombardment. All over the streets lay dead horses with distended stomachs and legs stretched skywards. A stink of decay and corruption hovered over the village. Down in a cellar we located the staff of Grenadier Regiment 10. Major von der Goltz briefed my commander on the situation: the French had attacked in strength, captured the First Position and were heading for Assevillers... The battalion was to link up with Zehner's Platoon, occupy the Second Position south of the village and hold it at all costs... The staff headed for the Second Position, via the Goltz-Weg [Goltz Way]. There was no sign of the enemy and our companies had not yet arrived... Accompanied by a runner, I rushed off to find Zehner's Platoon. Two guns of a battery were still firing from Füchsbau-Wäldchen [Fox Covert], which ran through the Second Position. Numerous dead gunners lay around in smashed trenches. North of Fox Covert, I came across two sections of Zehner's Platoon and linked up with its commander. When I returned to the staff which had occupied a half-completed dugout south of Fox Covert, the companies arrived and took up their positions."

In much the same way, reserves were assembled from Grenadier Regiment 10, other companies of Fusilier Regiment 38 and machine guns from Reserve Infantry Regiment 7, so that gradually the Second Position was turned into an increasingly viable defensive line, as other detachments from Grenadier Regiment 11 and Grenadier Regiment 101 were fed forward. The defenders were a very mixed bag. These emergency measures led to a terrible intermingling of unrelated subunits, but collectively they did at least form a recognisable line of defence, which would be ready the following day to do battle. In the meantime, the surviving artillery continued to play as much of a role as the damage they had suffered would permit.

*Oberleutnant Niemeyer Commander 4th Battery Reserve Field Artillery Regiment 40[81] 14.*

"During the afternoon the battery fired constant defensive and harassing fire... which had to be suspended briefly from time to time to preserve the barrels. Because there was a total lack of information concerning the state of the infantry in the sectors to our front, about 8.30 pm Unteroffizier Gerth and Gefreiter Ludwig were sent forward along the Hantelmanngraben [Hantelmann Trench] to the tower in Estrées, in order to obtain a situation report on the battle and to see who was manning the so-called 'Z' Position there. To the front of the gun position, a group comprising one leutnant and fifteen men was found to be occupying a fifteen metre length of trench. Further to the right they discovered that there were no infantry at all to be seen. After 9.00 pm, the general area and the gun position came under gas attack once again then at 10.30 pm the position was subject to drumfire by 150 millimetre field guns, which set fire to a large proportion of the ammunition, which had only just been driven forward that afternoon. Plans to recover and bury the fallen that night had to be abandoned due to constant fire and the total exhaustion of the men..."

Gradually this momentous day drew to a close. In some places, bitter fighting continued late into the night. Elsewhere, especially where it was obvious that the Allied attacks had failed utterly and that the survivors posed no threat to the German defenders, unofficial truces and other humanitarian gestures occurred. Up near Beaumont the final attacks had been beaten back by the men of Reserve Infantry Regiment 119 by 1.00 pm. One regimental humorist from Tübingen is said to have wiped the sweat from his brow and remarked in broad dialect to his

* Fox covert was located 750 metres south of Asseviliers.

mates, 'Well that's got the dust out of the weapons!'[82] Pausing to take in the scene before them they saw a No Man's Land bleached by 'White Star' gas. Hundreds of khaki-clad corpses were piled up in front of their wire. The area of the massive new crater on top of Hawthorn Ridge was littered with British dead and encircled by the fallen of the 7th, 9th and 12th Companies. The trenches were flattened; the dugout entrances all buried by white chalk, metres high. Then, suddenly between 1.00 pm and 2.00 pm, a hole appeared next to the edge of the crater and out came Reserve Leutnant Renz and a few of his men. After five hours of ceaseless labour, they had escaped from their tomb, just as the air was about to run out. **1.**

They were greeted joyfully by their comrades, one of whom, Landsturmmann Schneider, who had a perfect command of English, noticed that some of the 'dead' British soldiers were lifting their heads from time to time. He shouted to them to come into the German trench. They would not be fired on and would be well treated. After some delay and further coaxing, a group of unwounded British soldiers carried their seriously wounded lieutenant over to the trench. As wounded men nearby saw that this group was received correctly, as promised, they put their hands up and called for help. Men of the 9th Company then went forward and, with the aid of British soldiers, who had been playing dead out in No Man's Land and who now surrendered, they managed to rescue thirty-six wounded soldiers, including five officers, one of whom, a battalion adjutant, was carrying important documents. There was no firing by the defenders during this drawn out operation, though they noted with disgust that the adjacent 10th Company was under constant fire from a British battery throughout.[83]

Further to the north, the men of Infantry Regiment 169, who had fought like men possessed earlier that day, were both appalled at the sight before them and moved by compassion for the suffering the day's battle had produced.

### Unteroffizier Otto Lais Infantry Regiment 169[84]   3.

"Evening falls. The attack is dead! Our own casualties are severe; the enemy casualties are unimaginable. In front of our divisional sector lie the British in companies, in battalions; mowed down in rows and swept away. From No Man's Land, the space between the positions, comes one great groan. The battle dies away; it seems to be paralysed at so much utter misery and despair. First aid men hasten around the area. A complete British medical team with many stretcher bearers and unfurled Red Cross flags appears from somewhere. It is a rare and deeply moving sight in trench warfare. Where to begin? Whimpering and moaning confronts them from almost every square metre. Our own first aiders, who are not required elsewhere, go forward to bandage the wounded and deliver the enemy carefully to their own people..."

1.   Hauptstaatsarchiv Stuttgart M107 Bü 42/103
2.   Gerster: History RIR 119 p 53
"White Star' was a 50:50 mixture of chlorine and phosgene.

3.   Kümmel: History RIR 91 p 211
4.   Wißmann: History RIR 55 p 111
5.   *ibid.* p 111
6.   *ibid.* p 115
7.   Kümmel: History RIR 91 p 212
8.   Lais, *Die Schlacht an der Somme* pp 16-18
9.   This is a staggering number of rounds to fire through a single weapon in one day. The weight alone of such a quantity of ammunition is around one ton, yet several similar contemporary accounts exist.
10.  Hauptstaatsarchiv Stuttgart M201Bü 200
11.  Holtz: History RIR 121 pp 33-35
12.  Gerster: op. cit. p 53
13.  Hauptstaatsarchiv Stuttgart M107 Bü 42/103
14.  Hauptstaatsarchiv Stuttgart M107 Bü 42/103
15.  Hauptstaatsarchiv Stuttgart M43/19 RIR 99
16.  Kriegsarchiv München HS 2205 [Bram]
17.  Kriegsarchiv München HS 2205 [Bram]
18.  Soden: History 26 Res Div p 110
19.  Kriegsarchiv München 8RIR Bd 4
20.  Hauptstaatsarchiv Stuttgart M43/19 RIR 99
21.  N.B. These were not raw recruits; rather they were soldiers who had completed their basic training in Germany and were undergoing advanced battle training before taking their place as individual reinforcements for the regiments of the division. Such companies could be, and often were, used as normal troops in an emergency.
22.  Klett: History Württ. Res Drag R p 100
23.  Kriegsarchiv München HS 2205 [Bram]
24.  Hauptstaatsarchiv Stuttgart M410 Bu 239
25.  Hauptstaatsarchiv Stuttgart M410 Bu 239
26.  Hauptstaatsarchiv Stuttgart M410 Bu 239
27.  Kriegsarchiv München HS 1984 [Wurmb]
28.  Kriegsarchiv München 8RIR Bd 4
29.  Wurmb: History BRIR 8 p 69
30.  Hauptstaatsarchiv Stuttgart M410 Bü239
31.  Hauptstaatsarchiv Stuttgart M410 Bu 239. In fact, as has already been noted, the first of the men of the 36th Division were in positions overlooking Grandcourt very much earlier. They came under fire from the Second Position and the guns of 2nd Battery Reserve Field Artillery Regiment 27 were engaging them from their positions near the 'Ruined Mill' over open sights from mid morning. See History RFAR 26 - 1st July 1916. This is a good example of the extreme difficulty faced by commanders of the period, who frequently had to make important decisions based on incomplete or out of date information.
32.  Wurmb: *op.cit.* p 70
33.  Kriegsarchiv München 8RIR Bd 4
34.  Kriegsarchiv München HS 1984 [Wurmb]
35.  Kriegsarchiv München 8RIR Bd 4
36.  Stosch, *Somme-Nord I Teil* p 41. Captain Craig was the MP for South Antrim. He was wounded and captured, as described, on 1 July 1916, whilst serving with 11th Bn Royal Irish Rifles. He is known to have been interned in Holland on15th June 1918. He may possibly have been sent there by the Germans because his wounds rendered him unfit for further service. He was later repatriated to the United Kingdom on 4th October 1918.
37.  Soden: op. cit. p 111
38.  Hauptstaatsarchiv Stuttgart M410 Bü 239
39.  Kriegsarchiv München HS 1984 [Wurmb]
40.  Here Wurmb is quoting from verse three of *Das Grab im Busento* [The Busento Grave] by the German romantic poet August von Platen (1796-1835) '*Allzu früh und fern der Heimat mussten sie ihn hier begraben / Während noch die Jugendlocken seine Schulter blond umgaben*' [All too soon

and far from home they had to bury him here / Whilst his fair, youthful locks were still cascading down around his shoulders.] It sounds better, if somewhat sentimental, in German.

41. Hauptstaatsarchiv Stuttgart M410 Bu 239
42. Müller: History RIR 99 p 104
43. Kriegsarchiv München 8RIR Bd 4
44. Hauptstaatsarchiv Stuttgart M410 Bü 239
45. Hauptstaatsarchiv Stuttgart M410 Bü 239
46. Stosch: op. cit. p 43
47. *Die Wacht am Rhein* was a stirring, patriotic soldier's song, which includes the couplet '...*Lieb' Vaterland, magst ruhig sein, Fest steht und treu die Wacht am Rhein*.' ['Dear Fatherland be calm; all will be fine. Faithful and firm stands the Watch on the Rhine'.]
48. Hauptstaatsarchiv Stuttgart M410 Bu 239
49. Haupstaatsarchiv Stuttgart M410 Bü 260
50. Kriegsarchiv München HS 1984 [Wurmb]
51. Hauptstaatsarchiv Stuttgart M43/19 RIR 99
52. Müller: op. cit. pp 108-109
53. Hauptstaatsarchiv Stuttgart M 99 Bü 142
54. Hauptstaatsarchiv Stuttgart M 99 Bü 142
55. Vischer, 'Das 10. *Württ. IR 180 in der Somme-Schlacht*' p15
56. Vischer: History IR 180 p 37
57. Soden: op. cit. p 111
58. Stosch, 'Somme-Nord' p 53. N.B. The Commander was affected by the poisonous gases produced when a normal high explosive shell detonated and not by British 'White Star' gas [50:50 chlorine and phosgene]. The British army had no gas shells at the time.
59. Anon: History RIR 110 p 125
60. Frick *Erlebnisse* p 9
61. Bachelin: History RIR 111 p 102
62. ibid. pp 291-293
63. Frisch: History RIR 109 p 126
64. Bezzel: History BRIR 6 pp 91 - 92
65. ibid. pp 111-112
66. Zastrow: History FAR 50 pp 156 - 157
67. Denizot, *La bataille de la Somme* pp 83-84
68. ibid. p 84
69. Kriegsarchiv München 6 RIR Bd 2
70. Bezzel: op. cit. pp 117-119
71. History FAR 6 p 126
72. Schoenfelder: History FAR 42 pp 139-140
73. History FAR 6 p 131
74. Bieren: History RFAR 40 pp 103
75. Cron: History IR 60 p 141
76. ibid. p 144
77. Schütz: History Gren R 10 p 127
78. ibid. pp 127-128
79. ibid. p 129
80. Burchardi: History Füs R 38 pp 207 - 208
81. Bieren: History RFAR 40 pp 103-104
82. Gerster: History RIR 119 p 54
83. ibid. p 54
84. Lais: op. cit. pp 24 - 2

# CHAPTER 5

# 2nd – 31st July 1916

O n the 2nd July the early fighting claimed another victim. Generalmajor Grünert, Chief of Staff of Second Army, was relieved by General von Falkenhayn, during the latter's visit to Army Headquarters at St Quentin. Ostensibly this was because Grünert had, contrary to Falkenhayn's policy of not giving up ground, acquiesced to a request from General der Infanterie von Pannewitz to shorten his line along the front of XVII Corps near Herbécourt, following a partial French breakthrough south of the Somme.[1] Others, most notably Crown Prince Rupprecht, were not taken in.

*Crown Prince Rupprecht of Bavaria – Diary Entry 3rd July*[2]

> "Quite apart from the fact that it is inappropriate to change a Chief of Staff at a moment of supreme crisis, such a measure also amounts to lack of confidence in the relevant commander, who does in fact bear the ultimate responsibility for any decisions which are taken. This, in turn, diminishes the commander in the eyes of his subordinates. As I have already noted, the blame for what happened lies at the door of the Army High Command itself, which did not arrange in time for reinforcements to be allocated to Second Army."

Grünert had to go, being replaced by Oberst von Loßberg, a defence specialist who, during the coming days, was responsible for the general adoption of a more elastic form of defence. That change of policy still lay in the future. In the meantime, doubtless with Falkenhayn's words ringing in his ears, Commander Second Army lost no time in issuing a related order.

*Second Army Order I a 575 (Secret) dated 3rd July 1916*[3]

> "The outcome of the war depends on Second Army being victorious on the Somme. Despite the current enemy superiority in artillery and infantry we have got to win this battle. The large areas of ground that we have lost in certain places will be attacked and wrested back from the enemy, just as soon as the reinforcements which are on the way arrive. For the time being, we must hold our current positions without fail and improve on them by means of minor counter-attacks. I forbid the voluntary relinquishment of positions. Every commander is responsible for making each man in the Army aware about this determination to fight it out. The enemy must be made to pick his way forward over corpses.
>
> General von Below"

Meanwhile, in response to the heavy fighting on the opening day of the battle, reserves were being rushed forward to make good the losses incurred and to ensure that the dents made in the German line did not become break-throughs. Within ten days, no fewer than fifteen fresh divisions were either committed to the battle or moving towards it. In the first hours, however, the load was borne by those closest, who were force marched into position to replace the depleted units. Inevitably, in all the confusion and given the generally unfavourable tactical situation at the points most at risk, casualties mounted rapidly amongst these reinforcing units. The experience of men of Infantry Regiment 186, split up and deployed all along the front from Beaumont Hamel to Fricourt, is typical. The 3rd Battalion was sent forward to relieve Reserve Infantry Regiment 111 during the evening of 2nd July. After a brief but hard fight against the odds, they were almost all killed or captured, along with the remnants of Reserve Infantry Regiment 111.

*Reserve Leutnant Ballheimer 12th Company Infantry Regiment 186*[4] **1.**

"The march through the shot-up wood was extremely awkward. In Bazentin we went past the Divisional Headquarters. The companies were issued hand grenades, but most of them had no detonators. There was a total lack of clarity about the situation in the Headquarters and the commander of Reserve Infantry Regiment 111 did not know either. Once maps had been found, Hauptmann Kade gave out orders...On the way forward, 11th and 12th Companies soon split up, because we had to force a way through a small gap in a hedge. 12th Company eventually reassembled at a destroyed battery position by Mametz Wood. British artillery fire was coming down everywhere. We found our way along a communication trench and bumped into the 11th Company once more. A short section of occupied trench was followed by an almost totally destroyed communication trench, which ran along a completely smashed wood. Finally, we moved across country to a dressing station where we met up with the 11th Company, which was soon moved further west. Eventually I came across an officer in one of the dugouts, who told me that the company needed to move further right. I attempted this, approaching from the rear, but we went wrong and had to retrace our steps to the left. I went back and found another officer, who directed us to a different trench, then disappeared. A vizefeldwebel of the Machine Gun Company of Reserve Infantry Regiment 111 gave me a cursory description of the position, then wanted to pull his machine gun back out of the position. I told him that he should wait until our machine gun arrived. He insisted that he had orders for immediate withdrawal and that the other machine guns had already pulled out.

"To my right and as far along the trench as possible, was Ravoth with his platoon. Further over again there were some British, but our rifle fire drove them off. We were not in contact with the 11th or 9th Companies.

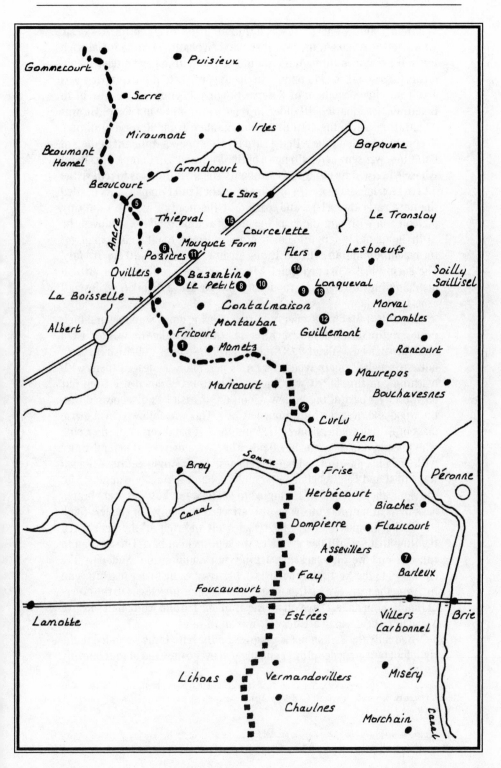

The trench simply ended. It was not more than thirty centimetres deep. To the left was Rauch, then Gallbach and Gebhardt. Leutnant Gallbach was soon wounded through the shoulder. He went to have it tended and, on doctor's orders, had to remain in the dugout. Left of the company was a still unrelieved platoon of Reserve Infantry Regiment 111. I went to Battalion Headquarters in order to report to Hauptmann Kade. He was negotiating with the battalion commander from Reserve Infantry Regiment 111 about the relief. Leutnant Quietmeyer, Adjutant of the 3rd Battalion, was sent to obtain news of the 11th and 9th Companies, about whose whereabouts nothing was known. The intention was to relieve the 111th men left of me with a platoon from the 10th Company. As I exited the dugout, Feldwebel Freund arrived at the head of a 10th Company platoon and with him the machine gun of Leutnant Freise. I moved the 10th Company straight into position and, with Leutnant Freise's help, got the machine gun into a fire position. Meanwhile it was 7.30 am 3rd July. The enemy had remained quiet. To our west we could see the British manhandling boxes around the farm,* but we drove them off with small arms fire.

"Towards 8.30 am the enemy started to bring down shrapnel and high explosive fire on the hollow behind us. Gradually the fire was adjusted onto the trenches. About 9.00 am we saw dense lines of British infantry move through Mametz Wood. As far as possible we engaged them with machine gun fire, but it was not possible to bring down fire from our position over part of the hollow. Soon the British had disappeared into the wood and over the hill to our left rear. This was followed by a dense mass of British soldiers emerging from the left hand corner of the wood, who pressed down on our left flank. They were driven off several times with machine gun fire and hand grenades. In this fight Leutnant Rauch was killed and Feldwebels Freund and Gebhardt seriously wounded. To the right, the British also attempted to get forward, but they were beaten back by Leutnant Ravoth. They also attacked frontally. On the left flank the British advanced, throwing grenades left and right of the trench. All the time that we still had grenades we kept them at bay. These began to run out and we also lacked machine gun ammunition. Suddenly the entrances to the Nestlerhöhlen [Nestler Caves]† came under machine gun fire from the rear. Gradually our situation became hopeless. On the orders of Hauptmann Kade, I fired off all the available red and white flares to give a signal to the German artillery. It was all in vain!

"Gradually the British made progress on the left. I was wounded in the right foot by a grenade splinter and handed over command of the company

---

*On modern maps, this farm is named 'Ferme du Bois'. It is situated 300 metres northeast of the Fricourt German Military Cemetery. German trench maps do not give it a name, but the History of Reserve Infantry Regiment 111 calls it 'Fricourt Farm'.

†The Nestlerhöhle was a major mined dugout located just to the south of the track running east-south-east – west-north-west, between the most northerly section of Bois de Fricourt Est and Bois de Fricourt Ouest.

to Feldwebel Schmidt, so that I could have the wound dressed. As this was happening and I was giving Hauptmann Kade a report, Leutnant Ravoth arrived with a member of Reserve Infantry Regiment 111, who had been waving a white flag. He maintained that he was doing this on orders from the dressing station! Leutnant Ravoth was shot through the chest just in front of the dressing station. I went up again and discovered that the company had evacuated the trench to the right of the approach track. I collected some courageous men in order to reoccupy this trench and asked Leutnant Quietmeyer to assume command of them, because I could hardly walk. Leutnant Quietmeyer approached, but came under a hail of hand grenades, so he had to pull back. When I wanted to report to Hauptman Kade that further resistance was hopeless, a great mass of British arrived and Hauptmann Kade surrendered the position."

*Ersatzreservist Joseph Würz 12th Company Reserve Infantry Regiment 111*[5] *1.*

"Around 8.00 am on 1st July 1916 the 12th Company was stood to and distributed amongst the companies holding the position. I stayed at Battalion Headquarters as a runner. Towards the evening the Battalion staff pulled back to the Nestlerhöhle. As it went dark, I was ordered by Feldwebel Kaufmann to go to [Fricourt Chateau] Park and collect the leather pouch which contained the nominal roll book. Musketier Freitag went with me. We took it carefully, because we were not sure if the British had occupied the Park. I went into the dugout and fetched the pouch. As I turned to leave, I heard groaning. I went to the other side of the dugout, where three wounded men were lying, apparently overlooked. My mate Freitag and I took one back to the Nestlerhöhle [Nestler Cave] and I reported in. The other two were collected by stretcher bearers. On 2nd July we could see the British in the direction of Mametz. Our casualties mounted. Between 2.00 am and 4.00 am on 3rd July we were reinforced by 3rd Battalion Infantry Regiment 186. It was not long before this unit was exhausted as well. Towards 10.00 am the commanding officer of this battalion summoned the officers from Reserve Infantry Regiment 111 and said, 'You are relieved, but I should be grateful if the men of Reserve Infantry Regiment 111 would stay and help us. Above all we must clear the way to the rear, because the British have already pushed on behind us in the direction of Contalmaison. How are we off for machine guns?' Reserve Infantry Regiment 111 had none left. A few of those of the 186th were still working, but most of the ammunition was gone and there were no hand grenades left. We of Reserve Infantry Regiment 111 had had nothing to eat or drink for two days and were exhausted. The battalion commander summoned Dr Frank and asked him about numbers of dead and wounded. The doctor replied 'Hauptmann we have no dressings left. I can give no guarantees. The men are likely to bleed to death.' At that the commander said, 'Right we shall have to surrender. If we are captured you, as a doctor, will be exchanged. When you get home, go to the Regiment and explain how things stood here.'"

It was not only the German army which was facing problems. Despite the territorial gains made by the Allies, the plain fact was that neither the hoped-for breakthrough, nor even the reduction of the German First Position, had occurred on 1st July. The extra two days which the bombardment had lasted had reduced stockpiles of artillery ammunition, especially heavy and super-heavy calibres, considerably. Even if the British army had not been pre-occupied with reorganisation after the trauma of the first day of the battle, in the short term there was no possible way of providing artillery support for another attempt at a general advance. Haig's solution was to maintain the pressure by means of limited local attacks, concentrating mainly on exploitation of the gains made south of the Albert – Bapaume road, in order to prepare the way for a general attack against the German Second Position, along the rough line Contalmaison – Delville Wood. In the prevailing circumstances, it is difficult to see what else he could have done in order to maintain the pressure and thus keep faith with the French. However, the decision committed the British army to a slow advance across terrain which, though not ideal, offered the determined German army considerable scope for defence. The names of the woods in the area: Mametz, Trônes, Bernafay, Delville and Foureaux [High] would soon become extremely familiar, as two months of that summer were given over to the fight for their control.

Elsewhere, the battles, though not always so critical, continued almost without interruption, imposing enormous strain on both sides and testing their discipline, resolution and powers of endurance to the limit. Some idea of the conditions for the infantry and the artillery respectively, may be obtained from the experiences of the soldiers of the Bavarian Reserve Infantry Regiment 6 who survived the 1st July disaster, when they were employed as replacements near Curlu early that month and those of the men of Field Artillery Regiment 6, battling against the odds down near Estrées.

*Reserve Leutnant Gruber Machine Gun Company Bavarian Reserve Infantry Regiment 6*[6] 2.

"On the morning 4th July, we moved forward from the Intermediate Position to relieve the troops in the front line. Twelve of us were wedged into a narrow slit trench in a very weak dugout that was barely splinter proof and so low and narrow that it was hardly possible to sit upright in it. Silent and resigned, we sat it out as fire of all calibres roared overhead. It increased from about 4.00 pm and by evening it was simply terrible. The fire crept nearer until a shell landed one metre away from the dugout entrance, spattering us in the face with earth and splinters of rock. We were deafened by the fire, terribly tired and indifferent to our fate. Wedged in tight, with our knees drawn up, we waited for nightfall and entertained ourselves – by discussing dying. Whenever a shell landed nearby we felt a blow to our backs, but everything continued to fall beyond us. In the unbelievably stifling July heat there was not a drop to drink. For days, therefore, thirst meant that we had not eaten anything either. My faithful batman, Wolf, hauled a carboy of tea from the field kitchen for three hours through the heat and the fire. Blue in the face and bathed in sweat, he had just arrived on our hill when the carboy was smashed by a shell splinter and the precious liquid ran away. He was determined, however, that the men had to have something to drink, so he returned once more and this time was more successful. Every man received a carefully measured beaker of tea.

"A direct hit crushed the dugout where one of my machine guns, the one commanded by Unteroffizier Krämer, was kept for safety. Several men of the infantry battalion were killed, some were buried alive and the gun was put out of action by earth and sand. Ignoring the continuing heavy fire, Krämer and his men set about rescuing the buried men. In this they were successful, then, despite the fire, they stripped down their machine gun, cleaned it and set about getting ready for action. After a few hours they were able to report that it was back in working order, which delighted us all, because we felt that the enemy would soon be coming."

*Major von Mellenthin Field Artillery Regiment 6[7]* **3**.

"We could see about twenty captive balloons over there and aircraft circled over every battery. With my field guns I could do nothing to drive them off, even if I had wished to, but in any case our targets lay elsewhere than in the blue skies above us. We had our hands full. The barrels steamed, no one could touch them. The gunners had to open and close the breeches with pieces of wood. We cooled the barrels with wet sand bags and poured water through them if we could. There was still some water in the village of Estrées, but in the other positions there was none to be had anywhere. It did not take the aviators long to discover our new positions. One gun after another was knocked out, or failed mechanically. Just remember we were firing 2,000 – 3,000 rounds per battery per day. The French sent over incendiary bombs and gas shells as well. Everything caught fire: the guns, the rations, the mens' equipment. Some of the gunners were buried alive and others, stupefied by gas, suffered for hours or even days. Add to this, constant hard work and strain, physical and mental, which went on for days. From time to time gas shells simply rained down. The gas masks offered good protection, but because of all the hard work and deep breathing, it was impossible to prevent all the gas from entering the organs of the body. When things got really bad, the men wanted to keep their masks on, but get out into the open air, but I forbade it. They would have been totally without protection, so I made them stay in the gun positions..."

Further north, desperate fighting continued. Fricourt, as has been noted, was evacuated in the early hours of 2nd July and La Boisselle finally fell, after a tough fight, twenty-four hours later. At 5.10 pm, 2nd July, 26th Reserve Division issued a warning order by telephone, "Reserve Infantry Regiment 110 is pulling back via La Boisselle. Infantry Regiment 180 is to hold Ovillers to the last man."[8] This was further clarified in a written order, which arrived at 9.30 pm, "Infantry Regiment 180 is to defend Ovillers to the last man. It is not to take a single step backwards from its current positions without an order from division. The regiment will be reinforced this evening by the Machine Gun Company of Infantry Regiment 186, which is on the march to Regimental Headquarters in Ovillers."[9] Despite everything that was thrown at it, this outstanding regiment did just what was asked of it, until it was relieved by the Fusilier Guards and elements of Reserve Infantry Regiment 15 four days later.

Another first class regiment that was pitched into the battle early in July was the élite Lehr Infantry Regiment. Plunged into the thick of the fighting in the Pozières – Ovillers area, it contributed greatly to holding the southern shoulder of the 26th Reserve Division area, but the cost to its irreplaceable high quality officers and men was simply enormous. Within a few days it had been ground down, largely by artillery fire, was incapable of fighting on and had to be replaced. The sacrificial devotion to duty of Grenadier Regiment 9, the Fusilier Guards and the Lehr Infantry Regiment bought valuable time for the defence at a critical moment, but the fact that the Germans were forced to squander the 3rd Guards Division in this way, is a measure of the pressure to which they were being subjected. Well might Oberst Paul von Mülmann, the historian of the Lehr Infantry Regiment, lament, "What enormous sacrifices this battle demanded of the German infantry!"[10] He might have been describing the entire battle, but this was still the beginning. He continues as follows:

> "On 3rd July, 1st Battalion Lehr Infantry Regiment arrived on the Second Position in Pozières and on that day did not suffer any casualties. So there remains only the outcome of just over four days of fighting to be counted. The calculation presents an appalling picture! What a state this superb battalion had been reduced to as a result of these few days of battle of changing fortunes under the violent fire of enemy heavy artillery! The battalion commander, Hauptmann von Schauroth, was wounded, but still with the troops. His Adjutant, Reserve Leutnant Kohbieter, was dead and left lying on the battlefield. His replacement as Adjutant, Reserve Leutnant Cann, was wounded and still at his post. From 1st Company, Landwehr Leutnant Verholen was wounded, Leutnant Behnke was wounded and missing. Offizierstellvertreter Staudtmeister was wounded. In addition there were twenty-two dead, eighty-nine wounded and ninety-two missing. From 2nd Company, Leutnant Pielock was dead and Leutnants Collinge and Langhoff were wounded. There were also forty dead, seventy-five wounded and twenty-five missing. From 3rd Company,

Reserve Leutnant Graw was wounded and there were thirty-eight dead, fifty-one wounded and seventy missing. From 4th Company, Reserve Leutnant Burghardt was dead and Leutnant Finkenstedt wounded. To these must be added thirty-four dead, fifty-one wounded and ninety-eight missing.

"So in four days and not counting losses in the Machine Gun Company, the total amounted to nine officers, one officer deputy, and 685 other ranks. Again and again the questions were asked: 'Where is this soldier? Where was so and so left? Who saw him last and where?' - Yes where were they, all those whose name had to be entered in the nominal roll under that unholy heading, 'Missing?' That was a dreadful word for the parents and siblings, for all relations whose thoughts back in the homeland were directed day by day and hour by hour, waking or dreaming, towards the hoped-for safe return of their father, uncle, brother, son, husband or grandson.

"'Missing!' in other words, 'We do not know what has become of him. Perhaps he is lying in a hole in the ground, torn apart by a shell, perhaps he has been killed while acting as a runner and carrying a message through a hail of shells, maybe he was a signaller and died isolated and alone while out repairing a cable. He could have been buried alive beneath the ruins of a house or down in a dugout, which did not withstand the shock. Perhaps he sank exhausted into the wet clay. Possibly he was wounded and fell into the hands of the enemy when he had no means of returning. The hopes of many were concentrated on this last possibility and certainly one or two families were lucky enough to be reunited after the war with those who went missing on the Somme. But, sadly, it is certain that many of the missing never returned, could never return, because, soldiers brave to the last as they were, they had already spent years slumbering somewhere beneath foreign soil.'"

During the incident in which he was wounded, Hauptmann von Schauroth was witness to several courageous acts by men of Infantry Regiment 190, who were supposed to be withdrawing, having been relieved. As soon as he was well enough to do so, he sent a full description to the commanders of 1st and 3rd Battalions Infantry Regiment 190, in order to ensure that those deserving of medals received them.

*Hauptmann von Schauroth Commander 1st Battalion Lehr Infantry Regiment[11] 4.*

"In what follows, I wish to draw to the attention of the battalions to the outstanding courage shown by some of their officers and men during the Battle of the Somme. Unfortunately I do not know the names of the officers and men concerned, but perhaps they may be established. During the morning of 7th July 1916, I requested permission from the commander of Grenadier Regiment 9, to whom I was then subordinated, to advance with the remnants of my unit, 1st Battalion Lehr Infantry Regiment (two platoons), from Pozières to La Boisselle via the Lattorf Trench, in order to come to the aid, or at least to prevent two of my companies, who were deployed in the area of 1st and 3rd Battalion Infantry Regiment 190 and who were outflanked on both sides by the British, from being taken prisoner. It was around midday when, at the head of my small reserve, I met up with my two companies, as well as those of 1st and 3rd Battalions Infantry Regiment 190, who were retiring slowly and in perfect order along the line of the Lattorf Trench between Cross Trenches II and III. After long and courageous resistance, they had had to yield to the British pressure on both flanks.

"When I began to let the small brave band move through to the rear, so that I could push forward with my two fresh platoons, several officers and men of 1st Battalion Infantry Regiment 190 stayed with me on their own initiative and made known their firm intention of advancing with me towards their former position, in which they had passed hard days with many casualties. The situation was extremely threatening for all of us. The enemy was advancing towards us along the Lattorf Trench and were only about twenty paces from us. The trench was under constant heavy artillery fire on both sides and the left flank was wide open for around 1,000 metres to Jägerhöhe [Hunter's Hill].

"In an effort to gain the line of Cross Trench II, we threw hand grenades at the British in Lattorf Trench and soon we reached this, our first objective. Suddenly to our left flank and in rear of us, a line of enemy infantry, in about two company strength, appeared from the direction of Contalmaison. It was hardly one hundred metres away. They closed to within fifty metres and 150-200 metres to our rear along the line of the light railway, before we were able to halt them temporarily with hand grenades. The British then took cover and brought rapid small arms fire down on our badly shot up trench. At this moment of extreme danger, a bugler of 1st Battalion Infantry Regiment 190 climbed up on the parapet of the trench and blew 'Advance at the double!' several times. Unfortunately it was not possible to get this man's name. I also lacked the time to discover the names of two officers of 1st Battalion (an Oberleutnant and a Leutnant), who were near me the whole time in the Lattorf Trench and constantly displayed outstanding bravery. From what I observed, both these officers and the bugler merit the award of the Iron Cross First Class. I should like to stress that the courageous behaviour of these two officers and the bugler inspired us all and increased the will of our small group to resist. As a result, we succeeded further through a constant fire fight, which brought us ever closer to the British, in holding them off, so that, with the exception of the wounded, whom we had to leave behind, we were able to escape from encirclement and to resume our resistance in front of Pozières.

"To my regret, I did not see the officers or the bugler again after we reached Pozières, so I assume that they fell dead or wounded into the hands of the enemy.  Should they still be alive, I wish to bring their courageous behaviour to your attention.  It may help identification if I mention that I was wounded in the head in the Lattorf Trench by a shell splinter which was bandaged on the spot by an Unteroffizier of 1st or 3rd Battalion Infantry Regiment 190.  This individual was also very calm and brave in his actions and is worthy of a decoration too.  Finally I wish to mention that my two company commanders, whose companies were operating in the areas of 1st and 3rd Battalion Infantry Regiment 190, reported unanimously that the remnants of these battalions fought superbly during these severe battles."

It is known that at least one of the officers concerned received his medal and on Monday 14th August 1916, Regimental Orders had the following entry:

"May the shining example of these courageous men inspire us all to similar heroic deeds, so that we shall truly merit the honour of belonging to Infantry Regiment 190.

Signed von Rogister<br>Oberstleutnant and Commander Infantry Regiment 190"

Having beaten off minor assaults in the days following 1st July, on 6th July, it was decided to remove, once and for all, the British pocket of resistance which was still holding on near Thiepval in the 'Meisennest' in C2.* The attack was mounted jointly by men of Bavarian Reserve Infantry Regiment 8, Reserve Infantry Regiment 15 and Infantry Regiment 185, who attacked from three sides following a preliminary 'German field-howitzer concert'.[12] The attack went in during the early hours of 7th July and after a short but hard fight, the pre-1st July line was once more in German hands.  Several prisoners were taken, including Lieutenant Lewis H. Neville, Machine Gun Officer of 1/5th Battalion York and Lancaster Regiment, who drew their attention to the presence of his commanding officer, Lieutenant Colonel F.H.S. Rendall, who was lying wounded in the trench. The Germans were amazed that the defence of such a tiny section of captured trench had been the responsibility of so senior an officer. This small, but sharply contested, action had cost a number of casualties on both sides:

*Leutnant Petersen Reserve Infantry Regiment 15*[13] **5.**

"Amongst the dead were two extraordinarily capable officers. Leutnant Fred Rauschenbach, who in the tranquillity of the Logeast Wood in premonition of his death, had passed me greetings to his girlfriend and to Leutnant Kaiser. He returned on 10th [July]. He had been wounded by two bullets to the head. Enthusiastically he described the assault, his eyes shining. Then he fell silent and reflective. He thought about the severe casualties of his company and his friend Fred. Suddenly he began to suffer

---

* 'Meisennest' was a small strongpoint in the front line, approximately 500 metres south of Saint Pierre Divion.

a searing headache. His eyes were burning. He had been hit harder than he had realised. On 16th our fine comrade died at the field hospital in Vélu. With his passing, the Battalion lost a model officer, a cheerful comrade who was always ready to help others, its sunshine..."

To the south of Thiepval the battle continued to rage with great ferocity. The high attrition rate amongst the defenders continued to sap the strength of the reinforcing units, so with one crisis fusing into the next, the situation became extremely confused. Pushed to the limit of human endurance, somehow the defenders hung on grimly. Discipline held up, courage was not lacking. The men holding this vital area did their best and for a while their best was good enough to prevent further progress either against the village of Pozières or Thiepval ridge.

*Leutnant Wernich Reserve Infantry Regiment 15[14]* **6.**

"The higher staffs press, urge and commit. But we know all about Pozières. During these days, signallers, repair teams and runners were all fully aware of their duty to their comrades and worked brilliantly. Their dedication, their faithfulness, their tenacious skill, saved the sector from falling. Our main concerns were resupply of munitions, water and food and casualty evacuation. The commanders of two medical companies came forward each evening to be briefed. At the main dressing station at Courcelette Chateau, which had been commanded by our Regimental doctor, Oberstabsarzt Dr Köhler, since 7th July, work went on at an exhausting pace day and night. Casualties streamed there from the artillery and all the reserve positions. There were always casualties from the troops who came forward at night to dig and amongst the carrying parties, so that each day the stretcher bearers had to search the entire battlefield. A great deal was demanded of the quartermaster's staff, so they too understood what a major battle meant!... More and more units were subordinated to us...gradually we incorporated six battalions from 2nd Guards Reserve Division, until by the 18th the entire front line of our sector was held by three unrelated battalions..."

*Hauptmann von Forstner  Reserve Infantry Regiment 15[15]*  **6.**

"[During the night of 6th-7th July] we were stood-to about six times. The terrain from Ovillers to Hardécourt was under drumfire. The fiery battle, fought out under cloudy skies, was grotesquely beautiful. The concentration of fire was quite remarkable; the shells spewed out long red fiery strands constantly. Where had these tens of thousands of shells come from? Not the slightest clue could be discovered; apart, that is, from the spectral flashes lighting up the horizon. Then as it became light, captive balloons began to ascend: five – ten – fifteen – twenty! Could it really be possible? Then came wing upon wing of aircraft. Towards 6.00 am things begin to get lively around us. The whole sector comes under fire. Around

8.45 am thick clouds of smoke appear. Smoke shells! They are trying to mask their attack! 'Bring down the defensive fire!' Leutnant Maier, that most likeable Württemberg Artillery Liaison Officer, who has supported the battalion magnificently, fires off red signal flares. In the drizzling rain the first few fail. At long last one ignites! And slowly, like the first heavy raindrops of a thunderstorm, shrapnel shells start to whiz over our heads, to explode in the clouds over there. Gradually they increase in intensity, until, after about ten minutes, they have gradually won the battle. That was just in time! The Tommies did not even risk leaving their trenches! Patrols which tried to attack in the early morning were beaten off with hand grenades. Now the main attack has been nipped in the bud.

"Two companies advanced on the Bavarians to our right and have been destroyed. During the day the enemy makes seven separate attempts to use smoke to disguise an assault, but the links to the artillery are maintained constantly. To the left is 1st Battalion of the *Maikäfer* [Cockchafers].[16] There is bitter fighting in that area. Around 1.45 pm comes the news that the first trenches have been overrun by the enemy, who are continuing the advance. No hand grenades or reserves are available! So launch everything that is to hand – two thirds of the 7th Company Infantry Regiment 185 and a platoon of Bavarians, with all the spare hand grenades! A hasty stop line facing south is manned by the last machine gun, one third of the 1st Company and sixty engineers. Around midday Major von Delius and Oberstleutnant Krause speak over the last surviving telephone line. 'Almost all the officers are dead or wounded. Reserves cannot get forward. The enemy is occupying the second trench of the Lemberg Position. Casualties are enormous...' At that, two companies of Infantry Regiment 186 are despatched to advance to Thiepval South via Thiepval North. This essential communication takes place during the moments the line is still operating. It is all thanks to the superhuman repair work of the signallers.

"Brigade orders: 'The Hindenburg Position is to be recaptured tonight!' Oberstleutnant Krause counters: 'If I am to hold out, I need two fresh battalions!' Late that evening all is quiet, as quiet as a graveyard. Leutnant Maier estimates that we have fired 36,000 shrapnel shells! We feel that we have done our duty! The order to the company of Infantry Regiment 186 goes out at 2.30 pm, but 7th Company Infantry Regiment 186 does not arrive until the following morning at 5.00 am. The company commander of the 8th Company reports one hour later, 'His men are at the end of the tether! They have been on the march for twenty hours! The 7th Company has occupied the dugouts allocated to him by 1st Battalion and refuse to vacate them!' Understandable! We take care of his dead beat men as best we can..."

It was the same story south of the Albert - Bapaume road and on the southern bank of the Somme, where the French army continued to exert pressure. The policy of not yielding territory and immediately counterattacking any Allied gains was causing casualties to rise alarmingly. Dog tired, battered endlessly by the artillery directed from the air and harassed by constant local probing attacks, the infantry held on grimly everywhere. It was an especially torrid time for Infantry Regiment 89, which was deployed down around Barleux in mid July and which succeeded in checking French progress in this sector, albeit at heavy cost.

*Grenadier Siegel 8th Company Infantry Regiment 89[17] 7.*

"[On 9th July] a direct hit landed between the right flank of the 8th and the left flank of the 7th Companies. The bloody consequence was a total of fifty comrades killed or wounded. It was an appalling sight as we worked feverishly to get the wounded into the dressing station dugout."

*Unteroffizier Normann 11th Company Infantry Regiment 89[18] 7.*

"It was 10th July and the French were battering our position heavily. In an outstanding manner, their artillery had ranged in on our trenches, so that very soon first here, then there, direct hits were landing in the trenches. We sought shelter in the small foxholes, which certainly kept splinters out, but were collapsed under the weight of direct hits. In this way the French were able to land two rounds in our section's stretch of trench and level it. During all this heavy fire a reservist, Hans Glockow, was on sentry duty and observing the enemy activity. All of a sudden, a shell which buried two of our comrades landed near him. Taking a swift decision, he grabbed a spade and, totally ignoring the explosion of shells around him, dug down until he freed the men; all this without even letting his pipe go out, then he calmly returned to his observation post and kept a sharp look out. The enemy launched an attack. Loudly and firmly he alerted the men to man the fire step, indicated the target and engaged the enemy with effective fire. The attack was beaten off easily. For his coolness under fire, Glockow received the Military Service Cross 2nd Class."

It had become clear that Gommecourt was once more a quiet sector, so, with the battles around Mametz Wood consuming reserves fast, 1st Battalion Reserve Infantry Regiment 91, which was resting out of the line in Bucquoy, was ordered on 10th July to move south, where it took part in an over-optimistic, ill-fated counter-attack on the 12th. Attacking south out of Bazentin Wood with only two companies on a front of 800 metres after a perfunctory preparatory barrage, it stood little chance of success. The northern edge of Mametz Wood was by now firmly held by the 38th (Welsh) Division, so as soon as the attack was halfway across the open ground between the two woods, a hail of British rifle and machine-gun fire stopped it in its tracks. Nothing had been gained and losses to the 2nd and 4th Companies were severe. The survivors then joined a miscellany of units which

German Artillery units parading across Pariser Platz near the Brandenburg Gate, Berlin: Summer 1914.

The Kaiser and Crown Prince Wilhelm, dressed in the uniform of the Totenkopf-Husaren (Death's Head Hussars) review troops about to depart for the fighting in France and Belgium.

German infantry confidently advancing to contact in France in late summer...

...only to be cut down in their thousands by the concentrated fire of 75mm field guns, machine guns and rifles.

The first shallow trenches and dugout command posts appear along the front: autumn 1914.

The first rudimentary protective equipment against gas: spring 1915.

By 1916 German trenches on the Somme were fully developed, forming a formidable and complex defensive system.

Generalleutnant Freiherr von Soden, the brilliant Commander of 26th Reserve Division, who was the primary architect of the bloodiest day in British military history.

German miners at work: autumn 1915.

A German mine exploding in the Dompierre area: autumn 1915.

A giant mine crater near Fay which has been incorporated in the German front line: early 1916.

NOTICE

BOCHE · TRENCHES · CAPTURED · BY
BRITISH · H · S · W · OF · BAPAUME · JULY·1ˢᵗ·TO·14½
FRONTAGE · 16 KILOMETRES DEPTH 8 KILOM⁵
12000 HUNˢ · PRISONERS · 60 GUNS TAKEN
5 · 21 C·M·MORSERˢ MORE ᴛᴏ FOLLOW
GOD · SAVE · KING · GEORGE · V.
SUCCESS ᴛᴏ OUR ALLIES

A British trench notice captured by Bavarian Reserve Infantry Regiment 12: August 1916.

French infantry attack north of the Somme: summer 1916.

At a forward aid post battle casualties were assessed and given emergency first aid prior to being evacuated.

Front line trench near Montauban being defended by 2nd Foot Guards: August 1916

By summer 1916, interlocking machine gun fire was a mainstay of the defence.

Allied prisoners being conducted to the rear by a cavalry escort.

German prisoners and their machine guns, being marched to the rear.

A classic portrait of a young Sommekämpfer.

Hauptmann Willy Lange Commander
2nd Battalion Infantry Regiment 27: a
man who drew inspiration and
strength from his religious beliefs.

Hauptmann Wilhelm Kellinghusen
Reserve Infantry Regiment 92, who
rallied his men with readings from
Blücher.

A dog fight during the air superiority battles. Note the man falling to his death.

The new command team. The Kaiser accompanied by Fieldmarshal Hindenburg and First Quartermaster General Ludendorff

A seriously wounded man is evacuated in a makeshift stretcher constructed from a wooden pole and a tent half or groundsheet. This was a standard front line procedure.

A member of Leibgrenadier Regiment 100 resting in a small foxhole in a front line trench near Vermandovillers: September 1916.

Exhausted men of Fusilier Regiment 35 attempting to sleep in a muddy shell hole Grandcourt: November 1916.

A sentry from Reserve Infantry Regiment 74 in the Morval area: September 1916. Note the use of full body armour.

A German prisoner captured during the final days of the Battle of the Ancre: November 1916.

were holding the line from west of Bazentin Wood to Longueval. The stage was set for Fourth Army's attack against the Longueval Ridge, scheduled for the early morning of 14th July. "The 'Position' presented a dismal sight", wrote Reserve Leutnant Steuerwald of Reserve Infantry Regiment 91. "It had been laid waste by the drumfire of the past few days. The line of the trench could barely be seen. Only through superhuman efforts could the entrances to the remaining dugouts – there were no more than six or seven for the whole sector – be kept open. There was insufficient cover for everyone, because it was also home to elements of: 3rd Battalion Bavarian Infantry Regiment 16, Infantry Regiment 184, two sharp shooter groups and the 8th Company of Reserve Infantry Regiment 77. There was not a trace of a wire obstacle."[19]  In close proximity of Reserve Infantry Regiment 91 were also men from 3rd Battalion Infantry Regiment 165, the Recruit Company of the Fusilier Guards and part of 3rd Battalion Infantry Regiment 190. Together they formed a brave front, but hardly offered a cohesive defence to the forthcoming onslaught.

*Reserve Leutnant Borelli Machine Gun Sharp Shooter Troop 106*[20] **8.**

"During the night 13th-14th July, the enemy increased his fire to previously unknown intensity, eased up between 1.00 am and 3.00 am, then around 3.30 am opened a terrible drum fire once again. I ordered immediate readiness and everyone lay in waiting in the entrances to the dugouts. Just before 4.00 am I realised that the enemy was lifting his fire rather more to the rear. The sentry fired a flare and in the same second bawled, 'Get out, here come the British!' Everyone took up position in the shell craters. The enemy had advanced to within twenty to thirty metres of our position. They were surprised by the sudden burst of machine gun fire and our infantry made use of the opportunity to throw hand grenades into the shell holes to our front. All three machine guns were ready to fire in a trice and, by the light of illuminating rockets, we could observe their extraordinary effect. The enemy assaulted in about six waves. These were not dressed lines of infantry; rather they were concentrated groups of soldiers.[21]  My machine gun crews suffered heavy casualties because the British, who were sheltering in the craters directly to our front, could not be brought under fire and so were able to throw grenades with impunity into the area of the machine guns.

"Our shortages of grenades and flares made themselves felt and it was not until after dawn that we could see the individual groups of British troops lying on the ground and seeking cover in the shell craters. Because our ammunition was already running short, we were restricted to firing at large groups only, but we observed that we were having a good effect. The remainder of the unwounded British attempted to flee towards Mametz Wood. Apparently there were some British soldiers who wished to come over to us, but our men did not recognise this, so they were shot down. It seemed that the British carried large stocks of grenades on their waist belts because we saw that often our bullets were causing explosions. The attack could be regarded as having been completely and bloodily driven off. We could not, however, have dealt with a further British attack in similar strength, because both the infantry and my guns had fired off their stock of ammunition...Two machine guns had each fired 6,000 rounds and one gun 5,000 rounds. Just before the end, this machine gun was knocked out by hand grenades.

"Fifteen minutes after small arms fire in our area had died down, a British aeroplane was spotted. It had descended to about 100 metres over Bazentin le Grand. This drew our attention to the left and we noticed that, unfortunately, the enemy must have broken through in the region of Bazentin le Grand, because entire columns of British were moving up in this area. Soon after this we heard small arms fire to our rear, coming from Bazentin Wood and the hamlet itself. We were surrounded. The infantry attempted to drive the British out of the wood, by means of a bayonet attack. Heavy British machine gun fire prevented this. As a result, our men pulled back to the western edge of the wood, but they were unable to hold out there for long. At that my machine guns were completely isolated, so I ordered my gunners to remove the working parts and to withdraw under cover. Throughout the battle the gunners performed brilliantly, serving the guns all the time that they were unwounded. Of the twenty men who were with me in the final position, only one was unwounded when we withdrew. The machine guns proved their value, because I estimate the strength of the attacking British soldiers to have been more than two battalions. Our artillery fired well initially, but failed to observe the breakthrough in the area of Bazentin le Grand, due, I think, to poor visibility."

*Reserve Leutnant W Steuerwald Reserve Infantry Regiment 91*[22] **8.**

"During the morning of 13th July, the artillery fire eased slightly. Hauptmann von Rauchhaupt ordered that the part of 1st Company under Reserve Leutnant Kaufmann, which was still on the northern edge of Bazentin Wood, to move forward to the position, to extend the line of 4th Company and to attempt to link up the Sector of Major von Kriegsheim (3rd Battalion Lehr Infantry Regiment). The move succeeded. Manning our front line now were 1st, 4th and 2nd Companies... Could the position be held until 15 July?... Artillery fire came down heavily around 11.00 am. The troops had suffered casualties from the fire during the move forward and the attack which followed. Hour by hour the casualty list grew. How would we fare in the event of an attack which seemed to be ever more likely? It would be extremely difficult to move forward the Reserve Company or other support through the artillery fire. The same applied to trench stores and ammunition.  Our men had been rationed for three days, but the shortage of water was already making itself felt. There was still a well in Bazentin, but every time it was cleared out, it was hit by fire once more. The 3rd Company had made a huge effort to get water forward, but it was just a drop on a hot stone. The mineral water store in Bazentin, as well as the complete engineer depot, had been destroyed by enemy shelling.

"There was a dressing station for the wounded, but this had almost been wrecked by several direct hits...There was constant telephone contact with the Artillery Liaison Officer, but that was not worth much, because counter battery fire had almost completely accounted for our artillery. The Sector Commander, Oberstleutnant Kumme of the Lehr Infantry Regiment, was only reachable by telephone from time to time. All other information had to be passed using runners, who often did not reach their destinations. Only one single runner got through from Brigade and he brought – a Divisional order concerning administrative matters in the battle area! The situation was further worsened by the fact that Kriegsheim's men were relieved by two companies of recruits. Towards 1.00 am, the companies demanded material to construct a barbed wire entanglement, signal flares, hand grenades, ammunition and water. 1st Company had forty-five to fifty men left and the 4th Company reported around one hunded, some of whom were from 2nd Company. 2nd Company had sixty and the 3rd Company 120 men.  The company commanders all felt that a further attack on Mametz Wood had absolutely no prospect of success, but they hoped to be able to hold their positions if they had time to work on them.

"On the 14th July, the French national day, an attack by their British allies was entirely likely. The activity of the enemy artillery made this almost a certainty.  Fire increased to extreme intensity and involved all calibres.  It was dreadful.  8th Company Reserve Infantry Regiment 77 was reduced to its commander (Reserve Hauptmann Denicke) and his runner.  Our artillery had no chance of taking on the enemy batteries. It could not even seriously counter the forward move of the British troops. At around midnight strong patrols were detected moving forward.  The position was occupied.  No attack took place, but around 3.00 am 2nd Company observed strong infantry forces on the edge of Mametz Wood. The company was stood to, followed shortly afterwards by 4th and 1st Companies.  The enemy advanced in strong waves, occasionally even in assault columns.  Small arms fire and grenades were directed against the British ranks.  Three waves of attackers were beaten off.  One machine gun from Sharp Shooter Troop 77, which fired to the last round, caused the enemy heavy casualties.  Fresh masses pressed forward and there was heavy hand to hand fighting.  It was possible to hold the left flank of the position until about 4.00 am, but by then strong enemy forces had broken though to the left. They reached Bazentin le Grand, then soon afterwards Bazentin le Petit where, between 5.00 am and 6.00 am, Oberstleutnant Kumme was captured. As a result 4th and 1st Companies were rolled up from the left and even the rear.

"2nd Company managed to hold on and beat off all frontal attacks until 6.00 am, then they ran out of ammunition and hand grenades and, in addition, the enemy was through in the sector of their right hand neighbours. 3rd Company could not withstand the weight of the attack alone. It fought on holding the northern edge of Bazentin Wood until 8.30 am, then it was surrounded. At 2.00 pm the Battalion staff and that of 3rd Battalion Bavarian Infantry Regiment 16, with which it shared a Headquarters, was captured. The Battalion, which was right up to strength on 9th July, was in ruins. The three company commanders: Kaufmann, Milz and Lohse were dead and with them many of the best. Amongst the officers were numbered Leutnants Schnare, Scherrer, Wirtjes and Feldwebelleutnants Boß, Glaenzer and Schweitzer. Only Leutnant Blasberg and Feldwebelleutnant Bartels made it back and both were wounded. Six officers and 200 men went into captivity...At a Divisional Headquarters attempts were made to interrogate us. Again and again we were asked, 'How could it be that when we attacked after hammering the trenches for days on end, there were still battleworthy troops manning them?...'"

Just as the men of Reserve Infantry Regiment 91 detected some signs of British activity during the period which led up to the assault, so too did Bavarian Regiment 16, which was holding the longest stretch of the front to be attacked and which had patrols forward. The 16th was the last of the regiments of the Bavarian 10th Infantry Division, which had been moved north of the river in late June, to be involved at the main focus of the battle, but it had already suffered heavily during the fighting around Mametz and Trônes Wood. By 14th July, their 3rd Battalion, for example, was reduced to six officers and 230 men.[23] The attack, when it came, was every bit as traumatic as that directed against its sister regiment, Bavarian Reserve Infantry Regiment 6, on 1st July.

*Reserve Oberleutnant F. Gerhardinger 7th Company Infantry Bavarian Infantry Regiment 16[24] 9.*

"It was shortly after 3.00 am [14th July] when I was awakened by sudden drumfire. As the company commander and I scanned the area to our front there was nothing to be seen but smoke and fountains of earth. The enemy was bringing down fire of all calibres and shrapnel on the trenches and obstacles, but the sentries were all manning their posts. Those who fell were immediately replaced by their comrades. Our listening post forward succeeded in returning to the trench and reporting the advance of strong British columns towards our obstacle. From the noise which our patrol observed before the drumfire began, the entire hollow in front of the position appeared to be full of British soldiers. We called for defensive fire and the few guns that could still fire replied, but then the fire was lifted to the rear and great masses of British soldiers appeared in front of our obstacle. They took cover when the garrison fired at them... then Unteroffizier Hofer arrived from our left flanking platoon and reported that the British had broken through in the sector of the 6th Company and were already pressing forward to Longueval and round to our rear...[I was ordered to go to the threatened place] and, putting on a waist belt festooned with stick grenades and taking volunteers with me, I arrived on the right flank, where the courageous defenders had already gained a breathing space. They had already shot down more than half a dozen grenade throwers of a British Highland battalion, (absolutely first class human material) and were continuing to fire at the enemy, who were cutting the obstacle in front of the position and also those who were advancing in dense masses to Longueval...The men, especially the daring members of the patrol, some of whom were standing on the parapet, were pouring fire into the massed British ranks. The courageous Vizefeldwebel Stiedl was shot through the leg doing this...

"I shouted at the gunner of a heavy machine gun of the 6th Company, that he should bring down fire on the British soldiers who were heading for Longueval, but he did not respond. So I dashed from the trench to the gun. (My men meanwhile kept the heads down of the British in front of the obstacle with heavy small arms fire). I threw myself down by the gunner and saw that he was dead, shot through the temples. Hardly had I prised his cramped grip off the handles of the gun, pushed him to one side and tried to fire at the British platoon in the hollow road, than the weapon jammed. It had been hit in the breech by a rifle bullet. I yanked the belt out of the gun, grabbed another from the ammunition box, wrapped them around me and raced back to the trench through the fire of the British infantrymen, who were only twenty-five to thirty metres away in front of the obstacle... Meanwhile the British were firing at us from windows and holes in the roofs of Longueval. A super-heavy shell which impacted in the embankment of the road to Guillemont about three or four metres away, sent me and another man flying, but fortunately it was a dud...We then shot down a few sections of British infantry near Longueval from a range of eighty to one hundred metres. All these activities took place within ten minutes...then things got very serious. [At one point in a hand grenade battle] I was standing behind a parapet, when simultaneously British grenades landed on the parapet and the edge of the trench and fell down into the trench next to me. I only escaped from this hopeless position by instinctively grabbing the grenades which had fallen in the trench and hurling them out. They were still in the air when they exploded..."

The 7th Company was fortunate to be fighting at the extreme south-east tip of Longeuval, where there was a reasonable obstacle and good fighting positions. Nevertheless, after desperate fighting lasting throughout the day, it was obvious to Gerhardinger and his company commander, Oberleutnant Sheuring, that, outflanked as they were, to stay in their positions any longer would mean that they would all be killed, without achieving any useful further service for the defence. They decided, therefore, to abandon Longueval and to withdraw via Ginchy towards Guillemont. At 8.00 pm, they made their move and succeeded for the most part in dodging artillery fire and a hail of machine-gun fire from Deville and Trônes Wood. Eventually, after a hair-raising journey, they managed to reach Gueudecourt, where they dropped off a wounded man and Gerhardinger had a shrapnel ball removed from his hand. Part of the way along their route, they passed two recruit companies which were hastily attempting to dig a stop line and Gerhardinger remarks that, 'that was all that remained of the German line here and had the British pushed on from Trônes and Delville Woods at midday, via the sugar refinery and north-east towards Ginchy and Lesboeufs, not only would the fate of our company, but also that of those two places have been sealed.[25] That opportunity, if such it was, only existed momentarily. As the steam went out of the attack, everywhere there were small signs, such as the arrival of the recruit companies mentioned above, that resistance was stiffening. By that same evening, men of Infantry Regiments 27, 163, 165 and Grenadier Regiment 9 were moving rapidly to reinforce the battered remnants of Infantry Regiments 26 and 184, who, together with Landwehr Brigade Ersatz Battalion 55, were stretched out in a weak line east and west of Foureaux [High] Wood.

Further to the west, almost the entire Bavarian Infantry Regiment 16 was killed or captured, but there were exceptions. Two members of the 1st Company, which fought just to the south-east of Bazentin le Grand, had a miraculous escape. By midday the tactical situation was hopeless. Casualties had been heavy, there was no more ammunition left and the company, like the remainder of the 1st Battalion, was surrounded. One man, however, was determined to take his chance. All around him men were taking off their equipment, tying white handkerchiefs to their weapons and holding them above the parapet.

*Vizefeldwebel H. Gareis 1st Company Bavarian Infantry Regiment 16[26]*

"I suggested to Leutnant Süssenberger that we should try to break out to the rear. Even if some of us were killed, it was better than being captured...[but] nobody would volunteer to accompany me...Leutnant Süssenberger, likewise my friends Vizefeldwebels Krämer and Wälisch, tried to dissuade me...but the thought of capture was unbearable. There was no end to the war in sight, I knew that my application for a commission was being processed and that my military career would be over if I were to be captured... I made ready and, leaving my knapsack and helmet behind, I wore only a cap and had a dagger and a pistol on my belt...My friends having tried and failed once more to prevent me from going, called out, 'break a leg!' and I took my leave...[On the way] I met a friend, Vizefeldwebel Resch [who agreed to accompany me] and we headed back along the communication trench...At 3.00 pm came the decisive moment, when we crossed the Bazentin-le-Grand – Longueval road. We agreed on a direction and hared across. We had hardly covered one hundred metres when we received machine gun fire from our right and rifle fire from the rear. I dived into the next shell hole, then a second later Resch joined me. He had been hit, but fortunately only in his right boot heel...We decided to wait for nightfall...We made a small mirror with my dagger and Resch's cigarette tin and observed the British digging in our second trench...and in front of Longueval...The hours until sunset were a torture; we expected to be discovered at any minute, but twilight came like a blessed relief.

"At about 10.45 pm we crept on towards the next hill, but found ourselves in a witch's cauldron. Small arms fire was flying in all directions, flares were going up. It was impossible to distinguish friend from foe...In the flashes we could make out the outline of Foureaux [High] Wood to the left and Longueval to the right. To get to Flers we had to pass between them, so we raced on. Flares went up again and we saw four figures appear in a cornfield to our front. 'Don't shoot, we're Bavarians!' we shouted and by the light of another flare we realised from their helmets that they were British. There was no way of avoiding them, so we rushed them bawling, 'Halt!' I pointed my pistol at them from about twenty metres, as did Resch. I fired twice and four rifles were thrown down. Before we had fully recovered our wits, the British were clinging to us, begging for mercy. We were the masters of the situation, so leaving behind in the cornfield one man who had been shot, we set off with other three. Resch, who could speak English, questioned the British corporal, who said that they had recently arrived from England, that they had deployed 1st May and that they had been sent out on patrol...They had a dreadful fear of the German 'barbarians'. One of them, a very young lad, asked me if they would now be shot, or if they would become prisoners and be set to work. He pressed his cigarette case into my hand, but I did not have the heart to take it...

"Carefully we made our way back to Flers. A flare suddenly went up, accompanied by the word of command 'Feuer!' [Fire!]. We threw ourselves down and a hail of small arms fire went over our heads. Together the two of us bawled repeatedly, 'Don't shoot. We're Bavarians!' Some time later things went quiet. Resch and I stood up and shouted once again not to shoot and that we were Bavarians. This brought more fire from the right. We took cover again and were fired on once more by the people to our front, as though we were part of an advancing enemy line. We were less than one hundred metres from the German lines and could tell from the words of command that we had Prussians in front of us. During the next pause in the firing, we stood up and shouted, this time in a dreadful rage, 'Don't shoot, we're Bavarians!' Then a voice replied, 'Anyone can say that.' We replied, 'We're Bavarians and we have three British prisoners.' Resch made the three of them stand up and now we were greeted with shouts of joy. Some of the Prussians rushed up to us and led us through their lines to their company commander.

"After a confrontation with the Prussian platoon commander, a reserve leutnant, who had given the order to fire and to whom I gave a piece of my mind, so forcefully that in other circumstances it would have led to a court martial, we explained the situation to the front...The prisoners and we were led to Regimental Headquarters...where we were congratulated. One of the officers asked us if we wished to conduct the prisoners to the rear, or if we wished to leave it to them. We agreed to this – something which we later regretted bitterly –[27] because we were so dog tired that we were grateful only to have to drag our own bones to the rear...[In] Flers we heard that the Regiment was assembling in Le Mesnil. Utterly exhausted, hardly able to put one foot in front of the other...we found them in Le Mesnil. We were the last to return to the Battalion..."

When the remnants of Bavarian Infantry Regiment 16 finally assembled in Beaulencourt on 15th July, it was established that its total casualties during the two weeks of fighting, amounted to seventy two officers and 2,559 other ranks.[28] Hauptmann Killermann assumed command temporarily and issued a Regimental Order, which included a message of praise from Generalleutnant von Lindeqist, Commander of the 3rd Guards Division, for the performance of the Bavarians. Then he sat down and produced a short report to the Commander 10th Bavarian Infantry Division, which summarised the state to which the Regiment had been reduced:

"Beaulencourt, 15 July 1916, 9.15 pm

"After obstinately defending the position between Bazentin le Grand and Longueval for the past fourteen days, the Regiment was more or less wiped out during the course of yesterday. The remainder, following the arrival of fresh troops and reinforcements, pulled back to Beaulencourt and will move tomorrow to Le Mesnil. Missing are: the Regimental Staff, the staffs of the 1st and 3rd Battalions, the Machine Gun Company (plus its weapons) and Machine Gun Sharp Shooter Troop 87, which was subordinated to the 1st Battalion. In addition the Signal Platoon is missing.

"The current fighting strength is as follows:

| | |
|---|---|
| 1st Battalion | One officer and 147 other ranks |
| 2nd Battalion | Six officers and 365 other ranks |

| 3rd Battalion | One officer and 111 other ranks |
| Machine Gun Company | Twenty-one other ranks |
| Machine Gun Troop 87 | Fourteen other ranks |
| Machine Gun Troop 44 | One officer and thirty other ranks |

"I have assumed command of the regiment for the time being. Oberleutnant Scheuring is commanding the 1st Battalion, Oberleutnant Schwub the 2nd Battalion and Hauptmann Hunglinger the 3rd Battalion. Almost all of the men listed above returned minus their equipment and some do not even have a weapon. They include many who are lightly wounded or suffering from the effects of gas. I assess the battleworthiness of the combined forces listed above as extremely low after the unbelievably strenuous and destructive fighting since 1st July...Because nothing is known of the fate of Headquarters 20 Infantry Brigade, which was also located in Bazentin, this report is not being sent via the normal channels...I have neither received direction on how to proceed, nor do I expect any, from Headquarters 3rd Guards Infantry Division...I request instructions concerning reorganisation and future tasking...'[29]

Amidst all the fighting, for many soldiers the Somme experience was one of having to endure, impotently, endless artillery fire, heat, hunger and thirst without being able to respond in any way. The experience of the men of Reserve Infantry Regiment 15, engaged during the middle of July in a see-saw battle for Pozières, is typical.

*Reservist Rabe 11th Company Reserve Infantry Regiment 15*[30] **6.**

"Because there were no dugouts, we sheltered in shell holes. With the help of a mate, I dug mine down a bit deeper. Lying flat out, we carefully lifted thistles and other shrubby weeds, which we planted around the rim of our shell hole to give us cover from view. We lay in this hole for three and a half hours, unable, because of the heavy fire, to move or be relieved...Frequently we also sheltered in foxholes with our legs drawn up, or we would scrabble our way from shell hole to shell hole, linking them together. The water was green and full of muddy clay, but we had to use it to brew coffee, because the ration parties could not get through to us. We were always short of bread. On one occasion the section was able to share a bottle of wine. Once came the shout 'Tommy is attacking!' We waited in painful impatience, and looked forward to giving him a warm reception, but not a single Tommy appeared! What a shame, what a bloody shame! I had dug myself in so well and was equipped with piles of hand grenades and ammunition. We felt very certain of ourselves. On the 21st we were relieved and made our way back in small groups to a rendezvous between Ligny and Thillois [sic], having negotiated a gas attack on the way. There we received our first hot meal. It comprised a porridge of barley with baked fruit. The band played: 'Victoriously, let us defeat the French!

Let us die a brave hero's death.' We were down to a strength of about four
sections and when the losses dawned on us, many of us shed a tear."
By mid July it had become clear to General von Falkenhayn that the intensity of the
fighting and the number of formations to be handled meant that the span of
command was too great for Second Army Headquarters alone to handle. No fewer
than twenty divisions were now involved. The front was reorganised, von Below
becoming responsible for the forces north of the river at the head of a new First
Army, based at Bourlon, whilst, south of the river, General der Artillerie von
Gallwitz was appointed Commander of  Second Army and simultaneously was
made Commander of 'Army Group Gallwitz', which combined the two. Although
in the event, this was a temporary arrangement, which was superseded when
Crown Prince Rupprecht assumed the role of Army Group Commander in late
August, von Below, naturally enough, had immediately taken issue with the
implications of the proposal and it has been suggested that Falkenhayn had
originally intended to place von Below in overall charge.  Gallwitz, however, was
senior to Below, so he refused to be subordinated to Below and Falkenhayn, who
needed the services of Gallwitz, felt obliged to acquiesce to his demand.[31] Crown
Prince Rupprecht was once more not impressed.

*Crown Prince Rupprecht of Bavaria - Diary Entry 17th July 1916*[32]

> "General von Below is justifiably sickened by this slight. The guilt for
> the reverses which his Army has suffered lies with the Army High
> Command, not him.  They ignored his reports and took no account of his
> requests for reserves.  When, at long last, reserves did arrive, it was too
> late. They arrived in dribs and drabs and had to be deployed immediately
> to plug gaps.  As a result there has been such a mixing of formations, that
> nobody knows what is happening."

This complex mixture of units in the line did indeed make life complicated for all
levels of the defence.  Administration of the engaged forces became a nightmare for
those involved.  Field kitchens to support men of the Fusilier Guards, as well as
Infantry Regiment 185 and Reserve Infantry Regiments 15, 77 and 91 were all
clustered together to the north of Courcelette, so carrying parties not only had to
dodge British harassing fire, but also compete for space in Stockachergraben
[Stockacher Trench], which was the only one leading forward still fit to use.
Stumbling around in the dark, with heavy loads to deliver to groups almost
randomly scattered in the forward positions, was extraordinarily difficult.
Nevertheless a sense of humour generally prevailed.  The stock reply to all
questions relating to the whereabouts of particular sub units was, 'I'm afraid I'm a
stranger here myself!'"[33]

Confusing by night and muddled up by day, the nature of the fighting in mid-
July led to all sorts of strange encounters. "Reserve Leutnant Eggert captured a
British second lieutenant [near Pozières] during the night 19/20th July.  This
officer had entered our trenches during a British hand grenade attack, when he

suddenly came across Leutnant Eggert. The latter had the presence of mind to intimidate him by shouting loudly and to wrench the pistol out of his hand. The British second lieutenant followed him willingly as a prisoner, explaining away his conduct by saying that he was only just nineteen."[34] Meanwhile the battle for Pozières continued to intensify and to cost the defence an increasingly large casualty list.

*Unteroffizier Klußman 5th Company Reserve Infantry Regiment 77*[35] **11**.

"Wounded and soldiers coming towards us looked like mud men. From top to toe they were covered in filth... In Flers we witnessed an appalling scene: an engineer company, which was being issued with grenades whilst taking cover from aerial observation under a clump of trees, received a direct hit. A bloodcurdling shriek rent the air! The horse of the transport commander, Unteroffizier Louis Deppmeyer, was hit by a splinter and stampeded... around Pozières fire of the heaviest calibre was falling on our trenches. We sat huddled in our dugout smoking pipes, cigars and cigarettes by the feeble light of a candle to calm our overstrained nerves because, with one hit, we could all be killed. The overhead cover received five direct hits. It held firm, despite the fact that the earth trembled and shook. Things did not go so well everywhere. The commander of 7th Company, Reserve Leutnant Reusche, was buried alive three times in an hour and a half, but on each occasion he was dug out in the nick of time by his men... The air was foul, decomposing corpses spread a disgusting stink..."

While the battles for Pozières were still raging, the French army was also involved in heavy and costly fighting around Barleux. Finally, on 20th July, they succeeded in driving in the German position. It was a desperately sad day for the men of Infantry Regiment 89, who lost some of their very best leaders and men during the course of the fighting.

*Offizierstellvertreter Schlacht 2nd Company Infantry Regiment 89*[36] **7**.

"Leutnant von Oertzen fired standing unsupported at the assaulting enemy and shot them down until eventually he met his death.[37] With his passing we lost one of our finest. He was a courageous officer who was always to be found at the point of danger and never flinched at the bullets. We mourned him sincerely, even though we were never able to recover his body. We missed him badly in later battles. He always put the company before himself. Closely linked to him was his runner, Gefreiter Almstädt, a carpenter from Schmadebeck. The two of them were inseparable; they went everywhere together. Whoever could not pull back during this attack was either killed or captured by the French. An awful fate awaited Reservist Wilhelm Lange, a shepherd from Güstrow, who, having been captured, was conducted away by the French. He was severely wounded during this process and was left lying between the lines. For several days he had to stick it out amidst the artillery and mortar fire, with nothing to eat or drink. Eventually comrades from 3rd Battalion heard his cries and finally rescued him from his desperate situation."

Once Trônes Wood finally fell to a determined assault on 14th July, the battle line was pushed forward to the proximity of Guillemont, with the first determined attacks beginning almost immediately. From the very start, the fighting in this area was amongst the most savage and drawn out of the entire battle.

*Reserve Leutnant Richard Sapper Artillery Liaison Officer Field Artillery Regiment 116[38] 12.*

"'I am reporting for duty as artillery liaison officer to the Battalion!'[39] Somewhat breathlessly, I reported thus during the early morning of 20th July 1916 at the Battalion Command Post in Guillemont, because the last 500 metres of road that I had covered were under heavy artillery fire. In an endless series, heavy British shells had torn up the road surface or had landed left and right of it, boring down into the soft soil of the fields, exploding with ear-splitting detonations and sending razor-sharp fragments and heavy clods of earth in all directions. The command post of the Saxon battalion[40] to which I had been sent was on the eastern edge of the little village of Guillemont. It was located in a mined dugout seven metres deep, which was equipped with two entrances and was approximately 500 metres behind the front line which ran along the western edge of the village. A table stood in the passage way which was one metre twenty centimetres wide and at it the battalion commander and his adjutant were poring over maps and plans by the light of a smoky candle. I was allocated a tiny workspace at the table. Crouching on the floor, three artillerymen and three infantrymen manned the telephones. Half a dozen runners and Headquarters personnel squatted on the stairs of the dugout, so the place was completely packed. There was nowhere to stretch out and sleep. Only the commander had a box-like bed, an amenity that he was able to use only once for a few minutes during my four-day stay with battalion. For the first day of my attachment the battalion medical officer, who had been severely gassed, occupied this bed. Like all the other wounded and sick, he could only be moved to the rear during the night.

"Around midday the enemy artillery fire slacked off a little. The only exception was the stubborn firing of the British 'Big Bertha', a 380 millimetre shell, which, with extraordinary endurance and punctuality, hurled its coarse greeting at the village every four to six minutes. This had been going on for days, every four to six minutes, day and night. Every four to six minutes the ground shook with the terrible impact and detonation of this giant shell. With a hellish crack, an enormous cloud of smoke and dust was shot skywards, followed by the clatter and crash of collapsing masonry. In our dugout, the light was extinguished and the nails loosened in the walls, so that caps, coats and weapons were flung in all directions. It was clear that even our seven metre deep dugout could not withstand the destructive power of this shell. After each impact, which did not crush our protection, we were conscious of relief that fate had granted us another four to six minutes before we might be forced to turn our back on life, having been buried alive, charred or suffocated. The temptation to concentrate on this thought to the exclusion of all else was so great that it took every ounce of willpower to keep working and to stay calm. Every day near misses by the 380 millimetre shells buried the entrances to our dugout, so that we had to go to work as quickly as possible with pick and shovel to regain our air supply.

"The earth heaved once more. A new thunderclap hurt our ears and two men came gasping down the stairs together. Their hair and beards had been burnt off; the jacket of one of them was still smouldering. They were gripped by fear and they struggled to speak. 'E-e-veryone's dead! E-e-veryone's dead!' they croaked through distorted lips. It was two of the personnel of our telephone exchange, who had been based in a mined dugout, also seven metres deep, beneath a house directly opposite us. The last round had smashed the dugout and twenty-three men lay buried seven metres deep beneath the rubble. The two survivors had been up at the entrance of the dugout when the disaster occurred and had received the flash of the explosion in their faces. The rescue team, which was despatched immediately, could only recover a soldier's boot with the remains of a charred leg. The presence of carbon monoxide gas, which overcame one of the team, prevented further progress into the collapsed entrance. The twenty-three men in the dugout were lost.

"The day dragged by slowly and endlessly. With fixed stares men listened to the rising noise of battle. From one corner came the tortured breathing of the man from the rescue squad who had been poisoned and this sound blended with the quiet whimpering of the men from the telephone exchange, who had collapsed completely. Now and again the runners appeared; their faces drawn and unrecognisable with the shock and strain. They handed over the reports from the front line wordlessly and were sent out again with orders. My telephone contact with the Artillery Operations Centre had been destroyed beyond repair long ago. I had to use my telephonists as runners. By the end of the first day two of them had become gas casualties and not until two days later did I receive a man from a Prussian regiment and Kriegsfreiwilliger Hofer of 6th Battery as replacements.

"Towards evening, enemy artillery fire of all calibres increased to drumfire. Doubtless the enemy was about to launch an assault, just as he had against this point morning and evening for days past. Because there were no telephone links to the rear, I rushed up the stairs to the entrance of the dugout with a signal pistol and red and green flares. All hell had broken loose up there! Shells were landing everywhere with deafening crashes, enveloping the collapsing houses with their black clouds of smoke, boring down into the ruins, ploughing through heaps of rubble and sending showers of rock and pieces of metal flying into the air. Shrapnel shells burst with sharp cracks and flashes of light, smashing tiles with their showers of lead. Beams began to burn and above the flames countless white flares lit up the sky, their light casting grotesque silhouettes of the smashed and ruined houses. And there – Yes here we go! – searchlights came on, machine gun and rifle fire crackled along the trenches. I fired my red signal cartridges and from the trenches red flares were fired above the white ones calling for defensive fire. Angrily our field guns opened up to our rear and our mortars and howitzers joined in, hammering and banging away. Now at last the whole orchestra was present. I listened with glee to the whistling, roaring and gurgling of our shells, which crashed down amongst the British. Great work you gunners. Fire! Fire! Give them everything you've got! After about an hour the fire slackened. Reports arrived from the companies and the neighbouring battalions. Everywhere the attack had been beaten off, though it was a matter of hand to hand fighting in places.

"The following morning I accompanied the battalion commander round the trenches. Carefully we clambered over the ruins of the houses and through the countless craters which the shells had torn in the street, or panted away inside our gasmasks through the poisonous fumes of the gas shells, which the British had used in great quantity.[*] Again and again bursts of machine gun fire whipped along the destroyed village street, crackling peculiarly as the small bullets cut through the air to bury themselves in splintered timbers, or crash loudly into, or ricochet off, ruined walls. Then we came to the trench! – Trench? What trench? It was just an area of torn, ploughed up ground. In small holes, dug out with spades, crouched clay-covered grey bundles with weatherbeaten, lined faces and sooty hands. In some places lay long rows of dead covered with groundsheets, which provided additional cover. Enemy small arms fire thudded repeatedly into their lifeless forms. One man, screaming terribly, was pulled out from beneath the rubble of a buried dugout; another sat in a puddle of filth singing. His matted hair was plastered to his forehead; madness stared from his bulging eyes. As we passed, he gabbled to us that he had seen the Devil, yesterday, every day. It had been really comical – ha-ha! – he had even danced with him – and he cackled and clicked his tongue...

"A young man came up to me. His whole body trembled and he stammered repeatedly, again and again, the same question, 'When are we

---

[*] The British artillery had no gas shells at this time, so either Sapper is confusing poisonous fumes from normal high explosive shells with the contents of chemical shells. Or the French artillery was firing at the village.

going to be relieved?' Utterly exhausted, these brave men had held out under terrible fire in the front line for fourteen days, without relief, without sufficient food and had beaten off daily the most violent attempts at breakthrough by the British."

Alarmed by the turn of events, which now saw the British army pressing hard in Delville Wood and before High Wood, General von Below issued a secret amendment to his order of 3rd July on 17th July:[41]

*Supplement to Army Order I a 575 (Secret) dated 17th July 1916*

"Army Order

Despite my ban on the voluntary relinquishment of positions, apparently certain sectors have been evacuated without an enemy attack. Every commander is responsible for ensuring that his troops fight to the last man to defend the sector for which he is responsible. Failure to do so will lead to Court Martial proceedings.

This Army Order is to be made known to all commanders.

von Below"

Being forced to endure heavy shelling and assault by infantry was one of the two major experiences at trench level during the battle, but the other was that of counter-attacking, or advancing across open ground under fire, to bring succour and relief to hard-pressed comrades. On 25th July, 12th Company Infantry Regiment 76 was sent forward, together with 4th Company Grenadier Regiment 8, to try to reinforce Infantry Regiment 12, which had suffered heavy casualties during the fighting in the Delville Wood area since 20th July. An anonymous member of the company left a vivid description of what it meant to attempt such an operation during daylight hours.

*An Unknown Ersatzreservist 12th Company Reserve Infantry Regiment 76*[42] **13.**

"At approximately 3.00 am 25 July, guides arrived from Infantry Regiment 12. They reported that the British had broken into their position and that they had to have support. We were ordered to, 'Get ready' and so we were, in a matter of a few minutes. Hand grenades were distributed. A leutnant from Infantry Regiment 12 urged us to hurry. Our company commander leading, we set off in single file across country and through trenches to the Second Position... Here we dropped our knapsacks, fixed bayonets and on we went along a sunken road* which contained our dead and wounded. The barbed wire obstacle was still more or less intact. The ground rose a little and, in a few moments, we reached the crest, from which we had a good view over the battlefield. To our front was Delville Wood and, by the right hand corner of the wood, a few houses of Longueval were in sight. There was no time to enjoy the view. We doubled forward and, having been spotted by the enemy, came under

---

*This was probably the track which runs north from the area of the New Zealand Memorial to the ground between High Wood and Flers. The crest referred to is almost certainly the area of the memorial.

heavy fire. Shrapnel rounds burst near us, claiming several victims. They lay still or tried to pull back; there were more and more of them, some of whom sought cover in shell holes. A destroyed machine gun lay on the ground, half covered with earth. We ran on without stopping, lungs and legs giving it everything they had. We urged each other forward with shouts, as though it was a competition. Our orders were crystal clear: forwards, ever forwards, ignoring the wounded and those who had fallen. We had to come to the aid of our comrades forward. Without really being aware of it, we stumbled on half-right towards the village. Half-left of us, dug in on the corner of the wood, was an enemy machine gun, which fired on our ranks. This would be about 11.00 am. It grew hotter and it seemed to me that we must have come a kilometre at least.

"The company visibly melted away and finally we could see nobody. To our right was a shallow trench; probably the former communications trench between the first and second trenches. It ran north-south, parallel to the edge of the wood. We took cover in it, our platoon commander leading. Here, too, lay some of our men, dead and wounded. The wounded begged us for water, but their pleas fell on deaf ears. Although it was painful to us, we ignored them; we could not stay and help them. Our platoon commander shouted, 'Halt! Take a quick drink from your water bottles, then on my command we head for the wood.' A quick headcount revealed that there were twelve of us altogether, all that were left of 3 Platoon. Our platoon had been the last to advance. The other two had gone ahead, but where they were we could not discover. I had lost my water bottle, but got a swig from a mate. Across country, with another man, came the company commander, who had been at the head of the company. He saw us in the trench and called out to our platoon commander, 'S. Why don't you get forward?' In a flash the hunt was on again. Completely winded, we raced forward several bounds, taking cover between each in shell holes. After a few rushes our platoon commander was wounded. Another sprang to take over command, but we did not get much further.

"We stayed down in the shell holes, not really knowing where we were meant to go. A few members of the company were to our front, but we could not make ourselves understood above the racket. It was quite clear, however, that they knew as little as we did. The fire from the right had not let up and thudded into the ground, whilst the shrapnel balls whistled and flew through the air past our ears. I had found a fairly deep crater, which I shared with three others. We felt reasonably secure, but what were we to do? We were more or less opposite the village, so I felt that we needed to move as far to the right as possible. In the meantime we could tell from the increased artillery and machine gun fire that our fourth platoon was in a fire fight. A few raced across to join us, until there were thirteen of us sheltering in this shell hole. A gefreiter assumed command of this little group. Where should we head? We were 300-400 metres from the wood. That was certainly our objective. All our leaders were wounded and we knew nothing of the battle situation. The few men in front of us had apparently got too little protection, so the wounded and the two remaining fit men came running back. Had they stayed they would have been shot. The wounded attempted to get further to the rear and the serious cases lay where they were.

"We sorted ourselves out in the shell crater, taking turns to observe. In this way we saw a line of infantry advancing west of the wood. They were almost in step, their rifles under their arms and apparently hardly being shot at. That was partly explicable...The troops approaching the wood from a westerly direction were shielded from view by it and could approach it almost unnoticed... The wood was under heavy fire, but I could not make out who was doing the shooting. Branches and twigs were flying everywhere. Enemy aircraft were operating all over the battlefield. Flying fairly low, they gave horn signals from time to time. They were clearly indicating the whereabouts of thickly occupied shell holes to their artillery, which increased its rate of firing. We decided to act dead if they came our way, in order to conceal the fact that there were fourteen of us. It was about 6.00 pm. The fire had eased slightly...We were hungry and thirsty, but where could we find anything? Our equipment was in the second trench. The heat was unbearable. We had something to smoke which consoled us somewhat and allowed to forget our ticklish situation, despite the fact that nothing had really improved. Would we receive support? How many of our company could be left? Of course nobody could give a satisfactory answer.

"After lengthy consideration, it was decided to attempt to reach the communication trench a short distance behind us. Here we could organise ourselves better and also have more chance of contacting the others. We had a short distance to run across country, but that was no great problem. One by one we carried out this manoeuvre and most of us made it. We spread out along the trench, but in fact there were too few of us to defend the trench effectively in an emergency. We searched the equipment lying around for water, but without success. Either the bottles had been shot through, or they were already empty. The wounded lying in the trench here demanded water, but we had none ourselves. There was no way we could get them away from this shallow and fragmented trench. We could not help them, so we withdrew, crawling and dashing to the second trench. We placed ourselves at the disposal of the commander of another company, but he could not employ us and directed us to go to the Sector Commander. So off we went, taking a few of the wounded to the dressing station with us..."

The experience of the men of Infantry Regiment 76 was entirely typical of this period of the fighting – for both sides. Time and again during the fight for the woods, there would be a weak effort by a battalion or less. The units would be launched in attack or counter-attack, gain some ground, then be vulnerable to artillery fire in the salient that they had just created, or to further counter-action. In a battle, allegedly on a large scale, often only very small groups of men would actually be involved at the forward edge of the battle area and these would frequently be acting independently; almost randomly. This situation was to the advantage of the German defenders. It enabled them to make best use of their much depleted and over-committed artillery and allowed them for several weeks to continue the contact battle with the relatively small reserves that they had available. It was far from a neat and tidy method of conducting a defence, but it was effective and it enabled them to maximise the value of the superior battle experience of their men, even when their command structure was shaken by heavy casualties. At about the same time as Infantry Regiment 76 was disputing possession of Delville Wood, Infantry Regiment 72 was called upon to carry out a similar mission against Foureaux [High] Wood.

*Reserve Leutnant Störel 11th Company Infantry Regiment 72*[43] **14.**

" ...A runner arrives from battalion. 'The company is to send a patrol forward immediately to reconnoitre the situation.' The mission is given to Vizefeldwebel Kreuzmann and three men. They set off for the right hand corner of the wood. We watch until the four of them disappear in the haze. New order from battalion: '11th Company is to launch an immediate counter-attack against the edge of the wood!' After I have allocated troops to tasks and launched the widely-spaced first wave, the company commander, Leutnant Bornemann, appears. I brief him quickly on the situation... and he resumes command of the company... Suddenly Vizefeldwebel Kreuzmann appears by our right flank, being assisted by another man. There is blood streaming from his mouth and nose. He reports: 'The enemy has broken into the wood. The 12th Company is holding the edge of the wood. The right hand corner is unoccupied!' He himself has been caught in the blast of a heavy shell and buried. Now we know enough. I depart with the next group in the direction of the right hand corner of the wood. Just before we get there we catch up with the first wave. We have taken no casualties from high explosive shells or shrapnel. It is now broad daylight. Right of the wood the ground is blanketed with fog. Some rifle shots crack over our heads, but we can see nothing. From the line of riflemen comes the shout: 'The company behind us – go left!' Half left of us the edge of the wood is still occupied by German soldiers. We can see them in groups of two and three, engaging targets from the first of the trees. We need look no further, for our enemy is to our front. Soon we reach the edge of the wood. My bugler gives a short groan and collapses, shot through the heart! There!... suddenly there are British troops to our front! Like lightning we drop on one knee. I give a quick order and everyone pumps off several rounds into the fog.

"A cluster of men comes into view. 'There they are!' someone shouts. 'Go!' and with a '*Hurra!*' we fall on the Tommies. With raised rifle butts or rifles ready to fire, we plunge at the nonplussed British soldiers. They make one quick attempt at resistance, but quickly throw down their arms and gather in a small group. In no time we have them surrounded. With trembling hands, some pull money, others cigarettes, out of their pockets and offer us their treasures. Judging by the few shilling coins which one young lad wants to press into my hand for my consideration, it doesn't appear as though the poor devils place a very high price on their lives. 'Hey, what am I meant to do with that money?' laughs one of my men. 'Hand over your cigarettes!' Soon we are all enjoying a smoke. Musketier Stollerz, a tough old warhorse and simple soul from Upper Silesia, passes me a complete handful, beaming broadly and offers me a light, which of course I accept. The British are visibly relieved that none of them have come to any harm and their faces light up into broad grins. What must they have been told about the German barbarians, the Huns? When the rest of my men appear, there are a few long faces on the other side. Two German sections were opposing thirty British soldiers. Now of course it's too late! Gefreiter Amm and three men, one of them slightly wounded, march them off.

"In the meantime the sun has risen in the sky and the fog has disappeared. On the rising ground in front of us no British troops are to be seen. Occasional shells fall in the wood. Somewhere in the distance can be heard the tack! tack! of a machine gun. Otherwise all is quiet! 'Hey, that was fun!' I hear someone observe, laughingly. The determined faces of my men, bristly with unshaven beards and unwashed for days, are lit up in the morning sun. We need to get on. The wood is full of suspicious rustlings and cracklings. Carefully we creep along paths which lead diagonally forward into the wood. A shot!.. A British soldier has loosed a round off at us and leaps over a tree trunk to make his escape. I bring my rifle up into the aim... and he tumbles head over heels into the next shell hole. Another tries to take cover in a hole, which a heavy shell with a delay fuze has made in the root plate under a tree. He dives head first into the hole, but his hips get stuck and he hangs there, caught up in the splintered but tough tree roots, helplessly presenting us with a view of his backside. Laughing, some of us drag him out by the seat of his trousers and set him off in the direction of our rear area. Numerous dead British soldiers lie in the shell holes, or behind tree trunks, which the hurricane of shells has turned into matchwood.

"Our route takes us round a curve to the right and leads to a small clearing. On the right hand edge and hidden by undergrowth is another detachment of British soldiers. They do not seem to be a united team, because they are all talking at once and waving their arms around. In the middle, a very lanky Tommy is trying to calm them down. Unnoticed, we creep up to them then, with a determined spring and a shout of '*Hurra*', we surprise this careless group. They throw away their arms and put their hands up as one. Simple young lads, they turn their shocked faces towards the lanky chap who is their leader. Then the whole business with money and cigarettes begins all over again, just like the first time. Whilst we are checking them for hand grenades there is a small incident which could have had serious consequences for us if we had not been dealing with such obvious beginners at the art of war. Twelve Germans against twenty-five British troops is not exactly good odds, even though we are armed. One of us seems to get a bit close to one of the British, or perhaps the prisoner misunderstands him. Anyway there is suddenly a loud exchange of words which looks as though it might come to blows. The Tommies become restive, perhaps in fear, perhaps with the intention of resuming resistance. 'Get back!' I shout to my men, 'take aim!' Twelve rifle barrels are trained at the enemy. That works! The leader pacifies his men and finally succeeds in calming them down. Then he turns to me and holds forth about comradeship amongst enemies.

"I make him understand that I share his view. If only all the British thought the same, things would be fine. As it is we need to check them for hidden weapons. He accepts this and asks for a field dressing for a wounded man lying behind a tree trunk. I hand him mine and he bandages him. The leader is an impressive man. He is clean shaven and is wearing gold-edged pince nez spectacles – I am amazed that he has not already lost them. He resigns himself to the inevitable and asks me where he his men should go. With a heavy heart, I allocate three men as escorts, because I am now down to nine men, but I dare not let them proceed alone. There are enough weapons of dead British soldiers lying around the wood to equip a complete company. With heads down, they set off down the woodland path.

"What now? There is no sign or sound from our company. Probably it has been deployed elsewhere after it went left at the wood edge. There is still the crackle of rifle fire to our front. Perhaps some Germans are still holding out in the old front line on the front edge of the wood. After a short council of war, during which Stollerz displays great talent as a field commander, we decide to move forward. In a small group we head across a clearing, where things get tricky. The British artillery seems to have been concentrating on this section of the wood and tree trunks are laying higgledy piggledy everywhere; some of them with their root plates torn out of the ground. Splintered branches and shell craters of enormous diameter block our way, but we plough on. Tripping, scrambling and jumping we make our way forward. Now we are in amongst an abandoned German howitzer battery. Forward. We are just climbing over a thick tree trunk when we receive a burst of machine gun fire that sends muck, splinters of wood, leaves and ricochets whistling and cracking past our ears. Like lightning we drop back into a shell hole and stick our noses back up to see what is happening.

"Immediately another burst flies overhead. Then someone shouts 'They're Germans!' Now we stick caps and helmets on our rifles and wave them, whilst exchanging cries of '*Hurra*!' The fire ceases. Shouts such as 'Come on!' and 'It's about time!' are heard. Delighted to find German comrades so far forward, we press on carefully. The wood thins and, there on the edge of the wood, are a few Germans and a machine gun in a fire position. A few more heads pop up. They all wave and shout: 'Extend the line to the left, but be careful, there are British troops over there!' We run the final twenty to thirty metres. A few grenades explode to our left. Too short! To be on the safe side, two British soldiers take flight. Breathlessly, we jump into the holes to our front. Thank heavens! We've made it. The joy of the gallant crew who have stuck it out here is enormous. They are from Infantry Regiment 165. For hours they have been battling against encirclement and against snipers who have been trying to pick off the machine gunners from shell holes. They cannot give me any information about the situation. All they know is that the British attacked after a short bombardment and broke into the wood. Their officers are all dead. Further right all is quiet, but they are not in touch with other troops. At least we have arrived at the right moment."

Leutnant Störel and his little band, having succeeded in reaching the front line, stayed to reinforce the survivors from Infantry Regiment 165. Within a short time, Störel, Stollerz and three others were wounded, but not before the precarious situation had been partially stabilised. Not all such efforts lacked success. Aided by the fog of early dawn, 1st Battalion Infantry Regiment 62, which was Divisional Reserve of the 5th Infantry Division at that time, launched a very successful counter-attack on 21st July. In his report, its commanding officer stated, **14**.

"At about 11pm on 20th July, 1st Battalion Infantry Regiment 62 received the order to recapture Foureaux [High] Wood, which had been lost the previous day. The order circulated rapidly round the Battalion, which was in reserve and occupying the cellars of a monastery in Eaucourt l'Abbaye [a monastic grange rather than a monastery] about 1,000 metres behind the front. According to the order the wood, which dominated our positions, was to be captured the following morning. I was to receive detailed orders from the Headquarters of a regiment [Infantry Regiment 72] of the Saxon-Altenburg Division, which was unknown to me, though the ground to be assaulted was familiar. In the darkness and under heavy enemy artillery fire, I left the shelter of the monastery cellars with my Battalion.

"The darkness and enemy fire made assembling the Battalion difficult...and it was not until 3.00 am that all were together. I moved forward to the appointed village[44] to receive my orders. The place was under very heavy artillery fire, because the enemy expected that it would be used as an assembly area for fresh assault troops. In the meantime, the Battalion was issued with ten grenades per man from an engineer depot. The artillery fire had eased somewhat and, in the grey of dawn, the area was blanketed by fog, which was of the greatest value for my attack. The frontage of the wood was about nine hundred metres. One hundred metres in front of it and more or less parallel to the newly gained position which the enemy had occupied, was a fold in the ground. I directed two companies, the 1st and 3rd, to attack and kept the remainder in reserve about six hundred metres from the edge of the wood. During the firing I got the troops to exploit the fog and to edge forward in groups. By now I and my staff had reached the Headquarters of the battalion we were going to relieve, where we were greeted with enthusiasm...The commanding officer was amazed that I had already given out my orders and that I intended to assault without a detailed reconnaissance and a full scale bombardment.

"Although we were only four hundred metres from the wood, it was invisible in the fog. I obtained valuable local information here. The assault group had by now arrived, so I briefed them fully about the situation and the enemy position they were to take. All surrounding friendly forces were informed about the attack which was to take place. As a final step, I reinforced the two assaulting companies with an additional platoon of the Reserve Company. Still under cover of the fog, we reached the fold in the ground and the temporary trenches which it contained. The fog lifted gradually. It was a beautiful July morning. After a short pause, the first wave crept up to within forty metres of the enemy. Everything was absolutely still, apart from artillery fire which fell behind us. The order to attack spread like lightning amongst the troops and, in a few seconds, the two companies had reached the enemy position and, in hand to hand fighting, had pushed on a further one hundred metres through a further two well-defended positions. I had immediately reinforced each of my flanks with a further platoon. Only the left hand corner of the wood remained in enemy hands after the initial assault. Here the enemy had constructed a regular little fortification, which had several machine guns built into it. The daring men of the 1st Battalion stormed the fortification repeatedly, until after fifteen minutes and, sadly, at the cost of heavy casualties, the enemy was defeated in an heroic close quarter battle. By 5.50 am the entire wood was ours and with it a large haul of machine guns and other small arms, not to mention around one hundred prisoners. News of the success of our assault caused great elation within higher headquarters and when I returned to Battalion Headquarters I received telephoned congratulations. The Battalion had only a few men killed. The number of wounded was somewhat higher, but still relatively light. So ended the glorious morning of 21 July."[45]

The attempt of the Australians to capture Pozières had at last been crowned with success on 23rd July, when the 1st Division finally succeeded in wresting control of the village from the defenders. Summoning reserves, the German launched a series of counter-attacks, one of which involved Infantry Regiment 157 on 25th July. This degenerated into bitter close-quarter fighting for the Schwarzwaldgraben [Black Forest Trench] and the north-west tip of the village.

*Unteroffizier Wabnik 3rd Company Infantry Regiment 157*[46]  11.

"During the afternoon the British succeeded in by-passing us. We now fought on two fronts. We threw hand grenade after hand grenade ceaselessly. We fired round after round from the rifles, until the barrels glowed red hot. Our courage began to falter in the face of overwhelming enemy strength, but Reserve Leutnant Neugebauer shouted loudly at us to hold on and threw one grenade after another at the British. Our casualties were high; one comrade after another fell to the floor of the trench, shot through the head. The little group of fighters shrank steadily. Some of the men were gripped with trench frenzy and launched themselves at the enemy with spades, only to be beaten to death with rifle butts. In front of us and behind us our dead and those of the enemy heaped up. Things continued like this until darkness fell. Then the enemy pulled back a bit and we could take a breather for a few moments... There were about twenty of us forced, because of the British attacks, into a fifty metre section of trench.

"We were surrounded on all sides by the British. Obstinately we hung on to our position and would not allow ourselves to be ejected. We could not have lasted very much longer, however. We had almost run out of ammunition and we had very few hand grenades. Our one and only machine gun had been knocked out long before. The British called on us in German to surrender. We replied with hand grenades. After it became somewhat quieter, we realised how serious our situation was. There could be no question of rescue; where would it come from? We prepared ourselves to be marched off to London. We destroyed the bolts of the weapons and waited. Morale was not exactly rosy. Leutnant Neugebauer, who was with us, tried constantly to keep us going. Suddenly the sentry on the right flank of the trench reported that a German soldier was crawling towards our position. It was a runner from Reserve Infantry Regiment 11 who was lost. Our comrade from Reserve Infantry Regiment

11 had made use of a shallow ditch in front of our position and so could close right up to it. We decided to make use of this ditch to make our escape. We discovered that altogether that sixteen of us, including Leutnant Neugebauer, were still unwounded. We agreed to crawl back at five metre intervals. Initially all went well, then the men began to get nervous and to run back bent double. The British spotted us and directed machine gun fire at us. We then simply ran back. Some of the men were killed or wounded. Physically completely drained, we landed in the reserve position of Reserve Infantry Regiment 11. We were down to eleven men. Five had fallen victim to British fire."

The intensity of these small-scale actions was such that the entire battlefield in and around Delville Wood, High Wood and Pozières was littered with corpses and seriously wounded men sheltering in shell holes. Towards the end of the month, 8th Company Reserve Infantry Regiment 76 from Hamburg was holding a roughly constructed line near to Longueval.

*Reserve Leutnant Walter Schulze 8th Company Reserve Infantry Regiment 76* [47] **13.**

"This morning [25th July] two British soldiers came over to us. As dawn broke, I saw a man about twenty metres away crawling towards us. He was working his way forward with his arms, with his legs dragging behind him. He must have been very severely wounded. Somewhat to the right of him a second was crawling gingerly towards our line. He seemed to have been shot in the leg, but soon arrived in our trench, whilst the other was still pulling himself forward in agony. I took a firm grip of my revolver. You never know! It was important to be careful. Finally he reached us. A weak smile creased his grey, pain-wracked face. His look of anxiety and trembling fear spoke eloquently, arousing sympathy. He was not dangerous. I reached out a hand and pulled him into the trench.

"Our medical orderly, Kühl, who had just arrived, bandaged him up and I questioned him. He implored us to give him a drink and though we had little ourselves, we gave him one. Then he lay back and is sleeping the deep sleep of total exhaustion. When he awakes, he will ask for another drink. The poor chap is at the end of his tether. As for his wounds, which were all over his body, they have got dirt in them, and are already suppurating. They stink dreadfully. He comes from Kent, is married and has four young children. Smiling happily he pulled a grubby, faded photograph out of his breast pocket and showed me a picture of his family. He was pleased and grateful to be allowed to be with us and not to be coming to any harm. The people opposite us had been taught to fear the 'Huns'. He presented me with a shoulder title with the letters in brass 'RWK' (Royal West Kent)...

"On 27 July another wounded British soldier arrived. In the grey dawn he was standing upright about thirty metres in front of our trench. We waved him away and shouted, 'Go back!', because we did not want to be bothered with him. Transportation to the rear is so problematic and we were having enormous difficulty evacuating our own dead and wounded. But he was deaf to our entreaties. One of the senior soldiers fired at him in his excitement. The man was quite helpless. Thank goodness the shot missed. We were very sorry for the chap. He must have been lying out there amongst his dead comrades, severely wounded and in agony, between the lines for a long time with nothing to eat or drink; beyond all help. So we waved him towards us and straight away he stumbled towards us, arms raised. He collapsed down into the trench and lay there motionless. To reach us had used up his last reserves of strength. We got a drink inside him and gradually he came round. He was an old soldier, with six years service at the garrison in Kent behind him. He was riddled with wounds from shell splinters, which were in a terrible state. He could barely move a limb and it was a complete mystery to him how he had managed to make his way to us. He asked me to reach in his pocket and take out two cap badges. They were the badges of the Royal West Kents, a unicorn reared up on its hind legs. I kept one cap badge myself and gave the other to an NCO...

"It was foggy this morning [29th July]. After the sentries had been relieved I had sheltered in a corner of the front wall of the trench and slept a little. To one side, in the early dawn, I could hear someone speaking about machine guns, dead British soldiers, bread pouches and razors and I woke up. There was a thick layer of fog all around. The half company had left the trench and crossed the cover in front of the position. I climbed up to join them. We looked around at the dead British soldiers. Most of them had appalling wounds, which had been made worse by the ceaseless drumfire of the past few days. Some skulls were only partly there. Stomachs and chest were torn open and ripped apart. Arms and legs lay all over the place. Many bodies had received direct hits and were reduced to shapeless lumps of flesh. Dreadful sights met our eyes everywhere we looked. Most of our soldiers were there to cut the ration pouches from the dead. It was well known that the British had good things, such as binoculars, cut-throat and safety razors that we did not just want to leave lying around in the clay.

"I extracted some biscuits from a pouch, which was lying on the ground and a spoon and fork to replace my cutlery which had gone missing. I also took a tube of hand cream, but I could not bring myself to cut ration pouches off the dead like the others. One man from 7th Company was about to cut a ration pouch from a British soldier lying in a crater, when he suddenly moved. Horrified, the man fled as though he had seen a ghost, but he came back with several others. The apparently dead man was, in fact, severely wounded. He had been out there between the lines since the last British attack during the night of 23 July. The fear that we would kill him had kept him and probably others, from attempting to reach our trenches. The cause of this was the fact, as explained to us by a British soldier whom we captured, that they had often been given an order not to take prisoners. They feared, therefore, that the situation would be similar with us. The 7th Company men carried him in unconscious and the first thing he asked for was a cigarette. A weak smile of joyful thanks spread across the anxious face of this severely wounded man as he was given one. How many such had died between the lines, without help and in unspeakable agony? Earlier, the day after we had carried out our relief in the line, the first platoon of the company came across a wounded and totally blind member of the 63rd, who had apparently been abandoned to his fate by his comrades, in their haste to escape this hellish place. Our ration party transported this poor unfortunate to the rear."

The early weeks of the Battle of the Somme were marked by total Allied air superiority, which made life almost intolerable for the defenders. Whatever they did, wherever they went, they were, or at least felt they were, under observation from the crews of balloons and aircraft which circled over them, directing artillery fire, or attacking them directly. Occasionally, very occasionally, they managed to turn the tables on their tormentors.

*Reserve Leutnant Seydel, Commander Machine Gun Sharp Shooter Troop 107*[48] **15.**

"At 6.00 am on 25 July, as I was standing outside my cellar in Courcelette, I saw a British bi-plane which was flying low from south to north over the western exit of Courcelette. I immediately ordered that a reserve machine gun from Machine Gun Company 157, which was situated at the other entrance of the cellar, be prepared for firing. The bi-plane had, in the meantime, disappeared off to the south once more. The machine gun was barely ready to be fired when I saw the same aircraft coming straight at me from the direction of Martinpuich at a height of about one hundred metres. I moved to the machine gun and, lying on my back, fired about fifty rounds at it. Shortly after I had fired, I saw the aircraft bank steeply away to the west and then crash vertically. As it fell, I fired a further twenty rounds at it. The machine was lying about one hundred metres from me, in a farmyard south of the village street. The pilot had been shot five times in his chest, head and liver and had been killed instantly. The observer had only been creased on the head and was slightly wounded. Both were soon taken away by some gunners. The bi-plane had been made by a firm called Ruchon, which was based in Lincoln, England. It had a four bladed propeller and was armed with two machine guns. There were three hits in the engine cowling and fourteen in the pilot's seat."

For his decisive and prompt action, Leutnant Seydel received a written commendation from Oberst von Weise, Commander of 233 Infantry Brigade and Machine Gun Sharp Shooter Troop 107 received prize money of 350 Marks. Unfortunately for the German army, such successes were few and far between. Elsewhere, as July drew to a close, their lot was to hold in the face of overwhelming firepower and constant attacks. The deep shelters, with which they had begun the month, were, for the most part, a distant memory. Clinging on to lines of shell holes, roughly joined by narrow trenches, their casualties mounted, but naturally, amongst all the death and destruction, there were fortunate escapes.

*Reserve Leutnant Walter Schulze 8th Company Reserve Infantry Regiment 76*[49] **13.**

"29 July. 'To thee be thanks, almighty and great Father! Thou hast held a protective hand over me, as a father shields his child!' Tonight at stand to I was once more wearing the steel helmet which the carrying parties had brought forward to us.[50] We were standing in the beaten zone of the treacherous guns which are always bringing down rapid surprise fire on this area. Shrapnel balls were flying just over our heads, hissing and whistling devilishly. Suddenly, with a great clanging thud, I was hit on the forehead and knocked flying onto the floor of the trench. I had stars in front of my eyes and there was an appalling roaring in my head. Cautiously I felt up at my helmet and, there at the front, was a deep dent. I took my helmet off and, thank heavens, there was no head injury. In fact nothing had happened to me. A shrapnel bullet had hit my helmet with great violence, without piercing it, but sufficiently hard to dent it. If I had, as had been usual up until a few days previously, been wearing a cap, then the Regiment would have had one more man killed.

"Initially we had all been reluctant to wear the heavy iron helmets. This showed how useful they were. I felt dizzy and my head was spinning for a while, but I sat in the trench and marvelled at my deliverance. After a few moments all was forgotten and I resumed my alert position. An unteroffizier was leaving his post and I called out to him to come over to me. I wanted to show him the miracle of the helmet, so I turned slightly sideways and – clang! I was thrown once more sideways into the trench. Two balls, whose impacts on the side of my helmet I felt very clearly, had knocked me over and left a dent on the left side of my helmet. These two did not seem to have much energy left. I had been saved for a second time. A warm feeling of thankfulness spread through me. What a miraculous escape; yet this sort of occurrence was absolutely terrifying...

"This afternoon [29th July] the British laid on another murderous bombardment. Our own artillery had been firing short during the morning and had damaged the trench. Now the British were trying to make a more thorough job of it. We ducked down behind the clay walls to get what shelter there was. Bruodereck and Unteroffizier Schnell arrived, somewhat agitated. Blood was streaming down Bruodereck's face. Schnell was shot through one arm and had a splinter wound in the other. I took his field dressing off him and bandaged him up. I then went over to Brudereck, where another comrade was bandaging up his head wound. He also had splinter wounds to the chest and back. When the fire eased a bit, the two of them set off for the dressing station. That was another two men gone. How quickly the little band shrank. Fewer and fewer of the old hands were still around. Shortly afterwards, the feared British aircraft, 'Number 10' appeared. He flew so low over our lines that we could easily see the figure '10' underneath his wings.

"Within seconds our trench was under fire by heavy artillery. Shell after shell came down, well directed and dangerously close. We thinned out to one side and fled to the right flank of the company position to escape the fire. As it eased, we returned to our original positions. Wartemann and Knoblauch were with me. Wartemann said that it might be best to take cover in the trench which linked us with 7th Company and which was only fifty centimetres deep, if we wished to avoid being buried alive by the great masses of earth thrown up by the heavy 280 millimetre shells. He might have been right, but down came the fire once more: a shell to the left, one to the right and one behind us. I was on the left. Wartemann, Knoblauch and Leifering had ducked down five metres from me in Paul Wendt's shelter; he having fled to the right with the rest of his section. I looked for cover in my old shelter. Then there was an appalling crash. From the smoke came a piercing, whimpering scream. I quickly got up and looked for my comrades. All I could see was a mound of earth, out of which came desperate cries for help. At first I could only see Knoblauch at one corner of the heap. His eyes stared in terror from his distorted white face. He was only buried up to his waist, but he could not extract himself. With an enormous effort I released him.

"Terrified shouts were still coming from the heap of earth. They had recognised me. 'Dig, Walter, dig! Walter, help us quickly, for God's sake help us! Quicker Walter, quicker, we're suffocating!' they implored me desperately from the earth. My blood ran cold at the shouts of fear. It was simply dreadful. At least Knoblauch was free, scrabbling at his legs which were still trapped under the earth. I worked fast with a spade that luckily was still there in the trench and undamaged. Digging carefully, we searched. Yes! there is a helmet, a head. Leifering is freed as far as his chest. He was bent double and trapped the same way. His face was white as a sheet from the terrible shock and fear of the incident. Now there is only one left – Wartemann. He is still shouting, but weaker now, as though he is expiring, suffocating. I am gripped by fear. I call over two men from 7th Company who had appeared a few steps away. They set to, to help and I run to summon further assistance from the right.

"Nobody dares risk passing through the appalling fire which is coming down at twice the former intensity. I am at the end of my strength, completely exhausted. I have dug at all corners of the heap and found no trace of the buried man. Worried moments pass. All is quiet from the heap, as quiet as the grave. I know that I am now likely to dig out a corpse. In the tortured anxiety and bitter desperation of the effort, I have rubbed up three great blood blisters on my right hand. I am consumed by the unspeakable concern that I have not been able to save the poor chap. I scramble on top of the heap, so that I can throw the soil to the side and shrapnel bullets whistle around me. It's all the same to me. I have lost all feeling for the danger which hovers all around me. I just want to help the unfortunate man down there, to dig him out. The two lads from 7th Company go to work with a will, digging at the side of the heap. 'A hand', shouts one. Yes, it is a human hand. We shudder, but yes, it is attached firmly and we feel along it, further up. Yes, hair, a head! We dig on carefully with our hands. Oh what a fearful sight! I have known this man the whole time I have been in the field, but I don't recognise him now. We have cleared his face, but it is all puffy. Blue lips, wild staring eyes, seemingly mad, the nose fat and bloody. But at least his upper body is now free.

"Instinctively I try artificial respiration, press down with his hands on his stomach then lift them back over his head. I repeat this several times. He begins to breathe. Consciousness seems to be returning. His eyes begin to focus. Thank heavens he seems to be coming round. I loosen all his clothing and give him little sips to drink. After a few seconds I call out to him. He recognises me, though apparently weak and only semi-conscious. 'Walter, is that you? What's happened to me?' I explain to him that he has been buried. A spark of life is still there. Then suddenly he has a fit of madness. It's all we can do to restrain him. He wants to climb up the walls and out of the trench. Moaning, he shouts in a hoarse voice, 'Throw me overboard. Just throw me overboard.' It is simply dreadful. I cool his forehead, temples and chest with coffee and now he is speaking more sensibly.

"Suddenly he coughs up a clot of blood, then another. The thick dark blood spills from his mouth between his distorted lips. I stay with him constantly, feeling suddenly a warm sacrificial love for this unhappy man, who up until then was really a stranger. And he thanks me again and again from deep down inside. 'You are so good Walter, so very, very good. Did you dig me out? Oh Walter, my poor...' He slurs his words like a child who has bitten his tongue... I soothe him and say. 'Take it easy Otto. Try to sleep. Once it goes dark, we'll get you out of here then things will be better.' The very helplessness of the man is deeply moving. I have to pull myself together, or all the misery before me will have me crying like a child. He sleeps a little. Now and then he stirs and mumbles something incomprehensible... In the corner of the trench his heavy laboured breathing never ceases. Feverish phantasies flit through his brain. Finally, night falls, the ration party arrives and places him in a groundsheet to carry him back. 'Get well soon! Keep your chin up!' 'You too, Walter.' Thank heavens he is away from this hell. Hopefully the poor chap is not beyond help..."

The Army Group Commander, General der Artillerie von Gallwitz, was quite clear that the month of July had not gone well for the forces under his command. They had generally fought in a disciplined manner and with outstanding courage, but the fact remained that ground had been yielded. In order to rally all the Ottos, Walters, Karls and Heinrichs, upon whose individual performances the overall integrity of the defence rested, he issued an order of the day.[51]

"Army Group Gallwitz 30th July 1916    I. Nr. 155

The enemy is expected to attack in strength during the coming days. The decisive battle of the war will be fought out on the battlefield of the Somme. It is to be made clear to all officers and men in the front line how much is at stake for the Fatherland. The utmost attention and sacrificial action is to be paid to ensuring that the enemy does not gain any more ground. His assault must be smashed before the wall of German men.

The Commander in Chief
von Gallwitz, General der Artillerie"

The Regiments and the men belonging to them were only too well aware about what was at stake. They had indeed thrown themselves into the breaches in the wall; thus far with a fair degree of success, but the cost in high grade officers and men was already crippling. The German army was overdrawing its resources, incurring losses it could never hope to make up. Let one young officer's eulogy for his fallen commanding officer, Hauptmann Rausch, speak for them all.

*Leutnant Wolfgang von Vormann 2nd Battalion Infantry Regiment 26* [52]

The death of Hauptmann Rausch 16th July 1916

"With the death of Rausch, a man is gone from us whose personality and powers of leadership were incomparable. Self contained and justifiably self confident, his influence was felt way beyond the bounds of his own Battalion, with which he had a special bond. He was a man apart in the way he rallied his men around him and what an ability he had to make his portrayal of the role of the carefree warrior the centre of his being!

"He is not dead. He lives on in the ranks of his 2nd Battalion, which is stamped with his personality and imbued with his spirit. Rausch lies buried in Le Transloy, but his soul finds no rest there, rather it soars in the still of the night over the battlefields. Many men must be born, live and die before a new Rausch appears. His like will rarely be seen and seldom will one such have the opportunity to exert the influence that he did.

"'To all of us, especially those of his 'Iron Battalion', he remains unforgettable...'"

1. The opinion of General von Falkenhayn concerning rigid retention of terrain, is quoted in the German  Official History: *Der Weltkrieg 1914 bis 1918,10. Band. Die Operationen des Jahres 1916* p 355 as follows: 'The first principle of positional warfare has to be not to yield a single foot of ground and if a foot of ground is lost, to launch an immediate counter-attack with all forces, down to the last man'. There are those, including Ernst Junger, (*Storm of Steel* p 110) who attribute this to '...Prussian obstinacy with which the tactics of the line were pursued to their logical conclusion'. Writing in *General Headquarters 1914-1916 and its Critical Decisions* (passim, but see especially pp 35-38), Falkenhayn repeatedly implies  that the psychology of the average German soldier, shortage of manpower and consequent lack of reserves forced this  policy on the German army; there being a constant concern that if lines were allowed to crumble and ground were to be yielded too easily, it could be extremely difficult to seal off and counter the inevitable breakthroughs.  Despite the consequent high loss rate, there is something to this argument.  Certainly it is easier to drum a policy of 'no retreat' into the minds of defending soldiers, than to allow the idea to spread that there is some discretion in the matter.  Even when, later in the battle, flexible defence in depth was introduced as a tactic, the decision to relinquish ground voluntarily was retained at Army level.
2.  Kronprinz Rupprecht *Mein Kriegstagebuch* Vol 1 p 495
3.  Kriegsarchiv München 8 RIR Bd 21
4.  Pfeffer: *History IR 186* pp 67-8
5.  Bachelin: *History RIR 111* pp 295-6
6.  Bezzel: *History BRIR 6* pp 102-3
7.  Anon: *History FAR 6* pp 138-139
8.  Soden: *History 26th Res Div* p 113
9.  Vischer: *History 10. Württ. IR 180 in der Somme-Schlacht* p 21
10. Mülmann: History Lehr-IR pp 289 - 290
11. Fasse Collection: *Bericht an das I. und III. Bataillon IR 190 5 Aug 16*
12. Wurmb: *History BRIR 8* p 77
13. Forstner: *History RIR 15* pp 313-14
14. *ibid.* p 333
15. *ibid.* pp 316-17
16. Maikäfer, literally May beetles = Cockchafers, was the nickname of the Fusilier Guards.
17. Zipfel: *History IR 89* p 246-47
18. *ibid.* p 249
19. Kümmel: *History RIR 91* p 216
20. Wohlenberg: *History RIR 77* pp 204-06
21. This represents an interesting change of tactics from those used only two weeks earlier during the first day of the battle.  It is, perhaps, a further example of the innovative skill of the Kitchener divisions.
22. Kümmel: *op.cit.* pp 216 - 217
23. Wohlenberg: *History BIR 16* p 44
24. Kriegsarchiv München HS 2105
25. Kriegsarchiv München HS 2105
26. Kriegsarchiv München HS 2106
27. Gareis does not provide any more details about the prisoners, but the implication must surely be that they were shot by the Prussians and that Gareis got to hear about it later.
28. Lutz: *History BIR 16* p 47
29. Kriegsarchiv München IR 16 Bund 3
30. Forstner: *op.cit.* pp 335-6
31. Möller: '*Fritz von Below*' p 53
32. Kronprinz Rupprecht '*Mein Kriegstagebuch*' Bd1 p 503
33. Kümmel: *op.cit.* p 227
34. Wohlenberg: *History RIR 77* p 199
35. *ibid.* pp 194-5
36. Zipfel: *op.cit.* p 253
37. In tribute, Reserve Hauptmann Dr Stratmann said of him, 'The heroic death of Leutnant Otto Helmut von Oertzen was an especially painful loss for the Regiment.  He embodied not only the 1st Battalion, but also the entire Regiment, with his honourable uprightness, his energy and his courage.'
38. Staehle: History FAR 116 p 66
39. Sapper does not identify the unit, but it was probably 1st Battalion RIR 107.  The 2nd and 3rd

Battalions were at that time heavily involved in the fighting for Delville Wood, where they were intermingled with men of IRs 26, 52 and 153 into one amorphous group.

40. It is quite possible that this command post was located in the dugout which still exists near the church at the south-east corner of the village.

41. Kriegsarchiv München 8 RIR Bd 21

42. Gropp: *History IR 76* pp 168-170

43. Gruson: *History IR 72* pp 244-247

44. This was probably Martinpuich.

45. Reymann: *History IR 62* pp 100-02

46. Guhr: *History IR 157* pp 116-117

47. Gropp: '*Hanseaten im Kampf* pp 158 - 161

48. Guhr: *History IR 157* p 118

49. Gropp: *op. cit.* pp 159 & 161-5

50. It is interesting to note that the German army was relatively late to issue steel helmets to its soldiers. Part of the problem was the sheer number to be produced. Initially they were issued where the need was greatest, so during the first half of 1916, that meant Verdun. For a while they were handed over as trench stores during relief. The majority of soldiers, arriving on the Somme from quiet sectors for tours of duty at the front, were issued with helmets on arrival, or, as in this case, after they had actually deployed. The shortage lasted for some months. Crown Prince Rupprecht, by then an Army Group Commander, noted in his diary on 5th September 1916, 'The Army High Command is sending us 200,000 steel helmets, which should prove their worth brilliantly.' *Mein Kriegstagebuch* Bd 2 p11. So even at that late stage of the battle the shortage was still causing concern.

51. Düssel: *Das RIR 17 während der Sommeschlacht* p 18

52. Vormann:

p 513

# CHAPTER 6

# August 1916

B y the beginning of August the German army felt that although the operational situation was still extremely serious, it was over the immediate crisis. A breakthrough was as far away as ever. The Allied advance had slowed to a crawl; everywhere they were contesting each village and wood with dogged determination. As part of the process of taking stock, questionnaires concerning the performance of the French and British forces were circulated down to regiments at the end of July. The responses were then collated and passed back up the chain of command for information. Oberstleutnant Bram, commander of Bavarian Reserve Infantry 8, which had followed up its successful recapture of Schwaben Redoubt on 1st July with the obstinate defence of the front from Thiepval to Saint Pierre Divion, provided his Brigade Commander with a very detailed report.

*Oberstleutnant Alfons Bram Bavarian Reserve Infantry Regiment 8* [1]

"The Regiment was locked in battle with soldiers from Ulster from 1 – 3 July [*sic*] and Yorkshire from 3 – 7 July. Both formations belonged to Kitchener's Army. The British infantrymen were, without exception, personally courageous and daring and through these characteristics they contradicted the underestimate which we had generally made concerning the members of the young Kitchener Army. The fact that the first major attack on 1 July took place in dense masses which walked forward, demonstrates the boundless trust that each individual placed in the ability of their artillery to make reality of the concept of occupying our trenches without a fight. Traces of hand grenade splinters on almost all the entrances to the dugouts prove that there was systematic clearance of all trenches and dugouts within the boundaries of the attack. Thanks to excellent artillery defensive fire and the alert trench garrison, later attacks on a large scale on 2 and 4 July were dealt with in good time. Some were nipped in the bud in the jumping off positions; others broke down in No Man's Land under the combined fire of our artillery, machine guns and rifle fire.

"During individual battles, which quickly developed because of our counter-attack of 1 July against Schwaben Redoubt, the general situation and later clearance of British pockets of resistance, the British soldiers displayed great courage, coolness under fire and a striking reluctance to take cover. Their main strength in this type of fighting was their masterly use of grenades, with which they had evidently trained with sporting enthusiasm and their numerous machine guns. Cooperation between hand grenade throwers, weapons carriers and grenade carrying parties was designed and organised down to the last detail. The enemy never seemed to run short of grenades. They generally only gave up their nests [of resistance] if they perceived themselves to be threatened from several sides simultaneously. In this case they sometimes sought escape by running back across country without stopping, but on other occasions they withdrew slowly, fighting constantly. We actually observed the first during the battles of 1st July when, in the final phase of our attack on the Schwaben Redoubt, the pressure exerted by our numerically inferior assault groups was such that it almost induced panic among the very much stronger enemy. The other method was seen during the battles to clear the enemy out of the sections of trench which the British still held after 1st July. There were no fundamental differences between the Ulster soldiers engaged on 1 July and the Yorkshiremen between 3 and 7 July.

"There were no infantry attacks after 7 July. It was striking that, from this day on, the infantry which was garrisoning the British trenches adopted a very quiet posture; it was possible to move around in the open in full view of the enemy. Now and then there was some enemy machine gun fire. It created the impression that, from 7th July, the British had decided to deploy worn out troops on those sections of the front where there was no infantry activity. Towards the end of July, British corpses from the battles of 1– 4 July still lay near to the enemy trenches. From all of this it can be seen that the British have succeeded in taking their young soldiers, who physically are almost all young powerful men, the great majority of whom are drawn from the working class (clear from examination of their pay books!) and turning them into effective fighters. British morale was good. No deserters were encountered. However cases have been reported and from statements of German soldiers, who were captured and subsequently escaped, it seems that the British have plundered captured and dead soldiers.

"The standard of training is good. Very specific drills for attack and defence appear to have been practised during training. This may account for the fact that men were ill-prepared for unexpected situations and, therefore, took to their heels when under pressure. It was clear that the greatest attention was paid to painstaking organisation of resupply; soldiers were minutely drilled in their respective roles. To this must be added the fact that the British administrative authorities have issued their soldiers with first class equipment. Although the British infantry did not achieve a successful attack, the main reason for this is that, although care had been taken with their training, it was not possible to reinforce the favourable results obtained through the instillation of battle experience. The officers and NCOs appointed to command the men lacked

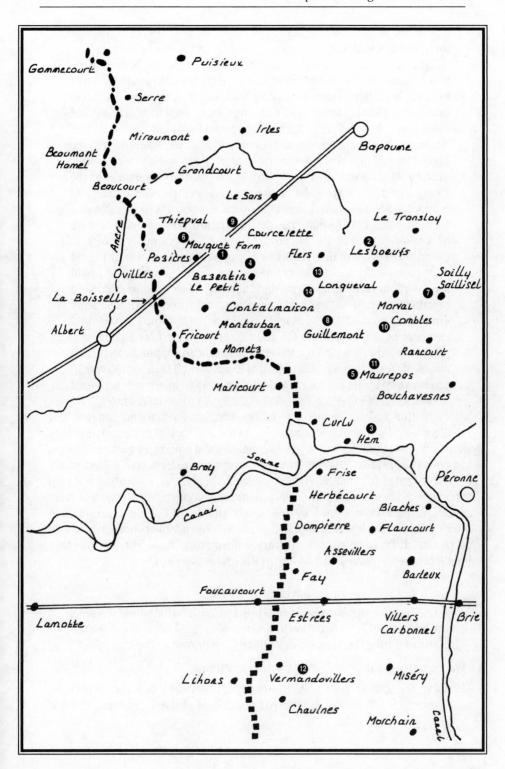

experience of war and the ability to react swiftly to new, changing and unexpected situations.

"The personal behaviour of British officers in battle is beyond all praise. They are fearless and brave, providing their soldiers with a shining example of soldierly bearing. They are oblivious to danger and disdain to take cover. They lay importance on being seen by their men in battle and many times they were observed moving upright in shrapnel and shell fire. According to the statements of prisoners of war, the soldiers have the highest regard for the personal courage of their, mostly very young, officers. Against this must be set the lack of military awareness of the young officer in unexpected situations. He ceases then to be a leader and is as much an individual fighter as his subordinates. It is noticeable that the British officer lacks thorough, detailed training; he appears to be more of a sportsman. The British do not seem to expect much ability to command in battle of their subaltern officers. They appear usually to send more senior officers to the front line to carry out duties which we should leave without further consideration to a junior officer. So, for example, a captain was detailed as leader of a reconnaissance patrol which the enemy directed against C2 (St. Pierre Divion) on 5 July. During the final clearance of the trenches of C2 and C3 (British nest near Meisengasse [Titmouse Alley]) on 7 July, the commander of the approximately 150 metres of trench that was still in British hands was a [Lieutenant]Colonel,[2] accompanied by his adjutant. The NCOs are young, equally inexperienced in command, but they are also possessed of great personal courage..."

Naturally this type of report was of considerable background interest, but intelligence staffs required much more detailed and topical information if they were to be able to prepare intelligence summaries and reports for the commanders and operational staffs. Prisoner interrogation appears to have been a particularly fruitful source of information. It seems clear that only scanty attention was paid at the time to the question of resistance to interrogation. In fact, so much of value appears to have been gained by completely simple and straightforward field interrogations, that it would appear that those taken prisoner frequently felt no particular duty to withhold military information from the enemy. One intelligence report issued on 2nd August illustrates this clearly:

"Interrogation Report

Of several Australians of 25th, 26th and 28th Battalions (7 Brigade) and a captain of 23rd Battalion (6 Brigade) of the 2nd Australian Division captured during the morning of 29th July, north west of Pozières.

- War organisation of 6 and 7 Brigades was confirmed.

- History: The 2nd Australian Division was, until fourteen days ago, in position near Armentières. It was partly relieved by battalions of the Hampshire and Royal

West Kent Regiments (? Div)
– The Division entrained in the area of Bailleul.  After a short journey by train to Amiens it was rested for a few days in the area, then marched, with rest days interposed, via Rubempré, Herissart and Barlo* [*sic* probably a garbled version of Warloy-Baillon] to the Albert area.

– Battlefield activity:  On 27th July, 6 and 5 Australian Brigades relieved the battalions of 1st Australian Division, which were holding the line.

– The position of the 6 and 5 Australian Brigades on 28th/29th July was detailed as follows:

"On the extreme left flank of the Australian 2nd Division (southwestern end of Cantergraben)  and adjoining the 48th Division, was 23rd Battalion of the Australian 6 Brigade. To the east of it was 21st Battalion, 6 Australian Brigade, then on the right flank 22nd and 24th Battalions 6 Australian Brigade.  Further to the right again and on the Albert-Bapaume road, were elements of the Australian 5 Brigade.  22nd and 24th Battalions of 6 Australian Brigade did not participate in the attack.

"7 Australian Brigade was moved up to Pozières during the evening of 26 July and took part with three battalions in the attack. The 25th, 26th and 28th Battalions of 7 Australian Brigade passed through the sector of 22nd and 24th Battalions of 6 Australian Brigade in four waves.  The 27th Battalion of 7 Australian Brigade remained behind in reserve.

"The attack failed utterly. The prisoners were of the opinion that serious errors were made during the attack.  The British artillery had the mission of bombarding Cantergraben which was not occupied by us, but was the objective of the attack.  When signal rockets were fired, the fire was to be lifted to the rear.  Because the assault battalions had come under very heavy artillery and machine gun fire from the start, they suffered serious casualties; all the officers were alleged to have become casualties just as the attack was launched. The consequence was that no signal could be given to the artillery to lift the fire.

"The Captain, who believed that he was one of the very few surviving officers, confirmed in general the statements of the prisoners from 7 Brigade.  The casualties were unusually high because the British artillery had fired on their own men in Cantergraben.  In the general confusion it was not possible to locate the men who were carrying the rockets intended as signals for the artillery.  He was soon wounded and unable to move.  In his view the higher command and control must have been extremely poor, because the troops on the right flank of 48th Division obviously had no information regarding the Australian attack and had fired at the advancing Australians, whom they must have mistaken for Germans.  It is to be assumed that the Division will almost certainly be due for early relief...The companies within the battalions have about one hundred men each, with three or four officers. There have been no large-scale reinforcements recently.

"The few prisoners, who had already fought at Gallipoli, were of good military bearing. The majority had arrived as reinforcements during the past three months and, militarily, almost without exception, they leave a rather lamentable impression. Apparently they only volunteered for military service because it offered a cheap way to see something of the world and the chance to play at soldiering on the side. Many declared that they had had enough of the reality of war and were happy to have been taken prisoner. Some of the older men were very downcast and regretful that they were ending their relatively long war service as prisoners. The captured officer explained further, conversationally, that he had heard that the 4th Australian Division had been deployed in the area of Armentières and that it was said to have suffered significant casualties, but he was unable to provide exact timings."

By the time the contents of this report and many others like it had been processed and recirculated as official enemy assessments, the German army had discovered that the Australians were, in fact, truly formidable opponents. The village of Pozières was, by now, firmly in Allied hands, but the Germans certainly did not accept that was how the situation was going to remain. Whilst the weight of Allied attacks swung north towards Mouquet Farm, German counter-attacks continued to be launched against the captured village. One such failed attempt, launched during the night of 5th / 6th August, involved the 12th Division, the formation which had taken a terrible beating during the pre-1 July bombardment east of Mametz.

*Leutnant Zinnemann 1st Company Infantry Regiment 63*[3] **1**.

"We set off towards evening in the direction of Pozières...Warlencourt was behind us and we approached a very dangerous place. I ran up to the commander. 'Herr Major, I urgently advise that we get off the road. We took casualties here three days ago. The enemy tries to destroy ammunition columns at this point.' – 'Yes you have a point. OK, get over to the left and advance across country by platoons.'...Off we go, leaning forward slightly, chin straps of our helmets tightened under our chins, eyes directed towards our objective. Shells hurtle over us, to burst in the houses of Ligny-Thilloy, in Warlencourt, over to the right in Pys and forward left in Martinpuich. Pillars of earth, black as night, fly up skywards everywhere. There is a fearful racket, sometimes too close for comfort. The German artillery fires, sending greetings over and preparing for the assault...The groups of shadowy figures push forward. The first shells are coming down. We must be near the objective. We do not know exactly where we are. It is the very worst sort of feeling. We are effectively blind, yet we feel that we are near, that they are lying in wait for us. So far all has gone well, no casualties. A piece of luck – or is fate biding its time? We shall soon know.

"We run the next one hundred metres. Illuminating rockets cast a spectral light on the terrain. Yes there's a sunken road – take cover, halt along the embankment and have a breather...The Commander arrives and 1st and 4th companies dash forward another one hundred metres...The assault is due to take place at 1.30 am. And now comes a decision. 'August, if should die, farewell. I thank you for your faithful comradeship.' 'Leutnant, you should not talk like that.' – 'August I feel it in my bones. It's nearly over. This time it will be tough they say. Tonight it is going to happen – anyway enough of that, get the platoon commanders over here!' They arrive at the run. 'Gentlemen, the attack goes in at 1.30 am, but we only push forward until we have passed that flat-topped rise to our front and we halt with our right resting on the road. To the right, the 2nd Battalion is attacking. OK, break a leg.' We rush forward 100 metres to the first position.

"'Let's, go! Jump to it, go, go!' – Everyone leaps forward, bent double. – Over there one, two flares. 'Take cover! Stay still!' To our front is churned up earth, craters, rifle fire. – Bullets crack past us at short range. Go on! Jump! Throw! A few more bounds forward and we reach the remains of a freshly- dug trench. There are figures lying around. Are they dead? Alive? Machine gun fire rips past us. What a racket it makes! They have seen us, heard us! Not only that, flares are being fired everywhere. The front is nervous and on the alert. That's bad. This isn't going to work! Assaults must have surprise...We all have hand grenades ready. It's nearly 1.30 am! The safety caps are unscrewed and we grip the sticks tightly. The enemy must be right in front of us and a little higher. We can judge it when a flare goes off. The direction is firmly imprinted in our minds. Now our artillery fire is landing in tight groups just to our front. We close in on each other. Our trench is very shallow. Men gather in groups wherever there is a crater. Heads tucked in, our helmets are down on our shoulders. I check my watch, a flare goes up. It's 1.30 am! At that same moment the German fire lifts – flares go up – we rush forward, our grenades exploding in a wide arc in the enemy position. – There is quick succession of explosions, shouting, the flash of bayonets, more flares.

"'Forward! Go! Go!' Piercingly shrill '*Hurras*', shouts and roars fill the air – then comes a shower of enemy hand grenades – they burst and men fall – the battle is joined! We are on top of the enemy. It is truly terrifying. Figures flit before us, right and left of us come huge bursts of fire – bullets fly everywhere – a British machine gun rattles away. In the harsh light of the numerous flares, Germans can be seen going down. Cursing, moaning, the last of the grenades are thrown in the direction of the machine gun.

The man on my right pulls one out, raises himself and prepares to throw. Then there is a crack, a thud, a shriek and he collapses, shot through the arm. My batman tears the grenade out of his cramped hand and throws it away from us. We duck and it explodes – it could have killed us all! The attack has only progressed twenty metres. We are caught in the open and take cover in shell holes, whilst machine gun fire scythes through the air just above our heads. Enemy artillery is bringing down heavy shells behind us. It does not get us here. We are at grenade range from the enemy. The arm is bound up. August has sacrificed the belt of his trousers. The man is quite chirpy and wants to head back. No chance of that. We are completely pinned down and cannot lift our heads one single centimetre. Spades out! We scrabble at the ground sweating. Tonight will bring death and tomorrow? What then? We shall be wiped out here. OK, spades to the rescue. Soon we have dug a shallow channel and we lie along it one behind the other.

"To our front we make progress and soon our upper bodies are in cover, but our legs are still damn well out in the open. The men in rear dig round the legs of the man in front and carefully we make our trench deeper and deeper. Bullets crack through the air above us, shells crash down and splinters fly. They can't get us that way, but they could be through us suddenly with a bayonet charge. There are very few of us here forward. The majority are dead or wounded; we can hear them. We can't help hearing them and it grates on us. Towards dawn we are sufficiently deep down that we can crawl around, so we branch out and begin to link up. I crawl in the direction of the road, pushing past the men. Everywhere it's the same. Grey faced soldiers digging in and bloodied men groaning. I give out orders that the wounded are to be got back to Martinpuich before it gets light. Whoever can crawl has to set off along the trench. There is nothing else for it, even if they are in great pain. Once day breaks, there will be no possibility of evacuation.

"Everyone realises this and they pull the groaning men along the trench, lifting them over themselves whilst lying in the trench. It is incredibly strenuous, but anxiety about the coming of day acts as a spur. I have managed to get to the road, to the trench by the road, which is totally cratered. Trees lie across it, offering some protection from small arms fire. I take an NCO with me. We are not linked up here and that won't do. The enemy could simply roll us up from the right. So, let's go. We must make contact with the 2nd Battalion. We move along the Road trench, keeping a close look out on the other side of the road. Suddenly we hear voices. They are Germans. We leap across the road [Pozières-Martinpuich road] and get down in the trench quickly. We are in luck. It's the left flank company, which is still occupying the start line. We, however, are rather further forward. The Battalion was shot to a standstill and now they are back in the original position.

"I find a commander and we agree that we must get a channel dug in the road, then a trench forward to link with us. Immediately the picks get to work on the damaged cobbles of the road. Stones fly, but it is hard to create a trench in such a place in one hour. A crater in the road helps. We dig into the embankments and throw up earth walls. It's going to work. Now I need to return to my men. They must not be without their commander, or they will feel my absence and with justification. I find that they have worked with a will in my absence. The trench is now about one metre deep in parts. That is a great help. Back at my own position, I find that things are so far advanced that certain men are already in sentry positions. A new trench system is being developed..."

After a lively journey back to his company, Zinneman set about organising the survivors for defence. This was far from easy, because they spent the entire day under heavy direct and indirect fire. Zinneman, who was in any case exhausted from previous exertions and whose nerves were not in good condition, was blown up by a shell which landed nearby and was badly winded. Finding no puncture wounds, he was persuaded to try to rest for a while and get some sleep in a small foxhole, which his batman had produced whilst he was away, but events conspired to prevent even that small degree of relief:

*Leutnant Zinnemann 1st Company Infantry Regiment 63*[4] **1.**

"I am indescribably tired. I crawl into a tiny hole, my aching knees pulled up tightly and my arms folded in close. My eyes are burning with tiredness and I am tortured with thirst...I am half asleep, drowsy and yawn deeply repeatedly, instinctively holding both hands in front of my face. Then suddenly, for a fraction of a second, I hear a howl and, at the same moment, an indescribably heavy leaden thud on my skull. My bones must be broken, my skull caved in. I am falling down a great hole, my senses are reeling and my brain aches terribly. I can see nothing but stars. Then from somewhere comes a roaring sound, silent tears then ice, really terrible cold ice. Then I lose consciousness. Then the tears come again. I am looking up into a great milky sky. My heart pounds terribly. I am lying, but everything is so heavy, so terribly heavy on me, and cold. I am being choked. A great weight is crushing me. I feel light headed. I am going to die. It's all happening so quickly. The good Lord has made it swift – rest, so tired – 'Leutnant! Leutnant! Are you still alive?' Right above me, so close that it makes everything dark, are two piercing eyes, a very wide forehead and drops of water are falling in my face. All I can see is water. It's flowing over me and rises around my head. With a jerk I am back in the land of the living. Life has reached out to me, pulled me back from the valley of the shadow of death: it calls out, 'For God's sake, live!'

"Suddenly molten lead is flowing along my spine. I regain my limbs and the power of speech: 'August! August!' I shout. I realise that I cannot get free. I am completely buried in the earth. Only my head is free. August can see that I am alive. Seized by the Furies, he tears at the earth with his bare hands, pulling out clods. 'Hey, Antek, Get over here, the Leutnant's buried!' I am wide awake now and am freezing cold. Things feel lighter, then I am free. They pull me clear and lay me along the shallow, damaged trench. I stretch out and gasp for breath. I am freezing cold and I ache and hurt in every limb. What has become of me? I must be going mad. Is my back broken? my legs? I find myself weeping uncontrollably. I can't bear to cry, but the tears roll down. I'm lying on ice. Then someone else arrives. Puffing and panting he pushes alongside me. I feel something wet and stinging in my mouth, stinking and burning. I try to see what is happening. I am at the end of my strength – It's all over. 'Leutnant! – nant – nant – errr – ummmm.' 'Leutnant, you're going to be all right. I'm the first aid man.' I heave myself upright. I can see again. That feels a bit better. 'Leutnant, you've got to crawl to the doctor. I'm going to help you.' He turns me on to my stomach and I feel him massaging my knees.

"OK, it's going to be all right. Then the tears come again. I just hope my men can't see them! Come on man, pull yourself together. Just crawl.I move like a whipped dog, moving slowly on trembling hands and knees, on all fours, forwards. There is no question of standing up, the trench is too shallow. With the last reserves of strength I get to the end of the communication trench at the entrance to Martinpuich. The first aid man gives me a hand and, with enormous energy, heaves me to my feet and supports my weight. For the first time since yesterday evening I stand upright at long last. But my legs have had enough, I am about to collapse. I cling desperately to his neck then I slip down again. I am freezing - then once again I feel OK and lie down on the hard stones of the village street. But I've got to go on. Get up! Yes that's possible. I haul my exhausted body upright and sway around. I feel terrible. What has happened to me? The brave man comes trotting back again, with a second, then they support me and, with my feet dragging on the cobbles of the village street, we make it to the cellar entrance, where the white flag with its red cross hangs right across the street..."

Zinneman was lucky. After sedation and rest in the dressing station, he was able to rejoin his company and carry on in command. Others were not so fortunate. During the early part of August, although most operations were small-scale, for those directly involved they were costly in terms of casualties, nerve-shattering and exhausting. The battle did not seem to be leading anywhere, yet metaphorically and often literally the entire area from Pozières to Hem was constantly in flames, as the opposing artillery fired bombardments, defensive fire and counter-battery missions.

*Leutnant Thieme Field Artillery Regiment 75[5] 2.*

"The fountains of clay leap upwards. Because the infantry keeps demanding defensive fire missions in quick succession, we have not time to change our position. Suddenly Unteroffizier Raap comes stumbling past. 'The dug out by the 'Bertha' has been crushed. There are four men down there!' The rescue squad is immediately in action with picks and shovels. Siegert, wearing the oxygen apparatus belonging to the medical unteroffizier, collapses unconscious into the dugout. We haul him up and away and he recovers later. Other masked individuals are also affected by the gas which has filled the dugout and they begin to reel about. Nevertheless they are able to establish, with certainty, that the ceiling timbers have broken and that the entire weight of earth is pressing down on the four missing men; so there is no hope for them. The exit is unusable, so they will have to be dug out from above. Everyone sets to and a boot is seen sticking out of the earth, but at that exact moment, fire comes down once more in torrents, landing only a few metres away. We fling ourselves to the ground, whilst splinters and clods of earth fly in all directions. For the time being we have to break off our sad work. They must have met their deaths swiftly. During the night, we pulled back to our old position."

*Unteroffizier Hundt Reserve Infantry Regiment 17[6] 3.*

"The shells came over in great salvoes, exploding with ear-splitting detonations. Then bits were flying in all directions: clods of earth, stones, pieces of wood and also showers of loose earth which came down everywhere, like rain. It was about 4.00 am, the heavy shells were falling ever closer. I was on the left flank of my section, when... there was an almighty explosion right next to me, which seemed to get me right in the stomach and innards. I was seized by its irresistible violence and flung into the air. When I came round I had been thrown three metres into a hole and covered with a light layer of earth. I jumped to my feet and saw a huge shell crater right next to me. A man of my section, who had been shot through both legs, was being carried off. Despite the most energetic efforts, no trace was found of three of my men, the four others were rescued by men of the company. In the meantime there was no let up in the intensity of the fire. Those who were still able to fight crouched down in the knee-deep trench, rifle and grenades next to them and waited the launch of the infantry attack. To do this in the face of such fire demanded great willpower and self control."

Hundt, a young eighteen year old section commander, was describing the process of softening up, which preceded further French attempts to wrest control of the high ground around Hem from its increasingly battered defenders. The bombardment went on for days, being interspersed with infantry attacks which, because of the willingness of the French troops to 'hang on to their barrage', often achieved a fair degree of surprise and led to hand to hand fighting.

*Unteroffizier Hans Herbst 11th Coy Reserve Infantry Regiment 17*[7] **3.**

"...It was about midday [on 7th August] and once more there was a crash and a bang. I saw and heard nothing more, just a ringing in my head. It must have some time later when I came round and sat up. To my amazement, I was not injured. I took a few paces to my left and was met by an appalling sight. A shell had exploded on the edge of the trench. Wehrmann Spelsberg lay dead, Lettau was wounded. Krieger was wounded and buried by earth. Christmann and Leutnant Loos were able to free themselves. Leutnant Loos now gave the order to move to the right. At this precise moment came a hail of rapid fire. An aircraft circling above us had spotted our movement. There was no escape and blow followed blow...'I'm hit', screamed a man who was mortally wounded. Next to me a group of bandaged wounded were moaning. The drumfire continued with increasing intensity until 6.00 pm. Suddenly we heard rifle fire to our right. We lined the trench and observed a line of Frenchmen appear to emerge out of the ground, whilst their artillery maintained the fire on our trenches. They had crept up on us right behind their own fire. What were we to do now? They were already fighting hand to hand on the right flank of our platoon. Feldwebelleutnant Schönberg was bayoneted to death. Leutnant Loos was severely wounded by a grenade. Leutnant Kranepuhl – who deserves the highest praise! – fought on until the enemy had pushed round one side and into our rear. Then we were attacked again from the front and, before we could rearrange our defence, hand grenades were flying around our heads. In no time they were on the edge of our trench and firing a volley at us. Then they leapt over us and began digging in one hundred metres from us. I had had my share. A bullet had hit me in the shoulder and emerged out of my upper left arm as a ricochet. Feldwebel Högel lay in the trench, never to move again. Flöttman was shot through both arms. A few moments later came the second wave. Those who were walking wounded were conducted to the rear. We moved across country and frequently had to take cover in the craters...."

*Leutnant Korff 9th Company Reserve Infantry Regiment 17*[8] **3.**

"The 7 August was a sunny day with only desultory artillery fire landing between the Marsh and Brauner Graben [Brown Trench]. During the afternoon, the main weight of fire moved further right. Soon everywhere was cloaked in smoke. Enemy aircraft were flying low. Because we could observe movement in the French trenches on the far side of Monacu Farm, we placed strong forces on the northern edge of the wood. We soon saw smoke on the hill and, immediately, three enemy machine guns opened up on the Marsh from the south and one from the west. They were in action throughout the attack, causing great problems to our men. Then an attack was launched at the area of the Bahnwärterhaus [Platelayer's Shed]. I observed as machine guns were moved forward. Our fire brought the enemy to a halt and forced him to take cover in shell holes, from which he did not subsequently move.... Other troops, 1,000 metres to our north, were brought under fire. The first wave of the enemy must have closed up under cover of the smoke and surprised the 11th Company. To what extent infiltration played a role I cannot say. I saw one enemy section running back as a result of our artillery defensive fire and small arms fire and believed that the enemy attack had been defeated by a counter-attack, but then a detachment was seen moving in single file and, through the telescope, I was able to make out that those involved had no weapons or equipment. At its head were three men dressed in German officers' caps and greatcoats. They were in a line, the centre man being supported by the other two. He was apparently severely injured. One of those next to him had a bandaged hand. When our men shot at the detachment, they all took cover. I ordered an immediate ceasefire. During the attack our wood was under constant artillery fire. We had numerous wounded and four men killed. Leutnant Lunow was wounded and handed over command of the Company to me... I am convinced that the enemy cannot approach us without a thorough bombardment of our wood. We are covered on the left by a machine gun. This has not opened fire during the attack, in order not to betray its presence. For the time being, there is no chance that the Platelayers' Shed can be by-passed. It seems to me suspicious that the enemy has not attempted to push past the wood from the west. In any case, in view of all the firing, they are probably not clear about the extent of the garrison here. Perhaps the weight of our fire has put them off. In order to deceive them for the time being I shall fire no more signal cartridges."

Immediately south of the river, the previous two weeks had seen heavy fighting in the Biaches-La Maisonette area, just to the west of Péronne. Casualties had been heavy amongst Infantry Regiments 160 and 110 on the right and Infantry Regiments 31, 75 and 29 in the centre and in front of La Maisonette and, according to the Regimental historian of Fusilier Regiment 40, 'the whole position was just one great field of corpses.'[9] The weather was hot, there was little water to be had and over everything there hung the appalling, sickly-sweet stench of decomposition. Something had to be done, so the men of Fusilier Regiment 40, which had also lost heavily during the past few days, were given the grisly task of removing as many of the fallen as possible and taking them back to Péronne for interment. Picking their way through heaps of bodies, French as well as German, men from the 8th Company came across a complete machine gun crew from Infantry Regiment 75, whose members were lying dead over their weapon, as though trying to protect it. Beside it lay the body of Leutnant Bornemann, still clutching his telescope.

The fiery sun had burnt his face black and the gaze of his dead, glazed eyes summed up the entire ghastly experience. Choking and gasping, the fusiliers – two men to a corpse – wrapped the dead in tent halves and attempted to head for Péronne. Many did not make it that far. Stumbling and lurching under the weight, dizzy and utterly nauseated by the filthy smell, they often had to set their burden down and recover. In addition, the French did not cooperate, keeping them under harassing fire throughout and adding to the toll of casualties. Many of the bodies ended up being buried around La Maisonette Copse, but, through an heroic effort, on 8th August alone, seventy six men, thirty five German and forty one French, were recovered across the river for decent burial. Ten of the bodies were not identified.

| | |
|---|---|
| *Wer wird es wohl sein?* | *Who can it be?* |
| *Drüben am Waldesrand* | *There on the wood edge* |
| *Ein Holzkreuz allein -* | *A lonely wooden cross -* |
| *Es trägt keinen Namen* | *That bears no name* |
| *Wer wird es wohl sein?* | *Who can it be?* |
| *Irgendwo am Rhein* | *Somewhere along the Rhine* |
| *Drüben in Deutschland* | *Back home in Germany* |
| *Weint still eine Mutter:* | *A mother weeps silently* |
| *'Wo wird er wohl sein?'* | *'Where can he be?'* [10] |

Up and down the line it was the same story. Trenches with well made dugouts were a distant memory. The weight of artillery fire remained prodigious, whilst the accuracy was of a high standard, thanks to the presence from horizon to horizon of Allied observation balloons and aircraft, which directed the fire. Infantry Regiment 68 took so many casualties from machine-gunning aircraft that it was forced to issue directions that men occupying shell holes were to dig out foxholes for themselves, or cover themselves with earth, to provide cover from view. They even changed the orders for sentries who, conventionally, were required to keep a constant lookout throughout their period of duty. 'Sentries are to remain absolutely still during the day, so that they cannot be observed either by aviators or from the enemy trenches.' For the defenders, it was a period which tested their ability to endure to the full. The men of Reserve Infantry Regiment 15, returning for a second tour of duty in the Martinpuich-Bazentin le Grand area after a difficult and costly initial deployment, found it a hard trial of stamina and determination.

*Leutnant Spielmann 4th Company Reserve Infantry Regiment 15[12]* **4.**

"Everyone had to make do with what they had brought forward in their bread pouches and water bottles. An attempt during the morning of 7th August to supply the company with food and water cost several lives and succeeded only in delivering three loaves, some pieces of bacon and ten bottles of mineral water. By the third day the thirst was unbearable. Every last man was involved in sentry duty, because there was no barbed wire obstacle and the location of the position, just behind a fold in the ground, meant that the enemy could have taken us by surprise at any time. There were saps a short distance forward of the two platoons, which were the scene of several grenade battles. The proximity of the enemy and the reverse slope position did not, in fact, protect us from artillery fire, because the trench could be enfiladed from Bazentin le Grand. In addition, two heavy mortars were deployed [by the enemy]. Airmen, who shot at anyone who moved, made work by day impossible. In any case there was a lack of material. During the afternoon of the 9th alone, thirty to forty men were buried alive, but the majority were dug out still living. Some individuals were buried three times by masses of earth. Up until we were relieved, all the company could do was to bury the dead and keep the trench passable. It suffered twelve killed and thirty two wounded, amongst whom were Leutnants Seeger and Schäfer and Offizier-stellvertreter Hinrich."

By the middle of the month, French pressure around Maurepas was reaching a critical stage. The 8th Bavarian Reserve Division, less Bavarian Reserve Infantry Regiment 23, which was already deployed down near Barleux, had been operating in the area since 23 July. They had inherited a totally smashed up position from the 123rd Infantry Division and had clung on to a crater field, in the face of determined French assaults, during the following two weeks. As the Divisional casualties mounted, Bavarian Infantry Regiment 23 was summoned hastily from a short rest after its efforts south of the river and placed in the line on 30th July to replace worn out subunits of Bavarian Reserve Infantry Regiments 19 and 22.[13] Over the next few days, the Bavarians beat off attack after attack but, finally, the end came on 13 August, after thirty-six hours of almost constant fighting. This assault was part of a joint Franco-British attack, originally scheduled to fall on the sector from Faffémont Farm, south to the river, on 11 August, but postponed until the 12th. Significantly, possibly due to battlefield obscuration, the artillery failed on this occasion to support the defending infantry. The result was the loss of the southern part of the village and the cemetery.

*Oberleutnant Dehner 12th Company Bavarian Reserve Infantry Regiment 23[14]* **5.**

"From 10.00 am to midday, [on the 13th] the enemy kept remarkably quiet. Enemy aerial activity increased and, after midday, we came under drumfire from all calibres of high explosive and gas shells. When I [later] refused to answer his questions, a French staff officer who interrogated me in the citadel at Amiens, asked me sarcastically, 'How did the French 260 millimetre shells and the new gas shells suit you?' In a short while we suffered heavy casualties. With great care, a number of the most severely wounded, who had been sheltering in foxholes, were moved into my dugout, which was quickly filled with dead and dying men. A shell, which burst right outside it, broke one of the props, filling the dugout with suffocating smoke and large quantities of sand. As a result, I despatched a report, 'Heavy drumfire on the entire position. Have been buried. Am remaining with the Company.' Towards 5.00 pm, I sent a further report, which stated roughly, 'Drumfire noticeably heavier. Own casualties heavy. Enemy attack possible. We are ready for them.'

"Subsequently the enemy concentrated fire even more on the dugout. Numerous French aircraft flew over the position at low level, dropping bombs and bringing machine-gun fire down on flattened trenches and craters...Towards 5.00 pm it was possible to detect sporadic rifle fire. I ordered the craters to be occupied, which was done quickly. From that moment on, until I was captured, I fired an almost unbroken stream of red flares calling for defensive fire, as well as aiming from time to time directly at the swarms of enemy aircraft that came at us from all directions. Gefreiter Straüsl handed ammunition up to me from the dugout. Altogether I fired off the contents of two full sandbags (approximately one hundred rounds). During the entire attack our artillery failed to fire one single round.

"The enemy attacked in dense waves. I counted at least ten of them, at fifty metre intervals. After a short, but heavy, pounding with mortars, they quickly overran the 9th Companies of Bavarian Reserve Infantry Regiments 22 and 23. A few pockets of resistance still held out; I observed them firing red flares for a further half an hour. To our front, the first wave closed to within fifty metres, but was halted by our heavy fire, flooded to the rear and disappeared into shell holes. After the enemy, trying for a second time, had been beaten back – largely by Unteroffizier Zürl – and had pulled back about one hundred metres to await reinforcements, at the third attempt, they broke through in the area of Pillhofer's Platoon and, thrusting into Maurepas, exploited out left and right, bringing down machine gun fire on us and attacking us from the rear. Before this occurred, I quickly scribbled a note with blue pencil on waterproof paper, 'Enemy attacking and has broken through left and right of me. Ammunition, grenades and reserves forward!'

"Our casualties were heavy. Reserve Leutnant Kraus, firing to the last, was killed next to me, shot through the head, as was Vizefeldwebel Schmidt to my left. Vizefeldbel Dotter was wounded by a grenade to the right of me. Finally, the battle was being carried on by only four unwounded men.   Lightly wounded men scrabbled about to locate ammunition and hand grenades, which were mostly buried in the foxholes, to replace our dwindling stocks.  I myself continued to use the signal pistol, shooting flares in all directions at the attackers, but we were soon overwhelmed by the enemy, a mixture of alpine troops and Zouaves, who robbed us of all our possessions, before we were sent to the rear.  As far as I could tell, French casualties before our position were very great; certainly our, mostly wounded, men were made to transport them to the rear.  Right up until the last minute, I hoped to see our longed-for reserves and, with that thought, I ceaselessly encouraged the few men still capable of fighting."

Naturally the battles continued to rage around this area over the coming days, as the Germans, who had succeeded in maintaining their positions between Maurepas and Cléry, launched repeated counter-attacks.  The other division of I Bavarian Reserve Corps, 5th Bavarian Reserve Division, had been rushed forward in the wake of the 13 August fighting and over the next few days its units struggled to maintain the integrity of the defence.  It was a brutal and bruising battle, with heavy casualties on both sides.

*Reserve Leutnant Georg Will 3rd Company Bavarian Reserve Infantry Regiment 7*[15] **5.**

"[On the 17th and 18th] The enemy hammered us with all calibres up to 280 millimetre. We were effectively defenceless against it, but the 2nd Company got off lightly, suffering only five killed and thirty wounded. It was a different story for the 3rd Company, which has been hit terribly badly. More than twenty men are lying dead in the trench, many of whom had been buried alive by heavy shells and suffocated. The walking wounded are happy with their lot. Only E., whose arm has been torn off by a shell splinter, takes it badly: crying and moaning like a little child. The destruction of the 3rd Battalion forward in Maurepas... seems to be complete.  Hundreds of guns of up to super-heavy calibre have been bringing a storm of steel, of hurricane proportions, down on the village for twenty four hours now. The landscape is enveloped in one great cloud of dust. Signal flares cannot be seen through it and it seems as though all signs of life have been snuffed out. We send patrols forward. It is now evening and the order arrives for the companies at readiness to move up to Maurepas to reinforce and support. It is extremely difficult to get the men out of the trenches and to maintain an overview of proceedings, because shells keep exploding all over the place. Heavy suppressive fire threatens to prevent us from getting forward, but we succeed and extend the right flank of the 3rd Battalion, until we make contact with our neighbouring Regiment.

"During 19th and 20th August we find ourselves in the front line. There are no trenches, so we occupy shell holes, seeking shelter behind piled up banks of earth. Everyone tries to edge forward, as close to the enemy as possible, to escape from the shelling. During the hours of darkness we dig as hard as we can to link up the craters. The whole place is a charnel house, defying description. The earth is reduced to dust and ashes, the trees are uprooted and smashed, the houses have been swept away, the air is poisoned by smoke, gas and the reek of corpses. Countless pieces of equipment, of all sorts, lie strewn everywhere and in between them are the corpses of the fallen, blown up and distended. Some of them had been hastily buried, but ploughed up once more by the shells. Here and there limbs are sticking out of the ground or just lying around. The sunken road of Maurepas! No worse place can exist! A doctor has taken a photograph of it, which will show more than I can relate. We had laid the courageous Leutnant Beckh in a shell crater, intending to recover his body during a quiet moment, but he was hit by a 280 millimetre shell, which ripped him apart and flung the pieces up in the air. During the afternoon I lay for several hours on the back of a dead man without noticing. The corpse was covered up, but the ground gave under the pressure of my knee, just as if I was on boggy ground. When I sought the reason and scraped away some soil with my hand, I came across the jacket of a dead man.

"I assume command of the 3rd Company... During the day the infantry suffers terribly from the depredations of the aviators. Although doubt is sometimes cast on the assertion that aircraft descend to twenty to thirty metres to attack the infantry with grenades and machine guns, here we are experiencing it as the bitter truth...The doctors' work is endless. Leutnant Beckh was killed, shot through the head. His helmet did not save him. The bullet pierced his forehead and exited behind as a ricochet. Despite that, he lived for a short while. Oberleutnant Erndl fell, shot through the stomach. Whilst he was being carried away, he was wounded again by several splinters. Reserve Leutnant Löwel was also killed by a rifle bullet. Reserve Leutnant Barnewitz, the little man from Saxony, was hit by a shell in front of the command post in the Artillery Hollow. Reserve Leutnant Vollrath was killed by a tiny splinter which pierced his helmet and entered his brain. Reserve Leutnant Krauß is missing. That was not all. To our front, very close to the enemy lines, there was an intact dugout. I went inside and found the body of a dead Jäger officer. An army of flies swarmed round the corpse, which had been lying there for days..."

The surviving Bavarians were extremely grateful to be away from the pestilence of Maurepas when they were finally relieved on 23rd August. Meanwhile, some fifteen kilometres to the north-west, the struggle for domination around Mouquet Farm was in full swing.

*Leutnant Tschoeltsch 10th Company Infantry Regiment 133[16]6.*

"I led my Company, with only light casualties, through the defensive fire. The remains of a light railway showed us the way forward. In single

file, by sections, we moved through the mixture of light and dark caused
by a combination of illuminating and signal flares. In front of us there
was little artillery fire. By chance, I bumped into a runner from 11th
Company which we were due to relieve. It had been hit badly. Hauptmann
Klöppel, Leutnant Boehme and Leutnant Schultze were wounded.
Leutnant Kühn, the most junior of them all, commanded what was left.
There was no trace of a trench. Everyone was located in a straggling line
of shell holes, which was, in fact, considerably better. Now there was
plenty of work to do. Defence sectors had to be allocated to the platoons
and sections. That is no easy task in the dark. The 11th Company heads
out. We had come forward at a moment when a British attack had just
been beaten off. The 8th Company, sent forward by the 2nd Battalion,
also pulled back, leaving us as the sole company guarding the right flank
of the regiment.

"Dawn breaks, a new day begins. My runner and I dig in in a large shell
hole and cover ourselves with a groundsheet to avoid detection by enemy
aircraft. It starts to rain. It is getting rather cold, but at least the airmen
cannot pester us continually. Now we are on our own resources. We take
up our spades and dig, until we make contact with our neighbours. In this
way we produce a sort of substitute trench. Despite the poor weather,
firing continues, but we notice clearly that it lacks direction. Aviators and
captive balloons can see nothing today. Here, out in front, we really feel
fine. We know exactly what we have to do; we only have to hold our
position and not be sent from pillar to post, as is the case for reserve
companies behind the front. Here we are left in peace and, in particular,
the enemy fire is hopeless today. My casualties, including those sustained
in the Sunken Road at Courcelette, amount to about forty men. Luckily
many of these are only slightly wounded. I request the forward despatch
of the reserve platoon left behind in Warlencourt under the command of
Leutnant Winkler. We still have communication to the rear. The telephone
is working once more.

"I have Prussians to my right. I personally made contact with them.
Behind me are the ruins of a proud farm, Mouquet Farm, upon which the
enemy has had his eyes for a long time...To my left is our 9th Company,
then comes 12th Company. The entire Battalion is gathered here; only the
11th Company had to stay in the Sunken Road. Because it is on slightly
higher ground, the farm dominates the surrounding area. We realise that
last night's attack will not be the last; that it will in all probability be
repeated in greater strength, because possession of the farm is vital. I take
a look around the area, naturally with the intention of deploying my
company so that it suffers as few casualties as possible. I notice that this
could best be done if I temporarily evacuated the trench in front of
Mouquet Farm, which was being held by my 1st Platoon. In any case,

since the wounding of its brave commander, Offizierstellvertreter Öhme, it was insufficiently secure there. The main point of course, was to ensure that the section of trench was reoccupied immediately at the moment of attack. Otherwise the British would be sitting in the farm and we should be captured. This undertaking demanded men of decision and spirit, but fortunately I had sufficient of them in my company.

"Together with my batman, Löbel, a metal worker from Chemnitz, I crawled to my right. The further we went, the heavier the fire. This part at least had to be evacuated, otherwise all the reserves allocated to me would be destroyed. I crawled to the Prussians to explain my plan. My neighbouring company commander was in agreement. We took the decision on our own responsibility. If anything went wrong, we should look stupid. But then nobody would be able to call us to account, because in that event we should be dead, but would have at least have died knowing that we had saved valuable lives. If, on the other hand, our plan succeeded and we cleared this sector and reoccupied it at the right moment, then the British would not get Mouquet Farm today. The main thing was to evacuate the area unnoticed. We agreed that the signal for immediate reoccupation would be two green signal flares. I then crawled back, drawing my right flank back in echelon, whilst the Prussians did the same with their left flank. This would, of course, have been simple, had it not been for the enemy fire.

"The battle now became tense again. We rejoiced at every shell the British landed in this gap to our front. He fired, fired and fired again, until he had utterly wrecked this wonderful part of the fertile Somme countryside. We had to keep a sharp lookout. We had to spot the launch of the attack immediately, so that we were not too late in occupying the gap. I stayed with my batman on the right flank. The drumfire never ceased that day. Only when the sun went down was there the daily one hour pause. There was much to do. I had lost more than one hundred and twenty men, so a platoon of the 1st Battalion of my Regiment was deployed forward. Its commander, a Vizefeldwebel Günther from Zwickau, was killed by a shell splinter right in front of me, as he reported his platoon present. Volunteers attempted to fetch food. The Battalion Adjutant, Leutnant von Wolffersdorff, came forward bringing cigars and chocolate and also a few 'cigarettes' of the 'Hand Grenade' brand. Pull the pin and throw them away. It was better than nothing and we did, in fact, receive some food in the carriers. I did not eat any; I had other things in my mind. Would I be able to hold this shot-up company together through the night?

"Enemy fire increases once more, coming down particularly heavily on the evacuated sector in front of Mouquet Farm. About midnight a reserve platoon arrives, at long last, as reinforcement to me. I distribute it throughout the entire company sector in order to compensate for the casualties. Drumfire continues throughout the night. Morale sags. In the morning, as dawn breaks, yet another reinforcing platoon arrives. Everything is in chaos. The wreck of my wonderful company forms the ribs of the defence. Will the men be able to hold off an attack? The final remaining reserve platoon arrives; unfortunately it has already been hit badly on the way from Warlencourt. But its commander, Leutnant Winkler, arrives with it, so, at long last, I have another officer forward with me. This means that I can place an energetic, reliable commander on the right flank. The enemy brings down drumfire without ceasing. His assault columns can be seen marching past the Windmill in Pozières. Things are bound to start tonight. There is no evening pause, he shoots on without stopping. Darkness falls. This is the most dangerous moment. Once again I go round the craters, perhaps for the last time. Then I suddenly note that the appalling fire has been lifted from our position; that it is being moved more and more to the rear, where it forms a steel curtain across all the routes that lead to us. There can be no retreat for us; no way forward for reserves. I realise that the attack is about to begin.

"Quickly, as agreed, I fire two green signal flares. We have enough time to close the gap. Red flares follow immediately and our artillery defensive fire missions are fired. The first line of enemy closes with us. Our artillery, which has remained silent all day and which we cursed, fires brilliantly, but the apparently unstoppable attack continues. Flares almost rain down from the sky. Numerous attacking columns join the flood. They are determined finally to capture the farm and the sunken road. Now the machine guns under Leutnant Nebgen join in. The infantry fire like men possessed and hand grenades explode - can we do it? I head off to the right with my subordinates Löbel, Badstübner, Hüttel and the other brave men, through the craters. It is no problem moving upright now that there is no artillery fire coming down and we close the gap.

"Our plan has succeeded. We have saved valuable mens' lives. More attacking waves keep streaming forward. The first of them are long since destroyed, but the attack is pressed home with cool daring. Finally, just before Mouquet Farm, the masses begin to stall. Here no resistance had been expected, but exactly here we gave them a hot reception. Red flares continue to demand artillery fire – just keep it coming! After an hour, the attack was effectively beaten off. The enemy had hardly reached our line of craters, even though we had no barbed wire. I sent my reports into Battalion. The following morning we were relieved while it was still dark. We left the place reluctantly. Here the finest of my company had shed their blood. Officers and men were joined by a solid band of comradeship. Each had had unshakeable trust in the other and so had achieved victory."

At the beginning of the month, the vital Ginchy-Guillemont-Maurepas sector was being defended by the 27th Infantry Division. For the men of Infantry Regiments

120, 124, 127 and Grenadier Regiment 123, it was to be the sternest trial of the entire war.  They were in action constantly; the days and nights of incessant battering by the artillery being punctuated by grimly-fought infantry battles, as the British army attempted to force its way eastwards and the German army to deny it.  Amidst the general level of combat, certain days stood out as being particularly hard fought.  One such occurred on 8th August. 7.

*Generalleutnant Otto von Moser Commander 27th Division: Diary Entry 8 August* [17]

"At 6.00 am a report arrives. 'Large scale British attack for the past hour!' Into the car and race towards Sailly!  There I receive some happy news:  Regiments 123 and 124 have beaten off the attack, which was mainly directed towards Guillemont.  There, in the grey dawn, numerous dense waves of attackers were bloodily repulsed after bitter hand to hand fighting.  Already the great courtyard of the farmhouse adjoining Divisional Headquarters is full of prisoners, including several officers.  The British soldiery are a real mish mash: some of them have the faces of low criminals, obviously the scum of the population, others, both young and old, look to be far more agreeable types.  They are from a 'freshly-shaved' division; that it to say, apparently they only moved out of rest yesterday evening to take part in the battle.  This is a great advantage for the British and the French.  Because of their numerical superiority, they can repeatedly withdraw their divisions from the front, allow them to rest, recuperate and train for weeks at a time, and then redeploy them, fully refreshed; which for us is completely out of the question.  It makes the performance in battle of our troops all the more amazing.  Incidentally, the prisoners are unanimous that a British victory is assured, because the Germans are out of food and manpower.  Just wait and see!

"A second enemy attack on Guillemont, launched after a heavy bombardment, occurs between 9.00 am and 10.00 am.  It, too, is repulsed bloodily.  The number of prisoners rises to over 300.  Deeds are reported which will live on in the histories of the Regiments.  The most striking is that of a Battalion Commander from Grenadier Regiment 123, the gallant Uhlan Major Landbeck [a cavalry officer serving with the infantry] who, together with the small garrison of his dugout, a few men armed with a single machine gun, intervened personally in the close-quarter battle, linked up with an advancing assault troop from Infantry Regiment 124 and forced between one hundred and two hundred British soldiers to surrender.  It is a great battle and a day of honour for the 27th Infantry Division.  The Corps Commander, who hurried to meet me at Sailly, congratulated me heartily and I in turn, pass on my own congratulations to the brave Regiments 123 and 127 in particular..."

On 14 August, the sixteenth day of fighting for the 27th Division, an example of British cunning was captured near to Guillemont. It was a printed sheet of paper, dated 25 June and signed 'Fraser, Captain, Adjutant 9th Battalion Royal Scots', which contained phrases designed to trick the German defenders. On approaching the German lines, the British soldiers were supposed to shout, *'Ganze Kompanie kehrt, marsch!'* [Company! About turn! Quick march!]. On patrol, the recommended sentence was, *'Hier ein Mann verwundet, brauche Hilfe, kommt näher.'* [There's a wounded man over here. I need help, come closer.] Full marks for imagination, but only an optimist could presume that the Jocks would be able to remember, or get their tongues round, those sentences and only an extreme optimist would expect Scotsmen to fool, in this way, Schwabian regiments, whose own accents and dialect were a great challenge to the remainder of the German army.

By the middle of the month the pressure was building up further. Casualties in Infantry Regiment 127 were so high on the 16th that it had to be relieved. The only possible way of achieving this was to send forward individual battalions of Infantry Regiments 123 and 124, which had only been out of the line for four days, following a severe mauling. Nevertheless, this was done and the fighting raged on, being directed by Generalleutnant von Moser from his bed, where he was suffering from a high temperature and a racing pulse.[19] An enormous weight of fire was maintained against the lines in general and Guillemont in particular and then, on the 18th, by which time casualties within the Division had risen to ninety officers and 3,500 men, came an extremely heavy attack, launched by the British 24th Division.

*Dr J. Forderer Medical Officer Infantry Regiment 120*[20] **8.**

"Dawn broke on 18 August. The enemy began the morning by bringing down a hellish drum fire. The battle line was held by tired, agonised, half-starved and severely decimated German troops. But the fighter of the Somme knew his duty and at moments of danger he would be wide awake and ready for battle... From the rear, Guillemont appeared as a great cloud of dust, above which a huge wing of enemy aircraft cruised in circles in a clear blue sky. A hail of shells was coming down on the village. The defenders had to endure a terrible hammering and repeatedly to change their positions. Fire of all calibres went on until 3.00 pm. The British then believed that they had extinguished all trace of life and assaulted in dense masses, but no sooner were the enemy attacking waves visible out of the dust, than they were engaged by machine guns firing from the gravel pit in front of the village. Each man excelled himself in the heroic struggle which followed. There was no need for orders. One shot, another threw grenades, a third stormed with the bayonet, but the enemy did not give up easily. Again and again he stormed the gravel pit and was always repulsed bloodily. On the right flank, the station was lost. The Reserve Company, despatched forward, took a beating from the enemy artillery and only small groups got through. They were, however, sufficient to prevent the enemy from pressing forward. South of the gravel pit, the enemy also broke into our lines. The 4th Company threw them back with grenades and cold steel. Wherever the British were in the rubble of the village, they were finished off in hand to hand fighting. Our losses were bad, but the enemy suffered far more... The communiqué of the Supreme Army Headquarters for 21st August stated: 'Bitter fighting took place for possession of the village of Guillemont. The Württemberg Kaiser Regiment victoriously beat off all attacks and the village remains firmly in our hands.'"

Just to the north, much the same artillery preparation was directed against Ginchy, which was being defended by Infantry Regiment 125. The bombardment during the 17th and the morning of 18th took a heavy toll on the defenders of the front line, who were clinging on to a series of roughly connected shell holes. When the infantry assault came in, hard up behind the barrage at 3.45 pm, almost all of the nine remaining machine guns were buried or damaged. There was inadequate artillery defensive fire and the result was predictable: the forward positions were driven in. Matters were critical, but thanks to the determined fire of 3rd Company and half of 12th Company who were manning the so-called 'Stutzpunkt Links' [Strongpoint Left], which ran alongside the Ginchy – Flers road and was thus not under direct attack, the assault force began to slow. At that moment, acting on his own initiative, Reserve Leutnant Schlenker brought a machine gun into action in the northwest corner of Ginchy, adding its fire to the one intact gun in the depth position. This finally brought the attack to a standstill, but left the attackers holding a line very close to the village. Oberst Stühmke, the regimental commander, was ordered by Brigade Headquarters to hold the Stutzpunkt and Ginchy at all costs. Two companies were moved forward, the 12th to reinforce the Stutzpunkt and the 9th the western edge of Ginchy.

Oberst Stühmke then decided to launch a counter-attack from the Stutzpunkt with two companies, to throw back the enemy. On being informed by the Artillery Liaison Officer of Field Artillery Regiment 65 that the requested artillery fire against the British line from 8.00 pm to 9.00 pm was not possible and that his own Regiment, which was in direct support, was down to seven serviceable guns, he nevertheless decided to press ahead, requesting release of his own 11th Company, which was the designated brigade reserve, to strengthen the attack. This decision, though understandable, was questionable. The British troops may have been unable to continue the advance, but they could certainly defend their gains. The commander of the attack describes its inevitable outcome:

*Reserve Leutnant Brunner 11th Company Infantry Regiment 125*[21]  **8.**

"I decided to advance in three waves from the Stutzpunkt. The first two waves closed to within one hundred metres of the enemy, but were then halted by enemy rifle and machine gun fire. I then tried to lead the third wave through a communication trench and to take the enemy in the flank.

As we left the communication trench, we were met by such a weight of fire that we had to pull back into the trench where, gradually, we were joined by the survivors of the first two waves. Linking up with 9th Company Infantry Regiment 119, we developed the communication trench as a defensive line."

There matters rested, although work to improve the defensive positions went on feverishly for the next few days, until responsibility for the sector was handed to Fusilier Regiment 35 of 56th Division on 25th August. The men of 27th Infantry Division from Württemberg had held on for an astonishing twenty five days right at the focus of the August fighting, withstanding several set piece attacks, constant bombardment and countless minor actions. It was an amazing achievement in the circumstances, but, eventually, they too had to be withdrawn for rest and recuperation – not so their artillery. There was a shortage of artillery throughout the battle. This lack was particularly acute until the suspension of German attacks around Verdun released units to be moved north. The intervening shortage was compensated for, much to the disgruntlement of the gunners, by keeping them in the line for far longer periods than the infantry, despite their fatigue and their losses. Field Artillery Regiments 13 and 49, for example, who were associated with 27th Division, remained unrelieved for an eight week period, during which time they lost fourteen officers and 304 men, not to mention 160 guns which broke down or were destroyed by enemy counter-battery action.[22]

It was asking much of the gunners; too much, according to the historian of Reserve Field Artillery Regiment 18, who complained, 'In complete disregard of the extraordinary performance of the artillery, at that time the Higher Command was still under the false impression that the artillery was less in need of relief than the infantry. The cause of this may have been the fact that only a few artillery officers succeeded in making a career in the General Staff [!]. These higher commanders, who had received a narrow and one-sided infantry education, believed, in all seriousness, that the artillery had less to endure, simply because it was stationed a few kilometres behind the front line.'[23] Perhaps he had a case. During the regiment's tour of duty from 25th July to the end of September, it suffered forty killed and 153 wounded and no fewer than 206 sick. Fifty-one field guns and twenty light howitzers were destroyed, or suffered mechanical failure, during the firing of over 500,000 rounds.

*Leutnant Adolf Obermüller Infantry Regiment 120*[24] **8.**

From a letter home, 23 August 1916:
"We have been pulled out of the front line as lords and masters of Guillemont. If you believe that so-called street fighting is taking place in and around Guillemont, you are very much mistaken. Guillemont is just one great heap of stones, not a single wall remains standing."

*Leutnant Ernst Jünger Fusilier Regiment 73*[25] **8.**

"It was the days at Guillemont that first made me aware of the overwhelming effects of the war of material. We had to adapt ourselves to an entirely new phase of war. The communications between the artillery and the liaison officers were utterly crippled by the terrific fire. Despatch riders failed to get through the hail of metal, and telephone lines were no sooner laid than they were shot to pieces...There was a zone of a kilometre behind the front line where explosives held absolute sway...Every hand's-breadth of ground had been churned up again and again; trees had been uprooted, smashed and ground to touchwood, the houses blown to bits and turned to dust; hills had been levelled and the arable land made a desert...I cannot too often repeat, [battle] was a condition of things that dug itself in remorselessly week after week and even month after month...The terrible losses, out of all proportion to the breadth of front attacked, were principally due to the old Prussian obstinacy, with which the tactics of the line were pursued to their logical conclusion. One battalion after another was crowded up into a front line already over-manned, and in a few hours pounded to bits. It was a long while before the folly of contesting worthless strips of ground was recognised. It was finally given up and the principle of a mobile defence adopted...Thus it was that there were never again such bitterly-contested engagements as those that for weeks together were fought out round shell-shot woods or undecipherable ruins."

Naturally, it was the men in the fighting line and on the gun positions who bore the brunt of the attritional fighting of August, because this was essentially an artillery battle. Dominance of the skies above the battlefield provided the Allies with an enormous advantage and their overwhelming superiority in guns and ammunition enabled them to control the depth, as well as the contact, battle. Every aspect of life in and behind the German lines was dominated by this fact, which manifested itself throughout the area as a dangerous, disagreeable, but inescapable fact of life.

*Leutnant Tschoeltsch 10th Company Infantry Regiment 133*[26] **9.**

"I lay with my company in the Sunken Road [probably the modern day D107] near Courcelette. The shells which flattened everything, dominated everything and destroyed everything had done the same thing here, so to talk of a sunken road seemed almost like a bad joke. We had had to spend the entire day tucked away in our rabbit holes. Now that it was evening, we could stick it no longer. We wanted to stretch our stiff limbs. We were tired out. We wanted to breathe freely again, after almost suffocating in these tiny holes while the shells whizzed past. As the shadows of the shattered trees began to grow towards infinity, it was possible to risk some movement. The crack of the guns had changed to barking and coughing. They were hoarse and needed to get their breath back. The suspension of fire, which occurred every evening at about this time, seemed to be on schedule today as well. It usually lasted about an hour, then the hammering continued against the thin front. We had to exploit this hour, because it was followed by twenty three more which offered no such respite.

"So there began all the hustle and bustle of a city, which we had observed so often behind the front, at the most important points of the reserve position. The ammunition wagons came galloping up, carrying new ammunition for new battles. Every muscle straining, the drivers sat astride the horses, their gaze directed at the commander, who rode a few paces ahead in the inky blackness, keeping an eye open for craters in the road. Behind the columns came the field kitchens which brought us food and mail. How happy we were when the mail arrived! On those days all the strain was child's play and we took up the fight again with glee. Then came the engineers with piles of material and equipment, to feed this monster of a war which, tireless and never satisfied, swallowed everything which came its way: barbed wire, posts, planks, sandbags, boards, ammunition etc.

"It was just like a busy city, right down to the rushing and the haste. Between all these columns appeared now and then a wounded man who was strong enough to limp to the rear on his own. In between were the sections which had been relieved, which were returning from hell. In between were the sections, heading forward to hold the front. Fresh German blood was coming to stem the advance of the enemy. Runners rushed around. Patrols set about restoring broken down telephone links. Motor vehicles transported to the rear those of the wounded who could go no further. Many of these heroes – for they were heroes all – succumbed on the journey back to the field hospital. We, however, we who were caught up in the middle of all this, doffed our helmets to them.

"Now all was activity on the Sunken Road, but it was hurried; it was limited to an hour. Speed was all. When this hour was over, the guns began to thunder and roar once more, snuffing out all signs of life. We get back in our holes, the columns flood to the rear. Drumfire begins again, heralding the next upheaval. Human life was cheap, and worth less with each day. Just don't think about it – that way lies despair. Our God in heaven, can you really, possibly, wish for all this murder? Our artillery too fell silent at this time and took a breather. When all is said and done, we had to leave our opponents in peace for a while, just as he did us. He needed this hour, just as much as we did. He was human too. This hour was needed so we could all gather strength for the next twenty three hours. Only then would this hour return...."

*Fähnrich Kölling Infantry Regiment 164[27]* **10.**

"Combles, which was situated in a slight hollow, must have been a charming little country village. Heavy shells had had a terrible effect on it. The entire frontages had been torn away from the beautiful large houses. Great stone buildings had collapsed like houses of cards. Cupboards and beds hung out of the opened up rooms. The entire place was permeated by the stink of corpses. Dead inhabitants lay in the rooms. Many had been overcome, when asleep, during the terrible night of 24th-25th June by some of the 3,000 high explosive and gas shells which rained down on the unfortunate place."

*Leutnant Freiherr von Salmuth 6th Company Grenadier Guard Regiment 3[28]* **5.**

"The march [towards Bouchavesnes] was via Allaines, to the west of the road Bapaume-Péronne. Before we reached Allaines we split into platoons, because the whole area of the village near our German battery positions was under fairly heavy fire. The intersection of the track Allaines – Cléry and the Bapaume – Péronne road was known as 'The Place of Death', because fire of all calibres came down on it, with only short pauses. There was no way of avoiding it, because it lay between a canal and a quarry. When we neared it, we waited for a pause in the stream of 155s and shrapnels, then doubled across the ploughed up junction. The grenadiers looked only briefly to their left and right, but in shell craters here lay ammunition, ambulances, trucks and complete light railway trains all piled up in tangles. The only item still more or less upright was a wayside calvary, but the top half of that was shot away. All this presented a ghostly scene, as the flashes of guns and exploding shells briefly lit up the dark night. As we dug and prepared the positions, shells landed behind us every five minutes. During the night 20/21 August the defending infantry in front of us called five times for artillery defensive fire. It was really brilliant to see how alert our artillery was. Barely had the initial red flare gone up, than the first shells were roaring over our heads...

"From our hill in front of Maurepas we had a good view of the area to our rear, through the middle of which ran our second (Forest) position. Throughout 26 August this was under extremely heavy drumfire. There were no dugouts any more and the trench was partially flattened. The smallest calibre the French were using seemed to be 150 millimetre, the largest 380 millimetre, with the majority of the shells being 210 or 280 millimetre. The drumfire went on endlessly; at least ten shells were landing each second. Our ears rang, our senses were reeling. The French were amazed by our new position, but because it was tucked in tight behind the crest line, they could not bring their artillery to bear properly. They had closed up so tightly themselves that they were in danger of hitting their own trenches. The plain behind us looked utterly bleak.

There was not a trace of green, just overlapping craters.

"The village of Leforest was simply one heap of ruins. A nearby copse was no more than a mass of splintered wood. The shattered stumps stood out like ghostly beings. The area was like a lunar landscape. Bodies and bits of bodies lay strewn everywhere. It was the foulest sight I ever saw! This battle was even worse than the famous one in Champagne. Ceaselessly, the Frenchmen hammered away at our positions, our brains and our nerves! At night it continued, but a little easier. Everywhere the night sky was split by the flashes and red hot splinters flew all over the place. We, however, maintained a sharp look out in case they came but, apart from patrols, they did not come!"[29]

For obvious reasons, protection against the endless shelling remained a major preoccupation. Where they still existed, dugouts were used; but life inside these dimly lit, claustrophobic places was no bed of roses and, in the unlucky event of a direct hit, they could become death traps. Small wonder, then, that by this stage of the battle some experienced men preferred to avoid them.

*Reserve Leutnant Pohl 5th Company Foot Guard Regiment 4*[30]  **11.**

"Because there was little in the way of props and shuttering timber, I had forbidden the men to dig more than half a metre below the surface of the road embankment. This was to reduce the possibility of being buried alive. The narrow, but deep, trenches provided excellent protection during the drumfire. We only suffered ten casualties, of whom Reserve Leutnant Müller was killed."

*Hauptmann Freiherr von Hodenberg Guards Field Artillery Regiment 3*[31]  **12.**

"On 17 August, the staff of 2nd Battalion Guards Field Artillery Regiment 3 relieved the staff of 2nd Battalion Field Artillery Regiment 42 in a dugout in Ablaincourt next to the village exit towards Vermandovillers. Once you had crawled backwards into the dugout, which lay six metres below the village street, you were immediately seized by an overwhelming feeling of helplessness and had only one desire, namely to return to the open air as soon as possible. The 'Monkey's Chest', as the dugout had been known since its initial construction, was three metres long and two metres wide. You could only gradually adjust to the atmosphere, which was composed of a mixture of all kinds of smells – alcohol, mould, acetylene fumes, tobacco and leftover food scraps. There was hardly room to move in this cramped space, so the handover/takeover took place by the entrance..."

*Unteroffizier Schnellrath 1st Company Infantry Regiment 88*[32]  **13.**

"At around midday one day [27th], an unteroffizier from the neighbouring battalion appeared in our shell hole and asked where the runners' dugout was. I explained that it was just in rear of our parados. Some time later he reappeared and stated that, although the battalion command post was next to us, there was no trace of a hole behind our parados. I climbed out of my hole and, sure enough, the runners' dugout had been hit and completely buried by a huge dugout-crushing shell. I immediately raised the alarm amongst my comrades and we rushed to the dugout, which was situated a little lower than we were, in order to dig out the entrance. In order not to endanger ourselves, we could not throw the earth up over the sides, but had to spread it within the trench. We soon dug down to a field grey towel, then a gale of foul air from the dugout came out at us.

"Five to six runners had been overcome within the dugout. We hauled them out and lay them along the trench. Opening their jackets, we set about resuscitating them. Gradually, with the exception of two who had already suffocated, they began to come round. We were still working hard on them when a second round landed right on top of the Battalion Command Post, blocking the entrance and once more covering up the rescued men. Now we had to work twice as hard. Taking great care, we began digging. Unfortunately the men who had been buried alive a second time did not survive, but we succeeded in rescuing the Battalion Commander, Major Broeer and his adjutant, Leutnant Zeh, unconscious, but alive. Gefreiter Schmidt, a clerk, was seriously wounded. During a later patrol along Foureaux [High Wood] Trench, I discovered that it was the same all along it."

*Reserve Leutnant Zeh Adjutant 1st Battalion Infantry Regiment 88*[33] **13.**

"During the entire night, the British had kept bringing down destructive fire with super-heavy calibre weapons on the entire length of the Foureaux [High Wood] Stop Line, where the battalion command post was located. This had caused a great deal of damage and had buried many dugouts. Our own dugout, which was mined out, had only one entrance and which was reached down a flight of sixteen steps, swayed around during the night like a rolling ship. After a short period of quiet during the morning, about midday the British resumed their shelling. A runner arrives from 4th Company, with the news that its popular and valued commander, Reserve Leutnant Sircoulomb, had been buried alive and killed. Still shaken by this bad news, we then hear that our runners' dugout has been buried. On the floor of the trench outside our dugout lie four or five men, some dead, the remainder unconscious, when another burst of shelling forces us to take cover. Suddenly there is a violent blow like that of a giant blacksmith's hammer. Our candles are extinguished; a torrent of earth falls in – night!

"I switch on my pocket torch and look round at the chaos. The lower end of our dugout has been wrecked by a heavy shell. The runners and telephonists, who were sitting on the steps there, must have been crushed and suffocated. Only we, my commander Major Broeer, Gefreiter Schmidt our clerk and I are left – hopelessly buried alive four metres below ground, in a tiny space about 1.50 x 1.20 x 0.80 metres. It is an oppressive, nightmarish situation for us. The commander has already lost consciousness. 'There is no hope left,' I say to Gefreiter Schmidt, 'We've had it!' 'Nothing of the kind', replies Schmidt, removing his jacket, taking a pick in his hands and beginning to attack the burnt and blackened earth. Then his pick penetrates the seat of the explosion and a green, poisonous cloud of gas hits him in the face, just as he has taken the point of the pick backwards. Almost instantly the stream of gas knocks him down and, by the greatest misfortune, he falls with the back of his head on the point of the pick and fractures his skull. I try to haul him upright because he is lying with his head downwards and it is streaming blood, but I feel my strength ebbing away. His head is lying in my lap, his warm blood running all down me and soaking me. Schmidt is groaning, but only weakly. I want to help him and to bandage him up, but I have no strength left and I am incapable of the slightest action. I am gradually losing consciousness, but once more the utter hopelessness of our bleak situation flits through my mind. Here we are, in this tiny air pocket, four metres below ground, which could collapse completely at any moment. But I have lost the power to resist. I am resigned to my fate, then I lose consciousness...

"I come to in the hospital in St Quentin. Good old Hoderlein had not left us to die and, despite heavy shell fire, kept on with the digging until we were rescued with barely detectable pulses. Apparently, as we were being transported to the rear in groundsheets, one of the stretcher bearers was wounded."

*Musketier Specht 4th Company Infantry Regiment 164* [34] **10.**

"4th Company, under Leutnant Bode, was occupying an advanced position on the site of an old smashed up battery [near Combles]. During the morning the tired out men of Godt's left forward platoon had laid down to get some sleep in their dugouts. Each of the entrances was occupied by a sentry who was observing to the front. Individual British soldiers were moving around in No Man's Land. Nobody had any thought of an attack. At, I suppose, about 9.00 am, pistol shots rang out at the dugout entrance. The sentry fell down the steps, shot through the chest and lay there unconscious. I was the only person awake on the steps to the right hand dugout entrance where I was cleaning my weapon. I swiftly wakened Unteroffizier Kolbig and the others. We raced up the dugout steps. A few tall British soldiers appeared right in front of the sentry Musketier Beißner. Unteroffizier Kolbig and the leading British soldier fired at each other simultaneously. Kolbig was uninjured, but the British soldier was winged. Leutnant Godt raced up the other set of steps and threw hand grenades amongst the British. The British who were surprised by the swift reaction, were confused, and ran to the rear. The heavy machine gun was brought up from the dugout and fired out to the left. It had barely fired a few rounds, when the gunner was hit twice through the arms and was unable to continue the fight. Initially the machine gun fell silent. About forty British soldiers, who had crept up from a flank unobserved, raced down through a hollow and up the other side. Fired at by the 2nd Platoon, the majority lay where they fell. Only a very few escaped to take cover in a fold in the ground. A little later, British medical orderlies crossed the hill but, because they were followed by an advancing line of infantrymen, we had to open fire. The enemy withdrew. During the evening a coloured flare landed to the left of 4th Company. At the same instant hand grenades exploded in our position. On the order of our commander we leapt behind the position and from there smoked the British out of the position."

During the final week of August, fighting reached a new peak of intensity as the Allies continued to press forward in a series of 'line-straightening' attacks, designed to prepare the ground for a further major joint assault with the French in early September. German losses during the past four weeks had been grave. Many of the defending divisions had been fought to a standstill, with heavy losses, before they were eventually relieved, frequently long after they should have been. Time was running out for the defenders of Delville Wood, whilst the Grenadier Guard Regiments, holding reverse slope positions in and around Maurepas-Le Forest had a very hard time at the hands of the French army.

*Leutnant Freiherr von Salmuth 6th Company Grenadier Guard Regiment 3*[35]**11.**

"The enemy drumming reached a peak of intensity from 4.00 pm [27 August]. The fire roared just over our heads to burst against the second position. We could not hear ourselves speak and were almost suffocating from explosive gases. The sickly stink was nauseating. We knew now that the French were going to attack! We crouched down in the trench. I had a signal pistol in my left hand and a grenade in my right. In front of me was my pistol and dagger! The French drumfire continued for another three solid hours. We were almost driven crazy. Our tongues were stuck to our palates and our eyes were burning, but if we lost our nerve, we should lose everything! Finally, around 7.00 pm, the fire began to lift to the rear. They must be coming! The first of the French were rushing over the crest, fifty metres away, with their bayonets fixed. Red flares roared into the air, the machine gun took post and opened up. Hand grenades from both sides exploded. There was the crackle of rifle fire and our artillery defensive fire started to come down. Dozens of high explosive and shrapnel rounds landed in dense clusters in amongst the French attacking waves. It all happened in a split second, as though all hell had broken loose. It looked bad for us. Naturally the machine gun was the main target. The gunner was badly wounded. His number two leapt into position and had his shoulder torn off. Leutnant Ziesing fell, shot through the jaw. I was hit on the helmet by a spent round, the NCO next to me was shot through the chest! As I rushed to take over the machine gun, a round came through its cooling jacket and boiling water squirted everywhere. I pulled it down and smashed it so that it could not fall into enemy hands. But the attack stalled and the survivors disappeared behind the crest line, whilst our artillery continued to fire. Only now did I notice eight French aircraft which descended to 150-200 metres to machine gun us and throw hand grenades. Now fate dealt us a severe blow. The non-stop fire of our batteries caused the range to shorten, until the shells were landing in and behind our trench. We had the enemy in front of us and our own artillery [landing rounds] overhead and behind us. Our situation was desperate. I fired one green flare after another, until things finally eased. We beat off a further attempted attack by the French, then, around 8.00 pm, things quietened down. After the appalling din of the past hours, the silence was strange and depressing. The losses of the Battalion had been dreadful..."

Nevertheless, the German troops clung to their positions here for the time being. Further north, High Wood was still being contested. On 27th, the capture of Delville Wood was finally completed, but in a continuation of the policy of counterattacking whenever and wherever possible, a German operation was planned against it on 31 August. It was to be conducted by units of the 56th Division and the 4th Bavarian Division and was to be directed as a pincer action against the northern and eastern sides of the wood. This was not a full two division attack, however. It was actually carried out by 3rd Battalion Fusilier Regiment 35, 2nd Battalion Infantry Regiment 88 and 1st Battalion Bavarian Infantry Regiment 5, each attacking two companies up.

*Reserve Leutnant Trobitz 7th Company Infantry Regiment 88* [36] **14.**

" 'So gentlemen, I repeat: Tomorrow afternoon, 31 August, at exactly 2.15 pm, 6th, 7th and 8th Companies will attack the enemy, which is holding the northern edge of Delville Wood. To our right, a battalion of Bavarians will assault simultaneously and, to our left, a battalion of Fusilier Regiment 35, equipped with flamethrowers. The assault distance is 400 metres.' These were the words of our battalion commander on 30 August in a briefing to the assembled company and platoon commanders in a farmhouse in Rocquiny. As it went dark, we were on the march up to the line. In a long column, we advanced via Le Transloy, Lesboeufs and Flers, across unharvested cereal fields. The approach march was nowhere near as bad as those at Verdun. There was only occasional British shrapnel fire. Not until we were within two kilometres of the front line did we notice that we were in the battle zone. We were soon standing side by side in the jumping off trench and surveying No Man's Land. Through the dawn we could gradually make out the outline of the wretched remains of the shattered Delville Wood, where battle was soon to be joined. The sun rose and lit up the scene to our front. We lay and looked down into the hollow. On the far side of it, we could see enemy trenches criss-crossing the so-called wood, which was so thin that we were able to see the ruins of the village of Longueval behind it."

There was one new feature which underlined the determination, or perhaps desperation, of Second Army to try to retake the wood and that was the use of the newly-formed Jäger Storm Battalion 3. This unit was one of the first to be converted from being a normal Jäger battalion into one which was specially trained in assault tactics and reserved for use in critical situations. Its exacting training had begun in mid June 1916. Large numbers of men deemed to be unsuitable for the new task had been transferred to normal line regiments and it spent July and early August on fitness training and mastering new tactics and weapons, such as the light mortars and flamethrowers, with which it had been issued. It arrived on the Somme on 20 August and was subordinated to Second Army. Some of its personnel were immediately employed on training and demonstration duties, but assault groups from the 1st and 2nd Companies were given the task of spearheading the counter-attack of Bavarian Infantry Regiment 5 and Fusilier Regiment 35 respectively.

The assault went in, as planned, after a bombardment which began at 10.00 am, but because of a poor performance by the German artillery, which completely failed to neutralise the British front line positions and the all-pervading mud, which rendered the flamethrowers inoperable, it made little progress.[37]

*Reserve Leutnant Trobitz 7th Company Infantry Regiment 88*[38] **14.**

"When the green flares went up, we rose as one out of the trenches and, no sooner had we set off, than the enemy artillery opened up, which wiped the smile off the faces of the succeeding waves. We ran and ran. But you have to bear in mind: first, the ground, which was completely covered with shell holes; second, the clay, which sucked at our boots; and third, the load we poor soldiers were carrying; assault order, rifles with bayonets fixed, bandoliers of rifle ammunition hung around the neck, revolvers, signal pistols, with flares carried in sandbags, ration pouches, filled water bottles and, finally, digging equipment. After perhaps fifteen minutes, we had possibly advanced about 300 metres without enemy interference. Then the British placed a machine gun in position and opened a slow rate of fire, but still we were not really close enough. With each step we drew nearer, until, silhouetted against the horizon, we must have presented a perfect target and they began to pick us off, one by one. There we lay; dead, wounded and unwounded, in shell holes, in the bright sunshine between the lines. Above us, enemy aircraft, some as low as one hundred metres, filled the sky and swooped down to machine gun us.

"Those who have not lain out wounded between the trench lines can barely imagine the situation. All sorts of thoughts run through your mind: tetanus, stomach wounds, wife and family. There is plenty of time for this, until you are enfolded by blissful unconsciousness. To awake is exquisite, you are still alive! The will to resist grows. One hand clasps the revolver, while the other clutches the wound. If they come, you will not make it easy for them. The enemy artillery has opened up, mainly firing shrapnel. A comrade in the same shell hole, so far unwounded, is suddenly hit on the collarbone by a shrapnel bullet. It is a blow like a box on the ears. Our spirits sink as he goes down. Once it goes dark, he will have to try to crawl off to get aid. The sun burns down unmercifully, torturing us with thirst. Minutes become hours. We exchange addresses. If one of us escapes, he will inform the relatives of the others. All too slowly the sun sinks. It is just 7.00 pm. Suddenly the comrade, who was hit on the collar bone, awakes from a deep sleep, feels his shoulder and discovers that the shoulder strap of his equipment has stopped the shrapnel ball. Apart from severe bruising to the shoulder, nothing has happened to him. He offers to go and get help. Another hour passes and the shadows are lengthening across the battlefield.

"Help will soon be on the way. The British are a noble lot. They will not shoot at stretcher bearers working under the Red Cross flag. I have witnessed this myself. The waiting becomes agonising. We have been lying here for six hours. Many, those who can still walk, have already made it back. Why should we not try it too? Initially it is very hard, but the emergency brings forth an iron will and the waiting has become unbearable. Supporting one another, or crawling on all fours, we move carefully from shell hole to shell hole and so towards safety. The first aid men have their hands full. Tirelessly they gather in the wounded, without being interfered with by the British. Sadly there were a great many victims. Perhaps the assault would have succeeded by night, perhaps not. From our trenches, there was no sign that the other two battalions had cooperated."

Despite the experience of Trobitz, there had in fact been some progress in places; thanks, in particular, to inspiring leadership by Reserve Oberleutnant Schmitt, company commander of 3rd Company Bavarian Infantry Regiment 5[39] and the performance of certain individuals from Jäger Storm Battalion 3. Gefreiter Dietrich, a noted grenade thrower from 1st Company, for example, succeeded in knocking out a British machine gun nest, which was holding up the advance, by landing a grenade right by the crew from a range of sixty metres. Another Jäger managed to save himself by grabbing and holding on to a British bayonet which was thrust at him. His assailant was quickly killed and, despite severe cuts to his hands, the man carried on.[40] The faltering attack was renewed, following a second period of artillery preparation at 5.00 pm, but once again the shooting was poorly directed. The Jägers managed to capture about 300 prisoners and a foothold was gained, but the attack could hardly be counted as anything but a gallant failure. As evening fell, the repulse of the 56th Division units meant that the Bavarians were coming under increasingly heavy fire and they pulled back from the wood.

*Gefreiter Renzing 7th Company Infantry Regiment 88*[41]  **14.**

"When, during the rainy evening of 29 August, we occupied positions in the Foureaux [High Wood] Stop Line [Tea Support], our spirits were not exactly rosy. Here we spent the following day sitting in the filth, being rained on and shelled heavily, prior to moving forward during the night 30th / 31st August. It kept on raining and it needed all our care and effort to maintain our weapons ready to fire. When, at about 9.00 am, the rain slacked off and the sun started to break through, we received orders that at 2.15 pm our battalion was to assault Delville Wood, which was about 500 – 600 metres away. Soldiers have a finely developed sense about the viability of missions which they are given and we were all of the opinion that we had been given a tough nut to crack. The terrain, which fell away into a hollow from the edge of the wood, could be entirely overlooked. Furthermore the distance was too great and our artillery fire was far too obvious. At exactly 2.15 pm the first wave, of which I was a member, went over the top and raced down the gentle slope which led to the hollow in front of the enemy position.

"Thus far the enemy had remained silent, but now they opened extremely heavy and effective fire. The entire edge of the wood seemed to be one single machine gun nest. After about 150 metres, I took cover to get my breath back. I was on the right flank of our 7th Company – to my right was the 8th Company, which took some time to catch up. Finally they arrived. Its commander, Reserve Leutnant Göhringer, together with two runners, leapt into a shell hole. During the attempt to leave the hole and get forward, both the runners were wounded. The company commander grabbed one of their rifles and, taking up a kneeling position in the open, engaged the enemy. He had hardly fired his second shot, when he was himself hit and he fell, killed by two bullets in the head. Once again I attempted to dash forward and I hurled myself down in a deep shell crater, which already contained two sappers who belonged to our first wave and who had also sought cover from the murderous fire. As far as we could tell, the entire assault line had been brought down by enemy fire. Here and there the attack flared briefly into life, as, for example, down at the foot of the hollow, where the courageous Vizefeldwebel Neuhaus of our 3rd Platoon was killed and where, later, wave after wave of the 35th [Fusilier Regiment] were mown down in rows. Any further advance meant certain death and useless sacrifice, especially when the enemy artillery joined in, plastering No Man's Land and our trenches with fire.

"So we prepared our crater for defence and the engineers laid their grenades out ready.[42] The following seven hours when I was trapped out between the lines, completely cut off, burdened by the thought that this enormous sacrifice had all been in vain and subject to overwhelming enemy artillery fire, were amongst the worst of my entire experience at the front. Anyone severely wounded here would have been better off had he been killed instantly, because there could be no aid by day and who would find him in the dark? Meanwhile the August sun burnt down from the sky. When, during the evening, we were ordered back to our start line, it was hardly recognisable. The trench was completely flattened; everywhere lay dead and badly wounded men – our mates, with whom, only a short while ago, we had formed one big happy band. Together we had marched side by side and passed many a happy hour. The entire company was shattered; its pathetic remnants gathered back in the assembly trenches, where we remained until 2 September."

As the month drew to a close, a combination of factors came to a head and the team of Hindenburg and Ludendorff replaced General von Falkenhayn in charge of the German Army. The campaigns in the east during 1915 had not been decisive, Falkenhayn's carefully crafted strategy, which had led to the attack on Verdun in February, had failed in its aim of bleeding the French army to death, inexorable pressure was being exerted on the German army astride the Somme and then, on 27 August, came the last straw. 'German Soldiers!' stated leaflets, which French airmen dropped all over the German lines 28 August, 'Romania, which was once allied to the Central Powers, has declared itself for our side. It has just declared war on Austria-Hungary.'[43] Like most such offerings, the only effect on the men defending the front line was to increase the supply of toilet paper dramatically, but it spelt the end for Falkenhayn. The King of Romania, who was a member of the German House of Hohenzollern and Colonel in Chief of the Prussian Infantry Regiment 68[44], had taken his country to war against Germany.

The pressure had been building on Falkenhayn for months, affecting his personal performance and making life extremely difficult for his staff.

"Colonel Bauer...in the Operations Section of the General Staff, records how unbearable the last part of Falkenhayn's regime was for the more intelligent and individualistic among his officers. 'From week to week...things became more desperate. Falkenhayn, formerly unruffled and superior, was visibly losing his calm and security... Colonel Tappen, the head of Operations Section [remained completely detached]... one day a junior officer was deputed by the others to approach me and to declare that it was my duty as next in seniority after Tappen to intervene. After some hesitation, I decided to approach the Minister for War, Wild von Hohenborn... I accordingly called on him, but without result. I next tried my luck with Plessen.

"At first Plessen was indignant at this peculiar step and it took some time for me to explain that it was only as a last resort that we had undertaken this unsoldierly measure. Finally I seemed to have convinced General von Plessen...A few days later we returned to Pless; the position continued to grow more difficult and we were in despair. On 27 August, when I was walking in the castle grounds at Pless with Freiherr von der Bussche of the Operations Section, we came across the Kaiser. He was calm and cheerful and told us that Romania would certainly not declare war... A few minutes later we received news in our office that Romania had already declared war. Next morning I approached General von Plessen once more, represented to him that the only man who could help us was Ludendorff and begged him to assist us. Soon afterwards I was informed that the Kaiser had been persuaded: Hindenburg and Ludendorff were sent for.'"[45]

The fall of Falkenhayn was no internal palace coup, however. For some time influential men near the centre of power had been manoeuvring against him.

*Crown Prince Rupprecht of Bavaria Diary Entries:*

5th July[46]

"...The dissatisfaction with Falkenhayn's performance is increasing everywhere. I myself have merely written a letter to Graf Lerchenfeld, requesting him to inform the Imperial Chancellor [Bethmann-Hollweg] that matters cannot continue as they are and that we shall be totally ruined through mismanagement, if Falkenhayn stays any longer as head of the Army Supreme Command. General von Nagel told me that throughout the entire army, even in Army Supreme Command circles, a strong movement against Falkenhayn is underway... There is also a general view in the Foreign Office that, because of the odium Falkenhayn has drawn down on himself, there is a need for another Chef of the General Staff before peace can be achieved."

7th July[47]

"During the afternoon I had a meeting in Tournai with the Governor General of Belgium, General von Bissing. He had had a discussion with Graf Lerchenfeld, who had briefed him about my reading of the situation and who had put it to him that, because matters could not continue as they were, the Kaiser had to be briefed about Falkenhayn. At more or less the same time and independently of Lerchenfeld, Herr von Lanken, Head of the Political Department in Brussels, had come to him and informed him that, in the opinion of many in Berlin, especially in the Foreign Office, he was the right man to open the Kaiser's eyes. Generaloberst von Bissing said to me that even though he would not shrink from such a step, a change in Chief of the General Staff at such a time would be seen askance abroad. Furthermore, the Kaiser would regard such a step as an invasion of his prerogative... The only possible successor to Falkenhayn was

Generalfeldmarschall von Hindenburg... Now General von Bissing asked me to give him my thoughts about Falkenhayn. I mentioned his disastrous intervention before the Battle of Ypres, his responsibility for last year's defeat at Arras, the crazy offensive at Verdun and the current defeat of the Second Army. As I concluded, Generaloberst von Bissing stated that he had not realised the situation regarding Falkenhayn was so bad; indeed, it could not be allowed to continue.

"At that he showed me an encoded telegram from the Imperial Chancellor, who in the meantime had also spoken to Graf Lerchenfeld and who now announced, 'No matter how desirable, because of the seriousness of the situation, a change in the person of Chief of the General Staff would be, if I, as a civilian, represent that to the Kaiser, the opposite of what is wished may happen. It can only be done by a military man, such as Bissing.'"

20th August[48]

"Now that I have waited long enough, perhaps too long, today I composed a letter to the Head of the Military Cabinet, General von Lyncker, in which I portrayed the sins of the Army Supreme Command, expressed the view that things could not continue as they were and [stated] that the Army no longer had confidence in General von Falkenhayn. In conclusion I requested General von Lyncker to acquaint the Kaiser with its contents the next time he briefed him."

29th August[49]

"At 5.15 [pm] a telegram arrived, announcing that General--feldmarschall von Hindenburg has been appointed Chief of the General Staff and General Ludendorff as First Quartermaster General! At long last!"

1. Kriegsarchiv München: 8 RIR Bd 3
2. Lieutenant Colonel FHS Rendall 1st/5th York and Lancaster Regiment
3. Kaiser: History IR 63 pp 137-140
4. ibid. pp 142-143
5. Berr: History FAR 75 p 326
6. Düssel: History RIR 17 pp 27-28
7. ibid. pp 37-38
8. ibid. pp 38-39
9. Führen: History Füs R 40 p 314
10. ibid. p 314
11. Pafferath: History IR 68 p 251
12. Forstner: History RIR 15 p 347
13. Bayerisches Kriegsarcihiv: *Die Bayern im Großen Krieg* pp 277-278
14. Roth: History BRIR 23 pp 73-74
15. Meier-Gesees: *Vater Wills Kriegstagebuch* pp 95-99
16. Niemann: History IR 133 pp 54-55
17. Moser: *Feldzugsaufzeichnungen* pp 216-218
18. ibid. p 221

19. ibid. p 222
20. Flaischlen: *Unser Regiment im Wandel der Zeiten* [IR 120] p 18
21. Stühmke: History IR 125 p 135
22. Deutelmoser: History 27th Inf Div p 46
23. Reimers: History RFAR 18 pp 58-59
24. Flaischlen: op. cit. p 18
25. Jünger: 'The Storm of Steel' pp 107- 110
26. Niemann: op. cit. pp 51-53
27. Anon: History IR 164 p 242
28. Rosenberg-Lipinsky: History GGR3 p 323
29. ibid. p 338
30. History: GR 4 pp 191-192
31. Collenberg:  History GFAR 3 pp 213-214
32. Rogge: History IR 88 pp 280
33. ibid. pp 280-281
34. Anon: History IR 164
35. Rosenberg-Lipinsky: op. cit. pp 339-340
36. Rogge: op. cit. p 285
37. Anon: History FüsR 35 p 182
38. Rogge: op. cit. p 286
39. Weniger: History BIR 5 pp 63-64
40. Lattorf: History Jäg Batl 3 pp 127-128
41. Rogge: op. cit. p 287
42. Although by this stage of the war most infantrymen had been trained in the use of grenades,
  engineers received special additional training in the use of both hand grenades and rifle grenades.
  This was an extension of their role in charge of grenade launchers and light mortars.  The likelihood
  in this case is that these engineers had been specifically included in this attack as specialist grenade
  teams
43. Studt: History IR 31 p 157
44. Pafferath: History IR 68 p 295
45. Tschuppik: 'Ludendorff' p 57
46. Kronprinz Rupprecht 'Mein Kriegstagebuch' Bd 1 p 497
47. ibid. 1. Band pp 498-499
48. ibid. 1. Band p 520
49. ibid. 2. Band p 1

# CHAPTER 7

# September 1916

D espite the momentous events which had been taking place at Supreme Headquarters, for the troops on the ground the fighting at the beginning of September continued with unabated intensity. Attacks and counter-attacks were a constant feature, just as they had been for the past two months as both sides struggled to achieve dominance, whilst, further to the rear, reinforcing units were being moved forward to relieve regiments worn down in the hard battles of the past few days.

*Hauptmann Reinhard Seiler Infantry Regiment 161*[1] **1.**

"In the meantime, the sector where the Regiment was due to carry out the relief was laid down exactly. It was between Guillemont and Ginchy. The front line was only to be occupied by five platoons. This meant that the battalion holding the line could provide its own depth and a further battalion was held in readiness behind it. What a difference this was from the situation during the Battle of Arras, where we were forced to face the enemy in one, single, thickly occupied line of defence, without any forces in readiness or reserve behind it and no further lines of defence.[2] 3rd Battalion Infantry Regiment 161 was designated to hold the line, with the 2nd Battalion at readiness and the 1st Battalion resting.

"On 3 September there was a service in the church at Maretz. The Divisional Pastor was late for the evangelical service, so, after a lengthy wait, the Oberstleutnant took over the Holy Office and got us to sing that defiant old hymn, 'A mighty fortress is our God, a sure defence and weapon...'.[3] Seldom have we agreed so strongly, or joined in so wholeheartedly. The golden light of evening flooded in through the narrow windows and played sparkling patterns on the armour of Joan of Arc, whose statue stood in the church and glowed throughout the sermon of the pastor, who in the meantime had joined us, until we all sank into the gloaming. Under the ever-increasing thunder of the guns, which rent the air and shook the windows, we all received communion and thus prepared for the battle, as Cromwell's 'Ironsides' had once been, and then we stepped out into the dark night."

South of Guillemont, the men of the 1st and 2nd Guards Divisions were battling hard west of Bouchavesnes, between Leforest and Cléry, where the French army was striving to gain ground, prior to the planned joint offensive later in the month.

*Leutnant Woigeck 1st Battery Guards Field Artillery Regiment 3[4] 2.*

"1st September was a critical day. Intense enemy aerial observation and heavy harassing fire from early morning were unmistakeable precursors of an attack. 1st Battery had another bad day. Between 1.00 pm and 7.00 pm we counted approximately 1,000 shells on our poorly constructed position. A 150 millimetre battery, accurately directed by a balloon, had made it its objective to destroy our four small field guns totally. Nevertheless it did not quite succeed. Two guns remained untouched; a dismal result, which did not justify the expenditure in ammunition. Because the battery had no battlefield mission I kept the men, with the exception of the sentries for whom we had hurriedly prepared shell scrapes, in the one remaining dugout. This heroes' cellar had very little overhead cover, but it did boast two entrances. It creaked and groaned alarmingly and many cast doubts over its ability to withstand the shells. One ceiling support cracked and broke very swiftly, but the bunker remained intact. With a speed that would have done credit to trained carpenters, a new roof prop was put in place. Hardly had this work been completed, than the sentry reported that a great pile of ammunition was on fire. With cold blooded courage, the men raced to it in the attempt to extinguish the fire by smothering it with earth. Kanonier Priemel also distinguished himself by digging out several men of the left flank gun who had been buried alive. Unfortunately he never received his well-earned Iron Cross, because he fell victim a few days later to a gas attack on the position..."

*Unteroffizier Bertram 11th Company Grenadier Guard Regiment 3[5] 2.*

"[1 September] Heavy and super-heavy artillery began to bring down systematic destructive fire on the position. It seemed as though a gun of 285 or 305 millimetres, directed by an aerial observer, was concentrating on our sector. The light artillery, on the other hand, performed poorly. Most of the rounds were overs that landed in the swampy ground without exploding, but the heavy shells were right on the mark. It was awful, the shells were bursting ever closer. The trench was so narrow that it was impossible to pass. In addition, it was covered with groundsheets as camouflage. The aviators must nevertheless have spotted the line, because the bursts were landing right next to each other. Wounded men from the left hand platoon started coming through our position. Unteroffizer Beck, an old soldier who was known throughout the company as a veteran of Russia, scrambled along the trench nursing a terrible arm wound and others followed, but we stayed where we were; there was nowhere else to go. Any movement would have betrayed our presence and brought down more artillery fire on us...Flank protection to the right was the main task, otherwise there could be no coherent defence

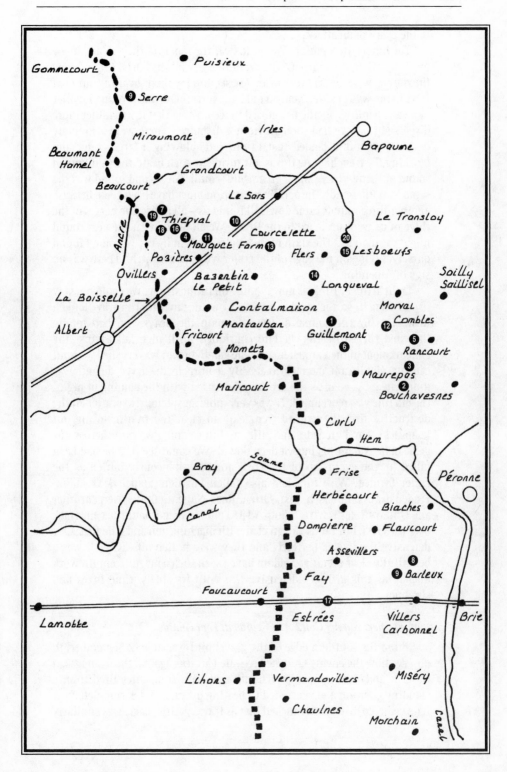

in the event of an attack.

"The bursts drew closer. We could hear the report of the gun and knew precisely when it had fired. The section to my left had been hit and now the rounds were getting very near. My section lay there awaiting our fate. Next to me was Fusilier Neu, an old Landsturmman, and a young Fusilier named Alberding. As the fire closed in we noticed that it was rather more dispersed than we had thought from a distance. There were also many duds. One round landed just to our left, blowing a large crater and blocking the trench. Now it was our turn! We each heard the well-known sound of firing. There was a great thud – dud! The second round was the same – another dud! The aerial observation must have been good, because another three rounds came down all round us – all duds. The nerves of the three of us were stretched to the limit. We all knew what the next round might mean to us. The sixth round exploded right by us. Neu and I found ourselves lying on the edge of the crater without a scratch. There was no sign of Alberding.

"Light artillery fire was now landing on the position. We could not stay in the trench, so the final section was withdrawn to a nearby Sunken Road. During the course of the afternoon the heavy gun had totally flattened the entire trench. Fire continued until nightfall against the embankment of the Sunken Road. One small dugout was crushed without causing significant damage to us. By a miracle the large dugout was untouched. As soon as the artillery fire eased with the coming of night, the old line was reoccupied. It was very quiet, suspiciously so, after all the destructive fire. We worked frenziedly to clear the trench, to dig out knapsacks, hand grenades and rifles and in so doing we came across our great mate Alberding, buried deep down. We could see that he had been killed by the explosion of the shell and simultaneously buried as the crater formed. With him had also fallen Fusiliers Stapel, Max Mann, Lindenstrauss, Roßbach, Just, Otten, Rose, Supe, Gefreiter Hergenröther and Unteroffizier Tewitz. About 11.00 pm the French launched an attack over the crest, but they were greeted with machine gun and rifle fire. Our defensive fire landed perfectly and they were beaten off easily. It was a beautifully clear evening. Seldom have I seen such a magnificent firework display as this artillery defensive fire with its shells, time fuzes and shrapnel..."

*Leutnant Freiherr von der Goltz 4th Regiment Foot Guards* [6] **3.**

"From the southern edge of the gravel pit I was able [2 September] to observe how the enemy launched repeated attacks against the frontages of the 5th and 6th Companies. The men of both companies fired from a standing position and succeeded in beating off each attack completely. A renewed French attack, launched just as it was getting dark, was similarly dealt with. At 11.00 pm the 5th Company reported that it was maintaining the full extent of its frontage, but that it needed reinforcements and resupply with ammunition, hand grenades and flares. The Saxons, who had been on the march for hours to reinforce us, had still not appeared, even though hour after hour had gone by. After it went dark, the French made a deep breakthrough along the Somme valley where the Bavarians were deployed. A French infantryman of the 57th Battalion walked by mistake into the gravel pit and was captured. He stated that the French 57th and 58th Battalions were already established in Cléry. A little earlier, Rittmeister Graf von der Schulenburg had gone to the rear to see about reinforcements for the companies and to bring them forward, but he was killed doing this. The Battalion staff and three sections of 5th Company under Feldwebel Schütte also brought down heavy fire on the French in Cléry..."

Almost seamlessly the Allied bombardments and pressure of the first two days of the month fused into a major day of battle on 3 September. The 4th Guards Division, deployed on the left flank of the Württemberg 26th Reserve Division to buttress the Thiepval ridge against further advance towards Mouquet Farm, found itself in action early, with a determined enemy armed with flamethrowers.

*Reserve Leutnant Krüger 8th Company 5th Regiment Foot Guards*[7][4].

"Towards 3.00 am, we noticed clouds of gas, which did not affect us, but caused me to bring the company up to the highest alert state. It was nerve wracking for everyone. Eyes and ears strained to observe No Man's Land, which was filled with the spectral light of flares. But nothing happened. The gas dispersed and the clock ticked on to 6.00 am. Tired, I lay down on the ground and had hardly dropped off into a deep sleep...when that faithful runner, Gefreiter Eickelmann, woke me with a shout. 'Leutnant, the British are coming!' I leapt to my feet and saw before me a sea of flame and smoke. Stinging fumes were getting into lungs and eyes. I could only see Eickelmann as a shadow surrounded by fog into which he was calmly firing. Tiredness disappeared instantly. I made the defenders move forward out of the trenches where the smoke was clinging and making breathing difficult, in order to keep up a calm rate of rifle fire.

"We were confronted by an amazing spectacle. As far as the eye could see, the sky was lit by innumerable flares. Red and green signal rockets fired by both sides cut broad arcs in the light of dawn. Machine guns hammered away ceaselessly and rifle fire rang out. Heavy and super-heavy shells crashed down and burst, whilst, over our heads, came the bright flashes of the devils brew from the flamethrowers, which splashed its liquid fire down on us, singeing clothing, beards, hair and skin. If the Tommies believed that they could crack us with this latest surprise, then they were deluding themselves badly. The Prussian Guards, battled tested and used to victory, were fighting here! Standing in thick smoke and surrounding by flaming blazes were the unshakeable Grenadiers, burnt and as black as chimneysweeps, but taking careful aim and calmly picking off the soldiers in their plate-like helmets as they leapt from shell hole to shell hole. The enemy soon saw that he was gnawing at granite here and he disappeared in short order into the dawn of Sunday..."

Fifteen kilometres away, just to the north of the Somme, the French army attacked at intervals throughout the day. The pressure built until, fighting hard to the last, men of the 'Elisabeth' Regiment [Grenadier Guard Regiment 3] were overwhelmed and the few remaining survivors were captured.

*Leutnant Ay 3rd Company Grenadier Guard Regiment 3[8] 5.*

"The Company had its three platoons in the front line. Vizefeldwebel Fröhlich's platoon was on the right, linking with 2nd Company. Leutnant Freiherr von Schrötter's platoon was on the left, but could only maintain contact with the Saxon regiment next to us by means of nightly patrols across the 150 metre gap. The enemy occupied the crest. 3rd Company was on the reverse slope, occupying foxholes and shell craters about fifty to one hundred metres lower down. There was a machine gun between von Schrötter's platoon and the centre platoon, but it took a direct hit during the night 2/3 September. The weakest point of the defence was on the left, in the area of von Schrötter's platoon, so the company commander stationed himself there.

"The losses during the morning of 3 September were bearable. The drumfire, some of which was of super-heavy calibre, deluged the Sunken Road on the left flank, so that the Saxon company to the rear of 3rd Company was completely overwhelmed and had to withdraw. Despite the drumfire, casualties up to 10.00 am were kept in reasonable bounds and the company still had around one hundred riflemen.

"At 10.00 am the enemy lifted the fire to the rear. Relieved, the company awaited the inevitable attack, but the enemy only probed forward with patrols, which disappeared once more when fire was resumed.

"At 10.30 am the drumfire began again. Clouds of dust made observation difficult and the fire was causing more serious problems. Towards 1.00 pm, the curtain of fire rolled towards the rear. About a company of light mountain troops stormed forward, but they were beaten off easily. Our men were in high spirits. About midday the enemy broke through on our left and penetrated about 600 metres in rear of the company on the territory of our neighbouring division. They then pressed on in strength to establish themselves on high ground behind us. The company turned about, set its sights at 700 metres and opened fire, with only moderate success, against the waves of attackers, who were not deflected from their advance. The situation forward became more serious. It was hard to see the enemy so, on the left flank of 3rd Company, the men moved out in the open and shot from a standing position, whenever the enemy attacked in packs. Because of the obscuration, the enemy managed to by-pass to the left without being observed and to set up a machine gun to the left flank of 3rd Company.

"From 3.00 pm, attacks from the front were countered, but the enemy pulling sledges with equipment round the flanks were not engaged. The enemy worked their way forward, a battle began with hand grenades, but by 4.00 pm they [our grenades] began to run short. The enemy did not want to take many chances, however. Two to three hand grenades was all it took to drive them off. The company was now completely surrounded and, as a result, at least the appalling machine gun fire ceased. The remainder of the company clung to the hope that, with nightfall, they might be able to break out. Calls for grenades and ammunition increased. The French attacked again at 4.30 pm with grenades, but did not follow up. They then demanded our surrender, but were met by shouts of anger from our ranks. We could not, however, overlook our casualties. The last remnants of the company closed in tightly around the company commander. Towards 5.00 pm an enemy aircraft circled low above our pocket of resistance. We could not shoot at it, because the company had fired off all its ammunition. There was then a complete pause which lasted about half an hour until, at about 5.30 pm, the enemy launched a surprise attack in about company strength, complete with drummer, from short range at our left flank, which overran the last of us. Including lightly wounded, only about a dozen men plus the company commander were taken prisoner."

This situation was serious enough, but further north disaster was looming in and around Guillemont. Guillemont! The village which had been defended so well and so obstinately for so long, was not destined to remain in German hands for much longer. The survivors, of whom there were comparatively few, wrote numerous accounts of the day's fighting, which provide a vivid impression about the intensity and brutality of the fighting over a place for which both sides had sacrificed so much. The German army took the loss of this place particularly badly. For weeks it had symbolised the totality of the defensive effort and now it had been lost.

*Reserve Leutnant Wetje 2nd Company Fusilier Regiment 73⁹* **6.**

"On 2 September, 2nd Company was at readiness in the cellars of Combles. That evening, towards 11.00 pm, we marched forward to relieve the 9th Company. We had several casualties from artillery fire during the move, nevertheless we completed the relief correctly. I carried out thorough checks and discovered that the position was in a worse state than ever. On the right the Sunken Road, blasted to a shallow hollow, offered no cover at all. On the left flank the trench was mostly flattened and nowhere more than one metre deep. The company dug in anew. I and my runners occupied a dugout in the Sunken Road which had two entrances and one to two metres of overhead cover. I also held one section and one machine gun and its crew as a reserve in the dugout. Two machine guns took post on the position. There was artillery fire throughout the night. The Sunken Road on the left flank was kept under constant fire. The gap to the neighbouring regiment was about 300 metres wide and was constantly under heavy fire. Fähnrich Wohlgemut established contact with Infantry Regiment 76. Vizefeldwebel Kormann took a platoon into the gap and the 8th Company also established sentry positions there.

"After dawn, the artillery fire increased, peaking at about 8.00am. Enemy airmen flew low over us, machine gunning the position and giving their hooter signals. One entrance to the dugout was crushed. The artillery fire continued relentlessly, high explosive being mixed with shrapnel fired by the flanking batteries. Casualties were already considerable. Despite all our efforts, we could not maintain contact on the flanks. At about 1.00 pm, the second entrance to the dugout was crushed, so, for a time, I was cut off from the company. We worked with all our strength to reopen the entrance and succeeded. As a man crawled through he shouted back, 'The British are here!' Everyone pressed forward to get out. The British, who in the meantime had overwhelmed the trench garrison, immediately killed each man as he crawled out of the dugout. As we pulled their corpses back into the dugout, hand grenades exploded in the entrance, producing fire and smoke. The other entrance was blocked by beams and earth. Resistance was impossible. I and the few men who were with me were called on to surrender by an officer. Captured, too, from the company were one NCO and about fifteen men, almost all of whom were wounded. I found out that when I was cut off the British suddenly appeared from the rear and both flanks. Finally they also assaulted from the front. Leutnant Gievers was killed as he fired red signal flares to call for our artillery. Gefreiter Bartels, the last man from the left flank still alive, reported that Leutnant Vogel was surrounded with the remainder of his men and fell, revolver in hand, after putting up a brave defence. As I was conducted to the rear, I knew from the casualties that the British had suffered that the company had done its duty to the last."

*Oberleutnant von Hornbostel 1st Company Fusilier Regiment 73*[10] **6.**

"During the night 2/3 September, 1st Company relieved the 12th Company in the second line near Guillemont. Enemy artillery had damaged the trench badly. All the so-called dugouts in the centre had been crushed, but were roughly repaired, prior to the company being allocated shelters. The morale of the men, who had arrived at the trench without casualties, was good. The officers went to the flanks. I myself was on the left. We did not succeed in establishing the link with Infantry Regiment 164. Artillery fire continued throughout the night, increased in intensity the following morning and reached a peak around midday. Numerous dugouts were wrecked once more. The artillery fire that we had called for with signal flares was not fired. There was much aerial activity, which made observation difficult, even over our own sector.

"Suddenly came the report: 'The British are outside the dugout!' At the same instant hand grenades detonated and, with the exception of Unteroffizier Brand, all the occupants of the dugout were dead or mortally wounded. I myself suffered multiple wounds. On my order Brand left the dugout. Resistance was pointless and impossible and he was captured. The remainder of 1st Company put up an energetic fight. With a few exceptions, the entire trench garrison was killed, both leutnants amongst them. I myself lost consciousness due to loss of blood. In the first hospital I was found to have been wounded twenty times, some hand grenade splinters were not removed until later. Until 7 September I was only conscious occasionally. In the hospital at Dartford men of the 1st Company said that the enemy who had broken through attacked from the rear."

*Ersatzreservist Tebbe 6th Company Infantry Regiment 164*[11] **6.**

"In the early dawn, [3rd September] the night sentries crept shivering into the dugouts. Thick smoke and fog filled the shallow hollow. Towards 9.00 am the sun broke through and it was a fine summer day. The fire had increased considerably, but our front line was due to be relieved that evening and we all hoped earnestly that our final day in the position would pass off successfully. About 10.00 am, Ersatzreservist Steding and I went on sentry in the middle sector of the 6th Company. We lay under a stretched-out tent half and observed the terrain to our front. As far as the eye could see, a lifeless, empty crater field stretched away endlessly. Unexpectedly, a British soldier with a dog appeared and moved steadily towards the German lines. Suddenly his dog began to bark. The British soldier hesitated, stood still, then turned away. Landsturmman Zotetzki set his sights at 150 metres fired and hit him. When Leutnant Patz asked 'What are we going to do with him?' the somewhat taciturn and reserved Zotetzki replied, 'I hit him, I'll fetch him!' He nimbly crawled off on all fours, picked him up and brought him in to the German position. The British soldier, who had been shot through the chest was bandaged up and cared for. He soon came round and was quite cheerful.

"Half an hour later the enemy attacked the left neighbouring company about 600 metres in rear. From the elevated position of 6th Company we could observe the advancing British in detail. Dense columns rose out of their trenches. Behind them came harnessed hospital wagons. The attack withered away in German artillery fire. Sentries changed over at midday. The relieved sentries disappeared into the dugouts, then, about 12.30 pm, the British artillery increased to heavy drum fire on our position. The platoon commander ordered, 'Stand to!' No sooner had the men spread out in the shell craters than it was, 'Here they come!' The British advanced in immense masses. After a few moments, the entire broad battlefield was covered with a great depth of advancing waves. The defenders opened up rapid fire, without getting many hits. Every shot needed to count. The German artillery fired very little. Only once did a heavy mortar round crash down on a dense column and sent an entire section of soldiers spinning into the air.

"When they were 150 metres to our front, the main force of advancing British soldiers turned to the right to assault the position of the 1st Platoon, which occupied block houses in a sunken road. No Man's Land was in dead ground. In the noise of the artillery battle, the British attack was a surprise. Suddenly the sunken road was full of British, demanding that the crews of the blockhouses surrender. The reply was a shower of hand grenades, but superiority of numbers told. In the cramped bunkers the British grenades caused a dreadful bloodbath, from which very few Germans escaped. In one blockhouse a shell had torn a hole in the rear wall. Ersatzreservist Garbe attempted to force his way between two planks. He was caught by his belt hooks, so pulled off his jacket and thus escaped the British hand grenades. Just as he emerged there was a British officer in front of him with a revolver, which he fired. The bullet hit him in the mouth, knocked out a row of teeth and exited behind his lower jaw. Garbe fell and played dead. Later a wounded British soldier took him to the rear. Subsequently Garbe remarked to us dryly that he had never had so many teeth pulled out at once or so quickly.

"British pilots flew so low over the central platoon that the smell of petrol fumes penetrated the trenches. They sprayed the trenches with fire and hammered the defenders in the shell craters. The dull 'Tack-Tack!' of their weapons died away. Vizefeldwebel Oschaz, Unteroffizier Rust and Gefreiter Winzel lay dead in their holes. Ersatzreservist Steding was wounded. The wounded crawled down into the dugouts. On the topmost step of the dugout sat Musketier Thies, whose lower jaw had been broken by a bullet. Without making a sound he read quietly and told his rosary. All the commanders were dead or wounded. Out of the whole of 2nd Platoon, only three men were still firing: Gefreiter Wienecke, Ersatz Reservist Blome and me. Blome, always calm, sensible and modest; who had always borne the hard lot of the front line soldier contentedly, showed here during this hour of danger the entire manliness and strength of a self-contained individual. He had already been wounded through the wrist. Every time he fired I could see blood streaming from his sleeve, but he kept on encouraging the two of us, 'Fire, fire, maybe we can hold them off!' Only when he was hit a second time, through the shoulder, did he collapse and crawl off to the dugout.

"As the mass of attackers surged towards those parts of the line from which there was less firing, the terrain in front of the 2nd Platoon became emptier. The bullets of the last of the riflemen were running out; their barrels were red hot. Gefreiter Wienecke and I crawled into a corrugated iron shelter. As we gradually collected our thoughts, the sheer hopelessness of our situation became clear. The hand to hand fighting had come to an end. To our right and left the enemy had made deep inroads. All contact to the rear had been severed. Behind us were masses of British, all around nobody but the dead and wounded. It seemed to be hopeless to try to break through to the rear. Suddenly a shell collapsed the corrugated iron shelter. We crawled out from under the debris and leapt into the nearest dugout entrance. It was full of wounded and out of the depths came groans. The uppermost steps were covered in blood. A little while later the first of the British grenades came flying down into the packed dugout. The second injured both of my eyes and initially I could see nothing.

"There was barely an unwounded man in the dugout. Terribly cramped, the wounded huddled together as deep as possible, helpless before the hand grenades. Then the wounded British soldier, who was down below in the dugout, became our saviour. He shouted up to his comrades, climbed the steps and explained that there was nobody in the dugout who was capable of fighting. Protectively, he stood in front of the Germans who had earlier treated him in a knightly manner. Slowly the Germans emerged without their weapons from the dugout. The lightly wounded assisted those who required help. The wounded Landsturmmann Deppe led me upwards. Covered in blood and clay the remnants of the 6th Company staggered off into captivity. In a sunken road we halted. British medical orderlies treated our wounds and gave us tea and cigarettes..."

*Reserve Leutnant Oschatz 7th Company Fusilier Regiment 73*[12] **6**.

"Gefreiter Preul came charging down the steps [of a dugout near to Faffémont Farm] yelling, 'Here they come!' Because we had been sitting there all day long with our equipment on, we were able to man the trench swiftly. As I emerged, I saw the British advancing in broad dense lines out of the hollow about 200 – 300 metres to our front. We fired the previously agreed red signal flares to call down our artillery fire and battle was joined. Because the men clustered around the two entrances to the dugout, Neckel and I made them spread out. Initially, in accordance with orders, I ran through the craters to ensure that the right hand platoon had stood to. I shouted briefly to Leutnant Dühr and hared back again. Bullets were flying everywhere and as I reached the dugout, I saw my old comrade Neckel, with whom I had passed many an hour, held in the arms of his batman with a serious neck wound. Blood was pumping in a thick stream from his severed artery; he was beyond help. I could not stop, duty called on the left.

"I grabbed my men, who were pinned down by heavy fire round the entrance to the left hand dugout and led them through the craters to the left so as to fill the gap there. Once I felt that we had gone far enough, I threw myself down and opened fire with a rifle that I had grabbed. Now for the first time in the full September sun I could see the battlefield that thus far I had only observed when it was dark. All around, as far as the eye could see, there was not a speck of green, just a broad brown crater field. In front of us, beyond the hollow, was the steep rise to the village of Maurepas, down which streamed dense enemy columns. There were countless aircraft in the air buzzing around just above the ground. To our front and advancing in short bounds, were the British. I could see how, on the hand signal of an officer, the whole line rose and rushed towards us. They were about two hundred metres away. Our artillery fire was coming down brilliantly; the black fountains of earth were springing up all around the enemy. I could see men spinning up into the air. We shot as rapidly as we could. It was just a wild crashing and clattering. I was the furthest left. Left of me there was nothing. Immediately next to me was Musketier Mehrle. We shouted to each other every time we thought that we had scored a hit. Suddenly we came under heavy machine gun fire from a rise to our left. I could see the muzzle flashes and the crew of the gun, so I shouted to Mehrle to indicate the target. I did not receive a reply and spun round to see that he was already dead, killed by a head wound. Now I was all alone and the machine gun fire was getting worse. I could not make up my mind if it was coming from the machine gun that I had spotted, or from one of the many aircraft that were still buzzing around overhead. The British attack had stalled. Individuals could be seen running to the rear. Suddenly there was another burst of machine gun fire and I received a heavy blow on the right thigh and noticed blood streaming down. I had just received a flesh wound. The bone was uninjured, so I was able during a quiet moment to make my way through the craters to the entrance to the dugout where I was met by our medical orderly Busse, who bandaged me up..."

Gradually the intensity of the battle died away as strong point by strong point, trench by trench, the defenders were overwhelmed. Most fought to the death, some made it back to positions in rear and some, a few, were captured and lived to recount their experiences, writing graphically about what they had lived through and the appalling sights they had witnessed.

*Reserve Vizefeldwebel Heinrich Warnecke 1st Company Fusilier Regiment 73*[13] **6.**

"I walked across a battlefield many times during the World War, but never did a place of battle leave so moving an impression on me as that of Guillemont on 3 September 1916. I, too, belonged to the 1st Battalion that shed its lifeblood here. I was captured in a hopeless depth position held by 1st Company and was led away with my comrades through the positions of the 2nd 3rd and 4th Companies. We advanced through a crater field and then we were standing on the edge of the Sunken Road in which our comrades had fought and suffered. What we saw took our breath away. The soldiers lay where they had died. Many hung there on the edge of the road in their firing positions, others had been thrown back onto the surface of the road and lay there, their dead eyes and white faces turned up to the sky. In one place, about a dozen of them had defended a large shell hole which had been torn out of the road. Firing to their front, they had been shot down from behind by the enemy who had by-passed the position. The fight in the 4th Company area must have been especially bitter, where our position ended and the Sunken Road was blocked by a sandbag barricade. There our dead lay, not individually, or next to one another, but piled up. Repeatedly, our men must have rushed to defend this vital place and again and again they fell as fresh victims, on top of those who had gone before. It was a living wall which could only have been broken by overwhelming enemy strength. Near this place lay the commander, Oberleutnant Engelbrecht, that ideal of front line officers, who had fallen amidst his men."

The fall of Guillemont came as a savage psychological blow to the German army, which had invested so much blood and effort in its defence. Infantry Regiment 76 from Hamburg published a detailed book later[14] which, apart from describing fully the course of events, devoted much space to a description of how the men of the Regiment had done all in their power to hold on, to explaining that their artillery support had faltered at a critical time and to putting forward the case that rigid defence here was pursued longer than it should have been. They really had nothing to apologise for. The losses on this appalling day were simply dreadful. 2nd Battalion Infantry Regiment 76 was utterly destroyed. The survivors of the 5th Company, having reached the rear assembly point, posed for a photograph. There were five of them. When, some years later, the time came to write their Regimental History, nobody at all was left from 3rd Company Fusilier Regiment 73, the regiment of Ernst Jünger, of 'Storm of Steel' fame, to contribute. They had all fallen in the defence of Guillemont. Struggling to do justice to their sacrifice, Major Seiler, their historian, hit on a possibly unique solution. One entire page carries, in bold typeface, a simple statement.

"3./73

Nobody from 3rd Company can provide a report – all the men were killed, as was every officer. We honour these courageous comrades symbolically through this silent page, believing that that the simple '3./73', is more eloquent than words..."[15]

Writing in the same history, Hauptmann (Retired) Louis Engelbrecht, grieving father of Oberleutnant Horst Engelbrecht, who was killed at Guillemont 3rd September whilst commanding 4th Company Fusilier Regiment 73, paid his own tribute to the fallen.

| | |
|---|---|
| *Den Helden von Guillemont* | *To the Heroes of Guillemont* |
| *Den Tag habt ihr gerettet* | *You men have saved the day* |
| *Mit eurem Heldenmut* | *Your duty nobly done* |
| *Nun liegt ihr still gebettet* | *Now you lie and take your rest* |
| *In letzter Sonnenglut* | *In the dying rays of the sun* |
| *Und über all' den Hügeln* | *And over all the hills* |
| *Des blutgetränkten Sandes* | *Above the blood-soaked sand* |
| *Schwebt wie ein Hauch des Himmels* | *Soars like the breath of heaven* |
| *Der Dank des Vaterlandes* | *The thanks of the Fatherland* |

Reserve Hauptmann Louis Engelbrecht[16]

On 5th September Hindenburg and Ludendorff travelled to France for their first detailed examination on the spot of the crisis in the west. After a brief visit to Crown Prince Wilhelm at Charleville, where the suspension of offensive operations at Verdun was confirmed and welcomed, the two of them moved north for a crucial conference at the Headquarters of Crown Prince Rupprecht in Cambrai. Arriving at 8.00 am, Field Marshal Hindenburg handed Crown Prince Rupprecht his Prussian Field Marshal's baton, then the serious business of the day began. Generals Ilse, von Kuhl and von Luttwitz, chiefs of staff of 4th Army, Army Group Crown Prince Rupprecht and Army Group German Crown Prince respectively, each gave detailed presentations concerning their sectors, but the main effort was devoted to an examination of the Somme battle. Ludendorff, after his experiences in the east, was less concerned about the loss of terrain *per se*, than with the cost in manpower terms that the rigid denial of ground was causing. Much of the detailed discussion, therefore, centred on obtaining clarity about rates of loss and force ratios, especially in opposing artillery and aircraft. This proved to be extremely difficult, but it was essential if informed future decisions at the operational and tactical level were to be made. There was also much detailed examination of current tactics and operational procedures.

*First Quartermaster General Erich Ludendorff*[17]

> "That which I learned in Cambrai about our infantry, its equipment and tactics was extremely valuable for me. It was certain that the infantry was fighting too narrowly and rigidly. They were clinging on to ground far too much and the consequence was high casualty rates. Deep dugouts and cellars were too often fatal mantraps. The use of the rifle had been forgotten. The hand grenade had become the primary weapon and the equipment of the infantry with machine guns and other direct fire weapons had fallen way behind the measures which the enemy had taken. Initially the Field Marshal and I could only ask that, in principle, the front line positions be more thinly manned, the deep mined dugouts be destroyed and that all trenches or areas of terrain not essential for the overall defence be relinquished, if their rigid defence meant that particularly heavy casualties would have to be endured. We would tackle the further questions concerning training and equipment of the infantry at a later stage..."

The Cambrai conference was not only significant at this relatively low level. Summing it up later, General Ludendorff recorded, 'The Cambrai conference produced much that was valuable. The silent grandeur of the assembled commanders and chiefs [of staff], who had been engaged for almost two years in great defensive battles here in the west, whilst the Field Marshal and I had been able to win daring offensive battles in the east, made a deep impression. I was reinforced in my intent to get the government to recognise the war for what it was. Manpower, materiel and moral strength were the essentials for the army. The longer the war lasted, the more urgently must these needs come to the fore. The more the army demanded, the more the homeland must provide and the greater the task of the government and especially that of the Prussian Ministry of War.'[18] It was a pivotal conference. It led to sweeping changes on the battlefield and the decision to begin the construction of the Hindenburg line twenty miles to the east. More significantly, it produced the germ of the idea which became reality as the Hindenburg Plan. Designed to marshal all the resources of the German nation for total war, it became ultimately the catalyst for disaster and ruin.

Meanwhile, on the increasingly muddy and devastated Somme battlefield, pressure continued to be applied everywhere as the Allies prepared for the major offensive, planned for mid-September. On 9 September Ginchy finally fell. Holding it for that length of time had pushed some of the best regiments in the Germany army almost beyond the limits of endurance. For example, the company commander of 10th Company Infantry Regiment 88, which was then located close to Ginchy, felt on 5th September that he had to bring his concerns officially to the attention of the chain of command. Writing that day to his battalion commander, Reserve Leutnant Speikermann stated,

> "The Company has now spent nearly twelve days in the line (the seven hour stop over in Rocquiny does not count as rest) and during this time

the men have had no rest at night and hot food only on occasional days. The men are so weakened as a result that they can no longer be used as fighting troops. The state of morale is such that if the relief promised for yesterday does not take place tonight I cannot take responsibility for the consequences."

This report was then forwarded to higher authority by Hauptmann d'Heureuse as follows:

"Eleven days facing the enemy, without a single rest day, the 10th Company has suffered particularly from heavy artillery fire. A total lack of dugouts means that it has also suffered from the bad weather conditions. The bearing and morale of the men has declined so clearly that I can no longer be held responsible for their physical and mental condition." [19]

Despite its plight, nothing could be done and the company was deployed even closer to Ginchy itself on the morning 6 September, where it was later to take part with the 9th Company in a counter-attack. Remarkable to relate, discipline and morale held up. The troops attacked as ordered, but were extremely grateful to be relieved later in the day.

*Reserve Leutnant Hoffman 10th Company Infantry Regiment 88*[20] 1.

On 6 [September] both companies, 9th and 10th, were moved forward into the so-called Reserve trenches, 300 metres from Ginchy. The sky was full of aircraft. Heavy artillery fire of all calibres was coming down, as was enfilading machine gun fire from the left, while the companies advanced in three waves. Amazing to relate, the trench which was shot up and only usable here and there, was reached without significant casualties. Hardly had we arrived in the trench, however, than it came under heavy large-calibre fire and many men were buried alive. One shell alone buried three complete traverses. The company commander, Reserve Leutnant Speikermann, had only just arrived at the trench, when he was wounded in the left upper arm by a grenade splinter. At that, I assumed command of the company about 2.00 pm. The 9th Company also arrived and took up position on our right. Because the commander of 1st Company had been killed, I amalgamated the 1st and 10th Companies and added in a ration party from the 7th Company and some engineers... Suddenly I heard that the enemy had forced a way into Ginchy. Working with Reserve Leutnant Reymann, commander of 9th Company, we decided on a counter-attack. 9th Company despatched one and a half platoons and I sent the same number and the remainder of 1st Company. The rest of the troops were launched later. Because our artillery was late, not coming down until we were actually advancing, we had to endure a lot of enemy machine gun fire and shrapnel rounds. The seriousness of the situation meant that the physical and mental exhaustion caused by constant heavy artillery fire and the exertions of the past twelve days were put aside. The soldiers were re-energised and, with cries of 'Hurra', the enemy in Ginchy were ejected out of the far side of the village...Reinforcements from Infantry Regiment 104 filled out our depleted ranks, so I was able to send more than a platoon back to our original trenches, then that evening Leutnant Reymann and I withdrew with the remnants of the 9th, 10th and 1st Companies..."

Holding positions in and around the so-called 'Entenschnabel' [Duck's Bill] between Delville Wood and Ginchy, the men of 1st Battalion Bavarian Infantry Regiment 19 were battered constantly by artillery fire as they observed the life and death struggle for Ginchy unfolding a few hundred metres away.

*Hauptmann Ewald Weisemann-Remscheid 1st Company Bavarian Infantry Regiment 19[21]1.*

"Dawn broke on the morning of 8th September. Hardly had the last of the troops who had been relieved moved to the rear, than British guns of all calibres began to spew out a destructive drumfire on the forward and reserve lines. We were established in the Entenschnabel [Duck's Bill]. It had once been a meadow, now it was ploughed up with trenches, holes and shell craters. Heavy enemy fire poured downs on us, sending pillars of mud, as high as houses, up into the air and showering our steel helmets with hard clods of earth. The drumfire grew and grew in intensity. It seemed as though the trench, which could hardly be described as such anyway, was going to be buried totally. We dug down, but we found it difficult to go deep, because as we dug we kept finding newly-buried British corpses, whose stench of decomposition poisoned the air. No chloride of lime was available. A feeling of nausea rose in our gullets! The sun climbed higher and higher. We heaved the corpses of the Tommies up in front of the trench. To have attempted to move to the rear would have meant certain death, so the medical orderlies threw our fallen comrades into the shell holes behind the position. There they lay with distorted faces and glazed eyes staring up at the sky.

"Gradually the situation became clear. Ginchy was occupied by the enemy, but our men were holding on to shell craters and dugouts just by the eastern exit of the village...Night fell on the 10th September. Courageous runners raced to the rear. Would they reach their goal? There was no change in the situation on 10th or 11th September. On one occasion food got through to us, but the stink of the corpses had robbed us of our appetites. We smoked to keep the sickly stench at bay. But the more we smoked, the greater our thirst. We longed for water or coffee. More runners made their way to the rear through the dense curtains of the drumfire. Would they be successful? It was now 12th September. With half the company now casualties, how long would we still have to wait before the British attacked? The situation became ever more confused; uncertainty wore down body and spirit. Shellfire continued to hammer down on our shell holes. We scrabbled and dug until the enemy finally came. It was a relief to us!

"It was afternoon by now. Towards 5.00 pm the British guns fell silent. All was deadly quiet. The exhausted fighters knew what was coming. It did not remain quiet for long. Aircraft buzzed around over the trenches – British ones, who sprayed us with machine gun fire. Everyone who was still capable of fighting took up rifle and grenades and lay in wait. Yes, over there! In the gap between Delville Wood and Ginchy, the British stormed forward in dense columns on a broad front. They bore down on the German trenches like a wall. Would this human wave force a way in? The nerves of the men defending the Duck's Bill stiffened. They allowed the wave to approach until it was within 150 metres, then fire orders were given, weapons were raised and the enemy was hit by volley after volley. They hesitated, took cover and were dashed to pieces by the fire of a German company. Victory was ours! We had withstood the drumfire of the Somme. But what is happening half left? The enemy, whom we had not noticed when we were fully occupied with dealing with a frontal attack, has pushed forward beyond the eastern edge of Ginchy. It seems as though our men have been overwhelmed or buried alive in their trenches and dugouts. The Tommies are outflanking us. Should we pull back?

"In such situations of uncertainty and high tension, it is best to remain calm. We pull back our left flank and open enfilade fire on the enemy. It hits him at the moment of maximum weakness, which always occurs just after an attack. He halts his advance and heads back into dead ground near Ginchy, where our fire cannot touch him... During the night 12th/13th September we are relieved. The 1st Company assembles in its accommodation and counts its casualties. Of the 130 men who marched forward into the Duck's Bill, ninety eight are dead or wounded..."

The constant operations continued to take a toll of the strength of the defending regiments. Even though it had been weeks since there had been a concerted attempt to assault the Thiepval – Saint Pierre Divion sector directly, the continual artillery fire smashed up the defences and wore down the companies manning them, so that well known places such as Goat or Schwaben Redoubt were, in reality, reduced to battered earthworks manned by small garrisons, who were clinging on to shell craters, foxholes and the remnants of the earlier dugouts. During the first week in September, Infantry Regiment 66 was ordered forward to relieve the units in the front line.

*Vizefeldwebel Collet 4th Company Infantry Regiment 66[22] 7.*

"4th Company Infantry Regiment 66 arrived at Schwaben Redoubt in thick fog. We advanced along a trench which had been dug hastily and urgently during the course of one short night. In places it was only knee deep, in others chest deep. We lay in a simple zigzag communication trench with no dugouts and no other form of cover. There was no trace of an obstacle to our front; so there we were, completely exposed in an open trench – and this called itself the Schwaben Redoubt. We all felt that we should not be able to stay here, that to do so would mean certain death from shellfire. But then along came our battalion commander, Hauptmann Niemeyer, who urged us to dig in quickly, because as soon as the fog lifted fire would be brought down on the new trench. So there was nothing for it but to dig in and endure whatever might come. Everyone in his place, working in pairs as far as possible, we rushed to deepen the trench.

"Gradually the fog cleared and the sun broke through. Then suddenly shells and shrapnel rained down. We dived into our holes, where we were literally flattened. One after the other we fled this evil length of trench and soon it was completely abandoned. To stay was simply impossible; it would have been certain death. Once this frenzied fire lifted, the commanders gathered their men together again and reoccupied this dismal trench. As far as possible the holes were dug out once more and developed, but the British kept a sharp look out and brought down another hail of fire and iron on us. In next to no time, everything had disappeared into one of the holes, or elsewhere, until the concentration was over... Finally it was evening and the enemy was quiet, but we continued to work flat out. Wood was brought onto the position and the dugouts progressed ceaselessly, step by step, ever deeper into the earth, until it was broad daylight. Everyone gave it their all. Company commander relieved rifleman and rifleman the platoon commander with pick and shovel. At no time during the entire war did we work as hard as we did from 5th – 13th September 1916 in the hell called the Schwaben Redoubt. It was a hell, where we worked each night liked men possessed, then from morning to night we despaired as shells poured down on us.

"The fire was at its worst on 7th and 9th September. The British had spotted our work on the new dugouts, despite all our attempts to conceal it. At a slow tempo, the British brought down shells on our heads, which were intended to bury us in our holes or crush us. They used shells with delay fuzes, which bored down two to three metres into the earth before exploding and crushing their surroundings. I lay with twenty others, packed like sardines, in the staircase of a newly-begun dugout. We had six metres of overhead cover. Light shells and shrapnel crashed and clattered on the surface above like angry dogs, but without doing us any damage. In between, however, from the far distance, we heard a loud firing signature, followed by a dangerous rushing in the air which, as it grew closer, became a gurgling sound. Everyone knew from the sound that a monster was directly on the way towards us. We listened intently, nerves on edge, to the dull thud and huddled together. There followed an explosion and a short shockwave which made every joint in the wooden framework creak...

"How was it possible for the 4th Company to hold out from 5th to 14th September? Here the old catch phrase applied, 'Words teach, but deeds impress'. Our battalion commander, through his actions, gave his men an incomparable example of devotion to duty. Day and night he lay forward amongst us in shell holes, wherever the fight was hottest. He held on when all around him failed. The fact that the Schwaben Redoubt held out during those days was due to the devotion to duty of our battalion commander, Hauptmann Niemeyer. I well remember that there were times when only he and those closest to him held on forward in a shell hole, the remainder having fled. When the fire slackened, we used to lead forward the soldiers as unobtrusively as possible, so that he would not notice anything. He really put us to shame and in so doing earned the total loyalty of all his soldiers to their commander."

The scale of operations was altogether more subdued south of the river during the summer. This did not mean that the defending units had an easy time of it, however. They tended to stay in the front line for longer periods, absorbing constant punishment from the air and concentrations of artillery fire and, in addition, French attacks, when launched, could frequently be of great intensity whilst they lasted. For every account describing how easy it was to repel French infantry advances by means of throwing a few grenades, there are many others which tell a different story. Barleux had been the scene of repeated moves and countermoves for weeks on end. Arriving in the area on 9th August, Grenadier Regiment 89 defeated all French attacks during the next month. On 4 September the French army launched a fresh thrust, which was duly countered. This was the fifth major day of battle around Barleux for the Regiment.

*Hauptmann von Heimburg Commanding Officer 3rd Battalion Grenadier Regiment 89[23] 8.*

"The shout, 'Here they come!' got us all out of our shelters. It was a relief, that after days of intensive bombardment, the fire directed at us had slackened and the artillery was engaging targets to our rear. From the parapet of the trench the French attack could be observed and, once I saw that the enemy had reached the forward trench, I gave Leutnant von Platen, who was standing next to me, the order to launch a counter-attack with the one and a half platoons of 9th Company, who were immediately available. Leutnant von Platen launched his attack with daring impetus, but sadly lost direction and so supported the 2nd Battalion, rather than 10th Company. The enemy had established themselves in the quarry and had made a further penetration on the left flank between 11th Company and Regiment Bremen [Infantry Regiment 75]. When I saw that Barleux was occupied by the French and that they were working their way more and more round our left flank, I rushed forward every available man - the remains of 9th Company, batmen and runners, altogether and regardless of rank.

"Officer or grenadier, they all headed for Barleux, rifle in hand. Assistant Medical Officer Dr Theodor, tore off the Red Cross brassard from his arm and joined the attack. Once the worst of the danger was passed, he returned to tending the wounded. We did not make much progress. The French brought machine guns into action, so I gave the order to dig in and to bring down deliberate fire on Barleux. I personally moved with my batman to the Battalion Command Post, where the first of the prisoners was arriving. I made contact, with 2nd Battalion and requested the use of any reserves available. Two sections were put at my disposal and were ordered to attack Barleux from the north. This was carried out skilfully and the attack was continued using the remainder of 3rd Battalion. Almost simultaneously at 5.00 pm, support from the neighbouring regiment, Infantry Regiment 75, made itself felt, the village was cleared and a number of prisoners was captured. Around 5.30 pm contact was re-established with Infantry Regiment 75.

"The quarry was still in the hands of the French, who had barricaded both sides. When the Reserve Company (12th Company Grenadier Regiment 89) was allocated to me at 7.30 pm, I ordered it to recapture the quarry. Leutnant von Platen, who had just arrived at my location, asked to be allowed to take command of the operation, because he knew exactly where the French had dug in... After about ten minutes a great round of '*Hurras!*' could be heard in the forward trenches. The quarry was back in our hands and all the Battalion internal links were re-established. Number 3 Platoon of 12th Company, under Feldwebel Dahl, had especially distinguished itself, being first into the quarry and capturing thirty nine prisoners. I regard 4 September as a special day of honour for the 3rd Battalion. After a heavy nine day bombardment, the companies were brilliantly victorious. The same will and thought was shared by all. 'The enemy shall not break through.'"

A few days later, the 58th Infantry Division from Saxony arrived in the Barleux area to relieve the worn out troops who had endured for so long. By this stage of the battle a great deal of experience had been accumulated concerning the problem of resupply of the forward troops. Gefreiter Hartisch of Infantry Regiment 106, which was deployed on a six hundred metre frontage running south west from Barleux, towards Belloy, was co-opted on arrival to carry out this duty for 9th Company.

*Gefreiter Hartisch 9th Company Infantry Regiment 106*[24] **9**.

"We were off to the Somme! How can I describe the feelings, the thoughts that raced through our minds? It was not exactly pleasant. We had been following the fighting for months from newspaper reports and accounts of our comrades who had been engaged there...It was dark when we arrived and I do not know the name of the place. We had coffee and a hot meal, then were loaded into trucks and headed for the drumfire which continued to thunder and roar, boiling like a witch's cauldron...We arrived at Devise and spent the night sleeping in the open, wrapped in our groundsheets, our rifles by our sides and our heads pillowed on our knapsacks. Some dreamed, others could not sleep, but some snored and grunted as loud as sawmills. Before daybreak we were up and away to another place called Athies.

"During the afternoon of 13 September rations, grenades and signal cartridges were issued. Each platoon had to nominate a ration party. Who wants to do it? Everybody really wanted to stay with the company; nobody wants to cut themselves off from that which the other comrades will experience, will have to experience. Our company commander made it clear what it meant in the present circumstances to bring forward essential food under fire and in bad weather. Men were selected and this included me. We still had no real idea about the danger and the strenuous nature of what awaited us. We marched forward for an hour in lashing rain that poured down continuously and soaked us completely. That was a fine start! In addition, the guns roared and the drumming went on ceaselessly. Didn't those miserable sods over there want to take a break?

"We crossed the Somme marshes, then the canal, almost all at the run, because this is a dangerous place sought out by the heaviest of the fire. Shell hole after shell hole, crater after crater, filled us with horror. I had seen a lot; I had been in the field since October 1914. I had taken part in everything that the regiment and company had done, but this was way beyond all normal experience. The artillery fire never ceased, but there was nothing for it but to traverse these places. We reached the Halbmond [Half Moon Trench spanning the present-day D148 north of Villers-Carbonnel] position and here we were to stay to carry out our function every evening. The Company still had a fair way to go before it reached the front line. 'Good night lads, mind how you go and dig in hard when the French come!' 'Good night rear details!' they chorused back. Yes, rear detail. I did not think badly of those who called that out, because the following days and nights taught us all what it meant to be numbered amongst the rear details. We were always under fire and they were not just dropping stuffed pancakes!

"'Commanders and carrying parties report to the tunnel at 9.30 pm!' We were bang on time. Oh Hell! Would our waggons be able to get forward through this fire? It was non-stop. But listen! There was a rumbling and rattling, as though a wild animal was charging and through and over the shell holes, right across a six metre wide mine crater, came our ration wagons. It was a long column, one for each company. It was scene of frenzied activity. Horses were snorting, voices shouting; 'Tenth!' 'Eleventh!' 'Ninth, over here!' In between was the crash and crack of our batteries, the endless roar as enemy shells exploded around us and shrapnel rounds burst overhead. Right, over we go to the 9th company waggon! We collect everything that our comrades forward need after they have already been hanging on for a day and night without resupply. Great big bottles of coffee, cases of mineral water, sandbags full of bread, preserves, butter, cheese, the inevitable jam, chocolate, sugar, lights, cigars and matches. Loaded up, off we set, wondering how we shall we get on. I lead, so that we do not go wrong and, behind me, one by one, come the men, puffing, panting and sweating with the effort of carrying the valuable loads. Twenty, twenty-five minutes we head across country, until we reach the so-called Totenschlucht [Dead Man's Ravine, present-day Vallée des Singes], which did not get its name for nothing.

"Suddenly there is another concentration of fire! Here's a large crater! Jump in everybody! Men and boxes, bottles and sacks; all lie tightly packed together, but care is taken to ensure that nothing is broken or mislaid. Then crack! – a shell splinter hits a large carboy containing the brown liquid men are longing for and twenty litres have gone to the Devil. Then it's up and away! We reach the ravine! Thank God! The worst is behind us. We have a short, but well-earned breather, then continue on. We are now following a trench, if this pathetic 'thing', shattered by artillery and mortar fire, deserves the name. But what's this? A long procession is coming the other way – wounded, some of them being carried. There's nothing else for it. Ration party out of the trench and we stumble along the top until the wounded pass. Then we muddle along forward again. We deliver everything to one of the platoon commanders, who signs for it all. As well as collecting the latest gossip, we load up with empty containers, boxes, rifles, knapsacks, coats and other equipment belonging to the dead and wounded. Then, moving as quickly as possible, we head back to the Half Moon position, bathed in sweat, dog tired and nerves on edge. We report in that everything has been delivered and that the carrying party is back in one piece. Only then can we eat and relax, knowing that we have done our duty."

Routine, their work may have been. Certainly it was essential and definitely it was dangerous. It is hard to conceive of routine in the context of such a titanic life and death struggle, yet without administration, all is lost in battle. Without regular reports, no overview may be had of conditions in the front line, nor may requirements in terms of reinforcement and replenishment be established.

Nevertheless it was yet another burden on the hard-pressed junior leadership, which already had to deal with a flood of correspondence with bereaved relatives.

*Rittmeister von Krosijk 2nd Battalion Field Artillery Regiment 78²⁵* **10.**

"At 3.00 am the daily report had to be submitted, in order to arrive promptly by midday at Second Army, having passed through the Artillery Brigade and Division. At 2.00 am the constantly heavy rate of fire generally slackened until 7.00 am to 8.00 am, so for the front line troops, especially the infantry, it was always felt to be an unpleasant fact of life that the few quiet hours of early morning was when the 'paper battle' was in full swing, placing considerable demands on the front line officers, who were forced to complete a great deal of paperwork."

Amongst the need for reports and returns, which burdened all participating armies equally, the battle went on ceaselessly, involving the 45th Reserve Division in constant minor actions in and around Courcelette and Martinpuich where, in mid - September, Reserve Infantry Regiment 211 was fighting to maintain its position in the Hammer Riegel [Hammer Stop Line]. This trench straddled the Albert – Bapaume road about one and a half kilometres south-west of the present-day D107 which links Martinpuich and Courcelette.

*Feldwebelleutnant Weinert 8th Company Reserve Infantry Regiment 211²⁶* **11.**

"Whilst the grenade battle was still in full swing, two Bavarian soldiers arrived in our trench carrying a full food container. They were from the neighbouring Bavarian Regiment which was deployed to the left [south-east] near Martinpuich. Completely amazed not to find their own men, only now did they realise that they had gone wrong. 'What's going on here?' they asked. 'We are just about to eject the Tommies who have broken into our trench', we replied. 'OK. We'll join in!' they said, putting down their container, festooning themselves with a goodly number of grenades and very shortly afterwards joining in the battle with our men. Shortly before the close quarter battle was broken off, one of them fell, mortally wounded by a machine-gun bullet. Saddened, the other took his identity discs and small personal possessions, took one final glance at his faithful friend, and retraced his lonely steps to rejoin his comrades. In the heat of battle it was unfortunately not possible to get the names of the two brave men, but both of them, the dead man as well as the survivor, deserve our thanks for their truly comradely behaviour...

"If we now felt that we deserved some peace and relaxation, we were mistaken [Weinert continues]. Heavy artillery fire was soon coming down on the position. We did all we could to dig out men who had been buried alive in destroyed sections of trench. Sometime we succeeded, sometime we did not. Most of those dug out were unable to fight on, their nerves were shattered. We had enemy airmen above us who had a detailed knowledge of the dugouts in the Bayern Riegel [Bavarian Stop Line, a trench running from southwest of Courcelette to Hammer Riegel]. The entrances with their wooden frameworks were obvious, despite attempts to camouflage them, so they directed the fire of their batteries exactly on to them. Soon only two dugouts offered any sort of protection; the remainder were destroyed. Fire continued even at night, increasing from time to time on 12th September to drum fire. Yet again a dugout fell victim to the carefully directed fire of a 280 millimetre shell. There was nothing left of those inside. We were successful in concentrating most of the remainder of the personnel in the one undamaged dugout, but some had to stick it out in the open under fire. The last deep and strong dugout sheltered the remnants of the 8th Company, who by now were pitifully few. Some shells impacted overhead, without damaging the dugout significantly. Just an ominous creaking in the timber supports made us think, 'How much longer?'"

The men of 8th Company were enduring the worst bombardment for weeks, as were those of Field Artillery Regiment 221.

*Hauptmann Freiherr von Steinaecker 2nd Battalion Field Artillery Regiment 221*[28] **12.**

"Today's fire was the worst ever. Oberleutnant Merks, Commander of 5th Battery Field Artillery Regiment 7, and I were together on the gun position. We moved deeper into the dugout to get away from the enemy shells, which were falling ever closer. Outside our own ammunition was constantly being blown into the air. The enemy artillery was firing brilliantly, directed from the air, of course. German aircraft were nowhere to be seen.[29] Finally a direct hit landed right in the entrance of our dugout, wounding me in the head. But my luck held. During the bombardment, a further three or four direct hits came down into the entrance. The overpressure extinguished the lights and, with each hit, we both thought that the dugout was going to collapse. It was quite impossible for anyone to venture outside. Impact followed impact as the enemy shells crashed down. During a quiet moment I sent two runners to [the Artillery] Group, informing them that I needed ammunition and replacement guns. The left hand gun had been completely knocked out by a direct hit. A shell landed right in front of the gun second from the right, blasting it with mud and earth. The breech could not be closed and the elevating gear seemed to be bent. The gun position looked dreadful – a crater field strewn randomly everywhere with charred shell-carrying baskets, torn open cartridges and duds. There were also enemy shell splinters and shell holes so large that they would comfortably have accommodated a complete gun, not to mention beams of wood and huge clods of earth. It was a scene of the most terrible devastation..."

After all this preparatory fire, the biggest offensive operation launched by the Allies since 1st July, began on 15 September. All the 'line-straightening' of the past few weeks, all the attritional struggles for tactical advantage during the battle for the woods and the villages of Ginchy, Guillemont and Maurepas throughout August, had been leading up to this day. This was to be a serious attempt to crush German resistance once and for all and to force a breakthrough. After a forty eight hour period of increasingly heavy bombardment, drum fire came down all along the line, concentrating especially on the area held by the Bavarian 3rd, 4th and 5th Divisions of the Bavarian II Corps. 'Martinpuich, Eaucourt l'Abbaye and Le Sars were cloaked in black smoke, through which the flash of shells exploding could be seen...infantrymen came running through the positions of the 3rd and 6th Battery, reporting that the British had already taken Flers... Immediately [the two batteries] brought down gunfire over open sights against the eastern end of Flers. All enemy attempts to push forward here were defeated by the guns...In front of the guns there was no fighting infantry at all... Reserve Leutnant Schneider 3rd Battery Bavarian Field Artillery Regiment 12 destroyed two British tanks advancing from Flers with direct hits, having laid the gun himself. He has the distinction of having been the first to destroy British tanks.'[30]

The Staff of Reserve Infantry Regiment 231, moving forward to link up with Infantry Regiment 17, found their greetings returned with, 'Keep quiet gentlemen! A battle is raging in the forward area.' One of their number, von Praetorius, witnessed the rest of the day's activities from a privileged position.13. He described the way events unfolded as being like a drama enacted on the stage of a theatre. 'The reports came pouring in. 'The British have broken into our forward trenches under the cover of the morning mist.' 'The front line trench is lost.' 'The British are working their way forward to the Second Position in places.' The new Foureaux [High Wood] Stop Line [Tea Support] has fallen.' 'The enemy is advancing on Martinpuich.' 'The enemy is pouring down the main road through Martinpuich in massive groups.' – then the line went dead...'[31]

Thick fog had blanketed the positions until 8.00 am, then, as it lifted, the British divisions were seen advancing in mass in the direction of Flers and Gueudecourt. In the case of the Bavarian 7th Infantry Regiment, the British, who were given overhead cover by twenty to thirty aircraft, advanced in dense columns, closely supported by two tanks. The Bavarians brought down a storm of small arms fire against the attackers, but to no avail. The front line of craters was broken through and, fanning out left and right, the individual companies were singled out and destroyed. By midday, the assault had pushed on to the Second Position, but was already running out of steam. The 3rd and 4th Companies, who were holding a final depth position with four machine guns, were not attacked. An attempt was made to counter-attack that evening, but it failed in the face of heavy Allied fire.[32] The picture was much the same all along the Bavarians' line.

*Leutnant Oeller 1st Company Bavarian Infantry Regiment 14³³* **14.**

"About 5.45 am the British occupied trenches pushed forward from Delville Wood, both sides of the Longueval-Flers road. With our rifle and machine gun fire, we forced them to move back to their main trenches. About 7.00 am the British advanced from Delville Wood in the hollow to the left [east] of the Flers-Longueval road. They advanced in columns four to five men wide, with five to ten paces between the columns, each of which was about eighty men strong. The assault was accompanied by three tanks, one of which ditched attempting to cross the road. Once the attack had closed to two hundred metres range, British destructive fire came down and utterly smashed the company sector. The attack was spotted the instant it left the wood and from that moment, until the British troops broke into the position, an uninterrupted series of signal flares was fired, calling for defensive fire, but none came. Because there were only forty five men left who were still able to fight and to defend a 400 metre company frontage, I pulled back, along with every other part of the company who made it in time, to the hill to the right [west] of the Flers-Longueval road and brought down enfilade fire on the advancing enemy.

"Simultaneously, I sent back to the Second Line for support. I remained, together with some elements of 12th Company Bavarian Infantry Regiment 9, on the hill, until I was deeply outflanked on either side and was afraid that I should be cut off. At this moment I was also wounded in the shoulder. I gave the order to pull back to Flers, my men fighting briefly from the Second Line and between the Second and Third lines as they withdrew. I personally went back to Flers to fetch support. Pulling back further, I passed a battery of 210 millimetre guns in Gueudecourt, who had no knowledge of the attack. Because nobody was outside the dugouts, I raised the alarm. In answer to my question why the battery was not firing, I received the reply that there were no orders, because all the telephone links were destroyed. In my opinion, if artillery defensive fire had come down at the right moment the enemy attack would have been beaten back with heavy casualties".

As it was, due to the speed of advance, the shock effect of the new tanks and the number of German prisoners captured, the heavy casualties were on this occasion mainly on the side of the defenders. When the Bavarians were ultimately relieved, Bavarian Infantry Regiment 14, for example, had lost six officers killed, twelve wounded and twenty-six missing and 158 other ranks killed, 531 wounded and 884 missing. Although many of the missing were, in fact, captured, it was still a serious blow and typical of those suffered by the other front-line regiments that day. In the heat of battle, the number of killed was, perhaps, higher than it should have been. Doctor Blass, Medical Officer of Bavarian Infantry Regiment 9, who was captured near Flers, later reported, 'Straight after their capture, those prison-

ers who were unwounded or were only lightly wounded, were directed on their
way with hand signals. Despite the fact that there was no resistance, the New
Zealanders fired recklessly, or through sheer blood lust, at individuals and groups
of prisoners or wounded who were making their way back, killing a great many.
Witnesses to these events include Hauptmann Biermer 3rd Battalion Bavarian
Infantry Regiment 9 and Gefreiter Rügemer 9th Company Bavarian Infantry
Regiment 9, who were both shot in the back and Oberleutnant Golpert and
Leutnant Wohlfahrt of 3rd Battalion Bavarian Infantry Regiment 9, who narrow-
ly escaped the same fate.'

   A little to the north, on the right flank of II Bavarian Corps, Bavarian Infantry
Regiment 17, which was located north east of Martinpuich, was maintaining
contact with 1st Guards Reserve Division on its right.

*Reserve Leutnant Hermann Kohl Bavarian Infantry Regiment 17*[37]*13.*

   "During the early hours of 15th September, a forest of guns opened up
   in a ceaseless rolling thunder of fire throughout the Foureaux [High]
   Wood,-Flers-Martinpuich- Courcelette sector. A sea of iron crashed down
   on all the front and support lines of the area. The noise was terrible.
   Impact after impact. The whole of No Man's Land was a seething
   cauldron. The work of destruction grew and grew. Chaos! It was
   impossible to imagine that anyone could live through it. Square metre
   after square metre was ploughed up. The regimental witches' sabbat was
   upon it, as an unparalleled hurricane of fire blew over from the front. It
   was like a crushing machine, mechanical, without feelings; snuffing out
   the last resistance with a thousand hammers. It is totally inappropriate
   to play such a game with fellow men. We are all human beings, made in
   the image of the Lord God. But what account does the Devil take of
   mankind, or God, when he feels himself to be Lord of the Elements; when
   chaos celebrates his omnipotence?... From the direction of High Wood, we
   can hear the sound of voices and confused shouting, which persists until
   the few remaining survivors, wakened from mental confusion, find
   themselves shocked back into the reality of the moment and fight on,
   until the British flood overwhelms them, consumes them and passes on.
   Wave upon wave. An extraordinary number of men and there, between
   them, spewing death, unearthly monsters: the first British tanks...Our
   artillery does not fire a single round.

   "All links to the rear are totally disrupted. Feeble resistance is offered
   in the Sunken Road and on the outskirts of Martinpuich. Small infantry
   pockets of resistance fight on, sending despairing shots snapping and
   barking into the oncoming masses. It is all in vain, the enemy is
   impressively and overwhelmingly superior in men and material. The
   British break through on all sides. Breach after breach. The front line is
   overrun. The final survivors of Martinpuich fall into the hands of the

enemy... Over there, in the Sunken Road, is a soldier in a firing position. The barrel of his rifle is red hot. He is a giant amongst men, a true hero! He was the man who, on patrol and weaponless, captured some British soldiers. He has proved himself repeatedly. He was always the first in line when enemy attacks had to be broken. He is not about to call on the enemy for mercy today. He will stand and face them as long as his heart is still beating! That is what he believes in and that is what he will die for. Dozens of British troops go down from the lead he is firing. He knocks gap after gap in their ranks. He fires and fires. His comrades fall back, pleading and shouting at him to do the same. They can see that it is pointless to throw themselves under the oncoming steamroller. He is deaf to their entreaties, he stares death in the face. He knows what his fate will be. Greedily, threateningly, the enemy reaches out for him. He fires his last round, the last round of his life; then dies for the Fatherland! A hero to the last."

Despite all the efforts of those in the path of the initial onslaught who attempted to hold their ground, a significant penetration was made between the Bavarian 7th and 14th Regiments, then on the right flank of the 14th Regiment and to the west of Flers in the Bavarian 4th Infantry Division area. It is quite possible, as alleged, that the artillery failed to fire in support of the forward troops. The most probable cause, apart from a lack of telephone links, was that of battlefield obscuration. As always, the artillery did the best it could in the prevailing circumstances, as exemplified by the medal awarded to Gefreiter Ernst Hohberger of 2nd Battalion Bavarian Field Artillery Regiment 10, who received the Silver Bravery Medal for his work that day. In part, his citation reads "...on 15th September, all communication links between the 2nd Battalion and the batteries were destroyed... orders had to be passed by runner. Despite the heavy enemy artillery fire, which was being directed from the air, Gefreiter Hohberger brought orders to the 4th Battery to bring fire down on an armoured vehicle which was advancing from the direction of Guillemont..."[38] Whatever the true facts of the situation early in the day, it certainly fell to the artillery to save the situation and prevent the relatively minor penetrations from evolving into a major breakthrough.

*Rittmeister von Krosijk 2nd Battalion Field Artillery Regiment 78*[39] **13.**

"On a day of heavy bombardment and British attacks, came a report from one of the batteries that an extraordinary vehicle was advancing in their area of responsibility. It was approaching the British front line. Initially, it was thought that it might have been an ambulance, because it was thought that a Red Cross flag had been seen, but that was not certain. I replied, 'Bring it under fire immediately.' In the meantime, another report from the next door battery came in, saying that they had just fired at the vehicle, because machine gun fire had come from it. After four rounds, the armoured vehicle was knocked out. The British soldiers, who emerged from the vehicle, were all shot down by the machine-gun fire of our infantry. That was the first appearance of the 'tanks' or armoured fighting vehicles, which, henceforth, were fired upon without permission being sought".

*Leutnant Klengel 1st Battery Field Artillery Regiment 77*[40]**15.**

"From 7.00 am on 14 September continuous fire from heavy and super-heavy calibre guns came down on the sunken road (Ginchy-Gueudecourt), on the Third Infantry Position (Gallwitz Riegel) [Gallwitz Stop Line] and on the village of Gueudecourt. First Section, known as the 'Sunken Road Section', was under heavy artillery fire, directed by aerial observers until it went dark. It continued throughout the night 14th/15th September...At about 6.00 am on 15th September, the fire continued to fall on the same sector, but with increased intensity...Gas shells came down on the Sunken Road at around 6.30 am. At about the same time there was a direct hit on the left hand gun in the Sunken Road, which knocked it out...The right hand gun was also hit at about 7.40 am. Its outer shield was penetrated; its optical sight and leather head rest were smashed. At about 7.50 am, the same gun was hit once more, wrecking the outer and middle shield and throwing the ready-use ammunition in all directions, but without setting it off. The gun crew was not injured...Sentries were posted to look out for signal flares. Suddenly Gefreiter Koch shouted, 'Leutnant, our infantry is pulling back!' Leutnant Kohl and I observed, using the telescope and saw not our own infantry, but British assault waves, which were soon deployed in battalion strength. The right hand gun was ready to fire. The left, as has been mentioned, had been knocked out by a direct hit.

"Leutnant Kohl sent Unteroffizier Schramm and the signallers to the 'Trench Section' (2nd Section 1st Battery, located in the Gallwitz Stop Line), carrying the information that the British were advancing from the hill in the direction of Ginchy. No German infantry pulled back in our direction, rather, if the hill is viewed from the Sunken Road, they moved sideways to the left [north-east towards Lesboeufs]. As a result, the enemy could advance unchecked in the direction of the Sunken Road. Not one single battery was firing at the hill. I had the sighting mechanism removed from my left hand gun and, with Leutnant Kohl's permission, sent it, together with the crew back to the 'Trench Section'; then, working with the other crew, I hauled the right hand gun out of its pit and set it up out in the open. Leutnant Kohl gave me my orders. We engaged the assaulting British infantry with sights set at 1,400 metres (too long), then at 1,000 metres (too short), before being on target for a short while at 1,200 metres. Because of its open position, we could engage a wide arc to the left [east] and the enemy was approaching our flank. The actual arc of fire of the Sunken Road Section was towards Flers [west]. Suddenly we were engaged with rapid small arms from the hill in the direction of Flers [Point 120]. Leutnant Kohl shouted, 'Enemy advancing from the direction of Flers! New point of aim! Direction Flers!'

"The Gun Commander, Unteroffizier Hoffman, hauled the trails round to the left and I engaged the hill in the direction of Flers over open sights at 800 metres, reducing the range as the enemy infantry closed in to 600, 500, 400 then 200 metres. The enemy was massing more and more to our front and flank. There was still no German infantry pulling back and no reinforcements coming forward to us! Our well aimed fire was slowing the enemy and causing confusion. Displaying toughness, the enemy commanders rallied their men and regrouped those who were falling back. They were all wearing the small British steel helmets and had fixed bayonets. We could clearly see the commanders giving hand signals for an assault on our gun which was still firing. The British suddenly moved forward, then crawled from one hundred metres to within close range of my quick-firing gun. We had already laid out revolvers and grenades. Leutnant Kohl, Unteroffizier Hoffmann and Gunner Schwindack killed several British soldiers, including apparently two commanders, with revolver shots. We were not put off by the torrent of small arms fire, then, whilst the three of them drove back the first of the British infantrymen, who were closing in from a flank on the other side of the Sunken Road, I ordered the firing of canister rounds, giving Gunner Piper hand signals to fire where the groups of British soldiers were densest.

"The first or second canister round burst in amongst a group of twelve British soldiers and obliterated them; helmets and rifles flew in the air. When we saw that, Leutnant Koch, the gun crew and I shouted '*Hurra!*' so loudly that the enemy must have heard it. Nobody else tried to approach our gun from the front! The British had taken a bloody nose! A British machine gun, which had been brought forward by three British soldiers, came into action near the left hand gun of the Sunken Road Section, opening fire on us. This did not prevent us from firing. Not until a second gun opened up on our gun from the left rear did Leutnant Kohl say, 'We'll have to pull back, none of our infantry is heading this way!...'."

The small group managed to link up with Regimental Headquarters in Gueudecourt. Leutnant Koch was wounded and, despite strenuous efforts, had to be left in No Man's Land. An attempt that night to recover him failed, when the patrol sent forward bumped into British resistance, so his ultimate fate is not known. Having reported in, Leutnant Klengel and the remainder of the survivors were sent to reinforce the other section of 1st Battery in the Gallwitz Stop Line, which also had an incident-filled day.

*Leutnant Klengel 1st Battery Field Artillery Regiment 77*[41]**15**.

"Towards 9.00 am the Battery telephone squad returned from the Sunken Road Section, with orders to engage the advancing enemy infantry. The canister rounds were prepared...All non-essential personnel were ordered by the Section Commander to collect grenades and weapons from a cache one hundred metres away and to deploy along the Gallwitz Stop Line, left and right of the battery position, in order to thicken up the meagre infantry presence there. This could only be carried out fully when the crew of the knocked out left hand gun of the Sunken Road Section arrived...The enemy attack continued...Just before 9.30 am, an enemy armoured vehicle drove in front of the battery position and, with its first shots, set on fire an ammunition wagon, which was parked close behind a forward howitzer position. With its third round, the right hand gun, directed by the Section Commander, hit the armoured vehicle at a range of 925 metres and set it alight.[42] Altogether there were about eight hits, some of them from the left hand gun...The left hand gun continued to fire against the constantly renewed waves of attackers, who drew ever closer.

"In the meantime, another armoured vehicle approached the position of 3rd Battery Field Artillery Regiment 77, which was located a short distance to our right rear. Because it was not engaged for a few moments and was threatening the 'Trench Section', the section commander decided, despite the infantry that were drawing ever closer, to pull his one remaining functioning gun out, with the help of some hastily-summoned Bavarian infantrymen and to deal with the vehicle. Just as the gunner took aim at it, it was hit by a first round direct hit from the 3rd Battery,[43] so the 'Trench Section' was able to return to engaging the infantry...Towards 11.30 am strong forces, shoulder to shoulder and echeloned in numerous waves, advanced from Ginchy and, almost unmolested, were heading for Lesboeufs. Once again the gun was pulled out and, taking the enemy in the flank at ranges from 3,200 to 2,400, we succeeded in tearing great holes in the ranks. Again and again the enemy advanced from the line Delville Wood – Flers, but thanks to the sure, calm work of Gunner Hoenig, the gun layer, the thoughtful assistance of the Gun Commander Böhme and the sacrificial efforts of the remainder of the crew and the Bavarian infantry, which are beyond all praise, this single gun was able to operate at a very high rate of fire, switch targets rapidly and so carry out the work of several guns...The enemy assault troops closed to within 300 metres and it seemed as though there was a danger that both gun and crew would fall into the hands of the enemy and that there would be a successful breakthrough of the Gallwitz Stop Line...But at that moment Vizewachtmeister Ditzen and Gunner Schwindack succeeded...in making the second gun ready to fire. Vizewachtmeister Ditzen acted as layer and brought down flanking fire on the advancing

British troops and the supply teams which were following up. Gradually the British attack stalled..."

The first appearance of the tanks came as complete surprise to the German defenders but, as has been noted, it did not take long for the vulnerability of these early models to become clear. From the start the artillery had no trouble in dealing with them – in fact there was considerable competition to do so and also money available for successful actions. Once claims for destroying tanks were confirmed, cash sums were paid. On 15 September, for example, 5th Battery Bavarian Field Artillery Regiment 10, (observer Reserve Leutnant Mayer), was credited with the destruction of one tank and, in accordance with a War Ministry Decree, received, in May 1917, a reward of 500 marks.[44]

Although the main effort on 15 September was directed against the Bavarians, the French assaulted to the south and, simultaneously, a major push was launched along the Thiepval Ridge. This involved men of the 45th Reserve Division in a sharp fight for the Zollerngraben [ZollernTrench], which ran north-east from Thiepval to Zollern [Goat] Redoubt.

*Leutnant Höllwig 9th Company Reserve Infantry Regiment 213[45]16.*

"The enemy artillery resumed its fire at daybreak. Initially individual heavy rounds came over but, during the course of the day, the fire was intensified. We officers did two hour tours of duty, which consisted in checking constantly that observation was being maintained and that the observers were still alive. After midday the fire was so intense that the sentries were relieved every ten minutes. During my duty I sat on the topmost step of my dugout and cleaned cartridges which had been found on the position...Towards 4.00 pm the sentry bawled down into the dugout. 'They're coming! They're coming!' The entire staircase was full of soldiers and the officers were below them. Leutnant Schmidt, Commander of 10th Company, went up and shouted that everyone should stand to, but above us the shells were still exploding all around. I forced my way up into the open through the mass of soldiery. Damn it! It was certainly not pleasant; everywhere there were terrible bangs and crashes. At first I ducked in against the side of the trench to avoid flying clods of earth, but I saw that the sentry was still at his post and waving, so I leapt up to him and saw a dense line of British infantry, about 600 metres distant, advancing diagonally past us in the direction of Courcelette. They obviously intended to broaden the gaps they had torn in the line the previous day.

"To our left was the wreckage of two companies of Reserve Infantry Regiment 210 and left again was a half platoon of ours from each of 10th and 9th Companies, with Unteroffizier Gildemeister. Now that I could see what the British intended, I realised that the 210th and our poor contribution would not be able to hold them off alone. We should have to do something to help them, despite the fact that our sector was still under fire. I took a rifle which was lying next to me and began to fire at the Tommies. Others left the dugouts and lined the edge of the trench. Leutnant Vité shouted in a stentorian voice, 'Half left, in front of the hill – line of enemy infantry. Sights at 600 metres. Rapid fire!' That worked! The order was relayed along the line from one man to another, our bullets were falling among the Tommies and some were falling. More and more British, in ever renewed lines, pushed constantly closer, but our artillery did dreadful execution. I felt completely calm and fired round after round. I could see that my bullets were often hitting and bringing down the men at whom I was aiming. The bullets fired by others were also striking home. Then came the fire of the German artillery, which tore great gaps in the assaulting ranks. However the enemy artillery was also still active and I could see numerous members of our team as they crawled to the rear with a bleeding head or arm.

"I lay with Vizefeldwebel Helmers in a shell hole just in front of the cover. Our senses were stretched to breaking point. Every moment I could see shells bursting, exploding with a thunderous crack. Then came a terrible crash, everything went black and Helmers went somersaulting through the air into the trench where he remained down on the ground. A huge shell had blown out a new crater right in front of us, which partially destroyed the forward wall of our crater. I was unhurt, but for the time being I was completely deafened. I could not tend to Helmers, because the assaulting British were advancing in strength. When I eventually turned round, Helmers was nowhere to be seen; someone had carried him away. I had only one desire: to shoot, to shoot and watch some of them go down. If I did not have a Tommy to fire at, I shot at the aircraft above me. I felt more animal than human. I rejoiced when I had a good target and shot well, very well in fact.

"Then someone was crawling around below me. I looked and Helmers was passing a rifle to me up on the parapet. Under his open jacket, I could see that his chest was covered in blood, which was dripping from numerous wounds. He did not seem to be able to use his left arm, but he insisted that it was not so bad and that he could load right handed. A few moments later someone bawled in my ear that Leutnant Vité was wounded. 'Badly?' 'Yes, his left eye is shot away. Leutnant Schmidt has dragged him away and is bandaging him up.'... that meant that I was now the company commander and the thought flashed through my mind, 'I wonder how long it will be before they're dragging me away?' Then Helmers collapsed, his sleeves and trousers were torn and blood flowed from him. He could do no more. Helmers nodded at me, then crawled away. The British were much reduced in numbers. Four of them still thought that they could advance, then there were none. Now and again one tried to crawl to the rear, but none got very far. The attack was beaten off.

"... I crawled from my hole. A splinter had hit me on the knee, so I could not use the leg properly. The artillery fire had previously eased slightly, but it became more intense. Of the trench, only a few sections were still intact. I ordered the men into the dugouts, which miraculously had survived the shelling. Leutnant Hermann and I remained outside then a dud smashed into the ground half a metre from me and covered me with earth...After an hour the British lifted the fire to the rear again and the sentry shouted once more, 'Here they come!' I jumped up onto the parapet. Yes, they really were coming, but this time not in line, but section columns. That really beat everything! We poured fire at them and they fell in droves. It was not much longer before the first of them started to pull back, but a British officer shot one of them down and the remainder resumed the assault. More and more troops came over the crest and flooded down into No Man's Land. The whole place was crawling with Tommies. But in front of them was a black wall of smoke where the German artillery fire was coming down. Those who managed to penetrate this came under direct fire from our weapons.

"Because there was no British artillery fire coming down on our trench, we were able shoot calmly, but our ammunition was limited and running out. I ran from one man to another, impressing on them only to fire when they were certain of a hit. I longed for the coming of evening, because we could not hold out much longer. The 210th had already been over to ask for ammunition, but I could only let them have the rounds that I had cleaned that morning. I kept twenty-five of them for myself and by the time it went dark I had fired twenty of them. Then no more Tommies were advancing, so I sent everyone into the dugouts with the exception of a double sentry position every forty metres. Using my rifle as a crutch, I hobbled along the length of the position. Everything was shot up. Scattered at random were items of clothing, corpses, pools of blood, dressings and smashed weapons. I divided the survivors into five sections. Leutnant Hermann commanded three of them and Gefreiter Hannemann the other two. Unteroffizier Gildemeister was also wounded, hit through the right arm. He came past me laughing and beaming with joy that we had wiped that lot out. He had enjoyed doing it, but he could do no more at present. I shook his hand wished him a swift recovery then I was on my own.

"From my original 150 men, I was down to not quite fifty, all quite exhausted who, with the exception of the few sentries, were sleeping the sleep of the dead. We had nothing left to eat or drink. We had barely twenty rounds left for the rifles and no signal flares. I had sent the last of the hand grenades, to the left flank. My dugout was full of wounded. Working tirelessly, our first aid man, Gefreiter Hupe, had bandaged them up and moved them into the shelter where they now lay. Now and then a terrible groan came from below. Gradually I was overcome by a dreary thought. 'If they come now, it's all over. You will have to surrender!' If only one of the four runners whom I had despatched, would return, so that I should know if they was any hope of support or ammunition resupply. But two of the men had not got far. Both of them had had their legs shot off. I had then sent Franz Sauermann, who had never left my side throughout the day, to the rear, hoping still to see him back.

"Then suddenly Gefreiter Hellwig, whom Leutnant Vité had ordered back earlier, arrived at the shattered trench and climbed down. 'Leutnant, here's the ration party,' he said. I was so overjoyed I could have thrown my arms round his neck. Then down they all clambered, heavily laden with boxes and crates. Their commander, Gefreiter Rohde, reported to me, 'Rations delivered, Herr Leutnant. On the way we met Franz Sauermann, who said that we ought to bring up some ammunition as well. So we have, because Franz also said that otherwise the Leutnant would have had it.' There was a case of food for every section and one for the company staff. My earlier reorganisation meant that everything went smoothly. The ration party had to take the wounded back to Zollernfeste [Goat Redoubt]. The first of them was an officer of the 211th, who was wounded in the lung... He shook my hand and thanked me for everything. Leutnant Vité had already departed, supported by his batman and Gefreiter Hellwig and I was not able to wish him well. Once they had returned to the Zollernfeste, the ration party had to make a second trip, carrying ammunition. The morale of my men was now brilliant. They had smashed two British attempts to attack; they now had something to eat and something to shoot with. No wonder they took fresh heart. I stayed on duty until 2.00 am then Leutnant Hermann relieved me..."

Down to the south, fighting, albeit at a slower tempo, continued around Barleux as the French army drove on towards the river bank. The men of the 58th Infantry Division held the line here from the middle of September until they were finally relieved on the night of the 29th/30th. They had barely reached their positions when they were involved in extremely heavy fighting, which flared up again seriously on the 17th.

*Vizefeldwebel Süß 4th Company Infantry Regiment 106*[46] **8.**

"We left our positions near Reims on 9th September and nobody knew where we were headed. Rumours circulated that we were destined for Romania and that our 2nd Battalion was already in Germany being re-equipped for a different theatre of war. Spirits were high because everyone knew that we should have no trouble finishing off the Romanians and that the men facing us would be no better than the Russians. Events turned out differently. Already by early morning we realised that the railway was taking us northwards, so there could be no question of any sector other than the Somme. The thunder of the guns could be heard from a long way off. Some of the men were elated, others left the train with heavy hearts and mounted the trucks that were to carry us the short journey to Athies in a sombre mood...[In Athies] we met up with the first of the lightly wounded from the 2nd Battalion, who did not paint too grim a picture of the situation at the front. It was no more dangerous than Verdun, but the battles around Lorette [near Vimy] had been worse as far as artillery fire on approach routes and the surrounding villages was concerned.

"Our 2nd Battalion, having faced an enemy attack, had suffered heavy casualties and required relief, which was carried out the following day by the 1st Battalion. The companies made their preparations and at 11.00 pm on 14th our Company set off to occupy the so-called 'Half Moon' position, 1,800 metres behind the front line. Before our departure we received plenty of rations which were to last us for four days. These included tinned meat, biscuit, butter and sausage. Our waterbottles were filled and each man had to carry a further glass bottle filled with tea, because there was no possibility of getting drinks forward by day...As at Verdun and Lorette, each man was given a grenade in his hand as we set off. The guides were in place. 11.00 pm struck. Then came the orders, 'Attention! Pick up your weapons! Forward!' With beating hearts, but firm step, the company moved off. Hardly an hour had gone by when we were ordered to 'Double March!' and all of us ran as quickly as we could. We were passing a place which was under constant fire. A short time later a load of enemy 'sugar lumps' came over and landed in the swamp behind us.

"Somewhat relieved, we could breathe again and we marched on until we came to a chateau which contained Regimental Headquarters. 300 metres later the whole company had to make haste once more to avoid enemy fire. Around 1.00 am and without casualties, the company reached the appointed position, where the relief took place without incident. As soon as dawn broke, the enemy artillery opened up, a sure sign that we were no longer in Champagne. Mortar fire was mixed in with it, reaching a peak about 2.00 pm. We were on the alert so that we could not be surprised by the French. The fire lifted to the rear trenches, showing that the enemy was about to assault. They did not in fact have much luck; only the odd man got into our trenches.

"We of the 4th Company, which was in reserve, got the job of clearing out the trenches. The order ran around from man to man like wildfire. Having previously allocated responsibilities within the company, the commander shouted, 'Follow me!' and we raced after him as fast as we could. As if in a wild chase we ran after one another. The older men were overtaken by the younger, who urged them on with a quick word as they passed. Parts of the communication trench were in good order; elsewhere it was flattened and we had to leap across open ground under shell fire. [By the time we arrived] the battalion commander had already had a report from an earlier assault force that the trench was free of enemy and that no reinforcements were necessary forward, but we remained in reserve near Battalion HQ and that evening we went forward for some hours to reinforce the 3rd Company.

"At 5.00 am 17th September we relieved the front line troops and by 7.00 am artillery and mortar fire increased in intensity, persisting until 11.00 am. Then the French attacked Reserve Infantry Regiment 120 and a few minutes later a small group of black soldiers assaulted us from the trenches opposite. The throwing of a few of our hand grenades drove them back to their own lines. With that, the first enemy attack failed totally. The artillery responded to red signal flares and fired to keep the enemy heads down. The French tactics here were quite unlike those used at Lorette. The difference was that here they brought down heavy artillery fire on a very small sector, then left their trenches and assaulted ours with weak detachments about twenty to thirty men strong. A second line did not follow immediately. Once the first wave was broken up by our artillery fire and partly destroyed with grenades, the men flooded back to their own trenches. The main French weapons were mortars, rifle grenades and egg grenades. The first affected our nerves and our morale badly, but the last caused our men far less anxiety because, unless a bomb hit directly, it only caused minor injuries. My men, who kept me informed in a loud voice of every minor sighting or change in the enemy situation, distributed themselves skilfully behind cover in the trench and kept a sharp look out for mortars. If these were seen soon enough, it was possible to run away from them, so here, as at Lorette, came the shouts, 'mortar right!' or 'mortar left!', so everyone could take cover. Only in this way was it possible for us to beat off enemy attacks and maintain our position until we were relieved...

"I had twelve men forward with me in the front line. The rest were dead, wounded or buried alive. We hung on in this flattened position. To our great joy, careful watchfulness enabled us to beat off the first enemy attack and cause them casualties. There was no rest for us, however, because we did not have to wait long for the second attack, during which I lost four of my men to grenade splinters. This left me with eight men, who, true to their oath on the colours, put their trust in me, stood by my side, obeyed my orders and so held on to win glory and honour for our company. Thanks to our hand grenades, which were always laid out ready, the enemy was unable to gain a foot of ground with his third and fourth attacks. It was also clear to us that each time only four to six men were

storming forward from the enemy trenches and that they turned back to
their own trenches whenever we threw grenades. Though it was nerve
wracking, stronger willpower prevailed and we held out in our crater
position until we received the order to close up to the side of the 1st
Company and to erect a barricade after the enemy had broken into the
trenches of Reserve Infantry Regiment 120. As it went dark and attacks,
artillery and mortar fire had eased, we were relieved by 1st Company and
returned to K3. Two days later the whole of the 1st and 2nd Battalions
were relieved and occupied quarters in Athies."

The artillery had also suffered badly on 17th September from counter-battery fire.
Everywhere the German lines and battery positions had been under an intense
hurricane of fire for hours, which caused many casualties, then suddenly, at 4.00
pm, came a call from the infantry for fire by Guards Field Artillery Regiment 3.

*Gefreiter König 6th Battery Guards Field Artillery Regiment 3*[47] **17.**

"There were two of us left to serve the gun. These were Kanonier
Böttcher, who was killed a few weeks later at Hyencourt, and me. My dear
friend Böttcher passed the shells up to me, from a trench dug between the
trails of the gun. I had to load, aim and fire. We kept this up for hours,
giving it our very last reserves of strength. We were under extremely
heavy fire the whole time. A hedgerow ran away to our right. All of a
sudden, whilst we were engaged in heavy firing, I saw twenty to thirty
Frenchmen run past us in their light blue coats. My first thought was that
we had been overrun. We prepared for close quarter battle, but it was
unnecessary; they were deserters. We carried on firing..."

Ever since Ovillers and Pozières fell, it was clear to the Germans that Thiepval's
days were numbered. Nevertheless, such was the nature of the terrain and the
ferocity of the defence of Mouquet Farm and the sector as a whole, that it took
twelve weeks of extremely hard fighting before the British army was in a position
to carry out a final assault on the village which had been the lynchpin of the
defence for a full two years. Forced to attack on a narrow frontage, attack after
attack had been beaten back at the cost of enormous casualties on both sides.
When the end ultimately came, the core of the defence of the ruins of Thiepval was
in the hands of Infantry Regiment 180, which having fought so heroically at the
beginning of the battle in defence of Ovillers, was reconstituted and deployed in
and around Thiepval from 26th July. So, for no less than two months, this superb
regiment, reinforced from time to time, beat off everything that was thrown at it,
without once being relieved. It was probably the most outstanding regimental
performance on either side throughout the battle.

*Oberstleutnant Alfred Vischer Commander Infantry Regiment 180*[48] **18.**

"On 26 September at 1.30 pm, drum fire came down along the entire
line Thiepval – Serre and Thiepval – Courcelette. This was immediately

followed by an infantry attack in an easterly direction on the southern
flank of Thiepval. The left flank of the attack, which was organised in
waves, was directed against C7 and the southern part of C6 at the junction
with the road Thiepval – Authuille. As could not otherwise be expected in
the event of so strong an attack, the advanced triangle Mauerweg [Wall
Way]* – C7 – Braunerweg [Brown Way]†, which was only defended by a
platoon of 2nd Company and sentries from 2nd and 3rd Companies, was
lost. The first determined resistance was offered at Braunerweg.

"The first wave of attackers was almost completely destroyed by rifle
and machine-gun fire before it even closed up to the obstacle. The second,
denser, wave flooded to the rear with heavy casualties. Suddenly an
armoured vehicle (tank) emerged out of Authuille Wood. It was followed
and flanked by a third wave, which succeeded in checking the withdrawal
of the second wave and, assisted by the tank, to work its way forward to
the obstacle. There the attack stalled. Attackers and defenders engaged in
a fire fight. The situation took an unfavourable turn when suddenly the
left flank and almost simultaneously, the left flank and centre of the 3rd
Company were attacked from the rear with hand grenades. The British
seemed to have forced their way into the south eastern and eastern fronts
of Thiepval and pressed with increasing strength from the direction of the
church and chateau to the south and south-west. Attacked from the front
and rear and threatened in the flank as well, the 3rd Company had to fall
back, echeloned from the left, on C6. The enemy did not succeed in
forcing a way via Mauerweg into C6 from the south, but he attacked
unopposed from Thiepval until, finally, after the toughest defence
possible, the barricade at the junction of C6 and Mauerweg had to be
pulled back in order to avoid encirclement...."

The tank referred to here was one of two allocated to the British 53 Brigade, which
advanced from hides in Blighty Valley. It should not be confused with the two well
known ones which moved forward from Thiepval Wood during the battle. One of
these, C5 'Creme de Menthe', played a key role in taking the chateau. During the
week following the fall of Thiepval, this third tank was the subject of a report
which Oberstleutnant Vischer forwarded to Divisional Headquarters. It seems to
have been a 'Female', [ie armed only with machine guns] but given the
inaccuracies in the rest of the report, that may not be correct.

10th Württemberg Inf Regt Nr. 180          4 October 1916
Nr. 427
To the 26th Reserve Division
Report Concerning British Armoured Vehicles based on Witness Statements.

During the attack on 26th September 1916, an armoured vehicle
moved across country with the first attacking wave via Brauner Weg
[Brown Way] against the south western section of Thiepval (Mauergraben)
[Wall Trench]. It advanced very slowly across the heavily shelled terrain,

*Mauerweg [Wall Way] was a section of the second trench line, running east – west and situated very close to what is
now the southern edge of the Thiepval memorial to the missing.
†Braunerweg [Brown Way] was originally a communication trench linking the first and second trenches in C7 a little
to the south of Mauerweg.

stopped before larger shell holes and attempted as far as possible to go round them.  It halted in front of the wire obstacle in front of Mauergraben and engaged the company stationed there with machine gun fire, paying particular attention to the machine gun.  It was impossible to establish if the mortar rounds, which during this time and later fell around the junction of the Schwabengraben [Schwabian Trench] and the second trench, came from the armoured vehicle.

"According to the statements of certain individuals, about forty men debussed from the vehicle. Others maintained that they did not debus; that they were merely following the vehicle. It was not possible to establish if the vehicle crossed the Mauergraben and continued on its way. Length of the armoured vehicle was five to six metres. It was egg-shaped. There was a four-cornered mounting set low on the vehicle, from which the machine gun fired. The number of these could not be determined. There were shovels in front of the armoured vehicle which pushed the earth aside. The witnesses can provide no information about the way the vehicle moved."

Had there been survivors of Infantry Regiment 180 from the fighting around the chateau itself, matters would probably have been somewhat clearer because, near there, the defenders got to close quarters with at least one tank.  A newspaper report provides a graphic description about what happened next.

Manchester Guardian: *27th September 1916*

"The exciting adventure of one of our landships must be mentioned here. On its own responsibility, it had chosen to head for an enemy trench below the village. So it arrived during its lonely advance at a deep and wide ravine, which apparently concealed soldiers. The tank intended to cross this trench in the usual way, but it suddenly got stuck. At the same instant, the Germans rushed out of their hiding places and swarmed around the tank like bees.  They displayed extraordinary courage. Although the hidden batteries of the vehicle showered them with fire, they attempted with desperate violence to storm the mobile armoured fort and to kill its crew.  Despite ceaseless machine-gun fire, they helped one another to climb onto the steel roof. They obviously hoped to find hatches and cracks in the monster's armour, but they might as well have been attacking a battleship with spades.  It was an indescribable sight, this battle of man against machine. The crew on the inside were filled with fury. Not in their wildest dreams had they considered it possible that they might be attacked. These Germans were driven on by blind determination. In the madness of the moment, they were willing to stake their lives. Finally British infantry attacked and drove the enemy back..."

Pressed in on three sides, the defences began to crumble.  All telephone links had long since been destroyed.  As a result, it was almost impossible for the higher headquarters to monitor the progress of the desperate fighting. At 6.30 pm on the 26th, a carrier pigeon arrived at Headquarters 26th Reserve Division. Its message read, 'One unteroffizier and seventeen men still occupying the dugout of the 1st Battalion [Infantry Regiment 180]. Cut off from all companies and surrounded by British soldiers. Signed: Gossers, Patrol Commander. Belthle, Battalion Drummer.'[52]

By the morning of the 27th, the remnants of the defenders were grouped together under virtually the last surviving officer of 1st Battalion Infantry Regiment 180, Reserve Leutnant Kimmich, who had been conducting a fighting withdrawal from one trench barricade to another in a northerly direction towards Saint Pierre Divion.

### Reserve Leutnant Kimmich 2nd Company Infantry Regiment 180 [53]19.

"Leutnant Mayer was wounded during the morning of 27th September and because Leutnant Engel had also gone, I took command of the remainder of the Battalion. Then a report arrived that the British, who were pressing hard against the barricade in the Hoher Steg, had brought down heavy machine gun fire from the rear and had caused heavy casualties. A heavy thrust from Thiepval north via Hoher Steg was underway. In order to avoid being cut off and with the agreement of Reserve Infantry Regiment 77, I ordered the front-line trench to be evacuated as far as Hoher Steg, but to hold Hoher Steg itself as long as possible. This would buy time for Marktgraben [Market Trench] to be prepared for defence. I took over the defence of the front-line trench and Marktgraben as far back as the second trench. I linked up on my left with Reserve Infantry Regiment 77. Because of a lack of hand grenades, I had to yield ground bit by bit in Hoher Steg, but the barricade at the junction of Hoher Steg and the front-line trench was held in the face of constant attacks. Marktgraben was under heavy artillery fire all day long, so temporarily it was impossible to install a strong garrison there. The enemy infantry were not very active that day, but in contrast there was a great deal of aerial activity. In order to permit my exhausted men some rest, I requested Infantry Regiment 66 to relieve me of Marktgraben during the evening of 27th September. This enabled me to house the remnants of the Battalion in a dugout...Because Infantry Regiment 66 had consumed all its iron rations and the fact that the serious situation precluded resupply, there was very little to eat on 26, 27 and 28 September. Above all there was a lack of water.

"During the night of 27/28 September I relieved Infantry Regiment 66 at the barricades and in Marktgraben once more. During the morning of 28 September the artillery fire increased until, by 1.30 pm, it was coming down as drum fire all over the position. At the same time the British began to storm forward in waves via Martinspfad [Martin's Way]. The first wave actually advanced in the drum fire. The machine guns had been taken into cover during the heavy shelling and worked excellently. I was wounded right at the beginning of the fighting. The British had already pushed forward in C3 to the junction with Burkgraben [Burk Trench]. I gave orders to break through them. We succeeded in dealing with them and started work immediately on new barricades. In the meantime our artillery lifted its fire from the edge of the wood onto the enemy who had been sighted advancing in column via Thiepval. As the attack stalled, I ordered the remnants of 1st Battalion Infantry Regiment 180, by now reduced in strength to no more than three sections, to withdraw and rendezvous in the tunnel at Saint Pierre Divion, where I had my wound dressed and received an order relieving me...Despite the great losses and the lack of food and water, the remnants of 1st Battalion Infantry Regiment 180 fought against an enemy hugely superior in numbers with fatalistic courage. The heroic defence of Thiepval was acknowledged respectfully by the enemy."

This last statement was nothing less than the truth. In its report of 27 September quoted above, the *Manchester Guardian* also stated, 'The past few days had already taught the Württembergers that they would not be able to hold out as one part after the other of the surrounding defensive chain had been destroyed. They said to themselves that, sooner or later, their own isolated position would have to be next and that it would be a life or death battle. "We knew it was useless", they said, "but we carried on fighting." And fight they did, just like the old infantry battalions at the beginning of the war. They were descended from that old army, which blew through Belgium and France like a gale, brushing all aside. The deep, vaulted cellars of Thiepval maintained their fighting power undiminished until their moment came. Yes, it was no easy thing to be able to break the spirit of Thiepval.' The fight for Thiepval Ridge, the village itself and Schwaben Redoubt were drawn-out slogging matches in the same mould as the earlier costly battles. In this case, however, the ground was sufficiently important to justify, in the terrible arithmetic of the day, the cost in human lives, but by this time that degree of doggedness was no longer the rule. The measures which had been taken energetically by the new Army Supreme Command were beginning to work by the end of September. The crisis in the battle had been overcome and the attacks, which of course continued in strength through to November, tended to be broken up early. Only here and there, where the Allies came up against troops which were insufficiently rested and reconstituted, did they succeed occasionally in gaining ground. As far as tactics were concerned, further effective developments had taken place. Frequently, for example, reverse slope positions were selected to provide protection for the infantry from observed artillery fire. As the weather worsened, hindering air operations, which by this time were not always going the way of the Allies, this was a useful gain. Although these locations had only short fields of fire, attackers were usually skylined as they approached the German positions, thus making them easy targets. It was of course necessary to ensure that the artillery observers were placed further back and sufficiently high up to be able to direct fire accurately.

Now that the suspension of offensive operations at Verdun had released a large number of German artillery regiments for service on the Somme, the role of the artillery, though constrained by a continual shortage of ammunition, became increasingly important. In the final two months of fighting the artillery was to play the major part in the defensive battle. Every effort was made to bring down destructive fire early on troop concentrations to break them up. The underlying idea was to try to prevent assaults from taking place at all and so avoid the waste of ammunition which the firing of pre-designated defensive fire missions often involved. Naturally the infantry was not terribly concerned where the artillery found the necessary ammunition, just as long as they received support when they felt it was needed. This was not always the case. At 2.00 pm 24th September, for example, a day when the 6th Bavarian Infantry Division was under considerable pressure and holding the Gallwitz Riegel [Gallwitz Stop Line] to the west of Gueudecourt, Hauptmann Bucher sent a typed one-page note from the Observation Post of 4th Battery Field Artillery Regiment 11 to the Commander 1st Battalion Bavarian Field Artillery Regiment 2 (who was presumably the coordinating authority), drawing attention to administrative deficiencies and complaining that the reasonable needs of the infantry for defensive fire were not being met.

*Hauptmann Bucher 4th Battery Bavarian Field Artillery Regiment 11*[55] **20.**

"The heavy weight of enemy fire, of both heavy and super-heavy calibre, which began this morning and which is being directed mainly against our trenches opposite Flers, has remained, right up until the time this report was written (2.00 pm), unanswered by any of our batteries. 4th and 5th Batteries Field Artillery Regiment 11 have fired thirty rounds each. All the remaining batteries are silent. In my considered opinion, this situation must be being regarded with bitterness by our infantry, who are suffering so much. On the other hand, the enemy infantry and especially its artillery are taking no casualties; we are simply acquiescing to enemy superiority.

"In view of the lack of ammunition, flanking fire may only be opened by batteries on specific command, or if the enemy attacks. This of course is only possible if the telephone lines are in order. Today's experience has shown, however, that despite the sending out of patrols repeatedly, the lines cannot be maintained over any length of time. In view of the increased enemy fire, this situation cannot be expected to be any less serious during the coming days. In order to be able to intervene effectively in this battle, in my view, battery commanders must have the delegated right to open fire independently. In order to meet the need for economy of ammunition, higher authority could limit the number of rounds available for fire mission on own initiative to one to two hundred shells per battery per day.

"I also request direction concerning the timings of defensive fire missions. As far as I am aware, timings and number of rounds to be fired are laid down for each battery. This information is not available for 4th Battery, because it only moved the day before yesterday into completely unprepared positions. Finally I request the issue of a 1:25,000 map, such as has been issued to all the other batteries. So far 4th Battery has not received one."

As the autumn days grew shorter, some aspects of the defence were being handled with increased efficiency, but there remained plenty of room for improvement if the German army was to be able to continue to fight a delaying battle and thus hang on for the coming of winter and the completion of the Siegfried Stellung [Hindenburg Line]. The Allies had made important gains during the month but, as October opened, the German defence was being conducted with undiminished ferocity. The impetus generated by the gains in mid-month, the fall of Thiepval and the thrust eastwards north and south of Morval, had stalled once more. More costly attritional fighting was the inevitable consequence.

1. Seiler: History IR 161 pp 124-125
2. This shift in tactical thinking plainly owed nothing to the overall change of command. Clearly the practicalities of the situation were already forcing changes on the army, before these became formalised by Ludendorff's new defensive instructions when they were distributed later.
3. *Ein fester Burg ist unser Gott* by Martin Luther (1483-1546). This is possibly his most celebrated hymn.
4. Collenberg: History GFAR 3 p 217
5. Rosenberg-Lipinsky: History GGR 3 pp 354-355
6. Reinhard: History GR 4 p 204
7. Stosch: History GR 5 pp 283-284
8. Rosenberg-Lipinsky: op. cit. p 364
9. Voigt: History FüsR 73 p 415
10. ibid. p 415
11. Anon: History IR 164 p 318-320
12. ibid. p 322-323
13. Voigt: op. cit. p 420-421
14. Nau: 'Guillemont'
15. Voigt: op. cit. p 417
16. ibid. p 395
17. Ludendorff: 'Meine Kriegserinnerungen' p 213
18. ibid. p 215
19. Rogge: History IR 88 p 297
20. ibid. pp 298-299
21. Weisemann-Remscheid: 'Wo der Krieg gehaust!' pp 18-19
22. Korfes: History IR 66 pp 213-214
23. Zipfel: History FR 89 pp 263-264
24. Böttger: History IR 106 pp 124-127
25. Funcke: History FAR 78 p 90
26. Fuhrmann: History RIR 211 p161

27. ibid. p161
28. Beyer: History FAR 221 p 98
29. This lack of friendly aircraft was a constant, enduring complaint. Earlier in the battle, General Armin's IV Corps had actually published an instruction relating to the use of aircraft which stated, inter alia, 'The aircraft of our squadrons are not suited to reacting to 'take off on call' operations. In addition, because the operational strength of these squadrons is insufficient to permit them to be used for constant defensive patrols, there is no way of fully preventing enemy aircraft from flying over our lines. The infantry and artillery must be responsible for their own low level air defence'[!] [See: Koch Die Flieger-Abteilung (A) 221 pp 27-28]. It is to be hoped that neither the contents nor the tone of this dismal paper were widely known to those front line troops who suffered daily at the hands of the Allied air forces, especially during the first three months of the battle.
30. Pfeiffer: History BFAR 12 pp 53-54
31. Anon: Festschrift 2. Regimentstag RIR 231 pp 8-9
32. Schaidler: History BIR 7 p 36
33. Anon: History BIR 14 pp 179 - 180
34. This may have been tank D7, commanded by Lieutenant AJ Enoch. See Pidgeon Flers & Gueudecourt p 74
35. Anon: History BIR 14 p 193
36. Kriegsarchiv München HS 2200
37. Kohl: Mit Hurra in den Tod! pp 128-130
38. Kalb: History BFAR 10 p 369
39. Funcke: op. cit. pp 93-94
40. Bolze: History FAR 77 pp 144-146
41. ibid. pp 149-151
42. This may have been tank D5, commanded by Second Lieutenant Arthur Blowers. See Pidgeon op. cit. pp 89, 90 & 101
43. This may have been tank D6, commanded by Lieutenant Reginald Legge. See Pidgeon op. cit. pp 89-92
44. Kalb: History BFAR 10 p 122
45. Tiessen: History RIR 213 pp 427-429
46. Böttger: History IR 106 pp 120-123
47. Collenberg: op. cit. p 224
48. Vischer: Das 10. Württ. IR 180 in der Somme-Schlacht pp 51-52
49. See Stedman Thiepval p 92
50. Hauptstaatsarchiv Stuttgart M99 Bü 142/833. It is strange that none of the witnesses drew attention to the tracks of the vehicle, because several of them had a good look at it. Vizefeldwebel Linder of 2nd Company saw it approach right up to the obstacle in front of Mauerweg. Gefreiter Grambusch and Hornist Hiller of 4th Company Infantry Regiment 180 were able to report detail such as, 'The armoured vehicle came from the direction of Authuille and headed towards the left flank of the 2nd Company. It had obvious difficulty in attempting to cross a large shell hole and only managed to advance at the third attempt.' See: Hauptstaatsarchiv Stuttgart M99 Bü 142/847.
51. Quoted in Grote: Somme pp 137-138
52. Vischer: op. cit. p 53
53. Hauptstaatsarchiv Stuttgart M99 Bü 142/807
54. Quoted in Grote: op. cit. pp 138
55. Kriegsarchiv München 2 FAR Bd 6

CHAPTER 8

# October 1916

In late September the Somme front received an unusual group of reinforcements. These were the men of the Marine Infantry Brigade, who had spent their entire war up to this point holding positions along the coast to the north of Nieuwpoort and east of the Yser. This had almost been a private war in the dunes, so it was something of a dramatic change of scenery, role and intensity of operations when they were ordered south. The marching in full equipment was hard going for them after such a long period on a static front, but they were, nevertheless, troops of excellent quality. The title 'Brigade' is somewhat misleading. Comprising Marine Infantry Regiments 1, 2 and 3, each at full strength, it was fully comparable with a normal infantry division. Furthermore many of its rifle companies had a Hauptmann in charge, assisted by three other officers, which meant that its overall officer strength and rank structure resembled far more an infantry division of 1914 than one of autumn 1916. After a couple of days when the Brigade was held in depth and used for digging duties, on 30th September they were ordered to relieve the 8th Infantry Division in the front line. For the next two weeks they defended the line of the Staufen-Riegel [Stuff Stop Line = Regina Trench], to deny any advance in the direction of Grandcourt or Miraumont. From the moment they arrived, they were under intense pressure as the Canadian Corps launched repeated attacks against them.

*Leutnant Wulf 3rd Company Marine Infantry Regiment 1*[1] 1.

"The time selected for the relief seemed to be favourable. The fire coming down on the position had become weaker, but the approach routes were still swept by shells and shrapnel. In single file my men followed me, whilst the Tommies brought down repeated concentrations of fire at short intervals in front of us on the shell-ploughed road, approximately where the shot down aircraft was located. We doubled past it and the majority of my platoon negotiated the danger zone safely. Nevertheless the artillery fire, which roared over our heads like a hurricane and exploded with ear-splitting crashes close behind us, constantly claimed victims. Sweating and with nerves on edge, we reached our designated sector. There was no trace of either position or trench! Smashed and buried dugouts, wrecked camouflage, a tangle of assorted equipment lying around, intermingled with all types of weaponry, told in very stark terms a tale of destruction and intense fighting. Had we not on the previous day observed what to us was an unfamiliar quantity of artillery fire crashing down, then at this moment it would have been brought home to us even more abruptly that we had entered into a completely new phase of large-scale warfare.

"Which is my sector? What are its boundaries? Where on earth are the soldiers whom we are meant to relieve? Previously we had been used to meeting up with soldiers due for relief gathered together at their start point. The front seemed to be empty of men; it was almost uncanny. If the Tommies had only realised that a little earlier they would have met with no opposition! Suddenly, following along the vague trace of a position, I stumbled across two men of Infantry Regiment 96. I asked about their company commander and had to repeat the question several times. They stared at me, wide eyed, disorientated and lacking all feeling. They could not give me an answer. The horror they had endured was almost tangible. How the poor lads must have suffered these past few days from the effect of constant drum fire, with no food or sleep for four days; just scenes of death and destruction unfolding before their eyes. The entire company was reduced to a handful of men. But the word 'Relief' electrified them, jerking them back to reality. 'Relief!' they babbled, with child-like happiness. Their bodies, which seemed physically and spiritually spent, grew visibly in stature and strength. 'Relief!' they breathed; it was their salvation. In no time at all, their equipment was fastened on and they headed as fast as they could for Baum Mulde [Tree Gully = Boom Ravine]*. I turned to my men and smiled. One of them muttered, *sotto voce*, 'In a few days we shall look just like that!'

"I felt my way forward through the darkness. There was no sign of anyone. There was an eerie stillness, broken from time to time by the crash of shells as they exploded on the road. My men, following me faithfully, were feeling uneasy; I could see it clearly. 'We haven't gone wrong; we're not blundering into the Tommies are we?' asked one. At that moment I arrived at a dugout, out of which a faint light could be seen. Soldiers were sitting on every step of the dugout, with their heads to one side, sleeping so soundly, perhaps for the first time for days, that they had not heard us coming. It was almost impossible to shake them awake. One of them, suddenly aware, sprang up and looked angrily at us as though he was in doubt as to whether we were friend or foe. Suddenly shocked into life, he asked, 'Are you our reliefs?' In an instant there was pandemonium as these utterly worn out, exhausted warriors grabbed for their equipment: officers and men alike. As soon as he found his, each raced to get away, as though driven by the Furies. The nest emptied.

"I made my way over to my predecessor to ask about the hand over of the position and to pick up suggestions and practical tips from him, which would have been very welcome to me. But he was in just as much a hurry as the rest. I grabbed him by the arm and told him forcefully that, in

---

*Boom Ravine was one branch of a deeply incised re-entrant, whose northern extremity was located midway between Miraumont and Grandcourt. Named Stallmulde [Stable Hollow], it twisted its way southeast for about 750 metres to where it forked. One branch, named Baum Mulde [Tree Gully] = Boom Ravine, ran east – west and the other continued as Stallmulde north – south for a further 500 metres to a final branch called Kleine Mulde [Little Gully]. On the modern map it is called Les Grands Royarts.

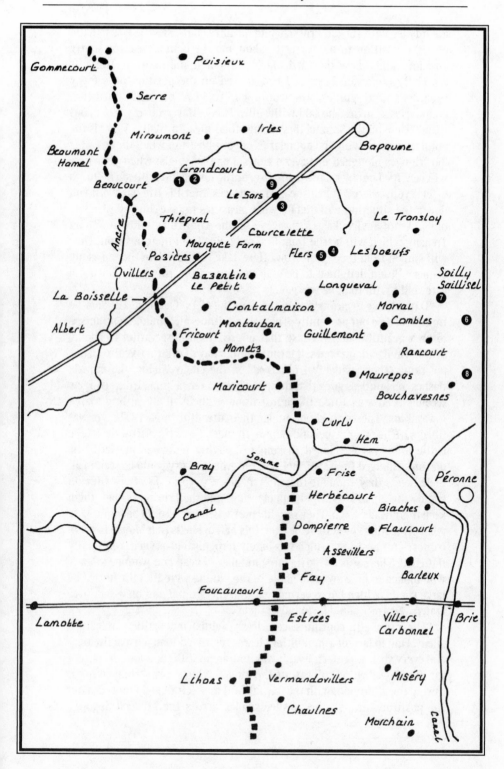

accordance with the old Prussian and military courtesies, he was to hand over the position to me correctly, show me the boundaries, the sentry positions and where the particularly vulnerable points were. This was especially important because I had arrived on the position on a foggy night, without guides. He would barely hear me out. 'Position, boundaries, sentries,' he said with sullen irony, 'Have you any idea about them? Here on the Somme they change their meaning daily. What is the point of you knowing the boundaries of your position when the so-called 'position' is ploughed up several times a day by shells; when your men will be wiped out by a day's drum fire, until you are left with a handful to defend your sector? When the enemy attacks after his fire has worn you down, the situation will dictate what measures to take. But I'll give you one piece of advice: keep a close eye on the sap [Allies called it Kenora Trench], which will be the Tommies' sally port from their position. They will launch from there tomorrow. Here, take this sketch of the sap as my bequest! I am delighted to be able to escape from this hell. Goodbye! Farewell!' With that, he was gone!

"Dawn broke to clear skies on the morning of 1st October. The Somme front stretched out peacefully. There was stillness all around. It promised to be a beautiful day. Because that offered good observation to enemy aviators and balloon crews, it meant another day of destructive fire on our positions. Then suddenly I observed, on the enemy's side, the muzzle flashes of countless guns that lit up the horizon on a broad front. In a few seconds there was a roar like a hurricane as shells of all calibres roared towards us. The earth shook under their dreadful impact. The air was filled with bursts, crashes and claps of thunder. In no time at all the whole battle area was enveloped in smoke. Roughly jerked from sleep, the marines emerged from their holes in the ground. Fury could be seen in all their faces; they thought that the enemy was going to attack. But an endless stream of bursting shrapnel rounds and shell splinters made them keep their heads down. They sought cover wherever it could be found. But what protection could there be from this hail of shells that landed in every corner? Our position, which was barely recognisable as such, was totally flattened. There was already a large number of dead and wounded. Many who looked to hide away in a hole in the ground were literally buried by large shells, which bored deep down into the ground and blew out large craters. No trace could be found of them...

"The drum fire continued ceaselessly, whilst our artillery remained silent. Due to lack of ammunition, it was restricted to defensive fire only and every shell was precious... It was now about 2.00 pm. Full of concern for how I was going to beat off the attack, which was certain to occur during the afternoon, with the few faithful men left to me, I moved about the position through the powder smoke, across the crushed dugouts, tangles of wire and all kinds of equipment. There were dead and wounded men everywhere, screaming and shouting... all the Furies of War were in full cry. British aircraft flying at thirty metres directed their artillery onto every sign of life in the shell holes and dipped forward like lightning to machine gun, or even throw grenades, at anyone moving around. During my tour I came across Gefreiter Kröning, one of the most faithful and courageous members of my platoon. He was crouching in a crater forward of the position and was observing the enemy. I was absolutely delighted to see him keeping guard so watchfully. I clapped him on the shoulder and said, 'I knew that I would find you out here; that you would not be cowering behind cover, just awaiting the arrival of a heavy shell which would carry you off to a hero's death.' His indomitable reply was, 'We few survivors of the proud 3rd Platoon are not going to yield to our fate, before we have defended our position to the utmost. The Tommies are bound to come today, but they will find us ready. If the weight of the attack falls on us, we shall sell our lives as dearly as possible and take a lot of them with us, Leutnant!'

"Crouching down together, we chatted about home, parents and family, so as to take our minds off our surroundings. All the while the hail of shells continued to crash down on our sector... Suddenly the enemy artillery altered its tactics. It was exactly 4.00 pm. The fire lifted abruptly behind our lines, falling on the reserve position, Boom Ravine and Miraumont. The intention of the Tommies was clear and the thought raced through my head: the enemy do not want to endanger their own troops and they are trying to interdict our reserves as they rush forward. I jumped up to a place of observation, where what I saw made my blood run cold and momentarily robbed me of my powers of decision. An unprecedented sight met my eyes. Eight or nine assault waves were advancing up the gentle slope towards our position. I regained my senses and red flares were soon emerging from my signal pistol; the sign to our artillery that the enemy were attacking. It is to the honour of our gunners that they responded promptly. With mighty yells, Gefreiter Kröning and I raised the alarm.

"Our sector came to life. The emptiness of the battlefield filled up as my men crawled out of craters and holes in the ground. Amazingly, these shelters had protected them from the murderous fire. The attack came as a relief from the destructive fire. They were ready to do their duty. All they wanted was for the enemy to attack, so that they could vent their pent-up rage. We were set and ready for the Tommies. I rushed to the right flank of my sector, to the entrance to the sap where the machine gun was located. In no time it was in position and it opened a destructive fire on the enemy, who went down like cornstalks before the scythe. But too many dogs mean the death of the hare. My little band was too few; the number of

Canadians too great, despite the enormous casualties that their repeated attacks caused them. In addition, the enemy were advancing through an area that was in dead ground to the machine gun sap, so that they could only be engaged with rifle fire. Pressing forward, following each other closely, they pushed past the sap towards our defensive line. I had to reckon with a breakthrough and at all costs prevent the great danger of being rolled up. It was to counter this very risk that I had put together an assault troop before our 'excursion' to the Somme and had posted it here the previous evening. Giving my men a quick briefing about the threatening danger, I made them load up with grenades then, placing myself at their head, we launched ourselves at the enemy with battle cries of 'Hurra!'

"Having practised this type of attack, we threw our grenades into the ranks of the attackers according to plan, as though we were on exercise. Caught in a pincer movement, they suffered terrible casualties and had to pull back. We pursued them, throwing grenades and forcing them back into the second half of the sap. There they were reinforced and we had to yield to their superior numbers. Our grenades had all been used and our action had caused us casualties. Marine Sager fell, killed by a shot to the head and Gefreiter Mielitz lost an eye. The flood of enemy continued to break against our position. Again and again I called on my men to follow me. Repeatedly we threw ourselves against overwhelming odds. The effect of our grenades was devastating. Frequently we came across five or six Tommies piled up on top of each other and we literally had to climb over their corpses. We fought for every foot of ground against our gallantly fighting enemy, who caused us bitter casualties. Adler was killed, Rudolph wounded, but the Tommies could not resist our assault. We pushed forward and were able to free our comrades Olin and Klempke, who had been overrun and captured when the enemy stormed the sap. Reinforced by them, we pushed on towards the trench which separated us from the enemy. There we were met by several hand grenades, which were thrown over the barricade. There was nowhere to run. They blew up amongst us, wounding almost all my remaining faithful band: Schmidt, Kröning, Olin and Müller. Almost miraculously, Winterkamp, Witte and I were unwounded. Reduced in numbers and out of grenades, we had to pull back to our main defensive line...[2]

"Although the Canadians must have realised that in us they were up against thoroughly obstinate opponents, who were prepared to defend their position to the last drop of blood, they made no attempt to withdraw. They no longer presented us with standing targets as they had during the first attacks; they had become more cautious. Leaping from crater to crater, they tried to work their way forward to our position, but we were equal to them. Our 'Pattern 98' rifles may have lost some importance with the introduction of modern close quarter weapons, but they resumed their place of honour against an enemy outside the range of our grenades. As soon as the Tommies dashed forward, they were met with well-aimed fire. Vizefeldwebel Lietz, a noted shot, excelled. 'Keep calm lads, every shot must count', he encouraged the men. 'See that tall man there? He's mine.' The shot rang out, the British steel helmet described a wide arc in the air, but its wearer fell. Following this example, my men dealt with every opponent who approached our position.

"Further attacks lacked the necessary impetus. The battle ebbed away. There were not even any more thrusts from the sap, against which the enemy had concentrated the main effort of the initial attacks. By throwing grenades, which Mieltiz and Olin, despite their severe eye injuries, passed up to us, we kept the enemy at bay. At it went dark the attack finally petered out..."

Having evacuated their wounded, the Marines settled down as best they could, determined to hold off future attacks. The fact that they were occupying a good reverse slope position was a great advantage. Despite the difficulty the Allied gunners had in bringing effective fire down behind the crest line, they lost a steady stream of casualties to artillery fire, but thanks to judicious rotation of forward companies and the fact that resupply was possible on a nightly basis, they were able to maintain their positions until they were relieved.

*Feldwebel Stahlbock 5th Company Marine Infantry Regiment 3[3] 2.*

"The company was split into four platoons and I belonged to the fourth. Our duty was to carry forward food, water and ammunition. We were quartered in Bihucourt, in a rather damaged barn containing straw. Each evening as it went dark, the 'Goulash Gun' [field kitchen] arrived and we of the carrying party, with sandbags tied around our legs and armed with stout sticks, fell in behind it and went forward. Replacements rushed past us. The familiar cry, 'Get over to the right!' announced the arrival of a lorry carrying all sorts of ammunition and matériel forward. We halted in Pys and the food was transferred to carrying containers, which we slotted along a pole carried by two carriers, one in front and one behind. The heavy sack of bread was carried in turns by two men. The NCO carried the butter, cheese, cigars and cigarettes. The remainder carried coffee and containers of schnaps and off we went to find the company, with our leader out in front.

"'Keep up!' comes the shout from the front. 'Keep hard right!' Suddenly the track is swamped with water, but we must continue. The leader tests the way forward carefully to ensure that nobody sinks in a shell hole and we wade through, knee deep in water, before stumbling up a slope and sliding down the far side with the sack of bread. There is considerable muttering in the party, but all we get is 'Forwards! Come on! Keep up!' as our commander keeps us together. The fire becomes heavier and heavier. We take cover in shell holes. As the fire dies away and the hurricane is over, we continue. There are signs of life in front of us – the company! 'The ration party's here!' shout the sentries down into the dugouts. The food is brought down to the platoon commanders and divided up. Mail is collected and taken back for despatch. One man per platoon reports to the company commander to collect the mail. The commander of the carrying party takes his leave and we return to the rear as quickly as possible."

On 8 October an even larger-scale attack was launched against Regina Trench. This involved British as well as Canadian formations, but although it enjoyed initial surprise, ultimately it was no more successful than the attack on 1st October had been. The Marines recovered quickly from the shock of the first assault and fought back hard. Their quality as fighting soldiers was fully proven; they were well organised and well-supplied. The result, despite the heroic efforts of the assault force, was another serious mauling for the Allies.

*Lt Otto Tuercke 4th Company Marine Infantry Regiment 3*[4] **2.**

"My battalion relieved the troops in the front line during the evening of 7 October. Fortunately my company reached its positions without casualties, despite the unpleasant harassing fire. During the night it was peaceful, but it was the calm before the storm. At 5.30 am the storm broke out in accordance with the British custom of attacking early in the morning. There was drum fire for about two or three minutes, then it lifted to the rear and the cry went up, 'Here they come!' In the white light of the flares, we could see a swarm of men in flat steel helmets in front of the barbed wire. Our artillery, alerted by the firing of coloured flares, opened up and brought down superb defensive fire right in front of our trenches, which caused the enemy serious casualties. That, coupled with our small arms fire and grenades, was sufficient to beat off the attack completely. Where the enemy had broken into the position to the left and right, he was thrown out again in short order following courageous counter- attacks with grenades.

"As it became light we could see what heavy casualties the enemy had suffered. I had taken over the company following the wounding of the company commander. We had to launch a further local attack to clear out the enemy in front of our wire, including a group of about twelve with a machine gun who were occupying a nearby shell hole and causing us problems. This attack brought us about seventy prisoners and three machine guns. It was then quiet for a while. Even the enemy artillery seemed to be unsure of the location of their troops and so it was not until the afternoon that fire came down with its previous intensity..."

*Vizefeldwebel Schneider 10th Company Marine Infantry Regiment 1[5] 1.*

"At 3.00 am on 8th October, 10th Company advanced from Pys via Miraumont, Boom Ravine and the Courcelette road past a shot down aircraft, to take up positions in Regina Trench. The sky was cloudy and there was not much artillery fire. My platoon was company reserve and I occupied the Dessauer Riegel [Dessau Stop Line = Desire Support], which was located about a hundred metres behind the front line. Around 6.00 am I wanted to deploy my platoon, so that everyone would know where to go in the event of an attack. Initially we grabbed our spades, with the aim of linking the holes into a trench. Just as I wanted to give the order to deploy, a murderous drum fire was opened on us, whose din prevented me from making myself understood. Everyone dived into cover in the earth which was shaking under the impact of the heavy shells. What was happening to our front? As dawn broke, everything was obscure. A slight fold in the ground in front of my crater blocked the view, so Sergeant Dähne and I leapt forward fifty metres, before diving into another crater. In front of us and along the road to our right, shadowy figures could be made out. Who could it be? Finally I believed that I had detected flat steel helmets through the binoculars. Dähne confirmed my impression. The enemy must have overrun Regina Trench! On the road the enemy had advanced to within forty metres of my reserve position. We immediately opened fire and the enemy took cover. Gradually it grew lighter and we could soon see how the waves of enemy were advancing to our front. More and more groups set out. None got as far as the first wave, which must have been lying out in front of our wire during the night.

"Suddenly Sergeant Dähne collapsed, shot through the chest. With the words, 'I'm dying,' his life ebbed away. My last grenade landed in the crater from which the shot had come. I was boiling with anger. I grabbed for my rifle and, standing next to the edge of the crater, so as not to represent a target negligently to my own people, I shot the opponent. I estimated that there were about twenty enemy and four machine guns on the road, so I disappeared back into my crater, pinned down by streams of machine gun bullets. Soon an enemy aircraft appeared, spraying us from very low level with its machine gun. If only we could dig deeper. Lacking a spade, we were forced to use our bayonets. After a lot of trouble I succeeded in scrabbling out a hole one foot deeper and so offered the aviators a smaller target. During the quiet moments the last of the bullets were fired. One last look at my dead comrade, then I returned to my men, who had long ago given me up for lost. A little later Hauptmann Oldermann appeared carrying a walking stick and with his usual cigar in his mouth. He ordered us to attack. Because of the four machine guns, a frontal attack was out of the question. If the operation was to enjoy success without too many casualties, the enemy flanking position would have to be pushed back and that could only be done by a surprise attack launched from my observation crater.

"A few volunteers would have to suffice to tackle the twenty British [*sic* – more likely to have been Canadians]. Unteroffiziers Lange and Schulz, Marine Biergatz and an Unteroffizier from another company volunteered. In order to be as mobile as possible, I dropped my personal equipment, shoved a few hand grenades between the buttons of my uniform jacket and grabbed Sergeant Dähne's rifle. Our dash [forward] succeeded and in a few seconds we were in my observation shell hole. A shot creased the back of Biergatz's head, but it did not prevent him from fighting on. We wanted to launch our attack and left the shell hole. There we saw the British, but instead of the estimated twenty, we were opposed by at least seventy to eighty riflemen with fixed bayonets. Back into the crater! What now? Retreat would be no less dangerous than attack. As we made ready, we heard cries of '*Hurra*' in the distance. That gave us the needed impetus. Coming to a swift decision, I leaped out of the crater and threw two hand grenades in the middle of the enemy. There were four others with me. With loud battle cries, we hurled ourselves at the enemy. They hesitated, leaderless, then hared off towards Regina Trench, pursued by fire from their own machine gun. Three British soldiers were cut off and sent back, unescorted, as prisoners. The road was strewn with weapons. Three machine guns fell into our hands. In the heat of battle I approached too close to Regina Trench and suddenly felt a sharp blow on my upper left arm, which in no time at all turned blood red. My artery had been severed by a splinter from a British grenade! My arm was hanging in shreds. Two faithful comrades carried me the 800 metres back to the dressing station in Boom Ravine. The doctor could hardly credit that I had returned from the front with a wound to an artery, but my three British [prisoners] had to confirm it, whether they liked it or not..."

*Vizefeldwebel Fock 10th Company Marine Infantry Regiment 1* 1.

"Suddenly a heavy shell landed on the dugout. The violent shaking extinguished the light. My friend's leg was virtually torn off. He lost his footing and fell down fifteen or twenty steps. I raced after him to give him first aid, but he could not be saved. Whilst I was kneeling next to him, I heard strange voices. The British had arrived. Swiftly I jumped over the wounded man and took cover behind a corner as four or five hand grenades were thrown down. Most of the fragments hit the wounded man, who never moved again. The other two of us were unwounded. Then our flares caught fire. I put on my gas mask at once, but my comrade, who did not have his to hand, collapsed silently. Fairly soon the wood of the dugout also caught fire and I had to emerge. The British lunged at me with fixed bayonets, so there was nothing for it, but to drop my equipment rapidly and raise my hands. A British soldier roared, 'Bloody Marines! This is revenge for Ypres!' and looked as though he was going to stab me with his bayonet. Luckily a small British soldier jumped in between us, so nothing happened to me.

"Then a shell landed amongst us. The overpressure threw me to my right, but the man who had shouted at me had both legs torn off. The small soldier grabbed me and off we went towards the British lines. Our numbers grew as we were joined by eight or nine wounded men. A whole group of our wounded lay together in a shell crater unable to move. A British soldier stood on the edge of the crater and shot one man who stirred slightly in cold blood. Shocked by such cruelty we turned away. Because there was a lot of artillery fire, we began to run across country. It then appeared that our escort had become disorientated, because we approached our own position once more. Unfortunately a British officer spotted what was happening. He pointed a pistol at my chest and asked something. Because I could not understand English, [yet he had understood the English of the would-be bayoneter] he waved at our escort and let us pass on our way. A machine gun opened up and we had to take cover in a shell hole. Suddenly our escort collapsed to the ground, shot through the forehead with a bullet. So there we were, lying just short of the British lines. What now? The British had suffered heavy casualties and it was not much better for us marines. Hardly had we decided to make our way back, than the British launched another multi-wave attack.

"Suddenly a British soldier jumped into our crater and looked us up and down. Because I was unwounded, he moved opposite me and released the safety catch of his weapon. I should have preferred it had he pulled out a cigarette case, because I was longing for a smoke. Soon he had taken a good look at me and I held out my hand. At that he put his weapon aside and, to the great joy of all, about fifty cigarettes appeared. In no time we were all smoking to our heart's content and chatting animatedly. Soon he found his voice too and explained to us that this mother was German. Then suddenly he jumped up and disappeared. In order to appear wounded, I took out my field dressing and dipped it in the blood of a dead man. Having done that, I noticed a British soldier waving a white flag and gathering in the wounded. 'Right', I thought to myself, 'you can do that too.' I undid the package of a dressing and waved as well. The firing simply ceased. We linked arms and headed off in the direction of Boom Ravine; the British allowed us to withdraw unmolested. Our hearts full of joy, we reported in to Leutnant Schoeller, who had taken over as company commander when Hauptmann Oldermann was wounded..."

For the time being Regina Trench was to prove too tough a nut to crack for the Allies. In fact it did not finally fall until almost the end of the battle, on 10th November. Although it had originally been dug to provide a route to the rear from

Stuff Redoubt, as it happened it was located along a reverse slope to attackers assaulting from the south. This gave the defenders a considerable geographical advantage during the fighting here throughout October and into November and was in sharp contrast to the situation along other parts of the German line, where the defenders were forced to attempt to hold a series of bludgeoning assaults from inadequate shell-hole positions, crudely linked together and under heavy fire. The proximity of Boom Ravine, with its excellent shelters and dugouts, also made the forward placement of reserves a relatively straightforward manner. The timely arrival of the fresh Marine Brigade undoubtedly contributed to the successful defence of the area which, although under constant fire and probing attack, was not subject to another major assault until 21st October. By then the marines had been relieved. Withdrawn to the Cambrai area, they formed two composite battalions, which took part 19th October at a parade for the Kaiser at Escadoeuvres, northeast of Cambrai. The Kaiser praised them for their devotion to duty, which had come at a high price. Marine Infantry Regiment 2 had lost 106 killed, 533 wounded and forty-seven missing.[6] Losses in the other two regiments were somewhat higher, reaching 41per cent in the case of Marine Infantry Regiment 3, but they had fully earned the praise heaped on them from commanders at all levels. The Army Commander, General von Below, remarked on one occasion to Generalmajor Graf von Moltke, the Brigade Commander, 'You have superb troops in your Brigade; looking at them, you could take them for the 1st Foot Guards!'[7]

The Marine Infantry Brigade was certainly exceptional, in that its manpower was first class and, perhaps more important, it was on its first tour of duty. By early autumn, many of the formations which had suffered badly in the early battles in July had been rested, reinforced and had returned for a second tour of duty. Some felt that their performance the second time round was only a shadow of that which they had achieved previously.

*Leutnant Wolfgang von Vormann Infantry Regiment 26* [8]

"We have been terribly mauled once more, even worse than the last time. It is hardly to be wondered at, because then we were a superb unit, welded together by the experience we gained during the hard days of small-scale action we had fought around the slag heaps of Saint Pierre. Commanders and men knew and trusted one another absolutely. This time we were simply a mob of soldiers. We received good reinforcements from Germany, but the interval between the first and second deployments was just too short. We lacked the proven junior commanders: NCOs and officers, who could hold the troops together. We enjoyed good success this time too, but we were not brilliant. We beat off about ten attacks, causing the British huge casualties, but we had to yield five hundred metres of ground. By then we were at the end of our tether, but we were relieved just in time..."

Elsewhere, the month of October opened with a heavy bombardment of the Eaucourt l'Abbaye – Le Barque – Ligny Thilloy area, as the British army continued to slog forward in the direction of Bapaume. The 6th Bavarian Reserve Division had been holding this sector since 26th September, taking a great many casualties from the artillery fire. During the night 2nd/3rd October Bavarian Reserve Infantry Regiment 21 was relieved in its positions near Eaucourt l'Abbaye by Bavarian Reserve Infantry Regiment 16, but in this case the fall of Eaucourt l'Abbaye could not be prevented. 3. The Bavarians remained in the line, but the constant pressure took an enormous toll on the ability of the defenders to endure both the conditions and British attacks. They launched several minor counter-attacks and helped to beat off a major assault launched by the British all along the line on 8 October. However, already by 5 October, the commanding officer of 1st Battalion Bavarian Reserve Infantry Regiment 16 was reporting,[9] 'The troops have naturally been severely affected by the extraordinary battlefield conditions. Morale is generally acceptable; nevertheless there are numerous factors which are having a negative effect on the men: the cold rations disagree with many of them and the violence of the artillery fire is getting on their nerves. The men are suffering especially from the fact that for days our own artillery has been landing shells on our own positions. Morale is also being badly affected by the regrettably large number of casualties and by the fact that a great many corpses, over which the men have to pass or step constantly, are strewn unburied along the tracks and in the trenches.'

The weather continued to be cold and rainy. Exhaustion, the lack of shelter from the elements, poor food and total lack of hygiene caused a great increase in non-battle casualties, with one quarter to one third of the manpower of the companies suffering from severe diarrhoea. The commanders at all levels were calling for relief, but there were no reinforcements to be spared. In desperation, the commanding officer of the 1st Battalion made a formal report to the regimental commander.[10] 'The daily returns of the past few days have seen a great increase in the number of reports stating that the strength of the troops is declining. Quite apart from the number of direct battle casualties, the number of sick, those rendered unfit to fight after being buried alive, the cases of diarrhoea and those suffering extreme depression are mounting to such an extent that I regard it as my duty to bring this matter to your attention. There is a danger that future enemy attacks will not meet with the resistance necessary to maintain the previously excellent and successful [defence]'. The regimental commander was only too well aware of the risks, but he could do no more than represent the situation to higher authority and redistribute his dwindling manpower, so as to be ready for the next attack.

By 12th October, when the next major blow fell, the fighting strength of the companies averaged a mere thirty five riflemen. A few hundred rifles and eighteen machine guns, manned by men worn out through strain and lack of sleep, weakened by dysentery and physically and mentally exhausted, was all he had at his disposal to defend an area 1,000 metres wide by 1,500 metres deep. Nevertheless, as was generally the case up and down the line that day, the danger and the demands of the moment when the assault was delivered during the afternoon of 12 October were such that this battered remnant succeeded in beating the assaulting forces back and ejecting them from their single minor penetration in the area of 7th Company. Filthy dirty, with hollow cheeks, but shining eyes, the survivors were eventually relieved by Reserve Infantry Regiment 181 during the early hours of 13 October.

*Reserve Leutnant Adam Blersch 2nd Company Bavarian Reserve Infantry Regiment 16* [11] **3.**

"It took the British five days to bring up further fresh troops. In the meantime we had to endure another five day bombardment. The battleworthiness of the Company sank visibly; relief was postponed day after day. During the night 11/12 October we were 'relieved', moving from our old ploughed up trenches to the newly-dug 'Spatny-Riegel'*, located fifty metres behind the 'Engländernest' [British Nest], which was intended to secure the most vulnerable place. It was a fine autumn day. The presence of balloons and aircraft, together with the impact of super-heavy calibre shells fired by flanking guns, led us to believe that an assault would take place during the next few hours. The endless crashes and ceaseless trembling of the tortured earth, coupled with the choking stink of powder smoke and corpses, had such a paralysing effect that nobody bothered to seek cover anymore. Those who were not on sentry duty slept; those who were hit lay where they fell. Our faces were pale and dirty grey, our eyes red-rimmed. Long periods of forced wakefulness and readiness had induced general torpor. The destructive fire reached a peak of intensity, involving flat and high trajectory fire, mortars and long-range guns. From Le Barque came a new message, 'Just hold on a few more hours. You will be relieved tonight!' Relief? There was a lightening of the atmosphere as the news was shouted from crater to crater.

"Two British officers knelt down a short distance away and orientated themselves with maps. A few well-aimed shots, a shout and their tall bodies hit the ground. A low-flying enemy aircraft dived over our heads, seeking out victims. It was greeted by desperate fire and, hit by a lucky shot, crashed in front of our position enveloped in fire and smoke. The ensuing joy was short lived! Dozens of other machines were cruising in the sky, preparing the way for the fatalistically courageous British infantry attacking towards our trenches. It was the same scene as five days previously. Once again the exhausted apathy fell away as the dense masses rose up from the earth before us. Once again the attack was checked at grenade range. Only in the left neighbouring sector was all life

---

*The Spatny Riegel [Spatny Stop Line] was located to the east of Eaucourt l'Abbaye, just south of the road Eaucourt l'Abbaye – Le Barque. It was dug as a replacement for Rutzgraben [Rutz Trench], which by this time formed a dangerous salient in the Gallwitz Riegel [Gallwitz Stop Line] and it usefully shortened the length of front-line trench which had to be held.

extinguished. There the enemy succeeded in launching an attack from the 'British Nest', penetrating and establishing themselves in the sunken road which ran alongside us back towards Le Barque. It was out of the question even to consider driving the enemy back. The last runners which we had despatched to the battalion with situation reports did not return.

"Night fell around us and our spirits drooped. At about 10.00 pm, the moon broke brightly through the clouds and we suddenly saw the British pulling back in long bounds to their start line. Luck was on our side again. The remainder of our Regiment, which had already gathered in Bapaume for relief, was once more brought forward through the artillery fire to help us in our dangerous situation. The British, who had not failed to spot the movement, decided to withdraw under cover of the night, pursued by our last bullets and hand grenades. We were saved and were able that same night to hand over the position to 8th Company Infantry Regiment 181. Our field kitchens stood steaming on the eastern edge of Bapaume and we assembled there for the first time in twelve days. From 130 men, barely a third remained. Lacking ammunition and personal equipment, rifles slung around necks, men straggled in – one grazed here, one with a cut there – all of them with a look in their eyes that can only truly be understood by someone who has also spent twelve days in a forward position on the Somme."

Just to the east of Gueudecourt there was also hand to hand fighting on 12th October, where the force of the British assault had produced minor penetrations at various points in the line. During the previous two weeks the Germans had combed out their forces holding positions around Verdun, in order to thicken up the defences between the Ancre and the Somme. These emergency measures, coupled with the tactic of holding counterattack forces in close proximity to thinly-held forward positions, were paying dividends, as in this instance when Infantry Regiment 64 launched a counter-attack with limited objectives, to restore the line after a British thrust had made progress on both flanks.

*Reserve Leutnant Meyer 3rd Battalion Infantry Regiment 64[12] 4.*

"Well equipped with hand grenades – the previous night 5,000 had been brought forward to the battalion staff – I went with some men of 10th Company to the left. One hundred metres this side of the sunken road we met up with the last man of the company. We took it a step at a time, always after having thrown several grenades. So gradually we worked our way forward until we could reach the sunken road with our grenades. After we had thrown half a dozen, panic set in amongst the British who were packed in there tightly. Without offering resistance, they attempted to flee the sunken road and were shot down by fire from all sides; we then left a small party to guard the sunken road. Because this had been so successful, we attempted to do the same thing on the right flank of the battalion in the 11th Company area. Step by step, the trench was rolled up. The only difference was the fact that hardly a man who attempted through flight to avoid the hand grenades escaped with his life. The machine guns, which were back in action, shot down from the flank all who attempted to get to the rear. Only the first British soldiers that I met attempted to resist. Out of a group of about twenty Tommies who were sheltering in a tight group behind the parapet of an intact section of trench, most raised their hands. The commander, on the other hand, fired his revolver at me without hitting me. A few hand grenades swiftly put an end to resistance. In a rather cowardly way those who had not been hit by grenade splinters also surrendered. Further on around the right flank of the old company position, we did not need to use grenades any more. We just shouted 'Hands up!' and they raised their arms high and surrendered. The 11th Company trenches were now thinly reoccupied."

Well pleased with the course of events, on 12th October, the following day, General von Below, Commander First Army, published a special Order of the Day.[13]

"For days the enemy has been trying to wear us out with artillery fire. Numerous attacks on narrow fronts against Thiepval, Sailly and St Pierre Vaast Wood have been carried out in preparation for the large-scale attack which was planned for 12th October. Yesterday the enemy stormed the entire front between the Ancre and Bouchavesnes. North of the Ancre, his intentions were signalled by gas attacks and very heavy fire. Between Courcelette and Lesboeufs alone, five newly assimilated divisions were launched into the attempted breakthrough. Around Sailly and Rancourt the French troops, who were fighting there earlier, have been replaced by fresh divisions. Once again on 12th October the attack was smashed to pieces against the iron wall of First Army. We hold our positions today just as they were before the attack. The defeat the enemy suffered during this attack amounts to a total victory for our defence.

"Every member of First Army will one day be able to look back on 12th October with pride. But the enemy's will to attack remains unbroken. He will bring up more ammunition and fresh troops to replace the old ones. The battle will continue until the enemy has bled to death in the face of heroic German resistance. For now we must gird our loins for new battles and new storms. We must improve damaged positions and finish off new ones. We must save ammunition during quiet days, so that we can counter later enemy attacks with huge quantities. We too shall be bringing up fresh troops, so that the brave fighters of the past weeks may have a well-deserved period of rest and recuperation in quieter places. With firm belief in final victory we shall continue to carry out our duties faithfully during the hard battles to come. British and French prisoners are now referring to the battlefield as, 'The Hell of the Somme'. We are going to make it our business to ensure that the British and French armies are smashed in the Hell of their own creation."

Amongst those faithfully carrying out their duties in the second half of October were the men of Infantry Regiment 24, who were occupying positions near Gueudecourt. The 8th Company was manning trenches either side of the road Thilloy – Flers. Its commander was Oberleutnant von Brandis, whose principal claim to fame was that he had been given the main credit for the storming of Fort Douaumont, Verdun on the 25th February 1916. Despite the fact that he entered the fort a full hour after the first penetration was made, he received the Pour le Mérite for his action and boundless public acclaim, fuelled by the books he wrote subsequently about his actions. His account of events on 16th October provides a vivid image of a quiet day on the Somme that autumn.

*Oberleutnant Cordt von Brandis 8th Company Infantry Regiment 24*[14] **5.**

'Artillery fire near Gueudecourt, otherwise nothing to report'

"During the morning of 16th October, we were sitting on the steps of our dugout. The runners were down below and Leutnant Glanz was sitting above me. The two of us had slept for a couple of hours. Now it was the turn of the others. I was reading *River Pirates of the Mississippi*. I cannot remember how I came by this trashy old book, but I shall never forget it; it kept me occupied during the worst of the shelling. As usual we were being 'blessed'. 'Whoosh – whoosh' roared the heavies, in between the hordes of lesser calibre. We had developed a fine ear for where each individual shell was going to land. This one was going over, that one was too short and as for this one...involuntarily we hunched our heads down into our shoulders and bit down on our cigars or pipe stems. A roar, the earth heaved and clods of clay fell from between the supports. 'Where did that land?' The sentry springs up and takes a look. 'Amongst the Second Platoon!' – 'In the trench?' – 'Looks like it!' – 'First aiders, stretcher bearers, go right!' comes the call from the collapsed holes. Someone comes bounding over a few minutes later. 'Oberleutnant, a dugout containing four men has been buried. We need someone to give us a hand with the digging.'

"We were quickly on the spot carrying spades. Glanz had the strength of a giant and the clods flew through the air. Each man dug flat out for about a minute then another stepped forward to take his place. Finally we came across the first of the beams. We wrenched it out, a man appeared, took a deep breath and gasped, 'Here, here, to my left was where Unteroffizier Stöflin was sitting.' We laboured, our faces dripping with sweat. 'Ping – ping', went the shrapnel balls. If only they would ease up for a while. I pulled my watch out. Not until seventeen minutes had passed did we reach him. He was slumped forward, not crushed, but his legs were pinned down by shuttering timber covered with earth... I ordered artificial respiration and we carried him to our dugout, placed a knapsack under the small of his back, pulled his tongue out and pressed down on his lungs, one, two, three and release; one two three. The breath whistled in his air passages, but there was no sign of life returning. We kept it up for twenty-five minutes as his body grew cold under our hands. He was one of our very best comrades.

"The enemy had the exact position of our hollow, which used to be a trench. During our attempts at resuscitation, a dud of the same calibre had thudded down a mere five paces from us. We resumed our places on the steps, smoking in short puffs. I went on reading *River Pirates of the Mississippi*. Glanz, who usually had a smile on his face, looked at me grimly. Suddenly there was a roar, a hiss and a crash. My cap flew off, hitting Wilhelm, who was asleep, in the stomach. The entrance went black. Buried alive! was my first thought, but no, black smoke had blocked the light and fouled the air with its stink. 'Are you in one piece Glanz?' – 'Yes.' But to one side, pitiful cries were coming from the smoke. Oh God! What has happened? Glanz was already outside, with me hard on his heels. We could see, diagonally to our front, that the neighbouring dugout had been wrecked, its timbers strewn crookedly forward. Blood was coming from between the baulks, accompanied by dreadful screams. I immediately turned to one side and took a firm grip on myself. Our medical corporal, whose conduct was beyond all praise, crawled between the convulsed men. Two were dead, the other had a serious hip wound, which only the clay was staunching; he died a little later. Another had suffered traumatic amputation of an arm and a leg and was severely wounded in the stomach. Sheds of cloth and clay had staunched his bleeding. 'Carry him away at once Biedermann; show the Red Cross flag.' At that time the British were respecting it. But Biedermann shook his head. 'He will bleed to death as soon as I lift him', he whispered, waving his hand and shaking his head. 'He's beyond help!' The wounded man slipped into unconsciousness and we made him as comfortable as possible.

"'Keep a good look out for the British!' The sentry was down in the trench, but popped his head up every minute or so and took a look forward. They were not coming! The cowardly dogs! We were seized with anger. That [shell] had come from America, from the Bethlehem Steel Company and our U Boats must have let it through. We sat down again on our stairs, just as the wounded man came round above us. 'Where is my arm? First aider – first aider! Oberleutnant!' He kept calling me until I was at his side. 'Oberleutnant, where is my arm? I can't feel it anymore. My leg! What have they done to me?' he groaned, but we could do nothing for him. Poor, poor chap! The barrage continued to roar. Heavy shells rained down. A runner arrived from the 1st Platoon across the road. 'Leutnant von Quast requests permission to disperse to the right. The situation is impossible by the road!' 'Yes, but some cover must be left there. If there is an attack, rush back again, machine gun on the left flank!' 'Yes Sir!' and with that he was gone. Once more there was a call for medical orderlies. This time the machine gun team had been hit. The Unteroffizier was the sole survivor. 'Where is the machine gun?' 'Buried.' 'It must be dug out. Get going and take the runners with you!' They brought it over a short while later. 'The third section has disappeared entirely,' reported one of them. The machine gun, our hope and support, lay between us, carefully wrapped in tent halves.

"A wounded man came over from the left. 'Where are you from?' – 'Leutnant I can't take any more.' – 'Show yourself! – That's just a scratch! Get straight back to your section!' 'The gefreiter is dead!' 'That is no reason to be wandering around just as you feel like!' He trudges shamefacedly back where he came from. We should have preferred to send him away, but we were all bleeding somewhere. Hardly any of us were without cuts or gashes.

"The number of wounded increased. Some were badly hit, but could not be transported to the rear. They were brought to us and clustered in the furthest recesses of the inadequate dugout. The dying man up above whimpered, 'Leutnant, Leutnant!' – 'Yes what's the matter?' – 'Please some coffee. So thirsty, so thirsty.' Glanz puts a water bottle to his lips. 'Oberleutant!' – 'Yes here!' 'Oberleutnant!' until he catches sight of me. 'Help me, oh God, what have you done to me?' We try once more to get him away. Then he turns angry. 'You dogs, leave me alone. You don't really want to help me, you dogs!' Below us the wounded moan. Wherever the gaze falls there are shocked, fearful eyes.

"The fire eases slightly. Gottschalk, a splendid young man, is on sentry duty. 'Gottschalk, what's happening? Are they coming?' – 'Get the machine gun into a fire position, clear the way!' 'Get cracking!' bawls the unteroffizier. 'Pass me the signal pistol. Is it still working?' – 'Yes' – 'Oberleutnant!' shouts the sentry, 'everything's ready!' – 'Are there many balloons up?' – 'They couldn't get any more into the sky!' All the fit men laugh, cut off a slice of bread and reach for the bottle of coffee and listen. 'Let's hope the British don't catch us napping!' says the big man, chewing away. 'They won't do that', says one man, rubbing his wrapped machine gun affectionately, 'as long as this has room to operate!' The wounded man above us calls out loudly, then in a murmur for his mother. It's still not midday, if only it was evening! Or if that lot want to come on over, it would be a relief if they did! ...The wounded man laughs out loud as the lumps of clay fall on him. The remainder below just moan. That is unbearable. 'Come on Glanz! Let's go and sit in the trench.' If we are going to get it, then preferably in the open under the great blue vault of sky, with its beautiful big white clouds.

"During a pause in the afternoon, I rushed along the line to see my other sections. Three dugouts were still intact. In the first a dead man lay on the top step, with his arms folded, his head forward on his chest and a gaping hole in his helmet. Below lay the vizefeldwebel, severely wounded. 'How are you Melzow?' He grins, 'Fine, thanks! Everywhere the faces look the same, the expressions are a mixture of powerless anger and resignation...Frequently their weapons are no longer intact. 'Where's my gas mask?' 'Is the machine gun still OK?' 'Does the signal pistol work?' The seconds drag by. The neighbouring company sends a runner over. 'Dear B.', it says on the message card, 'How are things with you? It's pretty bad over here. If those blackguards come over, bring enfilade fire down in front of my company.' Now we have to send a runner to the Battalion Headquarters in Luisenhof[15], to brief them and request that they bring down overhead machine gun fire to support us as soon as they see our red signal flares. If only we could rely on our artillery in the same way. Mercilessly, endlessly, the howling and growling [of the shells] continues. The dying man has had the last of the coffee and is begging for something to drink. Three times we have tried to carry him away, but it was impossible. His voice grows quieter. 'Leutnant, Oberleutnant!' [Earlier], if we did not reply immediately he became threatening, but now he has sunk into delirium. 'Gentlemen, gentlemen. The dogs! They are shooting at us...'

"Before us the landscape is desolate and dead. No British appear. Had they done so, they would have suffered. We should have torn them apart in our boundless stored up anger. The British knew that. So far we had only been four days in the line and they needed ten to batter German soldiers down. You wretched riff raff! You calculating swine! If only the hour of vengeance would come, as come it must – the hour when, faithful to the memory of our fallen, we shall unleash the pent up anger of the long drawn out defensive battle like a storm of dreadful revenge on you British. Slowly evening falls and as the daylight fades, so does the shooting, with the exception of insignificant harassing fire. Night calls us to work once more. Ration parties race rearwards to Ligny-Thilloy. Supply groups stagger forward, weighed down by wooden props. We strip off our jackets and work in shirtsleeves to make a connection with the neighbouring dugout, a matter of a good ten metres. Driven on by the urgency of the work, we place thirty-nine props during the night. I was reminded of school, when an approaching deadline meant that more was achieved in five minutes than in two normal hours of work. As the sun rose the final spades full of soil were thrown over the top. There can have been no greater joy when the Simplon Tunnel broke through than there was here down below when our two parties met. That was one day under fire. That evening the Army communiqué stated: 'Artillery fire near Gueudecourt, otherwise nothing to report.'"

In the midst of the impersonal industrialised killing during these battles of attrition, some incidents still had the capacity to shock and appal at an individual level. Life was cheap and survival, maiming, or death was reduced to mere chance. The state of mind of Fahrer Langkutsch and the effect on morale of the next two incidents is almost impossible to imagine.

*Gefreiter König 4th Battery Guards Field Artillery Regiment*[16] **3.**

"During the afternoon 10th October, there was direct hit on the left hand gun. Unteroffizier Langkutsch was blown to pieces, Kanonier Würtz was seriously wounded and Kanonier Schröder was shell-shocked. That evening Langkutsch's brother arrived. He was a driver for the battery ammunition column. He wanted to give his brother a pleasant surprise, so he had brought him some cigarettes. All we could do was to give him his brother's bones, which we had collected and wrapped in a groundsheet and which he transported away in his waggon."

*Leutnant Kröcher 1st Battery Guards Field Artillery Regiment*[17] **3.**

"At 1.00 am [18 October] a gas shell landed just in front of the space where our men were sleeping. In the darkness the men, suddenly shocked out of sleep, did not don their gas masks quickly enough and Kanoniers Priemel, Wypchol, Götz, Sobczak, Keller, Gremmler and Waldow collapsed unconscious in the suffocating fumes. Despite rescue attempts with the oxygen equipment which were begun immediately, Kanonier Priemel expired an hour later and Kanonier Wypchol on the way to the field hospital in Bertincourt. The waggon that brought post and rations in the early dawn took the others away to the field hospital in Douchy. Here Kanoniers Götz and Sobczak died the same day and Kanonier Keller succumbed to his serious gas poisoning the following day."

In the circumstances, it is small wonder that many members of this God-fearing army drew comfort and strength from their religion. Although few were as overtly devout as Hauptmann Willy Lange of Infantry Regiment 27, his thoughts, expressed in a letter to his wife Dora, just before the Regiment was plunged in early October into the thick of the fighting around Gouvernement Farm, located just to the east of St Pierre Vaast Wood, were shared by many.

*Hauptmann Willy Lange 2nd Battalion Infantry Regiment 27 6.*[20]

"I am entering this new battle completely calm and peaceful, trusting myself and my men to the care and mercy of the Lord. Pray for me that I shall be a good leader to my men and, above all, a transparently devoted and effective witness of our dear Lord. The Lord will provide; only through Him can I do my duty. Alone, I am quite helpless and powerless..."

Hauptmann Lange fell in May 1918, but his calmness under fire was legendary amongst the men of his Battalion. Gefreiter Ernst Bieler, one of his runners, describing an incident during the Battle of the Somme, later wrote, 'I had to take a report to Nurlu and brought the mail etc. back with me. There was already heavy fire coming down in Manancourt and it was difficult to make progress through the mud. I could hear large explosions and, as I passed through a [nearby] copse, I could see that Gouvernement Ferme was being plastered with heavy shells. I intended to traverse this dangerous area as quickly as possible but, as I emerged from the wood into the open area, I met our Hauptmann coming towards me. He got everywhere. He waved and asked if I had any mail for him, which indeed I had. I thought, 'He can't possibly be going to read his mail here in this hail of fire!' But he did. He opened the letter, which must have been from a member of his family and let the fire do what it would. I had to wait. With each successive explosion, more of the building collapsed. After a while I was free to go. I intended to head straight across country, but the Hauptmann said that I should stay on the road, because the enemy would soon lift the fire. It happened just like that and I emerged in one piece from the witches' cauldron.' [19]

Other equally dedicated commanders drew upon their history to fortify themselves and their men for the trials to come.

*Reserve Hauptmann Wilhelm Kellinghusen Reserve Infantry Regiment 92*[20]

"To keep my spirits up, I tucked into my pocket that well-known book *The Liberation 1813-1815* by Tim Klein. It contained the charming and refreshing campaign letters from Blücher to his wife, his 'Dear Malchen', as well as first class accounts of other great men from that period when Germany was fighting for its freedom. I had no idea what excellent service this book would provide, not only to me, but also to many other comrades. We all rejoiced and drew strength during pauses in the battle when, gathered together in the crater field, I read aloud from it to those around me items such as the superb appeal of King Friedrich Wilhelm III, 'To my people', which was received with great enthusiasm by the peoples of East Prussia and Silesia, who had arisen, thirsting for freedom; or the paeans of praise in poetry and prose of the Liberation writer Moritz Arndt. His 'Catechism for the German Territorial Soldier' was especially good and not least did we appreciate his inspirational songs, 'The God, who gave us Iron, does not want to see us as Serfs' and, 'Heart of Germany, Fail not.' We also enjoyed Theodor Körner's song, 'Arise, my People, the Torches are Ablaze!' Never had we found these songs so true to life or powerful than in the crater fields of this battle. They were a real source of strength at that time. But without any doubt, cares were eased and spirits rose the most as a result of reading the simple, but almost hypnotically-inspirational, speeches of Blücher to his soldiers, as well as his war letters to his 'Dear Malchen', in which he described the experiences of war, his cares and his hopes with such original, fresh and natural strength, that they read as though they were the words of a man chatting about the events of the previous day with his wife over their morning coffee..."

Down in the French sector, efforts continued throughout the month to outflank Péronne from the north. There was no alternative. Despite the relative ease with which the original main positions had been overrun, the swampy valley of the Somme effectively ruled out further progress south of the river. However, the importance of Bouchavesnes, Rancourt, Sailly-Saillisel and St Pierre Vaast Wood, in particular, was equally clear to the German defenders, who fought desperately to prevent any advance in this crucial area. Every piece of ground was disputed here. With major battles fought on the 13th and 14th and then again from 17th – 23rd October, enormous losses were incurred by both sides. In the face of bitter fighting, advances were few and far between and were always followed by counter-attacks. These could sometimes be launched too hastily, as in this case, when an attack by men of Infantry Regiment 160 west of Sailly Saillisel failed during the early hours of 4 October. There was inadequate intelligence about the French dispositions; there had been no reconnaissance and completely inadequate artillery preparation. Its commander, Leutnant von Pelser-Berenberg, though saved by his helmet, was wounded badly in the head.

*Leutnant von Pelser-Berensberg 10th Company Infantry Regiment 160* **7.**

"I led my company forward. At first all was quiet. Not until we had left Mesnil did shells begin to strike left and right of us. The plod of the weary soldiers quickened. Shortly before Saillisel, things got rather unpleasant. The way forward was dreadfully shot up. Here lay dead horses, over there a waggon shot to smithereens; ammunition was piled up at the side of the road where it had been hastily thrown. Once we reached the village of Saillisel, things got critical. The entire road had been torn up by giant shell craters. Shells came roaring in from all directions and, in some cases, exploded very near to us. The way forward was hellish. We had to get through five distinct belts of fire before we could reach the front line trench, or what passed for it. However, luckily I got everyone forward to the jumping-off point for the attack, which was a row of shell holes two hundred metres west of Saillisel. Then everything fell apart. The company had shaken out in the shell holes and was awaiting the order to attack, when out of the darkness appeared shadowy figures. It was the garrison of our front line trench, who had just pulled out of their position. What now? I was supposed to be attacking to the left, but there was nobody on my right. Because the situation appeared crazy to me, I ran back through heavy shellfire to Battalion Headquarters, which was co-located with three other battalion staffs in a cellar in Saillisel village. After a lot of argy bargy, the order to attack was confirmed, so once more I returned through the increasingly heavy fire to the front and once again I got through in one piece. It was nearly time for the assault and the artillery fire grew in intensity. The only way I could get the men of the company to advance on the enemy was to put myself at their head and lead them forward. So we advanced and for 500 – 600 metres all went well... but the enemy were not where our higher staff had predicted and where our artillery had been trying to engage them for several days. Instead they were dug in about 400 metres nearer to us, with the result that we came upon the enemy quite unexpectedly, were pinned down by machine gun fire when we thought that we were still some distance from their positions and there the attack stalled."

The new tactics of defending forward with reduced numbers of infantry placed great responsibility on the artillery to respond quickly and accurately to break up attacks, but this was far from easy. The huge weight of Allied artillery fire, directed from the air, meant that reliable telephone communications were a dream and all depended on flare signals being spotted in the battery positions. But the difficulties did not end there. Field Artillery Regiment 25, located 300 metres west of where the roads Nurlu-Péronne and Moislains-Templeux-la-Fosse met, was tasked with providing defensive fire in the area of St Pierre Vaast Wood, some 5,000 to 6,000 metres away. The guns themselves were in fully open positions, rendering them vulnerable to counter-battery fire. In addition, the range to the targets meant that shooting had to be predicted from the map, that the beaten zone of the guns was extremely large[22] and that it was impossible to avoid dropping some shells short into the German positions, no matter how carefully fire was controlled and the guns were laid. Other technical problems included the fact that shortage of raw materials meant that steel was now being substituted for brass in the manufacture of shell cases, leading to frequent stoppages during periods of rapid fire. Nevertheless, during these critical weeks, the Regiment fired between 2,200 and 4,700 rounds per day. One member of the Regiment describes a typical night action.[23] 8.

"'Defensive fire!' bawls the observer at the battery. There is a bustle around the guns and the sentry races to the dugout, shouting down 'Defensive fire!' which is the one phrase which unfailingly rouses you even when you are soundly asleep. Then the man races to the gun and slips the safety catch off. A swift pull on the trigger and the first shell disappears into the night with a crash and a flash of red light. The gunners tumble out of the dugout dressed just as they were. The gun commander runs along, buttoning up his jacket. 'Illuminate the aiming mark!' he shouts and one man runs over with the dark lantern. The gunlayer is already sitting in his seat checking the sight mechanism. The second round leaves the barrel with a roar, before the first has reached its target.

A fresh round is passed to the man on the loader's seat. A swift action, the round is in the chamber, the breech swings shut and, at the same instant, there is the crash of another round going off. Whilst the barrel is still recuperating, the breech is flung open once more. Powder smoke fumes upwards, a second later a further round is loaded and the shells roars on its way. In the meantime one shell basket after another is passed over. The basket is emptied and laid to one side, the safety pin is removed from the round and it is handed to the loader. The barrel gets hot, the powder smoke stings eyes and irritates throats; nothing can be heard above the hellish din; eyes are dazzled by the endless flashes. Then there is a roaring sound coming towards us, followed by a resounding crash. The ground trembles and something whistles by, a hairsbreadth away. Clods of earth rain down. All this takes just one second. The enemy is responding! It is a proud feeling to be serving the gun under enemy fire. The loader works calmly and carefully. Another round is fed into the breech. The gunlayer, who concentrates constantly on the panoramic sight, checks his sight settings one last time. Then there is a crash and the shell flies out towards the area, from which the flickering light of the flares, the flash of enemy guns and those of our exploding shells can be seen over the gun shield. Another incoming shell lands, this time behind the gun. Stones fly at the gun trails and a splinter lands in an empty shell basket. From the right comes a shout which can hardly be made out above the din, 'Increase the rate of fire!' and shot after shot rings out. The breech locking lever is so hot that it is almost impossible to touch it. The heap of empty shell baskets grows ever higher. The men only take cover for an instant at a time when shells land and splinters fly. The sound of battle dies away to the front. There are fewer flares to be seen. 'Fire at slow rate!' and then 'Cease loading!' The barrel is cooled. It hisses when a wet cloth is laid on it..."

At times the intensity of shelling was so great that it was nothing short of a miracle that infantry – artillery contact could be maintained, or that even rudimentary flare signals could be sent and received.

*Georg Queri Infantry Regiment 163*[24] **7**.

"The telephone is down – all the lines are cut. We'll have to make ourselves understood by means of flares...but the cartridges are buried. Two heavy shells, landing simultaneously, have thrown huge masses of earth on top of the dugout which leads to the flare store. It would be the work of days to clear the entrance to the dugout. Gefreiter Schönau [of the 7th Company] heads off to fetch some signal cartridges. The first part of his task is to wait and study the impact patterns of the falling shells for five minutes, in order to see if there is a regular gap in the curtains of death through which he could slip. Ah, it appears that initially it will be possible to follow a diagonal course for the first hundred paces. All goes well, very well in fact. Now it's a matter of sheltering in a shell hole to work out the next moves – head not too high! Splinters are flying in all directions. Then it's off once more, rolling like a barrel from one shell hole to the next, with the splinters whizzing by only a hand's width above. Dive into another shell hole, then one more. Things nearly went wrong there. That thing crashed down damned close. Now it's possible to move in a number of proper bounds.

"Time for a quick breather, further observation, then the move is sideways to the fourth crater on the right. Over there at about two hundred paces distance is Sailly, or rather a number of piles of rubble which offer plenty of cover. That will certainly be needed, because everywhere is being swept by machine gun and rifle fire. So it's on with the dance, as the bullets crack by a couple of feet higher. Now it's possible to crawl – quick, quick, quick! – Crump! That bloody thing was close! That wasn't in the programme! Better wait and see if there are more to come! No? OK then, off to the village, which is burning, smouldering, stinking and collapsing with loud crashes and splintering sounds. But here, at least, it is possible to hide away from the small arms fire and make some progress. Now the area is open once more – start running! The shells are not landing so thickly here. Now sniff out the headquarters of the 2nd Battalion. The first part of the mission is complete and it's time to take a proper break, because the return journey with a sack of cartridges will be harder. But there is a pleasant surprise for them up front. The Company is to prepare to be relieved! What a lucky day. Everything the Devil can throw has been negotiated successfully...Fortunately the Regiment had many such men – men who were ready to lay their lives on the line without hesitation if the good of all demanded it. All commanders know how much the troops owed to the work of the runners. For many, life as a runner was life on Death Row, but even when the seemingly impossible was asked of them, they had only one response: 'Yes Sir!'"

After days of unrelenting shelling and incessant attacks, the arrival on the scene on 6th and 7th October of men of Infantry Regiment 68 and Reserve Infantry Regiment 76, back for second tours of duty after hard days near Thiepval and Longueval respectively in late July and early August, came as a relief in every sense of the word to the exhausted soldiers holding the remains of Sailly Saillisel. Reserve Infantry Regiment 76, which relieved Infantry Regiment 163, also belonged to 17th Reserve Division, but Infantry Regiment 68 deployed as the leading element of the newly arrived 16th Division.

*Offizierstellvertreter Hugo Gropp Reserve Infantry Regiment 76*[25] **7**.

"Sailly was under heavy, destructive fire, but the company got through more or less unscathed. As darkness fell we were defending the front line battle position. Most of the position comprised shell craters, linked with communication trenches. Here and there a start had been made on dugouts, which soon had to be used for the wounded. The enemy had still not located the position exactly. The ceaseless fire kept landing just behind us on the edge of the village where he suspected we were. The ground was continually ploughed up here. In front of Sailly there was a wall of smoke and fountains of earth were being thrown up. Every few minutes, shells of the heaviest calibre roared overhead. We could hear the guns fire a few seconds earlier amidst all the uproar then, because we were in the direct line of fire, we could actually make out the final phase of the trajectory of these black monsters before they landed with an enormous crash which made the earth shake....These hulking great things, which rained down incessantly and punctually, almost to the second, in our rear, remained our main concern. On the 10th the fire increased to ever greater intensity. 'Big Billy', as Tedje Staack had christened this great monster, beat out the rhythm. We took less account of the remainder of the contributions. Behind us Sailly was a dancing mass of rock; shells, stones and beams were continually flying through the air...Along with Tedje Staack, our proven stretcher bearer and two runners, I lay in a crater somewhat to the north of the road. Two pit props gave us at least the illusion of protection. One of us kept a look out at all times. Thank heavens that casualties were still fairly light; they were much worse during the first few days at High Wood.

"I had just returned from a quick tour of my platoon sector, when there was a roar like a hurricane, an appalling crash then the earth poured over us – buried us – the end. Not quite – I was still alive – and one comrade could shout to me in reply despite being deafened. With a desperate struggle we wormed our way out – success – saved – in one piece – thank heavens!

"But where were the other two? They lay still and crumpled up on the floor of our hole in the earth. Death had swept them away swiftly and painlessly. Tedje had a broken neck; our Tedje was no more. Our hole in the ground became his grave. With his passing went one of the Regiment's finest. Strong as a bear, hard as iron, unshakeable, ever-ready to help; armed with spade, rifle and grenade he would as easily stand up to any man as he would his plaster casts. I quickly crawled along the trench. Over a thirty metre stretch the whole thing had collapsed. Pulling together the few survivors of the sections which had been stationed here, I moved them off to the right before the next monstrous beast could land on us...Then I went off to report to the company commander, Leutnant Noebel, who heard me out. He was possessed of a quite extraordinary calm.

"The hail of iron continued to pour down us without pausing; the casualty list grew shockingly. Peters dead, – Jönsson dead, – Unteroffizier

Krützfeld wounded, – Nagel dead. 'First aiders! first aiders!' but there were none left. As far as possible I bandaged up the poor lads myself. One of them had the entire length of his arm torn open. Bloody strips of flesh and pieces of his jacket hung from the exposed bones. Deadly pale, the man stared up from the floor of the trench. 'He's had it,' I thought, but I bound him up anyway out of sympathy and to calm him. I used a dozen field dressings on him and a he thanked me with a silent glimmer in his eyes. Adolf Lemmerman and I took turns to keep a look out: a jump up onto the parapet, a swift look round then down again. The drumfire continued. Crashes, whines and whistling of all pitches and volumes filled the air. We pressed in as hard against the wall of the trench as we could. Our tongues stuck to the roofs of our mouths. Thirst, thirst, thirst! Everything drinkable had long since gone, with the exception of a small reserve of mineral water for the wounded, who lay helplessly on the floor of the trench or in shell holes. Nobody here could do anything for them. They just had to stick it out to the bitter end.

"My wounded man with the appalling arm wound was still alive. How was it possible for any man to endure such a thing? It was impossible to know how things stood in the remainder of the company sector. The entire place was one heaving, hellish mass. During the afternoon the fire seemed to be worse, but we couldn't give a toss. Just as before, we took turns to observe. We were seized with a peculiar unease. We knew in our water that they must be about to come over. Each man knew it and each was ready. Suddenly there was a different sound in the air. The enemy had lifted the fire. – 'Here they come!'

"In no time everyone had stood to and the French were greeted with a dense hail of iron. Red signal flares shot into the sky. Hardly had they hit the ground than our artillery defensive fire was landing in amongst them, reaping a dreadful harvest in their ranks. All enemy attempts to renew the assault and gain ground failed in the face of our defence...Not until several hours had passed did an uneasy calm descend. The pause in the enemy fire was used to move the wounded to the rear. The walking wounded had to help the serious cases to the rear. I was rendered speechless as my man with the wounded arm jumped up and made for the rear briskly with long strides. (I found out later that when the artery was torn, it twisted itself luckily into a knot which prevented the wounded man from bleeding to death.)..."

Although the fighting was of extraordinary intensity and violence during these October days, the situation in the air was swinging away from the Allied dominance of the early battles. By October the Germans had stationed over three hundred aircraft in the area and, which was worse for the Allies, the new Albatross fighters were superior in every respect to the best machines in the Allied inventory. Ludendorff's decision to establish two fighter wings on the Somme was beginning to bear fruit. From his arrival on the scene, Hauptmann Oswald Boelcke, commander of Fighter Squadron 2, had a meteoric, if brief, period in command. He fell as a result of a mid-air collision with Leutnant Erwin Böhme, a pilot of his own squadron, during a dogfight over Pozières on 28th October. By then he had shot down forty allied aircraft and inspired others, such as Manfred von Richthofen, to even greater glory.[26]

Offizierstellvertreter Gropp of Reserve Infantry Regiment 76 noted on 5 October, 'From our reserve position, we witnessed a gigantic air battle. Over fifty aircraft – ours and the enemy's – were locked in a dogfight. Our hearts soared at the sight. It was hardly possible to distinguish friend and foe amid the turmoil, which presented an ever-changing picture, until the enemy was finally forced back over his own lines. This battle had an electrifying effect on us, giving us confidence that, unlike the first time round, we should not be thrown back on our own resources.'[27] The fight for the skies north of Péronne continued to draw in scores of aircraft as the battle for air superiority was fought out during the indifferent autumn weather. In mid-October Infantry Regiment 68 felt that, 'The aerial plague was less intense. Our fighter wings hurled themselves into the attack and thus succeeded in ensuring that the enemy aviators could not intervene so cheekily and unmolested, as they had around Thiepval, when they made the life of the infantry so difficult. The soldiers on the position noted that there were still German airmen, or at least that they had reappeared. It was a question of the greatest importance for morale. In the first Somme battles the infantry had considered themselves to have been betrayed and sold out in this respect'.[28]

*Fliegerleutnant Johannes Fischer Air Wing 8*[29]

"Our next few flights took place in bad weather. Autumn storms swept through, bringing black clouds and slashing rain. Operating with our heads almost touching the clouds, we hunted back and forth at three hundred metres above the positions, which were barely discernable. We fired off recognition flares and the infantry responded between Lesboeufs, Morval and the south-western corner of St Pierre Vaast Wood...During the evening of 7th October we attempted to launch an operation with the entire wing, but we were defeated by the clouds and the weather. The other aircraft landed, but we pressed on alone. Battles were raging the entire length of the northern Somme front. In the gathering gloom, the countless flashes of the guns and exploding shells played on the cratered landscape like sunshine glittering on snowflakes. From east of Lesboeufs to St Pierre Vaast Wood, a front of nearly five kilometres, our infantry fired recognition signals at us; the palette of coloured flares giving this entire sector a fairytale appearance, in sharp contrast to the hopeless dark brown of the crater fields...The following morning we were surprised to be greeted by enemy small arms fire south-west of Sailly. These were probably fresh troops, who were not yet accustomed to the special means we employed against their positions...The walls of Sailly were only recognisable as small remnants between shell craters and trenches. An endless stream of shells continued to gobble up these remains. Sailly-Saillisel disappeared off the face of the earth...

"Aerial activity increased on both sides [after 16th October]. In order to demoralise the enemy, we demonstrated our power by machine gunning their positions. We swooped down to below two hundred metres over the troops occupying trenches south-west of Sailly-Saillisel...There, where once the church bells had rung out over old Sailly and the surrounding fertile area, fading into the distance and echoing in St Pierre Vaast Wood, there where fruit trees had cast shadows in verdant hedged gardens and where country cottages had lined roads and tracks, craters jostled one another for position. There were no houses, no trees and no tracks. No walls rose out of the ploughed up earth. From a dark patch on the ground, streaked with the powder of smashed tiles, it was just possible to make out where Sailly-Saillisel lay buried... Over the smoking desolation of shell craters, enemy and German air forces clashed. Real air battles developed. [Aircraft] fell like flaming torches to the ground. Whirling wings glittered in the sun. Here and there planes came down, landing luckily, or unluckily, after desperate attempts to control them. The enemy was forced back. The battle continued during the coming days and we forced the enemy back into their own airspace... There were two hundred and nine aerial combats during the day. In the Despatch could be read, 'Aerial activity was intense during the clear weather of 22nd October 1916. German aircraft flew over five hundred sorties. There were two hundred and nine aerial battles when the enemy was attacked. Sixteen enemy aircraft were confirmed as shot down and more must have carried out emergency landings behind their own lines...'."

Pressure of events meant that the 16th Division had to endure exhausting days of digging the so-called R. II Position* prior to being moved up into the line. It was hardly the best preparation for such a severe trial. The 30 Brigade order stated, 'Six companies are to be employed simultaneously on digging duties. In accordance with Army orders, work on dugouts is to go ahead ceaselessly in shifts by day and night. It is recommended to adopt an eight hour shift pattern.' Generously, it continued, 'The remaining companies are at the disposal of the Regiment for training or to improve the bivouac site.'[31] From utterly inadequate bivouacs in an open muddy field near Gouzeaucourt, therefore, half the Division each day was split into three eight hour working shifts and marched forward fifteen kilometres to their places of work through the driving rain, carrying full assault order, weapons and ammunition, in case a battlefield emergency occurred whilst they were away from their bivouac. On 7th October, for example, a group comprising two companies from each regiment set out at 4.00 am. They eventually got back to their bivouacs at 8.30 pm, tired out, cold, hungry and

---

* The R II, or Armin Position was located about two and a half to three kilometres in rear of the RI, or Allaines Position, which in this area ran to the west of Le Transloy, then southeast to the east of Sailly. The divisional place of work was south of Le Mensil, where the line ran in an arc to the south, then east towards Manancourt. It was designed to give depth to the Sailly-Saillisel-St Pierre Vaast area.

soaking wet. There was no means of drying clothing and equipment, but this rota continued day on, day off until, wearing their newly-issued steel helmets, they were moved forward to relieve the exhausted troops in the front line.

The Divisional warning order to the troops, issued 8th October, makes interesting reading. 'Just like the days of honour and glory at Thiepval and Mouquet Farm, it is equally essential not to allow the enemy, this time Frenchmen, to advance as much as a foot. I am absolutely certain that the Division will be equal to this mission. Our artillery and our airmen will support us. Signed: von Zaborowski.'[32]

At first glance, it might be thought that no account had been taken of Ludendorff's directions on flexible defence, but that would be a false reading. It was important that the French army was denied progress in this area and, clearly, 'Hold on regardless' was a simple message for the soldiers to understand. The actual deployment was much more subtle. The Operation Order, issued on 10th October, included this paragraph, 'Because it must be assumed that 16th Infantry Division will only be relieved after a lengthy period, despatch of troops to the front line is to be very sparing and there is to be considerable deployment in depth. Because of the significance of the village of Sailly-Saillisel, it is necessary to hold a sufficiently strong force, equipped with machine guns and commanded by an energetic and forceful commander, in reserve in the R I position. In the event that the enemy captures the village itself and attempts to advance eastwards, this force is to launch a counter-attack immediately.'[33]

The tactical situation which the Division was to inherit was extremely complicated and serious. The forward line of own troops was ill-defined; there was confusion over the precise location of the left hand junction point between Infantry Regiment 68 and its neighbouring formation; whilst French assaults and well-directed artillery concentrations had already rendered the central area to the south of the straggling village virtually untenable. Later this was to lead to a major controversy with Bavarian Infantry Regiment 2, when 1st Bavarian Infantry Division finally relieved 17th Reserve Infantry Division. However, that dispute was still in the future when the men of Infantry Regiment 68 moved forward to take over their positions.

*Unteroffizier Feuge 6th Company Infantry Regiment 68*[34] **7**.

"Towards evening we put the finishing touches to our equipment. Our knapsacks had already been left behind in Equancourt. As it went dark we moved by sections into Le Mesnil, where we assembled, pressed up against the ruins of the left hand row of houses. Shells were crashing down on the village. 'Break step, advance!' The company moves off somewhat sluggishly. The further we get inside the village, the faster our pace becomes. Rubble everywhere! Not one house intact! Some houses have disappeared altogether. The road has been torn up by shellfire. We branch off to the left around the corner of a house. 'Double march!' This is a dangerous place where shell after shell comes down. After two or three minutes, we emerge unscathed out of the village. To our right is an orchard and we march along its edge. In fact we really ought to have kept running, because this place was getting a pasting as well, impact after impact. But it is not possible to run all the time and this way we learn to be nonchalant and indifferent [to fire], which in turn builds self-confidence. Once again we turn half right, heading across country between Mesnil and Sailly. This area has been under a terrible weight of fire. There are shell holes everywhere. Cartridges, duds, items of equipment and wire lay all around.

"An evil smell is carried on the wind from the front. It's the stink of powder and the stench of corpses. After another half hour we come under shrapnel fire. Luckily we have no casualties; the enemy is just bringing fire down at random on the approach routes. We take two short breaks in sunken roads, then we are on to the final section, crossing an embankment about four to five metres high and then it's three hundred metres to the trenches. 'Single file. Quiet!' We stumble from shell hole to shell hole and some men fall in. We are sweating freely and working hard. Just keep as quiet as possible! If the Frenchmen detect that a relief is taking place, all hell will break loose. At long, long last, 'Here we are!' But where are we? 'Get in this trench', says our commander. We drop down into it. A few minutes later, the Frenchmen become active. Towards morning I cast a glance around our battle area. We are not manning a continuous line; each section has its own discrete trench. Ours contains eight men, the Leutnant and two runners. Immediately to my front is a shell crater, so large that it could hold a waggon and horses. It contains a dead comrade. Sixty metres further forward I catch sight of a lonely tree stump, with piles of earth to its left and right. Suspicious! In the grey of dawn I can make out about half a dozen steel helmets behind them...Two hundred metres to my left rear are the remains of houses and charred rafters. The French call these ruins Sailly. The most interesting view, I discover, is to be obtained when I lean out of the trench a bit and look to my right. The entire landscape from Sailly to Bapaume can be observed as it climbs gently away... On both sides of us the roadside trees have been shot away, but our trench has not been spotted..."

In a very short time, however, all the formations of 16th Division were to be drawn into the battle as Infantry Regiments 68 and 28 threw in repeated counter-attacks in response to thrusts by the French army as far forward as the church in Sailly. The German artillery played a key role in breaking up these attacks, but there was continual and costly hand to hand fighting, as the defenders maintained their positions. Having beaten off a series of determined assaults during the morning of 12th October, the Germans were then subjected to artillery fire of staggering intensity.

*Unteroffizier Feuge 6th Company Infantry Regiment 68*[35] **7**.

"Towards 2.00 pm, the French opened up drum fire on us once more. The fire increased to such a hellish racket that we could only communicate by shouting as loudly as possible to each other. We jammed together into a dugout. Red hot splinters flew all around us, but amazingly nobody was hit. Hour after hour the spectacle continued; initially at a low tempo, but then worse and worse. Finally, at about 7.00 pm, the French fired gas shells at the trench, so that we had to mask up. 'Stand to!' Something must be happening there in front of Sailly... The night dragged by slowly; we were under drumfire throughout."

Despite the pressure, the defenders managed to cling on to their positions throughout the day. It was no mean achievement, but it came at a high cost in casualties, Infantry Regiment 68 losing twenty-six killed and seventy-six wounded. In recognition of the excellent performance of Infantry Regiment 68 and Reserve Infantry Regiment 76, around Sailly-Saillisel, both were mentioned in the official Army Despatch for 12 October.[36]

"Western Front. Army Group Crown Prince Rupprecht. Fighting continued astride the Somme. A great weight of artillery fire came down along the entire front between the Ancre and the Somme. British infantry attacks northeast of Thiepval as well as along the line Le Sars – Gueudecourt were largely brought to a halt with defensive fire. Towards the evening, strong attacks developed forward of the line Morval – Bouchavesnes, continuing until the early hours of the morning. Six separate attacks were launched against the positions held by Infantry Regiment 68 and Reserve Infantry Regiment 76 in the Sailly area. All attempts were in vain and we maintained our positions intact."

Infantry Regiment 68, recently arrived, had to fight on, but four days under constant fire, followed by the large scale fighting of the 12th, was the final effort of Reserve Infantry Regiment 76. They were withdrawn, to be replaced by Bavarian Infantry Regiment 2.

*Offizier-Stellvertreter Hugo Gropp Reserve Infantry Regiment 76*[37] **7**.

"A little later the news raced through the position that we were to be relieved that evening. Hardly had we completed our preparations than the relief was on us. There was not much to hand over. We loaded the last of our seriously wounded into tent halves for transport to the rear and we buried our dead swiftly in shell holes – Quick, quick before the enemy resumed his drumfire. We pulled back skirting Sailly, because the village itself was still under heavy fire and we halted in a rear reserve position. There our ration party awaited us. I couldn't eat a thing, but I drank and drank. I swallowed two complete mess tins full of tea and rum in one great draught then fell down asleep."

Two days later, Crown Prince Rupprecht of Bavaria paid a visit to Reserve Infantry Regiment 76 to congratulate its officers and men. He noted in his diary for 14 October, 'This afternoon I visited the excellent Reserve Infantry Regiment 76 (Hamburg), which had distinguished itself greatly in the midst of the recent fighting. The hands of its commander, a very forceful man, trembled very badly, so much had the continuous strain taken out of him.'[38] The fighting on 12th October had obviously also taken its toll on the ability of the men of Infantry Regiment 68 to resist and to fight on. From the very first day, an argument began with the Bavarians over responsibility for covering the gap between their positions. This dispute was to come to a head after 17th October, when the French wrested the Sailly end of the village from the defenders, but for the next few days, precarious though the situation was, the Regiments succeeded in holding the line against further furious attacks, albeit at the cost of casualties which rose alarmingly. The main French attacks tended to be delivered during the afternoons after preparatory fire; that of the 14th October being especially violent.

*Unteroffizier Feuge 6th Company Infantry Regiment 68[39]* **7**.

"Shell fire started coming down about 1.30 pm, increasing during the following ten minutes to such a degree that great clouds of powder smoke swirled over desolate terrain, like thick banks of fog. I observed the impact of the shells for hours. Soon things livened up to our rear. Flashes came from behind every fold in the ground, as our artillery responded well. The racket got steadily worse and the villages soon disappeared in the powder smoke. Le Transloy was in flames. By 3.00 pm, the fire had reached hurricane proportions and it stayed like that until 6.00 pm. It was ghastly. Every piece of ground which appeared suspicious was systematically ploughed up; the embankment along the road coming in for particular attention, because the enemy suspected German positions there. It was an appalling scene, which was utterly nerve wracking. Towards 6.00 pm I felt tired, so I covered myself in my groundsheet and tried to get some rest. It was impossible to get to sleep, rather I was day dreaming.

"'Man the weapons!' Was I dreaming, or was I awake? Someone tugged at my groundsheet. I leapt up, grabbed my rifle, arranged my ammunition and took up a firing position. I was confronted by a scene, to which even an artist could barely have done justice. The horizon glowed blood red with the muzzle flashes of the guns and hundreds of flares rose all along the enemy front as far down as Gueudecourt. Countless stars shot out above the fiery traces and competed in brilliance with the few stars of the night sky. 'That is the French signal for the assault.' For a few moments all was still, then our flares soared upwards as well: the artillery was to bring down defensive fire. Within a few seconds, shells were crashing down in front of the enemy trenches. The French men joined in and a truly hellish concert got under way. At the same instant, things started to happen round the tree stump to my front. About half a dozen figures rose from behind the fire. Some dashed forward and tried to get over the edge of the trench. 'Fire!' My neighbour and I fired in unison. I counted, 'One, two, three, fire! One, two, three (load, aim) – crack!' Soon bullets were whistling past us. Left and right, behind us and in front shells came down, causing us casualties. Machine guns began their Tack! Tack!

"After only ten minutes, the Battle of the Somme was working away like a giant machine. Everything operated with a terrible rhythm. I could not make out a single patch of ground where things were not exploding. There was no time for fear. There were the enemy. Here were we and it was a matter of sticking it out. We shot ceaselessly, until our barrels were hot. There was still a lot of activity in the enemy trenches. Apparently some of them had started to crawl forward. 'Fire low!' I bawled at my neighbour. Now we were firing without counting. Everything possible poured out of the barrels. Still some leapt forward, but others were crawling back. To be ready for anything, I laid out hand grenades. Some shells burst right behind us. Splinters clattered against our steel helmets, but we took no notice. An attack absorbs all the senses. Suddenly my neighbour nudged me and pointed to the left. Our next door section had fixed bayonets and was climbing out of the trench. 'Are they mad?' Suddenly all was clear. To our left dense waves of French soldiers, ignoring dreadful losses had closed right up to the German lines. There, their courage failing them, they had flung themselves to the ground and they were now crawling to the rear. Thinking that they might be able to break in, Unteroffizier M. got his section to fix bayonets, in order to come to the help of his neighbouring section. 'One more good charge and they would have been in amongst us', one comrade said later.

"So the Frenchmen had had a bad experience here too. They had paid the price in blood and seen nothing for it. After an hour, the attack had been smothered all along the line. Gradually things quietened down. The battlefield resumed its dreary look of boring desolation. In the moonlight three Frenchmen were still staggering around the area. Two of them, an officer and a sergeant major, were disarmed by a comrade and brought in half-drunk. The third escaped. We got back down into our trench and tucked into some bread, because we had become hungry and even thirstier. 'That was great!' said my neighbour, 'Let's hope it always goes as well'...He had come through his baptism of fire well."

The defenders did not have it all their own way. Their casualties were mounting and resupply was becoming very difficult. Their own artillery, unsure about the forward positions and fearful for the fate of Sailly, continually fired short. The evening report by Infantry Regiment 68 on the 14th estimated that no fewer than 50 per cent of all the casualties were being caused by this. There was still a lack of clarity about responsibility for the gap between the Prussians and the Bavarians and the almost inevitable consequence was a penetration into Sailly on 15th October, which, despite frenzied attempts at counter-attacks, led to the loss of this part of the village on 17th October.

*Vizefeldwebel Dülz 8th Company Infantry Regiment 68[40]* **7**.

"From 12 to 15 October we were manning positions near Sailly. Initially I was commanding First Platoon of the 8th Company, but on the 13th I assumed command of the Second Platoon as well, when its commander was wounded. We beat off several French assaults on 13th and 14th. At about 6.30 am on 15th October 1916, my position was attacked by the French in battalion strength, supported by a machine-gun company. The trench was totally wrecked, so we were manning a line of shell holes. To my left there was a seventy metre gap. Then there was a platoon of 5th Company commanded by Leutnant Wallmann, who was in contact with the Bavarian troops. To my right there was another gap, which had been caused by our own artillery. I shot flares to call for artillery support, but unfortunately it came down too late, so the French had already pushed on for two hundred metres to my left and right, as far as Sailly itself. At this time I was down to about thirty men and at that moment two French reserve companies arrived on the scene and surrounded us. We continued to defend ourselves as best we could with grenades, but in the end we were captured. In addition to my thirty men and me, about ten wounded men were also captured, along with Leutnant Wallmann and the remains of the men of his company."

Catastrophe! There were several brave but vain attempts to push the French 152nd Infantry Regiment back out of Sailly during the next forty eight hours. This Regiment was awarded an Army Citation on 4 December 1916 for its capture and defence of Sailly,[41] but on the German side the recriminations started. How could it have happened? Infantry Regiment 68 devoted fifty-eight pages of its regimental history after the war to making the case that the loss of Sailly was due to their taking over a compromised position, to being hit hard by their own artillery, to confusion over the tactical situation, the orders given and to mapping ambiguities. The Bavarians of Infantry Regiment 2, to their right were incandescent with rage at the turn of events, holding what amounted to a Regimental Enquiry on the spot and placing the blame squarely on the Prussians. The daily reports and statements of officers closely associated with the events were collated and despatched to higher authority.

*Leutnant Nirschl 9th Company Bavarian Infantry Regiment 2[42]* **7**.

"12 Oct 16 – 11.45 pm. According to the briefing officer from Infantry Regiment 76, Infantry Regiment 68 should link up with my right flank on the road Sailly – Morval. I have already deployed almost a complete platoon north of this road, but the gap is still not closed."

"13th Oct 16 – 10.30 pm. According to the statement of the officer from Infantry Regiment 76 who handed over to me, my right flank should extend as far as the road Sailly – Morval. I have now extended two hundred metres to the right, because Infantry Regiment 68 refuses to move its left flank as far as the road on the grounds that the gap is being fired on by their own artillery. They definitely have enough men to fill the gap and close up to the road.

"14 Oct 16 – 8.45 pm. It is urgently imperative in the interests of justice that the neighbouring regiment be prevailed upon to reoccupy the section which their predecessors vacated irregularly.

"15 Oct 16 – 8.30 pm. A breakthrough occurred in the area of Infantry Regiment 68. After the attack only two sections were still to the right of us. It has now been established that Infantry Regiment 68 is only occupying the line as far as two hundred metres to the right of us. Apparently link up is complete again throughout Infantry Regiment 68.

"15 Oct 16 – 9.50 pm. Contact with Infantry Regiment 68 exists. It is located a further two hundred metres to the right of our right flank. It is not clear if the gap has been closed once more.

"15 Oct 16 – 11.45 pm. It has just been reported to me that Infantry Regiment 68 has once again evacuated the sector adjoining us to the right. I am about to have it temporarily re-occupied by a platoon (2nd Platoon 11th Company. A liaison team from this platoon is with me), but urgently request that Infantry Regiment 68 be persuaded to relieve the Platoon this evening. It is an area where I suffered the majority of my casualties yesterday (immediately to the north of the road Sailly – Morval). The morale of the men of Infantry Regiment 68, who at 7.00 pm this evening were still in this sector of trench, gradually deteriorated. Some of them had to be forced at pistol point to continue.

"16 Oct 16 – 2.30 am. The French have pushed into the Prussian gap and are pressing on my right flank. The entire wood behind is said to be occupied by the French, who pulled back there from the village of Sailly. I refuse to accept responsibility that the position of my right flank can still be held.

"16 Oct 16 – 11.30 pm. Various men of Infantry Regiment 68 fraternised with the enemy and were finally moved away as prisoners."

*Leutnant Märklin 6th Company Bavarian Infantry Regiment 2*[43] **7**.

"17 Oct 16 – 10.00 am. One company and two machine guns of Infantry Regiment 68 have just launched an attack on the French nest of resistance along the Bapaume-Péronne road south of Sailly. The men of Infantry Regiment 68 have no officer in charge of them; the machine guns are being commanded by an Offizierstellvertreter.

"17 Oct 16 – 10.20 am.  Detachments of the company of Infantry Regiment 68 which attacked are streaming backwards in disorder.  The commander has apparently lost control over his men.

"17 Oct 16 – 10.30 am.  It appears that Infantry Regiment 68 has completely run away to the rear.

"17 Oct 16 – 11.00 am.  An order from the commander of our neighbouring battalion of Infantry Regiment 68 has just arrived at the Infantry Regiment 68 machine gun which is subordinated to us, 'The Prussian machine guns are to pull back as soon as the Infantry Regiment 68 battalion withdraws.'  Such an order, which was also overheard by our men, has had a sorry effect, to put it no more strongly.

"17 Oct 16 - 12.00 am.  Patrols sent out in a north westerly direction could not make contact with Infantry Regiment 68."

*Leutnant Steyr 3rd Battalion Bavarian Infantry Regiment 2*[44] **7**.

"As 3rd Battalion Liaison Officer, I frequently had the task of discussing the situation with Hauptmann Soltmann, who was the commander of 2nd Battalion Infantry Regiment 68, which was the unit to our right.  These discussions were made difficult because there was an almost complete lack of communication between the front line and the Infantry Regiment 68 Battalion Headquarters.  There were practically no reports from the front line, so Hauptmann Soltmann often knew less about the front line of Infantry Regiment 68 than we did.  During the afternoon of 14th October I was in Battalion Headquarters 2nd Battalion Infantry Regiment 68 for the first time, in order to regularise the arrangements for the junction point between 2nd Battalion Infantry Regiment 68 and our right flank.  Hauptmann Soltmann promised that the designated junction point would be re-established once it went dark.  During my visits to Battalion Headquarters Infantry Regiment 68, I was repeatedly told by Hauptmann Soltmann that he was not in a position to conduct large operations, because his companies had suffered too severe casualties and furthermore that he had no officers left.  In the Battalion dugout, apart from his adjutant there was a captain and three or four other officers. On 16th October Hauptmann Soltmann personally visited Battalion Headquarters 3rd Battalion Bavarian Infantry Regiment 2 twice (morning and afternoon) and received orders from Major von Berchem. With great daring, Hauptmann Soltmann had attempted personally to reconnoitre the situation in Sailly, but it was obvious that he did not enjoy the full cooperation of his officers.  Officer casualties in Infantry Regiment 68 were also said to be very great."

*Leutnant Eder 12th Company Bavarian Infantry Regiment 2*[45]  **7**.

"About 2.00 am 16th October I was informed by Major von Berchem that the 9th Company had reported that the French have broken through immediately to our right and have forced their way into Sailly. At the same time I received the order to take my two platoons to the HQ of 2nd Battalion Infantry Regiment 68, to brief the commander on the situation and to place myself and my platoons at the disposal of the relevant commander charged with the clearance of the village and the closing of the gap. The command was obeyed. The commander of 2nd Battalion Infantry Regiment 68 did not, however, believe the report of our 9th Company; informing me that it had been reported to him by his companies that the French attack had been beaten off completely and that everything was in order. He refused the assistance of my company on the grounds that it was not needed. At this decision, I hurried back to 3rd Battalion Bavarian Infantry Regiment 2 and reported to Major von Berchem that our offer of assistance had been refused and informing him about the views of this battalion of Infantry Regiment 68. Major von Berchem, however, convinced that the 9th Company report, which I read myself, was correct, now ordered me to make an independent attempt, without the cooperation of Infantry Regiment 68, to drive the French out of Sailly, but it transpired that my company was too weak for the task."

There was, of course, never any love lost between to the two contingents and there is no evidence that the Bavarians made any allowance for the extra time the Prussians had spent in the line, the losses they had suffered and the strain to which they had been subjected. There was indeed confusion over where the front line was meant to run, Infantry Regiment 68 had specific orders not to commit too many men forward at any one time, which made the filling of gaps problematic but, as has been noted, their performance in the early days of their deployment was sufficiently good to merit a unit mention in despatches. With hindsight it seems clear that Sailly was taken because the French army exerted so much pressure that the defence was eventually found wanting. In the circumstances, it would probably have happened when it did regardless of who was holding the critical area. Serious though the loss was, Sailly was only an outer work of the defences. The remainder of the village remained in German hands for some time to come and St Pierre Vaast Wood still stood as a firm bastion, preventing any crumbling of the German position from north to south. The surviving defenders pulled their lines in tighter and hung on grimly until they were relieved. Crown Prince Rupprecht noted in his diary 24th October, 'From the point of view of artillery observation, it would be a good thing if at least the northern section of Sailly could be recaptured. Such an attempt could not be made until after the arrival of XV Army Corps. Both General von Below and General von Boehn share the view that the power of attack of our troops has been greatly reduced and that the lack of officers means that there is no future prospect of raising it.' [46]

*Unteroffizier Feuge 6th Company Infantry Regiment 68*[47] 7.

"At long last, at 1.00 am, came the happy news: three hours to go! At 2.30 am I slid on all fours like a frog through mud and filth, crawling out of the trench in order to carry out the mission of leading our reliefs, a platoon of Bavarians, forward. With swimming movements, I managed to gain twenty or thirty metres to the rear, had a quick breather, then I crawled away. Uppermost in my thoughts was the need to avoid the enemy noticing anything. One hundred metres in rear of the trench I was able to move bent double and, within five minutes, I arrived at the sunken road. I stressed to the Bavarians to keep absolutely quiet...What a state I was in by the time I had moved to the rear a second time in the way described above. This time there were no halts. Moving in small groups across country, we ran and stumbled, sweating profusely, from the Sunken Road to Mesnil. We were pursued by French shells and surrounded by bursting shrapnel... On and on we marched as the sky grew lighter. The number of exploding shells reduced and with that the feeling grew: 'You're saved!' We walked more slowly and the odd joke was exchanged. Our spirits were not exactly high; we were too hungry, thirsty and tense for that. There was not a trace of our uniforms to be seen. They were all covered with mud as thick as a finger...But we were certainly relieved. We had escaped the destruction. The roaring hell behind us concerned us not one bit. The driver of an ammunition waggon gave us a lift. Such was the jolting that a cavalryman amongst us felt sick, but we finally reached Equancourt where, lying wrapped in blankets on an attic floor, we soon forgot about the stress and strain."

It was not only the Germans who were feeling the stress and strain of continuous operations by the end of October. The weather was increasingly wet and cold, which transformed the whole area into one vast sea of mud. Mere survival against the elements demanded increasing amounts of energy, which left little in reserve to press attacks home with the necessary impetus. Exhausted men, plodding up to ill-defined start lines, cold and soaked to the skin, were hardly going to charge forward with élan when they saw the very occasional tank that they may have been allocated wallowing hopelessly in the mud, unable to move, or as the preliminary barrage, predicted off the map, fell in the wrong place. Despite the renewed French offensive at Verdun on 24th October, which interfered with the transfer of additional German formations to the Somme, there had already been a transformation of the situation as far as guns and aircraft were concerned. Allied gunnery techniques may have been improving, but deteriorating weather and interference with spotting aircraft removed the edge which the gunners had previously enjoyed. Their guns were wearing out and the gunners themselves were tired. Small wonder, therefore, that defenders, stretched as they were, suffering heavy casualties as they had, were able repeatedly to rebuff all attempts by the British Fourth Army to make progress eastwards. They were well aware of Allied problems and knew that they had only to force a delay of a few more weeks and winter would finally come to their rescue.

The intention to carry out a major offensive in the last week of the month against, successively, Regina Trench, the Ancre Heights, Beaulencourt and the Butte de Warlencourt was washed out by torrential rain before it could be launched. Not that this postponement was evident to the men of the 24th Infantry Division from Saxony, who were clinging on to positions around Warlencourt and floundering in the mud. 1st Battalion, Infantry Regiment 179 reported, 'Everything possible is being done to maintain the collapsed and unconnected trench system. But the term 'trench' is illusory. A line can barely be detected. The entire garrison, down to the last man, is fully occupied in ceaseless work to dig out what little remains. Those involved are literally stuck fast in the mud, so the useful work obtained, in proportion to the energy expended, is only slight. The gluey mud sticks to the shovels and is difficult to shake off... The streaming rain yesterday has left the trenches in an appalling condition. Everyone is up to their knees in mud and water. Even the best and most willing men can barely be motivated to hang on in the trenches. The companies have no grenades. Those in the front line are coated with mud and unusable. Patrols could not be sent to the site of the explosion, because the men can barely stay on their feet...The company requests that the field kitchen sends no more hot food; its transport forward is out of the question in the bottomless mud...'[48] The utter, squalid misery for all the participants of the Battle of the Somme in late autumn is summed up in the words of an NCO, sent forward for a spell of duty at the end of October.

*Gefreiter Fritzsche 6th Company Infantry Regiment 179*[49] **9.**

"We are lying in mud holes. There is filth on our clothing, in our food, all over our hands. Firing goes on ceaselessly. Everyone is exhausted by the approach march. The route followed the main road in the direction of Le Sars. Headquarters of the forward battalion is located in the ruins of some houses at the crossroads of the Ancre Position and the Warlencourt – Le Barque road. To our right, the ruins of the village of Warlencourt loomed out of the darkness; to the front was the valley of the Ancre. We picked our way across the rubble thrown up around a mine crater, along the wall of a house and over fallen trees, broken twigs and branches. Finally the going became a little easier, but this area was being pounded with shrapnel. We climbed down into and out of a mine crater, which was made more difficult by the wearing of gasmasks that we had had to don because of the gas shells. Once more the way was barred by fallen trees but, once past, there was a good track as far as the hand grenade dump. Unfortunately it was under heavy fire. We ran as fast as we could. Behind the dump was a chaos of craters. It was almost impossible to move across country here. We sank in the saturated morass, disappeared suddenly into unseen shell holes and forced a way up and out, only to tumble into another hole, where we would fall heavily on our faces and hands. It was impossible to see anything.

"We lost our way and wandered in confusion, not knowing the location of the front line. Sweating heavily we pressed on, until we could hardly haul our tired legs out of the clinging mud any more. Shells crashed down and shrapnel shells burst ever more frequently. Suddenly there was a flash of light directly overhead as a shrapnel burst, followed by shrieks of pain. There were killed and wounded. Duds thudded down alongside, showering us with dollops of mud. Somewhere around here some infantrymen were hiding in shell holes. After much searching up and down, getting lost, falling over, hauling ourselves upright once more; after an extraordinary expenditure of energy, we came across the comrades we were to relieve. Sometimes it happens that nobody arrives. The old sentries assume that they are relieved and depart. The new ones search around and finally push a new sentry post forward. That is to say, the section commander posts a man in a shell hole, a few more ten metres or so further on, and so on. If their luck holds, they will eventually be found once more in the darkness, the front line will have been occupied more or less correctly and nobody due to be relieved will be overlooked.

"Our entire bodies are boiling hot after the exertions of the approach march. With tired eyes we seek out the enemy, whose shells whiz over to explode around us. Rain falls ceaselessly. Twice already I have had to dig myself out of the clay; already it is collapsing again. I shall soon be crouching in wet mud. I try to prop up the wall with two shell racks and hang my groundsheet from them. It starts slowly to become light and extremely chilly. I rejoice that at least I have cover from the air. Two comrades, who have been occupying a place which has been sprayed with shrapnel and duds[50] constantly, join me in my hole. We stretch out another groundsheet against the persistent rain and reinforce it with a rifle, which forces it upwards. Nevertheless it also concentrates the water into every rill, so that it first pours down someone's neck, then in another's boots, but always into the hole, which becomes fuller and fuller, until we are squatting in a pool of wet mud. The weather clears around midday and hordes of enemy aircraft appear. Now we have to remain absolutely still; the slightest movement could betray us.

"The firing increases in intensity. Shrapnel rounds burst and shells explode sending columns of mud flying into the air. The giant 'coal boxes' of the naval guns roar past overhead. Steel fragments whiz through the air and we are deluged with clods of clay. We sit there and stick it out. Suddenly one of us falls dead, pierced through the chest by a shell splinter. Time passes agonisingly slowly. We realise that the enemy could appear at any minute. During the evening we try to improve our holes and to establish a link with our neighbours...Further to the rear is the village of

Avesnes, where the Second Position runs. Our heavy artillery is located here. When it fires, the houses creak and the walls crumble. The air is full with countless enemy shells, which are seeking out the guns. There are still some rooms in these houses, even though the windows and doors are smashed and there are shell holes in the walls. These rooms provide at least the illusion of security and those holding out in mud-filled or smashed dugouts or lying in the filth and squalor of the front line long for them; for what is danger to us!"

1. Kinder: History MIR 1 pp 261-262
2. See Reid: *Courcelette* pp 82-84 for the Canadian version of this anecdote.
3. Tannen: History MIR 3 p 152
4. ibid. p 160
5. Kinder: op. cit. pp 278-279
6. Goetze: History MIR 2 p 100
7. Kinder: op. cit. p 290
8. Vormann: History IR 26 Band 3 pp 603-604
9. Solleder: '*Vier Jahre Westfront*' p 246
10. ibid. p 247
11. ibid. pp 25-260
12. History IR 64 pp 174-175
13. Tannen: op. cit. pp 165-166
14. Brandis: History IR 24 pp 295-296
15. Luisenhof was the place where the aeroplane of Major Lanoe Hawker VC DSO, commander of 24 Squadron RFC crashed after a protracted fight with Manfred von Richthofen on 23 November 1916. He was buried by the Germans at the crash site, although his body was not found after the war.
16. Collenberg: History GFAR 3 p 231
17. ibid. p 225
18. Lange: *Hauptmann Willy Lange* pp 126-127
19. ibid. p 127
20. Kellinghausen: *Kriegserinnerungen* pp 518-519
21. History IR 160 pp 141-142
22. Variables such as the precise weight of a shell and its propellant charge, barrel wear and meteorological conditions mean that artillery pieces, like machine guns, deliver rounds which are dispersed around the precise aiming point: the greater the range, the greater the dispersion. The total area upon which rounds fall is termed the beaten zone.
23. Bickel: History FAR 25 p 164
24. Ritter: History IR 163 p 180
25. Gropp: *Hanseaten im Kampf* pp 186 - 187
26. This incident is covered in detail in Hart: *Somme Success* pp 204-208
27. Gropp: op. cit. p 184
28. Pafferath: History IR 68 p 311
29. Fischer: Zwischen Wolken und Granaten pp 42-52
30. Apart from the strange method of counting aerial battles, which presumably must relate to the number of individual German aircraft involved, this report is probably reasonably accurate. 22nd October was a bad day for the Allies, with the RFC alone reporting aircrew losses on the Western Front of two killed, four wounded and thirteen missing. See Cole: *Royal Flying Corps 1915-1916*' p 294.

31. Pafferath: op. cit. p 297
32. ibid. p 298
33. ibid. p 299
34. ibid. p 305-306
35. ibid. p 309
36. ibid. p 310
37. Gropp: *op. cit.* p 189
38. Kronprinz Rupprecht: *Mein Kriegstagebuch II Band* p 46
39. Pafferath: op. cit. pp 315-316
40. *ibid.* pp 319-320
41. *Illustrated Michelin Guide, The Somme Vol 1*  p 89
42. Kriegsarchiv München 2 IR Bd 7 Akt 3
43. ibid.
44. ibid.
45. ibid.
46. Kronprinz Rupprecht: *'Mein Kriegstagebuch'* II Band p 52
47. Pafferath: op. cit. pp 332-333
48. Goldammer:  History IR 179 p 135
49. ibid. , for example  pp 136-137
50. The proportion of duds, or apparent duds, increased towards the end of the battle.  Writing of the situation around Grandcourt in early November, Reserve Leutnant Enemark Reserve Infantry Regiment 91 commented, 'It was, however, a piece of good fortune that at the very least half of all shells fired were duds.' See Kümmel: Res.Inf.Regt Nr. 91 p 248.  Leutnant Schicketanz, an observer with Reserve Infantry Regiment 106, noted, 'It was very welcome to us that the British ammunition included so many duds.  For example, on 11th November during one half hour period, I counted thirty five duds, which landed about one hundred metres to the right of the observation point.'  See Böttger: History RIR 106 p 150.  Manufacturing faults were still largely to blame, but the condition of the battlefield also had two negative effects.  The first was that in the days before the arrival in service of 'graze' fuzes, the impact on swampy ground was frequently insufficient to set off the detonation chain.  The second was that some shells were not actually duds at all.  They had sunk so far into the morass before they detonated that their explosions were smothered by viscous clay and mud.

# CHAPTER 9

# November – December 1916

**B**y 1st November, the men of Bavarian Infantry Regiment 20 had been in the line for several days of hard fighting in vile weather conditions. Above all they hoped that there would be no further major attacks, but in pouring rain that turned the battlefield into a filthy brown sea, the French attacked the R I position hard from the south. Ground was lost, positions were driven in and the companies were soon in serious trouble as the latest thrust enveloped them. About two hundred, including eight officers, were captured.

*Reserve Leutnant Heimpel 6th Company Bavarian Infantry Regiment 20*[1] **1.**

"The dugout trembled and creaked in every joint. The candle, which from time to time we tried to light, kept being blown out by the overpressure. Suddenly there was a particularly violent impact and a torrent of earth came down the stairs, burying the sentry. We were thrown about in all directions and partially buried, but we dug around with bare hands and bayonets and soon we freed the man. It was not so easy to clear the entrance. The air in the dugout was almost unbearable, because we also housed ten wounded men, one of whom was so severely wounded that his legs were already going gangrenous. The will to live trebled our strength and so a little while later, after an extremely strenuous effort, we were able to produce an air space. This did at least produce some fresh air. Gradually we had enlarged the hole so that it was possible for a man to crawl out...

"It was long past midday when a man suddenly dived in and shouted 'They're coming!' I leapt out, a signal pistol in each hand and fired one flare after another to call for artillery fire. Countless bullets impacted all around me and I could see that Frenchmen were already running over a rise to my left rear. Everybody out was the next essential, but as they emerged the first of them were immediately hit by bullets crashing in around the entrance. The enemy had a machine gun trained on it. There was nothing for it but to pull back from the entrance, because egg grenades were already rolling down. We heard the crash of their explosions and felt the explosive gases hitting us in the face and stinging our lungs. Men cried out, then suddenly all was quiet. The head of the man with the gangrenous legs was torn completely off his body. A few moments passed then another hand grenade came down. There was an agony of expectation, but it did not explode. Something had to be done if we were not to be smoked out or asphyxiated. I climbed up to the entrance. Outside was a Frenchman pointing a pistol at my chest. Numerous others also aimed at me. That was the end!"

Despite the losses of terrain and the general confusion, matters were not simple for the attackers and even the following day there were still groups of defenders holding out in a rough line of connected shell holes.

*Gewehrführer Ludwig Meyer 2nd Machine Gun Company Bavarian Infantry Regiment 20² 1.*

"At daybreak 2nd November we were able to see what had changed. The French had dug in about 300 metres from us. The old second line was now our front line. Our flanks were hanging in the air; we were on our own resources. There were no commanders and nobody knew where there was a command post, so we could not report on our situation. There was only one thing for it: to hang on, come what may. We had the French to our left and the British in front. Our 12th [Artillery Regiment] was firing at the new French trench; or rather, that is where they were supposed to be shooting. In fact we had to endure the effect of all this heavy fire. We fired flares to indicate our position to the artillery, but it did not alter its point of aim. Our artillery observers failed utterly here. We took out our handkerchiefs, looked longingly to our rear and waved to show that there were still men here. But it was all in vain. In the afternoon it got even worse, as the weight of fire increased. We exchanged language that was not exactly pretty and I shall not repeat it here. Towards 3.00 pm there was a direct hit in the trench from the 21st [Field Artillery Regiment]. Gollwitzer and Reitmeier, who were manning the second machine gun, were killed and several infantrymen wounded... Night fell once more. The artillery continued to shoot at us and so granted the French soldiers a peaceful night. The situation that night is beyond description. The artillery mixed tear gas in, making our eyes stream. Two runners from Infantry Regiment 24 were despatched to the rear to inform the artillery, 'All gunners and their guns might as well go on leave. We are not here to act as cannon fodder...'."

Fighting also continued around Sailly Saillisel and St Pierre Vaast Wood, but it was several more days before the French gained a significant advantage by taking Saillisel and even then St Pierre Vaast Wood, apart from a small section temporarily occupied, proved to be out of reach until the German army withdrew to the Hindenburg Line the following year. During the night of 31st October – 1st November, Infantry Regiment 172 had the task of securing the start line for an attack the following morning by the other regiments of the 39th Infantry Division – 126 and 132 – and then to hold itself in reserve. It was no sinecure. The weather was wet and cold; the Regiment, which was kept under constant harassing artillery fire, was also subject to a gas attack and lost a valued battalion commander.

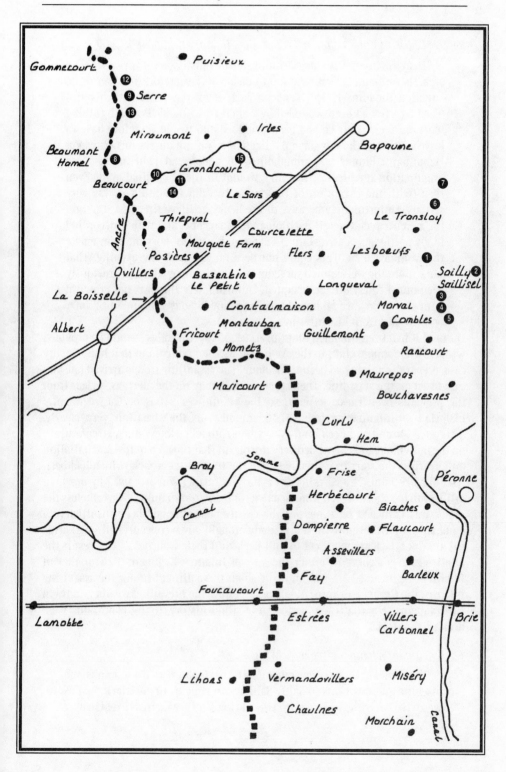

*Reserve Leutnant Kuby Adjutant 1st Battalion Infantry Regiment 172[3] 2.*

"Heavy artillery fire started coming down, mostly on the forward battle area. Hauptmann Finner went out of the dugout, therefore, to observe the situation for himself. He was soon back down the stairs with his arm bleeding. He had been wounded by a shell which landed close by. Along with the regret that he had been wounded and would therefore have to leave us for a while, was general relief that it was not too serious. But soon Hauptmann Finner was complaining of abdominal pain and a close examination revealed a tiny entry wound in the abdominal wall. Even then (with the exception of the doctor) we did not think it was very serious. Unfortunately because of the heavy artillery fire, which fell on the area between the R II position and Manancourt and which, according to my battle log, persisted until 5.15 pm, it was not possible to evacuate the wounded man. This could not be arranged until the evening. That same night the well-known surgeon, Doctor Ahreiner, who had previously been our medical officer, operated. Unfortunately this was not crowned with the success we all hoped for. The following day Hauptmann Finner was released from his sufferings..."

For once it had been intended that the attack of 1st November, would be provided with close air support but, in the event, bad weather put paid to that hope. In any case, preparation time had been inadequate. The assaulting troops arrived late and exhausted on the start line. The French were already on the alert, as is clear from the previous eyewitness account, so the result was a fiasco. The regimental historian of Infantry Regiment 126 summed up the situation very clearly. 'Saturated ground and deep mud everywhere, pitch blackness, the extreme strain on the individual and enemy artillery fire meant that the men of the 2nd Battalion only reached the start line shortly before the time of the attack, which had been fixed for 6.30 am. The Forming Up Place was further compromised by our own artillery firing short, which wounded two company commanders. Nevertheless the attack was launched on time, but the enemy positions had been insufficiently bombarded. Furthermore the alert enemy brought down concentrated small arms fire on the attackers, who had to pull back into their trenches... As a result the attack never got going in either the area of Infantry Regiment 126 or that of Infantry Regiment 132.'[4] Not knowing about these difficulties for the assaulting infantry, the German air force did its best, despite the prevailing weather, to fly in their support. For that early period in aviation history, flying conditions were decidedly marginal.

*Fliegerleutnant Johannes Fischer Air Wing 8[5]*

"At 6.51 am on 1st November 1916, we took off to drop bombs and machine gun positions in Sailly-Saillisel, in support of an attack. Just as we arrived over the target, a covering of cloud at fifty metres closed in over the positions. It was just as though the enemy had programmed natural protection into their plans. The enemy position was covered in cloud to the west as far as the eye could see. This bank of cloud slowly drifted eastwards, like a great white towel, blocking off any view of the ground. We loitered for half, then three quarters of an hour and, finally, an hour above the low cloud, continually looking to the west to check if any of the ground could be seen in that direction. We climbed to 2,100 metres to increase our field of view and so as to have a better overview of the weather. There did not seem to be any chance of improvement. We picked our way carefully back to our own aerodrome, which was also totally obscured by cloud, landing shortly before the arrival of a bank of ground mist. We were grounded throughout the day by the weather, but the following day brought us flying weather once more.

"Heading out over the lines, we encountered a French twin-engined Caudron biplane, which banked sharply away under our machine-gun fire. It dived away into cloud firing and we lost sight of it. We concentrated our reconnaissance efforts that day on enemy artillery positions and were able to establish that there had been a considerable amount of regrouping. With the aid of our one and a half metre camera, we made a series of overlapping photographs of the entire terrain, which would enable a type of map to be built up from the strips of photographs. The entire area between Lesboeufs, which had disappeared completely and the ruins of Le Transloy was one mass of craters... After our return there was the usual hustle and bustle about the aerodrome... Suddenly an aircraft was gliding in at a steep angle. We could tell at a glance that something was not in order. After a swift turn, it landed and rolled to a halt. A group of mechanics was amongst those who ran towards it. One called to another, 'Get the first aid men!', and its seriously wounded pilot was lifted out of his cockpit. During a dogfight he had been shot through the back by a bullet which had gone straight through his midriff. He lost consciousness as he was being supported by two mechanics. The seriously wounded man was laid on a stretcher, where he received first aid from our medical sergeant..."

For the next week the French maintained the most intense pressure on the regiments of 39th Infantry Division. Fighting flared up all along this sector as a supreme effort was made to turn Péronne's northern flank before worsening winter weather precluded further mobile operations.

*Hauptmann Tobias 1st Battalion Infantry Regiment 126[6]* **3.**

"The French attack began at midday [5th November]. The result was as follows: in the area of 1st Company, which had suffered less from the enemy artillery fire, the French were driven back to their trenches by rifle fire and grenades. It was not possible to follow up because the enemy trenches were full of reserves and machine guns. The position of 2nd Company, as well as the right flank and centre of the 3rd Company, was completely flattened by enemy fire. The surprise attack by the French was met only by the wounded, those buried alive and those deafened by the hours of drumfire. It broke through and pushed forward approximately 200 metres. Some members of 2nd Company had been withdrawn to the position of 1st Company by their company commander in order to avoid the drumfire. These men helped fight off the French attack on the front of 1st Company, prevent the French from advancing further towards Saillisel and began the occupation of a new stop line on the edge of the village south of the church. In front of 4th Company and the left flank of 3rd Company, the attack was spotted in time and simply beaten off with machine gun fire. The relatively undamaged rearmost of the 4th Company trenches were occupied and effective enfilade fire was brought down against the French, who had broken through the 2nd and 3rd Companies, thus preventing further progress...."

Attacks continued and losses mounted until, following extremely heavy artillery preparation, the French were able to exploit gaps which had appeared in the forward line held by Infantry Regiments 126 and 172 and there was a minor breakthrough in the area of Infantry Regiment 172, which led to the French occupying the north-east tip of St Pierre Vaast Wood, before being ejected a few days later by a German counter-attack. That evening Reserve Major Engel, commanding officer of 3rd Battalion Infantry Regiment 172, reported, 'The enemy has broken through, north of the road Rancourt – Gouvernement Ferme. Some of the attackers got as far as St Pierre Vaast Wood, where prisoners were taken. The extreme left hand assault group broke through the front line south of Point 1, rolled up the 8th Company and forced its way into of St Pierre Vaast Wood, which lies opposite, before digging in on the edge of the wood and appearing to extend itself to the left towards Saillisel. The entire garrison of the R II position has been moved forward to R I. 9th, 10th and 11th Companies are attacking the enemy from R I. The 12th is awaiting the arrival of the fourth platoons in R I. Corresponding orders were issued by 2nd Battalion Infantry Regiment 172 at 4.55 pm. In order to restore the situation, both Major Breslig and I consider it necessary that the battalion at rest (1st) be sent forward tonight to join in. I regard this as necessary because, firstly, the situation is unclear and secondly, the companies of the 3rd Battalion are totally exhausted and decimated by the drum fire which they had to endure yesterday and the day before that. The fighting strength of the 3rd Battalion is about 160 riflemen.'

Elsewhere the fighting had been intense, but the companies had at least succeeded in holding their positions.

*Gefreiter Geiß 2nd Company Infantry Regiment 172*[7] **3.**

"We advanced once more. This time 2nd Company moved forward to the well known sector of Sailly-Saillisel. That is easy to write; the reality was somewhat different. In single file, we left the château on a pitch black night. The way before us left much to be desired and was marked more by craters than solid track. Rather as a May beetle stretches its feelers out carefully, we groped our way forward, testing the next step with a stick. Despite all care, a great many of us made a thorough study of the inside of a crater. Finally we arrived at Saillisel, but all was in ruins. There was not even a cellar to serve as cover. We plodded on a further 300 – 400 metres to the south-west of Saillisel and then came the voice of my platoon commander, which I can hear to this day, 'OK lads this is our position. Split into threes and find yourselves a shell hole'.

"With two mates I immediately occupied a shell hole which contained the remains of a shed. There was no lack of water; it was half full. Because we could not get hot food forward, we had to eat the cold rations which had been issued earlier. It was all preserved meats and sausage, so it made us thirsty and there was insufficient coffee to go round. But we got by; there was enough water and we could slake our thirst. The night passed quietly and then we were able to get our bearings. It rained ceaselessly, so groundsheets and coats were soon soaked through. We clung to the edge of our crater, with mud up to our thighs. All three of us had given up any hope of coming through, because the artillery fire got worse with each passing day. Enemy aircraft were also very active, dropping bombs and grenades into our holes and making it very difficult to avoid flying splinters and clods of earth. Many of our men were buried alive, but they were on their own resources; the heavy fire ruling out any possibility of going to their aid by day. We longed for nightfall and were happy when it came and the fire eased a bit. We could breathe again, but there was much work to do, especially to dig out, as far as possible, our buried comrades. It kept on raining. The wind howled and we were frozen and soaked to the skin.

"It was about 1.00 am [on 5th November], when a line of figures appeared about forty to fifty metres in front of our line. As they came closer and we could make them out, we realised that they were French – members of a ration party, who had got lost in No Man's Land. They were heavily laden with red wine, white bread, biscuits and chocolate. There was even a sack of mail, which we thought was of little value. Anyway we had a good share out. The prisoners were conducted swiftly to the rear by men detailed by the company commander, Leutnant Altrogge. The night came to and end, day dawned and the enemy artillery fire increased again in intensity. It was a time that I shall never forget. During the afternoon enemy fire increased to drumfire and many of our comrades died the death of heroes because, although they were badly wounded or buried alive, it was impossible to go to their aid. So it continued. A direct hit landed on the crater next to ours and buried everyone within it. We just could not help them, it was simply too dangerous. Not until it went dark were we able to see what had happened and to establish that it was the hole which had sheltered Leutnant Bialkowski, his batman and his signaller.

"Leutnant Bialkowski was severely wounded, buried and unconscious. The signaller was dead, but his batman had escaped with bruises. It was essential to try to save our brave Leutnant. We prepared a makeshift stretcher then set off in pitch darkness for an extremely strenuous journey to the dressing station in Manancourt. I shall always remember it vividly. We had long since given up hope of delivering him alive, because there was not a sound from his lips, when one or other of us stumbled into a shell hole, but finally we arrived at the dressing station and laid our burden down."

It appears that Leutnant Bialkowski survived his ordeal. The troops in place were too weak to win back the lost ground, then, 'On 9th November a violent assault opened on a wide front between Bouchavesnes and the Ancre Valley. The Allies wanted to make a final attempt to achieve their aim and break through the front. In the north the British made a successful advance and the French broke into the trenches at Le Transloy, three kilometres north of Sailly. The situation was serious.'[8] Finally, 10th November, the 185th Infantry Division arrived to bring much needed relief to the 39th Division. Summing up the heavy fighting later, the historian of Infantry Regiment 126 wrote, 'The position which we had taken over at the end of October could be handed over to our successors without serious loss of terrain. Saillisel remained firmly in the hands of the Regiment. The slight territorial gains which the enemy achieved were out of all proportion to the enormous expenditure of artillery ammunition, including large calibre, or to the use of fresh assault troops, whose casualties were very heavy. Our losses were heavy too; amongst the command element they were particularly painful: nine company commanders, six of them killed. Total losses were twenty-eight officers (twelve dead, eleven wounded, five missing, one sick), 1,201 NCOs and men (199 killed, 604 wounded, 239 missing and 159 sick in hospital). No wonder that the mood was subdued as the Regiment left the blood-soaked field of battle. The ordinary soldier could not know what service he had rendered the Fatherland, as he fought with all his strength to hold his position and deny it to all assaults of the enemy. But this was not a matter of the fight for this or that trench. It was about holding Saillisel and the height where St Pierre Vaast Wood, which dominated it, stood. It was about holding the vital ground which the enemy needed if he was to break through.'[9]

In pursuance of this aim a major counterattack was planned for 15th November, to wrest possession of the captured section of St Pierre Vaast Wood back from the French.

*Offizierstellvertreter Hans Voigt Machine Gun Company Fusilier Regiment 73*[10] **4.**

"15th November 1916 dawned a fine sunny autumn day. Airmen and observers had excellent visibility and, by 2.00 am, the artillery fire had increased to drum fire. To our joy our own artillery was joining in. Its fire was coming down equally on the front line trenches and rear communications. Above all the fire of the field artillery was coming down precisely on the enemy trenches to our front. Extremely fearful, to our great and exuberant pleasure, just before the time for the assault - which was set at 4.48 am – French deserters, yelling for mercy, plunged down into our trenches and told us of the appalling effect of our artillery fire. From them we established that opposite us was the 9th Moroccan Zouave Regiment. These brothers in arms had had to endure what we had put up with at Guillemont and Combles...day after day of drum fire – then, when the storm came, to hold out to the last man and the last bullet! I let go of the grenades and the pistol which I had been grasping with cramped hands and look at my pocket watch – 4.30 am – the hands will creep round to 4.48 am then the die will be cast.

"The Frenchmen are nervous. Harsh cracks thud in against the newly turned earth on the parapet. A French machine gun maintains a terrible Tack...Tack...Tack.' 'Mount the parapet.' 'Comrade, let's exchange addresses. This is that of my parents. This is my fiancée.' 'That lot down there seem to have smelt a rat, they are shooting bloody accurately.' The French artillery is giving it everything it's got. With each salvo, they land shells closer to our trench. Steps are cut into the enemy side of the trench. 4.45 am – time is slipping by, it cannot be halted! Thank heavens, there's only three minutes to go – one way or the other. The machine gun goes on firing. 'Hang on!' A round from our own heavy artillery lands as a direct hit on the trench. No more flares may be fired, so as not to confuse our own artillery. The Frenchmen are still firing our signal for artillery support. 'First aid men, go to the left!' – 'Someone is seriously wounded.' 'Comrade help me!' There is not time. 4.47 am – crash – splat – mud is thrown up by the impact of machine gun bullets flies around our ears. 'Go!' 'Over the top! Go! Go!' 'Hurra!' Is the machine gun still firing? What about the artillery? To my left and right I can only see the assaulting troops. 'Over here! Keep together!'

"There is a short pause in the wire obstacle, but there is not much shooting. We're through. Here's the French trench. It's full of corpses; not one single living Frenchman. There is a Frenchman running back. He is indicating the way to the communication trenches leading to the rear. 'After him! Grenades ready! – Throw!' In a wide arc, thirty to forty hand grenades fly through the air to land in the communication trench. Further! Eight to ten Frenchmen appear from behind the next traverse. They have been hit in the back by grenade splinters. 'Mercy, comrades, mercy!' At a wave from us, they head off for the German lines. A seriously wounded officer comes towards us, supported by two men wearing Red Cross brassards. A finely drawn, waxy-yellow face peers out from behind a thickly padded dressing on his head. His uniform is completely soaked with blood. He tries to greet us, makes an effort, but cannot speak. 'Monsieur the Adjutant', explains one of the Red Cross men. Further! Tack... Tack... Tack! clatters the bloody machine gun, extremely close to our swiftly-ducked heads. Over there! It's hidden behind a thick tree trunk. The machine gun is firing from behind a heap of logs, bushes and piled up earth. We are already partially in rear of it. A few more steps forward, then it's, 'Ready! Throw!' The assault party is close up behind us in the trench. The hand grenades fly in small arcs. I see them explode immediately in front and behind the machine gun, which falls silent.

"Now the French emerge with raised hands from a shallow communication trench which leads to the machine gun post. A black man is in the lead. 'Mercy comrades, I'm only a poor Moroccan!' He falls to his knees and offers us a long cigarette case,'Fine cigarettes – Brazilian cigarettes.' What a pitiful wretch! We continue. According to our mission, we should ignore the machine gun and push on past into the reserve position. Everywhere the grey-blue clad figures of the trench garrison can be seen streaming to the rear. Our machine guns engage them from left and right. Large numbers raise their hands. Now we link up with the assault groups on both sides. As the same instant, a low-flying German aircraft buzzes overhead. We light a magnesium flare to indicate that the attack has been successful. The pilot fires off star-filled flares – 'Understood' – and disappears. We still have to hang on in the newly-won trenches for another three days, despite the fire, the mud and the cold! By day it rained. At night it froze. There is nothing worse than hanging on grimly like this after an attack. Such days demand endless heroism. Will history have anything to say about them?"

*Gefreiter Otto Fey 6th Company Infantry Regiment 390*[11] **4**.

"One overcast evening the platoon, which belonged to Infantry Regiment 390, was suddenly loaded onto trucks, driven forward as far as possible and then led into position. Orders had arrived directing that the enemy, which had occupied a considerable length of the German position, was to be ejected. The enemy had skilfully chosen this precise piece of terrain as the objective of their attack because it was of operational importance, providing as it did good views in various directions. Our platoon was allocated the centre of this attack, between the battalions of Fusilier Regiment 73, so that it could attack either to the left or the right and roll up the trench. After a few false starts, we eventually arrived in the line, or at least what passed for it, at around midnight. We dug hasty shell scrapes in our attack formation. Shortly after 11.00 pm, the German drumfire began to come down all over the sector. The French were not long in replying. Apart from a few wounded, we had no casualties, but we were regularly half buried and had to set to, to dig each other out. We constantly felt that it could be our turn next, but luckily it was usually just another clod of dirt that flew through the air to fall, not exactly pleasantly, against our skulls. At long last it was 4.40 am and the assault sections of our platoon emerged out of cover, looking as though they had been stamped into the earth. The cries of the wounded were drowned out by the noise of shells of light and, in particular, medium calibre, exploding, machine-gun fire and hand grenades bursting.

"I fired a flare from my pistol to indicate, 'Lift the fire further forward' and the German shells started to land beyond the enemy lines. In no time flat the assaulting troops were up to the French trench and the few machine guns that were still firing were put out of action. The captured Frenchmen were despatched to the rear. The storming of the position did not mark the end of our mission. Hardly had we entered the captured trenches, than an attempted counter-attack was launched from the French rear position. Rifle and machine-gun fire hammered against the enemy, who had attacked in considerable strength from the trenches. Several well-aimed salvoes ensured that the counter-attack soon petered out. In vain, the French officers attempted to drive their men forward. We stayed on in that position for two full days, whilst the French made our life extremely hard. My duties as a runner certainly were. If I managed successfully to negotiate one muddy hole, the enemy shells would make sure that I sank in the next one.

"Amidst constant danger, but with great care, I found my way back to Regimental Headquarters after several hours, where the first reports had been awaited for some time. I entered looking like a lump of clay and had to take off my helmet before anyone could recognise me. Highly delighted that they had, at long last, received the report of Reserve Leutnant Seib that the assault had been a complete success, someone poured me out two glasses of schnaps, which I drained gratefully. The following night I brought a Frenchman with me.We had fished him out of a shell hole in broad daylight, whilst he was trying to pull back. Initially he tried to give me the slip in the pitch black night, but after I had made him 'see reason', he became like a faithful dog, even helping me in a comradely fashion to find Regimental Headquarters, when he fell into the hole which was camouflaged with pine branches. Lying flat out, he called to me '*Ici, ici, Kamerad, j'ai trouvé le trou!*' [Over here, comrade, I've found the hole!].
Despite the dangerous situation, all I could do was laugh..."

Meanwhile on the opposite side of St Pierre Vaast Wood and occupying positions either side of the ravine (Vallée du Bois Brulé on the present-day map) which ran south-east from the wood to Moislains, were the men of Infantry Regiment 164. They contributed some troops to strengthen Fusilier Regiment 73 for this so-called 'Operation Hannover', which also involved Infantry Regiment 65, but for most of this tour of duty they were occupying a more or less static section of the front, taking casualties from incessant artillery fire, but suffering more from the exhausting effects of the weather and the heavy work load.

*Vizefeldwebel Mühlmeister 4th Company Infantry Regiment 164* [12] **5.**

"The cooks poured the coffee into twenty-five litre carboys, packed three loaves into a sandbag and tied two bags together. The food came in double-sided insulated containers of twenty litre capacity. Other sandwich making supplies were packed into platoon sandbags. During the afternoon everything was loaded into the wagons, until each was piled high. On top were groundsheets stuffed with wood shavings and the mail. The whole thing did not only look dangerous, it was dangerous, as it lurched from crater to crater. We were not forced to use a particular route, but somewhere along the way we always ended up in the filth, a somewhat mild expression and certainly not that of the soldiers, for liquid mud twenty five centimetres thick, flooded fields and other delightful spots. In about one and a half hours we were at the off-loading point, which was a fantastic hive of activity. Apart from the entire regiment's supply wagons, there were also columns loaded with mining supports and all manner of engineer stores. If the artillery fire aimed at the nearby battery position was added in then all hell broke loose.

"We were simply delighted to have distributed the food containers, carboys, bread etc. and that the carrying party had brought everything onto the position and had returned unscathed. All the tracks were in an appalling state; covered in disgusting filth. We were soaked from above and below. Our uniforms were soon completely coated with mud and saturated. Once the rations were delivered, we returned as quickly as possible, so as to return the empty food containers and carboys to the wagons. Then the men had to make a second journey, carrying props, hand grenades and other engineer stores forward and not getting back until midnight or 1.00 am. This meant that each night we had to cover fifteen kilometres, and a further ten fully loaded, along bottomless tracks and across muddy crater fields. That was a tremendous performance."

Operation Hannover secured German possession of St Pierre Vaast Wood for the remainder of their time on the Somme, but their almost simultaneous efforts to recapture Saillisel foundered in the face of determined French defence, mounting casualties and the introduction of fresh French assault forces during the morning of 15th November. This village was never fully recaptured and the Germans ended the operation holding a vague line of positions in shell holes on its outskirts.

*Feldwebel Henzgen 4th Company Infantry Regiment 161¹³* **3.**

"At midnight [14th November] I was called to go and see the battalion commander, Hauptmann Kleinekuhle. All the company commanders of the 1st Battalion were already present. We were briefed about the order to recapture at all costs the village of Saillisel from the enemy and all the necessary coordination was carried out. When I returned to the company I passed on the orders, then regrouped it in accordance with the needs of the operation. The 1st Platoon, which I was then commanding, had the task of overrunning the first two positions and then going firm along the street as ordered. The other two platoons were to occupy the positions which had been overrun and to be prepared to reinforce the front line as required. Once I had rallied the men and made it clear that the attack would certainly succeed, provided that each did his duty, Leutnant Bodenstedt, our company commander, returned with further information that he had been given by battalion. At the same moment the signal to attack was given. The flare had hardly gone up than I had dived into cover with my men. Loaded down with grenades, we made our way forwards from shell hole to shell hole. Leutnant Bodenstedt and I, who were in the lead, soon reached the first enemy positions. Leaving the garrison, which had apparently not yet noticed us, to the platoons which were following up, we pressed on to assault the second position.

"In the meantime, the situation became more lively and the enemy started to put up bitter resistance.Thus far it had been calm to our right, but now we began to observe the flash of exploding grenades there as well; a clear sign that an assault was taking place. Throughout the village, which had been very badly shot up, we had problems negotiating a great many obstacles, such as the remains of wire, piles of stones and all manner of other debris. The French offered particularly obstinate resistance behind an old threshing machine. Musketier Butscheid from Cologne collapsed next to me, his thigh shattered, but we still reached the nest of resistance, where a few well-aimed grenades recovered the debt. Some of the defenders put their hands up, others tried to escape. We pushed on with the assault. Those who had assaulted on the right got closer. The German battle cries of 'Hurra' were intermingled with the explosions of hand grenades, the rattle of machine gun fire and the crash of mortars. I suddenly saw figures appearing on the right. At first I was suspicious, believing them to be enemy troops, but I soon noticed German steel helmets. The first man I met was Vizefeldwebel Mohr of 2nd Company Infantry Regiment 161. He said to me that he had recognised me immediately from my voice. We then urged our men forward and went on to storm the Third Position. Although fresh troops were being fed in at the rear, our front line became ever weaker. Nevertheless we still made progress. By means of well-placed grenades we dealt with the garrison and took prisoners. Flares were then fired to show that the position had been taken.

"I still could not link up on my right. In the meantime dawn began to break. I noticed that we had come a bit too far and, pulling my right flank back about forty metres, made contact with 3rd Company Infantry Regiment 161. I placed two machine guns which had come forward, into favourable positions to beat off counter-attacks. But our occupying group was very weak. There were only ten to fifteen men manning alert positions. Nevertheless when the French, taking advantage of the morning mist, attacked, thanks to the courage of the trench garrison and the machine gunners, in particular, they were beaten back three times. They were, nevertheless, able to occupy trenches which we had initially captured but had then had to relinquish, so we were only about forty metres apart. As a result we suffered badly from enemy mortar and rifle fire, to which our dear Unteroffizier Lüttkenhorst fell victim, when we wanted to assess the situation and raised our heads out of our hole. He bled badly. We bandaged him up, but it was impossible to evacuate him by day and for the time being we had to leave him lying in the trench. Minor fighting flared up sporadically until it was almost evening, then more or less died away. I was buoyed up by the hope that we should soon be relieved and sure enough, just before 10.00 pm, they arrived. We took our seriously wounded with us and pulled back from the position by sections."

Desperate though the fighting in this area between the French and German armies was, there could still be lighter moments. At this time there was endless confusion behind the lines, because Bavarian Infantry Regiment 15 was deployed very close to Bavarian Reserve Infantry Regiment 15, which was operating in the R II (Allaines) Position. One day a member of a ration party from the latter got lost and found himself separated from his unit for days.

*Richard Mierisch Bavarian Reserve Infantry Regiment 15*[14] **6.**

"Those who did not know the area naturally asked where, 'the 15th' were located and they were frequently misdirected to the area of our sister regiment. Sometimes it was days before they found their way to the correct place. As a result, some of our men were always adrift and nobody could provide information concerning their whereabouts. This happened to Landsturmmann F. M. During collection of rations near to Barastre, there was a sudden shout of, 'Clear the way!' Everybody jumped to the left towards the field kitchens. Everybody that is, apart from F.M, who jumped to the right. There then followed an endless procession of ammunition wagons, some heading to the front, others returning. When, at long last, the traffic on the road ebbed away, F.M. could not find the field kitchens; they had disappeared. He was standing alone in the pitch black darkness, somewhere in the trackless desolation of the Somme battlefield. All around, muzzle flashes could be seen. He felt himself to be totally abandoned, took cover under a hay waggon that he came across in the middle of nowhere and settled down to consider his fate. It seemed to him that all the guns around him had come to a secret agreement to fire at him alone.

"What was a man in his position to do? He shouted for help! The ration party reported F.M as missing. Days went by; F.M. had disappeared. Then one morning the corpse of a tall man was found propped against the wall of our barn. He was stone dead and unrecognisable because he had been flattened by the passage of many wheels. The only form of identification was a shoulder title bearing the legend '15'. Could it be our F.M.? More days went by, then the 'dead' man was back among the living. Our Landsturmmann F.M. suddenly appeared amongst us, armed only with a walking stick. He was quite unharmed and his face shone with joy and happiness. In the place where he had shouted and bawled at the top of his voice for help, he had been found by some artillerymen, attracted there by his cries. What they thought and what he told them, following his miraculous rescue, we never discovered. At any rate he received a glass of wine and a quarter of a chicken as a restorative. He must have stumbled across particularly kindhearted helpers, because they kept him there for a week on light duties. When the Feldwebel then made it crystal clear to him that he was to take the next opportunity to head for his proper position, he retorted that he could not do that because he had no rifle. It was then explained to him in words of one syllable that he would have to fire with his stick, until he could find a rifle..."

Generally speaking, however, humour was in short supply during this, the fifth month of the battle. Conditions in the forward positions were appalling and dangerous; those in the villages just in the rear, hardly less so.

*Richard Mierisch Bavarian Reserve Infantry Regiment 15*[15] **7.**

"Although we had fewer lice in Bertincourt, we had flies in unimaginable numbers. They descended on us in swarms, covering furniture, walls and blankets in a solid grey mass, which measured several square metres. We attacked them with sulphur and burning bundles of straw, with some success, so that legions of these flies no longer flew, but crept and crawled all over the building. We then made fly swats by filling sandbags with newspapers and spent hours swatting the masses of insects until a bloody grey slime dripped from our sandbags and nauseated us. We then tried a different tack, sacrificing our packages of granulated sugar, which we spread all over a trunk in the left hand room. That attracted the flies, so that the other room of the house was, to some extent, free of flies. Sleep was only possible under a blanket and only then when all the pests beneath it had been killed. Countless flies, everywhere: in the cooking pot, in the knapsack, in the trouser pockets and even in the watch! – That was Bertincourt!"

*Reserve Leutnant Freter Reserve Infantry Regiment 94*[16] 4.

"Rain? It rained every day! The final village in which we bivouacked, namely Liéramont, which is where the clerical staff remained, gave a foretaste of what was to come. Most of the roads were almost impassable due to the mud. At the entrance to the village, some humorist had erected a shield bearing the words '*Moor und Schlammbad Ilmenau*' [Peat and Mud Bath Ilmenau (German health spa)]. This sort of gallows humour was bearable here where there were dry rooms and a roof overhead, but in the front line it would have been mental torture. The route forward led through Manancourt, which was constantly under fire, then ran from here to the front through woods and along tracks in total darkness. A journey which should have taken twenty to twenty-five minutes cost two to three hours. With each step men sank, literally, up to their knees in the mud, of which there were several types. The most bearable was thin mud, because it was less of an obstacle than the thick, clinging sort. Passing this latter type demanded great care, if boots were not to be lost – something which actually happened to some of our comrades. Those who had thus far not learned to curse and swear, certainly did during this approach march... There was not one square metre of terrain [of St Pierre Vaast Wood] which had not been ploughed up and turned over by shell fire, so it is no wonder that the constant rain turned everything into a foul slush. No trees, not even a branch, survived to indicate that this had ever been a wood. There were corpses and body parts everywhere. A head here, a leg there, an arm over there...It was by far the worst on the right flank of the Regiment. The whole place was a swamp, dotted with pools of filthy water. The dugouts were either smashed by artillery fire or filled with mud. It was simply impossible to use the remnants of the trenches... Every man had to cut off half of his coat and make a jacket out of it. The lower sections had become so encrusted with filth and mud that they were simply too heavy to move about in. In order to sleep there was no alternative but to sit on a baulk of timber with the upper body covered by a groundsheet. The only consolation was that it was every bit as bad for those opposite..."

Already by the middle of October, signs had been gathering that the Allies, whose progress eastwards was everywhere being checked by the defenders, were about to shift their efforts to the flanks of the Somme battlefield, concentrating especially on the British sector. Ludendorff later described the final stages of the Battle of the Ancre as '...a particularly heavy blow. We had not regarded such an outcome as possible, especially as our troops were still occupying good positions.'[17] Despite his remarks, at the time, the commanders on the ground all felt that something was being planned. Initially reports from agents provided the clues, but such was the build up of reserves and additional artillery, that the evidence began to accumulate rapidly.

*Crown Prince Rupprecht of Bavaria: Diary Entries* [18]

12 October

"According to a reliable agent, the attacks on the Somme are to be reinforced by an offensive on the British left flank (north of the Ancre). In informed circles, the word is that Sir Douglas Haig is going to strive to capture additional fortified points to the northwest of Thiepval."

18 October

"It is becoming ever clearer that enemy attacks are to be expected between Gommecourt and the Ancre. The enemy have deployed three powerful divisions on that front, have begun to range in their heavy batteries and have moved up thirty batteries of field guns near to the line Gommecourt-Serre."

28 October

"Four, rather than the earlier three, divisions have been identified between Gommecourt and the Ancre. Artillery fire has increased in this sector. There are heavy concentrations every morning, obviously with the aim of getting our troops accustomed to the practice, so that one day they may be surprised when the usual barrage is followed by an attack."

2 November

"General von Below stated [during a morning conference] that he was expecting an attack along the Gommecourt-Ancre sector, because the enemy had smashed all the trenches along this line...It is striking that the enemy is digging in vigorously on the high ground near Courcelette, Martinpuich and to the west of Delville Wood. This could well indicate that the enemy only intends to carry out an offensive with limited objectives, to capture our positions from Gommecourt to Bapaume and is considering spending the winter in these positions, security being provided by the trench line which has been begun from Courcelette to Delville Wood."

As usual, it was one thing to be in possession of compelling intelligence on the battlefield, quite another to be able to react when the whole front was still under pressure. There may have been a slight slackening off in the scale of infantry attacks, but the Allies continued to mount a huge artillery effort. German guns were now much more plentiful than they had been earlier, but there was a great shortage of ammunition, caused by further difficulties in the supply of raw materials, especially sulphuric acid. Concerns about the availability and quality of replacements led to the postponement or suspension of planned counter-attacks against Sailly Sailissel and other places early in November and there were no forces to spare to reinforce the threatened sector. The troops in place from the 12th

Infantry Division had to face the gathering threat as best they could.

On 24th October, Infantry Regiment 62 had been ordered to take over the Beaumont Hamel sector, which it did on 26 and 27 October. As an example of the strain, to which the German army had been subjected by four months of constant fighting, all of the rifle companies were very under strength. They entered their positions only eighty to ninety strong and by 10th November, the regiment had already suffered casualties of thirty eight killed, one hundred and thirty four wounded and three missing.[19] By the time of the final assault, they had been in the trenches for two full weeks. After being soaked through for days, almost all ranks were suffering from colds, chills and laryngitis; in some cases so badly that they could barely speak. Their clothes were permanently soaked and their boots had been wet for so long that the stitched seams were coming apart. The neighbouring formation, Reserve Infantry Regiment 55, was hardly better off. They had been holding the line to the south of Infantry Regiment 62 for ten weeks and their companies were reduced to an average of between 130 and 140 men.

The constant shelling eased a little around 11th November, so it was possible to carry forward rations and to replenish ammunition in the forward positions. During the night 12th/13th November the rain stopped and a full moon could be seen, clearly illuminating the scene of desolation. There was hardly any firing, which made the defenders suspicious about British intentions. As dawn approached a thick mist descended, rendering observation impossible. Sentries fired the occasional flare, but nothing was to be seen, then, without warning, at 6.45 am, a hurricane of fire came down on the forward positions and, almost simultaneously, up on Hawthorn Redoubt, a mine went off in sector B1, under a platoon of 11th Company Infantry Regiment 62. The British had succeeded in re-using the 1st July mine gallery. Four and a half months ago, they had enjoyed no success. Now, at the end of the battle, it was to be a different story, as a determined assault by the men of the 51st (Highland) Division swept all before them. Beaumont, so long an impregnable bastion of the defence, fell at last.

*Fähnrich Pukall 3rd Company Infantry Regiment 62*[20] **8**.

> "Huismann came up to me...and requested permission to fetch the mail. Three great sacks full were brought forward and I allowed each sentry to be relieved in turn, so that he could receive his mail. It was the first mail for three weeks, what joy! For many it was also their last! I restricted myself to opening my letters only, because the stillness outside demanded our closest attention. The mist was very thick and all was noticeably quiet. I went towards the hollow, where the double sentry post reported, 'Terrible fog, but all's quiet!' I then went back to the left flank, where Geisemeyer, who always was a very acute observer, called me over and urged me to listen, because something was happening out there today. I listened intently and could hear repeated muffled sounds. It could not be digging or wire cutters; the British must be moving forward! I stood my

platoon to and dashed over to the right flank, where the same sounds could be heard. 'Stand to! 'I ordered. 'Maintain high alert!'...It was essential to act before the Tommies did. I had to blow the mine and get the machine gun bringing fire down to the front. Why was the machine gun in the hollow not firing? I ran towards the hollow then, horrified, I staggered back a few paces. What was that? A huge pillar of flame and smoke was ascending skywards. The mist distorted and magnified its extent, making its exact location and size impossible to judge. Simultaneously a hail of machine-gun fire was opened along the front, and mortar bombs rained down amongst clouds of shrapnel. I raced back to my platoon. The sentries dived for cover – Attack!

"Hand grenades were swiftly issued and each man was given as much ammunition as he could carry. All were lined up on the stairs and I had a quick check of the bunks to ensure that nobody was neglecting his duties. I need not have worried. A picked NCO was on duty at each dugout entrance, armed with grenades and signal pistol, ready to raise the alarm the moment that the drum fire lifted. Our entrance was manned by the tireless and irreplaceable Schrott, a forester in his forties. A sentry up in the sap suddenly bawled, 'Here they come!' A shower of hand grenades landed in the trench. 'Everyone out!' I shouted. The occupation of the trench took place in an exemplary manner; beyond my wildest dreams. Left and right we threw grenades, then took post under cover of the explosions. Those who had further to go also threw grenades to clear the way, before taking up their positions and opening fire... The Tommies had been hanging on their barrage and they did not advance in lines, but solid groups... I saw red and white flares going up in the hollow, but due to the mist, they were mere pinpoints of light. I realised that if those to the rear had not heard the explosion, had not left their bunkers when they felt the shockwave and had not heard the sound of firing, they would not be likely to see my flares. I also thought it possible that Leutnant Walter still had the use of a telephone, so I fired my flares horizontally, so as to silhouette men advancing through the mist...

"After it became light we had to withstand a violent hand grenade attack, an artist's impression of which I later saw in a British magazine...I was on the extreme left flank and was caught in a very tricky situation, when a Lewis gunner suddenly appeared in front of me and grenades were thrown at me from my half right. Unteroffizier Belkner, rushed to my aid and, without hesitation, leapt out of cover to throw two hand grenades at the Tommies, who were lying down to our front. He could not hear my shouts to halt, because of the noise of battle. Before his grenades had exploded, the gunner fired another burst, hitting Belkner and throwing him backwards into the trench. I emerged unscathed...There was then a period of calm. To this day I can still see Ulka looking slyly at the dead and wounded to our front and saying, 'Fähnrich, I wonder if they have cocoa and schnaps on them?'

"The Tommies seemed to have been beaten off, so I was asked if there could be a return to the dugouts. It was out of the question, however, because I had noticed something inexplicable [earlier]. In the midst of the fog I had heard the sound of many voices endlessly shouting, 'Hurra' from the area of Beaumont. The voices were quite clear, but what possible role could there have been for our reserves there behind us? We needed them urgently! But in any case we had our hands full. At times the barrel of my rifle got so hot that I could hardly touch it and my arms were tired, so I stopped listening. Now that the fog had cleared, things looked different. Long lines of men in field grey were advancing towards us. Thank heavens! I thought, it is the reserves and an old gefreiter and I got up on the parapet and waved. At that, the first group which had been heading directly for us, veered away towards the 1st Company. I then saw that there were two British soldiers in front and behind them. I was sure that I was seeing ghosts, but then the gefreiter shouted, 'There are British soldiers with them!' I should have liked to have been able to rush over with a few men and free everyone, but our numbers had been thinned considerably and our reserves had not yet arrived from the second trench.

"Unteroffizier Schrott came running up: 'Fähnrich, just look at the Tommies on the right flank of the 1st Company!' I hung another bandolier of ammunition around me and raced to Schrott's position. I simply could not believe my eyes; wave upon wave of Tommies were advancing towards the 1st Company, without once ducking or taking cover. I had been told that the 1st Company did not have favourable fields of fire, but if we had had one or two machine guns, we could have brought down devastating enfilade fire. As it was we fired as fast as we could, out in the open, kneeling and firing from half right to right. The occasional British soldier came towards us with his rifle slung about him and one of us would give a fire order, 'Ready! Direction indicated! At the deliberate rate – fire!' Schrott, a former forester, never missed...I wanted to get hold of a machine gun, so taking a Gefreiter and our last five hand grenades we set off... but we had no luck... In the attempt some rounds tore through the Gefreiter's jacket collar, pieces of material fluttering down to the ground, but miraculously he was completely untouched.

"Then came a shout that Schrott was dead! ...He had been hit in the temple by a bullet. He lay there in front of me on the floor of the trench. He had been a friend to all; tirelessly he had worked for the common good. His experience had been indispensable, as had his presence in battle. Now he was no more. I did not want to believe it. But there was no time for mourning; I had to decide what to do. Our flanks were up in the air; there were British soldiers all around us. To our right, hordes of them were advancing down the road from Auchonvillers to Beaumont. We had to assume that the 2nd Battalion would launch a counter-attack, so we continued to wait. We were almost out of ammunition. We each had a few rounds left, which would probably have sufficed for troops pulling back. We went on waiting then it occurred to me that there were very few men left in the trench. I called out the names of individuals. 'They've had it,' came the reply. Even Huismann had been hit. Huismann: who was the most irrepressible of all. Tireless, always there when there was a need for endurance and courage; the one who could still laugh when others could hardly stand through tiredness. A comrade of rare quality, an enthusiastic patroller; a man always ready to lay his life on the line for others: he was no longer in his place...He limped past me, weak from loss of blood. We spoke briefly and he headed for the aid post. He waved and I had no idea that it was the last time we should greet one another...

"With my rifle at the ready I advanced along the trench. It was deserted! There was not trace of our right flank platoon. Suddenly I came across four British soldiers sitting in the trench. They immediately raised their hands. I called for Olbrich and the others, but there was no reply. The Tommies, who were unwounded, noticed this too, but I got back safely...I yielded to the opinion of Jakob and the Offizierstellvertreter that it was utterly foolish, in the circumstances, only to allow the Tommies to proceed over our nine corpses. At the time I felt like a whipped cur; I had to throw all my ideals overboard. I now believe this dreadful decision to have been justified, because the nine men who were still with me could be of far greater use to Germany alive than would be our bleaching bones in France...As the enemy approached, we lay down our arms."

Ground was also gained in the St Pierre Divion – Beaucourt area by the British 39th and 63rd (Naval) Division; Reserve Infantry Regiment 55 having been forced to withdraw to avoid encirclement and destruction in detail following the breakthrough in the area of Infantry Regiment 62. Here the attack came up against the survivors of Reserve Infantry Regiment 55, who had occupied the Schloss Stellung * as well as battalions of Ersatz Infantry Regiment 29 and Reserve Infantry Regiment 144 of the 223rd Infantry Division, which were still in the process of completing a relief in the line. The third regiment of the Division, Infantry Regiment 173, was initially in reserve, being called forward to man the Serre Riegel [Serre Stop Line]† during the early hours of 14th November.

*Reserve Leutnant Heckmann 2nd Company Infantry Regiment 173[21]* **9.**

"There was an enormous weight of artillery coming down to our front. All the approach routes were under very heavy fire. We double marched through Achiet le Petit. It was pouring with rain and the place was teeming with troops. Unluckily the company got caught behind an

---

*The Schloss Stellung [Chateau Position] guarded the western side of Beaucourt, running up the hillside towards Old Württemberg Redoubt.

† The Serre Riegel ran roughly eastwards, just to the south of Serre, until it linked with the II Puisieux Stellung [Position] which ran due north to Puisieux.

ammunition column. There were battery positions right and left of the road, which fired ceaselessly. This made life on the road very uncomfortable; it being hard to say if we were experiencing the sound of guns being fired, or enemy shells crashing down. To the front, near Puisieux, heavy shells were falling. The night was pitch- black; only from muzzle flashes was it possible to make out the surrounding area. We went into Brigade reserve behind Puisieux along the Kaiser Wilhelm Strasse. Nobody had a clue about what was happening."

Higher Commanders knew only too well what was happening. Ground had been lost to the south and south-east in the valley of the Ancre and it was crucial to contain, as much as possible, the British advance, which had already gained about two thousand metres. The next few days saw continuing fighting at local level as the British sought to consolidate their grip on the Beaucourt – Grandcourt sector. Heavy fighting during the morning of 14th November saw British artillery severing the links between the Schloss Stellung and Feste Alt-Württemberg [Old Württemberg Redoubt], but initial attempts to attack the Schloss Stellung, defended by Reserve Infantry Regiment 55, caused the British very high casualties. It is difficult to know how the Regiment would have fared in the event of a second massed attack from the west, because by mid-morning it had been outflanked, was under threat from the rear [east] and had to vacate its positions. There remained some doubt as to whether or not attempts were to be made to recapture Beaumont or Beaucourt, so Battalion Headquarters of 2nd Battalion Reserve Infantry Regiment 55 hung on in its dugout on the edge of the Artillery Hollow to the east of Beaucourt until late evening, even after it had been cut off, in order to ascertain if counter-action would be required. This led to several close encounters with the advancing British troops.

### *Hauptmann Minck 2nd Battalion Reserve Infantry Regiment 55[22]* **10.**

"From Battalion Headquarters, we could only look on as our senior Medical Officer, Dr Brummond, was led away by the British from a dugout, situated only 120 metres away. In the same way they ransacked a ration depot a mere forty to fifty metres from us. However the Unteroffizier in charge was able to make his escape through a second entrance and reached us safely. We kept the British at arms' length from us with rifle fire; then our own heavy artillery fire coming down on Beaucourt forced them to stay in cover. Because I still assumed that at least part of my Battalion was holding its original positions, I did not want to leave the Headquarters. At 11.45 pm, one of my runners, who had managed to sneak through, arrived with a copy of an order which made it clear that Beaucourt was completely in the hands of the enemy and that no attempt was to be made to regain it. The new defence line was defined [Kriegsministergraben-Fischergraben = Minister of War Trench - Fischer Trench], so there was nothing for it but to clear out of the dugout with my staff. We were the last out of Beaucourt at about midnight. We broke through the British lines, luckily without casualties, passing close to a double sentry position, which spotted us, but did not open fire."

Just to the south and east of Grandcourt the line was being held by Infantry Regiment 96. Attacks were launched from the direction of Stump Road, but did not enjoy equivalent success on 14th November. By mid-morning British attacks had petered out, as this report to the 2nd Battalion makes clear.

*Leutnant Spindler 6th Company Infantry Regiment 96*[23] **11.**

"The British attack which was launched this morning has been completely defeated. Not one section of trench has been lost. The Company performed brilliantly and I am proud to be able to lead such men. The lads shot as though they were on the range; frequently firing from standing positions in the open and cheering when the British attack collapsed. The British were then driven off with hand grenades. Ammunition resupply and the placement of the men in the recaptured trenches, was conducted with the greatest calm. It was as though we were out for a stroll and all the men are beaming with pleasure."

Luckily for the men from Thuringia, they were relieved before the final battle for Grandcourt. Up on the high ground above the Ancre valley, the Kriegsminister – Fischergraben position lacked every kind of feature to make it easily defensible. Infantry Regiment 25, which relieved the defenders up there  a few days later, commented, 'The positions that the Regiment held in 'Kriegsministergraben' and 'Fischergraben' had no dugouts at all, because earlier they were simply shallow communication trenches...Before the British broke in, they simply served as approach routes to the front line, which at that time was a long way off. A few destroyed artillery positions nearby had a few feeble dugouts. The majority of the companies lay in the open in shell holes, half full of water. The weather continued to be wet and cold and there were frequent night frosts.'[24]

It was a somewhat different story and altogether more successful for the defence a little to the north around Serre, where the regiments of 52nd Infantry Division were still holding the line. Compared with other parts of the Somme front, this particular sector had been relatively quiet since the early July battles, but it too was attacked during the battles of mid-November. Infantry Regiment 169 played a major role in the defence here, as did Infantry Regiment 66, returning to the front line for its third distinct tour of duty during the battle. The fighting, which was at close quarters, also began on 13th November, lasted for several days,  but ended with the repulse of the British army and with the Germans still in possession of Serre. In the initial confusion and thanks to the early morning fog, the first two trench lines of Infantry Regiment 66 were overrun to the north of the village – much to the embarrassment and annoyance of the battalion commander in that sector.

*Hauptmann Niemeyer 1st Battalion Infantry Regiment 66*[25] **12.**

"The whole business was very painful for me. I had not expected any such thing and I must admit, quite honestly, that my first thought was what on earth the Regimental Commander would have to say about this fine mess. I sat and considered my options. These were uncomfortable moments. Then I telephoned the Artillery Group, which was situated in rear on the western edge of Puisieux. This particular link was never interrupted at any moment during the Battle of the Somme. I conversed with the detachment commander for some time and ordered him to bring down destructive fire for ten minutes on the part of my two forward trenches which lay to the south of the Kaiser Wilhelm Hecke [Hedgerow]. I then briefed Kreidner, commander of the 4th Company, ordering him to launch an attack as soon as the artillery preparation was over and to eject the British from the Battalion sector. We watched as our shells came down on our own trenches. It was a painful sight. We then saw the men of the 4th Company climb out of the third trench and prepare to advance. We saw the short wiry figure of the unforgettable Kreidner, hurrying up and down in front of his company, exhorting and encouraging them, then the company launched its attack, with its commander way out in front."

*Offizierstellvertreter Collet 4th Company Infantry Regiment 66*[26] **12.**

"I lay with my platoon right and left of the Krosigweg [Krosigk Way]. Our company commander was with the Second Platoon, which straddled Borriesgraben [Borriesweg = Borries Way] and the Third Platoon was to the left on the Schüsslerweg [Schüssler Way]* in the third trench. The Third Platoon attacked around midday; going over the top in a truly heroic fashion, advancing astride Schüsslerweg into the midst of the battle that was raging to the front and capturing numerous prisoners. During this action Unteroffiziers Krüger from Magdeburg and Schmuhl from Halle proved themselves to be masters of trench fighting. At approximately the same time, our Second Platoon counter-attacked along the line of Borriesweg. Our new company commander, Leutnant Kreidner, left his mark here. He gave his men an incomparable example of courage and cold-blooded calm in counter-attack and close quarter battle. Our section of trench around Krosigkweg was under ceaseless heavy artillery fire throughout the entire day. It was no wonder that the British laid down their weapons to this little man. It was extremely hard work to get my platoon out of the third trench and to get them to advance fifty metres to where we lay completely unprotected. I led forward Vizefeldwebel Grund and two sections along the line of the Kaiser Wilhelm Hecke as far as the second trench, without the British noticing anything untoward to their

---

*These three trenches were all communication trenches, running roughly east – west, in the battalion sector just to the north of Serre. From south to north, the sequence was Schüsslerweg, Borriesweg and Krosigkweg. Schüsslerweg only connected the first three trenches, but the other two, which led back in the direction of Puisieux, were considerably longer. Collet's rendition of the names, which may have been from memory, is somewhat awry. The total attack frontage was about two hundred metres, but each platoon concentrated on one particular trench.

front. I left them lying there, having told them to wait until they heard my shouts of '*Hurra*' coming from the Krosigkweg. They should then join in and fall upon the British.

"Carefully I wormed my way with the remainder of my platoon along the hollow that was all that was left of the totally shot up Krosigkweg until we were just one good bound from the second trench. There we prepared for the final assault in a giant shell crater. Here I briefed my men that they were to bawl '*Hurra!*' at the tops of their voices, so as to create the impression that we were a large assault force. (The entire platoon comprised barely forty men). With a murderous yell, we fell upon the second trench. The effect on our opponents was catastrophic. The British jumped to the conclusion that they were utterly overwhelmed. They did not fire a single round. Swiftly we spread out along the trench as far as Kaiser Wilhelm Hecke and hauled the surprised British soldiers out of the dugouts. One of the first dugouts that I descended contained about twenty men. They stared at me as though I was a ghost. When I smiled, wished them a good evening and asked them what they wanted in our position, one man who could speak good German stepped forward as a spokesman and we soon understood one another. I was astonished to see two members of Infantry Regiment 170 emerge from around a corner. They had gone out early that morning to fetch coffee, but had been surprised by the attack and captured.

"We quickly extended our line to the left and made contact with our company commander who was coming towards us. We greeted each other joyfully. Then, collectively and making a great deal of noise, we launched ourselves at the front-line trench. I ordered every man to give orders in a loud voice and the entire platoon to make as much noise as possible. The British, deceived by this, thought that they were up against a powerful adversary and offered little resistance. It was not yet quite dark when I and my platoon had recaptured the entire sector. I had not lost one single man and at the same time the swift and decisive victory had filled my young soldiers with confidence that they were superior to the British. After this experience, I once more had command of an outstanding group of men, which made me feel myself to be master of the situation."

The performance of Infantry Regiment 66 earned them a mention in the Army Group Daily Report. 'The battle continues north of the Somme. From morning to night on 14th November, fighting went on in another in the series of major days of battle. Hoping to be able to exploit their initial success, the British attacked en masse north of the Ancre...at all other points along the wide frontage their attacks broke up in front of our positions with heavy losses. Infantry Regiment 66 from Magdeburg distinguished itself in particular by the way in which it beat off the enemy assault.'[27]

*Reserve Vizefeldwebel Spengler-Hugsweier Infantry Regiment 169*[28]  **13.**

"During the early morning [of 13th November]...fog lay thickly over everything, blinding us. Our eyes strained like daggers, trying to pierce this milky wall. There were four of us manning our machine gun, which was located five metres behind our front line trench. Ever since dawn, the enemy had been bringing down drum fire. All of a sudden it stopped, just as though it had been cut off with a giant knife. Our hearts were in our mouths, because we knew that they must come now! Outwardly we were calm. One of them was whistling through his teeth, another was pulling hard on a cigar, which he had not lit. I went below into the dugout and made some coffee. Without it everyone would have been collapsing from exhaustion. Finally the brown brew began to boil and I breathed in the aroma, in eager anticipation. Suddenly someone was yelling my name. I took one last glance at the coffee, which was now boiling over, then I was standing next to the gun, staring at ghostly figures who were there on all sides. They kept appearing then disappearing: in front, left and right and even in our rear! They had simply overrun the first trench, but my machine gun did a good job in all directions.

"The advancing figures checked, then fell back. Soon they were pressing forward once more, attempting to charge us with fixed bayonets. Then, damn it! At that precise moment I got a stoppage. We saw the triumphant gleam in the bloodshot eyes of the khaki-coloured soldiers who were charging at us. Did this mean that we had to resign ourselves to capture? Brave soldiers do not waste time thinking things like that; why else had we been issued with grenades? I felt quite calm and we rejoiced to see the British tumbling away [as the grenades exploded amongst them]. My men laughed out loud at each explosion. I could see a look of shame on their faces. We were but four and they were a great many. Bullets slammed in all around us. The thought ran through my mind, 'I wonder if I shall be killed instantly if I am hit?' My mind was a whirl as a multitude of images rose and fell within it. My life flashed before my eyes, as one grenade after another was pressed into the palm of my hand. I pulled and threw constantly; to the front, to the right and to the left! Crash, crash, crash! Were they never going to leave us alone? Were they simply going to wait until we had no grenades left?

"No, all of a sudden the whole lot disappeared into the fog like ghosts, the way they had come. I felt overcome by sleepiness. I could hardly move. Sleep, just let me sleep! It had been endless torture since June and now it was November! Now there was a new danger. The enemy artillery opened up again violently; impact after impact, crash upon crash: ever faster, ever heavier. We had to pull back out of it. We leapt up and ran, weaving, tripping and ducking from one shell hole to another. On one occasion I touched a shell splinter and burnt my finger. Shards of iron whizzed past our ears, we were out of breath. No words were spoken. The wide open eyes of my men spoke clearly enough. The race for life or death began once more. Breath whistled into our lungs through clenched teeth. Finally we were through the fire zone and saved. It was a miracle: God be praised!"

*Unteroffizier Otto Lais Infantry Regiment 169*[29] **13.**

"It was raining, it was freezing. There was fog everywhere: thick November fog. Each day brought its share of casualties. Every night the ration parties and the messengers ran for their lives; the food containers were usually half-empty as a result of the haste. One week had already passed at a high state of alert; a second was almost at an end. When would the enemy attack? At dawn on 13th November there was thick, absolutely dense fog. The daily bombardment began at 4.00 am. Were we deceiving ourselves, or was the drum fire heavier than ever? It came to a halt, at 7.00 am, just as it had on previous days...We emerged from the dugouts and tried to orientate ourselves. Fire was now falling only on and to the rear of Serre. It was impossible to see five paces to the front...After 9.00 am the fog thinned a little and it was possible to see about ten to twenty paces. From the front-line trench could be heard the sound of the odd burst of machine-gun fire or the occasional rifle shot, but then everything was still once more...One of the sappers felt a stirring in his bowels and settled down, with trousers unbuttoned, in a shell hole about twenty paces down towards the valley...Suddenly he appeared, running through the fog, bleeding from a wound caused by an infantry bullet which had grazed the back of his hand.

"'Unteroffizier, there are British soldiers down below us!' 'Don't talk rubbish, man. That was just a stray bullet. Have you seen any British?' – 'No.' – 'Have you heard small arms fire nearby?' – 'No.' Nevertheless he continued to insist that there were British soldiers down in the valley... I called on my gunner, Mall (from Sollingen)...'Hey you, come with me. Let's go and see what's happening.' We were both firmly convinced that the sapper had been wounded by chance and that the rest was imagination... We grabbed our gas masks and set off... By a stroke of luck we stumbled over a box of grenades belonging to the sappers. We placed two on our belts and set off, in twenty paces' visibility, along the trench carrying two more each... We could see nothing and hear nothing apart from the howling and growling of shells passing overhead to explode with dull thuds in the rear... We unscrewed the safety devices of our stick grenades. Thirty metres further on we found ourselves behind a shot-up parapet... Mall pulled me down by my belt and simultaneously we both shouted, 'Take cover!' We immediately threw our grenades half right, where they exploded, together with British ones which had landed all round us. Twenty paces half right we could make out the outline of flat British steel helmets behind the edge of a crater. We threw our remaining grenades and, taking advantage of the cover provided by the communication trench, we were soon back at our weapon.

"'Everyone out! – Stand to! – Pass me a sandbag! – Load!' The trigger is pressed then Tack! Tack! Tack!... rounds from the weapon crack out over the craters. The British did not follow up but, ducking down in the crater, threw grenades. As they later explained when we had captured them, they, like us, had become disorientated in the fog. Some of us threw grenades, whilst three others operated the gun. Sandbag up on the parapet – gun in position. First here, then there – Mount gun! – Keep your head down! – Raise the muzzle! Aim! Fire! Up in the air first, then bring the muzzle down gradually – spread the fire right across the craters! In the face of this hail of fire, the British soldiers crouch down in the deepest part of the craters. Quick, out of the trench and throw grenades before the belt is fired off. – Load with a new belt! Now the same again! – What's happening? Why are our grenades not exploding? – They have not been primed – pass the detonators – fit them. Our otherwise great sappers have fouled things up – Goddamn them! Thinking that back in the third and fourth trench, they were almost in the rear area, they had only primed one box of grenades. The remainder were not ready for use and, as a result, before we noticed anything we had thrown more than one salvo of them as duds into the surrounding shell holes. It was a nightmare when they did not explode.

"In no time the grenades are primed. Stand by! Muzzle up! Safety catch off! Fire! Lower! The earth kicks up all around the edges of the crater twenty metres away down the slope. Six of us, machine gunners and sappers, pull the initiation cords on our grenades... twenty-one... twenty-two... Up out of cover and throw – We are not beginners and we throw air bursts. The British are in cover too deep for normal ground bursts. In the meantime Mall hares six metres down the trench and turns off at the junction with the fourth trench. We see him briefly, silhouetted above cover, only a few metres from the thickly occupied crater. He throws two grenades in, one after the other then jumps back into the trench. Blam – Blam! – screams. With hands raised they all emerge. All of them are wounded, two seriously. Two are lying still in the bottom of the crater. It was a strong assault group. Köhler, our youngest member bandages them up then we place them below in the dugout. All around small groups are taking cover in both small and large shell holes. A few at a time, we reel them in. They are the best of British assault forces – Royal Scots – all of them totally lost in the fog. They did not just give in. They defended themselves bravely, but they were completely uncoordinated and got in each other's way. Our heavy machine gun, firing from such close range, demoralised them completely. As a result, our handful of defenders (eight machine gunners and six sappers) wiped them out, even though we were outnumbered more than ten to one.

"In the meantime the wind in the valley had dispersed the fog somewhat and we could see one hundred to one hundred and fifty metres. This enabled us to fire very precisely at individual craters. Emerging from the Heidenkopf [Quadrilateral] and from the battalion trenches, our infantry moved forward against them. They were surrounded and captured to a man. On all sides our hand grenade troops closed in on the British. As the visibility improved, the machine guns from the Heidenkopf joined in with us. The British were caught in a witch's cauldron. Unholy confusion prevailed amongst them. They wanted to break through but, caught in cross fire from three machine guns, they did not get ten metres. Taking cover in the crater field they cowered in the shell holes and, in their section groups, were wiped out or captured..."

On 18 November there was a further concentrated effort to capture Soden Redoubt and thus open the way to Serre from the south. Conditions were similar to those which had obtained four days previously and, in confused fighting, the British enjoyed some success. Countermoves, in particular vigorous use of artillery, prevented any significant advance and the fighting died down with fairly heavy casualties on both sides.

*Reserve Hauptmann Achilles 3rd Battalion Reserve Infantry Regiment 77*[30] **13.**

"At 7.00 am [18 November] extremely heavy drumfire came down south of Feste Soden [Soden Redoubt]...A report to this effect was passed by telephone to the Regiment, but then the line was destroyed. At 7.30 am the cry of, 'Gas Alarm!' went round, but it was false; the early ground mist had been mistaken for a gas cloud. Simultaneously the machine gun from Infantry Regiment 65, which was stationed on top of the Battalion command post, opened up rapid fire. Suddenly British soldiers appeared right in front of our command post. By the time the first attempt was made to reach the exit, hand grenades had been thrown in. The grenades silenced the machine gun and wounded, on the left, Reserve Leutnant Lüders and, on the right, Gefreiter Blume. Two men from Infantry Regiment 65 fell dead down into the entrance. An attempt was made to contact the nearby machine-gun officer, to request assistance, but this link was broken as well. There was no escape. The telephonists destroyed the telephone at the very last minute. We had to lay down our arms and, under the direction of the British Lieutenant Davidson of the Manchester Regiment of the 32nd Division, we were led across country through our own and the enemy's artillery fire, in the direction of Beaumont.

"We were accompanied by two battalion staffs which had already been captured, including Hauptmann Sattig from 2nd Battalion Infantry

Regiment 65. There were also several machine-gun officers. Moving across the battlefield, which was one mass of shell craters, the guides lost direction and ended up very near to Feste Soden [Soden Redoubt]. We spotted German soldiers in the trenches. The officers of the staff made a break for it individually and regained the German trenches. Later the other officers and NCOs were also freed. During this action those British soldiers, who had not been shot down on the way, went into German captivity, amongst them the Lieutenant.[31] Extremely heavy artillery fire was still coming down ceaselessly on the trenches... The Landwehrgraben [Territorial Army Trench], which linked Feste Soden and the Battalion command post, was cleared of small pockets of enemy by patrols of Infantry Regiment 121. We returned to the command post, but only came across stragglers and machine gunners, including two officers, from Infantry Regiment 169. There were still no telephone links. Because neither telephonists nor runners were available, at 1.00 am the battalion commander, accompanied by Leutnant Kohlhoff, went to Regimental Headquarters of Infantry Regiment 169 to make a report. The request to provide runners and telephonists, so that the Battalion command post could be re-established, was not agreed, because nobody could be spared. In addition, because 3rd Battalion Reserve Infantry Regiment 77 had already been subordinated to another Battalion staff, Infantry Regiment 169 released us to move to Courcelles [-le-Comte]. Lieutenant Davidson, whom we had escorted there, was handed over to Infantry Regiment 169."

Down in the valley of the Ancre, the final scenes of the Battle of the Somme were about to be played out as the British II and V Corps launched assaults. With sleet and snow blowing in an icy wind, the conditions were about the worst of the entire battle. The German 56th Division was in the process of relieving the 58th Division, so the situation was somewhat confused. One of the principal objectives on the right of II Corps was that of the 4th Canadian Division, which was to assault from Regina Trench, to storm and take a series of trenches leading northwards towards Miraumont. The German defenders failed completely to recognise that a great many Canadian troops were involved, so all their accounts simply speak of 'British soldiers.' The defensive layout here was complex, inherently strong and subtly arranged. Even the British Official History does not portray it quite correctly.[32] Located about 300 metres north of Regina Trench was the Alter Dessauer Riegel [Old Dessau Stop Line = Desire Trench]. This trench was only manned by patrols, whose business it was to deceive the Allies about the position of the front line, by firing off flares, light mortars and bursts of fire from time to time. As a result, during the build up, this trench was heavily pounded by artillery to no effect. An average of 150 metres to the north was another trench, dug more or less as an eastern extension of Kleine Mulde [Little Gully], an eastern branch of Stallmulde [Stable Hollow] located about 650 metres south of and parallel to Baum Mulde [Boom Ravine]. This trench was named Dessauer

Riegel/Leipziger Riegel [Dessau/Leipzig Stop Line = Desire Support]. A further one hundred metres to the north and parallel to Dessauer Riegel lay the Grimmaer Riegel [Grimma Stop Line], which was partially wired during the days before 18th November.

The final depth was provided by the Grandcourt Riegel itself [Grandcourt Stop Line = Grandcourt Trench] and machine gun positions along the line of Baum Mulde [Boom Ravine]. Leading forward to link all these trenches were three routes: The principal ones were Westweg [West Way] and Ostweg, [Eastern Way]. The Ostweg followed the line of the D107 from Miraumont to Courcelette and the Westweg the modern track about 500 metres to its west. In addition, just to the west of the Ostweg was the Courcelette Riegel [Courcelette Stop Line]. Despite a ferocious defence of the sector, largely on the part of Infantry Regiment 106, whose machine guns took a terrible toll of the attacking troops, the Canadian and British troops made some progress. In places the German defenders launched minor counterattacks but, by the evening of 18 November, Infantry Regiments 106 and 107 from Saxony, were largely out of ammunition, partially outflanked and had either been pushed back to the Grandcourt Riegel [Grandcourt Stop Line], or had been ordered to withdraw there.

*Leutnant Moltke 1st Company Infantry Regiment 106*[33] **14.**

"At 7.00 am we came under extraordinarily heavy drum fire, which lasted fifteen to twenty minutes. The trench sentries spotted, in good time that the British had advanced in large groups under its cover, to within seventy-five metres of our position. Our well-aimed rifle and machine-gun fire forced them back to Dessauer Riegel [Desire Trench]. From there they attempted until 10.00 am to renew their attack. At 10.30 am a patrol, which I had despatched...to Courcelette Riegel [Courcelette Stop Line], reported that the British were occupying positions two hundred metres to our left I handed over responsibility for left flank protection to Panzer's Section, which easily beat off an attempt at 2.00 pm to roll up our position from the left. Unteroffizier Krause had a very hard time of it out on the right flank, because the British attacked again and again from the Westweg [West Way]. The heavy fire of this group, who greeted each succeeding attack with, 'Here come the swine again!' nipped every attempt in the bud.

"As the pressure on my right flank increased and the British pushed forward in ever-increasing numbers in the neighbouring sector, I judged the moment to be right to despatch the machine gun under Gefreiter Albrecht to the right. His effective fire destroyed all further enemy attacking intentions in this area as well. During the afternoon, I sent several men back, requesting ammunition and reinforcements. By the time evening fell nothing had arrived, so at 5.15 pm I withdrew my three sections, the machine gun and a captured British soldier to the Grandcourt Riegel."

*Gefreiter Albrecht 1st Machine Gun Company Infantry Regiment 106*[34] **14.**

"At 7.00 am on 18 November drumfire came down on our position, which forced all the sentries into cover. At 7.30 am, despite the heavy artillery fire, I attempted to exit the dugout to see what the enemy was doing. I saw an extraordinary sight. The British were advancing on our trenches in section groups. The closest of them were no more than thirty metres from us. I immediately ordered my gun crew to take post and hurled three hand grenades at the first of the enemy columns, which brought their advance to a halt. In a few seconds the machine gun was set up and had opened fire. We laid down fire across the sector five hundred metres to our front and we also fired flanking fire half right of our position. To our left, we only had a one hundred metre field of fire, because the ground dropped away to the left.

"Once we had fired 500 rounds, I oiled the hot gun with the contents of two small tins of weapon cleaning grease. I covered all the working parts in this way and, because they were hot, the grease immediately melted and substituted for oil. In a short time we were ready to fire once more. After we had fired a further 500 rounds, the enemy to our front had been dealt with. I had already proposed to Leutnant Moltke that he send a section from his platoon to the right to occupy the Westweg and so prevent the enemy from advancing in this area. This he felt he was too weak to do, because he had received no reserves from the rear. But because the British had broken through in the area of Reserve Infantry Regiment 120 to the right [west] of the Westweg, I moved my machine gun 200 metres to the right and went into position along the Westweg. From here we brought down enfilade fire to the right [west]. Here, too, we were able to prevent any advance by fresh troops. We then had a dangerous stoppage (split cartridge case), but we were able to clear it quickly. Once we had fired off approximately 500 more rounds we had to change the working parts. With the firing of approximately 1,000 rounds, we caused the enemy heavy casualties and put an end to his desire to advance in this area... When it went dark, we returned to Leutnant Moltke's platoon, bringing with us the machine gun, two boxes of ammunition, the water container, as well as all the spare parts. Without having suffered any casualties, we easily made it back to the Grandcourt Riegel..."

*Unteroffizier Krause 1st Company Infantry Regiment 106*[35]

"The British had broken into neighbouring sectors to the left and right and attempted to roll up the 1st Company from the left and right. Due to their overwhelming strength, they had some success on the right flank, where the garrison had all been killed, wounded, or buried alive. On the left, on the other hand, the remnants of three sections put up spirited resistance. Towards 10.00 am, the British, by throwing in even more forces, succeeded in setting foot on the ground to the left [east] of the Westweg. Taking a swift decision, accompanied by Gefreiter Bischoff and two men, I charged them, threw hand grenades and immediately cleared the trench back as far as the Westweg. The British retreated en masse. Some went to the right [west] of the road, the remainder fell back to the former company commander's dugout, where they apparently attempted to reorganise. This offered us a superb opportunity to pour fire into this group: there must have been thirty to forty men altogether. Because of the casualties we inflicted...they pulled back in tactical bounds to the Dessauer Riegel [Desire Support], where they reformed.

"Towards midday the pressure on the right flank built up even more... The machine gun, which up until then had been located in the centre of the position, was moved to the right flank, where it continued to hold the British in check... The machine gun only engaged large groups, but we fired at individuals. Every single British soldier was fired at, including those who were escorting prisoners to the British positions. In this way large numbers of our men were released once more from captivity. The machine gun unfortunately suffered rather a large number of stoppages – the gradual lack of water being substituted by the use of red wine and schnaps from our rations...'

*Leutnant Schulze 1st Machine Gun Company Infantry Regiment 106*[36] **14.**

"Commanding three machine guns of 1st Machine Gun Company, I had occupied Baummulde [Boom Ravine] on 17th November. By then, however, it did not deserve its name, because only the occasional stump stuck up above the shell-ploughed earth... Upon receiving the alarm report from Reserve Infantry Regiment 120 that the enemy had broken into Dessau Riegel [Desire Support], I ordered my three weapons to take up fire positions. The first gun (Unteroffizier Schrödter) blocked Stallmulde [Stable Hollow], the second (Gefreiter Bodle) fired in enfilade towards Westweg and the third (Unteroffizier Schmalfuß) covered forward over the Grandcourt Riegel. Thick fog obscured the visibility. Towards 11.00 am, it cleared somewhat and we could make out troops massing in Stallmulde prior to moving towards us...As this was happening, we came unexpectedly under fire from the hill to our right rear, which had previously been occupied by Infantry Regiment 96. The right hand gun (Unteroffizier Schrödter) quickly cleared the endangered flank of the enemy, causing severe casualties but, by opening fire, we had betrayed our positions to the enemy. A few minutes later Baummulde heaved under the impact of super-heavy shells. Nevertheless we continued to man our guns. Our steel helmets proved themselves now. By evening a number had been dented, but none penetrated.

"Things became a little calmer, but then an extraordinary sight opened up before our eyes. Several British soldiers approached us under a Red Cross flag, but because it was being carried so close to the ground, it raised my suspicions and I directed all three guns to aim at it. I then sent a man towards the flag carrier. They allowed him to approach to within ten metres. Suddenly the flag disappeared and from behind it a cocked and loaded machine gun opened fire on us: only for a few seconds, because our machine guns joined in and soon silenced the enemy weapon...[37] For my men it was now a simple matter, once the machine gun had been dealt with, to keep the enemy infantry in Stallmulde under destructive fire and they were gradually forced back over the hill in front of the Grandcourt Riegel to the Kleine Mulde [Little Gully]..."

A little to the east, south of Pys, Infantry Regiment 88 also came under a great deal of pressure throughout the early stages of the attack. After launching a counter-attack, by evening it was occupying positions astride the Pys-Courcelette road and further forward. There it stayed until 7 January 1917.

*Reserve Leutnant A E Weber 1st Battalion Infantry Regiment 88*[38] **15.**

"On 17th November came the word that we were to move up into the line once more. One after the other, at a trot, we followed a narrow path during the evening through the ruins of the village of Pys. It was under heavy artillery fire, which was directed against its exits in particular. In this place, where there were already a great many dead, our guide from Infantry Regiment 107 was unfortunately killed. We had to hurry over him to get away from this place of danger. We relieved a company on the right, which was holding terribly battered trenches, but then we had to swap sectors, which meant that we got very little sleep during this moonlit night. On the 18th November the last great British attack took place. A hail of drumfire descended on us, but luckily we had managed to locate one mined-out dugout. The ground was absolutely ploughed up by shells, so that we thought every moment would be our last. Finally the British lifted their fire further to the rear. The infantry attack followed and we were able to beat it off. Only to our right were the Tommies able to break into our line and we moved over in that direction to reinforce [the garrison]. In the meantime, during the morning, the 2nd Battalion moved forward in open order across country downhill between Miraumont and Pys to occupy our position. Because of the muddy morass through which we had to wade, our weapons were almost all inoperable; only our grenades saved us. Despite heavy artillery fire, we launched a counter-attack, which drove the British back, at the cost of many casualties to ourselves. Finally, towards evening, we were pulled back from this area which was devoid of cover into the Grandcourt Riegel [Grandcourt Stop Line].

"Further minor line-straightening attacks by the Allies took place on 19th November, but all failed, shot to a standstill by artillery. Most of the day was given over to clearing the wounded from the battlefield; two full medical companies, supported by a large number of ambulances, being employed on the fronts of Infantry Regiment 106 and Reserve Infantry Regiment 120 alone.[39] After a lengthy period of trench duty and having performed well, Infantry Regiment 106 was happy to hand over to Fusilier Regiment 35. The loss of the forward positions on 18th November was rationalised later by the Regiment, who stated, 'A Divisional order directed that the Grandcourt Riegel was to be held as the front line, which meant that a very much better position could be handed over to Infantry [sic] Regiment 35, which relieved us, than the ploughed up, non-continuous line that we had taken over...Without the slightest difficulty, Infantry Regiment 35 assumed control of the sector on 20th November and after twenty-five hard days of fighting, the Regiment was withdrawn.'[40] Fusilier Regiment 35 had a slightly different version of the story to tell.

*Reserve Leutnant Kurt Schröder 9th Company Fusilier Regiment 35*[41] **14.**

"A guide was waiting for us near Miraumont. We followed in single file along a shell-damaged and muddy track. It was already past midnight by the time I was standing in the dugout of the company commander I was due to relieve. He was as relaxed as only a man nurtured in Saxony can be. 'We are here in the second trench', he declared. 'I have no idea where the front line is. It's probably a bit further forward. I have only been here for two days myself. I do not have a map. My left flank is hanging in the air. There are communication trenches leading forward from that point, which is where the runners are located. By the way there is a rumour that the company commander of the front line company has a dugout somewhere forward of the position. Well, I wish you luck. Good bye.' With that he was off, hard on the heels of his Saxons, who had long since disappeared.

"We were on our own resources for orientation; a hopeless undertaking in the dark. Patrols which were sent out returned without having accomplished anything. Apart from shell craters as deep as houses, they had been unable to locate a road, an adjoining company, or even the extension of our own trench. We just had to wait for morning. Just as the grey dawn began to break in the distance, there was a great burst of firing from the direction of the enemy. In our own area there were cracks, whizzes, rumbling and roaring which did not bode well...What's up? Nobody has any idea! To our front is a flat-topped rise, over which we cannot see and on the other side of the hill heavy artillery fire is coming down; the overs keep landing around us. Soon it becomes clear to us that there are Tommies, not Saxons in front of us. We had laid down to sleep in the second line and had woken up in the front line. 'Herr Leutnant! There is good observation from the communication trench twenty metres forward. Everywhere is swarming with Tommies. We must post sentries there!' reported Unteroffizier Weber. 'I'll come at once with you!' Swiftly I prepare a report for the Battalion, tell four men of the assault group to get ready then, with pistol and hand grenades at the ready, I head off.

"From here we could really see that the British were already digging in determinedly. A long stretch of what was now the enemy front line could be made out clearly. After the four men had been posted in positions of observation, I said to Weber, 'There had better be a leutnant and another full section here. We need to keep an eye on events. You cover out to the flanks and I will do the same to the front...' Then I came across a covered dugout. Pointing my pistol, I ripped off the groundsheet ...Germans! 'Where's your leutnant?' – 'Another fifty metres forward.' Further on. – Another covered hole. 'Where's your leutnant?' – 'Here right next to us.' Right, there was indeed another dugout there; before it stood a man with three hand grenades. I slithered down into the hole and found a bearded leutnant with a haggard face. I could see at once that he was unbalanced, hovering on the verge of madness. 'I'll give you a piece of good advice. Take your ten men and disappear. My company will take over the defence of this communication trench.' Highly indignant, he refused. He would stay and he could not be induced to move.

"Then something occurred which helped. Suddenly from above came the shout, 'Out, out, here come the Tommies!' The nest emptied like the wind. The Saxons were nimbler than I. In fact a few British steel helmets were approaching the trench. A few swiftly thrown hand grenades were enough to cover our return to where the sentries were posted. But where were they? Had they been taken off by the Saxons? Only Weber was still at my side but, hang it all, we were not going to buckle in just like that. 'Hold on the 35th!' I roared, 'Stay here!' At this a fusilier, admittedly only one, stood firm, grenades at the ready and waited for his leutnant. Now just think about it. He stood firm where his comrades had fled, where a dozen or more had run past him to the rear. That was worth a cross of iron. Swiftly the three of us blocked the trench. A knife rest lying near made a good barricade. Weber had to go further to the rear and move the assault group forward, because this point was valuable and had to be defended, even though it was a good two hundred metres in front of the position."

Apart from a final failed attempt on 22nd November by units of the British 96 Brigade to rescue the remnants of a company of the Highland Light Infantry, who were stranded in a section of Frankfurt trench, by 20 November the Allies had given up any further thoughts of continuing the attack, contenting themselves with holding on to their gains and continuing to nag away at the defence with artillery fire and psychological pressure. 'It has become known that British patrols are dropping letters to our front, in which soldiers in British captivity praise the treatment they are receiving. Similar letters are also being dropped by aircraft behind the front. These letters bear the real addresses of relatives of prisoners. The whole lot are forgeries. Their production-line origins are evident, because it can be detected that they are made by the use of a script-like printing process. A number of different letters of this type have been found in the regimental sector.'[42] Physically exhausted and emotionally drained, the poor unfortunate infantry of both sides held on in the clinging mud. Cold, icy winds knifed through sleet and driving rain, chilling them to the bone; almost beyond the will to live. It took almost all their effort to ward off illness and exposure and many succumbed. If they had any energy left even to think about their opponents, as often as not during these early winter days, they were thoughts of sympathy for the lot of their fellow sufferers. Down in the area of Grandcourt and Pys, the men of Fusilier Regiment 35 and Infantry Regiment 88 hunched down under their steel helmets and waited for the misery to end.

*Gefreiter von Stradonitz 9th Company Fusilier Regiment 35*[43] **14.**

"In order to look for markers amongst the confusion of shell holes for a planned patrol, I crawled out into No Man's Land in the early dawn, only to bump unexpectedly into an enemy advanced sap. I had the presence of mind to launch straight into a conversation with them in English, complaining bitterly about the filthy weather. This developed into an exchange of cigarettes and a conversation, during the course of which the two enemy sentries proposed that they would not take me prisoner if I gave them a German steel helmet, because, 'they were better than the British ones.' I took my leave of the Australians, saying 'All right' and went back to our trench, where I quickly explained to my company commander what was happening and returned with a somewhat battered helmet that was lying around. This I exchanged with the Australian sentry, who had now been joined by several others. I received a rather rusty British helmet for an epaulette button bearing the number '2' and I took careful note of the regimental insignia of the enemy, whilst wearing no regimental number myself. As a result, having returned 'home', the company commander of 9th Company Fusilier Regiment 35 was able to pass on a welcome report. So my swift recollection of the language saved me a night reconnaissance and brought me promotion to Unteroffizier that very night..."*

*Musketier Renzing 7th Company Infantry Regiment 88*[44] **15.**

"The front line was a roughly hacked-out trench. There were hardly any properly constructed positions. The weather was cold and rainy... so

---

* Stradonitz was lucky to be promoted. He certainly did not locate Australians. If the unit involved was not British, it must have been Canadian.

there was never any lack of chilly, wet conditions and clinging filth... The performance of our carrying parties... was beyond all praise. Even though trench duty was extremely hard in these awful weather conditions, it was far worse for our comrades, who had to make their way from our rest location to the front line and back, at least once per day. They had to endure rain, mud and constant artillery fire as they struggled forward with heavy loads of food, coffee and mail. One related incident has remained with me ever since. The 7th Company carrying party was under the command of the gallant Gefreiter Daniel Schmitt from Neckarsteinach. One evening the whole company pulled back to our rest position and we spent what was left of the night in a deep dugout. The following morning when I left the dugout, still groggy with sleep, hardly awake, I suddenly bumped into our brigade commander, Oberst von Dieringshausen. He asked me where the company carrying party was located. I led the commander to a dugout, which was barely more than a hole and which was so low that it was barely possible to sit upright in it. A groundsheet, from which two legs stuck out, covered the entrance. By pulling hard on these legs and shouting, I was able with some difficulty to rouse the sleepers who, utterly exhausted after the exertions of the night, were sleeping the sleep of the dead. Gefreiter Schmitt then paraded his section in front of the dugout. They stood there before their brigade commander, hollow cheeked, worn out, unwashed, unshaven, in the shreds of their torn and ripped clay-covered uniforms. He looked at them, shocked at their appearance, shook his head and said nothing more than, 'Boys, you are going to be relieved at the very first opportunity!' Neither the weather, the filth or the vermin were able to bring Daniel Schmitt low; he died of the flu after he returned to the homeland."

*Reserve Leutnant Kurt Schröder 9th Company Fusilier Regiment 35*[45]  **14.**

"It was a constant tough battle against rain, snow, mud and more mud. The battle line was dug along the line of shell craters, which filled up with water. All day long the men stood in the morass, their roof nothing more than tent halves. Their rifles, caked with filth and unusable, served as tent poles. The elements were a stronger force than discipline or the will of the commanders. The boots of many men were simply sucked off their feet and remained lost and beyond recovery in the mud. Many wore a look of total despair. Each platoon had to stick this out for forty eight hours at a time: an eternity. I arranged for cognac, as much as I could get my hands on, to be brought forward for the troops. I took a bottle and went from man to man, talking to them and consoling them with thoughts of relief. Was it any wonder, however, that one morning a sentry post was empty, that all that was left were two rifles and knapsacks? We commanders were content if we could just get our men to stick it out. Effective defence of the position was simply out of the question. It was fortunate that it was hardly better for those opposite. When the rain was simply too awful to bear, then peace reigned for a few hours in the two lines and friend and foe climbed out of their holes, at least to have a good stretch..."

*Reserve Leutnant Michaelsen 1st Company Fusilier Regiment 35*[46] **14.**

"Hardly has the weather cleared and the trench dried out a little, than the aviators come over and the shooting starts again. Is it better to wish for good weather and [artillery] fire or bad weather and bottomless filth? I cannot begin to describe our mud bath to you; it's hopeless. It rained again last night; it really would be best to pull out of the entire position and leave the mud to the Tommies. But it's just as bad for the Tommies. The infantry of both sides has given up doing anything to each other. It is all they can do to keep the mud at bay. In broad daylight, both we and the enemy climb out above our cover and nobody fires..."

It was almost impossible to maintain health and fitness in such conditions. In the closing weeks of the year, illness of one kind or another was almost universal. Little could be provided in the way of relief, even though in peacetime the great majority of the soldiers would have been on the sick list. Two short, but related reports from a regiment stationed near Serre in December sum up a widespread problem.

*Oberstleutnant Hoderlein Bavarian Infantry Regiment 4*[47] **9.**

*Reports to 8 Bavarian Infantry Brigade Concerning the Health of the Troops.*

*12 December 1916*

"The battalions have forwarded reports concerning the current state of health and I feel it my duty to bring these to your attention. The regiment has now been in the line without relief since 26th November. Because of the adverse weather all types of colds, chills and gastro-intestinal illnesses have appeared. Despite every effort to improve the lot of the troops, it has proved impossible to counter these illnesses, or to prevent them from spreading. The freezing wet and cold weather, wet dugouts, work in flooded trenches with mud a metre deep, extremely strenuous carrying duties to transport rations and trench stores, frequently over bottomless tracks across country, or through mud-filled trenches and not rarely in the face of extremely heavy enemy artillery fire, are all causes for the increased incidence of chills and hence illness, as is saturated clothing, underwear and boots which never dry out. The strength of officers and men in the front line has been greatly degraded by such illnesses. Warm food and the issue of red wine and schnaps are insufficient to counteract the essential warmth they need.

"It is also important not to overlook or underestimate what the troops, with good will and using all their strength have satisfactorily achieved.

Nevertheless their appearance is bad. The troops all complain of exhaustion, headaches and nausea. To delay [relief] until the men are at the limit of their strength, until their efficiency and morale is so lowered that the appropriate defence of the position is endangered, seems to me to be questionable. Serre is far too important a place for that. The influence and energy of my experienced and senior battalion commanders is beyond all praise. The continuing effectiveness of their troops is entirely due to them. I am putting forward their reports for notation because they provide a true picture of the condition of the troops. In the present situation and because of the very poor weather, I am of the opinion that the tour of duty cannot be allowed to exceed two weeks, even if part of the regiment can be rested from time to time. Therefore it is my duty as commander of the regiment, to make you aware that if the exhaustion and lassitude of officers and men increase any further, any enemy attack will not be countered with the necessary high degree of efficiency. I therefore request that the entire regiment be withdrawn to rest in a timely manner."

### 18th December 1916

"Even though there has not been a notable increase of men being evacuated sick, the condition of the troops in the position has deteriorated markedly. The lengthy period of duty has had a considerable effect upon their physical and mental strength. The morale of the officers, NCOs and men is generally sound, despite the fact that all are exhibiting signs of complete exhaustion, which is doing nothing to lift spirits. Good food is contributing to morale; it is certainly encouraging men to hang on in their positions and to give of their best. Today is the twenty eighth day of this tour of duty and, with the exception of the three companies pulled back in reserve, the cramped dugouts mean that in all that time the men have only been able to rest in a sitting position. The dugouts are damp and wet. The mens' uniforms, especially boots and trousers, are soaking wet and covered with mud, so that leather and cloth are beginning to rot on the man. It is impossible to clean anything on the position. Almost the entire regiment, from the youngest soldier to the most senior officer, is lousy and covered with matted filth. Every single man has a cold; only the severity varies. The current conditions are such that the duties a man has to perform with a carrying party or when digging trenches are extraordinarily hard, because men sink up to their knees with every step, frequently only being able to extract themselves at the price of their boots. (This has been especially the case for the fourth platoons of each company, who are acting as carrying parties).

"In addition to these physical exertions, it must also be stressed that prolonged duty on the position in the current conditions is wearing down both officers and men and it is extremely difficult to take measures against this. In my view a six day period in a rearward reserve position does not offer much in the way of rest and recuperation for the troops. The physical and mental strain caused by the marches to and fro on bottomless tracks, whilst subject to constant artillery concentrations, are enormous on troops in this condition. In addition, it has been reported to me that the accommodation in the rear is very poor, offering little in the way of recuperation. According to the commander of 3rd Battalion Bavarian Infantry Regiment 4, the essential delousing equipment at Gomiécourt was still not working on the third day of rest, with the result that the men could not be cleansed from the plague of lice and, further, that the reserve underwear, which the men had been keeping in their knapsacks, is now also lousy. I can provide no further detailed information from here on the position...The regiment is still holding the line, as it always has. However its ability to do battle or to attack is gradually sinking, as is the general resistance of officers and men, to such an extent that goodwill alone is insufficient to compensate."

This assessment was repeated in various forms elsewhere as fears rose concerning the long-term effects of this type of exposure.

*Reserve Stabsarzt Doctor Roeder Infantry Regiment 88*[48] **15.**

"In my previous report I stated my fear that because of the continuing extremely bad weather conditions in this sector [Grandcourt], if the same troops continue to be committed here, then a great many of those still on the position are likely to have to be permanently invalided out of the army. Many of the men are having to stand up to their knees in water. Because of the constant wet conditions, the dugouts are extremely unhealthy places, which lead to serious lung disease, rheumatism in the joints and to kidney infections. I can already prove on the basis of the sick list, which has still not diminished in size, that a large number of such illnesses has already appeared. In my capacity as a doctor I must make it quite clear that if the battalions which are currently deployed have to remain in their current positions, the consequence will be a considerable diminution in their value as fighting troops."

Despite the trials and tribulations of front-line duty in winter after months of battle, by the middle of December a general impression began to spread throughout the German army that the Allies had abandoned the attempt to break through, or even to continue their attacks through the winter. On 17th December, Crown Prince Rupprecht issued the following order:[49]

"Headquarters
Army Group Crown Prince Rupprecht of Bavaria
Operations Division Nr. 1812 Secret

"Operations appear to have come to a halt in the Battle of the Somme.

It is not clear when or if they will be resumed. I am making use of this pause to express my gratitude to and recognition of all commanders and troops.

The battle lasted almost five months. Exploiting their numerical superiority and deploying an extraordinary quantity of matériel, the enemy sought to break through and attacked repeatedly. In the face of the heroic courage displayed by the First and Second Armies, each attempt failed; the only gain being a narrow strip of utterly ruined terrain. Everyone who was there can be proud to have been a warrior of the Somme. The greatest battle of the war, perhaps the greatest of all time, has been won. Each individual man may be assured that he has the thanks of the Fatherland. It is entirely due to the fact that our front on the Somme remained unbroken that we have been able in the meantime to defeat Romania.

"My thanks are also due to the other fronts of the Army Group. Fully recognising the situation, the Sixth and Seventh Armies self-sacrificially kept their demands to a minimum, released every available man and item of matériel and accepted the greatest difficulties, so as to support the fighting on the Somme.

"I remain convinced that the front of the Army Group will continue to stand firm in the face of all future assaults."

For the most part, the German army had indeed been equal to the demands placed on it by its commanders, but the battle had taken its toll; a price had been paid. Allied pressure forced it to overdraw its resources and its political masters to adopt desperate and doomed expedients, such as unrestricted submarine warfare, which simply contributed to their ultimate defeat. 'The monster of the modern overwhelming machine of war gobbled up our finest men. Never again could these troops be brought to the same standard of battleworthiness, with which they began the Battle of the Somme...'[50] Ernst Jünger, writing later in *Storm of Steel*, used rather more colourful language to describe much the same sentiment, 'The names of the tiniest Picardy hamlets are memorials of heroic battles, to which the history of the world can find no parallel. There it was that the dust first drank the blood of our trained and disciplined youth. Those fine qualities which had raised the German race to greatness leapt up once more in dazzling flame and then slowly went out in a sea of mud and blood.'[51] Rather more soberly, General Hermann von Kuhl, writing in 1929, stated, 'There can be no doubt that the casualties suffered by Germany hit it harder than did those of the Allies. With each passing year of the war, it became harder for the Central Powers to compensate for their losses...'[52]

The Württemberg divisions, which had played such a prominent role throughout the previous two years, had performed exceptionally well during the main battle, but there were no illusions concerning the effect on them and, by extension, the remainder of the German army. Generalleutnant Otto von Moser, who had himself commanded the 27th Infantry Division with great success in the defence of Guillemont, summed the situation up at the end of 1916 like this: 'The formations which were deployed during the Battle of the Somme were very worn down physically and their nerves were badly affected. The huge gaps torn in the ranks could only be filled out by returning wounded, nineteen year olds who were too young or, by combing out from civilian occupations back home, men who to a large extent, due to their physical condition or mental attitude, could not be regarded as fully effective troops.'[53]

Although there continued to be artillery exchanges and numerous small-scale skirmishes during the next three months, there were no more major actions after mid- November and the battle wound down, stalled in the mud, with both sides temporarily exhausted. The Battle of Somme, as it unfolded, was a classic case of a battle which the British had to fight, rather than the one they wanted to. The French were the senior partners in the coalition, so the British had little choice but to accede to the choice of battleground and the timing of the commencement of operations. Neither was to the liking of Haig, who was only too well aware of the extent to which his army, from top to bottom, was deficient in both training and experience of battle on this scale. Despite these legitimate doubts, the demands of coalition warfare left the British with no choice at the end of 1915 but to agree to shoulder a greater burden of the continuing operations on the Western Front. Equally, events at Verdun in the spring and early summer of 1916 meant that the British simply had to start offensive operations earlier than they would have wished and so take some of the pressure off the French army, which deserves great credit for continuing to engage in the Battle of the Somme whilst the Verdun campaign was still raging. There is no doubt that its involvement came as a serious shock to the German Supreme Command, which in its planning had discounted any such possibility. In order to keep faith, the British clearly had to attack as agreed and (perhaps less clearly, despite pressure from Joffre) to go on attacking and supporting their French allies, even when the autumn rains and the churned up ground meant that the law of diminishing returns began to apply. That inescapable fact is really the only defensible reason for pursuing a military course of action which cost the two sides somewhere around one and a quarter million casualties in total and produced nothing of value geographically.

The argument is frequently advanced that the Allies and the British in particular, nevertheless gained more than the Germans as a result of the Battle of the Somme; that militarily the Germans were so worn down and the surviving British troops so improved as a fighting force that they would begin 1917 very much more evenly matched. In other words the collective overall experience was a beneficial and necessary stage in the development of the Kitchener divisions. Even if true, or partially true, that is a judgement based on hindsight. Any gains in military efficiency were a consequence of the battle and not the reason for fighting it. It was never a stated, or implied, aim beforehand. It glosses over the dislocation of British national expectations and appalling sense of loss it caused and it is additionally offensive, because it provides a fig leaf of dignity and respectability to the moral bankruptcy of attrition theory. The British did not invent the idea, which had already underpinned Falkenhayn's thinking when he launched his Verdun offensive, but they enthusiastically embraced it when the striven-for breakthrough on the Somme failed to materialise. The Battle of the Somme had to be fought, but to attempt to justify it on the grounds that the British army was all the better for it and that that somehow makes the cost in blood and treasure a price worth paying, is to stretch a point, to put it no more strongly.

If it was just a matter of gaining experience, then there are other ways to obtain it than to commit all available forces to a long series of bludgeoning frontal attacks, which cause your army over 400,000 casualties. The cemeteries of the Somme stand in silent reproach. It is not even as though the British army was the only one to learn lessons from the fighting. It has been repeatedly demonstrated in this book that the German army was endlessly analytical and self critical. Just as was the case for the British army, every single German unit and formation produced an after action report, complete with lessons learned, at the end of each tour of duty. These were then processed, staffed to a high level and redistributed for information and action. The early experiences gained on the Somme were absorbed and applied there during the later fighting; the overall lessons certainly informed the German style of defensive operations during the remainder of the war. Out went deep dugouts and continuous trench lines, to be replaced by concrete bunkers, surrounded by obstacle belts and sited for mutual support. Gone was the rigid holding of forward trenches packed with infantrymen. In came flexibility, defence in depth, a huge increase in infantry fire power, streamlined command and control and numerous tactical innovations.

It has also been claimed that the Allies won the battle because the Germans incurred irreplaceable losses and were forced to withdraw to the Hindenburg Line, rather than face a resumption of the battle the following spring. Not so, countered German historians after the war. The withdrawal did mean the relinquishment of a large area of occupied territory and the scorched earth policy it involved was highly controversial, even at the time. Nevertheless, the Allies set out to break through on the Somme and never succeeded. They attempted to smash the German army and destroy its morale. They failed completely in the first objective and it was the French, not the German, army that mutinied the following year. Militarily, at the time it was carried out, the withdrawal to the concrete emplacements of the Hindenburg Line was eminently sensible for a belligerent on the strategic defensive. In any case, if it was such a poor move, how come it took another eighteen months before it was finally pierced? If the Germans had suffered an irreversible setback, how come the war itself lasted even longer, not ending before the German army had delivered further serious shocks to the Allies?

Although even to talk of victory in the context of such a massive exercise in blood letting seems bizarre, the Germans are far from alone in claiming that, in battle, if the defenders are still holding the line, when the attackers cease to press home their attacks, they have won. Think of the Battle of Britain. Pyrrhic victories aside, after almost one hundred years, perhaps the time has come simply to recognise that none of the armies involved in this titanic struggle had any monopoly in courage or sacrifice; to stand in awe of their determination and endurance; to recognise their achievements as a triumph for the ability of human beings to rise above their surroundings and to view the Battle of the Somme as no more and no less than a gigantic European tragedy.

Reserve Leutnant Otto Ahrends, who was Adjutant, 1st Battalion Reserve Infantry Regiment 76 during the battle, kept a diary which was published after the war and of which Ludendorff wrote, 'The finest [account] I have ever read...was that written by a young officer of the tried and tested Hamburg Regiment. It is an heroic prose poem.'[54] Ahrends' message to his fellow countrymen was simple and straightforward, 'Homeland, dear, beloved homeland, whenever you see a fighter who was there at the Somme, bow low to the ground, because you simply do not know what he did for you.'[55]

1. Höfl: History Bav IR 20 pp 88-89
2. Hoffmann: *Das Kemptener Bataillon des KB 20 IR* pp 144-145
3. Wegener: History IR 172 pp 156-157
4. Glück: History IR 126 p 210
5. Fischer: *Zwischen Wolken und Granaten* pp 56-58
6. Glück: op. cit pp 211-212
7. Wegener: op.cit. pp 162-164
8. Seiler: History IR 161 p 186
9. Glück: op. cit. p 215
10. Voigt: History FüsR 73 pp 456-458
11. Schad: History IR 390 pp 18-19
12. History IR 164 p 345
13. Seiler: op. cit. p 201-202
14. Mierisch: *Beim Kgl. Bayer. RIR 15 im Felde* pp 28-29
15. ibid. pp 33-34
16. Richter: History RIR 94 pp 169-170
17. Ludendorff: *Meine Kriegserinnerungen* p 228
18. Kronprinz Rupprecht: *Mein Kriegstagebuch* Bd 2 pp 44-56
19. Reymann: History IR 62 p 117
20. ibid. pp 133-138
21. Kalbe: History IR 173 p 271
22. Wißman: History RIR 55 p 144
23. Bölsche: History IR 96 p 356
24. Hüttmann: History IR 25 p 107
25. Korfes: History IR 66 p 231
26. ibid. pp 231-232
27. ibid. pp 233-234
28. *Festschrift zum 1. Regimentstag des ehem. 8. Bad. Inf.-Reg. Nr 169* p 19
29. Lais: *Die Schlacht an der Somme 1916* pp 70-75
30. Wohlenberg: History RIR 77 pp 235-236

31. See Renshaw *Redan Ridge* pp 73-80 for the British version of this anecdote
32. Miles: *BOH 1916 from 2nd July* pp 514-519
33. Böttger: History IR 106 p 143
34. ibid. pp 144-145
35. ibid. pp 145-147
36. ibid. pp 147-148
37. The Regiment felt that this incident was atypical. Böttger: op. cit. p 140 comments, 'Our impression of the British was that they were courageous opponents, who behaved honourably towards the wounded. It is probable that the misuse of the Red Cross flag would not have met with the approval of the majority of British officers...'
38. Rogge: History IR 88 pp 315-316
39. Böttger: op. cit. p 150
40. Böttger: op. cit. p 140
41. History Füs R 35 pp 201-202
42. Rogge: op. cit. pp 312-313
43. History Füs R 35 pp 205-206
44. Rogge: *op.cit.* pp 314-315
45. History Füs R 35 p 205
46. ibid. p 208
47. Kriegsarchiv München IR 4 Bund 4 / 352 & 364
48. Rogge: op. cit. p 313
49. Lehmann: History Bav PiR p 461
50. Delmensingen: *Das Bayernbuch vom Weltkriege Bd I* p 89
51. Jünger: *Storm of Steel* p 110
52. von Kuhl: *Der Weltkrieg 1914-1918* pp 532-533
53. von Moser: *Die Württemberger im Weltkrieg* pp 62-63
54. Ludendorff: op. cit. p 109
55. Ahrends: *Mit dem Regiment 'Hamburg' in Frankreich* p 226

# Appendix 1

# German – British Comparison of Ranks

| | |
|---|---|
| Generalfeldmarschall | Field Marshal |
| Generaloberst | General |
| General der Infanterie | General of Infantry} |
| General der Kavallerie | General of Cavalry}   General |
| General der Artillerie | General of Artillery } |
| | N.B. The holder of any of these last three ranks was usually a corps commander or army commander. |
| Generalleutnant | Lieutenant General. |
| | N.B. The holder of this rank could be the commander of a formation ranging in size from a brigade to a corps. From 1732 onwards Prussian officers of the rank of Generalleutnant or higher, who had sufficient seniority, were referred to as 'Exzellenz' [Excellency]. |
| Generalmajor | Major General |
| Oberst | Colonel |
| Oberstleutnant | Lieutenant Colonel |
| Major | Major |
| Hauptmann | Captain |
| Rittmeister | Captain |
| | (mounted unit such as cavalry, horse artillery or transport) |
| Oberleutnant | Lieutenant |
| Leutnant | Second Lieutenant |
| Feldwebelleutnant | Sergeant Major Lieutenant |
| Offizierstellvertreter | Officer Deputy |
| | N.B. This was an appointment, rather than a substantive rank. |
| Fähnrich | Officer Cadet |
| Feldwebel | Sergeant Major |
| Wachtmeister | Sergeant Major (mounted unit) |
| Vizefeldwebel | Staff Sergeant |
| Vizewachtmeister | Staff Sergeant (mounted unit) |
| Sergeant | Sergeant |
| Unteroffizier | Corporal |
| Oberjäger | Corporal (Jäger regiments) |
| Korporal | Corporal (Bavarian units) |
| Gefreiter | Lance Corporal |

Musketier}
Grenadier}
Garde-Füsilier}
Füsilier}
Jäger}
Wehrmann }
Landsturmmann}
Landsturmpflichtiger}
Schütze}
Infanterist}
Landsturmrekrut}
Reservist}
Soldat}
Armierungs-Soldat}
Ersatz-Reservist}

N.B. These ranks all equate to Private Soldier (infantry). The differences in nomenclature are due to tradition, the type of unit involved, or the class of conscript to which the individual belonged.

| | |
|---|---|
| Einjährig-Freiwilliger | One Year Volunteer |
| Kriegsfreiwilliger | Wartime Volunteer |

N.B. These two ranks both equate to Private Soldier.

| | |
|---|---|
| Kanonier | Gunner} |
| Pionier | Sapper} |
| Radfahrer | Cyclist} |

N.B. These ranks all equate to Private Soldier.

| | |
|---|---|
| Fahrer | Driver} |
| Hornist | Trumpeter} |
| Tambour | Drummer} |

*Medical Personnel*

| | |
|---|---|
| Oberstabsarzt | Major (or higher) |
| Stabsarzt | Captain |
| Oberarzt | Lieutenant |
| Assistenzarzt | Second Lieutenant |

N.B. These individuals were also referred to by their appointments; for example, Bataillonsarzt or Regimentsarzt [Battalion or Regimental Medical Officer]. Such usage, which varied in the different contingents which made up the Imperial German army, is no indicator of rank.

| | |
|---|---|
| Sanitäter | Medical Assistant |
| Krankenträger | Stretcherbearer |

N.B. These two ranks both equate to Private Soldier.

*Chaplains*

| | |
|---|---|
| Pfarrer | Padre |

N.B. German padres were not given rank.

# Appendix II
## The German Army

In 1914 the army which Germany sent into the field was composed almost entirely of conscripts, who were divided into different categories. Visitors to German war cemeteries are often puzzled by the apparent plethora of junior ranks represented there. In fact, once the system is understood, it will be realised that the rank given reveals quite a lot of information about the individual. Every German man who was medically fit was subject to military service between the ages of seventeen and forty-five. He was not required for service with the active army until the age of twenty, but he spent the years until his call up as a member of the *Landsturm* [Home Guard], being referred to as a *Landsturmmann*. At twenty he began a military career which lasted for two years active duty if he was drafted to the infantry, or three years if he went to the artillery or cavalry. Thereafter he served seven years with the reserves, during which he might be recalled twice for periods of training. Having been a *Musketier, Grenadier, Füsilier, Pionier, Kanonier* or one of a wide range of cavalry private soldier-equivalent ranks, he then transferred to the *Landwehr* [Territorial Army] as a *Wehrmann* for eleven years, before completing a final seven years as a *Landsturmmann* once more.

In time of war there was no system of transfer between categories. Men could be called up prior to the age of twenty and, in theory, serve on until they reached the age of forty-five. The British system was in sharp contrast. Although long service regulars, who had signed on for seven years with the colours and five with the reserves, were automatically extended in service by one year when war broke out, thereafter they were 'time-expired' and due for discharge. In this way, up until the advent of conscription in Britain, men were allowed to leave the army, even though in many cases their units were short of manpower.

Prior to 1914, the Germans required approximately 300,000 recruits per year to meet the needs of the active army. This always left a surplus of men who, though fit for service, were not required. More than 50 per cent of those eligible and fit were not called up for any form of service and only approximately 20 per cent of any year group carried out active duty. However much of the surplus manpower was utilised in the *Ersatzreserve*. The men involved were placed in an additional reserve category for twelve years, during which time they were called up for training three times. After twelve years, they were placed in the *Landsturm* on the same basis as men who had completed service with the active army, reserves and *Landwehr*. Thus it was quite possible to be a *Landsturmmann* at the age of thirty-two. As a result of the existence of the *Ersatz* supplementary reserve, the German army could call on the services of an additional one million men in 1914 to fill up the ranks of the Reserve and *Landwehr* divisions. Because the German army deployed Reserve and *Landwehr* divisions alongside the active army when it mobilised and deployed in 1914, the bulk of its manpower reserves were committed from the start. As a result, many *Landsturm* men found themselves drafted into other parts of the army to replace the enormous losses of the early battles (1914 was the year of the heaviest losses in the German army).

Prior to the outbreak of war, there was a further important category of recruit. These were men of good financial standing and education, who were permitted to serve for one year only in the active army as an *Einjährigfreiwilliger* [One Year Volunteer]. Some individuals served for two, or even three years on this basis. There were provisos. They had to provide their own food and purchase

404

their own clothing and equipment but, at the end of their service, if they were judged to be capable and suitably qualified, they could then join the officers' reserve in the rank of *Fahnenjunker* [Officer Cadet]. Once they had completed two periods of training and passed an examination, they became reserve officers. Finally, once war was declared, it was possible for men over seventeen but under the age of twenty to volunteer for the duration of hostilities. These men were *Kriegsfreiwilliger* [War Volunteers]. They were frequently highly motivated, good quality men, but initially their training was often sketchy. Many of those shot down at Langemarck by the British army in October 1914, in what became known in Germany as the *Kindermord von Ypern* [Massacre of the Innocents of Ypres], fell into this category.

Despite the varying experience levels at the outbreak of hostilities, once fully trained or retrained and deployed into front line service, there was no practical difference in effectiveness between the categories of soldier, though naturally there was a distinct pecking order at formation level. These then were the men who filled the ranks of the German field army in 1914 and beyond. The twenty five peacetime corps, each of which, less the Guards who were based on Berlin, was territorially based and responsible for call-up, training and administration of recruits, were increased by the fielding of numerous reserve Corps, one of which, XIV Reserve Corps, played a key part in the defence of the Old Front Line during the following two years. This formation, which was composed of men from Baden and Württemberg in the south western part of Germany, was typical of those who formed the backbone of the defence of the Somme. In 1914 it was organised as follows:


26th Reserve Division (Württemberg)
51st Reserve Infantry Brigade (Infantry Regiment 180 and Reserve Infantry Regiment 121)
52nd Reserve Infantry Brigade (Reserve Infantry Regiments 119 and 120)
Württemberg Reserve Dragoon Regiment
Reserve Field Artillery Regiment 26
4th Company Engineer Battalion 4

28th Reserve Division (Baden)
55th Reserve Infantry Brigade (Reserve Infantry Regiments 40 & 109, Reserve Jäger Batalion 8)
56th Reserve Infantry Brigade (Reserve Infantry Regiments 110 and 111, Reserve Jäger Battalion 14)
Reserve Dragoon Regiment 8
Reserve Field Artillery Regiment 29
1st and 2nd Reserve Companies Engineer Battalion 13

To these main elements, must be added divisional and corps troops.

Despite the fact that the German army tended to retain formations in the same sectors for lengthy periods, by 1916 there had been various changes to the above order of battle. The Jäger Battalions, for example, were soon withdrawn from 28th Reserve Division for service elsewhere. For its part, the 26th Reserve Division lost Reserve Infantry Regiment 120 on 9th March 1915, but it still had four regiments, because Reserve Infantry Regiment 99 from Mönchengladbach, near Düsseldorf, had been operating with it since the previous September. What is more, Reserve Infantry Regiment 99 had four battalions, rather than the usual three. It lost its fourth battalion from time to time, when it was sent elsewhere in a reinforcing role, but by the time of the main battle in July 1916 it was a four battalion, sixteen company, regiment. Elsewhere within the Division there was great stability. Reserve Field Artillery Regiment 26, uniquely, was never fully relieved at any point from autumn 1914 to the end of the fighting in 1916.

The great majority of infantry regiments had three battalions, each of four companies numbered consecutively. In addition, most had one machine-gun company, but some had two. Early in the war a rifle company was commanded by a captain, who had four other officers, eighteen NCOs and 230 men under command. The company was split into three platoons, which were also numbered consecutively from one to twelve. The platoon was split into two half platoons. The number of eight man sections was dependant on the overall manpower available, but in peacetime, one platoon per company had nine sections, whilst the other two had eight each. It was usual to omit the battalion in describing a sub-unit, so, for example, 7./IR20 refers to 7th Company Infantry Regiment 20, which the reader can immediately tell is part of the 2nd Battalion of that Regiment. A similar system applied in the artillery. Horse artillery regiments operated 77 millimetre guns, but the field regiments were equipped with 105 millimetre guns. Initially a battery was equipped with six guns, but this number was reduced during 1915 to four. In addition the number of batteries per regiment declined from twelve to nine, organised into three battalions. As a result, in 1914, it would have been possible to find a sub-unit designated 7./ or 11./FAR2 [7th or 11th Battery Field Artillery Regiment 2] . Of these, the 7th Battery would have been part of the 2nd Battalion and the 11th part of the 3rd Battalion. By 1916, there were no batteries numbered 11 and the 7th Battery would have been part of the 3rd Battalion. Heavy guns of various calibres were the province of the foot artillery.

After the autumn advance of 1914 there was little call for independent cavalry formations on the Somme, so they were withdrawn and the majority of them were sent to the Eastern Front. However, cavalry units, originally allocated at the rate of two or three 150 man squadrons per infantry division, were usually retained, being used in the dismounted role to relieve infantry companies in the line, for despatch riding or prisoner escort duties. Machine guns were increasingly important to the defence. In 1914 most regiments had a machine-gun company, comprising approximately one hundred all ranks and armed with six machine guns and one in reserve. By 1916 these had been supplemented by independent machine gun troops and a few 'Musketen' companies, who were deployed in places considered to be particularly at risk. 'Musketen' were automatic rifles, equipped with a twenty five round magazine and operated by a two man crew. Such was the need for automatic weapons that at the opening of the main battle in July 1916, Reserve Infantry Regiment 99, guarding Thiepval and the Schwaben Redoubt, was reinforced by both types of unit and was deploying German, Russian, British and Belgian machine guns as well as 'Musketen'. Gradually, during the autumn of 1916, regiments began to be reorganised so as to have two machine-gun companies each and, by the following year, the light Maxim Model 08/15 was so widely available that it became a company weapon.

The infantry and the artillery, supported by the engineers, carried the main load of the Battle of the Somme, but one other type of unit began to make an appearance during the later stages of the battle, being used for the first time on 31st August 1916 against Delville Wood. These were the so-called *Sturmabteilungen* [Assault Detachments]. The first of these had been raised in late 1915 as *Sturmbataillon Nr. 5 Rohr* (It was named after the Hauptmann, who replaced its original commander, when the latter was sacked). The second, which was based on the reorganised Jäger Battalion 3, from which weaker individuals had been removed, began training in June 1916. Thereafter such units were all built up from selected cadres. They were highly trained élite units, equipped with flame throwers, 37 millimetre infantry guns and other specialised weapons and were excused normal trench duties; being used instead for training or demonstration purposes and to spearhead assaults or counter-attacks. They were the special forces of the day and, contrary to popular belief, there were very few such units. Even as late as 1918, they comprised a tiny fraction of the army. Used correctly they could achieve results out of all proportion to their numbers.

The German army awarded officer rank very sparingly. In 1914 a regiment was usually under the command of a colonel, with a lieutenant colonel as his deputy. At the outbreak of war surplus lieutenant colonels were used to command reserve regiments, often with a major as second in command. Initially majors generally commanded battalions, captains companies and subaltern officers, platoons. There was no system of temporary or acting rank, such as that which obtained in the British army and which ensured that a battalion commander would wear the rank of lieutenant colonel, even if his substantive rank was much lower. As a result, the expansion of the army, heavy early losses and an unwillingness to commission from the ranks or to promote officers in their substantive rank, meant that by the time of the Battle of the Somme, regiments tended to be commanded by lieutenant colonels. The commander of Reserve Infantry Regiment 99, Hans von Fabeck, who was a nephew of Generalfeldmarschall von Hindenburg, only held the rank of major, despite being a first class soldier and a former commander of the Guards Jäger Battalion. Most battalions were commanded by captains and companies were lucky if they had more than a single reserve second lieutenant in charge. The deficiencies amongst the officer ranks were compensated for by the creation of the rank of *Feldwebelleutnant* [Sergeant Major Lieutenant] and the use of a system of *Offizierstellvertreter* [Officer Deputies]. *Offizierstellvertreter* was not a rank, it was an appointment. This low proportion of officers to other ranks is one of the reasons why very few officers and hardly any above the rank of major are buried in German war cemeteries. The other main factor is that large numbers of identified bodies were repatriated to Germany after the war at the expense of their families and the families of officers tended to be better able to afford the cost involved.

This was the army which fought the Battle of the Somme. Drawn from the whole of German society, it was of good quality, well-trained, experienced and battle-hardened. It was always short of manpower and materiel, but it was an extremely effective fighting organisation.

# Appendix III
## German Historical Sources

A major obstacle to the study of any aspect of the imperial German army is the fact that a bombing raid on Potsdam by the Royal Air Force, on 14th April 1945, completely destroyed the Prussian archives. Because Prussian formations and regiments accounted for almost 90 per cent of the army during the First World War, the seriousness of the loss of these documents cannot be overstated. In some cases copies of Prussian documents still survive in other archives, such as those in Dresden, Munich, Stuttgart, Karlsruhe and Freiburg im Breisgau, but their presence in these places is a matter of chance. As a result, although information related to army units from Saxony, Bavaria, Baden and Württemberg is generally readily available in original form, the use of secondary sources is essential and unavoidable in relation to the Prussians.

Under the terms of the Treaty of Versailles, all branches of the German General Staff were to have been disbanded. However, in 1919, the Military History Department metamorphosed into the *Reichsarchiv*, which was staffed almost exclusively by former General Staff officers and which controlled access to the archives. Not only did this policy provide the *Reichswehr* with a clandestine source of General Staff reservists, it also influenced how the events of 1914-1918 were presented to the public post-war. Apart from the Official History, good examples of the flood of work produced by the Reichsarchiv are the series entitled *Erinnerungsblätter Deutscher Regimenter* [Histories of the German Regiments], the thirty nine monographs published as *Der Große Krieg in Einzeldarstellungen* [Episodes of the Great War] and the thirty-six volumes of *Schlachten des Weltkrieges* [Battles of the World War] which, in the space of 8,000 pages, mention the deeds of no fewer than 16,500 officers NCOs and men; the object being to inspire future generations by emphasising the heroism of the individual triumphing against enemies who were superior both numerically and materially. As far as the writing of the current book was concerned one bonus of this approach, which was echoed in other semi-official *Reichsarchiv* productions, is the fact that authors from the *Reichsarchiv* made much use of anecdote. However, one obvious question arises: to what extent can the content of such books be trusted? Quite apart from a natural human tendency to put the best gloss on past events, it is undeniably the case that what was produced was intended to chronicle a lost war in such a way that the reputation of the German military in general and the *Reichswehr* in particular, would be enhanced.

The question, in the view of this author at least, can be answered quite simply and positively. The work published by the *Reichsarchiv* generally matches other histories written and published privately by regiments who were not covered in the *Erinnerungsblätter* series. Furthermore, it is often the case that information concerning particular incidents also interlocks well with accounts written from an allied perspective. In addition, as a test, the author checked the contents and wording of several histories of Württemberg and Bavarian regiments against archival material held in Stuttgart and Munich respectively. No discrepancies were uncovered which, though not conclusive, certainly indicates that these secondary sources were produced with integrity and respect for the facts.

# Appendix IV

## German Order of Battle July – December 1916

| Formation | Commander | Army | Deployment Sector | Tour of Duty (Inf) |
|---|---|---|---|---|
| HQ XIV Corps | Genlt Stein (Genlt Fuchs from 29/10) | 2 | Bapaume | - |
| 2nd Gds Res Div | Gen der Inf Freiherr von Süßkind | 1 | Gommecourt | - |
| 52nd Inf Div | Genlt von Borries | 1 | Serre | To 27/11 |
| 26th Res Div | Genlt Freiherr von Soden | 1 | Beaumont Hamel | To 10/10 |
| 28th Res Div | Genlt von Hahn | 2 | Fricourt | To 7/7 |
| 12th Inf Div | Genlt Châles de Beaulieu | 2 | Hardecourt aux Bois | To 4/7 |
| HQ XVII Corps | Gen der Inf von Pannewitz (Genlt Fleck from 7/9) | 2 | Péronne | - |
| 121st Inf Div | Genmaj von Ditfurth | 2 | Dompierre | To 2/7 |
| 11th Inf Div | Genlt von Webern | 2 | Soyécourt | To 31/7 |
| 35th Inf Div | Genlt von Hahn | 2 | Chaulnes | To 8/9 |
| 36th Inf Div | Genlt von Heineccius (Genmaj von Kehler from 1/9) | 2 | Fouquescourt | To 13/10 |
| 10th Bav Inf Div | Genmaj Burkhardt | 2 (1 from 19/7) | Thiepval | 1-23/7 |
| 22nd Res Div | Gen der Inf Riemann | 2 | Péronne | 1-10/7 |
| 185th Inf Div | Genmaj von Uthmann | 2 | Pozières | 1-14/7 |
| Div Frentz | Genmaj Raitz von Frentz | 2 | Barleux | 1-8/7 |
| HQ VI Res Corps | Gen der Inf von Goßler | 2 (1 from 19/7) | Combles | 2-30/7 |
| 12th Res Div | Genmaj von Kehler | 1 | Guillemont | 1-18/7 |
| 11th Res Div | Genlt von Hertzberg | 1 | Maurepas | 3-24/7 |
| 44th Res Div | Genmaj von Altrock | 2 | Estrées | 2-11/7 |
| 3rd Gds Inf Div | Genmaj von Lindequist | 2 | Bazentin | 2-16/7 |
| 183rd Inf Div | Genmaj von Schüßler | 2 | Contalmaison | 6-18/7 |
| HQ IX Corps | Gen der Inf von Quast | 2 | Péronne | From 5/7 |
| 17th Inf Div | Genmaj von Minckwitz | 2 | Barleux | 8-28/7 |
| 18th Inf Div | Genmaj Bloch von Blottnitz | 2 | Estrées | 11-27/7 |
| 123rd Inf Div | Genlt Lucius | 2 (1 from 19/7) | Maurepas | 8-24/7 |
| Div Liebert | Genlt von Liebert (15 Res Div) | 2 | Péronne | 10-22/7 |
| HQ IV Corps | Gen der Inf Sixt von Armin | 2 | High Wood | 14-24/7 |
| 7th Inf Div | Genlt Riedel | 1 | Martinpuich | 12-25/7 |
| 8th Inf Div | Gen der Inf Ernst II. Duke of Saxony-Altenburg | 1 | Flers | 15-25/7 |
| 24th Res Div | Genmaj Morgenstern-Döring | 2 (1 from 19/7) | Guillemont | 14/7-1/8 |
| Div Dumrath | Genmaj Dumrath (29 Res Inf Bde) | 2 | Vermandovillers | 17-23/7 |
| 5th Inf Div | Genlt Wichura | 1 | Delville Wood | 20/7- 4/8 |
| 117th Inf Div | Gen der Inf Kuntze | 1 | Courcelette | 20/7-10/8 |
| 28th Inf Div | Genmaj Heidborn (From 19/8 Genmaj Langer) | 2 | Péronne | 20/7-4/10 |
| 8th Bav Res Div | Genlt Freiherr von Stein | 1 | Maurepas | 21/7-16/8 |
| Div Francke | Genmaj Francke (63 Saxon Inf Bde) | 2 | Soyécourt | 23/7-8/9 |
| 23rd Res Div | Genlt von Watzdorf | 1 | Cléry | 24/7-13/8 |
| HQ IX Res Corps | Gen der Inf von Boehn | 1 | High Wood | 24/7-10/8 |
| 17th Res Div | Genmaj von Zieten | 1 | Flers | 24/7-10/8 |
| 18th Res Div | Genmaj Wellman | 1 | Martinpuich | 24/7-10/8 |

| HQ Gds Res Corps | Gen der Kav Freiherr Marschall | 2 | Barleux-Estrées | 27/7-19/8 |
|---|---|---|---|---|
| 1st Gds Res Div | Genlt Albrecht | 2 | Barleux | 26/7-19/8 |
| 4th Gds Res Div | Genmaj Graf von Schweinitz | 2 | Estrées | 25/7-20/8 |
| HQ XII Saxon Res Corps | Gen der Art von Kirchbach | 1 | Combles | 30/7-12/8 |
| HQ XIII Corps | Gen der Inf Freiherr von Watter | 1 | Guillemont | 3-26/8 |
| 26th Inf Div | Genlt Duke Wilhelm von Urach | 1 | Ginchy | 4-26/8 |
| 27th Inf Div | Genlt von Moser | 1 | Guillemont | 31/7-25/8 |
| 16th Inf Div | Genlt Fuchs | 1 | Mouquet Farm | 9-25/8 |
| HQ XIX Saxon Corps | Gen der Kav von Laffert | 1 | High Wood | 10-28/8 |
| 24th Inf Div | Genmaj Hammer | 1 | Martinpuich | 9-27/8 |
| 40th Inf Div | Genlt Götz von Olenhusen | 1 | Flers | 9-28/8 |
| HQ I Bav Res Corps | Gen der Inf Ritter von Fasbender | 1 | Combles | 12/8-6/9 |
| 1st Bav Res Div | Genlt Soeringer | 1 | Cléry | 10-17/8 |
| 5th Bav Res Div | Genlt Ipfelkofer | 1 | Maurepas | 14-27/8 |
| 1st Gds Inf Div | Oberst Eitel Friedrich, Prince of Prussia | 1 | Cléry | 15/8 - 4/9 |
| 17th Inf Div | Genmaj von Minckwitz | 2 | Barleux | 18/8-3/9 |
| 18 Inf Div | Genmaj Bloch von Blottnitz | 2 | Berny | 19/8-9/9 |
| 1st Bav Res Div | Genlt Soeringer | 1 | South of Bapaume | 20/8-4/9 |
| Brig Scholz (32 Inf Bde Reinforced) | Genmaj Scholz | 2 | Chilly | 22/8-3/9 |
| 111th Inf Div | Genmaj Sontag | 1 | Guillemont | 23/8-9/9 |
| HQ Gds Res Corps | Gen der Kav Freiherr Marschall | 1 | Courcelette | 24/8-17/9 |
| 1st Gds Res Div | Genlt Albrecht | 1 | Courcelette | 23/8-9/9 |
| 4Gds Res Div | Genmaj Graf von Schweinitz | 1 | Mouquet Farm | 23/8-11/9 |
| 56th Inf Div | Genmaj von Wichmann | 1 | Ginchy | 25/8-9/9 |
| 2nd Gds Inf Div | Genmaj von Friedeburg | 1 | Maurepas | 25/8-11/9 |
| HQ XII Res Corps | Gen der Art von Kirchbach | 1 | Ginchy-Combles | 26/8-17/9 |
| HQ II Bav Corps | Genlt von Stetten | 1 | Martinpuich-Flers | 28/8-18/9 |
| 3rd Bav Inf Div | Genlt Ritter von Wenninger | 1 | Martinpuich | 26/8-17/9 |
| 4th Bav Inf Div | Genlt Ritter von Schrott | 1 | Flers | 26/8-17/9 |
| 23rd Inf Div | Genlt Bärensprung | 2 | Chaulnes | 30/8-11/9 |
| HQ 27 Saxon Res Corps | Gen der Inf von Ehrenthal | 1 | Bouchavesnes | 6-15/9 |
| 53rd Res Div | Genlt Leuthold | 1 | Bouchavesnes | 1-15/9 |
| 54th Res Div | Genlt von Knoerzer | 1 | Rancourt | 5-21/9 |
| HQ XXIII Res Corps | Gen der Inf von Kathen | 1 | Ablaincourt-Chaulnes | 16/9-20/11 |
| 45th Res Div | Gen der Inf Schöpflin | 1 | Courcelette | 5-19/9 |
| 46th Res Div | Genlt von Wasielewski | 2 | Chaulnes | 9/9-6/10 |
| 24th Res Div | Genmaj Morgenstern-Döring | 1 | Rancourt | 4-16/9 |
| 13th Inf Div | Genlt von dem Borne | 1 | Allaines | 9-21/9 |
| 5th Bav Inf Div | Genlt Endres | 1 | Ginchy | 6-18/9 |
| 11th Inf Div | Genlt von Webern | 2 | Vermandovillers | 6/9-8/10 |
| 15th Res Div | Gen der Inf von Liebert | 2 | Parvillers | From 8/9 |
| 10th Ersatz Div | Gen der Inf Freiherr von Gayl | 2 | Berny | 7-22/9 |

| | | | | |
|---|---|---|---|---|
| 185th Inf Div | Genmaj von Uthmann | 1 | Combles | 6-19/9 |
| 89th Res Inf Bde (207th Inf Div) | Genlt Schumann | 1 | Mouquet Farm | 10-20/9 |
| 58th Inf Div | Genlt von Gersdorff | 2 | Barleux | 13-26/9 |
| HQ XVIII Corps | Gen der Inf von Schenk | 1 | Moislains | 15/9-2/10 |
| 21st Inf Div | Genlt von Oven | 1 | South of Rancourt | 15/9-1/10 |
| 25th Inf Div | Genmaj von Dresler | 1 | Moislains | 15/9-1/10 |
| 50th Res Div | Genmaj von Petersdorff | 1 | Martinpuich | 15-29/9 |
| 37th Res Inf Bde (213th Inf Div) | Oberst von Triebig | 1 | Combles | 15-29/9 |
| 6th Bav Inf Div | Genlt Ritter von Hoehn | 1 | Gueudecourt | 6-28/9 |
| HQ XXVI Res Corps | Gen der Inf Freiherr von Hügel | 1 | Combles | 17-29/9 |
| 51st Res Div | Genlt Balck | 1 | Combles | 18-30/9 |
| 52nd Res Div | Genlt Waldorf | 1 | Lesboeufs | 18-30/9 |
| HQ IV Corps | Gen der Inf Sixt von Arnim | 1 | Courcelette | 17/9-2/11 |
| 7th Inf Div | Genlt Riedel | 1 | Pys | 18/9-2/10 |
| 8th Inf Div | Genmaj Hamann | 1 | Thiepval | 18/9-2/10 |
| HQ III Bav Corps | Gen der Kav Freiherr von Gebsattel | 1 | Gueudecourt | 18/9-2/10 |
| 212th Inf Div | Genmaj Francke | 1 | Allaines | 20/9-4/10 |
| 214th Inf Div | Genmaj Müller | 1 | Rancourt | 20/9-1/10 |
| 183rd Inf Div | Genmaj von Schüsler | 2 | Fresnes | 22/9-23/10 |
| 213th Inf Div | Genmaj von Bernuth | 1 | Sailly | 18-29/9 |
| 11th Res Div | Gen der Kav von Herzberg | 2 | Péronne | 24/9-7/11 |
| 12th Res Div | Genlt Dumrath | 2 | Barleux | 24/9-5/11 |
| 7th Res Div | Gen der Inf Graf Schwerin | 1 | Gueudecourt | 25/9-12/10 |
| 6th Bav Res Div | Genlt Scanzoni von Lichtenfels | 1 | Eaucourt l'Abbaye | 28/9-13/10 |
| 15th Inf Div | Genmaj Raitz von Frentz | 1 | Saillisel | 29/9-11/10 |
| HQ IX Res Corps | Gen der Inf von Boehn | 1 | Sailly | 29/9-26/10 |
| 17th Res Div | Genmaj von Zieten | 1 | Saillisel | 29/9-14/10 |
| 18th Res Div | Genlt von Wundt | 1 | Rocquiny | 29/9-16/10 |
| 113th Inf Div | Genlt Sontag | 1 | Moislains | 29/9-16/10 |
| HQ V Res Corps | Genlt von Garnier | 1 | Moislains | 2/10-17/12 |
| 9th Res Div | Genmaj von Dresler (25th Inf Div) | 1 | East of Bouchavesnes | 30/9-19/10 |
| 10th Res Div | Genlt Dallmer | 1 | East of Rancourt | 29/9-13/10 |
| Marine Inf Brigade | Genmaj Graf von Moltke | 1 | Courcelette | 30/9-17/10 |
| 23rd Inf Div | Genlt Bärensprung | 2 | Chaulnes | 2-27/10 |
| 4th Ersatz Div | Gen der Kav von Werder | 1 | Warlencourt | 1-15/10 |
| 206th Inf Div | Genlt von Etzel | 2 | Mont St Quentin | 5/10-6/11 |
| 29th Inf Div | Genmaj von der Heyde | 2 | Mont St Quentin | From 4/10 |
| 28th Res Div | Genlt von Hahn | 1 | Grandcourt | 6-24/10 |
| 44th Res Div | Genmaj von Völkersamb | 2 | Ablaincourt | 7-28/10 |
| 16th Inf Div | Genlt Fuchs | 1 | Sailly | 8-27/10 |
| 211th Inf Div | Genmaj von Lewinski | 1 | East of Rancourt | 9/10-7/11 |
| 6th Inf Div | Genlt Herhudt von Rohden | 1 | Gueudecourt | 9-26/10 |
| 35th Inf Div | Genlt von Hahn | 2 | Hallu | From 9/10 |
| 19th Res Div | Gen der Inf von Wartenberg | 1 | Le Transloy | 10-29/10 |
| 5th Ersatz Div | Genlt von Basedow | 1 | Pys | 11-30/10 |
| HQ XIX Corps | Gen der Kav von Laffert | 1 | Southwest of Bapaume | 15/10-5/11 |

| | | | | |
|---|---|---|---|---|
| 24th Inf Div | Genmaj Hammer | 1 | Warlencourt | 11/10-7/11 |
| 40th Inf Div | Genmaj Meister | 1 | Ligny-Tilloy | 11/10-6/11 |
| 1st Bav Inf Div | Genlt Ritter von Schoch | 1 | Saillisel | 13-30/10 |
| 2nd Bav Inf Div | Genlt von Hartz | 1 | East of Lesboeufs | 13/10-4/11 |
| 103rd Inf Div | Genmaj von Gabain | 1 | Moislains | 14/10-11/11 |
| 46th Res Div | Genlt von Wasielewski | 2 | Pressoire | 14-28/10 |
| 8th Ersatz Div | Genmaj von Stumpff | 1 | East of Bouchavesnes | 16/10-18/11 |
| 38th Inf Div | Genmaj von Schultheis | 1 | Grandcourt | 21/10-16/11 |
| 221st Inf Div | Genmaj von der Chevallerie | 2 | Fresnes | From 22/10 |
| 23rd Res Div | Genlt von Watzdorf | 1 | Beaulencourt | 24/10-7/12 |
| 36th Inf Div | Genmaj von Kehler | 2 | Chaulnes | 24/10-9/12 |
| Bav Ersatz Div | Genlt Kiefhaber | 1 | Le Transloy | 25/10-16/11 |
| HQ XV Corps | Gen der Inf von Deimling | 1 | Sailly | 26/10-18/11 |
| 30th Inf Div | Genlt von Gontard | 1 | Sailly | 24/10-20/11 |
| 39th Inf Div | Genlt von Bertrab | 1 | Saillisel | 28/10-12/11 |
| 58th Inf Div | Genlt von Gersdorff | 1 | Pys | 26/10-21/11 |
| 12th Inf Div | Genmaj Fouquet | 1 | Beaumont Hamel | 22/10-18/11 |
| 212th Inf Div | Genmaj Francke | 2 | East of Ablaincourt | 24/10-19/11 |
| 222nd Inf Div | GenmajKüster | 1 | East of Lesboeufs | 1/11-8/12 |
| 16th Res Div | Genlt Sieger | 1 | St Pierre Vaast Wood | 4-25/11 |
| HQ Gds Res Corps | Gen der Kav Freiherr Marschall | 1 | South of Bapaume | From 2/11 |
| 4th Gds Inf Div | Genmaj Graf von Schweinitz | 1 | Ligny-Tilloy | From 4/11 |
| 1st Gds Res Div | Genlt Albrecht | 1 | Warlencourt | From 5/11 |
| 1st Gds Inf Div | Oberst Eitel Friedrich Prince of Prussia | 2 | Péronne | From 2/11 |
| 2nd Gds Inf Div | Genmaj von Friedeburg | 2 | Barleux | From 2/11 |
| 111th Inf Div | Genmaj Sontag | 1 | Moislains | 7/11-19/12 |
| 185th Inf Div | Genmaj von Uthmann | 1 | Saillisel | 9/11-5/12 |
| 24th Inf Div | Genmaj von Morgenstern-Döring | 1 | Le Transloy | 10/11-16/12 |
| 223rd Inf Div | Genmaj Mühry | 1 | Grandcourt | 10-22/11 |
| 206th Inf Div | Genlt von Etzel | 2 | East of Ablaincourt | 13-27/11 |
| 208th Inf Div | Genmaj Heße (Genmaj vonGroddeck from 28/11) | 1 | East of Beaumont Hamel | 14/11-17/12 |
| 32nd Inf Div | Genmaj von der Decken | 1 | East of Bouchavesnes | From 16/11 |
| 56th Inf Div | Genmaj von Wichmann | 1 | Pys | From 16/11 |
| 50th Res Div | Genlt Freiherr von Ende | 1 | Grandcourt | 19/11-23/12 |
| HQ XIII Corps | Gen der Inf Freiherr von Watter | 1 | Sailly | From 19/11 |
| 26th Inf Div | Genlt Duke Wilhelm von Urach | 1 | Rocquiny | From 29/11 |
| 27th Inf Div | Genlt von Moser | 1 | Sailly | From 17/11 |
| Marine Inf Brigade | Genmaj Graf von Moltke | 1 | Warlencourt | From 19/11 |
| 22nd Res Div | Genmaj Ritter von Riedl | 1 | St Pierre Vaast Wood | 20/11-23/12 |
| HQ XVIII Corps | Gen der Inf von Schenck | 2 | Chaulnes | From 20/11 |
| 21st Inf Div | Genlt von Oven | 2 | East of Ablaincourt | From 22/11 |
| 25th Inf Div | Genmaj von Dresler | 2 | Chaulnes | From 5/12 |
| 14th Bav Inf Div | Genmaj Rauchenberger | 1 | Serre | From 23/11 |
| 214th Inf Div | Genmaj von Brauchitsch | 1 | Beaulencourt | From 29/11 |
| 5th Bav Res Div | Genlt von Ipfelkofer | 1 | Saillisel | From 3/12 |

# Select Bibliography

## *Unpublished Sources*

### Kriegsarchiv München

HS 1984:     Auszug aus dem Tagebuch des Führers der 5./16IR Hauptmann
             d.R. a.D. Karl Weber

HS 1984:     Auszug aus dem Kriegstagebuch des Generalmajors Otto Schulz,
             ehemaliger Regimentskommandeur bIR 22

HS 1984      Erinnerungen an die Eroberung der "Feste Schwaben" an der
             Somme am 1.7.16

HS 2073:     Auszug aus dem Kriegstagebuch des [Hauptmann] Grafen
             Armansperg Sep-Oct 14

HS 2105      Somme – Schlacht 1916  F. Gerhardinger, Oblt. d.R.

HS 2106      Erlebnisse in der Sommeschlacht 1916 nach
             Tagebuchaufzeichnungen von Dr. H. Gareis s.Z. Vizefeldwebel im
             1/16. Inf. Regt.

HS 2200      Bericht des Stabsarzt Dr. Blass über seine Erfahrungen in
             englischer Gefangenschaft

HS 2205      Plan für die Kämpfe bay. R.I.R. 8 vom 1.7.1916 Sommeschlacht
             1:5000

HS 2205      Anteil des bay.Res.Inf.Regt 8 an der Somme Schlacht

2 I.R. Bd.7:  Akt 3 – Gefechtsbericht der Kämpfe bei Sailly vom
              12.10 abends bis 19.10 Morgens 4.11.16:

4 I.R. Bd. 4:  Gesundheitszustand des Regts 12.12.16 & 19.12.16

6 RIR Bd 8:    General Kommando VI. A.K. Ia Nr, 1439/I.15 28.10.15

8 RIR Bd 3:    10. B.I.D. Ia No 2046 28.3.16

8 RIR Bd 3:    Regimentsbefehl 24.6.16

8 RIR Bd 4:    Kräfteverteilung C1 – C2 8.7.16 mit 13.7.16/ und15./16.7.16

8 RIR Bd 4:    Vernehmung des am 24.6.16 gefangenen Engländers des
               V.N.StaffordR.

8 RIR Bd 4:    Vernehmung von 2 am 28.6 morgens bei Beaumont gef.gen.
               Engländern
               vom I./Newfoundland-Batl. 88.Brig. 29. Div. 4 Armee.

8 RIR Bd 4:    Vernehmung des Ueberläufers (II./R.Fus. 29. Div. 86. Brig) Josef
               Lipmann, 23 Jahre alt, Tischler, seit 11.8.14 Soldat.

8 RIR Bd 4:    Gefechtsberichte 1& 2.Rekr.Komp./180 1. Juli 16

8 RIR Bd 21:   Armee-Oberkommando 2. Ia No 96 geheim 27.6.15

8 RIR Bd 21:   XIV Reservekorps Generalkommando Ia Nr 325 geheim! 7.3.16

8 RIR Bd 21:   AOK 2 Ia 575. Geh. A.H.Qu., den 3.7.16 & Zusatz den 17.7.16

8 RIR (WK):    Stellung des II./R.I.R. 8. vom 9.- 25.7.1916 M. 1: 2500

16 IR Bd 3:    [Meldung] An K.b. 10. I. Div Beaulencourt , 15.7.1916. 9.15
               Nachm.

2 FARBd 6:     Abschrift Beob.St.4/11 Luisenhof 24.9.16 2.50 nachm.

**Hauptstaatsarchiv Stuttgart**
M43/19 RIR 99
M99 Bü 141/2
M99 Bü 141/3
M99 Bü 141/91
M99 Bü 141/105
M99 Bü 142/833
M99 Bü 142/847
M107 Bü 41/22
M104 Bü 41/51
M107 Bü 41/119
M107 Bü 42/78
M107 Bü 42/103
M107 Bü 42/142
M201 Bü 200
M410 Bü 140/8
M410 Bü 140 Skizze 8
M410 Bü 239
M410 Bü 260

**Other**
Fasse Collection: Abschrift eines Berichtes des Hauptmann v. Schauroth (I. Lehr-Inf.-Rgt.) vom 5. August 1916 an das I. und III. Bataillon Inf.-Rgt. 190.

*Printed Works (German: Author known)*
**Ahrends, Otto,** *Mit dem Regiment 'Hamburg' in Frankreich 1914-1916,* München, 1929
**Bachelin, Major Eduard,** *Das Reserve-Infanterie-Regiment Nr. 111 im Weltkrieg 1914 bis 1918,* Karlsruhe
**Bathe, Rolf,** *Männer am Feind* Berlin, 1939
**Berr, Hauptmann Günther,** *Das Preußische Mansfelder Feldartillerie-Regiment Nr. 75 im Weltkriege 1914/18* Gräfenhainichen, 1934
**Beyer, Lt. d. Res. a.D., Dr. Walther & Scheitza Lt d. Res. a.D. Studienrat Erich** *Königlich Preußisches Feldartillerie-Regiment Nr. 221* Berlin, 1933
**Bezzel, Oberst, a.D. Dr. Oskar** *Das Königlich Bayerische Reserve-Infanterie-Regiment Nr. 6* München, 1938
**Bickel, Hauptmann a.D. & Strzemieczny Oberst a.D. von** *Großherzogliches Artilleriekorps 1. Großherzoglich Hessisches Feldartillerie-Regiment Nr. 25* Berlin, 1935
**Bierey, Oberst a.D. Rudolf** *Das Kgl. Sächs. Res-Feldartillerie-Regiment Nr. 40* Dresden, 1927
**Bolze, Generamajor a.D. Walther** *Das Kgl. Sächs. 7. Feldartillerie-Regiment Nr. 77* Dresden, 1924
**Bölsche, Arnold** *Sturmflut. Das Erleben des 7. Thür. Infanterie-Regiments Nr. 96 im Weltkrieg* Zeulenroda, 1935
**Bose, Königl. Preuß. Major, a.D. Thilo von** *Das Kaiser Alexander Garde-Grenadier-Regiment Nr. 1 im Weltkriege 1914-1918* Zeulenroda
**Böttger, Hauptmann Karl, Schönberg Oberst a.D. Kurt v., Wülsingen Generalmajor a.D. Georg Bock v. & Melzer Oblt. Walter** *Das Kgl. Sächs. 7. Infanterie-Regiment "König Georg" Nr. 106* Dresden, 1927

414

**Brandis, Hauptmann a.D. Cordt von** *Die von Douaumont. Das Ruppiner Regiment 24 im Weltkrieg* Berlin, 1930

**Broede, Major a.D** *Infanterie-Regiment von Stülpnagel (5. Brandenburgisches) Nr. 48* Berlin, 1935

**Burchardi, Oberst a.D. Karl** *Das Füsilier-Regiment Generalfeldmarschall Graf Moltke (Schlesisches) Nr. 38* Oldenburg, 1928

**Collenberg, Oberstleutnant a.D. Karl Freiherr von** *Das 3. Garde-Feldartillerie-Regiment Seine Geschichte* Berlin, 1931

**Cron, Oberstleutnant a.D. Hermann** *Infanterie-Regiment Markgraf Karl (7. Brandenburgisches) Nr. 60* Berlin, 1926

**Delmensingen, General der Artillerie Konrad Kraft von & Feeser Generalmajor a.D. Friedrichfranz** *Das Bayernbuch vom Weltkriege 1914 – 1918* Stuttgart, 1930

**Deutelmoser, Major a.D. Adolf,** *Die 27. Infanterie-Division im Weltkrieg 1914-18* Stuttgart, 1925

**Düssel, Oblt. d.R. & Fernow Major a.D.** *Das Reserve-Infanterie-Regiment Nr. 17 während der Sommeschlacht im Juli und August 1916* Oldenburg, 1925

**Eder, Offizier Stellvertreter a.D. Max,** *Das Preußische Reserve-Infanterie-Regiment 269* Zeulenroda, 1937

**Fischer, Fliegerleutnant a.D. Johannes** *Zwischen Wolken und Granaten* Berlin, 1932

**Flaischlen, General a.D. H.** *Unser Regiment im Wandel der Zeiten: Festschrift zur Feier der Traditions-Übergabe in Ulm Mai-1938* Stuttgart, 1938

**Forstner, Major a.D. Kurt Freiherr von** *Das Königlich-Preußische Reserve-Infanterie-Regiment Nr. 15* Oldenburg, 1929

**Frick, Leutnant d.L. Albert** *Erlebnisse in den ersten Tagen der Somme-Schlacht* Rastatt, 1916

**Frisch, Georg** *Das Reserve-Infanterie-Regiment Nr. 109 im Weltkrieg 1914 bis 1918* Karlsruhe, 1931

**Fromm, Oberst a.D.** *Das Württembergische Reserve-Infanterie-Regiment Nr. 120 im Weltkrieg 1914-1918* Stuttgart, 1920

**Fuhrmann, Major d.R. a.D. Hans, Pfortner Leutnant d.R. a.D. Otto & Fries Leutnant d.R. a.D. Nicolaus** *Königlich Preußisches Reserve Infanterie-Rgt. Nr. 211 im Weltkriege 1914-1918* Berlin, 1933

**Führen, Franz** *Die Hohenzollernfüsiliere im Weltkrieg 1914-1918* Oldenburg, 1930

**Funcke, Oberstleutnant a.D. von** *F.A.R. 78 Unser tapferes Regiment Das Königl. Sächs. 8. Feldartillerie-Regt. Nr. 78 im Großen Kriege* Leipzig 1931

**Gallion, Lt d.R. Dr. W** *Das Reserve-Infanterie-Regiment 40 im Weltkrieg* Karlsruhe, 1936

**Gerster, Matthäus,** *Das Württembergische Reserve-Infanterie-Regiment 119 im Weltkrieg 1914-1918* Stuttgart, 1920

**Glück, Generalmajor a.D. & Wald Generalmajor a.D.** *Das 8. Württembergische Infanterie-Regiment 126 Großherzog Friedrich von Baden im Weltkrieg 1914 – 1918* Stuttgart, 1929

**Goetze, Generalmajor a.D. von** *Das Marine-Infanterie-Regiment 2 im Weltkriege 1914/18* Berlin, 1926

**Goldammer, Lt. d.R. a.D. Arthur,** *Das Kgl. Sächs. 14. Infanterie-Regt. 179* Leipzig, 1931

**Gropp, Offizier-Stellvertreter Hugo,** *Hanseaten im Kampf. Erlebnisse bei dem Res.-Inf.-Rgt. 76 im Weltkriege 1914/18* Hamburg, 1934

**Grote, Hans Henning Freiherr** *Somme* Hamburg,1937

**Gruson, Oberst a.D. Ernst** *Das Königlich Preußische 4. Thur. Infanterie-Regiment Nr. 72* *im Weltkriege* Oldenburg, 1930

**Guhr, Generalmajor a.D.** *Das 4. Schlesische Infanterie-Regiment Nr. 157 im Frieden und im Kriege 1897 – 1919* Zeulenroda, 1934

**Held, Generalleutnant a.D. Karl & Stobbe Generalmajor a.D. Otto** *Das Königl. Preuß. Infanterie-Regt. Graf Barfuß (4. Westf.) Nr. 17 im Weltkriege 1914/1918* Berlin, 1934

**Hofmann, Major a.D.** *Das Kemptener Bataillon des Königlich Bayerischen 20. Infanterie-Regiments Prinz Franz im Frieden und im Kriege* Kempten 1928

**Höfl, Oberst Hugo** *Das K.B. 20 Infanterie-Regiment Prinz Franz* München, 1929

**Holtz, Hauptmann Freiherr Georg von** *Das Württembg. Res. Inft. Regt. No 121 im Weltkrieg 1914-1918* Stuttgart, 1921

**Hüttmann, Oberst Adolf & Krüger Oberleutnant a.D. Friedrich Wilhelm,** *Das Infanterie-Regiment von Lützow (1. Rhein.) Nr. 25 im Weltkriege 1914-1918* Berlin, 1929

**Ihlenfeld, Oberst a.D. v. & Engel Major a.D.** *Das 9. Badische Infanterie-Regiment Nr. 170 im Weltkriege* Oldenburg, 1926

**Jecklin, Königlich Preußischer Major a.D. Wilhelm v.** *Das Reserve-Jäger-Batl. Nr. 8 im Weltkriege 1914 – 1918* Erfurt, 1930

**Kaiser, Generalmajor a.D. Franz** *Das Königl. Preuß. Infanterie-Regiment Nr. 63 (4. Oberschlesisches)* Berlin, 1940

**Kalb, Oberstleutnant a.D. Georg** *Das K.B. 10. Feldartillerie-Regiment* München 1934

**Kalbe, Kgl. Preuß.Hauptmann a.D. Dr. jur Richard** *Das 9. Lothringische Infanterie-Regiment Nr. 173 im Weltkriege Teil II* Zeulenroda, 1938

**Keiser, Oberstleutnant von** *Geschichte des Inf.-Regts. v.d. Marwitz (8. Pomm.) Nr. 61 im Weltkriege 1914-1918* Privately published, 1928

**Kellinghusen, Hauptmann d. Res. Wilhelm** *Kriegserinnerungen* Bergedorf, 1933

**Kinder, Leutnant d.R. a.D. Theodor** *Das Marine-Infanterie-Regiment 1 1914-1918* Kiel, 1933

**Klaus, Major a.D. Justizrat Max** *Das Württembergische Reserve-Feldartillerie-Regiment Nr. 26 im Weltkrieg 1914-1918* Stuttgart, 1929

**Klett, Fritz** *Das Württembergische Reserve-Dragoner-Regiment im Weltkrieg 1914-1918* Stuttgart, 1935

**Koch, Dipl.-Ing. Arthur & Eberhardt Generalleutnant a.D. Walter von** *Die Flieger-Abteilung (A) 221* Oldenburg, 1925

**Kohl, Leutnant d.Res. a.D. Hermann** *Mit Hurra in den Tod! Kriegserlebnisse eines Frontsoldaten 17. bayer. Infanterie-Regiment 'Orff'* Stuttgart, 1932

**Korfes, Hauptmann a.D. Dr. Otto,** *Das 3. Magdeburgische Infanterie-Regiment Nr. 66 im Weltkriege* Berlin, 1930

**Kümmel, Leutnant d.Res. a.D. Studienrat Dr. Phil.,** *Res.Inf.Regt. Nr. 91 im Weltkriege 1914-1918* Oldenburg, 1926

**Kuchtner, Oberleutnant a.D. Dr. Lorenz,** *Das K.B. 9. Feld-Artillerie-Regiment* München, 1927

**Kuhl, General d.Inf. a.D. Hermann v.,** *Der Weltkrieg 1914-1918 Band 1* Berlin, 1929

**Lais, Otto** *Die Schlacht an der Somme 1916,* Karlsruhe

**Lange, Ernst,** *Hauptmann Willy Lange* Breslau, 1936

**Lasch, Lt d.R a.D. Dr. jur. Wilhelm** *Geschichte des 3. Unterelsässischen Infanterie-Regiments Nr. 138 1887 – 1919,* Saarbrucken

**Lattorf, Oberleutnant a.D. Claus-Just von** *Kriegsgeschichte des Brandenburgischen Jäger-Battalions Nr. 3 (Jäger-Sturm-Battalion Nr. 3) 1914-1918,* Berlin

**Lehmann, Generalleutnant a.D. August,** *Das K.B. Pionier-Regiment* München, 1927

416

Ludendorff, Erich, *Meine Kriegserinnerungen 1914-1918* Berlin, 1919
Lutz, Hauptmann Ernst Freiherr von, *Das Königlich bayerische 16. Infanterie-Regiment im Kriege 1914 – 1918* Passau, 1920
Meier-Gesees, Karl, *Vater Wills Kriegstagebuch* Bayreuth, 1931
Mierisch, Oberinspektor Richard, *Beim Kgl. Bayer. Reserve-Infanterie-Regiment Nr. 15 im Felde* München, 1937
Moser, Generalleutnant Otto von, *Feldzugsaufzeichnungen als Brigade-Divisionskommandeur und als Kommandierender General 1914-1918* Stuttgart, 1923
Moser, Generalleutnant Otto von *Die Württemberger im Weltkriege* Stuttgart, 1928
Möller, Hanns *Fritz von Below General der Infanterie* Berlin, 1939
Mücke, Kgl. Preuß. Rittmeister a.D. Kurt von, *Das Großherzoglich Badische Infanterie-Regiment Nr. 185* Oldenburg 1922
Müller, Major d.R Paul, Fabeck Oberst a.D. Hans von & Riesel Oberstleutn. a.D. Richard, *Geschichte des Reserve-Infanterie-Regiments Nr. 99* Zeulenroda, 1936
Müller-Loebnitz, Oberstleutnant Wilhelm, *Die Badener im Weltkrieg* Karlsruhe, 1935
Mülmann, Oberst Paul von & Mohs Oberleutnant, *Geschichte des Lehr-Infanterie-Regiments und seiner Stammformationen* Zeulenroda, 1935
Nau, Oberstleutnant a.D. W, *Beiträge zur Geschichte des Regiments Hamburg V. Guillemont* Hamburg, 1926
Neubronn, Leutnant Dr. Carl & Pfeffer, Leutnant d.R. Dr. Georg, *Geschichte des Infanterie-Regiments 186* Oldenburg, 1926
Niemann, Oberstlt. a.D. Johannes, *Das 9. Königlich Sächsische Infanterie-Regiment Nr. 133 im Weltkrieg 1914-18* Hamburg, 1969
Nollau, Oberstleutnant a.D. Herbert, *Geschichte des Königlich Preußischen 4. Niederschlesischen Infanterie-Regiments Nr. 51* Berlin, 1931
Pafferath, Leutnant der Reserve a.D. Fritz *Die Geschichte des 6. Rheinischen Infanterie-Regiments Nr. 68 im Weltkriege 1914-1918* Berlin, 1930
Pfeffer, Leutnant a.D. Dr Georg *Geschichte des Infanterie-Regiments 186* Oldenburg, 1926
Pfeiffer, Oberst, *Geschichte des ehemaligen Königlichen bayerischen 12. Feldartillerie Regiments* München, 1935
Reimers, Leutnant d.R., *Geschichte des Reserve-Feldartillerie-Regiments 18* Steglitz, 1919
Reinhard, Königl. Preuß. Oberst a.D. Wilhelm *Das 4. Garde-Regiment zu Fuß* Oldenburg, 1924
Reymann, Oberleutnant a.D. H *Das 3. Oberschlesische Infanterie-Regiment Nr. 62 im Kriege 1914 – 1918* Zeulenroda, 1930
Richter, Oberst a.D., *Das Reserve-Infanterie-Regiment 94 im Weltkriege 1914/18* Jena 1934
Richter, Oberleutnant der Reserve a.D., *Das Danziger Infanterie-Regiment Nr. 128 I. Teil* Zeulenroda, 1931
Ritter, Oberstleutnant a.D. Holger, *Geschichte des Schleswig-Holsteinischen Infanterie-Regiments Nr. 163* Hamburg, 1926
Rogge, Oberst a.D. Walter, *Das Königl. Preuß. 2. Nassauische Infanterie-Regiment Nr. 88* Berlin, 1936
Roth, Major a.D. Karl, *Das K.B. Reserve-Infanterie-Regiment Nr. 23* München, 1927
Rosenberg-Lipinsky, Hauptmann Hans Oskar von, *Das Königin Elisabeth Garde Grenadier Regiment Nr. 3 im Weltkriege 1914-1918* Zeulenroda, 1935
Rupprecht, Kronprinz von Bayern, *In Treue Fest. Mein Kriegstagebuch, Erster Band & Zweiter Band* München 1929

**Schad, Adolf,** *Infanterie-Regiment 390* Frankfurt am Main, 1929

**Schaidler, Hauptmann a.D. Otto,** *Das K.B. 7 Infanterie-Regiment Prinz Leopold* München 1922

**Schoenfelder, Generalmajor a.D.** *Das 2. Schlesische Feldartillerie-Regiment Nr. 42* Berlin 1938

**Schütz, Generalmajor a.D. von, & Hochbaum, Leutnant,** *Das Grenadier-Regiment König Friedrich Wilhelm II (1. Schles. Nr. 10)* Oldenburg, 1924

**Schwarte, Exzellenz Generalleutnant Max,** *Der Weltkampf um Ehre und Recht. Der deutsche Landkrieg Zweiter Teil,* Leipzig

**Seiler, Major a.D. Reinhard** *10. Rheinisches Infanterie-Regiment Nr. 161 – II Band* Zeulenroda, 1939

**Seneca, Oberstleutnant a.D. Adolf** *Geschichte des Königlich Preußischen 2. Unterelsässischen Feldartillerie Regiment Nr. 67* Karlsruhe, 1935

**Soden, General der Infanterie a.D. Freiherr von,** *Die 26. (Württembergische) Reserve-Division im Weltkrieg 1914 – 1918* Stuttgart, 1939

**Solleder, Dr Fridolin,** *Vier Jahre Westfront Geschichte des Regiments List R.I.R. 16* München, 1932

**Staehle, Leutnant d.R.,** *Das Württembergische Feld-Artillerie-Regiment Nr. 116 im Weltkrieg* Stuttgart 1921

**Stosch, Oberstleutnant a.D. Albrecht von,** *Somme-Nord I.Teil: Die Brennpunkte der Schlacht im Juli 1916* Oldenburg, 1927

**Stosch, Oberstleutnant a.D. Albrecht von,** *Somme-Nord II. Teil: Die Brennpunkte der Schlacht im Juli 1916* Oldenburg, 1927

**Stosch, Oberstleutnant a.D. Albrecht von,** *Das Königl. Preuß. 5. GardeRegiment zu Fuß 1897-1918* Berlin, 1930

**Stühmke, General** *Das Infanterie-Regiment 'Kaiser Friedrich, König von Preußen' (7. Württ.) Nr. 125 im Weltkrieg 1914-1918* Stuttgart, 1923

**Studt, Hauptmann d.R. a.D. Dr. Bernhard,** *Infanterie-Regiment Graf Bose (1.Thüringisches) Nr. 31 im Weltkriege 1914/1918* Oldenburg, 1926

**Tannen, Oblt. d.R., Illing Lt. a.D. Rudolf, Schütz Lt. d.R. a.D. Aug. und Forstner Major a.D. Kurt Freiherr von,** *Das Kaiserliche Marine-Infanterie-Regiment Nr. 3 in den Stürmen des Weltkrieges von 1914 – 1918* Zeulenroda, 1935

**Tiessen, Lt. d.R. a.D. Max** *Königlich Preußisches Reserve-Infanterie-Regiment 213. Geschichte eines Flandernregiments* Glückstadt, 1937

Vischer, Oberstleutnant Alfred *Das 10. Württ. Infanterie-Regiment Nr. 180 in der Somme-Schlacht 1916* Stuttgart, 1917

**Vischer, Oberst A** *Das Württemb. Infant. Regt No 180 im Weltkrieg 1914-1918* Stuttgart, 1920

**Voigt, Oblt. d. Res. Hans** *Geschichte des Füsilier-Regiments Generalfeldmarschall Prinz Albrecht von Preußen (Hann.) Nr. 73* Berlin, 1938

**Vormann, Lt. a.D. Wolfgang v.** *Infanterie-Regiment Fürst Leopold von Anhalt-Dessau (1. Magedeburg.) Nr. 26 Bd 3* Oldenburg, 1926

**Wagner, Oberstleutnant & Scheffel Oberst,** *Das Ober-Elsässische Feldartillerie-Regiment Nr. 15 im Großen Kriege 1914 – 1918,* Darmstadt.

**Waldenfels, K.b.Rittmeister a.D. Otto Freiherr von,** *Das K.B. 11. Feldartillerie-Regiment* München, 1931.

**Wegener, Hans,** *Die Geschichte des 3. Ober-Elsässischen Infanterie-Regiments Nr. 172* Zeulenroda 1934

**Weisemann-Remscheid, Hauptmann d.R. a.D. Dr. Ewald,** *Wo der Krieg gehaust* Nürnberg, 1930

**Wellmann, Generalleutnant a.D.,** *Mit der 18. Reserve-Division in Frankreich* Hamburg 1925

**Weniger, Generalmajor a.D. Heinrich, Zobel Oberst a.D. Artur & Fels Oberst a.D. Maximilian,** *Das K.B. 5. Infanterie-Regiment Großherzog Ernst Ludwig von Hessen* München, 1929

**Wißmann, Oberst von,** *Das Reserve-Infanterie-Regt. Nr. 55 im Weltkrieg,* Berlin

**Wohlenberg, Oberleutnant d.R. a.D. Rektor Alfred,** *Das Res.-Inf.-Regt. Nr. 77 im Weltkriege 1914 -18* Hildesheim, 1931

**Xylander, Oberst a.D. Rudolf Ritter von,** *Geschichte des 1. Feldartillerie-Regiments Prinz-Regent Luitpold* München, 1931

**Zastrow, Oberstleutnant a.D. Maximilian von,** *3. Badisches Feldartillerie-Regiment Nr. 50* Oldenburg, 1929

**Zipfel, Hauptmann a.D. Dr Ernst,** *Geschichte des Großherzoglich Mecklenburgischen Grenadier-Regiments Nr. 89* Schwerin, 1932


*Printed Works (German: Author unknown)*

**Bayerisches Kriegsarchiv,** *Die Bayern im Großen Krieg 1914-1918* München, 1923

**Offz. und Mannschaften der Kompanie,** *Die 5. Kompanie des Königlich Bayerischen Infanterie-Leib-Regiments im Weltkrieg 1914/18* München, 1934

**Offizier – Kameradenverein,** *Geschichte des Feldartillerie-Regiments von Peucker (1.Schles.) Nr.6 1914 – 1918* Breslau 1932

**Offiziere des Regiments,** *Das K.B. 14. Infanterie-Regiment Hartmann* München 1931

**Ehemaliger Offiziere des Regiments,** *Das Füsilier-Regiment Prinz Heinrich von Preußen (Brandenburgisches) Nr. 35 im Weltkriege* Berlin, 1929

**Feldzugsteilnehmer,** *Geschichte des Infanterie-Regiments Generalfeldmarschall Prinz Friedrich Karl von Preußen (8. Brandenburg.) Nr. 64 während des Krieges 1914/18* Berlin, 1928

*Reserve Infanterie-Regiment Nr. 110 im Weltkrieg 1914-1918* Karlsruhe

**Mitkämpfer,** *Geschichte des 9. Rhein. Infanterie-Regiments Nr. 160 im Weltkriege 1914-1918* Zeulenroda, 1931

**Mitkämpfer,** *Geschichte des 4. Hannoverschen Infanterie-Regiments Nr. 164* Privately published, 1932

*Festschrift zum 1. Regimentstag des ehem. 8. Bad. Inf-Reg. Nr. 169* Lahr 1924

*Festschrift zum 2. Regimentstag des Reserve-Infanterie-Regiments Nr. 231* Braunschweig June 1925

**Reichskriegsministerium,** *Der Weltkrieg 1914 bis 1918 Die militärischen Operationen zu Lande. Zehnter Band* Berlin, 1936


*Printed Works (French)*

**Ministère de la Guerre** *Les Armées Françaises dans La Grande Guerre Tome IV Deuxième Volume + Annexes et Cartes* Paris 1933

**Denizot Alain** *La Bataille de la Somme* 2002

**Laurent André** *La Bataille de la Somme 1916* Amiens 1996

**Miquel Pierre** *Les Oubliés de la Somme* Paris 2002

Printed Works (English)

**Cole, Christopher (Ed.)** *Royal Flying Corps 1915-1916* London 1969

**Edmonds, Brigadier-General Sir James E.** *History of the Great War. Military Operations France and Belgium 1916 Sir Douglas Haig's Command to the 1st July: Battle of the Somme* London 1932

**Falkenhayn, General Erich von** *General Headquarters 1914 – 1916 and its Critical Decisions* London

**Hart, Peter** *Somme Success. The Royal Flying Corps and the Battle of the Somme, 1916* Pen & Sword 2001

**Jünger, Ernst** *The Storm of Steel* London 1929

**Miles, Captain Wilfred** *History of the Great War. Military Operations France and Belgium 1916 2nd July to the end of the Battles of the Somme* London 1938

**Pidgeon, Trevor,** *Flers & Gueudecourt* Pen & Sword 'Battleground Europe' 2002

**Reed Paul,** Courcelette Pen & Sword 'Battleground Europe' 1998

**Renshaw, Michael,** Redan Ridge Pen & Sword 'Battleground Europe' 2004

**Stedman, Michael,** Thiepval Pen & Sword 'Battleground Europe' 1995

**Tschuppik Karl,** *Ludendorff, The Tragedy of a Specialist* London 1932

**Illustrated Michelin Guide,** *The Somme Volume 1* Reprint York 1993

In addition to the works listed above, which have been cited in this book, the following selected titles are indispensable to any person with an interest in the Somme:

**Brown, Malcolm,** *The Imperial War Museum Book of the Somme* London 1996

**Cave Nigel (Ed)** *The Battleground Europe Somme Guides* (Currently 22) Pen & Sword. Various dates.

**Farrar-Hockley, A H** *The Somme* London, 1964

**Gliddon Gerald,** *The Battle of the Somme* Stroud 1996

**MacDonald, Lyn,** *Somme* London, 1983

**Middlebrook, Martin,** *The First Day on the Somme* London, 1971 (Recently reprinted)

**Middlebrook, Martin & Mary,** *Somme Battlefields* London, 1991

**Prior, Robin and Wilson, Trevor** *The Somme* London, 2005

**Sheffield, Gary,** The Somme London, 2003

**Westlake, Ray,** *British Battalions on the Somme* Pen & Sword 1994

The best reference book to the imperial German army available in English is:

**Cron, Hermann (Tr. Colton C F)** *Imperial German Army 1914-18 Organisation, Structure, Orders of Battle* Helion & Company, Solihull, 2002

# INDEX